Sizing Up Rhetoric

David Zarefsky
Northwestern University

Elizabeth Benacka
Lake Forest College

WAVELAND

PRESS, INC.

Long Grove, Illinois

For information about this book, contact:
    Waveland Press, Inc.
    4180 IL Route 83, Suite 101
    Long Grove, IL 60047-9580
    (847) 634-0081
    info@waveland.com
    www.waveland.com

Contents

Editors' Introduction   1

Part I
Plenary Perspectives   5

---

1   One Size Doesn't Fit All: The Contingent Universality of Rhetoric   7
    Steven Mailloux

2   Rhetoric and Race in the American Experience:
    The Promises and Perils of Sentimental Memory   20
    Kirt H. Wilson

3   Religion and Rhetoric: Reason, Emotion, and the
    Sensory in Religious Persuasion   40
    Patricia Bizzell

4   Aphthonius and the Progymnasmata in
    Rhetorical Theory and Practice   52
    Manfred Kraus

Part II
Rhetorical Theory   69

---

5   Apuleius and the Forensic Genre in Antiquity   71
    Craig R. Smith

6   The Eulogy: Grief and the Wisdom of the Ancients   90
    Beth L. Hewett

7   "The Siren of Isocrates . . . Sappho's Lyre, or
     Some Other Power Greater Still":
     The Rhetoricity of Anna Komnena's *Alexiad*   101
     Susan C. Jarratt and Ellen Quandahl

8   Kenneth Burke and the Progressive Press   110
     Ann Dobyns

9   Intellectual and Conceptual Resources for Visual Rhetoric:
     A Reexamination of Scholarship Since 1950   118
     Lester C. Olson

Part III
Legal and Political Rhetorics   139

10   Sizing Up Legal "Rhetoric": Law from the Outside In   141
     Frances J. Ranney

11   Getting the Government Out of Farming:
     Sizing Up Eisenhower's Early Agricultural Policy Rhetoric   153
     Lora Cohn

12   Appealing the Divide: Logos, Ethos, and
     Contemporary American Presidential Campaign Rhetoric   173
     Marc C. Santos

13   Complexity and Ideology in Televisual War Rhetoric:
     The Ad War Over Iraq in Campaign 2004   181
     Stephen A. Klien

14   Receiving Rhetoric: Mayor Ray Nagin's Persuasion
     Regarding the Evacuation of New Orleans   200
     Karen Taylor

15   Into Dark Places: Violence, History, and the
     American Militia Movement   212
     D. J. Mulloy

Part IV
Rhetorics of Science   225

16   Bio(in)security: Rhetoric, Science, and Citizens
     in the Age of Bioterrorism—The Case of TOPOFF 3   227
     Lisa Keränen

17   The Biggest Rhetoric of All: Restoring the
      Tropological Heritage of Lacanian Psychoanalysis   250
      Christian Lundberg

18   Physicians Who Are Qualified; Women Who Are Not   265
      Barbara Schneider

19   Limited Prevention, Limiting Topos:
      Reframing Arguments about Science and
      Politics in the HIV Prevention Policy Debate   273
      J. Blake Scott

Part V
Rhetorics of Religion   285

20   In the Blood of the Word: Embodied Rhetorical Authority
      in St. Catherine of Siena's *Dialogue*   287
      Kristie S. Fleckenstein

21   Painted Sermons: Expanding the Scope of Explanatory Rhetoric   296
      Karen Rowe

Part VI
Nineteenth-Century Discourse   311

22   The Prophet of Abolition: Ambiguous Prophecy and
      Rhetorical Echoes in the Rhetoric of David Walker's *Appeal*   313
      David C. Bailey

23   What about Sex?: Reconsidering Histories of
      Nineteenth-Century Women's Public Reform Discourse   325
      Inez Schaechterle and Sue Carter Wood

24   Fortified Young Men: Comstock and the Force of Law   334
      Leslie Hahner

Part VII
Contemporary Rhetorical Cultures   353

25   Topoi of Identity: Rhetorical Practices in
      the Political Reconstruction of Poland   355
      Cezar M. Ornatowski

26   "Sorry Seems to be the Hardest Word to Say":
      Official Apologia and Rhetorical Agency in
      Contemporary Danish Politics   366
      Lisa Storm Villadsen

27   Rhetoric and Resistance in Lu Yin's Feminist Essays   379
      Bo Wang

**Part VIII
Rhetorical Pedagogy   391**

28   Transgressive Eloquence: bell hooks, Cicero,
      and the Aims of Rhetorical Pedagogy   393
      Antonio Raul de Velasco

29   Arguing War and Facing the Other:
      Critical Pedagogy in the Post-9/11 Classroom   398
      Kevin Kuswa and Briann Walsh

**Afterword
Remembering Wayne Booth   415**

30   Rhetoric, Criticism, and *My Many Selves*   417
      Gregory Clark

      Contributors   425
      Name Index   429
      Subject Index   435

Editors' Introduction

More than 500 scholars and teachers of rhetoric gathered for the twelfth biennial conference of the Rhetoric Society of America (RSA), which was held at the Peabody Hotel in Memphis from May 26–29, 2006. Included in this volume are 30 of the approximately 400 papers that were presented in 135 plenary and concurrent sessions there.

The conference theme was the same as this book's title: "Sizing Up Rhetoric." The ambiguity of this phrase was intentional. We meant it in the sense of taking stock of the status of rhetorical studies and its various subfields, and also in the sense of making rhetorical studies "bigger" by defining rhetoric more broadly or by taking on projects of greater magnitude and scope. We hoped that both senses of the conference theme would invite participants to reflect on the status and prospects for rhetorical studies. We were not disappointed.

Of course, a conference theme is not meant to constrain participants but to stimulate productive thought and interchange. As the papers in this volume illustrate, participants addressed the theme with varying degrees of directness. Some, such as Steven Mailloux's keynote, spoke directly to the question of the appropriate scale and scope for rhetorical studies. Some, like the plenary by Kirt Wilson and the essays by Lester Olson and by Frances Ranney, try to take stock of particular subfields within the domain of rhetoric. Other papers address the conference theme more obliquely. But whether they are theoretical essays, historical analyses, case studies, or practical applications, they contribute to the two senses of the conference theme. For example, the plenary by Patricia Bizzell encourages broader investigation of religious rhetoric and the plenary by Manfred Kraus seeks to revive interest in an ancient category of rhetoric and explore its relevance to rhetorical theory. The essay by Beth Hewett seeks to strengthen contemporary eulogies by recovering the wisdom of the ancients and the essay by Christian Lundberg pursues new directions in exploring the relationship between rhetoric and psychoanalysis. Indeed, *every* study in this volume contributes to the goals of understanding where we are and pursuing new directions.

From the papers submitted for consideration for this volume, we selected those that we thought evidenced the strongest scholarship and were ready for publication. We had to reject some that were still in embryonic form and others

1

that were deficient in argument or evidence. Although these were our only overt selection criteria, we serendipitously achieved two other results. This volume reflects the breadth of subjects that were addressed at the conference and it replicates the conference attendance by including contributions from people at every stage in their careers, from beginning graduate students to senior scholars.

Such a diverse collection of essays does not naturally organize itself, and there is no one right way to go about the task. Anyone so inclined could group these essays under other headings and thereby emphasize different dimensions and perspectives of rhetoric. The organizing scheme we have chosen seems reasonable and reflects many of the themes that emerged at the conference.

Part I presents the four plenary papers of the conference: Steven Mailloux's keynote address, Kirt Wilson's presentation at the National Civil Rights Museum, Patricia Bizzell's luncheon speech, and Manfred Kraus's public lecture that was associated with his conference seminar on Aphthonius and the progymnasmata.

In part II we include essays on rhetorical theory, both historical and contemporary. Included are Craig R. Smith's study of Apuleius and the ancient genre of forensic, Beth Hewett's treatment of the classical eulogy, Susan Jarratt and Ellen Quandahl's analysis of Anna Komnena's *Alexiad*, and two studies of contemporary theory—Ann Dobyns's account of Kenneth Burke and the Progressive press, and Lester Olson's survey of scholarship on visual rhetoric.

Part III is devoted to civic discourse—rhetorics of law and politics. It includes Frances Ranney's account of the rhetorical characteristics of legal writing, Lora Cohn's analysis of Eisenhower's agricultural policy rhetoric, Marc Santos's study of the blending of logos and ethos in American presidential campaign rhetoric, Stephen A. Klien's inquiry into televised political campaign advertisements regarding the war in Iraq, Karen Taylor's examination of Mayor Ray Nagin's appeals for the evacuation of New Orleans at the time of Hurricane Katrina, and D. J. Mulloy's reflections on the American militia movement.

Part IV addresses the rhetorics of science. Lisa Keränen offers a case study of rhetoric regarding bioterrorism. Christian Lundberg relates rhetoric to Lacanian psychoanalysis. Barbara Schneider reflects on how rhetoric establishes the authority of physicians in relation to their female patients. And J. Blake Scott studies the interaction of scientific and political arguments related to the prevention of the human immunodeficiency virus (HIV). Part V includes essays that address the rhetorics of religion. Kristie S. Fleckenstein examines rhetorical authority in the *Dialogue* of St. Catherine of Siena, and Karen Rowe studies explanatory rhetoric in visual sermons.

Several of the conference papers examined nineteenth-century rhetorical discourse, and this strand of scholarship is reflected in part VI. David Bailey examines prophecy in the abolitionist *Appeal* of David Walker. Inez Schaechterle and Sue Carter Wood study themes of sexuality in women's reform discourse. And Leslie Hahner is concerned with rhetorical texts that sought to regulate vice.

We were fortunate to have several papers at the conference that addressed rhetorical cultures and practices in other nations. Three of these are included in part VII. Cezar M. Ornatowski explicates rhetorical practices in the political reconstruction of Poland after the fall of communism. Lisa Villadsen examines the role of apologia in contemporary Danish politics. And Bo Wang looks at the interplay of rhetoric and resistance in the feminist essays of Lu Yin.

A recurring theme at RSA conferences and institutes is the inextricable tie between rhetorical scholarship and pedagogy. In part VIII, two papers focus on the pedagogical dimension. Antonio Raul de Velasco considers "transgressive eloquence" as an objective of rhetorical pedagogy, and Kevin Kuswa and Briann Walsh consider the role of critical pedagogy in the classroom in the aftermath of September 11, 2001.

Wayne C. Booth, a longtime friend of rhetoric and supporter of RSA, died in the year preceding the Memphis conference. A memorial program was held in his honor. One of the papers from that program, a personal remembrance by Gregory Clark, is included as an afterword in this volume.

Organizing the conference and reviewing the papers submitted for this volume has reminded us of the breadth of rhetorical studies, the interdisciplinary reach of many of our scholarly projects, and the health of our field. We hope that in reading these essays you share our judgment that this exercise in "sizing up rhetoric" offers cause for celebration.

David Zarefsky
Elizabeth Benacka
Evanston, Illinois
May 2007

PART I

Plenary Perspectives

One Size Doesn't Fit All
The Contingent Universality of Rhetoric[1]

Steven Mailloux

I will begin with two epigraphs. The first is from Hans-Georg Gadamer's "Rhetoric, Hermeneutics, and Ideology-Critique":

> The ubiquity of rhetoric, indeed, is unlimited. . . . No less universal is the function of hermeneutics. (318)

My second epigraph is a video clip, taken from the third season of the television series *The West Wing*, an episode called "War Crimes." In the clip, we see President Josiah Bartlet (JB) and First Lady Abigail Bartlet (AB), entering the White House after attending Sunday mass. They begin arguing about the sermon:

> AB: He feels the homily lacked panache. . . . It was a perfectly lovely homily on Ephesians 5:21: "Husbands love your wives as Christ loved the church and gave himself up for her." . . .
>
> JB: I have no problem with Ephesians. . . .
>
> AB: Then what is your problem?
>
> JB: Hackery. This guy was a hack. . . . He had a captive audience . . . and he didn't know what to do with it.
>
> AB: You want him to sing "Volare"?
>
> JB: It couldn't have hurt. Words, words when spoken out loud for the sake of performance, are music. They have rhythm and pitch and timbre and volume. These are the properties of music, and music has the ability to find us and move us and lift us up in ways that literal meaning can't. Do you see?
>
> AB: You are an oratorical snob.
>
> JB: Yes, I am and God loves me for it. . . . You can't just trot out Ephesians. Which he blew, by the way. It has nothing to do with husbands and wives. It's all of us. St. Paul begins the passage, "Be subject to one another out of reverence to Christ." Be subject to one another. In this day and age of 24-hour cable crap devoted to feeding the voyeuristic gluttony of an American public hooked on a bad soap opera that's passing itself off as important, don't you think you might be able to find some relevance in verse 21? How do we end the cycle? Be subject to one another.

AB: So this is about you?

JB: No, it's not about me. Well, yes, it is about me. But tomorrow it will be about somebody else. We'll watch Larry King and see who. All hacks off the stage, right now. That's a national security order.

I realize that it is somewhat dangerous to begin with the imperative "all hacks off the stage," but there you go.

My rhetorical goal in this talk is to size up rhetoric in the two senses illustrated in these verbal and visual epigraphs. In the *West Wing* clip, what President Bartlet does first is to size up, take stock of, then evaluate the rhetoric of the priest's sermon and the preacher is found wanting: he's judged a rhetorical hack. But the president's evaluation is opposed by a sizing up of the same sermon by Dr. Bartlet, the first lady, who goes on to size up the sizer-upper. She says to her husband: "You are an oratorical snob." But there is a second sense of sizing up that occurs in this scene: St. Paul's message in Ephesians 5:21 is sized up, enlarged, made more general: Bartlet interprets the passage not as just about husbands and wives, or Christ and his church, being subject one to the other. In his interpretation, it's about everyone being subject to everyone else. The specific examples Paul gives are sized up, by Bartlet, to cover all contexts of human interaction, rhetorical and otherwise, including the context of today's television consumer culture in the United States. "Be subject to one another." Can we not say that Paul's particular message has been sized up to be made universal? And universality is what the Gadamer quote is all about: rhetoric is ubiquitous, applies everywhere, and, thus, like interpretation, rhetoric is universal.

It is these two senses of sizing up, found in our conference call for papers, that I want to play off each other throughout my remarks. How does one size up the rhetorical turn: the return of rhetoric to the academic human sciences? Sizing up rhetoric (increasing its significance today) requires sizing up rhetoric (evaluating what it has been, what it is now, or what it could be). In what follows I will first size up rhetoric, then comment on its status and claims by doing a kind of practical and theoretical inventory. Then in a much longer second section I will size up rhetoric by suggesting one or two of its emergent projects for further development. Section one asks, where and how are we now? Section two, where and how will we go tomorrow?

Section One: Sizing Up as Taking Inventory

What do we now have in rhetorical studies? On the practical level, we have an interdiscipline that is often institutionally situated as a subfield (or sometimes simply a method) within various disciplinary departments in colleges and universities. I believe we should continue exploiting this double placement as subdiscipline and interdiscipline: We should work within our different departmental homes to develop rhetoric as historical tradition, theoretical perspective, and critical practice in the courses we teach and the scholarship we publish. In addition, we should be especially attentive to local opportunities for developing rhetoric as an interdisciplinary field, a field that combines different disciplinary methods and objects of study, a field that provides a transdisciplinary perspective on how disciplines do their business, a field that both explains and challenges traditional disciplinary boundaries.

The practical project of sizing up rhetoric (in both my senses) requires attention to a certain theoretical problem. Though some of you are understandably quite tired of talking about rhetoric's disciplinary imperialism, the globalization of rhetoric, and Big versus Little Rhetoric, these disciplinary and interdisciplinary debates still matter for the future of rhetorical studies at the local, national, and international levels. Thus, I would like to continue my sizing up of rhetoric by considering the objections brought against rhetoric's claim to universality. Specifically, I want to comment on three objections to the assertion that rhetoric can study everything because everything is rhetorical.

First objection: Some people argue that if rhetoric is everything, it is nothing because it can't be differentiated enough from other things to be distinctively treated. This is a logical objection, which can be answered by noting that though everything can be treated rhetorically (as persuasion or as figuration, for example)—and in that sense everything is rhetoric—it is still the case that such rhetorical universalism can be internally differentiated. That is, there are different rhetorics. For example, there are oral, visual, written, digital, gestural, and other kinds; and under written rhetoric, there are various genres such as autobiographies, novels, letters, editorials, and so forth; and under oratory, there are deliberative, forensic, epideictic, sermonic, and other types. My point is the logical one that a whole can have different parts; or that the one can also be made up of the many.

A second, more metaphysical objection to rhetorical universality is sometimes called antirhetoricism. This objection says: To claim everything is rhetoric denies that there is a nonlinguistic world. This is a charge brought against some poststructuralists and some postmodern rhetoricians. The rhetoricism charge is based on a confusion. Just because everything can be rhetoricized, or made an object of rhetorical attention, does not mean that there is nothing that is not rhetoric. Indeed, rhetoric depends on and acknowledges the nonrhetorical—whether the nonrhetorical is viewed as physical force or material context, Burke's scene, or Heidegger's background of practices. Derrida made this point in defending himself against Habermas's charges, and Rorty made a related point in preserving a distinction between violence and rhetoric in responding to Lyotard (Derrida 156n9; Lyotard and Rorty 584).

But there is a third objection to claims of rhetorical universality. Let's call it disciplinary. To see everything as rhetorical makes a specific discipline of rhetorical studies impossible. This objection has, I believe, more bite than the other two. If every human-science discipline studies something that is or could be rhetoricized, then what distinguishes a discipline of rhetoric? Here universality and particularity must be emphasized and interrelated: Yes, everything could be studied rhetorically, but some rhetorics are contingently better than others as objects of study. We can think of academic disciplines as institutionalized networks of practices, theories, and traditions for producing and disseminating knowledge (Mailloux, *Disciplinary Identities* 5). It is the task of every discipline to define and hierarchize its objects of study; that is, to form its traditions of interpreted objects according to its theories and practices. There are thus different kinds of rhetoric and some will receive more attention than others for different reasons at different times. Just as privileging is unavoidable in human behavior (where we have everyday phronesis, or practical wisdom, to help us), so too in academic fields (where we have disciplinary techne, or method, constituted by traditions of theory and practice). It's not a matter of choosing whether we should have a canon or not in rhetoric; we will always have one. Or, in words that I have used elsewhere, in rhetorical studies if there were no canon, we would have to invent one (71).

Section Two: Sizing Up by Sizing Down

Whether this practical and theoretical inventory has any persuasive force or not, I now want to turn to my second question: What next? The interesting thing about this question is that to answer it, we are led to something of a paradox. What next? We need to size up rhetoric, even super-size it, while trying to avoid the unhealthy side effects of academic Big-Macism. We need to move rhetorical studies more aggressively toward its transdisciplinary potential, to be part of every discipline as prolonged self-reflective moments (as their academic imaginary) even as rhetorical studies hovers precipitously above disciplines taking disciplinarity and particular disciplines as its subject matter. Rhetoric here can examine the academic/nonacademic divide as part of its object of study. That is, rhetoric should not only size up disciplines and interdisciplines, but also reevaluate the difficult relation between academic specialization and lay public spheres. Size it up.

At the same time, and perhaps paradoxically, rhetorical studies should super-size by down-sizing. "Down-sizing" here means becoming more ambitious, instantiating the universal, by getting more particular or more exactly foregrounding the particularity of the contingent. Let me give two extended examples of what I mean. I turn now to two interrelated topics that constitute emergent projects in rhetorical studies, projects that require a kind of sizing up by sizing down, a kind of universalizing that demonstrates, nevertheless, that in rhetorical studies one size does not fit all. I will look, first, at the rhetorical differences among types of intellectuals and, second, at the contemporary rhetoric of political theology.

In sizing up (enlarging rhetoric's purview), I have alluded to the academic/nonacademic divide, which includes the distinction between disciplinary expertise within the university and issues of more general public concern extending or originating beyond its boundaries. How might rhetorical studies elaborate this distinction between academic formations and lay publics?

At one time within Euro-American culture, the intellectual was seen as "the spokesman of the universal." In Foucault's words, "to be an intellectual meant something like being the consciousness/conscience of us all" ("Truth and Power" 126). In the 1970s, Foucault argued persuasively that universal intellectuals had been replaced by nonuniversal, specific intellectuals—magistrates, psychiatrists, doctors, social workers, lab technicians, sociologists—who used their specialized expert knowledge in specific political struggles related to their areas of expertise (e.g., penologists joining with prison reformers). As helpful as this distinction between specific and so-called universal intellectuals continues to be, it now seems time to ask: In the twenty-first century is there a need for a new kind of universal intellectual? I will return to this question, at least implicitly, but here I want to use Foucault to emphasize a different distinction: the academic versus the public intellectual.

Later in his career, Foucault described himself as "show[ing] people that they are much freer than they feel, that people accept as truth, as evidence, some themes which have been built up at a certain moment during history, and that this so-called evidence can be criticized and destroyed. To change something in the minds of people—that's the role of an intellectual" ("Truth, Power, Self" 10). Being widely recognized as a public intellectual, Foucault fulfilled the rhetorical function of his role—changing people's minds—partly by connecting his political activity in nonacademic settings with the research he did as an academic scholar and theorist. Besides speaking as a *public* intellectual, Foucault taught as a specific *academic* intellectual—the professor of the History of Systems of Thought at the Collège de France.

Academic intellectuals speak and write primarily for the professional disciplinary communities with which they identify. In contrast, *public intellectuals* not only rhetorically engage audiences beyond the academy but are recognized as doing so by both academics and nonacademics. As the example of Foucault demonstrates, academic intellectuals can become public intellectuals. Some of these hybrids rhetorically build on their disciplinary expertise in making their public interventions (e.g., the literary cultural critic Edward Said), while others tend to separate their principal disciplinary work from their sociopolitical criticism in the larger public sphere (e.g., the linguist Noam Chomsky).

Academic intellectuals in their teaching and research do have public effects, but such effects do not constitute them as public intellectuals according to the distinction I am making. That distinction can be further described in explicitly rhetorical terms: academic and public intellectuals differ in their primary intentions, chosen styles, and immediate audiences. Academic intellectuals wish to produce and disseminate new disciplinary knowledge using the tropes, arguments, and narratives of their respective disciplines and aim toward the specific disciplinary audiences with which they identify. Public intellectuals, in contrast, often translate their disciplinary knowledge in commenting on special topics and more general issues of concern to nonacademic publics using a rhetoric accessible to those publics.

Now we can develop this distinction between academic and public intellectuals to elaborate on an account more useful to rhetoricians examining various publics and counterpublics. What are some of the rhetorical functions of the hybrid intellectual, the academic who goes public with his or her thinking? Four overlapping roles include translator, commentator, inventor, and metacritic. *Translators* provide the lay public with interpretations of specialized disciplinary knowledge, making accessible not only the research that has direct, immediate applications to social issues and technological problems but also the speculative thought and practical philosophy generated from within the scholarly traditions that have less calculable but still discernible relevance to people's lived experiences. *Commentators* present the public with specific critiques and general explanatory models of society and its culture. Hybrid intellectuals are most often seen in the mass media fulfilling this rhetorical role. *Inventors* are creative thinkers who move beyond analysis of current public controversies and present alternative ways of thought. *Metacritics* comment on the rhetorical work of the translators, commentators, and inventors.

Rhetoricians have a special role to play as metacritics in their functioning as public intellectuals. They can analyze the audience specificity of the translation process; they can size up the persuasive success or failure of various rhetorical commentaries; and they can track the tropes, arguments, and narratives used in strategies of invention. Most generally, they can trace the rhetorical paths of thought in the public sphere. Rhetoricians can produce for various audiences analyses of how different agents think in public, their shared and different rhetorics of thought, as well as what they appear to think about rhetoric itself. This rhetorical self-consciousness, so crucial to a deliberative democracy, remains the major contribution rhetoricians can make as academic intellectuals who go public.[2]

There is one specific area where I believe rhetoricians can make a major contribution as both academic scholars and public intellectuals, one area that calls for sizing up rhetorical studies in both my senses. The return of rhetoric to the human sciences at the end of the twentieth century has been followed by another return in the twenty-first: the return of religion to the academy and its simultaneous reemergence (was it ever gone?) on the domestic and international scenes. There are many aspects to consider within the emergent topics of religion, but I will restrict myself to one: political theology.

What is political theology? It's the union of political practice with religious belief. More exactly, political theology is any theory articulating the historical relation between politics and theology, between worldly action within power relations and speculative thought about a world beyond.[3] Of course, the American version of political theology didn't begin in the Bush administration. It was present at the very origin of what became the United States. But for both domestic and global reasons, there seems to have been a rhetorical intensification of political theology since even before 9/11. There are many ways of examining the particulars of this intensification, but I will take one that emphasizes the continuity between one originary rhetorical moment in U.S. history and its reception in the current rhetorical scene at the national level.

On June 11, 2004, the funeral for President Ronald Reagan took place in the National Cathedral in Washington, DC. At the service, former President George H. W. Bush, father to the sitting American president, spoke movingly of the man whom he served as vice president for eight years. At one point, he said, "Ronald Reagan was beloved because of what he believed. He believed in America so he made it his shining city on a hill. He believed in freedom so he acted on behalf of its values and ideals. He believed in tomorrow so the Great Communicator became the Great Liberator" ("State Funeral"). The trope, the metaphor, of a shining city on a hill became a *leitmotif* at the funeral service. Its American genealogy begins, of course, in 1630 when John Winthrop delivered a sermon to a group of Puritans making their way to the New World. Near the end of "A Modell of Christian Charity," during his rhetorical performance of political theology, Winthrop reminded his listeners: "For wee must Consider that wee shall be as a Citty upon a Hill, the eies of all people are uppon us" (42).

During the Reagan funeral, Winthrop's sermon was quoted by Justice Sandra Day O'Connor of the U.S. Supreme Court, a Reagan appointee, and cited by Reverend John Danforth, a former senator and the Episcopal minister officiating at the funeral. Reverend Danforth reminded his listeners that Winthrop's source was the Sermon on the Mount: "You are the light of the world. A city set on a hill cannot be hid"; the same Matthew 5:14 passage was read by Cardinal Theodore McCarrick, Roman Catholic Archbishop of Washington, immediately before Danforth's homily. Like his fellow speakers, Reverend Danforth emphasized the positive political spin traditionally given the passage in applying it to the eulogized president. That America was a shining city on a hill for the rest of the world was, Danforth said, President Reagan's "favorite theme, from his first inaugural to his final address from the Oval office. . . . Winthrop believed that the eyes of the world would be on America because God had given us a special commission, so it was our duty to shine forth. The Winthrop message became the Reagan message. It rang of optimism, and we longed to hear it, especially after the dark days of Vietnam and Watergate." Later in his homily Danforth made the references contemporary as he affirmed to his audience, "You and I know the meaning of darkness. We see it on the evening news: terror, chaos, war. An enduring image of 9/11 is that on a brilliantly clear day a cloud of darkness covered Lower Manhattan." Danforth then asked, "What do we do when darkness surrounds us?" and declared, "St. Paul answered that question. He said we must walk as children of light [Ephesians 5:8]. President Reagan taught us that this is our mission, both as individuals and as a nation" ("State Funeral").

A rhetorician might comment on various aspects of this conjuring of an earlier American exceptionalism based on political theology. To track the interpretive and rhetorical elements of this repetition, I could adopt a rhetorical hermeneutic perspective, a kind of cultural rhetoric study that traces the rhetorical paths of thought across texts, events, and eras and their receptions. How is political theology thought of in the public sphere now and in the past? What is its rhetoric of thinking (what tropes, arguments, and narratives are used) and what is its thinking about rhetoric (what claims does its rhetoric make about rhetoric)?

There have been many answers to these questions given in the last few years, both by academic rhetorical critics and popular media commentators. Two especially rich examples of the former are Sharon Crowley's *Toward a Civil Discourse: Rhetoric and Fundamentalism* and Robert Ivie's *Democracy and America's War on Terror*. It seems to me that these two books speak to both academic and nonacademic audiences and thus illustrate the way rhetoricians can function as effective commentators at this critical moment of the explicit and implicit employment of political theology in the public sphere. But as rhetorical inventors I think that rhetoricians can do even more: they could, to return to my opening, develop a rhetorical ethics and politics of the neighbor: "Be subject to one another." I'm taking my cue here from several contemporary thinkers, some rhetorically self-identified, some not.

On the rhetorical side, Diane Davis and others are trying to develop a Levinasian nonappropriative ethics that emphasizes the nonhermeneutic aspects of rhetoric. A rhetorical ethics of the neighbor might adopt such a Levinasian rhetorical ethics and supplement a rhetorical hermeneutics of communication with a nonhermeneutic rhetoric that maintains a nonappropriative relation among conversants and thus continually acknowledges radical otherness, attempting perpetually to respect difference, not only in our neighbors but also in ourselves.

On the other hand, some political theorists are moving in the opposite direction toward a greater recognition of sameness, and it is with these thinkers I am in more sympathy. One nonrhetorical theorist of the postcolony, Achille Mbembe, has argued for a new (perhaps old) approach to conflict in the contemporary world. Commenting on his current situation in South Africa, Mbembe acknowledges the importance of postcolonial theory for understanding that situation: "In carrying out a radical critique of the totalizing thought of the Same, postcolonial theory enabled the positing of the foundations to think alterity, plural singularity even, this scattered multiplicity." However, Mbembe has now begun working against the grain of this theory, noting that "by insisting too much on difference and alterity" postcolonial currents of thought have "lost sight of the weight of the fellow human [*le semblable*] without whom it is impossible to imagine an *ethics of the neighbor*, still less to envisage the possibility of a common world, of a common humanity." Moreover, Mbembe continues,

> Insofar as postcolonial theory has considered the struggle between Father and Son—that is to say, colonizer and colonized—to be the most significant political and cultural paradigm in formerly colonized societies, it has tended to overshadow the intensity of the violence of brother towards brother and the status of the sister and mother in the midst of fratricide.

In passing, it has clouded our understanding of the relationship between sovereignty, homicide, fratricide, and suicide. (14–15)

Within his African context, Mbembe has not yet elaborated his alternative politics based on this ethics of the neighbor, but that ethics has begun to get more and more attention in the Euro-American context as an alternative to a political theology based on Carl Schmitt's enemy/friend opposition. In his recently published "Toward a Political Theology of the Neighbor," Ken Reinhard begins by juxtaposing two of Schmitt's assertions that have recently garnered perhaps the most commentary: First, from *Political Theology*, "The sovereign is he who decides on the exception" (4), and second, from *The Concept of the Political*, "The specific political distinction to which political actions and motives can be reduced is that between friend and enemy" (26). Reinhard explains how these theological concepts sustaining the political order function together: the sovereign within and outside the law determines an unstable friend/enemy opposition that is the essence of the political. Reinhard sees the instability of the friend/enemy distinction as leading to a symptomatic contradiction in Schmitt's political theology, but rather than abandoning that theory he uses Freud and Lacan to "push it further" into an alternative political theology of the neighbor (11).

Rhetoricians can immediately identify with much of this recent talk about friends, neighbors, and enemies. After all, we've been doing friend/enemy rhetorical analysis, Burkean or otherwise, for quite a long time now. Moreover, Reinhard in his important essay and others working on political theology often refer to Alain Badiou's philosophy of the event, and I suggest that Badiou's philosophy too could do with a recognition of current and past rhetorical theory, especially that which develops rhetoric's contingent universality. Here we have another opportunity for a double resizing of rhetoric, sizing it up as global universality while sizing it down by focusing on rhetoric's local particularity.

Simply put, Badiou's philosophy provides an account of universal truth as fidelity to an event that constitutes subjects. For Badiou, truth emerges in the subject's faithfulness to an event in the domain of politics, science, art, or love. In his remarkable book on St. Paul and universalism, Badiou argues that Paul's militant preaching, his proclamation of the Word, initiates the Christian subject who believes in the event of the Resurrection. In the hearing of this Good News, "There is neither Jew nor Greek, there is neither slave nor free, there is neither male nor female" (Galatians 3:28). The atheist Badiou writes admiringly: "[For Paul,] what matters, man or woman, Jew or Greek, slave or free man, is that differences *carry the universal that happens to them like a grace.* Inversely, only by recognizing in differences their capacity for carrying the universal that comes upon them can the universal itself verify its own reality" (*St. Paul* 106). The truth that emerges out of fidelity to the Christ-event is both universal and contingent: universal in that it is preached to everyone and for everyone, contingent in that the truth ends when the fidelity to the event ends. In his book on evil, Badiou raises the problem of a pseudoevent like the rise of Nazism (*Ethics* 72–77). Though Badiou does provide criteria for distinguishing between an authentic event and a pseudoevent, such as universal inclusiveness, I do think Badiou could use a rhetoric to supplement his ontology.

Such a rhetoric would need to begin by separating "essences" and "absolutes" from "universals." Universals are not metaphysical notions at all. They are empirical commonalities, rhetorically deployed in support of specific beliefs and practices at specific times and places. They are shared interests that get rhetorically and hermeneutically determined as common within and across different communities (Mailloux, *Disciplinary Identities* 119). In any particular case of appealing to contingent universals, such as promoting peace or ending torture, there are always interpretive and rhetorical questions: Can a universal be empirically established as such here and now? And even if it can, how might it be successfully invoked with this audience in this context? What, for example, are the contingent universals that might, at present in the United States, be successfully invoked, reconstituted, or invented to enable communication, and perhaps cooperation, across different groups of religious and nonreligious believers?

In elite and popular culture, in government documents and on television programs, human rights talk continues to pervade discussions animated by political theology. Rights to life, liberty, and the pursuit of happiness. Rights to be pro-life or pro-choice. Freedom of religious expression in relation to separation of church and state. Civil rights versus the right to security. I will conclude with one final sizing up by sizing down in relation to the last of these.

Rhetorics of security focus on product and process: the content of beliefs about security and the dynamic of securing those and other beliefs. Today, we see security as a local, national, and international obsession. Security as an anxiety has been super-sized to the global level yet it is lived and experienced at the local. We hear much about the insecurity of peace and the security of war. The United Nations Universal Declaration of Human Rights asserts that "Everyone has the right to life, liberty, and security of person" (Article 3). Article 24 of the Charter of the United Nations gives its Security Council "primary responsibility" for "the maintenance of international peace and security"; while newspaper articles declare: "The war we have just begun is absolutely necessary for the security of the United States, the stability of the world, and the good of the Iraqi people" (Pollack B17).

Rhetoricians, I believe, can contribute to analyzing the presuppositions and effects of these discourses. Indeed, they've already made useful interpretations of the belief content about security and the rhetorical dynamics of securing belief domestically and internationally. Earlier, I cited Crowley's and Ivie's books. Interestingly, both take up the rhetorical implications of Chantal Mouffe's "agonistic pluralism" for a renewed radical democracy, and, as Crowley points out, Mouffe herself invokes "the great tradition of rhetoric" as a resource for accomplishing her political goals (qtd. in Crowley 22). In the cases of political theology, rhetoricians can join intellectual historians, Foucauldian genealogists, and political commentators in tracking the rhetoric of thinking about security, and rhetoricians have even more to say about the rhetorical process of securing belief in security.

My final downsizing ends this talk with some pieces of rhetorical trivia: You'll remember that in my opening clip, President Bartlet ended his rant about the rhetorical and interpretive incompetence of the preacher by declaring: "All hacks off the stage. . . . That's a national security order." Not surprisingly, security rhetoric appeared again and again on a show that was about the rhetorical presidency of the twenty-first century. We might speculate about a more specific source for the *West Wing* security rhetoric. Before winning the Nobel Prize in Economics, could Bartlet have attended Foucault's lectures at the Collège de France from 1976 through 1978? One set of those lectures was called "Security, Territory, and Population," and another has recently been translated into English as "*Society Must Be Defended.*"

Now, the final episode of *The West Wing* series aired a couple of weeks ago: On the way to the inauguration, outgoing President Bartlet (JB) asks President-Elect Santos (MS):

> (JB): How's the speech?
>
> (MS): It's OK. A couple of good lines. There's no, "Ask not what your country can do for you," but. . . .
>
> (JB): JFK really screwed us with that one, didn't he? . . . Have you chosen a biblical quotation for the oath?
>
> (MS): Kings 3:9–11.
>
> (JB): "Grant thy servant an understanding heart to judge thy people"? . . . Good choice.

At the inauguration ceremony, the invocation by Cardinal Edward Doherty ends, "We pray that this good and generous country may be a blessing to the nations of the world and fulfill the hopes of our founding fathers." Then there's a blues rendition of "America the Beautiful" sung by Keb' Mo', and right after the lines: "America, America, God shed his grace on thee, and crown thy good with brotherhood from sea to shining sea," we watch the movers back at the White House packing up President Bartlet's personal items: a picture of his daughter, a bust of Kennedy, and . . . Foucault's lecture volume "*Society Must Be Defended.*" In its pages Foucault argues for inverting Clausewitz's famous aphorism, saying instead "that politics is the continuation of war by other means" (15). Searching for a more hopeful response to Foucault's suggestion leads me to give Kenneth Burke the last word, slightly revised, sized-down just a bit for my sizing up purposes: Not just his *Rhetoric* but rhetoric in general must lead us through the Scramble, the Wrangle of the Marketplace, the flurries and flare-ups of the Human Barnyard, the Give and Take, the wavering line of pressure and counterpressure, the Logomachy, the onus of ownership, the Wars of Nerves, the War. It too has its peaceful moments: at times its endless competition can add up to the transcending of itself. In ways of its own, it can move from the factional to the universal (23).

Notes

[1] I'd again like to thank David Zarefsky, Mike Leff, and the other RSA organizers for the opportunity to address the conference.

[2] For further discussion, see Mailloux, "Thinking in Public," where a version of the previous five paragraphs was first published after delivery of the present paper.

[3] See Scott and Cavanaugh; Davis et al.; Mailloux, "Political Theology."

Works Cited

Badiou, Alain. *Ethics: An Essay on the Understanding of Evil*. Trans. Peter Hallward. London: Verso, 2001.

———. *St. Paul: The Foundation of Universalism*. Trans. Ray Brassier. Stanford: Stanford UP, 2003.

Burke, Kenneth. *The Rhetoric of Motives*. Berkeley: U of California P, 1969.

Crowley, Sharon. *Toward a Civil Discourse: Rhetoric and Fundamentalism*. Pittsburgh: U of Pittsburgh P, 2006.

Davis, Creston, John Milbank, and Slavoj Žižek, eds. *Theology and the Political: The New Debate*. Durham: Duke UP, 2005.

Davis, Diane. "Addressing Alterity: Rhetoric, Hermeneutics, and the Nonappropriative Relation." *Philosophy and Rhetoric* 38 (2005): 191–212.

Derrida, Jacques. "Afterword: Toward an Ethics of Discussion." *Limited Inc.* Evanston: Northwestern UP, 1988. 111–60.

Foucault, Michel. *"Society Must Be Defended": Lectures at the Collège de France 1975–1976*. Trans. David Macey. New York: Picador, 2003.

———, with Alessandro Fontana and Pasquale Pasquino. "Truth and Power." Trans. C. Lazzeri. *Power*. Ed. James D. Faubion. New York: New P, 2000. 111–33.

———, with Rux Martin. "Truth, Power, Self: An Interview with Michel Foucault." *Technologies of the Self*. Ed. Luther H. Martin, Huck Gutman, and Patrick H. Hutton. Amherst: U of Massachusetts P, 1988. 9–15.

Gadamer, Hans-Georg. "Rhetoric, Hermeneutics, and Ideology-Critique." Trans. G. B. Hess and R. E. Palmer. *Rhetoric and Hermeneutics in Our Time: A Reader*. Ed. Walter Jost and Michael J. Hyde. New Haven: Yale UP, 1997. 313–34.

Ivie, Robert L. *Democracy and America's War on Terror*. Tuscaloosa: U of Alabama P, 2005.

Lyotard, Jean-François, and Richard Rorty. "Discussion Entre Jean-François Lyotard et Richard Rorty." *Critique* 41 (1985): 581–84.

Mailloux, Steven. *Disciplinary Identities: Rhetorical Paths of English, Speech, and Composition*. New York: Modern Language Association, 2006.

———. "Political Theology in Douglass and Melville." *Frederick Douglass and Herman Melville: Essays in Relation*. Ed. Robert Levine and Samuel Otter. Durham: U of North Carolina P, 2007.

———. "Thinking in Public with Rhetoric." *Philosophy and Rhetoric* 39 (2006): 140–46.

Mbembe, Achille. "*On The Postcolony*: A Brief Response to Critics." Trans. Nima Bassiri and Peter Skafish. *Qui Parle* 15.2 (2005): 1–49.

Mouffe, Chantal. *The Democratic Paradox*. London: Verso, 2000.

Pollack, Kenneth M. "A Dangerous Tyrant, A Hellish Fear: The U.S. Didn't Have an Alternative." *Los Angeles Times* 20 Mar. 2003: B17.

Reinhard, Kenneth. "Toward a Political Theology of the Neighbor." *The Neighbor: Three Inquiries in Political Theology*. Ed. Slavoj Žižek, Eric L. Santner, and Kenneth Reinhard. Chicago: U of Chicago P, 2006. 11–75.

Schmitt, Carl. *The Concept of the Political.* Trans. George Schwab. Chicago: U of Chicago P, 1996.

—————. *Political Theology: Four Chapters on the Concept of Sovereignty.* Trans. George Schwab. Cambridge: MIT P, 1985.

Scott, Peter, and William T. Cavanaugh, eds. *The Blackwell Companion to Political Theology.* Oxford: Blackwell, 2004.

"The State Funeral of Ronald Reagan." <http//:transcripts.cnn.com/TRANSCRIPTS/0406/11/se.01.html>.

United Nations. "Charter of the United Nations." <http://www.un.org/aboutun/charter>.

—————. "Universal Declaration of Human Rights." <http://www.un.org/Overview/rights.html>.

Winthrop, John. "A Modell of Christian Charity." *American Sermons: The Pilgrims to Martin Luther King Jr.* Ed. Michael Warner. New York: Library of America, 1999.

Rhetoric and Race in the American Experience

The Promises and Perils of Sentimental Memory

2

Kirt H. Wilson

On Tuesday, February 7, 2006, Bishop Eddie Long approached his podium and looked out on 10,000 people. He knew this space well—it was the focal point of his ministry. This day, however, the familiar faces of his affluent black congregation were seated next to poets, celebrities, senators, congressmen and women, and famous activists from the civil rights movement. Bishop Long could not see former President Bill Clinton and Senator Hillary Rodham Clinton, George and Barbara Bush, or Laura and President George W. Bush; they were seated on the dais behind him. No doubt he felt their presence as he called the audience to worship and remembrance (Copeland, "Thousands Pay Joyous Tribute"; Dewan and Bumiller). Whether or not he realized it, Bishop Long was, at that moment, officiating over the most prestigious memorial service the United States had witnessed since the burial of President Ronald Reagan. The funeral for Chief Justice William Rehnquist in 2005 brought together an impressive array of Washington's elite, but it did not compare to the assembly that gathered to pay their respects to Coretta Scott King.

The official service concluded memorial events that began the previous Saturday when Georgia Governor Sonny Perdue ordered that Mrs. King's remains be transported by a horse-drawn carriage to the rotunda of the state capitol. Her body lay in state throughout the day as 42,000 mourners braved a cold rain to pay their respects. Another 130,000 people viewed her casket on Sunday and Monday as she lay in repose at the Ebenezer Baptist Church (Chappell; Goodman). During the Tuesday memorial service, thirty-three speakers, including four U.S. presidents, stood to praise Mrs. King. Eight musical tributes, including performances by Stevie Wonder, Bebe Winans, and Michael Bolton, moved the emotions of the assembled audience. CNN, BET, and TV One broadcast many hours of the event, while highlights of the service appeared on all of the news channels and most of the nation's nightly news programs. For the recessional, several choirs, the Atlanta Symphony Orchestra, and the J. Berry Orchestra of Dekalb County joined forces for the *Hallelujah* chorus.[1] From start to finish, the entire service stretched to almost six hours in length (Copeland, "Thousands Pay Joyous Tribute").

How does one begin to understand this truly remarkable epideictic event? What, if anything, can it teach us about the status of rhetoric and race in the American experience? No doubt Professor Steven Mailloux would instruct us that our answers reside in the persuasive interpretations that surround the event. For the sake of time I will mention only two. A weeping 32-year-old woman, Rose Offord, explained to a reporter: "You know, [Coretta Scott King] was the queen of black America. . . . You never saw her in a situation where she wasn't polished and graceful. She was the most distinguished black woman I've ever seen" (Copeland, "Civil Rights Icon" 1). In this persuasive interpretation, the attention Mrs. King received amounted to the grateful outpouring of sentiment that subjects extend upon the death of royalty. If Rosa Parks was, especially in death, the mother of the civil rights movement (Wilson), then Coretta Scott King was its reigning monarch and the spectacle of her funeral was an official rite. Furthermore, one might claim that the presence of whites and blacks, presidents and people, celebrities and foreign dignitaries signaled the triumph of the civil rights movement. Perhaps this moment was the material fulfillment of Martin Luther King Jr.'s dream that "one day, on the red hills of Georgia, sons of former slaves and sons of former slave-owners will be able to sit down together at the table of brotherhood" (King Jr. 219).

This is but one interpretation of the funeral services for Coretta Scott King. An editorial by Wilbert Tatum that appeared in the *New York Amsterdam News* suggests a more ambivalent set of hermeneutical logics.

> The show was terrific and God must have sat somewhere in a very comfortable seat and asked himself, "Why did I let my people go?" White people were given license for everything they ever did against us by our civil rights leaders, not in the spirit of forgiveness but in the spirit of the songs that were sung, the heads that were bowed and the seats of honor for those who attended. One had to be impressed at the number of senators, presidents, cabinet secretaries et al. who attended, and one had to be amazed at the number of famous Blacks who chose not to come.
>
> A good time was had by all with every spiritual, with every amen, with every yes Jesus, with every note from that magnificently robed choir, with the messages being sent to those in the television audience and messages that were being received by those who were out there saying how wonderful, how wonderful. How good God is. How wonderful is this time and this place where our people lived and died. And now we celebrate their oppression, their lives and their deaths by sending another of ours home to the attention and the applause of the nation. (12)

In this persuasive interpretation, the aesthetics of the event turn the key to its meaning. The speeches, the songs, indeed, the memorial's performance, produce a feeling of "good times" that absolves the nation from past sin while it constructs a seemingly apolitical community. More important, however, is the sense that this interpretation suggests that all is *not* well. There is a hint of irony in the editorial that asks the question whether the funeral service signals the triumph of Dr. King's dream or its demise. The editorial's final words reinforce this tension: "The homegoing service sent Mrs. Coretta Scott King home in the style reminiscent of the March on Washington and with a prayer for our people. May God forgive us all" (12).

I have several reasons for beginning my talk this evening with the homegoing service for Mrs. King. It seems appropriate that we pay tribute to Mrs. King, as well as other recently departed civil rights greats like Rosa Parks and Shirley Chisholm. Too often, as many in this audience know, scholars have either ignored or minimized the significant contributions of women in the civil rights struggle. I agree with T. V. Reed that our attention to the public speeches of the movement, rather than the cultural or vernacular discourses of the movement, may be one reason why women like Ella Baker, Fannie Lou Hamer, Daisy Bates, and others do not receive their due attention (Reed ch. 1). Second, our current location, the National Civil Rights Museum, creates demands that I cannot ignore. The legacy of the King family is enshrined here, and although the museum celebrates the contributions of many (see Duncan and Smith), one cannot ignore how it pushes its audience forward toward a material and rhetorical climax, two hotel rooms that enshrine, as if suspended in time, the final moments of Dr. King. The third reason for relating the events of February 7, 2006, is that they illustrate well the increasingly complex environment that surrounds race in the American experience. Mrs. King's homegoing service is a synecdoche, a field of action that reveals not only the success and the failure of the civil rights movement, but also the problems that confront current activists who believe that our struggle for racial equality is not yet at an end.

I contend that since the early 1990s, the most sustained and frequent acts of public rhetoric about race in the American experience have taken place in explicitly epideictic moments that commemorate the civil rights movement. I argue, further, that one can read this commemorative discourse as a sentimental rhetoric. Of course, the sentimental rhetoric that frames our receptions of the civil rights movement does not match precisely the sentimentalism of the eighteenth and nineteenth centuries. It is not, for example, comprised of the overwrought details and elaborate metaphors of Daniel Webster's "Bunker Hill" oration (see Black). It is not the poetic romanticism of *Charlotte Temple* (Rowson), *Uncle Tom's Cabin* (Stowe et al.), or *Ruth Hall* (Fern) (for critiques of these novels see Hartnett; Tompkins). With a few notable exceptions, it is not the graphic representation of the racist violence depicted in Weld's "American Slavery As It Is" (for analysis see Browne). Comparative analysis provides a useful starting point; however, it is important to recognize that contemporary performances of sentimentalism invite affection and displays of emotional benevolence (Burstein 7) by using the cultural rhetoric of our age (e.g., the images of cinema and photo-documentary, the musical sound track and tribute, the decontextualized objects of museum exhibits, the melodrama of daytime television, and the ceremonial proclamations of public officials). Furthermore, as Nina Baym reminds us, "Sentimentalism is always in the beholder's eye. Like any other umbrella term, this one is plastic and ambiguous" (337). My point is simply this—it is critically *useful* to interpret contemporary civil rights memorialization as a form of sentimentalism. Furthermore, the evolving characteristics of nineteenth-century sentiment—the cultivation of sympathetic personal and social relations, a "ready emotionality," the use of cultural rather than explicitly deliberative discourses, and a rejection of those emotions that destroy empathy—are quite apt to the memorial rhetoric that is the subject of this paper.

In addition to claims about the *what* of civil rights memorial rhetoric, this essay offers the following arguments concerning its function. First, I contend that the sentimental act of civil rights commemoration is performative and constitutive. It invites non-black audiences to reexperience the movement as either sympathetic witnesses or as reformed, enlightened citizens. Second, it constitutes an ideal black audience that always offers whites forgiveness for the wrongs of the past in return for an affective state that diminishes but does not fully remove the pain, anger, hate, and despair so frequently produced by racism. Third, this rhetoric constitutes a sentimental society, a term employed to indicate not only the aesthetic and ideological aspects of this rhetoric but also its cultural/political appropriation of Dr. King's "the beloved community." Fourth, this sentimental rhetoric produces a sense of decorum that excludes symbolic acts that might disrupt the culture of sentiment and implies that either America is not fulfilling its moral obligations or that sympathetic relations are insufficient to solve racially based inequity. I conclude that unless we fashion a rhetoric that allows for *both* the epideictic celebration of civil rights' successes and the confrontational deliberative rhetoric of speaking truth to power, the future of black civil rights in America will be stymied by an increasingly anemic public discourse that celebrates the movement but only with language and styles that reinforce its death.

Now is the Time for Memorial

February's elaborate funeral services for Coretta Scott King are only the latest examples of a culture of commemoration that has evolved over the course of the last ten to fifteen years. It would be impossible to analyze even a small fraction of the commemorations that have transpired since the early 1990s, but to establish a sense for how frequent such acts have become consider the major memorial events of the last year. On February 20, 2006, The Sixteenth Street Baptist Church in Birmingham, Alabama, was designated as a national landmark to honor the four black girls who died there on September 15, 1963. In January, the National Park Service decided to transform the home of black historian Carter G. Woodson into a museum to celebrate his status as the father of black history. On December 1, 2005, President George W. Bush authorized the creation of a life-sized statue of Rosa Parks to reside in the Capitol's National Statuary Hall. Last November, Rosa Parks became the first woman and the second African American to lie in state in the United

States Capitol Rotunda. Mourners streamed past her body for twenty hours before it was transported to Detroit for her funeral. A portrait of Joseph H. Rainey, the first African American elected to the House of Representatives, was unveiled in a ceremony at the U.S. Capitol on September 21, 2005. On August 30, 2005, the post office released a 10-stamp series celebrating the civil rights movement, titled "To Form a More Perfect Union." Also in August, Congress authorized a gift of ten million dollars to help build the Washington, DC Martin Luther King, Jr. National Memorial. This monument, which is scheduled for unveiling in 2008, will be the first National Mall memorial dedicated to a specific individual who was not a president of the United States. Jackie Robinson was posthumously awarded the Congressional Gold Medal on March 2, 2005. Mississippi's largest airport, Jackson International, was renamed the Jackson-Evers International Airport to honor the slain civil rights leader Medgar Evers. And finally, last spring, Greenville County in South Carolina voted to observe the birthday of Martin Luther King, Jr., ending its dubious honor of being the state's only county that refused to observe the holiday.[2]

These events are only a fraction of the local, state, and national commemorations that have transpired in recent years. Since 1990 more than fifteen museums that commemorate the movement have opened (Romano and Raiford xii–xiii). Indeed, when one includes the numerous civil rights anniversary celebrations that have occurred since 1991, one might conclude that we have entered a period of remembrance that is similar to what followed the Civil War and Reconstruction (Blight). As with many cultural phenomena, the memorialization of the civil rights movement involves a commercial dimension. One can now find travel agencies that specialize in tours of civil rights' places. These tours are sometimes localized to a single city like Memphis, Tennessee, but they are often larger excursions, involving multiple cities and considerable travel time. If you are unable to take such a vacation, you can purchase *Save Our History: Voices of Civil Rights*, a 2005 Peabody award-winning video created by the History Channel. This documentary follows a busload of seventy journalists who, in 2004, visited 39 cities in 22 states over the course of seventy days. If bus travel doesn't thrill you no matter what its format, you can purchase *A Traveler's Guide to the Civil Rights Movement* (Carrier) or *Weary Feet, Rested Souls* (Davis). Both texts reinvent the guidebook genre to offer the independent traveler a rich set of history lessons as well as directions to the next civil rights monument.

According to Shaila Dewan, the growth of civil rights tourism has created its own set of controversies; many European Americans across the South are uncomfortable with an industry that highlights acts of racist violence and hatred. Resistance in some communities remains considerable, "particularly among whites who see no reason to dredge up the painful past or who fear that the motive is to assign blame" (19). Nevertheless, the prospect of money and the arguments of economic developers have swayed many municipalities to participate in the burgeoning industry. The civil rights museums in Birmingham and Memphis each attract about 150,000 people a year. The Martin Luther King, Jr. National Historic Site in Atlanta attracted 650,000 visitors in 2003, making it one of the most popular tourist sites in the South. Remarking on this tremendous economic opportunity, Dewan notes that "in 1993 there was not so much as a sign marking the bus stop in Montgomery where Rosa Parks was arrested," but today the success of civil rights tourism has prompted a shift in attitudes. Put simply, "The history of the 50's and 60's is a valuable commodity" (19).

So, what are we to make of this commoditization? Last year Myrlie Evers-Williams remarked that the U.S. government and its citizens continued to find new ways to recognize the struggle for which her husband gave his life. Reflecting on the commemorative stamps, she said,

> Children who would otherwise not know about the lunch-counter sit-ins in Greensboro, N.C., can and should be made aware of history's lessons, simply by looking at the stamp on their mail. . . . It is our job as educators and parents to bring these symbols to children's attention, to show them why they exist and why they're important. We must show them the scars of our past as a way of healing current wounds—and preventing new ones. (13a)

The rhetorical functions of education and prevention are, of course, central to the commemoration of the civil rights movement and memorials generally (Blair and Michel; Biesecker; Gallagher; Hasian). The National Civil Rights Museum in which we sit is just one example of an institution that serves these purposes. Now, I readily admit that I am sympathetic to this position. We probably all agree that the past is a hermeneutic resource for addressing the present. Furthermore, as the father of an eight-year-old child, I cannot express how excited I was when Cameron returned home from school one day and proceeded to lecture me on the importance of Rosa Parks. That said, we also must remember, "Museums are powerful rhetorical sites in which the past is selectively presented. Because of the limitations of symbol-use, museum exhibits can only cue us in to segments of history—they can never represent 'the' past in all of its social, cultural, and political complexity" (Armada 235–36). One should not naively reject the official symbols of our public memory, but we should think critically about the selective vision that memorials' symbols fashion. To accomplish this critical activity, we turn now to the concept of sentiment.

Constituting the Sentimental Society

"The eighteenth-century's inception of the cult of sentiment or sensibility constructed the figure of the 'man of feeling' as a male body feminized by affect" (Chapman and Hendler 3). Enlightenment philosophers like David Hume and, later, Adam Smith considered natural sentiment to be an essential component of moral judgment. Furthermore, sentiment and imagination were said to create sympathy between individuals, making civil society possible. Without the moderating influence that sentiment produced, the family and, perhaps, society as a whole might descend into chaos as the stronger emotions of anger, envy, jealousy, desire, and hatred overwhelmed the power of intellectual reason and prudential judgment. In *The Theory of Moral Sentiments,* Smith affirmed, "It is by the imagination only that we can form any conception of what are [the] sensations [of our brother on the rack]. . . . By the imagination we place ourselves in his situation, we conceive ourselves enduring all the same torments, we enter as it were into his body and become in some measure the same person with him" (qtd. in Chapman and Hendler 3).

According to Andrew Burstein, it would be difficult to overestimate the importance of sentiment for the founders of the U.S. government. "During the Revolutionary era, American citizens actively espoused a vocabulary rich in sentiment and productive passion that would distinguish them as a free and independent people with a special destiny" (23). To understand the ideal citizen of the early American republic, he suggests that we look no further than the main character of the popular 1782 novel, *The Man of Feeling* (Mackenzie). "A man of extraordinary generosity and sympathetic imagination who, in his travels, consistently thinks less of his own comfort than that of others. [Harley] is the embodiment of the eighteenth century's culture of sensibility, combining nature-given delicacy with self-conscious humanism, unable to turn from any person in need," states Burstein (xi). Advocates for the revolution argued that proper feeling was precisely what differentiated England from the colonies. The latter had maintained their capacity for sentiment; consequently, they were prepared to sacrifice their lives to protect their liberty and the community's future happiness. The former, England, and especially its political leadership, had grown cold, hard, intractable, tyrannical. Sentiment, at least in this theoretical configuration, provided the motivation for action and the structure of civil society.

Few national leaders have had a greater influence on the texture of civil rights commemoration than former President Bill Clinton. Since leaving his official duties as president, he has remained an active participant at the funerals of civil rights leaders and at the dedication services for new memorials. He has attended numerous civil rights anniversaries, both large and small. He remains, to this day, the most loved living president within the African American community; one need only reflect on the ovation he received at the memorial service for Coretta Scott King to appreciate his popularity among many blacks. On August 28, 1998, the president was invited to Oak Bluffs, Massachusetts to speak at a thirty-fifth anniversary celebration for the march on Washington.

After Clinton thanked John Lewis, Anita Hill, and Henry Louis Gates, Jr., he turned to the subject of the occasion.

> The summer of 1963 was a very eventful one for me, the summer I turned 17. What most people know about it now is the famous picture of me shaking hands with President Kennedy in July. It was a great moment.

> But I think the moment we commemorate today—a moment I experienced all alone—had a more profound impact on my life. Most of us who are old enough remember exactly where we were on August 28, 1963. I was in my living room in Hot Springs, Arkansas. I remember the chair I was sitting in. I remember exactly where it was in the room. I remember exactly the position of the chair when I sat and watched on national television the great March on Washington unfold. I remember weeping uncontrollably during Martin Luther King's speech, and I remember thinking when it was over, my country would never be the same, and neither would I. (1660–61)

Note, first, how President Clinton's remarks begin not with a narrative about the march or with reflections about the people who attended it. His initial four sentences frame the event in personal terms. If one were to read these lines without a sense of the occasion, one might assume that the speech's subject was the president and not the march on Washington. In point of fact, this story, and the speech as a whole, *is* about the speaker. In this text, the march on Washington is not so much a significant historical event as it is an affective experience. "Using his personal recollections of King's speech," write Shawn and Trevor Parry-Giles, "Clinton fuses his personal tale of the civil rights movement with the collective understandings and commemoration of those events" (422). The text casts the march as a persuasive invitation to the country, and Clinton makes the most of that invitation. He identifies so fully with the protestors he views on the "public screen" of his television that he ends up "weeping uncontrollably."

The passage above contains the sentence, "Most of us who are old enough remember exactly where we were on August 28, 1963." Not only does this sentence act as a transition, it also establishes memory as the primary hermeneutic method for interpreting the march on Washington. The absence of historical information in the speech and the heavy emphasis on Clinton's still emotional memories suggest that the historical details we learned in college—the importance of A. Phillip Randolph in keeping the idea alive, how the protest was intended to pressure the Kennedy administration, or how backstage negotiations forced John Lewis to alter his speech (Klinkner and Smith 243–44)—are secondary to understanding the event or its significance. What matters most for Clinton and his audience is how the moment *felt*, both then and in the speech's now. The primacy of this perspective is emphasized by the fact that the text shifts from the events located in Washington, DC to a small living room in Hot Springs, Arkansas. The room contains a chair, a television, and the future president of the United States. This is the scene of reception, a context of stark detail that will witness the transformation of a young seventeen-year-old boy, and, at least according to the text, an entire country.

The sentence that begins, "Most of us who are old enough . . ." also indicates that although he was physically alone when he experienced the transformation that brought about an "intense commitment" to the aims of the civil rights movement, Clinton was not the only person to be affected in this way.

Others had a similar experience. To understand this fact is to realize that although the affective reception of something like the march on Washington is an intensely personal or interior experience, it is also assumed to be strangely collective. According to the text, because of the march on Washington, "In very personal ways, all of us became better and bigger because of the work of those who brought that great day about" (1661). This negotiation between the personal and the collective is a fundamental aspect of sentimentalism. As the Adam Smith quotation I used earlier suggests, sentiment is about the negotiation between self and other, between what we feel with our senses, and what our imagination and sentiment allow us to experience from the lives of others. As we shall see now, this negotiation and the building of sympathetic relations is at the heart of President Clinton's interpretation of the civil rights movement.

As the text progresses, the president identifies three moral lessons that he learned from the civil rights movement. The fact that he articulates these principles as explicit moral lessons is not unusual. Bernard Armada's insightful critique of the National Civil Rights Museum demonstrates that moral lessons are frequently a part of memorialization (see also Blair and Michel). What matters, Armada reminds us, are the specific lessons we are taught. In Clinton's case, these lessons are "mutual dependence"; peace and nonviolence; and "love your neighbor as yourself." For the sake of time, I will describe how he teaches only this last, final lesson.

Again relying on his memories to guide his moral epistemology, Clinton reflects that when he first met President Nelson Mandela he felt compelled to ask him how he had summoned the courage to invite his jailers to his presidential inaugural. "You're a shrewd as well as a great man," Clinton said, "But come on, now, how did you really do that? You can't make me believe you didn't hate those people who did that to you for 27 years" (1663). The answer that Mandela gives, and the lesson that the text reinforces, is that in order to protect his mind and heart, Mandela had to forgive his oppressors. The president then drives the point home as an application for his immediate audience:

> And all of us—the anger, the resentment, the bitterness, the desire for recrimination against people you believe have wronged you, they harden the heart and deaden the spirit and lead to self-inflicted wounds. And so it is important that we are able to forgive those we believe have wronged us, even as we ask for forgiveness from people we have wronged. And I heard that first—first—in the civil rights movement: "Love thy neighbor as thyself." (1663)

These words express a core assumption of the cult of sentimentality. Beware the hardened heart, beware the deadened spirit. Cultivate the habits of forgiveness and love they neighbor. Then you will be performing the true spirit of the civil rights movement.

At this point, I would like to suggest that the president's central role in the remembered drama of the march on Washington is more than just further evidence of Clinton's considerable ego. We can read his textual placement and his actions as the ideal citizen that the text intends his audience to become. Just as the president's whiteness and geographical location in Hot Springs, Arkansas, were not obstacles to his participation in the march on Washington, so our racial diversity and our distance of both years and, in some cases, lifetimes do not prevent us from the transformative power of the civil rights movement. All we require is the appropriate prompt, the right rhetoric that will stimulate our imagination, and sentimental capacity. Once that moment arrives, as one might expect given the generic expectations of a memorial, the good citizen will embrace the appropriate emotions and become her own witness to the movement's powerful authority.

The peroration of Clinton's speech brings together the various strains of sentimentality that are woven throughout the text. In a rather ingenious rhetorical decision, Clinton chooses not to speak his own words but to quote at length from *Walking with the Wind*, a memoir written by civil rights veteran John Lewis (Lewis and D'Orso). The section of the book that Clinton quotes relates yet another memory. This time, because it is Lewis's and not Clinton's memory, the scene is rural Alabama in the middle of a violent storm that threatens the small tin-roof house where Lewis, his aunt, and twelve cousins reside. Holding hands with one another, the children move from one corner to another, always looking for the weak spot that is about to fly upward from the force of the wind. In the context of the book, this story is an allegory about people of conscience who struggle together in America for justice. In the context of Clinton's performance, the narrative retains Lewis's meaning, but it adds a whole new function that is grounded in the president's authority to claim this story as his own. That is, the mimetic appropriation performed by President Clinton helps to transform Lewis's story into an expression of the perfect American community. Still quoting Lewis but confusing the personal pronouns in a rhetorically effective way, the president states this is the story

> in essence, of my life, of the path to which I've been committed since I turned from a boy to a man and to which I remain committed today, a path that extends beyond the issue of race alone, beyond class as well, and gender and age and every other distinction that tends to separate us as human beings rather than bring us together. The path involves nothing less than the pursuit of the most precious and pure concept I have ever known, an ideal I discovered as a young man that has guided me like a beacon ever since, a concept called "the beloved community." (1663)

It is difficult to do justice to the stirring phrases that conclude the speech, but perhaps this imitation is sufficient to illustrate my point. The president is now the "I" of this passage, and he is talking about *his* own story. In a telling moment, the president explicitly invites his audience into this imagined community, stating: "This is the America we are trying to create" (1664). In point of fact, Clinton has created the community already. His own transformation, the lessons of sentiment that he outlined, and the stirring imitation of John

Lewis have, indeed, created a community. It might not be Dr. King's vision of the beloved community, but it is definitely a society of sentiment.

The Moral Education of Sentiment's Citizens

Mary Chapman and Glenn Hendler argue that "by the mid-Nineteenth Century... American sentimentality seemed to have become ensconced solely in a feminine 'world of love and ritual,' in 'the empire of the mother'" (3). Why "manly sentiment" declined and "feminine sentimentality" grew is a difficult question with several competing answers.[3] Fortunately for me, I don't need to resolve this history today. It is important, however, to recognize that patriarchy played a significant role in sentiment's evolution. As women produced and consumed increasing numbers of popular novels, this literature reflected a style that the nineteenth century associated with female identity. Often melodramatic, these novels invoked obligatory scenes of pleasant domesticity, expressive displays of emotional reconciliation, romantic heroes, and delicate, pious, self-sacrificing women. It was precisely these stylistic elements that caused traditional literary critics to describe such novels as immature, overly emotional, nostalgic, and politically ineffectual; furthermore, this literary aesthetic was reduced to the term "sentimental style" and the label was used as a social weapon by those "who feared that tendencies toward gender equality would undermine patriarchal power in the republic" (Burstein 313). Yet, as Jane Tompkins's study of *Uncle Tom's Cabin* illustrates, one can acknowledge the link between a feminized sentiment and women's novels while, simultaneously, interpreting these works "as a political enterprise, halfway between sermon and social theory, that both codifies and attempts to mold the values of its time" (126). Working from the gendered assumptions of the day, the "popular domestic novel of the nineteenth century" offered readers a moral education that was nothing less than "a monumental effort to reorganize culture from the woman's point of view" (123).

If one were to choose a single person who regularly enters the domestic scene in order to reorganize culture according to her own point of view, it would be difficult to find anyone more accomplished than Oprah Winfrey. Since the early 1990s, the *Oprah Winfrey Show* has reached almost 14 million viewers a day and 49 million each week in the United States alone. "No longer just a successful talk-show host worth $1.4 billion," she recently "has emerged as a spiritual leader for the new millennium, a moral voice of authority for the nation" (Oldenburg 1). In partnership with Habitat for Humanity, she helped construct a Houston neighborhood for the victims of Katrina, and she has promised to devote as much as ten million dollars to build additional homes. One media critic who has studied her book club credits her with transforming America's literary taste and bringing about the triumph of cultural democracy (Farr 99). What is important for this paper is that Oprah Winfrey is a frequent actor in national ceremonies that commemorate the civil rights movement. Furthermore, she has repeatedly used her television show and her public appearances to preach the gospel of racial reconciliation, a salvation that rejects the strong unhealthy passions of hate and anger for the more sentimental process of transforming shame and guilt into relief.

One episode of the *Oprah Winfrey Show* is particularly relevant, not only because of its significance when it was aired in 1996, but also because Oprah included it on her twentieth anniversary DVD box set published in 2005 (Terry and Winfrey). The episode is entitled "The Little Rock Nine, 1996," and it commemorates the integration of Central High School in Little Rock, Arkansas. For students and scholars of the civil rights movement, the episode, which she cut to ten minutes and thirty seconds in its DVD form, is a remarkable piece of television drama. The show begins with some obligatory images of Central High School and some historical information about the Little Rock Nine's heroic struggle. It mentions the Supreme Court's desegregation order, Governor Orval Faubus's abuse of power when he used the National Guard to resist integration, and President Eisenhower's decision to use troops to protect the nine African Americans who attended Central High. The political and legal history of this important civil rights event plays only a minor role in Oprah's drama, however. The center stage of the episode, indeed, the center stage of her set, is occupied by a different kind of morality play—Oprah Winfrey brings together, for the first time since 1957, seven of the original Little Rock Nine and three of their white tormentors.

Twenty seconds into the segment, a contemporary Oprah (2005) interrupts the show's back story to reflect on why this episode from 1996 was so "impactful" to her personally. As a young black girl, she says, she knew about the Little Rock Nine, but in the process of preparing for the show, "I realized how young they were. How young they were!" She then asks rhetorically, "When I was in the eleventh grade, would I have had the courage to do that? I don't know." As with our first case study, it is important to note that Oprah frames her civil rights subject, the Little Rock Nine, according to her own thoughts and feelings. She cannot help but feel moved as she prepares for the show's taping and these feelings lead her to a question that demonstrates her empathy—would *she* have done the same? At one level, this framing is a standard aspect of Oprah's rhetoric and persona. Sheryl Wilson argues that Oprah's "practice of sharing private experience . . . broaden[s] the base for a power that is political" (qtd. in Decker 171). Janice Peck agrees that Oprah employs an explicitly emotional aesthetic, but Peck is more critical, arguing that Oprah's power is not so much cultural as ideological ("Talk About Racism"; "TV Talk Shows"). Her rhetoric taps into America's civil religious faith and belief in individualism. Both Peck and Wilson offer persuasive arguments, but I suggest that at least this episode of the *Oprah Winfrey Show* subsumes or, more accurately, replaces an ideology of individual participation and rights with an emotional practice of sympathetic relations. Put differently, Oprah uses the fortieth anniversary of the integration of Central High School to conduct a secular-religious service in which the white students of that institution are granted the opportunity to atone for their sins and obtain absolution. The purpose of this service is not just to resolve past guilt for those who are present but also to instruct her television audience on the proper moral duties of the sentimental citizen.

Each of the three white students who appeared on the Oprah show was given an opportunity to apologize for her or his past actions, but the story of David Sontag is distinctive because he explained, or tried to explain, the reasons for his behavior. After Oprah introduced Sontag, Sontag explained that in 1957 he had harassed Minnijean Brown Trickey because some of his white classmates had dared him to do so. Sontag was remorseful, but he quickly explained that "it was not done, ah, it was not done out of hate. It was done out of ignorance, out of not understanding her plight." The video quickly cuts to a clip of the 2005 Oprah reflecting back on the 1996 episode. She says, "What is so interesting to me about that comment is that that is the root of all racism, actually." She continues, "I understood that it was all because of ignorance, and that is the sole reason why the Little Rock Nine could move on with their lives and forgive, because if it was just pure hatred there would be no way to forgive. . . . It is the same thing that Jesus said on the cross, 'forgive them for they know not what they do,' they know not what they do."

If, as Sontag evinces and Oprah reaffirms, the fundamental problem that the Little Rock Nine encountered when they integrated Central High School was ignorance, it might be useful for us to ask the question, what, precisely, was the source of that ignorance? Did the white students not hear about the famous *Brown v. Board of Education* decision? Did they not get the school memo that said, "Be prepared, we are integrating the high school next week?" No, of course not. The ignorance that allegedly caused a year of torment for the Little Rock Nine did not stem from a lack of informational knowledge. The answer to our question can be found if we ask a different set of questions. Since clearly Oprah's role is to resolve the show's conflict, that is, the ignorance that motivates racism, we might ask ourselves, "What is the lesson that Oprah is prepared to teach?" As the episode unfolds it becomes apparent that this instructor is not offering a history lesson, nor is she explaining the complex economic, cultural, and social systems that sustain racism. As numerous studies of her "therapeutic" rhetoric have demonstrated, Oprah's specialty is the emotions. Her expertise is with the cultural rhetoric of feeling. We can deduce, then, that the conflict that demands resolution, the "ignorance" that led to Sontag's racist behavior, was actually a deficiency in his emotional capacity, his emotive knowledge. Sontag lacked the appropriate level of sympathetic understanding. This, of course, is precisely the kind of education that Oprah can provide, and it, along with her reference to Jesus Christ and the lessons of forgiveness, situate her moral authority squarely in the realm of sentimentalism.

It is at this point that the staging of this drama merits discussion. At the episode's start, seven of the nine adults who integrated Central High School occupy the stage alone. Quickly, however, the show introduces a white student, then Robin Woods, and we are told that in 1957 this woman moved her desk next to Terrence Roberts to share her algebra book. Roberts, now a tall, distinguished-looking African American man, informs the audience that this benevolent act made Robin and her white family the targets of harassment. Robin Woods is, quite literally, the antithesis of David Sontag. In 1957, she demonstrated the socially appropriate degree of sentiment and acted accordingly, befriending at least one of the terrorized students. I posit that this moment is important for the show's moral drama. Prior to this point, the mostly white audience in Oprah's studio and those watching in their living rooms at home have no representation on the stage. They may feel some sympathy for the Little Rock students as they share their recollections of that first awful year, but, prior to this point, the white audience has no access to the stage, no place among the chosen seven. Now, though, with the arrival of Robin, the group on the stage shifts. Its "collective identity" is now interracial, and the white audience has the opportunity to rephrase the question that Oprah posed earlier, "Would I have had the courage to endure the taunts of my friends and support these black students as Robin did?" In addition to providing an opportunity for identification, Robin represents a citizenship that is analogous to the sentimental subjectivity that Bill Clinton embodied as a young boy of seventeen. She demonstrates the ideal, a level of empathy that others should strive to emulate. Additional evidence for Robin's past moral courage and sentimental nature can be found in a roundtable discussion that NBC aired in October of 1957. On that program she states,

> When Elisabeth [Eckford] had to walk down in front of the school I was there and I saw that. And may I say, I was very ashamed—I felt like crying—because she was so brave when she did that. . . . I think if we had had any sort of decency, we wouldn't have acted that way. But I think if everyone would just obey the Golden Rule . . . [that] might be the solution. ("NBC Roundtable Discussion")

If, as a virtual member of Oprah's audience, you think that you could say, "Yes, I would have behaved as a true citizen of sentiment, I would have reached out to these students despite the cost," then, like Robin Woods, you would gain access to the community, you would have a place on Oprah's stage. But what if your answer to the rhetorical question is, "No, I would not have supported these black students in their struggle for equality": What if in your honesty you admit that you would not have felt their pain or, at least, not sufficiently enough to act on the relational lessons that sentiment provides? Well, then you would be seated in the front row with the tormentors, not with the chosen on the stage. But even this status is not permanent, as we learn when Oprah's show moves toward its final resolution.

In the episode's climactic scene, Melba Pattillo Beals tells David Sontag that she had never forgotten his smiles, eyes, and catcalls. Oprah asks if Beals remembers him because he was "not nice" to her. Beals responds, "He was insidious, because he was continuous, he was like relentless, he never gave up, it wasn't like he did this one day, it was like every day. And he never really, ah, hit or anything but I always expected him to, and he was just always there and he had the most vibrant eyes and he really frightened me, because every day he was there, every day." As Beals is speaking, the television audience sees cut shots of Sontag's reaction to this testimony. His face is tight; his mouth wavers between a smile and a grimace. His eyes do look very intense, and he is clearly uncomfortable listening to the testimony that he caused real pain and terror to the students he harassed. Oprah then asks those who are seated on the stage, "Does his apology mean anything to you?" Minnijean Brown Trickey begins to respond, "Yes, a lot," but her reply is rendered mute. Sontag does not wait for an invitation, but, spontaneously, leaves his seat, crosses the stage, and embraces Trickey. The audience applauds and Trickey, who was crying earlier, pats him on the shoulders and says, "Don't worry about it; don't worry about it."

Here, in this emotionally honest yet staged moment, redemption is secured. Watching the episode it is difficult not to conclude that Sontag experienced real emotional turmoil and desired a personal reconciliation with Trickey and the other black students. At the same time, it is equally evident that this is the moment that Oprah and her producers have anticipated. The show's theme is both commemoration and reconciliation, after all, and Sontag faithfully fulfills the role required by this moral drama. He acts on behalf of not just himself but also on behalf of all "fallen whites," who once failed to fulfill the responsibilities of the sentimental citizen. Now, in the present commemoration of the past, another opportunity arises, emotional redemption is possible, and citizenship is renewed. Neither Sontag nor the white audience need fear the moment of reconciliation, because black Americans are forgiving and the emotional discomfort that accompanies an apology is only temporary. Afterward everyone has access to the stage.

There is a compelling backstory to the moment I have described. Although Sontag is the one who receives absolution from Minnijean Brown Trickey, it was actually Minnijean who paid the price. She never graduated from Central High School. In 1958, school officials expelled her for pouring a bowl of chili on the head of a white youth who had been torturing her. In fact, the original altercation for which she forgives Sontag was, ironically, an act of retaliation. Sontag targeted Trickey as a reprisal for her defiance. I doubt that the audience who watched the emotional reconciliation between this black woman and white man ever appreciated this part of the moral drama: It is better to control your emotions, to suppress your rage and forgive the individual who has wronged you than to resist and confront the evil of men.

The Rhetorical Norms of Civil Rights Commemoration

So, what can these case studies tell us about the present status of rhetoric and race in the American experience? Well, if they are isolated from the larger rhetorical culture then probably not much. But, if we are willing to entertain for the sake of argument that they are indicative of the kind of sentimentalism that now surrounds the civil rights movement generally, then perhaps there is much to say. In Edwin Black's famous critique of sentimentalism, he calls the form didactic. He says, "It not only elicits affective experiences, it also defines and delimits them. It enables the emotions to be given a recreation under sanctions auspices" (189). For Black, nineteenth-century rhetors used sentimentalism to escape the social realities that they feared to face. While I understand some of the concerns raised in Black's critique, I agree with Stephen Hartnett that sentimentalism is a complex productive expression of culture and moral authority that constitutes communities and prescribes action as well as pleasure. Sentimentalism was instrumental in the transition from U.S. colonies into a fledgling republic. It was a powerful force in the domestic and moral reform spheres of the mid-nineteenth century. It is being used today to project an interracial world of friendly relations where blacks and whites perform the rituals of commemoration and, in the process, overcome racism. My point here is not to reenact the traditional condemnation of sentimentalism, which is too often motivated by patriarchal expectations of what constitutes appropriate public argument, but to ask, "What sort of citizenry does the sentimentalism of contemporary civil rights memorial produce?" To begin to answer this question, I would like to return to the event with which I started.

In the days that followed the memorial service for Coretta Scott King, the news media buzzed with discussions about whether statements by Reverend Joseph Lowery and former President Jimmy Carter were inappropriate. In a section of his speech that addressed the war in Iraq, Lowery declared, "We know now there were no weapons of mass destruction. . . . But Coretta knew, and we knew there were weapons of misdirection right here." Later in the speech the civil rights veteran said, "Millions without health insurance, poverty abound. For war billions more, but no more for the poor." President Carter's comments were less direct. His claim that Coretta Scott King and her husband knew what it was to be "violated" by "government wiretapping and government surveillance" was interpreted as a critique of the administration's domestic surveillance program. He also added that the struggle for equal rights was not over. "All we have to do is remember the color of the faces in Louisiana, Mississippi and Alabama, those who were most devastated by [Hurricane] Katrina" (Torpy and Saporta 6). These sentences occupied barely a few moments of the many hours of the memorial service, yet in the days that followed the media and part of the American public began to take sides (Parker; Mathis). As this debate played itself out in the press, the primary question that everyone seemed to be asking was, were the comments indecorous, were they inappropriate for the epideictic occasion (Dewan and Bumiller; Noonan)?

I believe that how you answer this question depends, at least in part, on your position relative to the sentimental society created by modern civil rights commemoration. For those individuals who have invested in its ideas and norms of discursive behavior the comments of Lowery and Carter were indecorous precisely because they challenged the assumption that we have achieved a truly empathetic community or that such a community was ever the primary goal of the civil rights movement. Furthermore, Lowery and Carter's criticisms of President Bush transgressed an important rule of the sentimental society—one must not question the behavior or motivations of anyone who has declared his citizenship within the sentimental society. That kind of critique should be reserved for men and women who have not participated in the civil rights movement by embracing the emotional rituals that signal its triumph.

In a letter to the editor of the *Washington Post*, Franklyn J. Selzer stated:

> [A]s an active participant during the years of struggle for equality and civil rights and as someone for whom the outcome of that struggle meant a great victory, I watched the funeral ceremonies for Coretta Scott King with great interest and reverence. . . . The injection of mean-spirited political attacks by former President Carter and the Rev. Joseph Lowery clearly was out of place. It showed a tragic pettiness and lack of class. Martin Luther King and Mrs. King helped black Americans through love and wisdom, never by race baiting. Too many Democrats, to their shame, repeat the same tired lies over and over, lies that divide us—white from black. They distort history in an awful way. Race-baiting is ugliness of the worst kind. Its basis is false, and it had no place at a funeral for one of America's foremost protagonists for unity and equality. (9)

Although we do not know this individual, the words of his letter reveal him to be a full citizen of the sentimental community. The civil rights movement is a cherished part of his memory, perhaps because of his involvement it was successful in its aims and should be remembered fondly. Carter and Lowery's comments were inappropriate not just because they mixed the seemingly deliberative topic within an epideictic moment. They were "petty" and "classless" because they did not reflect the appropriate attitude and disposition that the sentimental community demands.

One significant problem with this editorial and with the sentimental society generally is that they don't provide a complete picture of what the civil rights movement was or even, for that matter, what its protagonists did. Coretta Scott King was a refined woman and a southern lady. At her funeral, many of the personal tributes of her friends and family emphasized how kind, loving, and forgiving she was. In 1970, for example, she visited Cesar Chavez after he had been jailed for defying a court injunction against boycotting. This, most certainly, is precisely the kind of action that a sentimental view of civil rights would embrace. But note that there was another side to Mrs. King. She also spoke to the United Farm Workers' Union about the problems that they faced despite a growing economy and prosperity. In that speech she said, "Social progress has always come when the people on the bottom, who in organized strength and from the foundation, shook the whole structure. Social change does not come from voluntary good will and charity from the top. It comes from motion at the bottom" (355). In this passage Mrs. King warns her audience that significant social change does not result from benevolence; it is not the consequence of sentiment.

Now, let's put our cards on the table, shall we? I happen to agree with Mrs. King; however, I want to add that benevolence and empathy are typically better than hatred and violence. I am sufficiently pragmatic as well as rhetorically savvy to respect the fact that the memorialization of the civil rights movement, even in its sentimental forms, reshapes our democracy in ways that we cannot see, but that is yet helpful. My point is not to reject sentiment or memorialization. It is, instead, to warn against its reign as the sole political language that the American public is willing to accept whenever race and politics are discussed. My concern is that the public is not only reluctant to listen to the hard yet essential critiques that resulted from the civil rights movement, but also that we have found a way to avoid those critiques while simultaneously embracing the movement through a sentimental experience of its memory.

Mrs. King once said,

> If this nation can produce a trillion dollars every year, it is a disgrace in the eyes of God that some people should be haunted by hunger and hounded by racism. The President of the United States should not gloat and take pride in a trillion dollar economy. He should be ashamed and mortified to acknowledge that abundance exists while the system producing it still cheats the poor. His days should be restless until the crime and violence of poverty is rooted out of the land rich beyond imagination. (356)

These are words that we still need to hear. May we never live in a democracy when such words and acts of brave confrontation are driven from the public forum in favor of sentiment and feeling.

Notes

[1] All details concerning the memorial service for Coretta Scott King have been gathered from newspaper reports and the service's official program. Although various copies of the program exist on the Internet, I have used the following: "Celebrating Her Spirit: Coretta Scott King."

[2] The events listed in this paragraph were determined by reviewing twelve months worth of the article "In Brief" as published in *The Crisis*. Not every memorial event identified in *The Crisis* was listed.

[3] Burstein argues that the decline of manly sentiment stemmed from at least three factors. The man of feeling was easily lampooned in an society that was democratizing. Sensibility had become boring because it was so conventional. Sensibility, at least at the individual level, was insufficiently pragmatic to thrive in an environment of economic competition (308–11).

Works Cited

Armada, Bernard J. "Memorial Agon: An Interpretive Tour of the National Civil Rights Museum." *Southern Communication Journal* 63.3 (1998): 235–43.

Baym, Nina. "Women's Novels and Women's Minds: An Unsentimental View of Nineteenth-Century American Women's Fiction." *Novel: A Forum of Fiction* 31.3 (1998): 335–50.

Biesecker, Barbara A. "Remembering World War II: The Rhetoric and Politics of National Commemoration at the Turn of the 21st Century." *Quarterly Journal of Speech* 88.4 (2002): 393–409.

Black, Edwin. "The Sentimental Style as Escapism, or the Devil with Dan'l Webster." *Form and Genre: Shaping Rhetorical Action.* Ed. Karlyn Kohrs Campbell and Kathleen Hall Jamieson. Falls Church, VA: Speech Communication Association, 1978.

Blair, Carole, and Neil Michel. "Reproducing Civil Rights Tactics: The Rhetorical Performance of the Civil Rights Memorial." *Rhetoric Society Quarterly* 30 (2000): 31–55.

Blight, David W. *Race and Reunion: The Civil War in American Memory.* Cambridge, MA: Belknap P, 2003. 512. <http://www.lib.umn.edu/slog.phtml?url=http://hdl.handle.net/2027/heb.03945>.

Browne, Stephen. "'Like Gory Specters': Representing Evil in Theodore Weld's 'American Slavery as It Is.'" *Quarterly Journal of Speech* 80 (1994): 277–92.

Burstein, Andrew. *Sentimental Democracy: The Evolution of America's Romantic Self-Image.* New York: Hill and Wang, 1999.

Carrier, Jim. *A Traveler's Guide to the Civil Rights Movement.* New York: Harcourt, 2004.

"Celebrating Her Spirit: Coretta Scott King." PDF file. The official program in celebration of the life of Coretta Scott King. 1 May 2006. <http://cobbnow.org/CorettaScott-King-CelebratingHerSpirit.pdf>.

Chapman, Mary, and Glenn Hendler. *Sentimental Men: Masculinity and the Politics of Affect in American Culture.* Berkeley: U of California P, 1999.

Chappell, Kevin. "Hail and Farewell to Coretta Scott King." *Ebony* 61.6 (2006): 186.

Clinton, William Jefferson. "Remarks on the 35th Anniversary of the March on Washington in Oak Bluffs, Massachusetts." *Weekly Compilation of Presidential Documents* 23 Aug. 1998: 1660–64.

Copeland, Larry. "Civil Rights Icon Dies at 78." *USA Today* 1 Feb. 2006, first ed., sec. A: 1.

———. "Thousands Pay Joyous Tribute at King's Funeral." *USA Today* 8 Feb. 2006.

Davis, Townsend. *Weary Feet, Rested Souls: A Guided History of the Civil Rights Movement.* New York: W.W. Norton, 1998.

Decker, Jeffrey Louis. "Saint Oprah." *Modern Fiction Studies* 52.1 (2006): 169–78.

Dewan, Shaila, and Elisabeth Bumiller. "At Mrs. King's Funeral, a Mix of Elegy and Politics." *New York Times* 8 Feb. 2006, late ed., sec. A: 1, 18.

Dewan, Shaila K. "Civil Rights Battlegrounds Enter World of Tourism." *New York Times* 10 Aug. 2004, late ed., sec. A: 1, 19.

Duncan, Alice Faye, and J. Gerard Smith. *The National Civil Rights Museum Celebrates Everyday People.* Mahwah, NJ: Troll Communications, 1996.

Evers-Williams, Myrlie. "A Long Way to Go." *USA Today* 23 Feb. 2005, sec. A: 13a.

Farr, Cecilia Konchar. *Reading Oprah: How Oprah's Book Club Changed the Way America Reads.* Albany: State U of New York P, 2005.

Fern, Fanny. *Ruth Hall: A Domestic Tale of the Present Time.* New York: Mason Brothers, 1855.

Gallagher, Victoria. "Remembering Together: Rhetorical Integration and the Case of the Martin Luther King, Jr. Memorial." *Southern Communication Journal* 60.2 (1995): 109–19.

Goodman, Brenda. "Mourners Line up for Mrs. King." *New York Times* 7 Feb. 2006, late ed., sec. A: 13.

Hartnett, Stephen. "Fanny Fern's 1855 *Ruth Hall*, the Cheerful Brutality of Capitalism, & the Irony of Sentimental Rhetoric." *Quarterly Journal of Speech* 88.1 (2002): 1–18.

Hasian, Marouf, Jr. "Remembering and Forgetting the 'Final Solution': A Rhetorical Pilgrimage through the U.S. Holocaust Memorial Museum." *Critical Studies in Media Communication* 21.1 (2004): 64–92.

King, Coretta Scott. "The Right to a Decent Life and Human Dignity." *The Rhetoric of Struggle: Public Address by African American Women*. Ed. Robbie Jean Walker. New York: Garland, 1992. 353–56.

King, Martin Luther, Jr. "I Have a Dream." *A Testament of Hope: The Essential Writings of Martin Luther King, Jr.* Ed. James Melvin Washington. San Francisco: Harper & Row, 1986. 217–20.

Klinkner, Philip A., and Rogers M. Smith. *The Unsteady March: The Rise and Decline of Racial Equality in America*. Chicago: U of Chicago P, 1999.

Lewis, John, and Michael D'Orso. *Walking with the Wind: A Memoir of the Movement*. New York: Simon & Schuster, 1998.

Mackenzie, Henry. *The Man of Feeling*. Litchfield, CT: Thomas Collier, 1790.

Mathis, Greg. "Honor King by Continuing Her Legacy." *Atlanta Inquirer* 18 Feb. 2006: 4.

"NBC Roundtable Discussion with Central High School Students." Little Rock, 1957. Transcript. Facing History and Ourselves 20 May 1996. <http://www.facinghistorycampus.og/CTP/ctp.nsf/All+Docs/CTP+Crisis+Connections+NBC2?>.

Noonan, Peggy. "Four Presidents and a Funeral." *Wall Street Journal* 10 Feb. 2006, eastern ed., sec. A: 18.

Oldenburg, Ann. "The Divine Miss Winfrey?" *USA Today* 11 May 2006, sec. D: 1.

Parker, Star. "Funeral Became Political Soapbox." *Cincinnati Post* 11 Feb. 2006, sec. A: 14.

Parry-Giles, Shawn, and Trevor Parry-Giles. "Collective Memory, Political Nostalgia, and the Rhetorical Presidency: Bill Clinton's Commemoration of the March on Washington, August 28, 1998." *Quarterly Journal of Speech* 86 (2000): 417–37.

Peck, Janice. "Talk About Racism: Framing a Popular Discourse of Race on *Oprah Winfrey*." *Cultural Critique* 27 (1994): 89–126.

———. "TV Talk Shows as Therapeutic Discourse: The Ideological Labor of the Televised Talking Cure." *Communication Theory* 5.1 (1995): 58–81.

Reed, T. V. *The Art of Protest: Culture and Activism from the Civil Rights Movement to the Streets of Seattle*. Minneapolis, MN: U of Minnesota P, 2005.

Romano, Renee Christine, and Leigh Raiford, eds. *The Civil Rights Movement in American Memory*. Athens: U of Georgia P, 2006.

Rowson, Susanna. *Charlotte Temple*. New York: Twayne, 1964.

Selzer, Franklyn J. "Letter to The Editor." *Washington Times* 9 Feb. 2006, sec. A: 20.

Stowe, Harriet Beecher, Raymond M. Weaver, and Miguel Covarrubias. *Uncle Tom's Cabin, or, Life among the Lowly*. New York: Heritage Press, 1938.

Tatum, Wilbert A. "And a Good Time Was Had by All?" *New York Amsterdam News* 9 Feb. 2006: 12.

Terry, Joseph C., and Oprah Winfrey. *Oprah Winfrey Show: 20th Anniversary*. DVD. Paramount Home Video, 2005.

Tompkins, Jane P. *Sensational Designs: The Cultural Work of American Fiction, 1790–1860*. New York: Oxford UP, 1986.

Torpy, Bill, and Maria Saporta. "A Portrait of Dignity: 1927–2006; Coretta Scott King; Political Jabs Pepper Funeral Oratory." *Atlanta Journal-Constitution* 8 Feb. 2006, sec. A: 6.

Weld, Theodore Dwight. *American Slavery As It Is: Testimony of a Thousand Witnesses*. New York: American Anti-Slavery Society, 1839.

Wilson, Kirt H. "Interpreting the Discursive Field of the Montgomery Bus Boycott: Martin Luther King Jr.'s Holt Street Address." *Rhetoric & Public Affairs* 8.2 (2005): 299–326.

Religion and Rhetoric

Reason, Emotion, and the Sensory in Religious Persuasion

3

Patricia Bizzell

Aristotle is supposed to have said, "No one uses fine language when teaching geometry." Actually, this does sound just like something you might say in the heat of the moment in class to clarify a point by shaving off the subtleties with which you usually hedge it around. Have you ever looked at your students' class notes? It can be a humbling experience! I've found that often, important words like "tends to" are missing—or even "not."

This saying of Aristotle's has come to emblemize the supposed conflict between rhetoric and philosophy. As this conflict is usually dramatized, rhetoric has only to do with "fine language," or superfluous ornamentation, whereas philosophy aspires to truths as certain as those of "geometry." Stanley Fish says rhetoric deals with "knowledge, which because it flows from some or other system of belief, is incomplete and partial (in the sense of biased)" and, because its object is primarily to promote one particular, partisan perspective, employs language that is either sinisterly manipulative or sportively playful (474). On the other hand, Fish says, philosophy aspires to "knowledge as it exists apart from any and all systems of belief" and employs language that only "faithfully reflects or reports on matters of fact" (474). As is well known, thinkers from Plato to Bishop Sprat have questioned the use of persuasive language in transmitting what are supposed to be absolute truths, whether philosophical or scientific.

However, if these truths migrate from one human head to another not via a Vulcan mind-meld but via language, then language is involved in how they are made to be understood. What is language to do in this instance? Only to convey so many things in so many words, as Bishop Sprat recommends? If so, this presumes that one needs to do no more than lay out the rational proposition clearly in order to induce adherence. But of course, history is full of examples in which eminently rational exposition did not win the day; I have just analyzed one such instance in a recent article on the Barcelona disputation of 1263 between Rabbi Nachmanides and Friar Pablo Christiani.

Indeed, nowadays the idea that any discourse could be purely rational is generally regarded as what J. J. Murphy has called the "Platonic rhetorical her-

40

esy" (qtd. in Olmsted 65). We don't expect language that only reports facts; we fully anticipate that all intellectual exchange will involve persuasion to some degree—even, as Thomas Kuhn has shown, in the natural sciences. Because we no longer oppose rhetoric and philosophy in the way I've just outlined, we are comfortable with the idea that all of our knowledge is essentially rhetorical. But here's something interesting: while we academics have no problem accepting that philosophical and scientific truths are constructed and conveyed rhetorically, many of us have not made the same adjustment concerning another set of once-absolute truths, namely, the truths of religion. Where the truths of religion are concerned, many of us are the most extreme, scornful skeptics—at least when we are wearing our mortarboards. When we don other hats, we may be religious believers ourselves. But the rhetorical analysis of religious belief processes has languished. I agree with Walter Jost when he says: "Arrival at religious belief involves the same sort of rhetorical methods and arguments as arrival at nonreligious belief and suggests the speciousness of the widespread academic dismissal of such religious faith as otiose (if not odious)" (101).

The function of rhetoric in religion, then, may not be merely to "convey" truths already established. A more complex view can be found from the foundational moment of Christian rhetoric, in the work of Augustine, as Wendy Olmsted has shown. Augustine is usually seen as subordinating rhetoric to religious truth, taking the view that, as she puts it, "Serious study of religion or theology or plain faith yields the truths that rhetoric must then propagate" (66). But Olmsted's careful reading of Augustine's *Confessions* shows that the development of his own religious faith was a highly rhetorical process. In Olmsted's words:

> Deliberation and consideration are pivotal for Augustine's discovery of religious faith in the authority of Scripture. . . . Rhetorical persuasion becomes an important instrument for Augustine in thinking through what can be believed and what cannot (75). . . . Deliberative conflict emerges into discovery only through the combination of reading, listening, meditating, and being moved rhetorically (78). . . . Augustine's insistence on the brief and often mediated character of the human knowledge of God emphasizes the need for rhetorical tropes through which to apprehend him. (81)

Augustine once desired to be as certain of the truths of religion as he was that three plus seven equals ten, a truth of geometry as it were (qtd. in Boyle 92)—but this was before his conversion. After it, he understood that religious truth, or perhaps we should say rhetorically warranted religious belief, was a matter of accepting probabilities. Jost has described Christian theology itself as a rhetorical activity concerning probabilities (see 105). To ask for certainty and to reject rhetoric as a proper theological method, according to Marjorie O'Rourke Boyle, "betrays a servile fear, the fear of punishment, of damnation, that error and sin provoke," thus leading the postulant to demand a "mathematical equation" as a "model for discourse" (92). Rather, she says, the believer learns to risk the mess of rhetoric, because "did not the Creator risk the mess of the Original Sin, then redeem it in divine charity? It was this spiritual generosity that found its methodological complement in the 'open hand' of rhetoric" (93).

Once rhetoric thus becomes an acceptable methodology for theology, it is not surprising that Christian thinkers following Augustine developed sacred rhetoric that conjoined, rather than opposed, rhetoric and truth, emotion and reason. Debora Shuger has amply demonstrated this tendency in sacred rhetorics of the Renaissance, about which she has this to say:

> The sacred rhetorics (and, in general, Augustinian Christianity) set affective inwardness over dispassionate intellection. Yet—and this is the crucial point—they do so in a way that links rather than opposes emotion and reason. That is, they do not treat rhetoric's power to move the heart and will as separate, or even separable, from the procedures of rational inquiry. . . . Rather, these texts typically insist on the ineluctable "interwovenness" of cognitive and emotional experience. . . . We feel fear, for example, because we judge that danger is imminent. Emotion is therefore bound up with argument; the orator moves by giving reasons. (54)

Jost has suggested that such an approach to religious persuasion does not refute the skeptics but rather, puts them in their "place, subsumed by a larger 'place' of publicly available criteria and acknowledgements" (118). Such rhetorical processes can proceed, he says, "in recognition of our always partial grasp of what we call the real, acknowledging others and the form of life and world we share, staking our all on them and it, while refusing to pretend to completeness or, skeptically, to despair about our limits" (119). The very process of judging the merit of good reasons is socially conditioned in this view, all we have, but, or therefore, sufficient to the task.

This lightning review of the ideas of some important contemporary thinkers on religion and rhetoric has been meant to introduce some analytic premises, to wit:

- Whatever the nature of the divine may be, it can be known only imperfectly by humans; we may believe, but we cannot know, the absolute truth about it.
- To arrive at a warrantable belief in religious truths, we may use rhetorical processes—indeed, this is our only pathway unless vouchsafed a mystical vision.
- These rhetorical processes require acknowledgement that rational appeals alone cannot effect commitment; the emotions must also be engaged.
- These rhetorical processes also require acknowledgement that persuasion takes place within human community, so that interlocutors' cultural frames of reference, psychological predispositions, and more must be taken into account.

So far, however, my examples have all been taken from scholarship on the Christian tradition of sacred rhetoric. In the remainder of my remarks today, I want to try to apply these premises derived from work on Christian rhetoric to Jewish religious rhetorical practice, and specifically, to the work of Moses Mendelssohn. I hope the example will enrich current discussions of sacred rhetoric, and enlarge our understanding of how to deal with religion in the academy as well.

First: who was Moses Mendelssohn? Born in Prussia in 1729, he was one of the first European Jews to receive a secular education. Influenced by Spinoza and the German Christian Enlightenment thinkers, especially Wolff and Lessing, Mendelssohn became a kind of poster boy for the Enlightenment contention that all humans—even Jews—had basic human qualities, abilities, and rights. Befriended by all the leading scholars, and noted for his own work on natural theology, Mendelssohn became the target of an increasingly aggressive program to convert him to Christianity. It was not credited that such an enlightened man could remain a Jew. In spite of his views on universal natural religion, however, Mendelssohn also remained committed to traditional Jewish ritual practice and the study of Talmud and Kabbalah; the great medieval rabbi Maimonides influenced him as much as his contemporary Enlightenment colleagues. Mendelssohn's major work of philosophy, published in 1783, three years before his death, is entitled *Jerusalem*, and it defends Jewish ritual observance as a necessary rhetorical process of faith keeping. (For a good introduction to Mendelssohn, see Meyer.)

Looking at the opening paragraphs of *Jerusalem*, I see intertwined the social and epistemological dilemmas Mendelssohn faced. He begins by talking about the difficulty of achieving the proper balance between civil and ecclesiastical power in the state. I imagine that he has in mind the situation of Jews in Enlightenment Europe, when secular authorities were moving, albeit by fits and starts, to accord full civil rights to Jews, whose religion stood as a bar to their full participation in the minds of many. This is a problem, to be sure; but in a way, it is a good kind of problem to have, because it means that the old restrictions are breaking up and people are groping for new ways of organizing their social life.

Mendelssohn transitions quickly to a discussion of the situation in which "despotism," whether secular or religious, holds sway. "It has," he says, "a definite answer to every question" (34). He is talking about total state control, admitting no political dissent, but, I think, also about that sort of moral universe in which all questions are answered, that is, the moral universe that supposedly existed before the Enlightenment undermined traditional sources of meaning. From his vantage point in 1783, he understands that the total political control and moral order that seemed to prevail once upon a time comprised only the calm that "prevails during the evening in a fortress which is to be taken by storm during the night" (34), and as a good son of the Enlightenment, he has to be on the side of the besiegers because they fight in the name of rationality and liberty. He notes, however, "as soon as liberty dares to move anything in this systematic structure, ruin immediately threatens on all sides; and in the end, one no longer knows what will remain standing" (34).

It is, indeed, unsettling to live in times when the old verities, along with the old social orders, are breaking up. Much as one may welcome the new opportunities, it also feels as if some sort of "ruin" is at hand.

To save religion from the potential "ruin" of the Enlightenment, Mendelssohn must be able to present its core values as rational. Thus, he divides religion into two main parts. One part comprises the "eternal truths" of religion that are accessible to all mentally normal humans in all times and places if they exercise their reason. Mendelssohn says: "I . . . do not believe that the powers of human reason are insufficient to persuade men of the eternal truths which are indispensable to human felicity and that God had to reveal them in a supernatural manner" (94). In other words, revelation cannot be necessary because such a state of affairs would not be fair: a just God must provide all humans access to the saving truths, not just those humans whom the prophets or messiahs have visited. Therefore, the universal human faculty of reason is called into service. And what does reason reveal? According to Mendelssohn, reason reveals the tenets of the "universal *religion of mankind*" (97, italics in original), one of which is that a God exists, "'the eternal, your God, the necessary, independent being, omnipotent and omniscient, that recompenses men in a future life according to their deeds'" (97).

Mendelssohn argued that this "universal religion" became apparent to people who used their reason to contemplate the human condition and the workings of nature—it's a sort of eighteenth-century version of the "intelligent design" argument. The argument is important to him in his time and place because it appeared to provide a common moral ground upon which adherents of all religions could stand, and if such a common moral ground did exist, then the legal exclusion of Jews from Christian civil society began not to make sense. Indeed, Mendelssohn's student David Friedlaender was so taken with the universal appeal of this outline of religion that he proposed to the chief Protestant theologian of Berlin that he, Friedlaender, be allowed to convert to Christianity (and thus escape the civil penalties still leveled against Jews) if he professed faith in this universal creed alone. The notion that Jesus was the Son of God, in Friedlaender's view, was a mere inessential dogma that could be discarded among intelligent people.

Mendelssohn, who died before Friedlaender pursued this course, would have been appalled to know about it. Mendelssohn had multiple concerns in his arguments about religion. Yes, he was interested in saving it from the potential "ruin" of the Enlightenment, instantiated, for example, in the vague, elitist panentheism promoted by Spinoza, whose work Mendelssohn knew well. He was therefore at pains to establish some basic truths about God and God's relationship to humans that, he believed, could be demonstrated rationally. In this he differs from the contemporary thinkers on religion and rhetoric whose work I sketched earlier, who typically regard the divine nature as unknowable. But Mendelssohn did not put his major emphasis on this argument. Closer to his heart, and to his own lifelong religious practice, were the ritual observances particular to Judaism.

Therefore, Mendelssohn devoted most of *Jerusalem* to examining a second essential part of religion, namely its dogmas and rituals. These, obviously, vary from time to time and place to place, and differ, as we see, in the world's different religions. In Mendelssohn's view, Judaism is relatively free from dogmas; that is, beyond the "eternal truths" recommended to all humans by their rational faculty, there is little that one must believe in order to be a good Jew. Judaism, however, does prescribe a panoply of actions via the ritual laws governing kashrut, Shabbat, etc. They are difficult to defend, not only because in many of their details they seem irrationally arbitrary, but also because they are the activities that most mark Jews out as different from Christians, inflaming the European climate of anti-Semitism in which Mendelssohn lived. The ritual laws literally separate Jews from Christians. Jews who observe kashrut cannot eat at a Christian's table; Jews who observe Shabbat cannot attend a business meeting on Saturday. Yet, fully aware of these difficulties, Mendelssohn exhorted his fellow Jews to uphold Jewish ritual practice. I believe his reason for doing so is essentially rhetorical.

Mendelssohn's primary defense of ritual observance is that it connects people to the eternal truths and thus serves a pedagogical function. If a ritual law does not in itself seem rational, nevertheless observing it may be the rational thing to do, if by doing so, one strengthens one's hold on the eternal truth it suggests:

> Although the divine book that we received through Moses is, strictly speaking, meant to be a book of laws containing ordinances, rules of life and prescriptions, it also includes, as is well known, an inexhaustible treasure of rational truths and religious doctrines which are so intimately connected with the laws that they form but one entity. All laws refer to, or are based upon, eternal truths of reason, or remind us of them, and rouse us to ponder them. Hence our rabbis rightly say: the laws and doctrines are related to each other, like body and soul. (99)

This argument seeks to attach a rational defense to ritual observance, but it also does more. Another kind of argument is going on here. Mendelssohn was also concerned with how people learn to use religion to make sense of their lives. He believed that people would have a much easier time of grasping the eternal truths that give life meaning if they were "reminded" of them and "roused to ponder them" via the concrete, social practices of ritual observance, which affect the minute details of daily life—such as how one prepares a chicken for the pot—and which are practiced communally—since one needs a more experienced cook to help prepare the chicken.

I noted earlier that Mendelssohn represented the central truths of religion as accessible to reason alone. But that is not quite right. Reason may access these truths without the aid of direct revelation, but this does not mean that it needs no aid at all. Indeed, in arguing against the use of excommunication as a punishment for heterodox ideas, Mendelssohn said:

> [T]he most essential purpose of religious society is *mutual edification*. By
> the magic power of sympathy, one wishes to transfer truth from the mind
> to the heart; to vivify, by participation with others, the concepts of rea-
> son, which at times are lifeless, into soaring sensations. When the heart
> clings too strongly to sensual pleasures to listen to the voice of reason,
> when it is on the verge of ensnaring reason itself, then let it be seized here
> with a tremor of pious enthusiasm, kindled by the fire of devotion, and
> acquainted with the joys of a higher order which outweigh even in this
> life the joys of the senses. (74, italics in original)

True, Mendelssohn is speaking specifically here about how participation in
communal religious life can edify the overly sensual person who needs the
energy of emotions such as "enthusiasm," "devotion," and "joy" to activate
attention to the "voice of reason." But such edification is offered by religious
organizations to all their members, not only the potentially apostate, making
me think that for Mendelssohn, this sort of assistance is useful for everyone,
not only those who are in some way deficient in their thinking. I would argue,
moreover, that it is essentially a rhetorical sort of assistance. "[Transferring]
truth from the mind to the heart" (as Mendelssohn describes the process of
achieving religious conviction) sounds much like the "[insistence] on the
ineluctable 'interwovenness' of cognitive and emotional experience" that
Shuger found in Renaissance Christian sacred rhetorics.

Moreover, committing to this sort of "edification" will involve one in
processes of "reading, listening, meditating, and being moved rhetorically,"
such as Olmsted discovered at the roots of Augustine's religious life. This
becomes clear when Mendelssohn lays out his theories about how people
acquire all kinds of knowledge. He argued that reason may assent to three different kinds of truths when each is accompanied by its own appropriate pedagogical approach, or what he calls, most rhetorically, its "means of
persuasion" (91). Does Mendelssohn realize that here he steps foot into the
ancient debate about the relationship between rhetoric and rationality? It
seems likely. Classical studies were much in vogue in the Berlin of Mendelssohn's day, and he made a name for himself as a scholar by publishing a
treatise on Plato entitled *Phaedon*. It becomes clear that Mendelssohn saw
rhetoric as a necessary concomitant of belief in any kind of truth.

Mendelssohn first discussed the types of "eternal truth" that are "*necessary*, in
[themselves] *immutable*" (90, italics in original). He called them "the propositions
of pure mathematics and of the art of logic" that are "immutable even for the
Omnipotent, because God himself cannot render his infinite intellect change-
able" (90–91). In effect, they seem to be built into the divine mind, in Mendelssohn's view. We again see here his commitment to belief in a class of absolute
truths that postmodernists might question, but notably, this category of truth
does not include the truths of religion. And even they, the most self-evident mathematical truths, require instruction. Mendelssohn advised the pedagogue that

> he should . . . dissect the ideas and present them to his pupil, one by one,
> until his internal sense perceives their junctures and connections. The

> instructions which we may give others is [sic], in Socrates' apt phrase, but a kind of midwifery. We cannot put anything into their minds which is not actually contained there already; yet we can facilitate the effort it would cost to bring to light what was hidden, that is, to render the unperceived perceptible and evident. (91–92)

This is perhaps the least invasive sort of persuasion, but, Mendelssohn thought, and I agree, it is a sort of persuasion nevertheless. Interestingly, it was here that he invoked Socrates, suggesting that Plato's arguments about rhetoric were much in his mind as he wrote. It appears that even when teaching "geometry," at least some "fine language" must be used.

Mendelssohn turned next to what he termed "eternal truths" that are "*contingent*," such as "the general propositions of physics and psychology, the laws of nature, according to which this universe, the world of bodies and the world of spirits, is governed" (90, 91, italics in original). As I understand him, he called these truths contingent because he wanted to allow for the possibility of miracles: he said that they had been created by God in a certain way, according to God's will, but could have been created in a different way if God had so chosen. To quote Mendelssohn: "[God's] omnipotence can introduce other laws in their place and can, as often as it may seem useful, allow exceptions to occur" (91). These truths, too, are accessible to reason, but not unaided reason, and again Mendelssohn advised the pedagogue: "[W]e must experience, observe, and test individual cases; that is, we must, in the first place, make use of the evidence of the senses; and next, determine by means of reason what many particular cases have in common" (92). Simply understanding the elements of these laws, unlike in the first case, will not be enough; we must see for ourselves that they are confirmed by the way the world works. At this juncture Mendelssohn described the scientific method and the pedagogical practice of today's laboratory science classes. Even here, however, Mendelssohn noted that we cannot confirm these truths from our own empirical experience alone. In addition to relying on our senses and on reason to comprehend these laws, we must also rely on testimony: "Our life span is not sufficient for us to experience everything ourselves; and we must, in many cases, rely on credible fellow men; we must assume that their observations and the experiments they profess to have made are correct" (92). A rhetoric of science is thus provided for in his system, with the concomitant need for the student to understand how to interpret and evaluate the testimony of other researchers.

The third type of truth that Mendelssohn discussed comprised of "*temporal, historical truths*; things which occurred once and may never occur again" (91, italics in original). A truth of this kind can be tested in a fashion similar to a contingent eternal truth—that is, by observation guided by reason—only if one happens to be present when it occurs. Mendelssohn said, "Everyone else must accept [these truths] on authority and testimony" (93). How do we do so? For one thing, it's likely that we will have to accept written accounts of what happened—an inferior mode of learning, in Mendelssohn's view, because it is not universal: "Sounds and written characters . . . are comprehensible [only] here and there" (93). In addition to being forced to deal through the slippery medium of language, we must evaluate the credibility of the person who narrates these events to us, without being able to test the veracity of the account as we usually can do with scientific experiments performed by others. Mendelssohn said that when God wants us to accept a historical truth, God confirms its narrator's authority by miracles; but again, that sort of proof works only for those who witness the miracles. Usually, the pedagogue will simply have to help the student learn how language works, how to decipher ambiguities, and how to assess the credentials of the witness who brings the word. This is rhetorical analysis.

This discussion of three types of truth and how we learn them immediately precedes Mendelssohn's assertion, which I quoted earlier, concerning the sufficiency of reason "to persuade men of the eternal truths" of religion (94). It seems to me that this assertion looks a bit different in the context that I have just explained. To be sure, reason is sufficient, and revelation is not required—but reason needs other aids. To the extent that the truths of religion resemble "necessary eternal truths," a student may still need a teacher to explain their inner workings. In other words, even the tenets of the so-called universal human religion, while accessible to the rational faculty, may not be easily accessible to the rational faculty working alone. As for the tenets of the second major division of religious thought that Mendelssohn created, namely the dogmas and rituals particular to each of the world's religions, these most resemble his third category of truth, that is the "temporal, historical truth," because since we garner them primarily from the religious texts that have been handed down to us, we have to accept these truths primarily on the testimony of others who witnessed the revelation at Sinai or Jesus's death on the cross or the inspired teaching of Mohammed.

Here, I believe, is where ritual practice derives its great importance for Mendelssohn. In his hierarchy of truths, the more one has to rely on language and writing to grasp the truth, the lower down he placed it. Highest are the necessary truths that require little (although something) in the way of exposition; next come the contingent truths that may require some reading of the results of others' experiments but can be tested by one's own senses; lowest come the historical truths that must be grasped from written accounts alone. Mendelssohn deplored the excessive reliance upon written knowledge in the modern world:

> We teach and instruct one another only through writings; we learn to
> know nature and man only from writings. We work and relax, edify and
> amuse ourselves through overmuch writing. . . . Hence, it has come to pass
> that man has almost lost his value for his fellow man. Intercourse with the
> wise man is not sought, for we find his wisdom in his writings. (103)

Indeed, in the pages immediately following this statement, he explained the genesis of written language as a degenerative process taking people further and further away from the certain truths of nature that can be apprehended by the senses, guided by reason (I might add, a view quite consistent with other Enlightenment thinkers such as Bishop Sprat). In the case of religion, putting truths into writing leads not only to error but to "idolatry," that is, to uncritical acceptance and rigid application (118). Mendelssohn specifically said: "In order to remedy these defects the lawgiver of this nation gave the *ceremonial law*" (118, italics in original).

Ceremonial or ritual law corrects the defects of written knowledge by reconnecting the apprehension of eternal truths to sensory experience, thus raising them in the hierarchy of truths, according to Mendelssohn's system. He lauded the fact that via ritual observance—such as preparing that chicken for the pot in a kosher manner—"religious and moral teachings were to be connected with men's everyday activities" (118). Shuger's analysis of Renaissance Christian rhetoric can help us understand how this works. The treatises she analyzed discuss the use of vivid images in sacred rhetoric. Others have deplored the use of images because they confuse aesthetic—read, sensual— pleasure with what should be a purer apprehension of the divine nature; but the homilists defend images because, as Shuger puts it: "Images make what is unseen accessible to both feeling *and* thought" (59, italics in original). Shuger notes that these sacred rhetoricians devise this defense of verbal sensuality from defenses of the Christian sacraments, actually experienced in the body. She quotes John Donne: "As rhetoric makes 'absent and remote things present to your understanding,' so the sacraments bring Christ 'nearer [to us] in visible and sensible things'" (58). For Jews, ritual practice performs the same function.

Mendelssohn also values the way ritual practice instantiates the eternal truths of religion because ritual practice preserves humans from overly rigid and uncritical adherence to these truths. Why? Mendelssohn said, "Man's actions are transitory; there is nothing lasting, nothing enduring about them that, like hieroglyphic script, could lead to idolatry through abuse or misunderstanding" (119). Mendelssohn suggested that for this reason, the rabbis long resisted writing down the Jewish law and attempted to restrict writing about it even after the traumas of exile forced them to do so. In this distrust of writing we perhaps see the influence of Mendelssohn's study of Plato.

For Plato, as for Mendelssohn, the ideal pedagogical situation brought teacher and student together face to face. Mendelssohn said this about the advantages gained by learning about religion not from reading books but from shadowing an adept at ritual practice:

> [The demonstrations of ritual practice] also have the advantage over alphabetical signs of not isolating man, of not making him to be a solitary creature poring over writings and books. They impel him rather to social intercourse, to imitation, and to oral, living instruction. . . . In everything a youth saw being done . . . he found occasion for inquiring and reflecting, occasion to follow an older and wiser man at his every step. . . . (119)

For Plato the glue that holds this relationship together is erotic attraction between pupil and teacher. Mendelssohn described the mature practitioner's relationship to ritual observance in rather erotic terms as well. When he wished to convey how one's understanding of and love for traditional observance grew the more one practiced it, he chose a metaphor invoking the groom's approach to the veiled Jewish bride: "[T]he more closely you approach it, and the purer, the more innocent, the more loving and longing is the glance with which you look upon it, the more it will unfold before you its divine beauty, veiled lightly, in order not to be profaned by vulgar and unholy eyes" (99). Mendelssohn had in mind, however, a more chaste relationship of mentoring between the mature practitioner and the student, which he described thus:

> What a student himself did and saw being done from morning till night pointed to religious doctrines and convictions and spurred him on to follow his teacher, to watch him, to observe all his actions, and to obtain the instruction which he was capable of acquiring by means of his talents, and of which he had rendered himself worthy by his conduct. (102–03)

The young student eagerly emulates the details of observance out of affection and respect for his teacher. At the same time, their social nature guarantees that a pedagogue is always at hand to explain their spiritual meanings to the student.

In summary, Mendelssohn's view of education issues is a nuanced defense of the second part of religion, the dogmas and rituals, as well as an enriched vision of how the first part, the eternal truths, are apprehended. For Mendelssohn, while reason required no divine revelation to arrive at the eternal truths of religion, it required other aid—and his subtle and complex rhetorical pedagogy provided it. Arguably, in Mendelssohn's pedagogical system, emotion and imagination must be enlisted to help the learner understand the eternal truths—and for him, this meant any learner, not only the mentally defective. Mendelssohn urged his Jewish readers to "adapt yourselves to the morals and the constitution of the land to which you have been removed; but hold fast to the religion of your fathers too. Bear both burdens as well as you can!" (133). It is a sad irony of Mendelssohn's historical situation that all of his children left traditional Judaism and several converted to Christianity. The composer Felix Mendelssohn, his grandson, was raised as a Christian. And as I noted above, Mendelssohn's principal student, David Friedlaender, also tried to convert—he didn't only because Provost Teller would not accept his offer to do so without affirming the divinity of Jesus.

In conclusion: Mendelssohn's defense of Jewish ritual practice points the way for several other scholarly projects. He helps us understand the union of reason and emotion in persuasion concerning not only religious truth but also other kinds of contingent or probable truth. He also shows how a rhetoric of the body operates in a religious context, with the physical actions prescribed by ritual law, such as walking everywhere one goes on the Sabbath, themselves teaching and persuading about religious matters. Most importantly, perhaps, he provides one more example to caution academics about overreacting to what Olmsted calls the "dangers of delight" (73). In discussing Augustine's religious evolution, she notes his concern that a notion of the divine might be only "what emerges when the human mind reifies its own fantasies in a conception of [the] cosmos" (72). If religious discourse is overly sensual and persuades by specious means, then, as Olmsted explains:

> The dangers of delight, then, are both rhetorical and religious. They are rhetorical inasmuch as delight, engaged in for its own sake, distorts rhetorical speech and argument by focusing attention upon language itself rather than upon some area of inquiry that would in time lead to truth. The dangers are religious in that delight may cause human beings to cleave to the transient rather than to the divine author of the whole. (73)

Perhaps we academics—when wearing our mortarboards—feel compelled to be so skeptical of religious discourse because we fear that it has succumbed to these twin dangers of delight. But we are able to deal with these dangers—that is, with the possibly obfuscating distractions of language and the requisite eternal vigilance about the unknowability of eternal truths—when we are dealing with secular knowledge. Perhaps we should be more willing to admit that practitioners of sacred rhetoric have considered these problems as well. There must be reasons why so many people are seeking meaningful religious expression in their lives today: can all these reasons be bad ones? Perhaps we should consider the possibility, as Walter Jost argues, that "any fundamental belief as a form of life can be said to have a rhetorical claim on us, calling us from something other than our momentary needs and desires, subsuming them into a greater reality that defines our own" (123).

Bibliography

Boyle, Marjorie O'Rourke. "Rhetorical Theology: Charity Seeking Charity." Jost and Olmsted 87–96.

Fish, Stanley. *Doing What Comes Naturally: Change, Rhetoric, and the Practice of Theory in Literary and Legal Studies*. Durham, NC: Duke UP, 1989. 471–502.

Friedlaender, David. "Open Letter . . . from Some Householders of the Jewish Religion." 1799. Rpt. in *A Debate on Jewish Emancipation and Christian Theology in Old Berlin*. Trans. and ed. Richard Crouter and Julie Klassen. Indianapolis: Hackett, 2004.

Jost, Walter. "Rhetoric, Conscience, and the Claim of Religion." Jost and Olmsted 97–129.

Jost, Walter, and Wendy Olmsted, eds. *Rhetorical Invention and Religious Inquiry: New Perspectives*. New Haven: Yale UP, 2000.

Mendelssohn, Moses. *Jerusalem: Or on Religious Power and Judaism*. 1783. Trans. Allan Arkush. Intro. and notes Alexander Altmann. Hanover, NH: UP of New England/Brandeis UP, 1983.

Meyer, Michael A. *The Origins of the Modern Jew: Jewish Identity and European Culture in Germany, 1749–1824*. Detroit: Wayne State UP, 1967.

Olmsted, Wendy. "Invention, Emotion, and Conversion in Augustine's *Confessions*." Jost and Olmsted 65–86.

Shuger, Debora K. "The Philosophical Foundations of Sacred Rhetoric." Jost and Olmsted 47–64.

Aphthonius and the Progymnasmata in Rhetorical Theory and Practice

4

Manfred Kraus

In this essay I will talk to you about big business. That, at least, is what Christy Desmet called it in her paper entitled "Progymnasmata, Then and Now," which was printed in the proceedings of the last meeting of this society. "By 2004," she stated, "the progymnasmata have become pretty big business" (186). She is indeed right. Even the most perfunctory Web search yields a considerable number of advertisements for various kinds of textbooks, Web sites, tutorials, and seminars undertaking the task of "developing excellent writers for our future: using the progymnasmata" (Selby). In the 1990s the progymnasmata were given a prominent place in Sharon Crowley's and Debra Hawhee's *Ancient Rhetorics for Contemporary Students* (320–66) and again in Robert J. Connors's fourth edition of Edward P. J. Corbett's *Classical Rhetoric for the Modern Student* (484–88). In 2000, Frank J. D'Angelo published his magisterial *Composition in the Classical Tradition*, which is in its entirety a revival of the ancient progymnasmata for the modern classroom. Obviously, it is possible today to earn money on a two thousand year old educational concept from ancient Greece. To be sure, in the public mind the progymnasmata are still associated with a kind of elitist education, with what is often referred to as classical or alternative education, or even Christian education. This kind of education enjoys such popularity among parents that some educators even feel the need to warn parents: "Nota bene: You will not ruin your child if you don't use the progymnasmata!" (Penzkover para. 1).

Only a decade ago, as Desmet points out, the situation looked quite different. At that time, a more occasional title such as "Progymnasmata Now and Then" might have been more appropriate. At that time the progymnasmata were rarely noticed in either higher education or academic research, and the name of Aphthonius—the author of the most popular and most widespread ancient textbook—was all but forgotten, perhaps even less known in Europe than in the United States. When I first started research on Aphthonius and progymnasmata about eight years ago, I was looked upon by some of my senior colleagues with feelings of pity if not scorn. I was going to waste my time, they maintained, on a subject completely devoid of attractiveness and scholarly reward: "Those are just uninspired, childish textbooks!"

But before long, this all changed. Scholarly interest in those ancient textbooks erupted almost simultaneously in many places and spread rapidly all over Europe, the Americas, and beyond. There was a Swedish research project on progymnasmata, conducted by Stina Hansson and richly funded by one of the biggest Swedish banks, eventually resulting in a major publication. Malcolm Heath has initiated an ambitious project in the Classics Department at the University of Leeds in Britain ("Preliminary Exercises"). Spanish scholars have started researching their country's particular Renaissance progymnasmatic tradition.[1] And even in a country as little interested in rhetoric as Germany, two or three scholars acting independently of one another began research work on the progymnasmata. Within just a few years, the ancient Greek textbooks were translated into English, French, Spanish, Portuguese, Swedish, and even Serbian.[2] Aphthonius's book is now available in no less than three different English translations—two of them are very recent[3] and the third is an updated edition of an earlier printing.[4] George A. Kennedy's *Progymnasmata* goes further and presents the first comprehensive English translation of all progymnasmata treatises preserved from antiquity.

Progymnasmata not only have become big commercial business, but also big academic business (and these do not necessarily coincide). They have become the object of international as well as interdisciplinary research. Historians of rhetoric, classicists, Renaissance scholars, educationalists, teachers of composition, and many others now happily collaborate in this field.

My aim in this essay therefore will not be to persuade you that the progymnasmata are an important feature within the history of rhetorical education—this I will take for granted—but rather to show you *why* they are important and why they deserve to be. My essay will have three main parts. In the first part I will try to give you an outline of the contents of ancient progymnasmata textbooks and of the pedagogical concept that underlies them, concentrating mainly on Aphthonius's manual. The goal of my second part will be to demonstrate the ways in which progymnasmata have contributed to the systematic development of rhetoric. In the last section I will sketch the fascinating history of the success of Aphthonius's progymnasmata in Western education.

Part I

The progymnasmata, or "preliminary exercises," as the term is best translated, form "a graded, cumulative sequence of writing tasks, manageable at each step, within an explicit rhetorical framework" (D'Angelo xiii). According to the most commonly accepted view these exercises were developed for classroom purposes in Greek rhetorical schools of the late Hellenistic period (second or first century BCE), although some of the individual exercises have a much longer tradition. They were organized systematically during the first century CE at the latest. In the Hellenistic Greek and Roman educational system, after students acquired the ability to read and write in elementary schools, they would be sent for higher education to a grammarian, with whom they would learn to read and interpret the works of the classical poets and writers. When they had acquired a certain ability in this respect, they would be passed on to a rhetor for education in rhetoric. Within this progression, the progymnasmata were located precisely at the transitional stage from grammar to rhetoric, and were thus charged with the pivotal task of providing a smooth passage from the reading of poetry to rhetorical education proper. They were basically written exercises, but occasionally were also delivered orally. They were specially devised for preparing beginners in rhetoric for the more advanced exercise of oral declamation.[5] This intermediary position, however, often led to professional rivalry among teachers. Quintilian, for instance, complained that in Rome grammarians were usurping substantial parts of the progymnasmatic curriculum, which was none of their business and rightly belonged to the rhetoricians (2.1.1–3).

Unfortunately, no rhetorical treatises survived from the Hellenistic period, so all we know about progymnasmata stems from late antique and Imperial sources. In that period, however, there is no shortage of pertinent texts. To learn more about the progymnasmata, it will be best to turn to the most popular of all ancient textbooks, the one written by Aphthonius.

Aphthonius was a Greek rhetor who lived and taught in the Syrian capital Antioch (which is now Antakya in Turkey) in the fourth century CE. About his life practically nothing is known. The only thing we know for certain is that he was a student of the famous rhetor Libanius. Aphthonius was neither the first nor the only writer to treat the progymnasmata. One Aelius Theon had composed a scholarly, comprehensive, and cumbersome handbook presumably in the first century CE (although Malcolm Heath in his article "Theon and the History of the Progymnasmata" tried to persuade us that he is a fifth-century man [141–58]). Earlier than Aphthonius, too, is the scanty manual erroneously transmitted under the name of the great rhetorician Hermogenes of Tarsus, which is best dated to the second or third century CE. The somewhat epigonous work by the fifth-century rhetor Nicolaus of Myra, however, postdates that of Aphthonius. We also have a handful of other names of Greek rhetors who were credited with having written progymnasmata textbooks, such as Harpocration, Minucianus, Paul of Tyre, Epiphanius, Onasimus, Ulpianus, Siricius, Sopater, and Syrianus. Only fragments of these texts survive, but they still testify to the great popularity and productiveness of the genre. In Latin rhetoric, too, we have Quintilian, who, in his *Institutio oratoria*, integrates the progymnasmata into his rhetorical curriculum in a manner similar to their treatment in Theon's handbook, suggesting the two men were contemporaries. Much later, in the sixth century, Pseudo-Hermogenes' textbook was translated into Latin and adapted to a Roman cultural background by the grammarian Priscianus.

Aphthonius's textbook is fairly short, only thirty-one pages in Kennedy's translation (*Progymnasmata*). It consists of fourteen chapters that describe fourteen individual exercises. Curiously enough, there is no introductory preface. Of the four extant Greek manuals, those by Theon and Nicolaus have a preface, while those by Pseudo-Hermogenes and Aphthonius do not. Either Aphthonius's preface got lost in the course of transmission, or else there never was one. In Aphthonius's order, the fourteen progymnasmata are as follows:

1. Fable
2. Narration
3. Chreia (or Anecdote)
4. Maxim (or Proverb)
5. Refutation
6. Confirmation
7. Commonplace (or Common Topic)
8. Praise
9. Blame
10. Comparison
11. Ethopoeia (or Speech-in-Character)
12. Description
13. Thesis
14. Proposal of a Law

Most of these should appear self-explanatory by their very name. But for die-hard nonprogymnasmatists, a few explanatory words will perhaps be in order for some of them (such as *Chreia,* which is a discussion of some wise saying or action by some famous person), to be elaborated on according to a set argumentative pattern. The same pattern is applied to the treatment of a *Maxim. Commonplace* (or rather *Common Topic*), in a progymnasmatic context, is an exercise in amplification of evil attributes of a certain stock type of wicked character (a drunkard, an adulterer, a murderer, etc.), which may conveniently be employed in any pertinent case. *Ethopoeia* (or *Speech-in-Character*) is a fictitious speech put into the mouth of some mythical or historical person in a particular situation. A *Thesis* is a discussion of a philosophical or ethical question of a general kind (such as, "Should one marry?" or "Should one learn rhetoric?"). Finally, the exercise called *Proposal of a Law* is a detailed argumentation for or against a law (often a fanciful law) that has been proposed.

The sequence follows a deliberate pattern that, generally speaking, advances from easier to progressively more difficult and demanding exercises. Accordingly, Aphthonius's chapters steadily increase in length, from a few laconic lines on *Fable* to half a dozen pages each for *Thesis* and *Proposal of a Law.* The exercises located at the beginning, such as *Fable, Narration, Chreia,* and *Maxim,* are still in some way related to what students would be acquainted with from the reading of poetry in grammar school, whereas the exercises at the end of the sequence unmistakably and steadily approach declamation. This is even more evident when the individual exercises are classified, as various ancient authors suggested, according to their respective affinity with different oratorical genres. Whereas the first four exercises clearly belong to deliberative speech, numbers 5 to 7 represent the judicial genre, and numbers 8 to 10 are attached to the epideictic. From this point of view, it appears that exercises 11 to 14 form a separate group of their own. Yet, in his exposition of *Thesis*, Aphthonius states that *Thesis* differs from a hypothesis (which is another expression for the topic of a declamation) in that it lacks individual speakers' characters and particular circumstances (i.e., specifications of place and time). Yet these are exactly the features supplied by *Ethopoeia* and *Description*. Once Character and clearly described Circumstances are added, a *Thesis* will be transformed into a declamation in the deliberative genre. To use Aphthonius's own example: A discussion of the question whether cities should be fortified is a *Thesis*. But the Lacedaemonians deliberating whether they should fortify Sparta in view of the Persian army advancing in 480 BCE will be a hypothesis or a declamation. For a declamation in the judicial genre, however, discussion of law is additionally required, and this is precisely what is practised in exercise number 14. Thus, it is this last group of four exercises that train the student in exactly those skills that will be needed for the composition of a proper declamation.[6] It may also be noted that only in *Thesis* and *Proposal of a Law* can the actual elaboration go either way, for or against, and thus allows for what in Latin is called *disserere in utramque partem* (arguing for both sides), which is exactly the common practice in full-fledged declamation. This of course presupposes advanced skill in argumentation and autonomous decision making on the part of the student, whereas in lower-rank argumentative exercises such as *Refutation* and *Confirmation* the outcome is built into the assignment.

Within the sequence, individual exercises may presuppose each other or be based on one another (for instance, any *Refutation* or *Confirmation* will necessarily contain a *Narration,* any *Blame* will make use of the *Commonplace,* and any *Thesis* or *Proposal of a Law* will necessarily contain elements of *Refutation* or *Confirmation*). In certain cases, particular exercises may even mutually presuppose one another (for instance, any *Praise* or *Blame* will contain a *Comparison,* but on the other hand any *Comparison* will also necessarily contain elements of *Praise* or *Blame*).

Each section of Aphthonius's text is divided into two main parts, theoretical instructions and a developed example. Each theoretical section is subdivided into the following stock components: (1) a concise definition of the exercise in question followed, if necessary, by an explanation of its appellation; (2) the indication of its characteristic features that distinguish it either from other related progymnasmata or from homonymous phenomena outside rhetoric; (3) a taxonomy of subclasses or kinds; and finally (4) instructions for the elaboration (*exergasía*) of the exercise in classroom practice, listing compulsory steps or elements, and sometimes specifying the proper stylistic level. In the case of *Narration*, for instance, it reads as follows (Heath, "Aphthonius" ch. 2):

(a) *Narration* is the exposition of an event that has occurred, or as if it had occurred.

(b) *Narration* differs from a narrative in the same way that poetry differs from a poem (the *Iliad* is a poem; the preparation of Achilleus's arms is poetry).

(c) *Narration* may be dramatic, historical, or political. The dramatic is fictitious; the historical contains a story from antiquity; the political is the kind that orators use in their disputes.

(d) *Narration* has six concomitants: the person acting, the action performed, the time, the place, the manner, and the cause of its performance. *Narration* has four virtues: clarity, concision, plausibility, and purity of diction.

All other theoretical sections in Aphthonius's work follow a similar pattern, with a single example for each exercise. The sole exception from this rule is *Praise,* which has two examples—praise of a person (Thucydides) and praise of a virtue (wisdom). The fact that *Praise* has two examples testifies to the major importance of panegyric and ceremonial oratory in Aphthonius's day.

It is these well-elaborated examples that make Aphthonius's textbook stand out among all progymnasmata manuals we know from antiquity, and they account for its unusual success (which will be discussed more later). In fact, as early as antiquity, there seems to have been quite a market for collections of worked-out progymnasmata exercises. The author of one of these was Aphthonius's own teacher, Libanius. His collection, and those of several other authors, is still extant.

One of the great assets of the progymnasmata that made them function as an ideal link between grammar and rhetoric was the fact that they were open to practical use on various levels. The first four exercises, for instance, could be used simply as either a textual basis for reproduction from memory upon hearing or reading, or for paraphrasing or translating into another language. On a slightly more advanced level they could serve as subject matter for various kinds of variations and modifications, particularly for expansion and condensation, and even for refutation and confirmation; this is the technique the Romans used to refer to as *pluribus modis tractare* (treatment in multiple ways). On the highest level, then, these same exercises could be worked out by the students as independent pieces of composition, involving a good deal of invention, disposition, and argumentation; this last procedure was the standard for the more advanced set of exercises.

A very peculiar exercise particularly associated with *Chreia,* but occasionally also with *Fable* or *Narration,* was the exercise of Inflection, and it operated on a purely grammatical level. As we learn from Theon's manual and from actual discoveries of scraps of students' assignments on papyri and tablets (Patillon 24–26, 33–34, 48; Kenyon 30), in this particular exercise the heading of a *Chreia* was to be recast into all possible grammatical cases and numbers, sometimes with bizarre results. For instance:

- Diogenes the Cynic philosopher once said . . . (nominative);
- There is a saying of Diogenes the Cynic philosopher . . . (genitive);
- The following saying is attributed to Diogenes the Cynic philosopher . . . (dative);
- They purport Diogenes the Cynic philosopher to have said . . . (accusative);
- O Diogenes, O Cynic philosopher, didn't you say . . . (vocative).

Subsequently, the whole series was to be repeated in the plural: "The Diogeneses, the Cynic philosophers, once said . . ." and so forth. And then even in the Greek dual form: "The two Diogeneses, the two Cynic philosophers, both said . . ." and so forth.

This variety of modes of treatment permits different degrees of complexity within individual exercises, and as their complexity increases or decreases, their place within the sequence of progymnasmata can change. Today we regard the sequence by Aphthonius as canonical, but it is just one of several options, and other arrangements are possible. Theon's manual, for instance, is oriented more toward grammar, and so its sequence is different. In Theon, it is *Chreia* (with *Maxim* as a mere variant) that comes first. *Chreia, Fable,* and *Narration* just serve as subject texts for various transformations and treatments, among them *Refutation* and *Confirmation,* which thus do not figure as independent exercises as they do in all later manuals. Moreover, both *Description* and *Ethopoeia* are ranked lower, and precede *Praise, Blame,* and *Comparison.* The only point of complete agreement with Aphthonius is that *Thesis* and *Proposal of a Law* come last. In a subsequent part that is lost in the Greek text, but fortunately preserved in an Armenian translation,[7] Theon further lists a number of basic modes of treatment, such as retelling a story from previous reading or listening, paraphrase, elaboration, and contradiction. Other contemporaneous authors such as Quintilian add even more grammatical kinds of exercises, such as the transformation of poetic texts into prose or translation from one language into another. From Pseudo-Hermogenes onwards, however, these purely grammatical exercises disappear, and the progymnasmata take on a distinctly rhetorical flavor. In antiquity the variety of progymnasmatic exercises and curricula was much richer and more diversified than the later Aphthonian system, with its subsequent dominance, would lead us to believe. It is in fact Pseudo-Hermogenes who first established the classical Aphthonian sequence of exercises, and Aphthonius merely improved on this by splitting *Refutation* from *Confirmation,* and by splitting *Praise* from *Blame,* so that two general exercises in Pseudo-Hermogenes (with two separate variants each) become four separate exercises. Aphthonius thus makes fourteen exercises out of Pseudo-Hermogenes' twelve.

Part II

I will now turn to the pedagogical concept underlying progymnasmata, or "gymnasmata" as they were originally called. The "pro" was only added later in the fourth century by the time of Aphthonius in order to keep the pre-liminary exercises clearly distinct from the rhetorical gymnasma proper—which was declamation itself.

The term "progymnasma" itself is a borrowing from the world of physi-cal education. Greek "gymnasma" literally means "an exercise in the nude." But relax—this is no longer a compulsory requirement in rhetoric. The back-bone of the pedagogical method behind progymnasmata is the idea that rhet-oric as a whole can be broken down into smaller parts that can be taught and practiced separately, before eventually being brought together to form a whole. The idea is that parts should be taught and mastered before the whole, small items before big ones, easy tasks before difficult ones. This is a method of acquiring practical skills that is well-known in areas such as sports, mili-tary drilling, fine arts, or craftsmanship. A proverb quoted by Theon says that an apprentice in pottery never will "learn pottery-making by starting with a big jar" (Patillon 1). Similarly, a beginner in rhetoric is advised first to work out single parts of a speech, concentrate separately on single tasks, and prac-tice acquired skills first on a very small scale before eventually combining all these, step by step, into a full-scale speech. This method uses the part as a pat-tern for the whole.[8] Our present conference of the Rhetoric Society of Amer-ica has taken as its theme "Sizing Up Rhetoric"; but I am afraid the whole progymnasmatic curriculum is instead an attempt in downsizing rhetoric to make it easy and teachable.

John of Sardis explained in his ninth-century commentary on Aphtho-nius that the progymnasmata are "miniature rhetoric" (qtd. in Kennedy *Pro-gymnasmata*). But this is just why we can find substantial parts of rhetoric as a discipline reflected in them. Let me therefore now turn to the question of what we can actually learn about rhetoric from the progymnasmata text-books. Let me just briefly address a few points of general interest.

I pointed out earlier that in antiquity the individual exercises of the pro-gymnasmatic curriculum were associated with the three genres of oratory and the five classical parts of a speech. So it is hardly surprising that students would make their first acquaintance with these basic taxonomies of classical rhetoric by attentively following step by step the development of the sequence of exer-cises, particularly so if their attention was guided by an experienced teacher.

Instruction in epideictic or ceremonial speech was conducted entirely on the level of progymnasmata, since no exercises in epideictic were available on the level of declamation itself. The entire job was to be done in progymnas-matic exercises such as *Praise, Blame, Comparison, Description,* and even *Com-monplace.* As a result, as panegyric oratory continued to grow in importance during the imperial period (and even in Byzantine and early modern peri-ods), so also did the progymnasmata grow in importance. In this respect it is interesting to note that Menander of Laodicea, one of the principal theorists of epideictic rhetoric in the third century CE, was credited with having written a commentary on the now lost *Progymnasmata* by Minucianus. He certainly knew where to find the fundamentals of his own discipline.

Another important rhetorical feature is Topics or Places of Invention. In progymnasmata handbooks students are given very detailed instructions on which questions to ask and where to look for suitable arguments in the process of invention. Especially in the most advanced exercises, *Thesis* and *Proposal of a Law,* students are invited to arrange their argumentation according to the so-called "final headings," or "headings of purpose" (*teliká kephálaia*)— Legality, Justice, Expediency, and Possibility—which would help them find proper arguments and lay out their speeches appropriately. The exercise of *Commonplace* also uses these same headings on a smaller scale, where they are augmented with two more headings of the Honorable and Potential Consequences. Even in the very rudimentary exercises of *Refutation* and *Confirmation,* students are asked to examine a given story according to the six categories of Clarity, Plausibility, Possibility, Consistency, Propriety, and Expediency. All this provided a convenient repertory of places of invention that could be prompted any time on demand.

These headings are helpful not only for *inventio,* but also they offer convenient schemes and patterns for *dispositio.* One of the most successful patterns contained in progymnasmata textbooks is the standard eight-step pattern set for the elaboration of *Chreia* and *Maxim.* In the genuinely rhetorical method of elaboration of *Chreia* as described by Aphthonius, the student is asked first to say a few words in praise of the protagonist of the anecdote, and then to paraphrase it in his own words. He then elaborates on the anecdote by producing a rationale, refuting the contrary position, describing an analogy, providing an illustrative example from myth or history, and citing the testimony of some ancient authority. He concludes with a summary of his information in a brief epilogue. This fairly rigid pattern continued to be used as a standard scheme of disposition in theme writing and composition in Western education through the eighteenth century and beyond.

Schooling in progymnasmata demonstrably will teach the student method and orderliness. By following the course of exercises, the student will learn step by step how to arrange his thoughts in an orderly way. It is this instruction in method that the humanists regarded as one of the main assets of progymnasmata.[9]

From progymnasmata, the student will also gain a profound insight into the persuasive power of ethos and pathos. It is the exercise in *Ethopoeia* (or *Speech-in-Character*) that proves particularly useful in this respect. The exercise as a whole was even subdivided into the two subclasses of ethical and pathetic *Ethopoeia.* And to judge from the numerous examples of elaborated ethopoeiae preserved, this could be an exercise in extremely pathetic speech. Therefore students would learn how to produce and how to use strongly pathetic language in their speeches.

The extremely powerful language and style of *Ethopoeia,* however, was counterbalanced by other exercises such as *Narration,* in which a somewhat sober and plain style was applicable. In the theoretical instructions provided for each exercise, precise advice was given regularly for choosing the appropriate stylistic level and linguistic means. Students had available the whole range of stylistic levels, from the plain and lucid style of the earlier exercises to the florid and elaborated diction of the more epideictic exercises such as *Praise, Blame,* and *Ethopoeia.* They would thus learn how to distinguish different levels of style, which linguistic features to choose, and which to avoid in any given situation.

Fluent ability in *elocutio* would be enhanced further by the fact that several of the exercises concentrated on amplification, which would, in the course of practice, strongly support the acquisition and development of *copia.* Thus, progymnasmata are also closely associated with training in elocution. In this respect it may be interesting to note that the earliest example we know of for the eight-part elaboration of a *Maxim* is found as early as the anonymous *Rhetorica ad Herennium* in the early first century BCE, but there it is included in the fourth book on *elocutio* where it is described as a method of stylistic amplification (*expolitio*). The treatment of *Ethopoeia* or *sermocinatio* as a rhetorical figure in *Rhetorica ad Herennium* also clearly betrays acquaintance with similar treatments in early progymnasmata manuals no longer extant.

But there is more in progymnasmata than just rhetoric. As the exercises are of a very general character and are clearly detached from any specific cases or circumstances typical of an actual speech, they have a distinct affinity with conventional literary forms and genres, and thus testify to the process of *letteraturizzazione* of rhetoric in the imperial period described by George A. Kennedy (*Classical Rhetoric* 5), who borrows this term from the Romanian critic Vasile Florescu. Features such as *Description, Praise, Blame,* and *Ethopoeia* developed out of progymnasmata handbooks into independent literary forms, thus enriching the classical canon of literary genres by a number of smaller forms. As the progymnasmata were basically exercises in written composition, their usefulness for the education of poets and writers was strongly felt at all times.[10] On the other hand, they were also converted into convenient tools for the analysis and interpretation of both poetry and literary prose. Perhaps the most striking example concerns the theory of narrative. *Fable* is described as a "false discourse" and *Narration* as the exposition of an event that either "has occurred" or "as if it had occurred." Together, these exercises provide a tripartite taxonomy of the true, the false, and the "as if"—clearly redolent of Aristotelian distinctions—that contains in itself the nucleus of the entire Western theory of narrative and fiction. For this reason the progymnasmata treatises are among the principal ancient sources that continue to be cited with respect to narrative theory.[11] The progymnasmata are even the ancient source for the six essential components of a good narrative—the person acting, action, place, time, manner, and cause—which many of us may recall having learned as parts of the mnemonic hexameter *Quis, quid, ubi, quibus auxiliis, cur, quomodo, quando.* All this, and much more, originates from progymnasmata.

Progymnasmata were useful not only for teaching writing and speech, but also for inculcating students with moral and cultural values that were implicitly conveyed by exercises such as *Fable, Chreia,* or *Maxim.* Furthermore, exercises such as *Thesis, Proposal of a Law,* or *Commonplace* involved the application of categories such as law and equity, thus laying the base for a certain kind of cultural and moral identity. The matter of identity was particularly important in *Ethopoeia*, which surprisingly was practiced often as a speech in a female character. Students were invited to cross borders of gender identity, an experience they perhaps would never again be in a position to explore, since antiquity had no real tradition of declamation in a female voice. Thus, schooling in female *Ethopoeia* could be addressed as an early exercise in cross-gender empathy, which would still seem commendable for our times, particularly since today the crossing of borders may go in either direction.

Part III

I want now to give a brief account of the tremendous success of Aphthonius's *Progymnasmata* in the history of higher education. There are two different reasons that explain why his textbook was so successful. The first reason is that Aphthonius provided models and examples that made available an additional mode of instruction, that of learning by imitation (which is certainly one of the best and most promising methods of pedagogy), that other manuals, as far as we know, were unable to provide.

The second reason for Aphthonius's predominance, however, was sheer luck. Some time during the first half of the sixth century CE, Aphthonius's manual was incorporated into the corpus of works by the rhetorician Hermogenes of Tarsus. This corpus was a group of four works that seemed to provide something like a full course in rhetoric (invention, stasis theory, a variety of elocutionary styles, and the method of the forceful style), but apparently lacked a progymnasmata. Since the Corpus Hermogenianum soon prevailed over all other competing handbooks, the *Progymnasmata* of Aphthonius was assured of its predominance.

In the Byzantine Middle Ages, during which the ancient educational system managed to survive until the eventual fall of Constantinople in 1453, and in which Hermogenes was the one and only undisputed authority in rhetoric, Aphthonius was enormously popular. A plethora of prolegomena, scholia, and commentaries to his little book were written from the ninth to the fifteenth centuries by outstanding scholars such as John of Sardis, John Geometres, John Doxopater, Maximus Planudes, and Matthaeus Camariota, to name only the most famous. A great number of collections of elaborated examples also appeared, adding mostly biblical or typically Christian examples.

In the Latin West, the situation proved more difficult. As the practice of declamation disappeared, the cleverly designed sequence of preparatory exercises seems to have broken apart, and the individual items were no longer addressed as rhetorical exercises, but rather as convenient means of amplification or as descriptive categories for the interpretation of literary texts. This is not to say that similar exercises were not practiced during the Middle Ages, but they were just no longer directly based on Aphthonius.

During the course of the fifteenth century, however, Aphthonius was reintroduced to the West, and to Italy in particular, by Byzantine refugees who brought with them their favorite rhetorical handbooks (i.e., Hermogenes and Aphthonius). George of Trebizond in particular seems to have been a pivotal character in this process.[12] Aphthonius's progymnasmata apparently fit very well with the educational ideas of the early humanists. Many outstanding humanist educators, such as Desiderius Erasmus, Johann Sturm, Roger Ascham, and Philipp Melanchthon, and later on John Brinsley and Charles Hoole, speak very highly of the progymnasmata and emphatically recommend them in their major educational treatises.

For proper implementation as a school textbook, however, Latin translations were absolutely needed, since no twelve-year-old schoolboy in the West could read any Greek. And indeed there was an immediate profusion of individual translations, and some of those translations ran into a considerable number of printings. Their time span ranges from the late fifteenth to the mid-eighteenth century. The figures given in Donald L. Clark's still valuable and groundbreaking article "The Rise and Fall of Progymnasmata" unfortunately are outdated (261–62). The new *Renaissance Rhetoric Short-Title Catalogue 1460–1700 (RRSTC)* by Lawrence Green and James Murphy gives much higher counts (27–32, 283, 293, 309, 344–45, 393), and my own counts, which go beyond the year 1700 and include printings attested in older sources and catalogues (although no extant copies have been located) are even higher. My counts yield about 400 individual printings of all attested translations and adaptations from the late fifteenth to the late eighteenth century (compared with 116 in Clark and 225 in Green and Murphy). It is hard to tell what these numbers would mean in terms of individual copies, but there can be no doubt that Latin translations of Aphthonius inundated Western grammar schools in hundreds of thousands of copies. All major European presses were involved in this gigantic process of adaptation of an ancient text, from the Aldine press in Venice and the Giuntas in Florence, to the great presses in Basel, Lyon, Paris, Leipzig, and Cologne, and to the Elzeviers in Amsterdam. In England the Society of Stationers soon took command of the enterprise. It is evident that in the fifteenth and sixteenth centuries the production and trade of Aphthonius translations was a huge commercial market and very big business indeed. This is especially attested by the great number of pirated editions found. There are many strange stories about less famous printers desperately trying to fake an expensive Elzevier printing but somehow getting the frontispiece reversed right-to-left, or listing the wrong first name of a legitimate printer, and so forth.[13] This is ample proof that fairly big sums of money were at stake.

Let us just look briefly at the impressively long list of individual translations, a list that includes many outstanding humanist scholars. Three main phases can be seen. The first can be called the pedagogical phase, from about 1475 to 1565. In this phase, there is no major interest in the Greek text itself, but mainly in the exercises as such. Commentaries, if any, are usually brief.

The earliest translation was made by the Dutch humanist Rudolph Agricola around 1478 in Ferrara, but it was first printed much later in 1532 by Alardus of Amsterdam. The first translation to appear in print was instead the one by the Italian Giovanni Maria Cattaneo (Catanaeus), printed in Bologna in 1507. There are two more early translations done by Italians, Antonio Bonfini (Lyon, 1538) and Natale Conti (Basel, around 1550), and an anonymous one edited by Gentian Hervet (London, 1520). Petrus Mosellanus and a Mallorquin named Antonius Lullus further contributed slightly adapted versions of Aphthonius. But the big successes clearly were the translations by Rudolph Agricola (twenty printings before 1583) and Cattaneo (twenty-five printings before 1559).

These latter two translations eventually were combined in 1542 (with a revised edition in 1546) by Reinhard Lorich, professor of rhetoric at the University of Marburg, to form the unrivalled hypersuccess on the Aphthonian market.[14] Lorich's edition was printed more than 150 times by presses all over Europe in countries as various as Germany, France, England, the Netherlands, Italy, and Switzerland.[15] The latest printing attested is from 1718. Not only did Lorich add a massive amount of exegetical scholia to the text of Aphthonius, but he also provided an enormous number of new examples, some original, some borrowed from ancient and early modern writers (thereby filling gaps left by Aphthonius's own examples), and adding some contemporary flavor. Lorich's work transformed Aphthonius's short text into an impressive compendium of 300–400 pages (but usually printed and bound in a compact handy format), which continued to be used in the grammar schools of Germany, Britain, France, Italy, and many other countries for over 150 years. In the seventeenth century it even found its way to New England and Harvard College, where the college's first president, Henry Dunster, is reported to have lectured on rhetoric weekly based on Lorich's Aphthonius.[16]

The second phase, the scholarly phase, ranges from about 1565 to 1650. Latin translations and commentaries were devised to explain the original Greek text, which was usually included. Examples of such richly commented editions are those by Joachim Camerarius (Leipzig, 1567), Burchard Harbart (Leipzig, 1591), and Anton Burchard (Stettin, 1607). But in the second half of the seventeenth century, pedagogy reasserted itself, and the Aphthonian text was progressively incorporated into large comprehensive handbooks on both sides of the confessional divide. Protestants included Christoph Praetorius (Frankfurt/Oder, 1655) and Johannes Micraelius (Stettin, 1656), while Jesuits included Jacob Masen (*Palaestra oratoria,* Cologne, 1659) and François Pomey (*Candidatus rhetoricae,* Lyon, 1661). Pomey revised his work as *Novus candidatus rhetoricae* (Lyon, 1668), and Joseph Jouvancy revised it again in 1710, carrying Aphthonius well into the eighteenth century. The latest attested printing of Jouvancy's revised *Candidatus* (1774) roughly coincides with the date of the abolition of the Jesuit order by papal decree (1773). It is thus the late eighteenth rather than the late seventeenth century, as Clark had insisted, that marked the end of the Aphthonian era in Western education (262–63).

The massive use of Aphthonius in grammar schools is also well attested by both Protestant school curricula and the Jesuit *Ratio studiorum*.[17] The writing of "themes" or "themata," as the exercises were commonly called, marked the intermediary stage between exercises in *copia* and letter writing on the one hand, and rhetorical education proper on the other.[18] But, as in antiquity, and especially in the period of the Reformation and Counter-Reformation, the progymnasmata were employed for political and religious indoctrination of students. At times even highly controversial political and religious issues were addressed in various model examples. Nevertheless, during the sixteenth century, in spite of its decidedly Protestant examples, Reinhard Lorich's edition continued to be used in Roman Catholic schools and was even printed frequently by Jesuit presses. But things changed with the outbreak of the Thirty Years' War. In Catholic grammar schools Lorich had to be used in "purged" editions until the Jesuits eventually produced their own progymnasmata handbooks. In Protestant manuals we can find a *Refutation* of dogmas of the Roman Catholic church, or a *Narration* proving that St. Bartholomew's Eve (the massacre of Protestants in Paris) was the greatest crime ever committed in human history (Micraelius). In corresponding Jesuit manuals there were examples of a sarcastically ironical *Praise* of Martin Luther, and a harsh and scurrilous *Blame* of Jean Calvin (Pomey), along with a genial *Ethopoeia* by a Jesuit adopting the voice of the reformer Martin Luther to criticize his own Roman Catholic church (Masen).

During the early modern period the progymnasmata could be used to accomplish almost anything. They functioned as a kind of universal text-producing machine that could produce any sort of text at any required length for any imaginable occasion. This observation takes us back to my introductory remarks about the contemporary renaissance of the progymnasmata in writing education. How are we to explain this development? Are we experiencing a new age of sophistry, in which versatility and virtuosity in handling language are regarded as superior cultural techniques? Or are we—to put it more sympathetically—witnessing the return of a new humanist age, in which texts and the ability to produce any sort of text easily and on demand are of supreme importance? Or are we finally, despite the apparently oral and visual character of present culture, fostering an ideology where the written text is the basis of everything and the spoken word of the orally delivered speech is only parasitical? This is a notion to which deconstructionists and advocates of "l'Écriture" would certainly subscribe. To be honest, I have no universal answer to this vexing question. Much research still will have to be done. Indeed . . . big business ahead for rhetoricians!

Notes

[1] Note particularly the work of Luisa López Grigera (University of Michigan), Elena Artaza (Bilbao), Alfonso Martín Jiménez (Valladolid), María Violeta Pérez Custodio (Cádiz), Jesús Ureña Bracero (Cáceres), and many others.
[2] For references, see Eriksson 203.

[3] See Heath "Aphthonius"; Kennedy, *Progymnasmata* 89–127.

[4] See Nadeau; Matsen, Rollinson, and Sousa 266–88.

[5] See Bonner 250 ff.; Hock and O'Neil 10.

[6] This particular distribution of the exercises to the three oratorical genres is of course not the only one possible. D'Angelo, for example, presents a slightly different one (18).

[7] Patillon 102–12. The text was meticulously restored by Giancarlo Bolognesi and published by Michel Patillon in his bilingual (or, for that matter, trilingual) edition of Theon's work.

[8] See D'Angelo xiii.

[9] On this topic, see, for instance, Jardine.

[10] See, for instance, Quintilian 3.8.49.

[11] See Calboli Montefusco.

[12] See, for instance, Monfasani 148–257; Kennedy, *Classic Rhetoric* 199–205.

[13] For similar reports, see, for instance, Margolin.

[14] The title of this pivotal edition is *Aphthonii Sophistae progymnasmata, partim à Rodolpho Agricola, partim à Ioanne Maria Catanaeo latinitate quondam donata: iam recens longè tersius edita, simul ac scholijs luculentis, novisque compluribus exemplis illustrata, per Reinhardum Lorichium Hadamarium* (Marburg: Christian Egenolff, 1542). *Eadem modò locupletata, atq; diligenter recognita* (Frankfurt a.M.: Christian Egenolff, 1546).

[15] For a list of 112 printings, see Green and Murphy (28–30). Clark (261–62) has only 73 printings.

[16] See Morison 172–77.

[17] For details, see Kraus 170–71, with notes 52–59; Baldwin II: 288.

[18] See Baldwin II: 288–90.

Works Cited

Baldwin, Thomas W. *William Shakespeare's Small Latine & Lesse Greeke.* Urbana: University of Illinois P, 1944. 2 vols.

Bonner, Stanley F. *Education in Ancient Rome: From the Elder Cato to the Younger Pliny.* Berkeley: U of California P, 1977. 250–76.

Calboli Montefusco, Lucia. "Cic. *Inv.* 1.27 and *Rhet. Her.* 1.12 f.: The Question of the tertium genus narrationis." *Papers on Rhetoric VII.* Ed. L. Calboli Montefusco. Roma: Herder Editrice, 2006. 17–29.

Clark, Donald L. "The Rise and Fall of Progymnasmata in Sixteenth and Seventeenth Century Grammar Schools." *Speech Monographs* 19 (1952): 259–63.

Corbett, Edward P. J., and Robert J. Connors. *Classical Rhetoric for the Modern Student.* 4th ed. New York: Oxford UP, 1999.

Crowley, Sharon, and Debra Hawhee. *Ancient Rhetorics for Contemporary Students.* Boston: Allyn and Bacon, 1994.

D'Angelo, Frank J. *Composition in the Classical Tradition.* Boston: Allyn and Bacon, 2000.

Desmet, Christy. "Progymnasmata, Then and Now." *Rhetorical Agendas. Political, Ethical, Spiritual.* Ed. Patricia Bizzell. Mahwah, NJ: Lawrence Erlbaum, 2006. 185–91.

Eriksson, Anders. *Retoriska övningar. Afthonios' Progymnasmata.* Nora: Nya Doxa, 2002.

Green, Lawrence D., and James J. Murphy. *Renaissance Rhetoric Short-Title Catalogue 1460–1700.* 2nd ed. Burlington, VT: Ashgate, 2006.

Hansson, Stina, ed. *Progymnasmata. Retorikens bortglömda text- och tankeform.* Åstorp: Rhetor förlag, 2003.

Heath, Malcolm, trans. "Aphthonius, *Progymnasmata.*" Ancient Rhetoric: An Introduction. <http://www.leeds.ac.uk/classics/resources/rhetoric/prog-aph.htm>.

———. "Preliminary Exercises *(Progymnasmata).*" Ancient Rhetoric: An Introduction. <http://www.leeds.ac.uk/classics/resources/rhetoric/progymn.htm>.

———. "Theon and the History of the Progymnasmata." *Greek, Roman, and Byzantine Studies* 43 (2002/03): 129–60.

Hock, Ronald F., and Edward N. O'Neil. *The Chreia in Ancient Rhetoric.* Vol. I: *The Progymnasmata.* Texts and Translations 27. Graeco-Roman Religion Series 9. Atlanta: Scholars P, 1986.

Jardine, Lisa. "Distinctive Discipline: Rudolph Agricola's Influence on Methodical Thinking in the Humanities." *Proceedings of the International Conference at the University of Groningen, 28–30 Oct. 1985: Rudolphus Agricola Phrisius 1444–1485.* Ed. Fokke Akkerman and A. J. Vanderjagt. Leiden: E.J. Brill, 1988. 38–57.

Kennedy, George A. *Classical Rhetoric and its Christian and Secular Tradition from Ancient to Modern Times.* Chapel Hill: U of North Carolina P, 1980.

———. *Progymnasmata: Greek Textbooks of Prose Composition and Rhetoric.* Translated with introduction and notes. Writings from the Greco-Roman World 10. Atlanta: Society of Biblical Literature, 2003.

Kenyon, Frederick G. "Two Greek School Tablets." *Journal of Hellenic Studies* 29 (1909): 29–40.

Kraus, Manfred. "Progymnasmata, Gymnasmata." *Historisches Wörterbuch der Rhetorik.* Ed. Gert Ueding. Vol. 7: *Pos-Rhet.* Tübingen: Niemeyer, 2005. 159–91.

Margolin, Jean-Claude. "Sur quelques exemplaires des 'Progymnasmata' d'Aphthonius conservés dans des Bibliothèques parisiennes." *Gutenberg-Jahrbuch* (1979): 228–40.

Masen, Jacob. *Exercitationes oratoriae ioco-seriae.* Cologne: Johannes Busaeus, 1660. 461–77.

Matsen, Patricia P., Philip Rollinson, and Marion Sousa, eds. *Readings From Classical Rhetoric.* Carbondale and Edwardsville: Southern Illinois UP, 1990.

Micraelius, Johannes. *Progymnasmata Aphthoniana.* Stettin: Jeremias Mamphras, 1656.

Monfasani, John. *George of Trebizond. A Biography and a Study of his Rhetoric and Logic.* Leiden: Brill, 1976.

Morison, Samuel Eliot. *Harvard College in the Seventeenth Century, Part I.* Cambridge, MA: Harvard UP, 1936.

Nadeau, Ray. "The Progymnasmata of Aphthonius in Translation." *Speech Monographs* 19 (1952): 264–85.

Patillon, Michel, ed. *Aelius Théon, Progymnasmata.* Paris: Les Belles Lettres, 1997.

Penzkover, Angie. "The Progymnasmata: Resources for Classical Writing." 2003. <http://home.wi.rr.com/penzky/progymnasmata.htm>.

Pomey, François. *Candidatus rhetoricae.* Lyon: Antoine Molin, 1661. 214–16, 290–91.

Quintilian. *Institutio Oratoria.* Ed. and trans. Donald A. Russell. 5 Vols. The Loeb Classical Library. Cambridge, MA: Harvard UP, 2001. 124–27, 494.

Selby, James. "Developing Excellent Writers for Our Future: Using the Progymnasmata." 2004. <http://www.classicalcomposition.com/>.

PART II

Rhetorical Theory

Apuleius and the Forensic Genre in Antiquity

5

Craig R. Smith

This article examines a case study of public speaking in the second century of imperial Rome to demonstrate that the forensic apologia was important to its success. The study is guided by Cicero's refinement of the *Rhetorica ad Herennium* inclusive of his advice on the use of humor as a performance enhancement. Cicero's writing dominated this epoch and helped speakers adapt to the expectations of the audiences in imperial Rome during a period when deliberative oratory had fallen on hard times but epideictic and forensic speech were still valued. The Romans had developed an extensive system of laws, and their forensic rhetoric, based on Greek origins, was carefully catalogued, particularly by Cicero. One particularly significant example of following the Roman rules of rhetoric was Apuleius's speech of self-defense.[1]

This study of that speech proceeds in two stages. First, it examines the development of forensic speaking during the imperial period of Rome. In the course of doing so, it reviews Cicero's much neglected theory of humor with an eye toward seeing how it enhanced the performance of the apologia. Second, the study analyzes an apologia by the noted speaker, philosopher, poet, and playwright Apuleius as a model of the time. To familiarize the reader with the case at bar and to determine how typical the speech might be, this section of the study begins with an examination of Apuleius's use of the stasis system. However, the analysis focuses on how Apuleius expands his style with humor, while also using it to undermine the credibility of his opponents.

The Development of the Forensic Genre

Observing the needs and practices in ancient Athens five centuries before Apuleius's time, Aristotle deduced three forms of public address in his *Rhetoric*: the forensic for legal battles, the epideictic for ceremonial events, and the deliberative for legislative arenas. Accordingly, the role of the audience helped to define each of these genres: the audience performed the role of judge or jury for a forensic speech; the role of observer for a ceremonial speech, e.g., an after-dinner speech or one celebrating a national holiday;[2] and the role of legislator for the deliberative speech. The forensic speech concerned a past act; the epideictic speech endorsed current moral and national values; and the deliberative speech centered on future action. The three forms of speeches differed also in terms of their subject matter: the forensic concerned accusation and defense; the epideictic praise or blame; and the deliberative examined ways and means, national defense, trade, and the pragmatics of government. Each kind of speech had a different end or aim: the forensic sought justice; the epideictic revealed honor or dishonor; and the deliberative aimed at making sure society functioned expediently to achieve contentment.[3] In short, the art of persuasion, that is, rhetoric, fell into three divisions or genres, each having its audience, concern with time, subject matter, and purpose.

Aristotle argued that forensic speakers needed to be knowledgeable in several areas. He advised them to know about such subjects as crime and its incentives, the state of mind of someone who committed crimes, and what kind of person was likely to be wronged or invite crime. He then divided the causes of human action into involuntary and voluntary. The involuntary causes, which are more excusable in court, include chance, nature, and compulsion. The voluntary causes, which are less excusable, include habit, reason (calculation), passion, and desire. This division of causes is reflected in Aristotle's advice that lawyers understand two different kinds of law: the particular laws of the state and the universal laws of nature.

The Roman Rhetorical System

With the decline of Greece and the rise of Rome, the development of rhetorical theory moved to the schools of the Roman Republic. The first major Roman rhetoric text is the *Rhetorica ad Herennium,* written about 90 BC by an unknown author who organized Greek rhetorical theory into five canons. The *Rhetorica ad Herennium's* most original contribution is its detailed study of organization in which we find the theory of stasis, a mechanism that greatly advances the forensic genre by serving both inventive and organizational processes. Though the system was first developed, as far as we know, by Hermagoras of Temnos around 150 BC, his text is not extant, nor was it as influential as the *Rhetorica,* for in the Latin work major questions are laid out that lead a speaker to generate arguments for self-defense or for the prosecution of another.[4] These include:

I. *What can be conjectured about basic aspects of the situation?*

   A. *Did the alleged act occur?* Evidence of violence or lost goods, testimony, etc., are used to establish this fact. In many trials this issue is stipulated, that is, agreed to on both sides.

   B. *Did the accused have a motive to commit the crime?* Evidence of motive is usually more subjective and in some cases it is based on the impressions of witnesses. This issue is hotly debated in many trials.

   C. *Did the accused have the character of one capable of committing the crime?*

II. *Can the act be defined as a crime?* While stipulating that a certain act occurred, a speaker may choose to argue that it was no crime.

III. *What is the quality of the act that lies behind the crime?*

  A. *Was the act justified enough not to be punished?* While admitting that he or she committed the act in question, the accused argues that what was done was justified. For example, a woman who was battered by her husband decides to take revenge or "strike back" and argues that she did so in self-defense.

  B. *Do mitigating circumstances excuse the act?*

   1. The most common defense in this category is temporary or permanent insanity.

   2. What occurred was an accident, not a premeditated crime.

   3. The accused is a product of a society gone bad. It is society that is responsible for the crime, not the individual.

  C. *Were there subsequent benefits of the act to justify it?* Perhaps there is no better example of this argument than Brutus's justification for the assassination of Julius Caesar from the play by William Shakespeare. Brutus joined other conspirators who stabbed Caesar as he arrived for a session of the Roman Senate. Brutus justifies the assassination before the Roman mob by claiming that because he loved his country more than he loved Caesar, he had to slay him. Caesar had become ambitious and tyrannical, thereby threatening the foundations of the republic. Preserving the republic, a clear benefit, reduces the evil of the assassination.

  D. *Was the criminal act necessary because the person attacked deserved to be punished?* In this argument, which is similar to the one above, the accused takes the law into his or her own hands not for some benefit to society or others, but because the victim deserved to be punished. The famed "Unabomber" used this defense in his apologia, which was printed in the *Washington Post* and *New York Times*.

  E. *Does the perpetrator deserve leniency?* If all else fails, the accused can argue that the punishment for the crime should be reduced or suspended. The plea for leniency can be based on the accused's otherwise good record, the charge being a first offense, the accused's lack of familiarity with the law, or on any of a series of arguments based on mitigating circumstances. Clarence Darrow's defense of Leopold and Loeb falls into this category since there was no question about whether a brutal crime had been committed. The question was whether the death sentence should be imposed.

IV. *Does the court being addressed have jurisdiction over the alleged crime?* A whole other series of arguments can be built around the question of proper jurisdiction. The accused in many cases seeks a change of venue to avoid the selection of a prejudicial jury in a locale where the crime was committed. Or the accused may argue that the court has no jurisdiction in a certain matter, or that another court would be better suited to the case.

V. *Has the case been brought in a proper procedural manner?* As if the defense did not have enough topics from which to build arguments, one more is provided that has proven crucial in many a court case: the issue of proper procedure. Was the accused informed of his or her rights? Was the evidence properly obtained? Has the statute of limitations lapsed?

These are the major questions that anyone putting together a speech of prosecution or defense would have to ask to find the available arguments for the case.[5] Few understood this better than Marcus Tullius Cicero (106–43 BC), who, using his skill particularly in forensic oratory, rose above his class by becoming a consul after being a senator with the group of leaders that included Pompey, Cato the Younger, and Julius Caesar.

Cicero's work on forensic speaking refines the *Ad Herennium* in several ways. He begins by wedding Aristotle's notion of character, which is based on being in the habit of making good decisions, with Isocrates' call for an understanding of civic virtue. For example, in *De oratore* Cicero claimed that "the wise control of the complete orator is that which chiefly upholds not only his own dignity, but the safety of countless individuals and the entire state."[6] Cicero also recommended incorporating national lore into a speech where appropriate if it would enhance the case being made by tying it to nationhood. Finally, Cicero retrieved Aristotle's notion of judgment as the ultimate quality of the good man (*vir bonus*). Aristotle believed the prudent ruler to be level headed and would take into account all possibilities, acting on them in a practical way that balanced courage with compromise. Cicero advanced Aristotle's conception of *phronesis* by arguing that leaders need to be copious in understanding causes of events and demonstrate moderation and self-control.[7] He argued that since education produced men who were active in practical affairs, oratory was essential to that education, as that education was essential to sound oratorical practice.[8] Only in this way can one exercise prudential judgment (*summaque prudentia*) or sensibility,[9] which achieves change within the context of historical advancement.[10] To hammer home this point, judgment is contrasted with rashness (*temeritas*), from *temere*, things that happen by chance instead of by calculation. The term implies a lack of forethought or impulsive action.[11]

However, Cicero did not stop there; he extended the notion of propriety to questions of ethical conduct, thereby specifically linking it to character; that is to say, one's credibility is the sum of one's conduct.[12] This linkage holds particular relevance for rhetoric as an art form: language choice is volitional and creative. It forces choice that reveals a sense of self. Apuleius's rhetorical dexterity would shape a person quite compatible with his forensic aims.

Cicero's speeches against Catiline are themselves legendary, as is his understanding of the stasis system used to construct his case. Like other Romans, Cicero relied on Hermagoras of Temnos to develop this system of stock questions. Cicero's *De inventione* summarized his stasis system this way:

> Every subject which contains in itself a controversy to be resolved by speech and debate involves a question about a fact, or about a definition, or about the nature of an act, or about the legal processes. . . . When the dispute is about a fact, the issue is said to be conjectural, because the plea is supported by conjectures or inferences. When the issue is about a definition, it is called the definitional issue, because the force of the term must be defined in words. When, however, the nature of the act is examined, the issue is said to be qualitative, because the controversy concerns the value of the act and its class or quality. But when the case depends on the circumstances that the right person does not bring the suit, or that he brings it against the wrong person, or before the wrong tribunal, or at a wrong time . . . the issue is called translative because the action seems to require a transfer to another court or alteration in the form of pleading. There will always be one of these issues applicable to every kind of case; for where none applies, there can be no controversy.[13]

The stasis system provides a way to invent lines of argument for the speech that concerns guilt or innocence, whether it be a summation to a jury or a sermon to a wayward congregation.[14] Cicero's system is so similar to that developed in the *Rhetorica ad Herennium* that there is no need to review it here; it is one of the many reasons he was thought to be the author of that work.

Cicero's comments on style in general are also relevant to the development of the forensic genre. Cicero, and after him Quintilian and Pseudo-Longinus, demonstrated how fruitful the joining of *inventio*, the finding of arguments, and *elocutio*, putting into language, can be. They vastly expanded the less detailed notions of "appropriateness" and "fitness of function" developed by the Greek Sophists[15] because they understood the infinite variety of choices humans have of words and sentence structures. Quintilian argued that an "impression of grace and charm is produced by rhetorical figures. . . ."[16] In his last rhetorical work, *Orator*, Cicero explained how style can be seen to run along a continuum:

> Metaphors are used in the plain style to make the meaning clear, not for entertainment. . . . [The orator] will avoid elaborate, contrived symmetry and repetition as well as the more powerful figures of speech. . . . Moderate vocal variety and slight gesticulation are typical of an orator speaking in the plain style. . . . The middle style is more robust. . . . Ornamentation is appropriate. Metaphor, metonymy, catachresis, allegory may all be used effectively. The orator using this style will present his arguments in detail and in depth. The [grand] style is described by the words full, ample, stately, and ornate. . . . Eloquence of this sort sways and moves an audience. Anyone who speaks only in this mode should be despised, since clarity and precision of the plain style and the charm of the middle

style must be used to prepare an audience. . . . That man is eloquent who can speak about ordinary subjects in a simple way, great subjects grandly, and topics between these extremes moderately.[17]

The interplay between *ornatus, decorum,* and *inventio* allowed Cicero and others to develop other stylistic tactics such as elaboration (expansion of an idea or argument), illumination (clarifying an idea or argument with an illustration), and paradox (catching attention with a striking contrast). These were the tools of self-fashioning on which Apuleius would rely.

Cicero on Humor

While the foregoing theories are well known, Cicero's exploration of the uses of humor has been given much less attention in our literature. This is ironic since his advice on humor seems as fresh today as it must have been during his lifetime. Book II of *De oratore* begins the discussion of humor in chapter 58. Cicero carefully divided his topic into five subheadings: humor's nature, its sources, whether it is appropriate to the speaker, the limits of license the speaker has, and a classification of things that are funny.[18]

Cicero claimed that humor is by nature unrestrained, by which he meant an audience *cannot help but laugh* if the words are selected and strung together in the right way. He claimed that the sources of humor included obnoxious or ill-mannered behavior and that which is ugly. The matter of appropriateness goes to the heart of what a speaker should joke about in a given venue. For example, radio host Don Imus once served as master of ceremonies at the prestigious White House press corps dinner. While President Clinton and the first lady were on the dais, Imus referred to the president's sexual escapades as a youth in a pickup truck, thereby insulting the presidency, the president, and the audience. If that were not bad enough, he went on to add an obscene twist to an affair one of the anchormen in the audience had with an intern. It was a terribly distasteful moment for those present. According to Cicero, the limits of humor include making fun of those who are weak, destitute, or infirm. One should not joke about serious criminal activity because it reflects badly on the speaker's values. Mocking of the helpless can make the speaker seem cruel or arrogant.

Those things subject to ridicule include flaws in those who are not respected or those who are unethical or guilty of crimes for which they have not been punished. Thus, when O. J. Simpson was found innocent of a crime to which DNA condemned him or when President Clinton escaped removal from office for lying about an affair with an intern they were fair game for comedians.

Humor can also be generated by looking at current events and other facts. Jay Leno of *The Tonight Show* is the master of using the day's newspaper stories to make jokes about contemporary matters. Humor can be generated by puns and plays on names. Taking words literally, using humorous quotations, and sarcasm are all part of Cicero's arsenal of humor. He also recommended the use of apt epithets and understatement to disparage an opponent. Humorous caricature of an opponent can also prove effective.

Cicero also included mimicry in his bag of tricks and recommended surprise, indecency, and making faces as weapons that could be used in a humorous manner if the speaker were judicious. As we know, Cicero not only recommended the use of humor in public speaking, he often used it himself in forensic situations.[19] His advice was widely imitated and very influential during the time of Apuleius, who resided in North Africa.

Apuleius and the Apologia

North Africa once housed the elaborate civilization of the Phoenicians, who built the walled city of Carthage in the region later known as the Roman province of Numidia. After the Punic Wars, however, Carthage was leveled (146 BC), which helped Alexandria rise as the new center of learning in nearby Egypt. Alexandria hosted a huge library of important manuscripts and several influential members of the Neoplatonic school. At the time of Apuleius's speech (c. AD 155), Christians were part of the philosophical fray along the southern coast of the Mediterranean. Rome was in almost total ascendance as the Pax Romana held firm. The literary movement of the period called for a flowery style that was intended to entertain audiences around the Roman Empire, especially in seats of sophistication such as the prominent North African cities. Thus, excessive verbal display was common, there being little other entertainment available.

Apuleius was born in Hippo (in the province of Numidia), which may explain Augustine's later identification with him. Apuleius's father was a judge, which may also explain Apuleius's adeptness at the law. The family eventually settled in Madaurus, Numidia, but Apuleius went to school in Carthage (as would Augustine) and then in Athens. After giving the speech examined in this study, Apuleius became a well-known philosopher and satirist. Apuleius's most famous works begin with the publication of *Apologia*[20] and continue with the rather ornate *Metamorphoses*,[21] then *On the World*, and *On the Philosophy of Plato*. His works were popular around the empire. Two and a half centuries later, Augustine mentions Apuleius frequently in *City of God* and shows respect for his knowledge of philosophy and rhetoric. Augustine particularly admires Apuleius's sophisticated understanding of Plato, which Augustine attributes to Apuleius's lesser known *The God of Socrates*.[22]

In the case of the present study, Apuleius chose to represent himself before the judge and the associate justices of the court (*basilica*) in Sabrata on the North African coast. In this court, the defendant was allowed one-third more time than his accusers, hence the four-hour length of Apuleius's speech. Representing oneself was standard practice; upper-class Roman citizens were educated to represent themselves and others in court. What makes Apuleius's apologia of particular interest to the modern reader is his reliance on humor and invective to win his vindication. His use of insults, name calling, lampooning, and sarcasm flows from the Ciceronian tradition.[23] The door to the use of these tactics was opened by his accusers, who had vilified him before the court. More importantly, the apologia reveals how these techniques create a dialectical tension between the accused and his accusers that will cause the judges and the observers to identify with the accused and become alienated from his accusers. Because Lucius Apuleius Afer was somewhat famous in the region—in fact, a cult would form around him that lasted into Augustine's time—a crowd of spectators was attracted to the case, as the text reveals at 001, 003, 098. Many came from Carthage, where Apuleius lived with his wife; her will was the proximate cause of the legal action by her son, who was represented by his uncle. These visitors provided Apuleius with a secondary audience to which he could play in order to put more pressure on the court. They were also the audience for which much of his humor was intended.

The general composition of Apuleius's speech matches the advice current at the time and derived from the *Rhetorica ad Herennium* as reinforced by Cicero and Quintilian. Apuleius's use of the stasis system would have made Cicero proud, as would the effective use of rhetorical questions. Cicero also would have liked the fact that the style was not so ostentatious as to detract from the message, but succeeded in dressing the apologia and made it entertaining. Arguments were adjusted to the primary audience, in this case the judicial panel, but were readily accessible to the observers.

In rough outline, the speech begins by attempting to allay hostility by confronting various rumors and building Apuleius's ethos (1–24). The early part of this segment also deals with procedural questions, as we shall see when we look more closely at the use of the stasis system in the address.

In the second division of the speech, Apuleius refuted the charges of seduction and use of magic (25–65). This section was lengthy because of Apuleius's reputation as a conjurer. His fascination with magic did, in fact, carry over into his most noted work, *The Golden Ass*. But in the present situation, he had to face charges that he had a store of potions and other magical items,[24] that he had cast spells on a young man and a lady, that he was involved in late night tribal activity, and that he had employed his magical power to gain the hand of Pudentilla, his wife and the mother of Pudens, one of his accusers.

The last major division of the speech dealt with a great deal of evidence that Apuleius read into the record to prove that he did not marry Pudentilla for her money (66–101), nor did he try to deny any of it to Pudens. There also were several pieces of real evidence, and inartistic proofs, such as statues and boxes that were brought before the court.

While this organization seems simple, it hides a more sophisticated strategy. Apuleius seemed well aware of Aristotle's astute observation that one genre can be used to mask another. In Apuleius's case, we have epideictic moments (i.e., passages of praise or blame) supporting a forensic thrust (i.e., passages of accusation and defense) by way of a dialectical division pitting an "us" against a "them." For example, Apuleius often emphasizes his own piety while castigating the ignorance and atheism of Aemilianus, the brother of his wife's first husband and Apuleius's chief accuser. This strategy, as well as many others we will examine, is pervasive in the speech. It occurs at paragraphs 010, 024, 034, 052, and 056, the last of which reads:

> Yet I'm aware that some people, Aemilianus being one of them, find it amusing to ridicule the sacred. What I hear about him from people in Oea[25] is that, to this day, he hasn't prayed to a single god, hasn't visited one temple, and if he passes a shrine he refuses to raise his hands to his lips to show respect. In fact, though he is a farmer, he doesn't offer the country gods anything. No cuttings from his earlier crops, none of his first ripened grapes, and no newly born animal in sacrifice. Yes, nothing for the gods who put food in his stomach and clothes on his back. Out at his place you'll find no shrine nor grove of trees dedicated to a god. (056)

The opening of Apuleius's apologia is deceptively simple, almost conversational in style. After only a few short pages, we are witness to Apuleius's ability to employ epideictic arguments (praise and blame) to assess the credibility (ethos) of the major players: Aemilianus, the uncle of Pudens, is deceptive, manipulative of his charge, and held in ill repute. Maximus, the judge, is wise and just,[26] a theme that continues throughout the apologia. For example, in section 064, Apuleius says, "Maximus knows I'm not making up anything, since he has mastered the concepts of supercelestial realm and the other-side-of-heaven in Plato's *Phaedrus*." For his part, Apuleius claims he has been put upon, and is doing the best he can to defend himself.[27] He uses the available means of persuasion to defend his reputation and to plead his innocence. Three important aspects of Apuleius's rhetoric characterize this speech: his profitable use of the stasis system; his style inclusive of humor; and his arguments based on ethos (credibility) and anti-ethos, which also includes humor.

Stasis

Only after his first pass at characterizing Aemilianus, Pudens (his wife's seventeen-year-old son by a previous marriage), Maximus, and himself, does Apuleius turn to the actual charges against him, using parts of the stasis system common in Roman rhetoric. In this way, he demonstrates his sensitivity to the audience and his sense of appropriateness. The first question that Apuleius draws from the stasis system is the one concerning proper procedure. He divides it into three parts. First, he argues that Aemilianus is hiding behind his nephew and should have brought the charges himself (002). Second, he argues that procedure has been fouled because Aemilianus has aroused public sentiment against Apuleius (001–003). And later, he claims that "the personal letters of my wife were unethically made public and inaccurately interpreted" (028). Thus, Apuleius begins his speech with the procedural question before moving to the weightier issues of guilt or innocence. This strategy gains sympathy for Apuleius while casting aspersions on the motive of his chief accuser. In this way, it sets the tone for the speech while allaying hostility in the audience for Apuleius. As we shall see in the investigation of style and ethos that follows, Apuleius's effectiveness often stems from his ability to accomplish two rhetorical goals at the same time.

Next, Apuleius refers to the charge of being a magician as an "old wives' tale" (025). He shows that the evidence in support of this charge is very weak and subject to ridicule. Finally, he issues one of the standard ploys of lawyers to this day—the "even if" argument: even if I were a magician, I did no wrong (028).

Later in the speech (068), Apuleius returns to the issue of the crime at hand and deals with it by recounting a long narrative that explains why his wife married him.[28] He also employs a letter written by the hand of his enemy and brother-in-law, Aemilianus, to support various points in the story.[29] This tactic allows him to conclude, "It's clear enough to anyone that I did not force her by magic to give up any stubborn determination to remain a widow" (071). He adds evidence that he was in no hurry to marry and has sections of letters of his wife read to show that she had been quoted out of context (082). Apuleius also quotes from the letters and incomplete will of her dead son Pontianus, who praises him. Finally, he makes an important distinction to deny directly once again the charge against him: "Knowing about these magicians is quite a different thing from being involved in the art of magic" (091).

Apuleius also considers the issue of motive. He denies that he lured Pudentilla into marriage in order to gain her wealth.[30] He claims that these charges are slanders (055).[31] Limited income does not induce evil; on the contrary, far from providing a motive for crime, his modest financial position contributes to his life of learning and reflection (18). He repeats this theme several times later in the speech (066, 090, 092), concluding that what really attracted him to Pudentilla was her "knowledge and higher values," not her wealth. He undercuts the monetary motive and further enhances his credibility by demonstrating that he talked his wife into making gifts of property and other objects to her sons. He saves his best evidence for last—only a few sections from the end—when he orders the breaking of the seal on his wife's will, which he helped write. By naming Pudens as heir, it demonstrates that Apuleius was not motivated by greed because he could have prevented Pudens from being so designated (99–100).

Throughout the speech Apuleius argues that he does not have the character of one who would act badly. That he writes poetry is no proof that he is a magician. Poetry of his type has been written by good men like Solon and Plato (009–010); in fact, Apuleius claims his poetry is about Platonic love (012). In like manner, he argues that possessing a mirror does not mean he is a magician, nor that it is used for constant preening (013–014).[32] Given that Apuleius spends some time on the argument, one suspects that he was either sensitive to it or had a reputation that supported the charge. He quotes from many philosophers, writers, speakers, and scientists to refute the point.

He also attacks the motive of his chief accuser, claiming at one point that Aemilianus had brought the case in order to establish a personal reputation, a long-standing tradition in Rome. However, Aemilianus's reputation is so poor as to make this an absurdity (066). So there must be some other motive. Apuleius claims that it is "envy" (067) pure and simple, and later that it is "good old-fashion greed" (099).

Recall that one of the major questions in the stasis system was: Can the act be defined as a crime? Apuleius uses this question to break down the charges against him. Beginning at section 025, he requests that his opponents "define for us just what a magician is." And even if they can do that, he argues that they should remember that Plato did not consider the practice of magic a crime, but as acceptable to the gods (028). Thus, the practice of magic is no crime.

Apuleius goes on to the supporting indictments against him on this count. He claims that the buying of certain fish is not necessarily proof that he is a conjurer. The fish could be used for medicine or for anatomical study. Apuleius then identifies himself with Aristotle and Plato, among others, who participated in similar research (041). As we shall see, this question allows Apuleius to demonstrate his devastating wit and style.

Next, he redefines the incident of a boy falling under a spell, which Apuleius was accused of casting. He says that there were no witnesses, and that the boy was unable to prophesy, proving he had not been cast under a spell (042). Furthermore, since the boy was impure, he would not have been an acceptable choice for the alleged spell. Finally, in fact, the boy was epileptic, and Apuleius claims that fourteen slaves, only a few of whom were owned by Apuleius, had witnessed his condition.

The same strategy is used to deal with the case of a woman who allegedly fell under one of his spells (048). Because she too was epileptic, Apuleius claims to have been examining her at the request of her doctor and in accord with Plato's writings (49–51). Apuleius concludes this major section of the speech by arguing that Aemilianus has only conjecture to support his other claims. He mistakes sacred objects for magical items (053–056 and 061–065). He relies on the testimony of Crassus, a man of bad habits who did not even show up for the trial and was bribed by Aemilianus using a middle man (057–060).

In this way, the stasis system provides an internal organization for the speech while assuring that it refutes each of the salient points made against Apuleius. It is efficient and lawyerly. However, it is the use of humor that distinguishes this apologia. Its relation to style and credibility take the speech to another level, a level that must have impressed the judges while entertaining the observers.

Style

That Apuleius was a master of style cannot be doubted by anyone who has read *Metamorphoses* (or *The Golden Ass*). But this speech is no literary work. Thus, when dealing with the legal questions above, Apuleius is wise at first to refute directly the charges against him using a middle style that is character-

ized by a heavy reliance on rhetorical questions but is not excessively ornamental.[33] However, when *ornatus* is needed, Apuleius not only uses it
effectively, he uses it to entertain. For example, throughout the speech
Apuleius launches a series of rhetorical questions meant to devastate his opponents and/or their charges against him. Consider this passage: "Aemilianus,
do you and your supporters hear the crowd's loud reaction against you? And
do you hear their response to your false testimony? Don't you feel the least bit
ashamed of all your slander?" (063). Rhetorical questions are also used to hold
interest and guide the judges through his arguments, a device that explains the
lack of a more obvious organizational structure.[34] The questions also serve to
make the observers part of the situation, opening them to Apuleius's humor.

Apuleius does not often use metaphor, perhaps because he does not want
it to get in the way of his arguments, or perhaps because he wishes to avoid
being accused of being too poetic. However, when he does use metaphor, it is
energetic in the Roman demonstrative sense. Early in the speech, for example,
he compares Aemilianus to a poisonous snake (003). Later he uses analogy to
ridicule Aemilianus by comparing him to the epileptic Thallus: "Thallus
twists his eyes, you twist the truth. Thallus draws his hands into a knot during
a fit, but you draw your cronies up into a clutch to plot your moves" (052). As
we have seen, Cicero recommended connecting metaphor and analogy to the
legendary figures and leading philosophers of Rome and Greece.[35] From Her-
cules to Archimedes, from the river Styx to Numidia, Apuleius not only provides illustrations for his points but enhances his credibility by demonstrating
his knowledge of science, geography, mythology, and philosophy.

Apuleius's rhetorical arsenal also includes other vivid imagery that
"brings the scene before the eyes of the listeners," as Aristotle recommended,
while being demonstrative in the Roman sense. We see birds picking the
leeches from the teeth of crocodiles (008). We see testimony go up in a "puff
of smoke" (060). We hear that the sons of one of his accusers are "horny
young bucks" (075), that within his stepson "the innocence of the green years
has mixed with the wickedness of the gray ones" (085). We learn that women
can be "dangled like a lure" (097).

Apuleius is also fond of turning the tables on his opponents. "I am innocent," he declares, "they are guilty of slander" (011). Later he quips ironically, "I interpret your attempt to insult me as a compliment" (022). This
tactic resembles the posing of a dilemma such as the one Apuleius uses to
escape the charge of being a magician: If they really believed that I was a
magician, they would not bring me to court for fear of what I could do to
them. Since they did bring me to court, they must not believe that I'm really a
magician (026, 046, 080).[36]

Apuleius's use of humor in various forms pervades the speech.[37] He takes
delight in painting Aemilianus as a "bumpkin" and a "light weight." Crassus is
described in terms of his various appetites. The verbal fireworks also include a
list of tropes and figures that hold interest, sustain the humor, and enliven the
arguments of the speech. While a description of each trope and figure is not

possible in the space allowed here, some of the standard devices include metaphor ("wine dark sea" [022]); simile ("Too much wealth is like an oversized rudder on a ship" [019]); apostrophe ("I ask the gods for help!" [078]); "Oh, Pudentilla!" [085]); exclamations ("I wish the gods would bring them to an end!" [035]); and paradox ("The person who wants very little will have as much as he desires" [020]). In the following passage, Apuleius also demonstrates a love of parallelism that is typical of the speech. It allows him to move into the periodic style while also demonstrating expertise to add to his credibility: "In Greek history we can see that having little led to the development of some good qualities in famous people: justice in Aristides, kindness in Phocion, vigor in Epaminondas, wisdom in Socrates, and eloquence in Homer" (018).

What is formidable about this speech is the use of these devices to attack his opponents with humor. For example, in one hyperbole, Apuleius is able to turn the tables on his chief accuser and do it while making a pun at the same time: "If you really want the truth, Aemilianus, you are the one who is epileptic . . . because you have taken a fall every time one of your slandering attacks has failed" (052). Following Cicero's advice on understatement, he issues an ironic rhetorical question that reveals a sophisticated understanding of style in language: "Once again, this is true because people enjoy seeing images of themselves. Can you give me any other reason why all those statues, busts, paintings, and reliefs of people have been put up?" (014); "Aemilianus began by asking me, 'Why have you tried to obtain certain kinds of fish?' So a gourmet doesn't need special permission to obtain fish for his dinner table, but a natural scientist does need permission if he is to do research?" (027); and, "Is the price paid for the little place enough to raise an eyebrow?" (101).

Sarcasm also pervades the speech: "What a success story for magic!" (102). Apuleius also plays with words not only to entertain, but to ridicule his chief accuser:

> Keep in mind, however, that it is just as foolish an argument to say that sea-creatures with sexy sounding names are sought for arousing sexual desire as it would be to say that the sea-comb is pursued for combing hair, or the hawk-fish for catching birds, or the boar-fish for hunting boar, or the sea-skull for luring skeletons out of the grave. (034)

Apuleius continues this line of attack for several paragraphs, reducing Aemilianus to one who mistakes puns for arguments. The strategy emerges during several arguments on various topics to show that Aemilianus is uneducated, unsophisticated, "senile," and "stupid."

By this juncture in the speech (034), one gets the feeling that Apuleius sensed that he had won the case, but now must provide a show for his listeners or they will go home disappointed. There is a wonderful passage near the end of the speech where Apuleius takes phrases that his accusers have applied to him and then refutes them with the same number of words. The building effect must have been quite humorous: "I quote your charges and my reply follows: 'Gleaming teeth,' dental hygiene; 'Using mirrors,' scientific curiosity; 'Writing poems,' allowed everywhere; 'Investigating fish,' like Aristotle; 'Icon worship,' Plato's suggestion; . . . 'Older wife,' nothing unusual" (103). In short, Apuleius's style enhances his credibility, while denigrating his opponents, demonstrating his mastery of knowledge and making the audience laugh. Aside from the entertainment, however, these attacks serve to reduce Aemilianus's ethos while enhancing Apuleius's. It is to the subject of ethos that this study now turns.

Ethos

Aristotle believed that credibility was the most potent constituent of persuasion.[38] Cicero linked ethos to civic virtue. Apuleius understood this, but he also knew that destroying the credibility of one's opponents and praising the character of the judge were also effective. Thus, he is following Aristotle's advice when he claims to be honorable (003), when he demonstrates that he comes from a good family (024), and claims that it is no sin to be handsome and articulate, insisting that these qualities are overrated by his accusers (004–005). He builds the argument for his good character in many other clever ways—for example, by quoting Statius Caecilius to the effect that "innocence itself is real eloquence" (005). Hence, the more eloquent he is, the more innocent he is.

Apuleius also enhances his credibility by demonstrating expertise in several unique ways. First, he shows that he knows the laws of Rome all the way back to the Twelve Tablets. Second, and more cleverly, he indulges in digressions that allow him to demonstrate his knowledge of philosophy, science, and literature from Aristotle to Zeno. In this passage, he sounds like a professor:

> As a footnote, I'll add briefly that advocates of the second theory disagree about what happens to the rays after they leave the eye: Plato says they flow from the pupil and combine with light outside it before they proceed to the object; Archytas believes that once the rays leave the eyes they don't mix with any other substance. (015)

In fact, displays of *episteme* are common in the address. A passage in section 038 proves typical: "The writings go on to show how nature distinguishes the *vivpari* (live-born) from the *ovipari* (egg-born) sea-life in respect to their anatomy and the reasons behind these differences. Please notice that I am the one who coined these two Latin terms to translate the Greek *zooticka* and *ootika*." Knowledge of history was also in Apuleius's arsenal: "We have a bit of history of our own. Around the year 200 BC we were an established town under King Scyfax" (024). The sentence leads into another digression that demonstrates just how knowledgeable Apuleius is on a wide variety of subjects.

Yet another strategy that Apuleius puts to good use is self-disclosure as a means of enhancing credibility. Self-disclosure remains an effective part of apologia, rearing itself in such well-known addresses as Nixon on Checkers, Kennedy on Chappaquiddick, and Clinton on Lewinsky. Apuleius uses a charge against him to reveal his rather Stoic existence: "I have a small house and relatively few servants because I eat lightly and wear plain clothing, and because I serve my guests rather ordinary food" (021). The parallel to Nixon's disclosure of his financial situation is hard to miss when Apuleius discloses his wealth: "If you don't know already, I'll state publicly that my father left my brother and me about two million sesterces. I have reduced my share a bit by extensive travel, years of study, and a number of gifts" (023). He also uses self-disclosure to deprecate himself humorously: "I was half-Numidian and half-Gaetulian. But I don't see what there is for me to be ashamed of. No more than there was for Cyrus the Great, founder of the Persian Empire, to be ashamed of being half-Mede and half-Persian" (024).

With regard to Maximus, the head judge, Apuleius has nothing but praise throughout the speech. He goes so far as to identify him with Aristotle and in the process identifies with him too: "Aren't you accusing me of the very thing which Maximus and I admire in Aristotle?" (041). He tries to please Maximus by identifying his case with Platonic thought. Being a noted Platonist himself, Apuleius could easily do this in a setting that was influenced by reports and writings that came from the Neoplatonic school at relatively nearby Alexandria. As we have seen before, we find further proof of an effort to flatter the judge when Apuleius says, "Maximus knows I'm not making up anything, since he has mastered the concepts of the 'supercelestial realm' and 'the other-side-of-heaven' in Plato's *Phaedrus*" (064). Finally, near the end of the speech, Apuleius relies on a letter of praise from the orator Lollianus, a man whom Maximus evidently admires (094–096) and who had preceded Maximus as governor of the province.[39]

Aside from building his own credibility and playing to the judges, Apuleius is adept at destroying the credibility of his accusers. He begins the process using an in-your-face rhetoric of accusation. Referring to Aemilianus, he says, "You shameless old rascal, you've been exposed! You didn't know that your letter was kept on file. And so you didn't imagine you'd be convicted by your own testimony" (070). In response to Pudens's claim that he knows of witnesses against Apuleius, he replies:

> Come on! Bring on these boys in whom you have so much confidence. Let's see them! At least tell us their names. . . . Say something! Why are you silent? What's the delay? What signals are you looking for back over your shoulder? Well—it seems I must address Aemilianus since Tannonius Pudens doesn't answer. (046)

This strategy seems to keep the opposition off guard while demonstrating that Apuleius is extremely confident and very much in charge of the situation. It also heightens the dialectic between identification and alienation for the audience.

In fact, Apuleius reinforces the negative picture he paints of his accusers with healthy doses of ridicule. His attack on the character of Aemilianus is sustained throughout the speech.[40] Aemilianus is accused of manipulating the public, using women to procure favor, and corrupting Pudens. Apuleius also tries to damage Pudens, the young charge who has brought the charges, by demonstrating that he is ignorant, corrupt, and a "little dictator" (098).[41] Apuleius blames Crassus and Rufinus for the boy's plight and in the process destroys their characters.

In regard to Aemilianus not allowing Pudens to testify, he says, "First, his age is no problem in his being a witness. Second, however, his deep involvement in the prosecution diminishes his credibility" (045). Next, the deposition of Crassus comes under attack: "He also claims that at that distance he recognized the smoke that was rising from his chimney. All this, of course, from 1,200 miles away! If Crassus saw the smoke from Alexandria, the man possesses the eyesight that goes beyond what the wanderer Odysseus hoped and prayed for to help him find his home again" (057). Crassus's absence at the trial is given no mercy:

> Has Crassus gone back to Alexandria because he's gotten bored at home? Or is he home scrubbing down the walls of his house? Or, more likely, is the boozer suffering today from last night's orgy? I certainly saw him here in Sabrata yesterday, hung over, making a pretty sight of himself as he carried on with you in the marketplace, Aemilianus, belching his way through the conversation. (059)

A few sections later, Herennius Rufinus comes into Apuleius's sights:

> I must in all honesty say he runs his house like a pimp. Everyone living there is a degenerate. Herennius Rufinus himself is a notorious rascal. His wife markets herself as a whore. Their sons take after both parents. Night and day, horny young bucks bang on the door of the house, their dirty songs rattle the windows. (075)

Once each of the accusers and their witnesses have been destroyed, Apuleius attacks the group as a whole, hoping to alienate it from the audience.

These sensational passages are combined with humor to keep the audience's attention during the long speech. In response to Pudens's charge that Apuleius used fish for his magic, the defendant replied, "If you had read Virgil, you would undoubtedly have known that other things are usually obtained for use in magic. As I recall, he names fluffy strands of raw wool, freshly cut olive branches, fine incense, and threads of many colors" (030).

Next, he demonstrates Pudens's ignorance: "Do you see what is going on? Virgil is speaking about a poison, but you are referring to a dish for the table. Where he mentions herbs and sprouts, you carry on about fish bones and scales" (030). He chastises Pudens that he will "never find the characters in Homer using anything related to the sea or to fish to work their magic" (031). He concludes by ridiculing Pudens's misunderstanding of the language: "My esteemed prosecutor couldn't express himself clearly. Finally, after some delay, he ignorantly and distastefully chose a term that sounds like a name of the male sex organ" (033).

With his opponents destroyed, and the audience warmed by his humor, Apuleius can afford to return to his own reputation near the end of the apologia. The unsealing of Pudentilla's will shows his largesse and lack of animus for his stepson. The reading of the will proves that he is a well-intentioned man falsely accused by his enemies to whom he had only shown charity: "As a stepfather, I stood up for my worthless stepson against his angry and disgusted mother, acting like a father standing up for his own worthy son against the boy's stepmother. And I felt that I hadn't done enough until I had put a limit on my lovely wife's big-hearted generosity toward me" (099).

Thus, for Apuleius ethos is a two-edged sword: It can be used to build character as well as tear it down. Both edges of the sword are important to Apuleius's apologia. As he says late in the speech, "Everyone there [Oea] has condemned Rufinus and praised me" (094).

Conclusion

Apuleius gave the impression of having completed a thorough defense of his honor as he began his conclusion, again relying on a rhetorical question to make his point: "[I]s there a charge that I haven't refuted?" (102). He then quickly summarized the arguments he made in his speech, undercutting the charges against him and showing he had no motive to do wrong. He once again praised the judge and reduced the charges with ridicule as he summarized each one (103).

His adroit use of the stasis system accounts for the argumentative success of the speech. The persuasive effort was also enhanced by Apuleius's effective use of style to keep the audience beguiled and the judges impressed. But what ultimately makes it unique, and what seals the persuasion, is the way Apuleius builds his own credibility while destroying the ethos of his accusers. If contemporary political strategists are correct in their advice to make negative attacks humorous, then Apuleius was ahead of his time. However, his use of humor to ridicule his opponents was born from a knowledge of Cicero's rhetorical theory and extant speeches.

The apologia of Apuleius is effective because it employs a direct style with flashes of imagery and humor that hold attention and entertain. It builds the character of Apuleius while destroying the character of his accusers. It successfully flatters the head judge, in part by relying on the man's favorite philosopher, Plato, and, to a lesser degree, on the accomplished Roman orator, Lollianus, who is in the audience, a man greatly admired by Maximus. Apuleius's *Apologia* relied on important questions in the stasis system to deny the crime, to undermine the alleged motive, and to question the procedures of his adversaries. In short, Apuleius provided us with a model of this genre that brings the scene alive before our eyes almost two millennia after it occurred.

Notes

[1] In the Roman system, the accused often had to defend himself. The apologia, a subcategory of forensic speaking, was a speech of explanation or self-defense, not an apology for action taken.

[2] This genre is also referred to as the panegyric. See, for example, Cicero's *De oratore*, trans. E. W. Sutton and H. Rackham (Cambridge, MA: Harvard University Press, 1988), II.lxxxiv.341.

3 For a survey of these aspects of rhetoric, see Donovan J. Ochs, *Consolatory Rhetoric: Grief, Symbol, and Ritual in the Greco-Roman Era* (Columbia: University of South Carolina Press, 1993), chapter 3.

4 Most of this information can be found in Book II of *Rhetorica ad Herennium*, trans. Harry Caplan (Cambridge, MA: Harvard University Press, 1954). Other references can be found in *constitutio*, the early Latin term for Greek stasis, and Hermagoras in the index. Cicero treats the same topics in his *De inventione*, trans. H. M. Hubbell (Cambridge, MA: Harvard University Press, 1959) in Book II under forensic speeches (*genus iudicale*). Quintilian deals with this subject most specifically in Book III, Chapter iv (entire) in *Institutio oratoria* (hereafter *The Institutes of Oratory*), trans. H. E. Butler (Cambridge, MA: Harvard University Press, 1920–22/1980).

5 These questions are extrapolated from Book II of the *Ad Herennium*.

6 I.viii.34. For a full discussion see I.ii–iv, viii, which are devoted to this topic.

7 Cicero's thoughts on the need for the orator to be erudite pervade *De oratore*: see especially I.xxxix.176ff, I.xlvi.201ff. His comments on the moderate and prudent judgment also pervade his work, see especially I.xv.67 on moderation and self-control, II.lxxv.347 on judgment, II.lxxiv.342 on wise management, and II.lxxxiv.342 on temperance. Quintilian concurs; see, for example, VI.iv.10, "Moderation, and sometimes even longsuffering, is the better policy. . . ." See also, VI.v.3, where Quintilian claims, "There is no great difference . . . between judgment and sagacity."

8 See especially III.xv.55–xxii.82. Throughout *De oratore*, Cicero claims that to accomplish this end one must have a solid education. See II.xiii.55ff, II.xviii.76, II.xii.92–94. This position influenced many important medieval and Renaissance thinkers, not the least of whom was Machiavelli.

9 III.xiv.55, also translated "supreme wisdom." See also III.xvi.60.

10 III.xv.55–xxii.82. See also Quintilian XII.i.3. At XII.i.19 *prudentissimos* is translated as "sensible."

11 See also the *Rhetorica ad Herennium*, IV.xxv.35, "*Temeritas est cum inconsiderata dolorum perpessione gladiatoria periculorum susceptio.*"

12 See Cicero, *Orator*, H. M. Hubbell, trans. (Cambridge, MA: Harvard University Press, 1962), at 70 and *De officiis*, H. G. Edinger, trans. (Indianapolis: Library of Liberal Arts, 1974), at I.144. Or see the Loeb edition of *De officiis* by Walter Miller.

13 Cicero, *De inventione*, H. M. Hubbell, trans. (Cambridge, MA: Harvard University Press, 1949), I.viii.10.

14 Perhaps the most systematic of the ancients on this subject was Hermogenes, *On Stasis*.

15 For example, see Quintilian, *The Institutes of Oratory*, Books I.vi (entire), II.xxiii.8–11, XI,i.82–83. See also, Charles Seltman, *Approach to Greek Art* (London: Dutton, 1949), p. 29.

16 II.xiii.11.

17 *Orator*, 82–100. I have condensed and simplified some passages for the sake of brevity here. The last thought reads, "*Is erit igitur eloquens . . . qui poterit parva summisse, modica temperate; magna graviter dicere.*"

18 Quantitative research into humor generally divides the causes of humor into release of tension, matching of incongruities, and types of trumping. For a summary, see John C. Meyer, "Humor as a Double-Edged Sword: Four Functions of Humor in Communication," *Communication Theory*, 10 (2000): 310–31. From a rhetorical perspective, theorists and critics tend to examine humor from a Burkean perspective. Kenneth Burke speculates on the comic frame and the burlesque in *Permanence and Change* (Los Angeles: University of California Press, 1984). An application of this theory can be seen in Michael P. Moore, "'The Quayle Quagmire': Political Campaigns in the Poetic Form of Burlesque," *Western Journal of Communication*, 56 (1992): 108–24.

19 Michael Volpe has demonstrated how adept Cicero was at taking his own advice in "The Persuasive Force of Humor: Cicero's Defense of Caelius," *Quarterly Journal of Speech*, 63 (1977): 311–23.

20 The best translation of the *Apology* can be found in S. J. Harrison's *Apuleius: A Latin Sophist* (Oxford: Oxford University Press, 2000). The most noted previous translation was H. E. Butler's, which is now available online at http://classic.mit.edu/Apuleius/Apol.html. For the purpose of this study, I used the universal section numbering system and retranslated several

passages since neither Butler nor Harrison seem to catch certain rhetorical nuances. See *The Apologia and Florida of Apuleius Madaura*, trans. H. E. Butler (Oxford: Clarendon Press, 1909; Westport, CT: Greenwood Press, 1970).

[21] *Metamorphoses* or *The Golden Ass* addresses transformations in the human much as Ovid's work by the same name had done a century and a half before. Among others, Boccaccio was influenced by this satire on vices that invokes the goddess Isis.

[22] See *City of God* (Garden City, NY: Image Books/Doubleday & Company, 1958), pp. 86, 162, 164–65, 173–74, 179.

[23] Apuleius is particularly hard on his brother-in-law. Several times he talks about his ugliness and lack of charm.

[24] His accusers claimed they found bird feathers and smoke-darkened walls in his home.

[25] Modern Tripoli was built over Oea. In fact, it was in Oea while Apuleius was staying with his friend and former student colleague Pontianus that he met his friend's mother, Pudentilla, whom he married, and whose will is the subject of this case. The trial was complicated by the fact that Pontianus for a time had supported his uncles against his new stepfather, but recanted this decision only to die before the trial.

[26] Claudius Maximus was in fact the governor of the province carrying the title *propraetor.*

[27] To establish this claim, Apuleius uses one of Aristotle's major topoi from the *Rhetoric*, the argument from more or less. At 003, Apuleius argued that since Aemilianus lied before he was likely to do it again. He was a man of "bad character."

[28] At the end of the story, even Apuleius admitted that this was a "digression."

[29] Aristotle refers to this as an "inartistic proof" in his *Rhetoric.*

[30] Apuleius's accusers exaggerated the difference in their ages. Apuleius was only a few years, perhaps seven at most, younger than Pudentilla, who was forty when she married him.

[31] See, for example, 055.

[32] To paraphrase Apuleius at 014, our love of sculpture reveals our love of images. To carry one's accurate image is no crime, therefore, it should be no crime to carry a mirror.

[33] Recall that Cicero spoke of the middle style as lying on a continuum between the grand or florid style and the plain or simple style.

[34] See, for example, 025.

[35] He compared himself to Paris (004).

[36] See also 046, 080.

[37] See 017, 048, 052, 059.

[38] In the *Rhetoric* at 1356a10ff.

[39] This moment again provided Apuleius with an opportunity to digress into his storehouse of knowledge: "Cato would find no fault with its responsible tone and approach. Laelius would approve of its flow and smoothness. Gracchus would praise its energy and forcefulness, Caesar its fire and passion, and Hortensius its clear and sensible plan" (095). The passage indicated that Apuleius was well read in rhetorical theory.

[40] See, for example, 003, 028, and 056, in which Aemilianus was accused of ridiculing the sacred.

[41] 030. Later in the speech at 086 he claimed that Pudens had no shame and had embarrassed his mother.

The Eulogy

6 Grief and the Wisdom of the Ancients

Beth L. Hewett

Nearly six years ago, my brother and his copilot were killed in an ultra-light plane crash. His was the first eulogy I had ever written. A year later, I wrote the eulogy upon my father's sudden death. Primarily because of the rhetorical principles I have learned, I was able to write the eulogies despite the shock and grief of these deaths. In contrast to these eulogies, my brother's copilot's family wrote and read a lamentation in the form of a letter that expressed their anger, shock, and pain at his choice to be a pilot. Because their letter addressed unfinished family business rather than praising their deceased loved one, its highly private message actually shut out many of the mourners who also needed this ceremonial occasion to validate their grief. The public nature of the family's grief-struck, disapproving feelings needed to be offset by a more standard eulogy that would console those gathered; instead, left standing on its own, the lamentation caused visible discomfort among those gathered for the funeral. Because the letter was so angry and did not involve "good words" of praise or blessing, it essentially did not honor their loved one in the ways that a more traditionally guided eulogy would do. The result was not simply that the gathered mourners were aware of the family's pain, which of course they were, but that the eulogy failed to comfort them. It was a missed opportunity for celebrating their loved one and for consoling each other in more positive and rewarding ways.

My observation as both a rhetorician and bereavement counselor has been that bereaved people generally feel unable to express themselves in words upon the death of a loved one. Indeed, whereas a clergy person might deliver a homily or a funeral professional might deliver a more formal, yet less personal eulogy, many bereaved people who want to honor their loved ones find themselves turning away from words and toward visual and audio media such as photographs, photo montages, video/CDs, and recorded music to represent their feelings about their loved ones. At a time when people naturally feel torn apart and inarticulate from grief, they also may feel verbally inarticulate or burdened by their own perception that they "can't write" and therefore cannot do justice to their loved ones. Yet, a genuine need to honor a loved one through the traditional form of a eulogy—of using words to memorialize the deceased—reveals a tension between desire and discomfort. Such tension makes the difficult day of the funeral still more difficult, unnecessarily adding stress to an already stress-filled time.

From the Greek, *eulogy* literally means "good words," and it often is translated as "praise" and sometimes as "blessing." These good words can have the positive effect of opening up the mourning process, or public expression and enactment of grief, for the bereaved. These good words also can affirm not only a person's or a family's values, but also those of a broader community. Unfortunately, few people feel truly comfortable with writing or delivering such good words; few people who are asked to give a eulogy would express confidence that the deceased is being honored with words that are fitting to the occasion. Instead, they may express fear and confess a poor ability to write or to speak publicly.

In this paper, I advocate a more publicly active role than contemporary rhetoricians may consider for educating and assisting the bereaved. Using the wisdom of ancient rhetoricians, as well as contemporary examples, I argue that the eulogy, though understudied (Kent "The Rhetoric of Eulogies"), remains important to how everyday people—private citizens—are mourned by the bereaved in funeral and memorial ceremonies. Further, I argue that the elements necessary for helping everyday people to develop a powerful eulogy already have been outlined by Aristotle, the precepts providing simple, time-honored, and proven steps for writing and presenting a contemporary eulogy.

This paper thus is divided into three parts. In the first, I review some of the recent literature about eulogies to make clear that basic rhetorical principles still guide eulogy writing. In the second section, I demonstrate how Aristotle's notion of virtue can assist writers in finding and developing words of praise that can console mourners, and I differentiate between the ideas of praise and of blessing. Finally, in the third section, I suggest how rhetoricians can and should become more active in publicly assisting eulogists who speak for private citizens.

Background

There is surprisingly little published literature about the rhetoric of the eulogy, particularly literature that regards the eulogy for the private citizen as opposed to the public figure. Three studies help to make my point that the ordinary person's eulogy can be guided by classical principles, many of which were articulated by Aristotle. As Michael L. Kent explains in "The Rhetoric of Eulogy: Topoi of Grief and Consolation," the ancient Greeks and Romans understood the eulogy to be primarily a consolation speech, which was offered for public figures rather than for private individuals. This speech, which Aristotle in *The Art of Rhetoric* considered epideictic and contained praise and blame for its subject (I.II.22.iii), traditionally was presented for a man who had died in battle or who otherwise positively represented the city-state. In this way, the eulogy was designed to console the bereaved, to affirm the community's values, and to exhort the audience to be virtuous. It had four main parts:

- *Prooemium.* A short introduction where the speaker would express approval of funeral customs, declare his unworthiness to make the speech, gain the audience's sympathy, and briefly praise the person being eulogized.

- *Epainos.* The section where the speaker would praise the deceased in terms of his (in ancient times) or her life, family, deeds, and other concerns of value for the community.

- *Paramythia.* The section where the bereaved were offered consolation and the audience was exhorted to live up to the values and deeds of the departed.

- *Epilogue.* The concluding section in which the speaker provided a final consolation, acknowledged his part in the funeral tradition, and dismissed the audience from the ceremony (Kent, "The Rhetoric of Eulogy" 109).

Historically, Cicero introduced these elements of the eulogy for public figures to Latin literature. Eventually, Christian eulogies developed, which differed from the classical tradition by emphasizing the praise of God over that of the individual or the state. Kent explains that the individual's worth was not ignored, but was placed as secondary to the higher power of God (109); thus, such eulogies have the flavor of a teaching homily more than a personal eulogy. It is not surprising that many contemporary Christian clergy adhere to this tradition and do not develop a funeral homily that praises the deceased, focusing instead on praising God and calling blessings upon the dead and the assembled mourners. More recently, the practice of a private citizen preparing and delivering a eulogy for another private citizen—the everyday person— parallels the tradition of honoring the famed public citizen or figure.

Kent continues his research with his dissertation into contemporary eulogia as presented by clergy members at a variety of funerals in "The Rhetoric of Eulogies: A Generic Critique of Classic and Contemporary Funeral Oratory." In this study, he is interested in the eulogy for the "everyday person," not the public citizen. He contends that the *a priori* assumption he and other rhetorical scholars have made that eulogies "to the exceptional (or 'great person') are representative of those to everyday citizens" is false, as is the notion that "only extraordinary citizens are deserving of eulogies" (17). Instead, he inductively studies contemporary eulogies to determine their focus and the topoi that hold them together. He finds that while a religious or spiritual component is integral to eulogizing, the focus tends to be more on the deceased than on God (63, 67–68, 70). Nonetheless, it is important to remember that the eulogists he studied were all clergy rather than secular speakers; thus, since a religious funerary service predisposes it to more spiritual topics and a homiletic nature, it is not surprising that these eulogies used a good deal of faith-focused topoi. Indeed—and again not surprisingly—Kent had few clerical survey respondents who saw the eulogy as having the classical function "to praise the deceased" (73). In terms of topoi for the eulogies that he studied, Kent finds a preponderance of language addressing belief in God; a focus on love, faith, and work, which led him to see these topoi as ones that transmit values of equal importance to belief in God (203); a concern for faith in God; and themes of soul, humor, and suffering, which are mentioned least frequently (199). He concluded that the common person's eulogy is not, by nature, developed using the classical model, necessitating a distinction between the contemporary eulogy of the public and the private citizen. Kent therefore believes that one area for future study is the development of "more sophisticated organizational structures that seek to incorporate multiple comforting topoi" (224). However, there is confusion here between the nature of a homiletic eulogy—as used in Kent's study—and one written and delivered by a private citizen. As the next study clearly shows, the structure that Kent seeks already exists in the classical eulogy. When employed by a private citizen eulogist rather than a clergy person who has the primary duty of acknowledging God, such a structure can be particularly helpful to developing a eulogy for a private citizen.

Adrianne Dennis Kunkel and Michael Robert Dennis in "Grief Consolation in Eulogy Rhetoric: An Integrative Framework" apply what they call a "new" analytical approach, one that involves the literature of death studies, or thanatology, to find common characteristics among eulogies for both public figures and private citizens. Interestingly, as the key characteristics fall neatly within the four classical categories that Kent outlines above, what is "new" appears simply to be the application of insights from death studies to rhetoric.

Classical Categories	Kunkel and Dennis Categories (Rearranged)
Prooemium	Credibility of speaker Self-disclosure of emotion

Epainos	Praise for the deceased
	Affirmation of vivid past relationship:
	   Notation of flaws (decreases reverence and raises appreciation)
	   Revelation to private insights and unique relationships

Paramythia	Problem-focused coping: suggestions for action
	Emotion-focused coping:
	   Positive reappraisal
	   Reference to afterlife
	   Appreciation of time spent with deceased
	   Appreciation of deceased's good life

Epilogue	Continuation of interactive bonds:
	   Addressing the deceased (second person "you")
	   Referring to the deceased in the present tense

Thus, the credibility of the speaker is based on building a case for his or her competence to speak in this ceremonial position, which is also a function of the prooemium. Anecdotes of the decedent's life affirm the speaker's relationship with the deceased, which is one way that the epainos works to reveal the decedent's lesser-known characteristics. Exhortations or suggestions for actions, such as calling for mourners to contribute to cancer research or to carry on the positive actions of the deceased, fall under the scope of the paramythia. The continuation of interactive bonds, wherein the speaker addresses the deceased directly ("You have no idea how much we'll miss you") or refers to the deceased as if she were still alive ("We know that you are with us even now"), belongs to the epilogue, wherein the speaker offers a final consolation to the mourners before dismissal. Kunkel and Dennis believe that such ways of addressing and referring to the deceased provide comfort by modeling and facilitating the new relationship with him or her (16). This rearranged division of their goals for a eulogy clearly demonstrates that a eulogy serves the same basic functions for the private citizen as it does for the famous public figure. Further, it suggests that the basic divisions of a classical eulogy can be used to assist everyday eulogists in discovering and arranging their material.

Eulogies for public citizens, such as politicians and celebrities who enjoy fame and wealth, tend not to stray too far from the classical model. Such eulogies, like that of Ron Reagan for his father, former President Ronald Reagan, and that of the Earl Charles Spencer for his sister Princess Diana, seem to have a blended classical-clerical form that elevates the dead and the occasion by praising the individual and his or her place within the state or broader society, as well as in relationship to God or a higher power. It is worth mentioning that such people are often eulogized by either professional speechwriters or through speeches that have been in constant development during the years of fame—or both. However, one might find a somewhat different expression in many clergy-offered services for the common, private citizen where, as Kent finds, there is attention both to the omnipotence of God and to the individual ("The Rhetoric of Eulogies"). As stated previously, the differences between the classical, homiletic, and contemporary eulogy lie in, respectively, the greatness of the person and his deeds and values; the decedent's relationship with God; and the ordinariness of the person as evidenced by such common visual media as photographic montages showing happy everyday people captured in everyday pursuits. Indeed, one might call the modern eulogy written by a private citizen for another private citizen the "eulogy of the ordinary" or the "common eulogy." It is this ordinary nature that rhetoric can both support and raise to a higher level. Not only can the organizational structure of the classical eulogy help those who are developing the good words, but rhetoric in particular can assist eulogists with the concept of praise found in the epainos. Praise, in its intention to confirm the deceased person's special qualities and actions, is somewhat antithetical to the ordinariness of contemporary private citizen eulogies.

Praise and Blessing

In the epainos, the eulogist's words traditionally invite others to reflect on their own mourning and to participate in a more communal experience of their grief. The eulogy becomes a part of the funeral ceremony that provides another meaningful time, place, and method for reflecting on the loss. Contemporary eulogies often provide opportunities for other people to rise and speak informally about their loss. On a broader social level, the eulogy actually inculcates values by instructing the gathered mourners about their common society's highest ideals and ethics. Through the selected details of the deceased's life, the eulogy writer illustrates those virtues, attitudes, and actions that the community expects, values, and—ultimately—praises as evidence of a life well-lived.

Praise can be grounded usefully in ancient rhetorical principles that recognize the essential qualities of personal virtue and those of noble activity. These qualities can then act as heuristics to help eulogy writers explore what to say about the deceased—in terms of praising him or her and relating that life to a broader community of fellow humans. For example, Aristotle noted that components of virtue include such qualities as justice, courage, self-control, generosity, magnificence, magnanimity, liberality, gentleness, prudence, and speculative wisdom (I.IX.1–7). Examples of noble activity include such actions that one recognizes as "good" for the family and the public: actions that are most useful to others; honorable deeds; unselfish behavior; acts of self-sacrifice, justice, and kindness; and those acts that bring credit to oneself or one's family in the eyes of the community and society at large.

When presented as a method of discovering what to say about the deceased, these qualities become tools for both exploring the person's life and providing unique personal qualities and past actions to talk about in the eulogy. Although anecdotal details like one's hobbies and jobs help to illustrate a person's interests, they also place the deceased solidly within the realm of the ordinary and fail to explore what is praiseworthy in one's life. However much people value the ordinariness of their lives, a eulogy is most memorable when it explores the deceased's life in terms of its deeper value and importance to those around him or her. Because the eulogy's content essentially determines and guides its other aspects, it is useful here to show how the rhetorical process works for finding ideas and focusing the speech itself.

Courage exemplifies a virtue of which Aristotle speaks, and it is a virtue often explored in the life of a famous public citizen. For example, in his eulogy for his sister in 1997, the Earl Spencer said of Princess Diana:

> All over the world she was a symbol of selfless humanity, a standard bearer for the rights of the truly downtrodden, a truly British girl who transcended nationality, someone with a natural nobility who was classless, who proved in the last year that she needed no royal title to continue to generate her particular brand of magic.

Spencer used the virtue of courage to praise Diana's greatness as a fighter for the rights of those unable to fight for themselves. Similarly, in 2004, Ron Reagan praised his deceased father, former President Reagan, by stating, "History will record his worth as a leader. We here have long since measured his worth as a man: Honest, compassionate, graceful, brave. He was the most plainly decent man you could ever hope to meet." In this eulogy, the younger Reagan lionizes his father as courageous.

But public figures do not have a monopoly on such virtues as courage. In the example below, one can see that there is much more to courage than the narrow contemporary perception that dangerous activity equals being a "hero," although this certainly is one valid meaning of courage. Courage can be applied to the common individual—the private citizen—who has lived his or her life in quiet but strong ways that address the world in a head-on manner.

A husband, who also was a father, has died unexpectedly. He will be greatly missed. How did his life exhibit the virtue of courage?

- *At the personal level*: Did he change his own life by prevailing over difficult childhood adversities—like losing a parent, or living in poverty, or attending many different schools, or putting himself through college? Did he fight a disease (successfully or not), battle with a mental disorder, or otherwise "take on" his own well-being by improving it somehow? Did he learn or teach any important lessons about acting bravely in the face of adversity?

- *At the family level*: Did he support his wife through her own struggles, choosing to stay with her when others might have left? Did he challenge authorities on the basis of his family's survival and well-being? Did he support his children even when doing so would seem unlikely or difficult, such as standing by a child who was in trouble with the law? Did he walk side-by-side with a child who struggled with drug addiction? Did he stand up for the rights of an elderly parent who needed an advocate?

- *At the community level*: Did he engage in courageous acts of civil obedience, where there was danger present in preserving the law? Or did he engage in acts of civil disobedience, where moral danger lay in following the law? Did he help to change a bad policy or create a good one when doing so might endanger himself or his family? Was he injured or killed in the "line of duty," or commit acts that illustrate the most common perception of courage?

- *At the societal level*: Was he a popular, famous, elected, or otherwise well-known individual that people could emulate for his courage? Was he unknown to others—not "born for fame"—but nonetheless earned local or broad fame because of an act of courage? For example, was he the first of his culture or ethnicity to face a difficult situation like segregation? Was his profession a conduit for courage? For example, was he a photographer who captured images that changed the world's view of poverty or crime or genocide?

How do these questions about courage lead to material for the epainos where praise is the theme? In the case of a famous, public figure, the answer might seem simple—fame makes for many things to say. Of course, not everyone gets to be a princess or the leader of a country, but it helps to remember that these titles and the celebrity that accompanies them do not by themselves necessarily reveal courage. For example, Christopher Reeve was one celebrity who was not particularly "courageous" at the height of his fame as an actor. When he acted in the *Superman* movies, his courage was not celebrated as much as his physical good looks and personal charm. His paralysis from a horse riding accident was not what made him courageous, either—even though it temporarily increased his fame. Instead, the acts that most demonstrated his courage were Reeve's nine-year quest for a good life as a paraplegic; his efforts to be a loving husband and father and to find meaning in personal tragedy; and his hard work to support advances in medical science's understanding of spinal injuries. At the most basic level, however, Reeve's courage involved the daily struggle to breathe in and breathe out. Sometimes, it simply is at that most basic level that a person reveals courage worthy of our praise and admiration. Using the above example of a private citizen husband and father, envision the following scenario:

As a child, he lost a limb in an accident. Imagine how he could have shown courage during his lifetime. What examples could look like courage to others?

- *To his parents,* his loss could have crippled his view of himself and his approach to life, but by surmounting that obstacle, such that others hardly noticed what he had lost, he showed courage.

- *To his children,* his courage might have come across as bravely ignoring what he could not do and instead focused on what he could do—it taught them that life does not have to be easy to be lived well.

- *To his wife,* his courage might have shown her that he would not let any obstacle get in the way of a successful marriage—it became a symbol of conquering adversity and the ability to build a satisfying life.

- *To his coworkers,* his courage might have revealed that he had the perseverance to get through even the toughest of jobs—it showed that they could trust his inner strength.

- *To his community,* his courage might have emerged in a city council fight for revitalizing the neighborhood despite very real financial and social obstacles—it gave others the audacity to continue this fight.

As one can see, one of the benefits of using the classical virtues to find ideas rhetorically is that it gives eulogy writers a heuristic, enabling them to speak to the most vital of human actions and qualities while personalizing the deceased beyond work and hobby-based anecdotes. In the examples above, only the virtue of courage is used to consider what one might say about a deceased father and husband. Obviously, the epainos could address additional or different virtues and noble actions to say more good words about the man, illustrating his life even more fully.

Another strength of this rhetorical heuristic of virtue is that it can be applied to honor almost anyone through a eulogy. While it is true that not everyone will have fully lived the virtue of courage—which is what makes courage special in human experience—most people will have exhibited a virtue like courage on one level or another at some time in his or her life.

- A woman who was both a divorced mother and a college student may have demonstrated her courage by working two jobs and taking a leave of absence from her college studies so she could support her children when her former husband, who still financially supported the family, became unemployed.

- A man who was an alcoholic might have shown his courage by not only giving up drinking, but also working hard to become a better person, eventually inspiring his best friend to quit drinking, too.

- A child who died as a toddler may have exhibited courage by fighting a series of infections without major complaints, while assuring her parents that even if she died, she knew she would be all right.

- A still-born infant, who never had the opportunity *to display courage* himself, may have given his parents the opportunity *to be courageous* in the face of their loss.

And so it goes. Even those deaths about which people are conflicted generally can lend themselves to discussing some virtue or noble action. For example, if a teenager committed suicide or overdosed on drugs or even caused the death of another person, the eulogist generally can find praiseworthy virtues and noble deeds that help to define the adolescent's life as a beloved child. As another example, if a parent was abusive, drug addicted, mentally ill, or otherwise emotionally or physically unavailable, the eulogy writer may find a single act of courage that speaks well of the deceased: perhaps a mother knew that her battle with schizophrenia was dangerous, so she tried to protect her daughter by teaching her the warning signs of an impending episode.

However, deaths related to difficult circumstances can create ambivalent feelings in mourners, so eulogists may benefit from understanding the notions of *praise* and *blessing* as different. It is possible to bless the deceased with good words and love even when the eulogist finds it difficult to praise a life. At its most basic, the act of praising connotes a comparison; one includes praiseworthy behavior and character in a eulogy, generally ignoring what is not praiseworthy because the funeral ceremony, with its purposes of enacting grief and comforting mourners, is not the time or place to explore these issues. On the other hand, the act of blessing connotes a nonjudgmental sentiment; everyone can receive blessing in death because of humanity's shared common nature. And, while a clergy person may bless with a sacramental authority, anyone can offer a nonsecular blessing intended to acknowledge and honor the decedent's life. The eulogist can bless by either invoking the decedent's understanding of God as a higher power or through other loving words that honor the life that has been lived. While blessing can take many forms, it can be commonly and innately understood as a blessing by those present. Thus, if a person's life ended in prison, if he committed suicide, if she harmed another person, if he acted in a way that family or society considered wrong, or if she simply was foolish, then blessing that life is especially important and validating to every mourner who attends the funeral gathering. The act of blessing a person in the eulogy shows respect for the human life that will be connected eternally to mourners. In difficult circumstances, if a life was cut short before all of its potential had been reached, sometimes blessing, not praise, is the most helpful content for the epainos.

Rhetorical Action

Like the funeral itself, the ritual of a eulogy provides a social space for mourning. By *speaking about the deceased* to the gathered mourners, the eulogist *speaks for the bereaved*—enumerating what people admired about the deceased, what they will miss about him or her, and how the deceased influenced the world. When it is well-written and delivered strongly, the eulogy brings the family and community together in a shared experience of mourning that ultimately is powerfully comforting. Such a eulogy both reinforces and broadens the community's view of the deceased. Eulogies offer other benefits to those who hear them (or even to those who later read them silently). The eulogist uses the funeral speech to articulate thoughts and feelings for the bereaved at a particularly inarticulate time. Hearing or reading a eulogy provides mourners with other words, new words, good words that suggest a wide variety of ways to express the loss. In ways different from visual media, the eulogy prompts and enables verbal and emotional expressions of grief, and even physical actions like crying, holding hands, or keening. These expressions can help the bereaved to articulate their private grief in the more public act of mourning. Like the viewing of a body, the eulogy provides a reality check; it clearly states that, *yes, this person is indeed dead, and yes, the mourning has begun officially.*

Kent describes contemporary eulogies given by clergy and funeral professionals as not applying classical virtues to everyday citizens ("The Rhetoric of Eulogies" 19) and he objects to an *a priori* reliance on Aristotelian rhetoric as a model for eulogies (21, 35). Yet, as I have shown, the classical approach has much to offer the private citizen's eulogy. Kunkel and Dennis cite other experts in death studies, stating that "the new paradigm of grief theory" is one that "re-emphasized the role of cognitive processes in emotional adjustment and recognized meaning reconstruction and 'relearning the world' as the central mechanism in grieving" (6). They see the value of the eulogy particularly as "the reconsideration of the relationship with the deceased, rather than its outright termination, [which] may be critical to the overall health of the bereaved" (6). In other words, they see "a process of accommodation" of the past relationship into the present context of death and separation (6). Indeed, the eulogist is especially important to providing "a 'positive spin,' or a different perspective, which provides a more acceptable understanding of the unalterable event" (12). Offering this perspective is the rhetor's job, and teaching how to develop that perspective into a powerful eulogy is the rhetorician's job.

At the first meeting of the Alliance of Rhetoric Societies in 2003, both keynote and breakout sessions called for contemporary rhetoricians to take responsibility for public outreach in civic and educational forums. Ceremonial occasions represent an area in which rhetoricians can use rhetorical knowledge and abilities to assist the general public—particularly in times of grief and mourning. For example, one of my professional goals is to complete a book called *Good Words: Writing and Delivering a Eulogy,* which is intended for private citizens and their bereavement careworkers to use when planning ceremonial praises and blessings for the deceased. To provide their own assistance in the practical work of giving the speechless a confident voice, I call on action-minded rhetoricians to do the following:

- Speak about the eulogy at professional conferences, such as those for hospice workers, bereavement counselors, and funeral directors;

- Collaborate with such specialists as thanatologists to discover more about the benefits of contemporary eulogia;

- Develop traditional and online course material for teaching ceremonial rhetoric—both the eulogy and encomium;

- Educate by speaking publicly about the value and importance of the eulogy to various groups (e.g., the media) upon the death of a prominent public individual or a high-profile private citizen; and

- Write about the eulogy and its relationship to virtues in particular for newspaper and magazine editorials, as well as for online media.

In a way, the eulogist becomes a teacher who leads the mourning community by putting his or her grief into words. Rhetoricians need to take an active part in that teaching process, thus enabling the everyday private citizen to find his or her own good words to speak when the time comes to mourn a beloved life.

Works Cited

Aristotle. *The Art of Rhetoric.* Trans. John Henry Freese. Cambridge: Harvard UP, 1982.
Kent, Michael L. "The Rhetoric of Eulogies: A Generic Critique of Classic and Contemporary Funeral Oratory." Diss. Purdue University, 1997. 20 Apr. 2006. <http://homepages.wmich.edu/~mkent/Index.html>.
———. "The Rhetoric of Eulogy: Topoi of Grief and Consolation." *Studies in Communication & Culture* 1.5 (Fall 1991): 109–19.
Kunkel, Adrianne Dennis, and Michael Robert Dennis. "Grief Consolation in Eulogy Rhetoric: An Integrative Framework." *Death Studies* 27 (2003): 1–38.
Reagan, Ron. "Eulogy for his Father." 12 Apr. 2006. <http://www.americanrhetoric.com/speeches/ronreaganeulogyfordad.htm>.
Spencer, Earl Charles. "Eulogy for Princess Diana." 22 Apr. 2006. <http://www.internet-esq.com/diana/index.htm>.

"The Siren of Isocrates . . . Sappho's Lyre, or Some Other Power Greater Still"

The Rhetoricity of Anna Komnena's *Alexiad*

Susan C. Jarratt and Ellen Quandahl

Over the past decade, feminist scholars have charted the contributions of women to the theory and practice of rhetoric. Cheryl Glenn, for example, has recovered female writers from Sappho through those of the early modern period who demonstrated rhetorical sophistication despite cultural restrictions. Notably absent from this new scholarship and from anthologies of women's rhetoric is the work of Anna Komnena, author of an epic history of her father, Emperor Alexios I Komnenos, who ruled the Roman Empire in the east, or Byzantium, from 1081–1118. When we began to read the *Alexiad* and to translate portions of it in our study group, we were immediately drawn to the text: a lengthy and learned work without parallel in the canon of women's writing in Attic Greek, a significant contribution to Byzantine history (Frankopan 67; Stephenson), and a text whose author draws attention to her rhetorical training and models. Scholarship on Anna's epic history is substantial (Buckler; Frankopan; Gouma-Peterson, *Anna Komnene*; Magdalino, "Pen of the Aunt"), and there is a growing body of work on Byzantine rhetoric (Conley; Hunger; Jeffreys; Kennedy; Walker). However, with the exception of one article on *ekphrasis* (Mullett, "Bohemond's Biceps"), we have found no extended treatments of the *Alexiad* with a specific focus on rhetoric.

What means of persuasion were available to this twelfth-century Byzantine princess? Was Anna bound by gender-based restrictions? What does her history reveal about her understanding of and attitudes toward rhetoric? In this essay we begin to explore what an explicitly rhetorical analysis of her history would look like, first, by pointing out rhetorically significant elements of Anna's intellectual formation, and second, by reading her reflections on her work as a historiographer in light of what has been called a signal feature of Byzantine rhetoric—the *eschematismenos logos* or "figured" discourse, a way of addressing readers indirectly (Ahl; Kennedy; Kustas; Walker).

101

What is known about Anna Komnena (1083–1153) comes to us primarily from four Byzantine sources. Anna, in the *Alexiad* itself, self-consciously reflects on her work as a writer of history and offers some details about her education, her life in the royal household, and the events to which she herself was eyewitness. Her contemporary Georges Tornikes, in a long funeral oration, offers details about her life from childhood on. And histories by John Zonaras and Niketas Choniates, one probably contemporaneous with Anna's and the other written some fifty years later, tell us a little about Anna at the end of her father's life. All attest to Anna's learnedness. Tornikes informs us that in her later life Anna commissioned commentaries on various writers, including Aristotle. From these sources we also know that, as a firstborn child, Anna was marked as future empress and betrothed to Constantine Ducas, the son of Maria of Alania, who was the wife of the two previous emperors. The boy Constantine had been co-crowned with Alexios. But the plan that would have led Anna to become empress was altered when Anna's brother John was born and designated as successor; Constantine died in youth and Anna was given in marriage to Nicephorus Bryennios. On Alexios's death in 1118, John claimed the throne, and perhaps because of a plan to overthrow John and rule with her husband, Anna was condemned to live out her days effectively under house arrest in the monastery Kecharitomene. Over the next three decades she wrote the *Alexiad*.

The purpose of the work was to record the deeds of Alexios and, scholars add, to praise him and his achievements (Hill 47; Scott 63). The history bears many features of the *basilikos logos* as described by Menander Rhetor, with each episode serving to show Alexios's eloquence, generosity, self-control, genius for battle formation, resourcefulness, piety, care for prisoners, commitment to education, and many other virtues. The "monumental figure" of Alexios dominates and unifies a fifteen-book text—a first in Greek historiography (Ljubarskij 133); he is figured as a healer and caretaker, taking control of a weakened empire whose infirmities, like those of the body, come from both internal and external causes (Sewter 381–82). Anna's composition during the reign of her nephew, Manuel I, as Magdalino ("Pen") and Stephenson have argued, appears to have aimed at refuting the panegyrics claiming that the descendant surpassed his ancestor.

This much is agreed upon by historians. But our research has uncovered, perhaps not surprisingly, gendered differences in judgments on Anna's work. These gendered readings begin with Anna's near-contemporary, Choniates, whose history starts with her brother John's reign. After relating that Anna's husband was too sluggish to carry out the plan to take power with Anna, Choniates inserts a remark about Anna herself, translated, with some liberties, by Magoulias to read: "It is said that Kaisarissa Anna, disgusted with her husband's frivolous behavior and distraught in her anger, and being a shrew by nature, felt justified in strongly contracting her vagina when Bryennios's penis entered deep inside her, thus causing him great pain" (8).[1]

More recently, male scholars have drawn conclusions based on the emotional tenor of the history. Anna's text frequently mourns three men—her father, her first betrothed, and her husband Bryennios. Pathos is without question a striking feature of Anna's rhetoric, with many passages referring obliquely, and some directly, to afflictions suffered in her own life. Our title passage occurs after Anna has detailed her informants and sources. She adds that she herself was present at many of the events she narrates and reports that she was beset by "troubles, afflictions, continual misfortunes." To write about "the enemies raised up against me by the wickedness of men, I would need the Siren of Isocrates, the grandiloquence of Pindar, Polemo's vivacity, the Calliope of Homer, Sappho's lyre or some other power greater still" (XV.vii; Sewter 459–60).[2] Anna's expressions of sorrow have been interpreted by several notable scholars as scarcely disguised bitterness about the failure of her bid for power. Gibbon, in *The Decline and Fall,* reads Anna's history as "betraying in every page the vanity of a female author" (qtd. in Sewter 11). More succinctly, Friedrich Schiller, an early translator, pointed out the "bad style and false taste" of the author (qtd. in Ljubarskij 127). Sewter's 1969 introduction to the Penguin edition of his work pulls no punches, averring that "when [Anna] wrote the *Alexiad . . .* she was full of self-pity, a disappointed old woman" (14).

While it is not our aim to refute every charge against Anna, we join a group of feminist scholars engaged in rereading the *Alexiad* (Hill; Mullett, "Bohemond's Biceps"), taking stock of Anna's achievements specifically *as* a woman writer by placing her within the context of her rhetorically charged imperial milieu, and then reinterpreting her rhetoric of mourning with reference to her many comments on the demands of history writing. Several features of the cultural context in which Anna came of age are notable as contexts for her preoccupation with rhetoric. First, as Paul Magdalino asserts, "There can be no doubt that rhetoric was the dominant element in Byzantine intellectual culture . . . never more so than in the twelfth century" (*Empire* 335). We know that elite women were educated in this period, but Anna's deep education in Greek rhetoric and letters was unusual. As Andrew R. Dyck argues, "Women of whatever position were not normally vouchsafed a classical education in Byzantium" (113). Despite rhetoric's prominence, the tension between rhetoric as a secular or pagan practice and Christianity—a dilemma since the era of Augustine, Jerome, and Libanius—reasserted itself in the eleventh and twelfth centuries and was partly driven by Alexios himself (Agapitos 191; Browning, "Enlightenment" 15). In the funeral oration for Anna, Georges Tornikes tells us that Anna's parents mistrusted education from outside the Christian tradition and that she managed to study the secular subjects of grammar and poetry secretly with a palace eunuch:

> [Anna's parents] looked suspiciously on education from without [that is, Greek/pagan letters, as opposed to Christian learning] as treacherous, just as wise child-nurturing mothers often look down on matchmakers lest they create in their maidens ignoble loves. . . . Taking care not to be perceived by the parents, with dignity [Anna] stole learning from the side from not unlettered servant eunuchs. Just as a maiden, seeing the bride-

> groom through some openings with secret eyes, so she secretly conversed
> with letters, when she was not with her mother. (Darrouzes 243–45)[3]

Some women with a literary or intellectual bent were less taxed by this tension, and most commonly focused on religious subjects. Examples include Michael Psellos's mother, whom we know through his amazing encomium (Walker), and Anna's own mother, Irene—who, Anna tells us, devoted herself to reading difficult theological texts (V.ix; Sewter 178) and later wrote the Typicon (or regimen) for the Kecharitomene convent (Thomas and Hero). In these two cases, we have women who encouraged or sponsored the rhetorical enterprises of the men around them—Psellos's mother supporting his secular schooling and Irene commissioning a history of Alexios from Nicephorus Bryennios, Anna's husband (Mullett, "Aristocracy")—but they themselves concentrated on religious subjects. As Diether Reinsch suggests, "With the great exception of Anna Komnene, the educated aristocratic women of the eleventh and twelfth centuries do not present themselves as writers, though certainly as persons who encouraged literature and to whom literature was addressed" (86).

Second, life at court has been described by Magdalino and others as a *theatron* for rhetorical performance (*Empire* 336–39; Mullett, "Aristocracy" 174–77). The court, as well as the homes of aristocrats and officials, were scenes of highly self-conscious play of word, gesture, and response among petitioners and performers of the new middle classes as well as elite patrons and the emperor himself. The stakes were high, and the power of rhetoric was manifest in these lively settings. As we will see, even the battlefield where Alexios fought was described as a place for high rhetorical calculation. Born into these rhetorical *theatra,* Anna was nourished by her close observations of her family's military, diplomatic, and conspiratorial activities, and through these early experiences came to see rhetoric as a comprehensive art of imperial power. Not only had Anna been designated in childhood to become empress, she also lived in an age when women helped emperors (including Alexios) come to power or legitimized their rule—her own grandmother and mother had ruled at court while Alexios was away in battle or ill. Barbara Hill has argued that Anna's attempted usurpation was well within the model that she "had been accustomed to all her life," with a husband to lead in battle and a woman in charge of the government at home (54). That is, she was positioned within a highly volatile scene of intellectual, religious, and family relations in which women's abilities and roles at court nonetheless were amply evident.

Within this extraordinary milieu, Anna produced an epic history preoccupied with rhetoric. In her preface, Anna overtly establishes her intellectual affiliations by saying that she is

> not without some acquaintance with literature—having devoted the most
> earnest study to the Greek language, in fact, and being not unpractised in
> Rhetoric and having read thoroughly the treatises of Aristotle and the
> dialogues of Plato, and having fortified [her] mind with the Quadrivium
> of sciences. . . . (Sewter 17)

Most critics note (with either admiration or suspicion) the detail with which Anna describes military strategies and armaments. But read from a rhetorical perspective, many battle scenes become evidence of Alexios's uses of persuasive speech and clever stratagems as alternatives to battle. From his very earliest experiences in the field at the age of fourteen, he demonstrated his wit and ingenuity, ultimately triumphing over his foes through devices "worthy of Palamedes" (I, i–iv; Sewter 32–36). In a single opening account, Anna presents the reader with three speeches by Alexios to two different audiences. In each speech, Alexios offers well-ordered, practical reasoning (along with gifts of money and land), proposing alliances and courses of action based on shared interests. As the action unfolds, Alexios remarks on the dangerous unpredictability of audiences of the lower order, noting like Aristotle that they are less susceptible to reasoned persuasion than those in positions of authority (with whom he was seeking to reach a deal). In re-creating scenes of high-stakes negotiation in which a leader had to be ready to use arms, arguments, promises of money, and still be prepared to elude the volatile crowd with trickery, Anna shows how the battlefield required of a Byzantine leader the same interplay of the rhetorical maneuvers found in the court:

> In my father's case the enemy was sometimes defeated by power, sometimes by a quick-witted move, sometimes by a shrewd guess and the nerve to act on it immediately during the actual combat. There were times when he had recourse to stratagem, at others he entered the battle in person. Thus many a victory was won, often unexpectedly. He had an extraordinary love of danger. . . . He faced them in different ways: by marching into them bare-headed, and coming to close grips with the enemy, or on occasions by pretending to avoid conflict and feigning terror. It depended on circumstances and the situation of the moment. (XV.iii; Sewter 477–78)

Recounting scenes throughout her father's life, Anna demonstrates her keen awareness of the multifaceted, rhetorical way of living that characterized her age. If Anna praises the effective rhetor and tactician, she equally blames those who are loquacious, who favor dialectic wrangling or who are untrained in rhetoric. In many episodes, the heroes of the *Alexiad* (including opponents worthy of Alexios) are described as educated, eloquent, and reasoning, while enemies (both military and religious) are rough, long-winded, and undisciplined. These episodes confirm Anna's investment in rhetoric as a class-distinguishing practice of the battlefield and court.

What we wish to emphasize here are the continuities between Anna's rhetorical context, her rhetorical education, and her rhetorical practices as a history writer. She positions herself within an august genealogy through her allusions to and imitation of classical historians Thucydides and Polybius. In a "conscious echo of the Polybian ideal of pragmatic history" (Dyck 115), Anna is careful to detail her sources of evidence—memories of events that she saw with her own eyes, reports from men still living, oral accounts from soldiers, and written records composed in simple, truthful language by

monks. But a stance of objectivity is made problematic by her personal investment in the history she recounts. Her response to this rhetorical dilemma is to
articulate self-consciously the tension between fact and encomium through
numerous first-person interventions, a characteristic feature of learned writing of her time (Magdalino, *Empire* 401). Her interventions bring Anna to life,
giving us a sense of her as a writer and of the arduous labor of the historian.
In a moment at dusk, when she is too weary to continue writing, she worries
that her text could become disjointed. She adds, "Ah well, 'tis no cause for
anger' to those at least who read my work with good will" (Sewter 412). As
Andrew Dyck has noted, Anna's quotation of a phrase from the *Iliad*
(III.154–58) "cloaks in a Homeric veil an idea that might offend if expressed
directly," that is, her own self-praise in comparing her written history to beautiful Helen (119). Moreover, Anna gently suggests that it is readers of good
will (and of sufficient learning to take pleasure in such figures) who will be
patient with the narrative disruptions required by her difficult subject.

Even more interesting to us is the link that Anna suggests between loss and
history writing. That is, to write history is also to mourn, to recall great losses,
the recollection of which threatens objectivity but is an inescapable element of
the work of writing history. In what is to us one of the most moving passages of
the work, Anna describes Alexios's battle with Malik-Shah, in which one of
her younger brothers was killed. Here she pauses to recall him in all of his
youth and physical perfection and promise (as we probably all do when we see
those faces of young men and women killed in Iraq on the NewsHour):

> He had just reached his young manhood, the most charming time of life,
> a daring soldier in war, but prudent too, with a quick hand and fine
> intellect. . . . His youthfulness, his physical perfection, those light vaults
> into the saddle—what do they mean now? My grief for him drives me to
> tears—but the law of history once more calls me back. It is extraordinary
> that nobody nowadays under the stress of great troubles is turned into
> stone or a bird or tree or some inanimate object; they used to undergo
> such metamorphoses in ancient times. . . . Had that been possible, these
> calamities would . . . have turned me to stone. (XV.v; Sewter 485)

Departing from the practices of her classical antecedents, Anna gives voice
here to the painful task of converting human loss into public memory.

In another passage suffused with sorrow, Anna describes the emperor's
generous treatment of a man when he is defeated and all but condemned to
death. She comments,

> My father was always like that, even if later he was repaid by all of them
> with ingratitude. In the same way long ago the Lord, Benefactor of the
> whole world, caused manna to rain down in the desert, fed the multitude
> on the mountains, led them through the sea dry-footed—yet afterwards
> He was rejected and insulted and smitten and finally condemned to be
> crucified by wicked men. But when I reach this point the tears flow before
> my words; I long to speak of these things and compile a list of these
> unfeeling men, but I check my tongue, bear with impatience and over and

over again quote to myself the words of Homer: "Endure my heart; thou
has suffered other, worse things before." (XIV.iii; Sewter 446–47)

There is much to comment on in this polysemous passage, in which Alexios's
beneficence and suffering are figured through a merging of Yewah, Moses,
and Jesus. Keeping to the boundaries of safe speech, Anna plays on the ambiguity of "unfeeling men," slipping from her father's suffering to her own,
using as her guide to forbearance Odysseus's words to himself as he endured
the insolent suitors sleeping with Penelope's women (Homer, *Odyssey*
XX.18). Couched within the reference to Alexios's generosity in the face of
internal threats to his rule, one might find Anna's reaction to the "unfeeling
men" who were responsible for her own long banishment from the rhetorical
theatron of public life. This life she finally describes at the end of the work:

> I pass my time in obscurity and devote myself to my books and the wor-
> ship of God. Not even the less important persons are allowed to visit us,
> let alone those from whom we could have learnt news they happened to
> have from others, or my father's most intimate friends. For thirty years
> now, I swear it by the souls of the most blessed emperors, I have not seen,
> I have not spoken to a friend of my father; most of them of course have
> passed away, but many too are prevented by fear because of the change in
> our fortunes. For the powers-that-be have decided that we must not be
> seen—an absurd decision—and have condemned us to a general execra-
> tion. (XIV.vii; Sewter 460–61)

Anna's protest at her exclusion from a life she had every expectation of
leading, we suggest, might be further justified by the fact that a number of
male conspirators (potential usurpers to Alexios's position), including not
only the minor governor of the previous passage but also his own nephew,
were welcomed back into public life after plots against them were foiled.

It is within the context of both historiographical conventions and Anna's
particular situation that we propose a shift in emphasis in the interpretation
of her frequent expressions of sadness. At the end of her father's "reign of surprising boldness and novelty" (XV.x; Sewter 504), Anna experienced loss on
three different levels: the personal loss of a father whom she held dear, the
loss of a leader whose example his successors failed to live up to, and the loss
of her freedom as a result of her supposed conspiracy against her brother
John. Focusing on the last of these three, the gendered readings we cited at
the outset seem not to grant the larger, public dimensions—the epic and historical dimensions—of the loss Anna narrates. At the end of her work, Anna
makes the point succinctly as she describes the "two-fold duty" of her task as
historian: "To relate the facts of the emperor's life and also to expose their
tragic nature. In other words, I have to give an account of his struggles and at
the same time to do justice to all that has caused me heart-felt sorrow"
(XV.xi; Sewter 505).

In sum, we suggest that to understand Anna's rhetorical achievement it is
necessary to read differently. Whereas Jakov Ljubarskij remarks in an essay

on irony in Byzantine literature, "Anna was a great writer but the text of her *Alexiad* is as it were one-dimensional . . ." (125), we see Anna's text as multi-dimensional, permeated with a "Patroclus-like" mourning. Anna several times uses this metaphor (e.g., Sewter 107) in reference to Briseis, who in lamenting Patroclus's death simultaneously grieves for her own inability to control her life (*Iliad*, XIX. 282–303).[4] Anna surely (and, we think, justifiably) mourns just such an inability, and much more. Noting that her father would rather have her composing elegies and dirges, Anna instead forges ahead with her monumental and burdensome history, insisting all along the way that the emotional work of mourning is an integral aspect of her intellectual and rhetorical task.

Notes

[1] A more literal translation of this passage demonstrates Magoulias's distortion: "It is said that the Kaisarissa Anna, disgusted with the weakness of her husband, because she suffered she was really provoked at and blamed nature for many things and put it [nature] under not a little blame, because it had cleft her groin and hollowed it out, and for Bryennios had stretched out his member and made him spherical" (Quandahl's translation of Van Dieten).

[2] All references are to E. R. A. Sewter's 1969 translation. See also Reinsch and Kambylis.

[3] Translation of Tornikes by Quandahl. See also Browning, "Unpublished Funeral Oration" 5.

[4] See Dyck for three examples of "Patroclus-like" mourning in the *Alexiad* (114–15).

Works Cited

Agapitos, Panagiotis A. "Teachers, Pupils and Imperial Power in Eleventh-Century Byzantium." *Pedagogy and Power: Rhetorics of Classical Learning.* Ed. Yun Lee Too and Niall Livingstone. New York: Cambridge UP, 1998. 170–91.

Ahl, Frederick. "The Art of Safe Criticism in Greece and Rome." *American Journal of Philology* 105.2 (Summer 1984): 174–208.

Browning, Robert. "Enlightenment and Repression in Byzantium in the Eleventh and Twelfth Centuries." *Past and Present* 69 (Nov. 1975): 3–23.

———. "An Unpublished Funeral Oration on Anna Comnena." *Studies on Byzantine History, Literature and Education.* London: Variorum Reprints, 1977. 1–12.

Buckler, Georgina. *Anna Comnena.* London: Oxford UP, 1968.

Conley, Thomas H. "Practice to Theory: Byzantine 'Poetrics.'" *Greek Literary Theory after Aristotle.* Ed. J. G. J. Abbenes, S. R. Slings, and I. Sluiter. Amsterdam: VU UP, 1995. 301–20.

Darrouzes, Jean. "Logos epi tôi thanatôi tês porphurogennêtou kuras Annês Kaisarissês." *Georges et Demetrios Tornikes: Lettres et Discours.* Paris: Editions du Centre National de la Recherche Scientifique, 1970. 220–323.

Dyck, Andrew R. "*Iliad* and *Alexiad*: Anna Comnena's Homeric Reminiscences." *Greek, Roman and Byzantine Studies* 27.1 (Spring 1986): 113–20.

Frankopan, Peter. "Perception and Projection of Prejudice: Anna Comnena, the *Alexiad* and the First Crusade." *Gendering the Crusades.* Ed. Susan B. Edgington and Sarah Lambert. New York: Columbia UP, 2002. 59–76.

Glenn, Cheryl. *Rhetoric Retold: Regendering the Tradition from Antiquity through the Renaissance.* Carbondale: Southern Illinois UP, 1997.

Gouma-Peterson, Thalia, ed. *Anna Komnene and Her Times.* New York: Garland, 2000.

———. "Gender and Power: Passages to the Maternal in Anna Komnene's *Alexiad*." Gouma-Peterson 107–24.

Hill, Barbara. "Actions Speak Louder Than Words: Anna Komnene's Attempted Usurpation." Gouma-Peterson 45–61.

Homer. *Iliad*. Trans. Richmond Lattimore. Chicago: U of Chicago Press, 1951.

Homer. *Odyssey*. Trans. Richmond Lattimore. New York: Harper and Row, 1967.

Hunger, Herbert. "The Classical Tradition in Byzantine Literature: The Importance of Rhetoric." *Byzantium and the Classical Tradition*. Ed. Margaret Mullett and Roger Scott. Birmingham: U of Birmingham, 1981. 35–47.

Jeffreys, Elizabeth M., ed. *Rhetoric in Byzantium*. Burlington, VT: Ashgate, 2003.

Kennedy, George. *Classical Rhetoric and its Christian and Secular Tradition from Ancient to Modern Times*. Chapel Hill: U of North Carolina P, 1980.

Kustas, George L. *Studies in Byzantine Rhetoric*. Thessalonike: Patriarchikon Idruma Paterikon Meleton, 1973.

Ljubarskij, Jakov. "Why is the *Alexiad* a Masterpiece of Byzantine Literature?" Studies Presented to Lennart Ryden on His Sixty-Fifth Birthday. Ed. Jan Olof Rosenqvist. Uppsala: Almqvist and Wiksell International, 1966. 127–41.

Magdalino, Paul. *The Empire of Manuel I Komnenos, 1143–1180*. Cambridge: Cambridge UP, 1993.

———. "The Pen of the Aunt: Echoes of the Mid-Twelfth Century in the *Alexiad*." Gouma-Peterson 15–43.

Magoulias, Harry J. *O City of Byzantium, Annals of Niketas Choniates*. Detroit: Wayne State UP, 1984.

Mullett, Margaret. "Aristocracy and Patronage in the Literary Circles of Comnenian Constantinople." *The Byzantine Aristocracy IX to XIII Centuries*. Ed. Michael Angold. Oxford: B.A.R. International Series 221, 1984. 173–201.

———. "Bohemond's Biceps: Male Beauty and the Female Gaze in the *Alexiad* of Anna Komnene." *Byzantine Masculinities*. Ed. Dion C. Smythe, forthcoming.

Reinsch, Diether R. "Women's Literature in Byzantium: The Case of Anna Komnene." Gouma-Peterson 83–105.

Reinsch, Diether R., and Athanasios Kambylis. *Annae Comnenae Alexias*. Berlin: Walter de Gruyter GmbH & Co. 2001.

Scott, Roger. "The Classical Tradition in Byzantine Historiography." *Byzantium and the Classical Tradition*. Ed. Margaret Mullett and Roger Scott. Birmingham: U of Birmingham, 1981. 61–74.

Sewter, E. R. A., trans. *The Alexiad of Anna Comnena*. New York: Penguin Books, 1969.

Stephenson, Paul. "Anna Comnena's *Alexiad* as a Source for the Second Crusade?" *Journal of Medieval History* 29.1 (March 2003): 41–54.

Thomas, John, and Angela Constantinides Hero, eds. "*Kecharitomene: Typikon* of Empress Irene Doukaina Komnene for the Convent of the Mother of God *Kecharitomene* in Constantinople." *Byzantine Monastic Foundation Documents: A Complete Translation of the Surviving Founders' Typika and Testaments*. Washington, DC: Dumbarton Oaks Research Library and Collection, 2000. 649ff.

Van Dieten, Ioannes Aloysius. *Nicetae Choniatae Historia*. Berlin: Walter De Gruyter, 1975.

Walker, Jeffrey. "'These Things I Have Not Betrayed': Michael Psellos' Encomium of His Mother as a Defense of Rhetoric." *Rhetorica* 22.1 (Winter 2004): 49–101.

Zonaras, John. *Epitome*. Vol. III. Ed. Th. Büttner-Wabst. Bonn: CSHB, 1897. 726–68.

Kenneth Burke and the Progressive Press

8

Ann Dobyns

From an early age, Kenneth Burke maintained a love/hate relationship with America. In 1922, he wrote Malcolm Cowley, "America I am coming to look upon as a responsibility. Like Mr. Sumstine, I must point out that the country is what we make of it. We cannot move out magnificently, like Stearns; for such a gesture leaves us with nothing but yammering" (Jay 122). And so, he often wrote about national problems, but when he did so, he addressed an educated and progressive audience. "[I]t is," he said, "no accomplishment to do as the representative progressive sheets (*New Republic, Freeman, The Nation*, etc.) and prove that the stupid are stupid, the trick is to prove that the elite are stupid; wherefore, you shall attack the elite. . . . But note: in attacking the elite, one must not be tricked into taking sides with the stupid" (116). Following his own advice, he addressed his public writings to the elite, the progressives whom he saw as responsible for shaping public discussions of political and economic issues, and he published these writings in the "representative progressive sheets." Concerned with subjects as diverse as humanism, capitalism, communism, the environment, the proliferation of nuclear weapons, war, American culture, as well as literary criticism, these essays show Burke "[using language] as a symbolic means of inducing cooperation" (*Rhetoric of Motives* 43). While exploring Burke's motives for entering the public sphere, this essay will argue that his public writings are powerful examples of Burke's notion of dramatism, particularly the scene-agency ratio. In other words, his attitude was shaped in response to the times, which led him to choose his methods of arguing. A comparison of essays written in the 1930s and the 1950s shows how changes in the antics in what he often called the "human barnyard" led him to rather different strategies of persuasion in his public writing.

William Rueckert comments on the role the Great Depression played on Burke's career, leading to his interest in social criticism. This historical situation manifested what Rueckert identifies as a "scientific, rational, technological, mechanistic, capitalistic orientation, which denies fundamental human need" (35). Burke's letters written to Cowley in the 1930s give much evidence of his attitude toward this orientation. A letter of August 1931, for example, indicates how strongly the times affected him as he describes his reaction to a visit to the city: "After the cocktails and the beer had worn off, even before I

110

had gone to bed, I all inside me sobbed, and I said, I am getting frightened. Big taxes on big fortunes—it is so obviously the method of reformation without revolution, I don't see how people can talk of anything else" (195). This kind of response must have compelled him to speak in the public arena. It was in these years that Burke wrote *Towards a Better Life, Permanence and Change, Attitudes toward History, The Philosophy of Literary Form*, his controversial speech to the American Writers' Congress, and also a series of essays in the progressive press, *The New Republic* and *The Nation* in particular. Rueckert argues that all of the works Burke wrote from this time on show what he calls Burke's "messianic urgency" to counter the "dangerously abnormal emphasis of the 'technological psychosis'" (35).

While not disagreeing with Rueckert about Burke's compulsion to address the dangers of technology, I find his essays from this period showing a strange optimism and consistently informed by a comic view. His approach in his early writings was, as he explained to Cowley in 1922, "to attempt a more constructive type of criticism, not merely to attack the existing, but to build up a counter-structure. . . . Thus, I do not modify my attitude but modify my method. . . . This can be done without growling" (119). That he maintained this essentially comic view can be seen in an October 1931 letter to Cowley, in which he talks of the rhetorical power of fantasy: "A work like *Gulliver's Travels* should be enough to remind us that fantasy is a fundamental weapon of extracurricular education, the only kind of education that is worth considering, since it is the only kind that does not uphold the powers that be" (Jay 199). And in May 1932 he claimed that "if you are to maintain [people's] attention upon things which are at bottom disagreeable, and which people wish were different, you can do this only by embedding them in literary happenings, only by making the story of corruption a beautiful and engrossing and fanciful thing" (200).

But the attitude expressed in his public writings was not always so comic. The second era that compelled Burke to speak with urgency, and now "messianic" seems the appropriate adjective, was from the mid-1940s through the early 1960s—with its progress, prosperity, cold war, and thus the danger of self-annihilation. As early as 1945, Burke was beginning to growl in apocalyptic tones, at least in letters to Cowley. In a letter written on the day the second atomic bomb was dropped on Nagasaki, Burke wrote his friend, "Has the recent inauguration of the new Power Age disgusted you as much as it has me? The era of the Mad Scientist of the B movie now seems with us in a big way. There seems now no logical thing to do but go on tinkering with this damned thing until they have blown up the whole damned world" (268).

This frustration and outrage seemed to build in the 1950s, which was, of course, the McCarthy era and the time in which Burke was denied a position at the University of Washington because of his leftist leanings. In 1953, commenting on the Republican cabinet, he exclaimed, "Jeez, how little they know! The stupidity of putting businessmen in those key jobs! Those jobs should be held by politicos who do the dirty business that the businessmen want done, and who take the blame for it whenever blame is being passed around" (316–17). This disgust with the political climate and his concern for human survival is certainly reflected in the rhetorical choices seen in his public writings of the times. Now his writing seems to turn darker, even apocalyptic. This is not to say that other factors did not contribute to his general mood and thus his manner of presenting arguments on public issues. In the 1950s Burke experienced illness, insomnia, and ailments he associated with aging, but his outrage at the dangers associated with progress seems almost palpable in his writings from this period. To illustrate the differences in Burke's method of attempting to induce cooperation in his public writing, I will look at three pieces—one from the 1930s, one from the mid-fifties, and an unpublished essay written in the late 1950s.

The first essay is "Waste—The Future of Prosperity." Published in *The New Republic* a year after the stock market crash of 1929, it is dedicated to "Mr. Henry Ford," and, in the spirit of teaching through fantasy, reads like an early twentieth century "Modest Proposal." After the dedication, Burke opens with a quotation about doubting, hope, and courage: "Perhaps the once-born is a man with a constant excess of some vital hormone; the twice-born, a man with an intermittent supply; the confirmed doubter, a man with a permanent deficiency. Perhaps hope and courage will some day be controllable by chemical or psychiatric means." This leads him to wonder whether someday a "constructive attitude can be maintained by a simple medical injection [of some vital hormone]?" Thus, "The day may come when a loss of financial confidence will be looked upon, not as a problem of economics, but as a lapse in hygiene." Then, with his tongue firmly in his cheek, he suggests that Mr. Ford's doctrine "that the well-being of the world rests upon the prosperity of increased production and increased consumption" is what he calls a "positive cause for hope—indeed the one overwhelming, undeniable and irrefutable cause for hope" (228).

The rest of the essay explores this "modest proposal" by projecting into the future and suggesting greater and greater absurdities of the implications of Ford's doctrine, to the ultimate consequence in which philosophers inherit the old models of everything imaginable with one great exception—the razor, which leaves them as unshaven symbols of progress. The final passage gives a good representation of his argument by means of fantasy, here burlesque, as he playfully employs figures that enact the essay's repetitive and progressive form, here with amplification, parenthesis, and anaphora:

> When heretofore could the philosopher without means—and was there ever a philosopher with means?—entertain such hopes of surrounding himself with all these manifold resources of man's industry? When heretofore could he entertain such hopes of paralleling, as it were, in external possessions that great wealth and accumulation which in the past he has possessed but within?
>
> One thing alone will he have to buy as it issues from the factory. Not pencils, for he can get them out of old cross-word-puzzle books; not post-

age stamps, for he can soak off the cancellation from used varieties; not inkwells, for the vast number of non-musical fountain pens made available by the combination fountain pen and music box, the Fountabox, will make inkwells unnecessary—but razor blades. A razor blade can never regain its usefulness, partly because of scientific deterioration and partly because it had so little to regain. So our indigent sage, rather than surrender, will probably not shave at all. What then will the well dressed philosopher wear? Quite simply—a beard soaked with Flit. (230–31)

The essay's final line shows Burke at his most playful. "Flit" was the brand name of an insecticide manufactured by the Standard Oil Company. In 1928, Standard Oil began a long-running successful ad campaign of cartoons that showed people being threatened by whimsical, menacing, insect-like creatures and included the caption, "Quick, Henry, the Flit!" These cartoons, by the way, were drawn by a young political cartoonist of the time, Theodor Seuss Geisel, before he began writing his Dr. Seuss children's books. Burke's use of the term "Flit," and the implied tagline, shows him playing with language in a way that appropriately ends his satire on conspicuous consumption by linking the old-fashioned beard with the contemporary ad campaign; it also recalls one of the consequences he had suggested in the essay—that rampant capitalism will beget a new priesthood of those who will sell or write the ads for the new commodities. And, with typical Burkean irony, he addresses the elite reader by implicating even the "indigent sage" in the scene he has constructed. And by alluding to the well-known phrase "Quick, Henry, the Flit!" he ends where he began, thus repeating the form with a twist: with a new "tribute" to Henry Ford, whose doctrine becomes reduced to the spraying of insect repellent.

Despite his appropriation of the generic characteristics of Swift's "Modest Proposal," Burke nonetheless maintains an attitude more like that given in the *Voyage to Lilliput*. As he suggests in his 1956 piece called "Recipe for Prosperity," he is more amused, perhaps outraged, but morose. After noting that his 1930 critique of conspicuous consumption was the only article he ever made money on, he takes up the issue once again and demonstrates the change in his attitude toward the dangers of technology. What he had considered a subject fit for a farce has become "material for an almost awesome tragedy (albeit a tragedy that lends itself, in flashes, to such shrewdly morose and wincing appreciation as can at times go with high comedy)" (191). And indeed a change in the times led to a different critique of human relations and motives, as evidenced by the climate of the 1950s: "Surely the greatest conceivable ironic twist of fate now hangs over us . . . the danger of thermonuclear, chemical, and bacteriological war. . . . This is an ironic danger, a fit theme for Greek tragedy, in that man's greatest cause for boastfulness is also the greatest threat to his survival" ("Art" 160). This seems to be the culmination of the evolution of progress he had warned of in "Waste," but with implications much more profound than he had anticipated in the 1930s.

Rather than "making sport" through burlesque of the persuasive techniques of advertising, his 1956 critique of the motives of business is presented in a shape more like that of the classical oration. He employs the techniques of tragedy as he demonstrates how the consumer ultimately loses because the goading of the higher standard of living increases his debt and therefore his ability to consume conspicuously. But this downward turn is balanced by an ostensibly upward and comic turn, albeit with "morose and wincing appreciation." In the first section, he delineates the appropriation of the ironic argument he had made in his 1930 article by two articles published in relevant issues of *Business Week*. After observing the contrast between the attitude expressed by the articles' "bright new asyndeton" ("Recipe for Prosperity") and the more somber admonitions of the proverbs of Poor Richard, he directly compares the blatant celebration of the way consumer excess contributes to the health of the national economy with his earlier parody. What was in his 1930 piece, the exaggeration of burlesque, "is now presented as the Ideal Norm" (192).

And so, instead of dramatic irony, Burke presents his critique in a more straightforward manner. He begins with rhetorical questions—instead of asking "What is good for business?" we should ask "What is business good for?"—and analogies—"The *Business Week* version of a business ethics would seem to be somewhat like the ethics of a tavern-keeper who thought it his business to get us all stinko drunk and keep us so" (192). Still the word man though, he engages in word play but now without the light touch of burlesque: for example, advertisers are "Nietzschean supermen of our modern sales philosophy" (192).

He then considers the causal implications of the *Business Week* articles' argument—that consumption is necessary for the health of the economy. Teasing out the causal chain, he finds the contradiction in the position. When consumers buy on credit, they probably buy goods they never would have purchased with cash, but, simultaneously, they eventually reduce the amount of money available for purchasing and thus cannot purchase as much. This observation of the inherent problem in the argument of the authors of the *Business Week* articles leads him to a deeper analysis of the motivation underlying the "assumption that this really is the Age of the Consumer" (192), and this is the comic turn. If the consumer really does have less agency, as Burke has just noted, which leads to what he calls the "Inevitability of Instability" (193), the place to explore motives is elsewhere. And so, he argues, perhaps there is a stability in another realm of the economy that is in the production of "goods not accessible to the fluctuations of the mass-market. ([He] refer[s] to such resources as investment by private corporations in plant expansion, but above all to the vast sums spent by government for the defense, rivers, harbors, dams, reclamation, highways, housing, crop subsidies, direct or indirect subsidizing of exports and the like)" (193). Though not the subject of the *Business Week* articles, spending on this other kind of production underpins the stability of the economy and provides the "motivational ingredients in our culture" (193). One outcome he suggests of this other kind of production may be seen in the danger that in times of peace the threat of sag in the economy may lead to someone inciting "international ill will" (193). Burke's analysis at this point may be comic, but the tone is certainly shrewdly morose and, in a typically Burkean sense, wincingly appreciative.

Despite the darkness of this argument, in 1956 he still holds out enough hope to end with the comic—by transforming the motive, albeit in a dream. After exploring the consequences of this ethical "transvaluation of all values" (192), Burke ends with a typical Burkean paradox in which the negative is transformed into a positive:

> [My] own fond dream whereby the federal government would undertake to reclaim our streams by equipping all towns and cities, and even private industries, with sewage disposal plants . . . to purify the very symbol of purification itself . . . then indeed technology could by its own technological devices transcend itself. . . . Far from being expended in a cult of waste, with the almost diabolical ingenuity that must sometimes be exerted to goad our citizenry into frantic efforts at exhausting our national resources as rapidly as possible, a vast project in national reclamation could be undertaken to the profit of us all.

Then with a Burkean ironic turn:

> And far from cramping the consumer, such improvements would but extend the range of opportunities for the consumer to disport himself, just as government-built dams but increase the opportunities for private enterprise. (193)

At a talk given at Bennington College on April 9, 1959, Burke spoke with his greatest messianic urgency and for once, constructed an explicitly deliberative argument. The essay, "Motion, Action, Words: The Cultural Implications of Technology and World Order," considers what he calls the central "'global' problem of the time, the possible end of such a world as we know it" while "the human race is now like a child playing with a live hand grenade" (1). His method of analysis is both dramatistic and apocalyptic. The form is tragic, ending with the now well-known "Old Nursery Jingle Brought Up to Date": "If all the trees were one tree" transformed to "If all the thermo-nuclear warheads/Were one thermo-nuclear warhead" and "What a splish-splash that would be" to "What great PROGRESS that would be" (18). A transformation to be sure, but one that we might call the downward way rather than the upward way.

Burke's view of the inevitability of apocalypse results in the sober tone and relative lack of word play and fable, and while he uses opposing terms, he does so without the possibility of transformation. The dialectical terms seem locked in static opposition:

> The major problem is that there is no essential difference between our swords and our plowshares, between the peaceful and the warlike use of these resources. The instruments of industry are, by the same token, usable for war. To talk of outlawing them for warlike purposes would be like trying to outlaw the fist while developing the resources of the hand. (3)

Likewise, his analysis of the language of the tensions between the United States and Russia notes the use of contrasting language, not to transform but to maintain opposition. "When we give [foreign aid], it's aid; when they give it, it's an offensive" (4). He analyzes the motives for the conflict in the advances in the physical sciences, "the sciences of motion"; the social sciences, "the sciences of action"; and the humanities, "specializing in words, or more generally, symbols" (2). In each case, the discipline is implicated in the conflict and inevitability of fated conflict. And, in each case, their research is supporting the inventions and attitudes that lead to conflict, the urge to perfection that goads all action. In an unusual move for Burke, he proposes a solution: A small hope may be found in confronting the conflict through cooperation through a "loosely federated organization, a body largely deliberative along the lines of the U.N." (12).

Finally, he employs paradox and dialectical opposition in an attempt to transform the apocalyptic moment into its own salvation. Recognizing that the promises of technology have become problems, that the elements of hope have become "property for men to wrangle over" (14), that art is expressing the attitudes of the time (but could contribute to a transformation through reminding readers of the tragic or comic pattern of the current situation), he nonetheless ends with lament and admonition (17) and with the transformed nursery rhyme:

> If all the trees were one tree
> What a great tree that would be.
> If all the axes were one axe
> What a great axe that would be.
> If all the men were one man
> What a great man he would be.
> If all the seas were one sea
> What a great sea that would be.
> And if the great man
> Took the great axe
> And chopped down the great tree
> And let it fall into the great sea
> What a splish-splash that would be! (*Language as Symbolic Action* 21–22)

Modernized, perfected, the form runs thus:

> If all the thermo-nuclear warheads
> Were one thermo-nuclear warhead,
> What a great thermo-nuclear warhead that would be.
> If all the intercontinental ballistic missiles
> Were one intercontinental ballistic missile,
> What a great intercontinental ballistic missile that would be.
> If all the land masses
> Were one land mass,
> What a great land mass that would be.
> And if the great military man
> Took the great thermo-nuclear warhead

And put it into the great intercontinental ballistic missile
And dropped it on the great land mass,
What great PROGRESS that would be? (21–22)

"Motion, Action, Words" was never published. The rationalization was that it didn't translate well from a lecture to a magazine article and "recent developments had taken some of the edge off the whole question of a runaway military technology" (McWilliams). And yet, the manner of presentation may have played an equal role in the rejection. In one of his letters to Carey McWilliams while *The Nation* was considering its publication, Burke put his finger on the tone that may have prevented its publication: "Alas! The investment in ill will still overhangs our entire economy. And unless the us-against-them attitude can be replaced by the all-in-the-same-boat attitude, there's no hope. And my ironic plea is, of course, in the all-in-the-same-boat mode" (Letter to C. McWilliams).

Whenever I try to write about Burke, I always worry that what he says about the universe applies to the enormous body of his writing. So, to quote Burke with a difference, we might say, "[Burke's writing] would appear to be something like a cheese; it can be sliced in an infinite number of ways—and when one has chosen his own pattern of slicing, he finds that other men's cuts fall at the wrong places" (*Permanence and Change* 136). Recognizing that my pattern of slicing is my own, I would argue that through his entire life, Burke found in academic journals and the popular press, as well as in the many letters written to friends and colleagues, different fora wherein he might employ his rhetorical perspective to seek the greater social good, but did so by applying his theories of the dialectical possibilities of aesthetic/rhetorical strategies to a not quite hygienic scene, and the scene always infected the agency.

Works Cited

Burke, Kenneth. "Art—and the First Rough Draft of Living." *Modern Age* 8 (1964): 155–65.

———. *Language as Symbolic Action: Essays on Life, Literature and Method.* Berkeley: U of California P, 1966.

———. Letter to Carey McWilliams. 14 Oct. 1959. Carey McWilliams Papers.

———. "Motion, Action, Words: The Cultural Implications of Technology and World Order." Unpublished manuscript, Carey McWilliams Papers, U of California at Los Angeles, 1959.

———. *Permanence and Change.* 3rd ed. Berkeley: U of California P, 1984.

———. "Recipe for Prosperity: 'Borrow. Buy. Waste. Want.'" *The Nation* 183 (1956): 191–93.

———. *A Rhetoric of Motives.* Berkeley: U of California P, 1969.

———. "Waste—The Future of Prosperity." *The New Republic* 63 (1930): 228–31.

Jay, Paul, ed. *The Selected Correspondence of Kenneth Burke and Malcolm Cowley: 1915–1981.* New York: Viking, 1988.

McWilliams, Carey. Letter to Kenneth Burke. 15 Dec. 1959. Carey McWilliams Papers.

Rueckert, William H. *Kenneth Burke and the Drama of Human Relations.* Minneapolis: U of Minnesota P, 1963.

Intellectual and Conceptual Resources for Visual Rhetoric
A Reexamination of Scholarship Since 1950

Lester C. Olson

In the United States, research into visual rhetoric has flourished in colleges and universities for over half a century now. Those of us who study visual rhetoric are in the midst of an intellectual movement that is both broad based and deep. By that, I mean that the study of visual rhetoric now spans multiple disciplines, and it often engages some of the most important technological developments of our lifetimes. Visual rhetoric scholarship is rich in its critical, philosophical, and historical ramifications across the humanities and sciences. In the United States, the following are the varied historical roots of the burgeoning interest in visual rhetoric since 1950: intellectual, technological, social, political, and economic.

Among the intellectual roots, Kenneth Burke's (1950/1969) *A Rhetoric of Motives* defined rhetoric as symbolic action in ways that raised several possibilities for visual rhetoric scholarship. Consequently, Burke influenced generations of intellectuals. In addition, a 1971 collaborative statement entitled "Report of the Committee on the Advancement and Refinement of Rhetorical Criticism" set priorities that further advanced scholars' contributions in visual rhetoric. The report commented on an intellectual movement underway in communication and speech departments across the nation. The report advised: "Rhetorical criticism must broaden its scope to examine the full range of rhetorical transactions; that is, informal conversations, group settings, public settings, mass media messages, picketing, sloganeering, chanting, singing, marching, gesturing, ritual, institutional and cultural symbols, cross cultural transactions, and so forth" (Sloan et al., 1971, p. 225). This statement, along with earlier intellectual contributions, set the academic scene for subsequent work by scholars on what today is regularly referred to as visual rhetoric.

Additional roots nourishing the development of visual rhetoric scholarship were political, social, and economic. During the 1960s and early 1970s, because of dramatic protest techniques employed across the United States and abroad throughout the Vietnam War years (when the 1971 report was written), rhetoric

This article will appear in *Review of Communication*, a publication of the National Communication Association. NCA and RSA have reciprocally approved the joint publication of the article.

scholars recognized that traditional definitions of and approaches to rhetoric were much too limited to account for contemporaneous endeavors to influence beliefs and actions in public life. More fundamentally, because of a proliferation of new, highly visual media technologies with profound ramifications for communication, academic interest in visual rhetoric deepened noticeably. Photography, film, television, the World Wide Web, and digital technology, for instance, transformed the ways in which speeches and other messages were recorded and conveyed to their audiences, while also making visual evidence—both archival and contemporaneous—readily available to communities of scholars. In the wake of such nineteenth- and twentieth-century visual technologies, academic researchers became increasingly interested in pictorial records, visual components of messages, and the culturally shaped practices of viewing them.

Further, some researchers recognized that attention to symbolic aspects of visual artifacts, sometimes referred to as vernacular or material culture, provided a way to document histories of the poor and working classes, African Americans and other racial minorities, women, gay men and lesbians, and other understudied populations and cultures. Histories of communication practices could be recovered by examining the symbolic objects that members of such social groups had used and left behind. For instance, consider a fresco thought to have been made sometime between AD 300 and AD 600 by an ancient Teotihuacan culture in Mexico.[1] It was made of mineral pigment and lime plaster and depicts a rain priest's speech rendered in pictorial symbols including sea shells and plants. The fresco reminds us that certain cultures' speeches were recorded pictorially, not linguistically. Another strong example of such artifacts consists of numerous symbolic belts from the Iroquois confederacy and other indigenous tribes and leagues. Constructed from white and purple beads made from oyster shells, these symbolic belts preserved records of speeches, treaties, and other historical events so that knowledge of them could be transmitted from generation to generation within these likewise quintessentially American cultures.[2] Artifacts such as these demonstrate that the study of visual rhetoric presents tantalizing prospects for rhetoric scholars, including those who still consider speeches and orations to be the central or defining focus of the discipline.

Attention to such artifacts and other sorts of material culture—objects that were not records of speeches—enacted a democratic impulse in scholarship that intensified in the wake of a centuries-long political process of broadening voting rights to include working-class men, African Americans, and women. These nineteenth- and early-twentieth-century political developments impacted ongoing changes in the demographic make up of college and university teachers, whose voices and perspectives now regularly emphasize messages produced by understudied populations and cultures. In addition, because race, sex, age, certain disabilities, and other factors are ordinarily visible features of individuals and demographic groups, some researchers' engagement with visual rhetoric scholarship has been enhanced by their interest in visible and invisible communities, or dominant and relatively vulnerable social groups—including diverse minorities' visual symbolism and social stigmas. A powerful expression of this interest with regard to race, for instance, is Shawn Michelle Smith's 2004 book, *Photography on the Color Line: W. E. B. Du Bois, Race, and Visual Culture*, even though she does not mention "rhetoric." Last, but not least, evolving understandings of "public" and "private" in the United States helped to make material or vernacular culture in the home and elsewhere captivating to scholars of visual rhetoric. As a related development, previously taboo and sensitive topics came into public consideration in numerous ways, including via visual rhetoric scholarship.

As a consequence of over half a century of scholarship since 1950, there is now a wide variety of ways of naming the terrain regularly designated by the recent expression "visual rhetoric." I am using that expression here as a shorthand to emphasize culturally shaped practices of seeing in their relationship to historically situated processes of rhetorical action. Like other ways of naming the terrain, "visual rhetoric" is not unproblematic, because, for instance, reading is a highly visual activity. Yet most visual rhetoric scholarship is concerned primarily with symbols other than words, even though words regularly are elements of the analysis and even though one important body of scholarship concentrates on word-image relationships. So I do not want to be misunderstood as implying either that there is a consensus on how to name the area of study or that "visual rhetoric" is evidently the best of all options. I am using "visual rhetoric" as a shorthand mainly because it is inclusive language and because, since the turn of the millennium, it appears with increasing regularity in recent research across a range of disciplines. "Visual rhetoric" does not appear to have been used frequently as a central, organizing term before 1990. During May 2006, an electronic search of the Communication and Mass Media Index located a total of 150 articles and reviews concerning "visual rhetoric," none of them with a publication date before 1964 (see http://www.ebscohost.com/ehost). Fully two-thirds of those articles and reviews (101 out of 150) were published after 2000. (Incidentally, of the remaining one-third published before 2000, almost half—24 out of 49 essays—were printed between 1990 and 2000; before 1990, only 25 essays used "visual rhetoric" as a featured term.)

In what follows, I will articulate a history of visual rhetoric scholarship by describing the nomenclature employed by speech and communication researchers for designating germane scholarship, by specifying some landmark moments in its history, and by identifying recurring patterns in intellectual and conceptual resources during the last half century. Because the pluralism of definition and emphasis is valuable for ongoing projects in visual rhetoric, I am less concerned with identifying a center that holds visual rhetoric scholarship together than I am with focal points for substantive conversations and dialogues to advance current scholarship with all its diversity and promise. Toward the conclusion, I will concentrate on the ongoing process of instituting the study of visual rhetoric in higher education. My concluding comments will suggest some open-ended questions that, I hope, will initiate collaborative, collective conversation among visual rhetoric scholars concerning components of one overarching question: How might the study of visual rhetoric be better positioned and developed within colleges and universities in the United States? I believe that collective engagement with that question might better position visual rhetoric in higher education while strengthening pedagogy in the area. I will endeavor not only to "size up" visual rhetoric scholarship, but also to "up size" it.

Nomenclature for Visual Rhetoric Scholarship Since 1950

Let me begin with the numerous, sometimes synonymous but almost always overlapping, names for visual rhetoric, to which I now turn in the spirit of sketching a necessarily broad history of the nomenclature, landmarks, and key concepts. At the outset, I want to acknowledge that my account will tend to foreground scholarship in speech and communication departments but that the story is more complex. I hope others will feel welcome to round out this preliminary sketch by reference to specific, additional essays and books that merit inclusion in a revision of this history-in-process. At present, useful perspectives on the development of visual rhetoric scholarship can be found in essays by Richard B. Gregg (1985), Diane S. Hope (2006), and Lawrence J. Prelli (2006), who discuss visual rhetoric scholarship against the background of symbolic inducement, visual communication, and rhetoric of display, respectively.

In 1950, Kenneth Burke employed the expression "rhetoric of symbolic action" in his influential book, *A Rhetoric of Motives*. The impact of this book on subsequent generations of scholars was deep and abiding. The bulk of visual rhetoric scholarship in the 1960s and 1970s certainly was influenced by Burke's writings, which continue to be useful today. His views on the comic and tragic frame, for instance, have been featured in Adrienne Christiansen and Jeremy Hanson's 1996 essay on ACT UP and the rhetoric of AIDS activism as well as Anne Demo's 2000 essay concerning the Guerrilla Girls' comic politics of subversion. My first publication on visual rhetoric in 1983 featured Burke's concept of identification to study Norman Rockwell's "Four Freedoms," while other scholars—both before then and afterward—have drawn on a wide range of concepts from Burke's writings. For instance, Gregory Clark's 2004 book *Rhetorical Landscapes in America: Variations on a Theme from Kenneth Burke* featured his concepts of identification and representative anecdote.

In the late 1960s, Phillip K. Tompkins wrote a book review essay on what he termed the "rhetorical criticism of non-oratorical forms." This naming had the disadvantage of defining an area of study by negation—by what it was not—not oratory. He began the essay, which concentrated on literature (specifically Truman Capote's *In Cold Blood*), with an apology for the "clumsy" language. He explained that he had "borrowed" the expression "non-oratorical works" from a recent convention program (Tompkins, 1969, p. 431). "Nonverbal rhetoric," another expression from this period, likewise had the disadvantage of definition by negation, but it appears to have had more frequent use than "non-oratorical forms" in publications during the late 1970s and early 1980s. It was featured in a 1971 book, *The Rhetoric of Nonverbal Communication*, a collection of readings compiled by Haig A. Bosmajian. The preface alluded to "the turn to ritual, ceremony, symbols, demonstrations; the dependence upon communication, which takes us beyond words" (p. vi). Of the 25 articles and reviews that featured "nonverbal rhetoric" in the Communication and Mass Media Index as of May 2006, more than half were published between 1969 and 1979 with only intermittent uses since then.

In 1974, Thomas W. Benson concentrated on what he initially termed "rhetoric of film." Later, in 1984, he broadened his nomenclature to "rhetorical dimensions of media," as did Martin J. Medhurst, his coeditor of *Rhetorical Dimensions in the Media: A Critical Casebook*. Dedicated to Burke, this landmark book consisted of 17 essays and concluded with a 40-some-page bibliography of germane books and essays. The quality of the publications listed in the bibliography was uneven and it often included books and essays that did not meaningfully engage rhetoric, pertaining as they did primarily to a particular medium. Even so, this bibliography is still useful to anyone wishing to become familiar with scholarship on visual rhetoric before the mid-1980s (pp. 365–407). The book and bibliography both organized the study of visual rhetoric by the type of medium: television, film, radio, graphic arts, music, magazines, public letters, and literature, suggesting strongly that the medium was especially fundamental to understanding visual rhetoric. As the essays concerning music indicate, the sense of rhetoric was capacious.[3]

The terms "symbols" and "symbolic" surfaced regularly in studies of visual rhetoric throughout the 1970s and 1980s. In 1974, for instance, Sol Worth and Larry Gross published an essay concerning what they called "symbolic strategies." In general, their essay inquired, "How do we distinguish 'natural' from 'symbolic' events, and how do we assign meaning to them?" (p. 27). By the early 1980s—probably before then—Richard B. Gregg employed the expression "symbolic inducement," a naming likewise influenced by Burke. This language identified the central focus of Gregg's 1984 book *Symbolic Inducement and Knowing: A Study in the Foundations of Rhetoric* and his landmark 1985 essay entitled "The Criticism of Symbolic Inducement," one of the few essays that provides a sustained historical account of the development of visual rhetoric and other symbolic studies.

In the early 1980s, other scholars were employing terms for visual rhetoric drawn largely from art history and designating specific art-historical techniques in the analysis of visual texts. In 1982, for instance, Martin J. Medhurst wrote an influential essay concerning film in terms of what he called "rhetorical iconography." Likewise borrowing from art-historical vocabularies, I devoted my 1984 doctoral dissertation, subsequent essays, and two books to what I called "rhetorical iconology" and the "rhetoric of material culture." Neither expression, "rhetorical iconography" or "rhetorical iconology," has surfaced much in subsequent visual rhetoric scholarship, perhaps because the language is too tied to art-historical approaches. Since then, however, there have been regular references to material or vernacular culture, motifs, rhetorical icons, and iconicity in visual rhetoric scholarship, about which I will say more later.

By the early 1990s, yet another broad expression used to name visual rhetoric was "rhetorical dimensions of popular culture," a naming that may be exemplified well by Barry Brummett's 1991 book with that exact title. Concurrently, still other names for components of visual rhetoric during the 1980s and 1990s tended to emphasize specific rhetorical processes or a certain medium or media. These emphases may be exemplified in Sonja K. Foss's scholarship, focusing as she did in 1986 on the Vietnam Veterans Memorial and in 1988 on Judy Chicago's *The Dinner Party*, an iconic work in the women's movement. Foss's scholarship was among the earliest visual rhetoric research to feature feminist subject matter. It was also among the earliest to concentrate on rhetorical perspectives concerning public memorials and memorialization, an especially rich line of visual rhetoric scholarship that has been taken up by several accomplished public memory scholars (Biesecker, 2002; Blair, Jeppeson, & Pucci, 1991; Blair & Michel, 2000). Recent visual rhetoric scholarship pertaining to public memory has extended to displays in museum exhibitions (Hasian, 2004; Hubbard & Hasian, 1998; Taylor, 1998, 2003) and to U.S. postal commemorative stamps (Haskins, 2003), among other settings and media.

In addition, certain elements of rhetoric—especially argument, figures, and devices—have received sustained attention in visual rhetoric scholarship. In 1996, two special issues of *Argumentation and Advocacy*, edited by David S. Birdsell and Leo Groarke, were devoted to "visual argument" with essays by several scholars, including contributions by David Fleming, J. Anthony Blair, Lenore Langsdorf, Cameron Shelley, and Gretchen S. Barbatsis. These special issues merit the attention of anyone interested in visual rhetoric, concentrating as the contributors do on a range of specific ways of conceptualizing visual argument. Margaret R. LaWare's 1998 essay examined visual arguments for ethnic pride, community activism, and cultural revitalization in Chicano murals located in Chicago. Cara A. Finnegan's 2001 essay explored what she called a "naturalistic enthymeme," employing language from classical argumentation that she drew on again subsequently in a 2005 essay defining "image vernaculars." Catherine H. Palczewski's (2002) keynote address at a major argumentation conference continued explorations of "visual argument," as did her 2005 essay concerning anti-suffrage postcards. A parallel body of research in visual rhetoric has developed around specific rhetorical devices and figures, especially pictorial metaphor. Arthur Danto's 1981 book entitled *The Transfiguration of the Commonplace* and Stuart Kaplan's 1990 essay illustrate sustained interest in pictorial metaphor (see also Edwards & Winkler, 1997; Olson, 1987). Additional researchers have concentrated on irony, metonymy, synecdoche, and other rhetorical devices or figures (Scott, 2004; Tom & Eves, 1999; Van Mulken, 2003; Willerton, 2005).

Other names for visual rhetoric scholarship exist and still others are now being promoted. Since the late 1990s, there have been essays by several writers on rhetorical icons or iconic images. For example, coauthors Janis L. Edwards and Carol K. Winkler's 1997 essay concerns what they call "representative form," a synthesis of iconic and ideographic features in readily recognized pictorial metaphors. A series of coauthored essays by Robert Hariman and John Louis Lucaites since 2001 concentrates on what they name "iconic photographs" (2001, 2003, 2004). In addition, Bryan C. Taylor's 2003 essay examines what he calls "nuclear iconography." Moreover, "material rhetoric" sometimes has surfaced in visual rhetoric scholarship since 2004 (Dickinson, Ott, & Aoki, 2006; Rohan, 2004). This nomenclature has the appeal of being less cumbersome than some earlier language, such as "rhetorical study of material culture" or "vernacular culture," which I mentioned in my (Olson) 1991 book. "Material rhetoric" has the appeal of concision, but it may have the disadvantage of reifying a process. Another recent name for germane scholarship is the "rhetoric of visual conventions," as in Charles Kostelnick and Michael Hassett's 2003 book entitled *Shaping Information: The Rhetoric of Visual Conventions*. Most recently, we have seen several titles that concentrate on digital media, as in Barbara Warnick's groundbreaking 2002 book, *Critical Literacy in a Digital Era: Technology, Rhetoric, and the Public Interest* (see also Warnick, 2005). Digital technology is currently generating extraordinary interest, to judge from the Communication and Mass Media Index.

Having now completed a sketch portraying changes in nomenclature over the decades since 1950, I would like next to turn attention to dominant patterns characterizing visual rhetoric scholarship since 1950, noting in the process some factors inhibiting its development.

Broad Patterns in Visual Rhetoric Scholarship Since 1950

Most visual rhetoric scholarship during the last half of the twentieth century consisted of conceptually driven case studies of historically situated events, featuring a particular medium and typically concerning a twentieth-century controversy or technology. Photography, television, and film have held the most attention over the decades, with the World Wide Web and digital technology rapidly emerging at present. Visual rhetoric scholarship regularly features special optical equipment and technologies ranging from stethoscopes and probes to ultrasound, MRI diagnostic imaging, and electron microscopes. Scholars' attention to technologies that enhance vision may be exemplified by Nathan Stormer's (1997) essay concerning fetal photography in a documentary film. Some research has underscored how the routine performance of scientific inquiry depends on visualizing inferences (or abduction), as in Cameron Shelley's (1996) essay concerning a process called "demonstrative visual argument." Whether visual rhetoric scholarship has examined the sciences, the humanities, or the arts, it has concentrated regularly on technological developments that have fundamentally transformed visual culture and communication practices.

Since 1950, most visual rhetoric scholarship has evinced an abiding and predominant interest in twentieth-century communication technologies, events, and controversies, usually centering in the United States. Scholars' interest in relatively recent history was emphatically expressed in the broad priorities set up in the 1971 report, presumably because of the widespread public unrest and civil disobedience that characterized the Vietnam War years. While identifying specific, academic priorities for the discipline, the authors of this report asserted "[t]he imperative we feel to study contemporary rhetorical transactions" (Sloan et al., 1971, p. 225). The authors averred, however, that "[t]he emphasis on contemporary criticism or on historical studies which can illuminate the contemporary is in no way meant to denigrate historical scholarship which is simply aimed at forming perspectives on the past; rather, it reflects a deep concern for the pressing problems of our time" (p. 225).

There is nonetheless a growing body of visual rhetoric scholarship that concentrates on earlier periods in history, especially the eighteenth and nineteenth centuries in the United States, but also sometimes investigates visual works and interpretive practices from earlier centuries and other countries. In certain instances, such scholarship combines attention to twentieth-century technologies and earlier periods in U.S. history. For example, Judith Lancioni (1996) has examined documentary film techniques for focusing on elements of archival photographs taken during the Civil War. Regardless of the time period featured, however, the predominant emphasis in visual rhetoric scholarship has been on the recent past in Western civilizations. Consequently, much could be gained in visual rhetoric scholarship were researchers to concentrate on communication practices in Eastern civilizations, intercultural symbols as they migrate across national boundaries, and ongoing processes of globalization.

Throughout the last half of the twentieth century, an immense body of scholarship named the rhetoric of a specifically named genre, medium, or space—usually depending on the historical period featured in the specific studies. In fact, several other relatively early terms pertained to a specific medium or media. By the mid- to late 1970s, for example, Bruce Gronbeck (1978) was concentrating on what he has variously called "celluloid rhetoric" or "electronic rhetoric," nomenclature that, at once, concentrates both on a specific range of media and a particular historical period. Gronbeck's early scholarship concentrated on what he called "genres of documentary," especially featuring programming on television and in film.

Benson's early work on "the rhetoric of film" likewise has this strength and limitation of featuring a specific medium and historical period (Benson, 1974, 1980, 1985, 1998; Medhurst & Benson, 1981).

A noteworthy shift in emphasis in visual rhetoric scholarship has placed interpretive practices of observing and seeing in the foreground rather than giving priority to the artifact or media. Although there has been a growing interest in the viewers' interpretive performances or interactions with symbolic expressions, there nonetheless has been a long-standing emphasis on contemporaneous viewers' diverse interpretations of visual artifacts during historical controversies, with attention to the timeliness of visual images as they circulated in specific moments. An emphasis on contemporaneous viewers' sensibilities and interpretive activities can easily be found in relatively early visual rhetoric scholarship in communication journals.[4] In fact, it would be difficult, if not impossible, to account for such scholarship detailing multiple perspectives on the exact same artifacts with attention to the eventfulness of pressing issues informing their uses at the time—in fact, struggles among contemporaneous partisans to shape various symbols' meanings—were earlier researchers unattuned to the diverse viewers' sensibilities and commitments as they actively interpreted whatever they saw.

In an influential 1994 essay, W. J. T. Mitchell describes the broad, cultural circumstances within which such visual rhetoric scholarship has flourished when he names "the pictorial turn" as a twentieth-century phenomenon. He asserts:

> In Anglo-American philosophy, variations on this turn could be traced early on in Charles Peirce's semiotics and later in Nelson Goodman's "languages of art," both of which explore the conventions and codes that underlie nonlinguistic symbol systems and (more important) do not begin with the assumption that language is paradigmatic for meaning. (p. 12)

Contemporary culture has become "totally dominated by images" (p. 15). Mitchell recognizes that the saturation of twentieth-century cultures with images has combined with anxieties concerning them, such as idolatry and iconoclasm, to make visual culture a preoccupation of contemporary life. Given Mitchell's thematic emphasis on audiences or spectators in characterizing "the pictorial turn"—"It is the realization that spectatorship (the look, the gaze, the glance, the practices of observation, surveillance, and visual pleasure) may be as deep a problem as various forms of reading" (p. 16)—it is unfortunate that his essay almost completely neglects germane visual rhetoric scholarship; the topic of "rhetoric" appears only in a list of germane disciplines in the introductory paragraph.

To be sure, it would be accurate to say that most of the early visual rhetoric scholarship tended to focus on a specific artist's oeuvre (e.g., Robert L. Scott's 1977 essay on Diego Rivera's murals) or a specific medium (e.g., Kathleen J. Turner's 1977 rhetorical perspective on comics). In recent years, there has been an increasing emphasis on the organizations and institutions that selected and circulated the images. For instance, Cara Finnegan's 2003 book *Picturing Poverty: Print Culture and FSA Photographs* continued a tradition of featuring a single medium (photography), but she underscored institutional factors in the Farm Security Administration, the various magazines that redistributed certain photographs, and the U.S. government. Visual rhet-

oric scholarship has sometimes featured pictorial images, or motifs, reproduced across an immense variety of media—mundane objects, high art, and
illustrated reading materials—as they recur across national boundaries to dis-
close broad patterns of partisan engagement with the media and contemporaries' underlying ideologies (Olson, 1987, 1990, 1991, 2004).

Recent visual rhetoric scholarship has tended to give greater attention to
powerful visual symbols performed, enacted, or circulated by members of
vulnerable communities. This attention is exemplified by Charles E. Morris
III and John M. Sloop's 2006 essay on the politics of what they describe as
"queer public kissing" between men. Among other images, their essay considers the graphic arts of a collective named Gran Fury (1988), whose
"READ MY LIPS" poster is now iconic in gay, lesbian, bisexual, transgen-
der, transsexual, and queer communities.[5] Further examples consist of recent
essays by coauthors Peter Ehrenhaus and Susan Owen (2004) and by coauthors Christine Harold and Kevin Michael DeLuca (2005) concerning the
lynching and murders of African American men. These two essays examine
such homicides as public, symbolic performances of white supremacist ideology and black political resistance, respectively. In addition, as an example of
visual rhetoric scholarship concerning both feminism and environmental
degradation, Phaedra C. Pezzullo (2003) focused on "toxic tours" in San
Francisco calculated to resist "National Breast Cancer Awareness Month"
insofar as it diverts attention from root causes of cancer.

Such essays illustrate relatively recent, burgeoning attention to the communication practices of women and feminists, sexual and racial minorities,
and other vulnerable communities. In addition, essays such as these exemplify
a broad trend in visual rhetoric scholarship that features "body argument" or
"rhetorical bodies," "performances," and "experiential tours" in symbolic
spaces, sites, or locations. In 1999, *Argumentation and Advocacy* published a collection of essays on "body argument" in two consecutive issues, which were
edited by Gerard A. Hauser. These special issues included contributions from
Kevin M. DeLuca, James L. Cherney, Thomas J. Darwin, Nathan Stormer,
Christine L. Harold, Kathleen M. Torrens, and Amos Kiewe. Likewise, Jack
Selzer and Sharon Crowley edited a 1999 anthology concerning what they
call "rhetorical bodies," which is also the title of their book.

Scholarship on visual rhetoric has been flourishing, however it has been
named, despite some difficulties, obstacles, or overt resistance, which I would
like to consider next in this necessarily brief historical sketch. Certainly one
factor that has obscured the half-century long history of visual rhetoric has
been the number of names, sometimes synonymous but almost always overlapping, such as: rhetoric of symbolic action, rhetoric of nonoratorical forms,
nonverbal rhetoric, rhetorical dimensions of media or popular culture, symbolic strategies or inducement, rhetorical iconography or iconology, pictorial
or visual persuasion or argument, pictorial metaphor, electronic or celluloid
rhetoric, rhetorical icons or iconic images, material rhetoric or rhetoric of
material culture, rhetoric of visual conventions, and digital rhetoric. Addi-

tional variations feature the rhetoric of a specifically named genre or medium, such as advertisements, architecture, atlases, cartoons, comics, films, maps, murals, paintings, photography, posters, prints, quilts, sculpture, symbolic bodies, television, and textiles, among many, many others.

Another factor inhibiting the growth of visual rhetoric scholarship has been the scattered range of disciplinary sites where the variously named versions of visual rhetoric scholarship have been produced. This has made it challenging to locate and use previous contributions to the germane literature. Among these disciplines are American studies, art history, communication, English and composition, history, media, rhetoric, speech, and visual studies. Across such varied disciplines, researchers have proceeded with more or less conscious awareness of rhetoric's rich and diverse history, which provides invaluable conceptual resources for analyses of symbolic action. While each distinctive disciplinary sociology has enriched visual rhetoric scholarship, the scattered pattern has resulted in researchers proceeding with less than ideal awareness of each other's scholarship. A predictable consequence is that it sometimes seems as though it has been necessary to reinvent the pencil before sitting down to write, or the stylus before sketching.

These last factors were exacerbated by the virtual absence of well-institutionalized concentrations on visual rhetoric in academic departments—not to mention the absence of interdisciplinary programs or centers—that could have brought such an extraordinary range of scholars into conversation. It is possible here and there to identify collaborative efforts among some people at the same place. Examples would be the Pennsylvania State University and the University of Pennsylvania throughout the 1970s and 1980s. But these are exceptions rather than the norm. The absence of academic concentrations not only limited the ease of intellectual exchanges among engaged visual rhetoric scholars, it also circumscribed the facility with which the next generations of intellectuals could receive substantive undergraduate and graduate training in visual rhetoric scholarship.

Last, but certainly not least, stiff resistance to the very idea of visual rhetoric may be illustrated by Donald Bryant's 1973 denunciation of the terrain as excessively broad and the 1971 landmark report as, in his words, "reckless" (especially pp. 16–17). The intellectual reservations that Bryant articulated at the University of Iowa and that other scholars enacted elsewhere probably constrained explorations of visual rhetoric at the institutions where such prominent, accomplished academic leaders influenced their peers and generations of students. The disciplinary background against which visual rhetoric scholarship grew in speech and communication departments may be concisely summarized by the book cover of the 1982 second edition of Bernard L. Brock and Robert L. Scott's *Methods of Rhetorical Criticism*, which, I imagine, needs no further comment for the reader.

Despite the difficulties, research on visual rhetoric has blossomed. In fact, it is now free-flowering. Recent years have seen several germane collections of essays concerning visual rhetoric. Charles A. Hill and Marguerite Helmers's

2004 anthology, *Defining Visual Rhetorics*, provides 14 essays by a range of established and newer scholars. This anthology has the value of bringing scholars from different disciplines, especially communication, composition, and English, into relationship with each other. Likewise, Diane S. Hope's edited collection entitled *Visual Communication: Perception, Rhetoric and Technology*, released in 2006, adds a wealth of materials in 13 interdisciplinary essays. Hope's introduction articulates a useful orientation to visual rhetoric scholarship against the backdrop of visual communication. Lawrence J. Prelli's *Rhetorics of Display*, which was also released in 2006, has a 20-page selected bibliography of visual rhetoric scholarship that I recommend as a useful resource. The collection's introduction likewise provides a useful orientation to a body of germane scholarship. More important, the 17 essays in Prelli's text range around the globe and over an immense variety of what he terms "rhetorics of display."

At present, myself, Cara A. Finnegan, and Diane S. Hope are in the process of completing a contracted anthology of essays

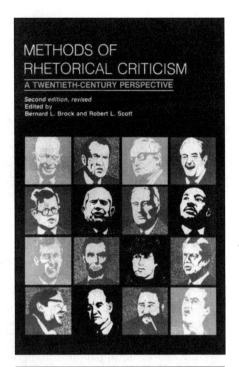

Figure 1
The book cover depicts 16 people in a four by four grid, from left to right, as follows: (first row) Dwight D. Eisenhower, Richard M. Nixon, Barry Goldwater, and Hubert Humphrey; (second row) Ted Kennedy, Nikita Khrushchev, Franklin D. Roosevelt, and Martin Luther King; (third row) Edmund Muskie, Abraham Lincoln, "Rocky," and Jimmy Carter; (fourth row) William Buckley, Jr., George McGovern, Fidel Castro, and George Wallace.

called *Visual Rhetoric: A Reader in Communication and American Culture,* which features key rhetorical actions: performing and seeing, remembering and memorializing, commodifying and consuming, confronting and resisting, and governing and authorizing. It is a testament to the vitality of the research on visual rhetoric that we found the selection process to be time-consuming and difficult. We have featured 20 carefully selected essays that we believe are especially instructive for learning about visual rhetoric. As we comment collaboratively in the preface:

> We elected to focus on rhetorical actions because we believe this is the most useful approach for students of communication and rhetoric. In

doing so we embrace what is now certainly a truism of rhetorical theory: that rhetoric is best characterized broadly as symbolic action. While individual instances of rhetorical practice might differ to the extent that they are more or less textual, oratorical, or visual, what is common to all rhetorical acts is that they all mobilize symbols to persuade.

Intellectual Resources in Visual Rhetoric Scholarship Since 1950

Precisely because visual rhetoric scholarship is flourishing, it is impossible in a single essay to identify an exhaustive list of key writers whose concepts and theories have enriched scholarship on visual rhetoric since 1950. Examples of recurring intellectual sources would have to include, in alphabetical order, Rudolph Arnheim, Roland Barthes, Jean Baudrillard, Walter Benjamin, John Berger, Kenneth Burke, Michel Foucault, Jacques Lacan, Suzanne Langer, W. J. T. Mitchell, Erwin Panofsky, C. S. Peirce, Susan Sontag, Barbara Stafford, Sol Worth, and, most recently perhaps, Michael Warner. Instances of key terms or concepts would include agency, appropriation, audience, author, body argument, circulation, commodification, consumption, display, dissemination, double binds, embodiment, enactment, fetishes, the gaze, genres, heterotopian space, icons and iconic, identification, image events, image vernaculars, interpellation, material culture, media ecology, metaphor, motif, panopticon, performance fragments, performative, pictorial indices, pictorial juxtaposition, production, public memory, reception, representative form, rhetorical bodies, scopic drive, semiotics, simulacrum, strategic ambiguity, surveillance, symbolic bodies, vernacular culture, and visual ideographs and ideology—to mention only a sample. As this list implies, visual rhetoric research is robust.

Some of these terms have multiple definitions and emphases in visual rhetoric scholarship. For instance, consider the terms "icon" and "iconic." Since C. S. Peirce's (1839–1914) early definition of icon (which, as you probably know, he distinguished from indices and symbols in that an icon entailed an element of resemblance), this term has surfaced with various meanings over the decades (see also Peirce 1992, 1998). Janis L. Edwards and Carol K. Winkler (1997), in criticizing me for my definition of the term icon, actually have a quarrel with Peirce, who coined the definition in question (p. 289); I never mentioned "resemblance" in my definition of icon. A more recent definition of icon in a series of important essays by Robert Hariman and John Louis Lucaites—whose forthcoming book, *No Caption Needed* from the University of Chicago Press, I await with great interest—treats icon as an image that is immediately recognizable by practically everyone throughout a culture (Hariman & Lucaites, 2001, p. 7). One possible problem with such a definition might be that it focuses, as a consequence, on mainstream, dominant culture, since powerful images produced from within vulnerable communities seldom attain that level of recognition: the poster by Gran Fury discussed above (Morris & Sloop, 2006, p. 11), or the HIV positive tattoos that Dan

Brouwer focused on so well in his 1998 essay, would not rise to iconic status in the definition offered by Hariman and Lucaites, however salient they are to certain vulnerable populations. Icon, as defined by them, tends to concentrate on mainstream, dominant culture. As this sustained example illustrates, it would be useful to reflect not only on the key terms in visual rhetoric, but the multiple meanings that those terms now have in the literature.

More important, it is my impression that, while we now have a wide range of conceptually driven and historically situated case studies, we do not have a substantive treatise that might accurately be described as a theory of visual rhetoric. Unless I am mistaken (and I might be), that important sort of scholarship lies ahead. I do not want to be misunderstood here. I am not saying that we lack rhetorical theories that are useful for studying practices of viewing and visual media. Nor am I saying that we lack theories of visual communication that are useful for studying rhetorical processes. Rather, to my knowledge, we do not at present have book-length, synthetic theorizing that centers on visual rhetoric. Where early scholarship tended to ask how, if at all, the resources of rhetoric were useful for analyzing, interpreting, and assessing visual media, more recent work has asked how understanding culturally shaped practices of viewing might be useful for reenvisioning rhetoric. I am inclined to think that it is important to hold those two questions in constant relationship to each other in the process of developing theories of visual rhetoric. If you believe, as I do, that the most important rhetorical theories of the past tended to engage the most consequential developments of their time, theorizing visual rhetoric holds considerable promise for the present and future.

Conclusion: Sketching a Future for Visual Rhetoric Scholarship

Having briefly sketched in necessarily broad terms an overview of the nomenclature and having identified some patterns, landmarks, and key concepts that recur in visual rhetoric scholarship, I would like to conclude by suggesting some open-ended questions that, I hope, will result in collaborative conversation concerning one overarching question: How might the study of visual rhetoric be better positioned and developed within colleges and universities in the United States? To my knowledge, this question has not received systematic consideration in any publication pertaining to the arts and humanities or liberal arts. An electronic search for germane materials pertaining to this question yielded only one essay (Brumberger, 2005), which concentrates on the curriculum of a business school rather than arts and humanities or liberal arts. There was, to be sure, an early 1982 essay by Sonja K. Foss, which developed a "resource unit" for teaching "rhetoric and the visual image" in one undergraduate course. Otherwise, to my knowledge, there is no extant scholarship concerning the matter of institutionalizing visual rhetoric in higher education. Here are some further questions concerning components of that larger concern:

1. What might a systematic curriculum in visual rhetoric include in higher education at the introductory and upper-level undergraduate levels, as well as the graduate curriculum for both the MA and the PhD?

2. What conceptual and theoretical resources might be most useful to students at these various levels as they are prepared for basic competence and advanced scholarship in visual rhetoric?

3. What training in archival research might be especially valuable to people who seek introductory and advanced training as experts in the history of visual rhetoric?

4. What education in the history of visual technologies and their uses is necessary to help undergraduate and graduate students understand and appreciate the ramifications of changes in visual culture over time?

5. How might concentrations on visual rhetoric be designed so that undergraduate and graduate students receive a systematic education that grounds them well in rhetoric, while at the same time makes them thoroughly familiar with cultural practices of viewing and interpreting images?

6. What varieties and constellations of faculty expertise would be particularly desirable in relationship to each other in instituting concentrations on visual rhetoric in academic departments?

7. How might the study of visual rhetoric be positioned advantageously in relationship to other components of departments as well as other entire departments, disciplines, centers, programs, and the like? For instance, how might we enter into meaningful conversation with scholars in American history and American studies who concentrate on what they often call "visual culture" and who seem to be interested in the symbolism, but who do not draw explicitly on rhetoric in their work?

Additional concerns around institutionalizing visual rhetoric extend to the need to hold regular conferences centering on visual rhetoric, and for journals that dependably feature the scholarship in ways that ground current work competently in its history. Instituting listservs, Web sites, blogs, and other online sources would improve the range of resources for training our students and for undertaking the research better ourselves. It would be prudent at this time for those who are interested in visual rhetoric to reflect on these and other aspects of the systematic institutionalizing of visual rhetoric because collaborative, collective work is likely to strengthen research, teaching, and general expertise in visual rhetoric.

In closing, I have no illusion that this essay has exhausted or definitively accounted for the range of nomenclature for visual rhetoric, its intellectual and conceptual resources, and landmark moments in its history. It is one person's perspective subject to revision. This account is partial in that it has tended to foreground scholarship in speech and communication departments in the United States. Certainly other disciplines have contributed to the study of visual rhetoric both in the United States and abroad. Moreover, as people like Colette Nativel are teaching us, there were earlier periods in the history of rhetoric wherein rhetoric ranged across the arts of painting and architecture—for instance, the Renaissance. Despite these and other limitations, I hope that this brief sketch of a historical perspective will spark a lively conversation among those of us engaged in remembering our past to get a sense of the present and to shape the future. I invite others to add their voices to underscore additional factors that a history of visual rhetoric scholarship might encompass. More important, as we look to the future, I hope that scholars will enter into substantive discussions that not only "size up" visual rhetoric, but also engage in conversation that has the potential to "up size" it by conscious reflection on the process of better institutionalizing the study of visual rhetoric in higher education.

Notes

[1] To view this artifact, please see the following Web site by The Art Institute of Chicago: http://www.artic.edu/artaccess/AA_Amerindian/pages/Amerind_4.shtml.

[2] To view some illustrative examples of particularly important wampum belts, please see http://kstrom.net/isk/art/beads/wampum.html. Numerous wampum belts are reproduced in photographic records available in microfilm (Jennings, 1985). Their ritual uses are discussed at length by an eighteenth-century American colonist, whose depictions reflect a white, British American's understandings of them (Colden, 1727/1755).

[3] Barry Brummett's 1985 book review of Medhurst's and Benson's anthology, which Brummett characterized as "a collection of media criticism done from a rhetorical perspective" (p. 274), suggests noteworthy institutional factors in colleges and universities at the time of its initial publication.

[4] For instance, the central objective of the 1971 report was expressly to call for a shift in the very definition of rhetoric scholarship away from featuring the types of artifacts or media studied toward concentrating instead on the perspectives taken toward the artifacts or media. The collaborative statement advocated "a shift in traditional emphases" in scholars' definitions of rhetoric scholarship from featuring the nature of the "material studied to identifying it by the nature of the critic's inquiry" (Sloan et al., 1971, p. 220).

[5] Materials pertaining to Gran Fury's poster and other graphic works pertaining to AIDS activism may be found in Crimp and Rolston (1990, p. 56).

References

Benson, T. W. (1974). Joe: An essay in the rhetorical criticism of film. *Journal of Popular Culture, 8*(3), 608–618.

Benson, T. W. (1980). The rhetorical structure of Frederick Wiseman's *High School. Communication Monographs, 47*(4), 233–261.

Benson, T. W. (1985). The rhetorical structure of Frederick Wiseman's *Primate. Quarterly Journal of Speech, 71*(2), 204–217.

Benson, T. W. (1998). Thinking through film: Hollywood remembers the blacklist. In J. Michael Hogan (Ed.), *Rhetoric and community: Studies in unity and fragmentation* (pp. 217–255). Columbia: University of South Carolina Press.

Biesecker, B. A. (2002). Remembering World War II: The rhetoric and politics of national commemoration at the turn of the 21st century. *Quarterly Journal of Speech, 88*(4), 393–409.

Birdsell, D. S., & Groarke, L. (Eds.). (1996). Toward a theory of visual argument [Special issue]. *Argumentation and Advocacy, 33*(1–2), 1–39, 56–80.

Blair, C., Jeppeson, M. S., & Pucci, E., Jr. (1991). Public memorializing in postmodernity: The Vietnam Veterans Memorial as prototype. *Quarterly Journal of Speech, 77*(3), 263–288.

Blair, C., & Michel, N. (2000). Reproducing civil rights tactics: The rhetorical performances of the Civil Rights Memorial. *Rhetoric Society Quarterly, 30*(2), 31–55.

Bosmajian, H. A. (1971). *The rhetoric of nonverbal communication*. Glenview, IL: Scott, Foresman.

Brock, B. L., & Scott, R. L. (1982). *Methods of rhetorical criticism: A twentieth-century perspective* (2nd ed., rev.). Detroit, MI: Wayne State University Press.

Brouwer, D. (1998). The precarious visibility politics of self-stigmatization: The case of HIV/AIDS tattoos. *Text and Performance Quarterly, 18*(2), 114–136.

Brumberger, E. R. (2005). Visual rhetoric in the curriculum: Pedagogy for a multimodal workplace. *Business Communication Quarterly, 68*(3), 318–333.

Brummett, B. (1985). Book review of *Rhetorical dimensions in the media*. *Communication Education, 34*(3), 274–275.

Brummett, B. (1991). *Rhetorical dimensions of popular culture*. Tuscaloosa: University of Alabama Press.

Bryant, D. C. (1973). *Rhetorical dimensions in criticism*. Baton Rouge: Louisiana State University Press.

Burke, K. (1969). *A rhetoric of motives*. Berkeley, CA: University of California Press. (Original work published 1950)

Christiansen, A. E., & Hanson, J. J. (1996). Comedy as a cure for tragedy: ACT UP and the rhetoric of AIDS. *Quarterly Journal of Speech, 82*(2), 157–170.

Clark, G. (2004). *Rhetorical landscapes in America: Variations on a theme from Kenneth Burke*. Columbia: University of South Carolina Press.

Colden, C. (1755). *The history of the five Indian nations of Canada, which are dependent on the province of New-York in America, and are the barrier between the English and the French in that part of the world*. London: Lockyer Davis. (Original work published 1727)

Communication and Mass Media Index. http://ebscohost.com/ehost.

Crimp, D., & Rolston, A. (1990). *AIDS demo graphics*. Seattle, WA: Bay Press.

Danto, A. C. (1981). *The transfiguration of the commonplace*. Cambridge, MA: Harvard University Press.

Demo, A. T. (2000). The Guerilla Girls' comic politics of subversion. *Women's Studies in Communication, 23*(2), 133–157.

Dickinson, G., Ott, B. L., & Aoki, E. (2006). Spaces of remembering and forgetting: The reverent eye/I at the Plains Indian Museum. *Communication and Critical/Cultural Studies, 3*(1), 27–47.

Edwards, J. L., & Winkler, C. K. (1997). Representative form and the visual ideograph: The Iwo Jima image in editorial cartoons. *Quarterly Journal of Speech, 83*(3), 289–310.

Ehrenhaus, P., & Owen, A. S. (2004). Race lynching and Christian evangelicalism: Performances of faith. *Text and Performance Quarterly, 24*(3/4), 276–301.

Finnegan, C. A. (2001). The naturalistic enthymeme and visual argument: Photographic representation in the "Skull Controversy." *Argumentation and Advocacy, 37*(3), 133–150.

Finnegan, C. A. (2003). *Picturing poverty: Print culture and FSA photographs*. Washington, DC: Smithsonian Books.

Finnegan, C. A. (2005). Recognizing Lincoln: Image vernaculars in nineteenth-century visual culture. *Rhetoric and Public Affairs, 8*(1), 31–57.

Foss, S. K. (1982). Rhetoric and the visual image: A resource unit. *Communication Education, 31*(1), 55–66.

Foss, S. K. (1986). Ambiguity as persuasion: The Vietnam Veterans Memorial. *Communication Quarterly, 34*(3), 326–340.

Foss, S. K. (1988). Judy Chicago's *The Dinner Party*: Empowering women's voice in visual art. In B. Bate & A. Taylor (Eds.), *Women communicating: Studies of women's talk* (pp. 9–26). Norwood, NJ: Ablex.

Gran Fury. (1988). *Read my lips (boys)*. Retrieved May 25, 2006, from http://www.queercultura lcenter.org/Pages/GranFury/GFGllry.html

Gregg, R. B. (1984). *Symbolic inducement and knowing: A study in the foundations of rhetoric*. Columbia, SC: University of South Carolina Press.

Gregg, R. B. (1985). The criticism of symbolic inducement: A critical-theoretical connection. In T. W. Benson (Ed.), *Speech communication in the twentieth century* (pp. 41–62, 380–383). Carbondale: Southern Illinois University Press.

Gronbeck, B. E. (1978). Celluloid rhetoric: On genres of documentary. In K. K. Campbell & K. H. Jamieson (Eds.), *Form and genre: Shaping rhetorical action* (pp. 139–161). Falls Church, VA: Speech Communication Association.

Hariman, R., & Lucaites, J. L. (2001). Dissent and emotional management in a liberal-democratic society: The Kent State iconic photograph. *Rhetoric Society Quarterly, 31*(3), 5–31.

Hariman, R., & Lucaites, J. L. (2003). Public identity and collective memory in U.S. iconic photography: The image of "Accidental Napalm." *Critical Studies in Media Communication, 20*(1), 35–66.

Hariman, R., & Lucaites, J. L. (2004). Ritualizing modernity's gamble: The iconic photographs of the Hindenburg and *Challenger* explosions. *News Photographer, 59*(4), 4–17.

Hariman, R., & Lucaites, J. L. (2007). *No caption needed: Iconic photographs, public culture, and liberal democracy*. Chicago: University of Chicago Press.

Harold, C., & DeLuca, K. M. (2005). Behold the corpse: Violent images and the case of Emmett Till. *Rhetoric and Public Affairs, 8*(2), 263–286.

Hasian, M., Jr. (2004). Remembering and forgetting the "Final Solution": A rhetorical pilgrimage through the U.S. Holocaust Memorial Museum. *Critical Studies in Media Communication, 21*(1), 64–92.

Haskins, E. V. (2003). "Put your stamp on history": The USPS commemorative program *Celebrate the Century* and postmodern collective memory. *Quarterly Journal of Speech, 89*(1), 1–18.

Hauser, G. A. (Ed.). (1999). Body argument [Special issue]. *Argumentation and Advocacy, 36*(1–2), 1–100.

Hill, C. A., & Helmers, M. (Eds.). (2004). *Defining visual rhetorics*. Mahwah, NJ: Lawrence Erlbaum.

Hope, D. S. (Ed.). (2006). *Visual communication: Perception, rhetoric and technology: Papers from the William A. Kern Conferences in Visual Communication*. Cresskill, NJ: Rochester Institute of Technology, Cary Graphic Arts Press, and Hampton Press.

Hubbard, B., & Hasian, M. A., Jr. (1998). Atomic memories of the *Enola Gay*: Strategies of remembrance at the National Air and Space Museum. *Rhetoric and Public Affairs, 1*(3), 363–385.

Jennings, F. (Ed.). (1985). *Iroquois Indians: A documentary history of the diplomacy of the six nations and their league*. Woodbridge, CT: Research Publications.

Kaplan, S. J. (1990). Visual metaphors in the representation of communication technology. *Critical Studies in Mass Communication, 7*(1), 37–47.

Kostelnick, C., & Hassett, M. (2003). *Shaping information: The rhetoric of visual conventions.* Carbondale: University of Southern Illinois Press.

Lancioni, J. (1996). The rhetoric of the frame: Revisioning archival photographs in *The Civil War. Western Journal of Communication, 60*(4), 397–414.

LaWare, M. R. (1998). Encountering visions of Aztlán: Arguments for ethic pride, community activism, and cultural revitalization in Chicano murals. *Argumentation and Advocacy, 34*(3), 140–153.

Medhurst, M. J. (1982). *Hiroshima, mon amour:* From iconography to rhetoric. *Quarterly Journal of Speech, 68*(4), 345–370.

Medhurst, M. J., & Benson, T. W. (1981). *The City:* The rhetoric of rhythm. *Communication Monographs, 48*(1), 54–63.

Medhurst, M. J., & Benson, T. W. (Eds.). (1991). *Rhetorical dimensions in the media: A critical casebook.* Dubuque, IA: Kendall/Hunt. (Original work published 1984)

Mitchell, W. J. T. (1994). The pictorial turn. In *Picture theory: Essays in verbal and visual representation* (pp. 11–34). Chicago: University of Chicago Press.

Morris, C. E. III., & Sloop, J. M. (2006). "What lips these lips have kissed": Refiguring the politics of queer public kissing. *Communication and Critical/Cultural Studies, 3*(1), 1–26.

Olson, L. C. (1983). Portraits in praise of a people: A rhetorical analysis of Norman Rockwell's icons in Franklin D. Roosevelt's "Four Freedoms" campaign. *Quarterly Journal of Speech, 69*(1), 15–24.

Olson, L. C. (1987). Benjamin Franklin's pictorial representations of the British colonies in America: A study in rhetorical iconology. *Quarterly Journal of Speech, 73*(1), 18–42.

Olson, L. C. (1990). Benjamin Franklin's commemorative medal, *Libertas Americana:* A study in rhetorical iconology. *Quarterly Journal of Speech, 76*(1), 23–45.

Olson, L. C. (1991). *Emblems of American community in the revolutionary era: A study in rhetorical iconology.* Washington, DC: Smithsonian Institution Press.

Olson, L. C. (2004). *Benjamin Franklin's vision of American community: A study in rhetorical iconology.* Columbia: University of South Carolina Press.

Olson, L. C., Finnegan, C. A., & Hope, D. S. (Eds.). (in press). *Visual rhetoric: A reader in communication and American culture.* Thousand Oaks, CA: Sage.

Palczewski, C. H. (2002). Argument in an off-key. In T. Goodnight (Ed.), *Arguing communication and culture: Selected papers from the Twelfth NCA/AFA Conference on Argumentation: 2001,* vol. 1 (pp. 1–23). Washington, DC: National Communication Association.

Palczewski, C. H. (2005). The male Madonna and the feminine Uncle Sam: Visual arguments, icons, and ideographs in 1909 anti-woman suffrage postcards. *Quarterly Journal of Speech, 91*(4), 365–394.

Peirce, C. S. (1992). *The essential Peirce, selected philosophical writings. Vol. 1 (1867–1893).* N. Houswer & C. Kloesel (Eds.). Bloomington: Indiana University Press.

Peirce, C. S. (1998). *The essential Peirce, selected philosophical writings. Vol. 2 (1893–1913).* Peirce Edition Project (Eds.). Bloomington: Indiana University Press.

Pezzullo, P. C. (2003). Resisting "National Breast Cancer Awareness Month": The rhetoric of counterpublics and their cultural performances. *Quarterly Journal of Speech, 89*(4), 345–365.

Prelli, L. J. (Ed.). (2006). *Rhetorics of display.* Columbia: University of South Carolina Press.

Rohan, L. (2004). I remember mamma: Material rhetoric, mnemonic activity, and one woman's turn-of-the-twentieth-century quilt. *Rhetoric Review, 23*(4), 368–387.

Scott, B. (2004). Picturing irony: The subversive power of photography. *Visual Communication, 3*(1), 31–59.

Scott, R. L. (1977). Diego Rivera at Rockefeller Center: Fresco painting and rhetoric. *Western Journal of Speech Communication, 41*(2), 70–82.

Selzer, J., & Crowley, S. (Eds.). (1999). *Rhetorical bodies*. Madison: University of Wisconsin Press.

Shelley, C. (1996). Rhetorical and demonstrative modes of visual argument: Looking at images of human evolution. *Argumentation and Advocacy, 33*(1), 53–68.

Sloan, T. O., Gregg, R. B., Nilson, T. R., Rein, I. J., Simons, H. W., Stelzner, H. G., & Zacharias, D. W. (1971). Report of the Committee on the Advancement and Refinement of Rhetorical Criticism. In L. F. Bitzer & E. Black (Eds.), *The prospect of rhetoric: Report of the National Developmental Project, sponsored by Speech Communication Association* (pp. 220–227). Englewood Cliffs, NJ: Prentice-Hall.

Smith, S. M. (2004). *Photography on the color line: W. E. B. Du Bois, race, and visual culture*. Durham, NC: Duke University Press.

Stormer, N. (1997). Embodying normal miracles. *Quarterly Journal of Speech, 83*(2), 172–191.

Taylor, B. C. (1998). The bodies of August: Photographic realism and controversy at the National Air and Space Museum. *Rhetoric and Public Affairs, 1*(3), 331–361.

Taylor, B. C. (2003). "Our bruised arms hung up as monuments": Nuclear iconography in post-cold war culture. *Critical Studies in Media Communication, 20*(1), 1–34.

Tom, G., & Eves, A. (1999). The use of rhetorical devices in advertising. *Journal of Advertising Research, 39*(4), 39–42.

Tompkins, P. K. (1969). The rhetorical criticism of non-oratorical works. *Quarterly Journal of Speech, 55*(4), 431–440.

Turner, K. J. (1977). Comic strips: A rhetorical perspective. *Central States Speech Journal, 28*(1), 24–35.

Van Mulken, M. (2003). Analyzing rhetorical devices in print advertisements. *Document Design, 4*(2), 114–128.

Warnick, B. (2002). *Critical literacy in a digital era: Technology, rhetoric, and the public interest*. Mahwah, NJ: Lawrence Erlbaum.

Warnick, B. (2005). Looking to the future: Electronic texts and the deepening interface. *Technical Communication Quarterly, 14*(3), 327–333.

Willerton, R. (2005). Visual metonymy and synecdoche: Rhetoric for stage-setting images. *Journal of Technical Writing and Communication, 35*(1), 3–31.

Worth, S., & Gross, L. (1974). Symbolic strategies. *Journal of Communication, 24*(4), 27–39.

PART III

Legal and Political Rhetorics

Sizing Up Legal "Rhetoric"
Law from the Outside In

Frances J. Ranney

Inspired by the Rhetoric Society's call for papers, I sat down one day to size up legal "rhetoric." I typed the word into the LegalTrac online database and, in a few seconds, found over 900 articles in law reviews and professional journals that included "rhetoric" in their titles, abstracts, or keyword lists. At first, the sheer number of results seemed beyond the scope of a short conference paper. But as I watched page after page of citations emerge from my printer, I had the beginnings of an idea: what if, I thought, I were to take the conference metaphor—sizing up—literally, while taking my research results metaphorically? In other words, what if, as a "seamstress" from way, way back, I were to talk about the kind of sizing one does to fabric, with the fabric in this case being my keyword search results? The pages emerging from the printer certainly had the look of reams of fabric rolling out of a loom: what if I were to "size" them as one sizes fabric, by applying a "solution" of sorts to the surface and allowing it to sink into the very threads of that fabric in order to give it a texture and shape that it would not otherwise have?

This heuristic took on a life of its own as I began the sizing process, looking at the titles of my findings with a rhetorician's eye. How did they use the word "rhetoric"? Was it paired or contrasted with other key terms? Did it appear in the title or (in later searches) anywhere in the body of the text? Where was the text published, in a law review, a newspaper, or in practitioner publications such as the *ABA Journal*, for example? Though I could have begun to (metaphorically) "cut and paste" the articles into thematic groups in my word processing program, I again chose to work literally on my metaphorical fabric, cutting 36 pages of findings into half-inch wide, 8½ inch long strips of paper, one citation each, and tossing them like so many strands of yarn into related piles. It took three hours, during which time my wrists began to ache, my dog began to whine, then snore, and my left index finger, on the cutting edge of the research, began to bleed. But at the end of this process I not only had several piles of "research strands," but a more fully developed idea of my own metaphor. I began to literally see and construct the texture of what was there before me, prior to the "solution" I had yet to concoct.

What I provide in this short paper is clearly not representative of all "legal rhetoric" or of all legal work claiming to be rhetorical work. Instead, it is a description of one swatch of legal fabric, a sampling of work called by its producers "rhetoric." It is the result of chance—chance created and enhanced by technology. Its derivation from chance does not, however, disqualify it as a valid sample for rhetorical analysis. As Aristotle maintained, quoting the poet Agathon, "Art loves chance, and chance loves art"—or, *tuche* loves *techne*, and vice versa (*Nicomachean Ethics* VI.4). The arts, and clearly rhetoric among them, capitalize on the chance, the opportunity, derived from "stumbling upon" an idea. In this case, having stumbled upon an unwieldy batch of work, I look at this fabric first and quickly from the outside, noting the relative width, texture, and thickness of various threads before moving closer to examine several strands in more depth to get a sense of what "rhetoric" looks like in legal scholarship.

I've been working either on or with the fabric of law for 28 years now, first as a paralegal practitioner, then as a graduate student, and now as a professor of rhetoric in a department of English. As such, I characterize myself as a professional rhetorician, a scholar devoted to the study and development of rhetoric rather than primarily of legal theory; as such, I also ally myself with what I here call "professional rhetoricians" in other departments of English and of communication, despite some characteristic differences in the way such professional rhetoricians approach their topic. As I review my "swatch" of research, I will be noting the lack of interest in much legal "rhetorical" scholarship in the work of professional rhetoricians more recent than the sophists, and will call for the use of such work—what I think of as "our" work—as a corrective to an ingrown and rather weak sense of rhetoric in legal scholarship. But I hope I will not be taken to be scolding the work of eminent legal scholars who cannot be expected to call upon the work of legal outsiders unless they accidentally stumble upon it themselves—or unless we make a concerted effort as a discipline to get ourselves underfoot.

Despite my long immersion in law and legal language, I was surprised by some of the characteristics of this one day's swatch. But not all—certainly, I was not surprised by the prevalence of many articles claiming to present us with the "rhetoric and reality" of various legal or political issues ranging from human rights (Forsythe) to welfare (Amuso), with the largest number invoking rhetoric in order to cast doubt on the reality of "legal reform," whether of Russian politics ("Legal Reform in Russia"), American divorce (Austin), immigration policy ("Forming Immigration Policy"), or the IRS (Guttman). Combined with articles that clearly called upon rhetoric in its "mere" sense (see Moris; Keogh) are those that purported to discuss the rhetoric of "X," where "X" could range from drugs (Zagel) to sustainable development (Verhoosel). There were so many that I found myself grouping the strands into bundles of 10, stapling them together at one end, and then stuffing these "skeins" into labeled plastic snack bags. Altogether, rhetoric in its impoverished sense constituted the theme of nearly 400 of the 900 threads in this swatch.

In the face of this large minority, this broad band taking up nearly half the swatch, I was at first surprised by a sturdy strand of practical advice drawing specifically upon this impoverished art in order to instruct practicing attorneys in the creation of opening statements and closing arguments (McElhaney), briefs (Bailey), and presentations (Wise). Here rhetoric is presented primarily as persuasion, and touted because, of course, it is effective—often through tropes, figures, quotation, and narrative. But why, on second thought, was I surprised? Rhetoric need not be "real" in order to be effective—in fact, one may believe it to be more effective precisely because one believes it is not real. And while those who write these articles believe attorneys can use rhetoric in order to "get past the barriers inside jurors' minds" (Lisnek), only one writer considered the possibility that creating reality through rhetoric for jurors might be contagious. Cautioning against the "sin of self-persuasion," this writer explained that "getting carried away with your rhetoric can be perilous" (McElhaney 92). But this writer is an exception: if rhetoric is overblown (Griset), irrelevant (Carelli), inflammatory (Gabor), reactionary (Futrell), inconsistent (Steuerle), irresponsible (American Judicature Society), or even felonious (Teepen), its accusers seem to believe "we," its users rather than receivers, can easily tone it down ("On Abortion"), shove it aside (Klooster), sift through it (Roberts), wade through it (Alexander), unpack it (Brown-Scott), swap it with the facts (Tuohey), and, above all, just get beyond it (Karcher; Hing).

Doth it appear these writers protest too much? Even if it is mere, maybe even because it is mere, as well as "merely" effective, rhetoric appears to be dangerous. And, indeed, a slightly larger band of colors in this multihued swatch attempts to take rhetoric seriously. In this band we find sincere efforts to examine the rhetoric of "X," of rights (Weston), of free speech (Cos and Snee), of difference ("The Rhetoric of Difference"), of slavery (Wiethoff), and, finally, Ed Meese (Moss). But again, from what I am calling a professional rhetorician's perspective, we run into snags in the fabric. Laufer's examination of the American court system's presumption of innocence, directed through the focus of legal pragmatism on the "disutility" of wrongful convictions, is a probing, insightful, somewhat dense analysis of the reasons why a court's failure to instruct a jury with regard to the presumption of innocence may be considered legally "harmless" if the jury has been told about the reasonable doubt rule. Because these instructions are redundant, Laufer suggests, there is no logical necessity for both of them (390); nevertheless, our general "reverence" for the presumption of innocence has caused a body of rhetoric to emerge in a way that is seriously "disconnected . . . from a true presumption of factual innocence" (388). Distinguishing factual innocence from legal innocence (which may or may not be "true"), Laufer argues that we need to bring substance to the rhetoric in order to substitute a presumption of factual innocence for the current presumption of legal innocence, thus providing it with real "meaning" (396–98).

Similarly, Warner and Gawlik speculate at the beginning of their article about the rhetoric of restorative justice in the victim's compensation movement that the provisions of the Tasmanian Sentencing Act calling for compensation orders may have been "just political rhetoric" (62). After some 12 pages devoted to discussing the impracticability of providing real and meaningful compensation to crime victims they conclude that, indeed, it is (74–75). Purporting in their titles to examine the rhetoric of "X," neither of these articles feels obligated to call upon any specifically rhetorical scholarship to do so, assuming that their understanding of the term is transparent and sufficient.

More radically, some serious attempts at rhetorical scholarship in law suggest that either law or a particular legal concept is, itself, rhetoric. I will deal a bit later in this paper with James Boyd White's substantive claims about the rhetorical nature of law itself; here I wish to point out that in two randomly selected articles that separately claimed "property" and "evidence" "are" rhetoric, the analysis was based in Charles Sanders Peirce's semiotic theory, which itself claims that a speculative version of rhetoric is the proper methodology for the investigation of signs. Thus, for Kevelson, property becomes a "rhetorical device or strategy" (189), while for Klinck, the reliability of evidence may be examined separately from its "persuasive or rhetorical force" (135). "Real evidence" in a narrow sense, says Klinck, "does not depend on mediation by some objective form of representation" (134)—thus, if we need to prove there was blood on a knife, we produce the "real evidence" of the bloody knife. But such evidence may be the "best" evidence at a "purely rhetorical level" as well, he says, because of what he calls "some culturally determined belief that 'oracular proof' is virtually infallible"—or, as he finally translates himself, "seeing is believing" (135). Meanwhile, Kevelson connects the world of things—objects of property, itself already identified as "rhetoric"—with the world of appearance. Though she draws on Chaim Perelman to contrast appearance with reality, she does not argue that appearance is thus less meaningful; instead, she argues for the role of rhetoric in creating property and properties as bearers of meaning in the human world (Kevelson 194).

I do not mean to question the value of these articles or the substance of their conclusions. However, I believe it is important to point out that Klinck seems to suggest that rhetoric is of the domain of icons, which he claims prove nothing, and that rather than being rhetoric, as his title has claimed, the use of evidence is simply "a significantly rhetorical process" (158)—a conclusion that hardly surprises the rhetorician. More significant to my purpose of "sizing up" legal rhetoric, I use these samples to point out the near dearth of reliance on what I am calling professional rhetorical theory. Both subsume rhetoric, without explicit justification of this move, into the field of linguistics, particularly that corner of linguistics known as semiotics; in some recognizable reliance on what I hold to be rhetorical scholarship, Kevelson mentions Kenneth Burke three times—once simply to contrast his definition of rhetoric with Peirce's—(194–96) and Stephen Toulmin once (202), while Klinck provides one sentence in a footnote about Aristotle's theory of natural and conventional signs (129 fn16).

Two other strands of "rhetorical" research in law are significant enough to merit mention before I provide a look at a number of law review symposia (special issues) and one anthology devoted entirely to rhetorical work on law. First is a very thin strand of classical rhetorical work, only 14 articles in the whole "bolt" of over 900, that draws on Aristotle, Cicero, and Plato or other classical sources. One of these 14, I should mention, is in French. The second strand is a fragile thread of rhetorical work within the larger "law and litera-ture" scholarship. It is simultaneously, however, a rather coarse thread, not so much in terms of its relative size (57 articles), but in terms of its assumptions about the nature of rhetoric (46 of these 57 articles reduce rhetoric to "narra-tive" or "story"). I have argued elsewhere, perhaps *ad nauseum*, that the "rhet-oric" of law and literature focuses far too narrowly on the reading or interpretation of text rather than on its production, which I have also argued is the unique capacity of rhetoric (Ranney 123). That argument provides my conclusion for this study as well. But first, I'd like to delve deeper into the fab-ric—not to apply my "solution" just yet, but to show what a serious, in-depth look at rhetorical legal scholarship can find.

These collections repeat the pattern evidenced in the less densely com-pacted categories of legal "rhetoric." In these specifically rhetorically focused collections, the most frequently mentioned source in classical rhetoric is Plato, via the *Gorgias* rather than the slightly more rhetoric-friendly *Phaedrus*; Aristotle appears much less frequently than either Plato or Stanley Fish, and often the reference is a mere courtesy, a nod to the first textbook on rhetoric that presumably is somewhat outdated. References to contemporary theory in these collections tend to draw on literary theorists (Wayne Booth, Michel Foucault, Jacques Derrida, and Roland Barthes, in addition to Fish) or on philosophers (Paul Ricoeur, J. L. Austin, Walter Benjamin, and Richard Rorty) for their conceptions of rhetoric. Clearly, when legal scholars put together collections on the rhetoric of law, they call first not just on legal scholars—we have to allow them that liberty—but on legal scholars who have developed interests and bodies of research in (no surprise here) literature and philosophy, not rhetoric. The one glaring exception in my (again, randomly chosen) swatch is a collection of short articles written by scholars in commu-nication (plus one legal scholar) that arose out of a panel on the rhetorical analysis of Oliver Wendell Holmes's decision in *Lochner v. New York* at the National Communication Association's annual conference. Though the pur-pose of my rhetorical exploration is not to make scientifically supported gen-eralizations, I feel safe in saying that the latter collection is unusual, and that only a very few rhetorical scholars in communication or English—the likes of James Arnt Aune and Stanley Fish—manage to publish in law reviews.

Two of the collections, law review symposia, focus almost entirely on the *Gorgias*. The first, a symposium published in the *Iowa Law Review* in 1989, truly stumbles upon rhetoric; it is the necessary consequence of talking about the *Gorgias* as a text about law, despite the claim of the keynote speaker, Ernest Weinrib (a law and classics professor) that the text is only "ostensibly" about rhetoric (788). The second symposium, published ten years later (1999) in the *University of Cincinnati Law Review*, was purposely fashioned as a symposium about "The Art of Rhetoric"; in this case, the keynote speaker, Anthony Kronman, then dean of Yale Law School, chose the *Gorgias* as a text that would allow him to mount a philosophical defense of rhetoric (693). Rhetoric, he says, fulfills what he calls (drawing upon the speech of Diotima in Plato's own *Symposium*) our "political longing" (695), our desire to join with each other through politics and law. Rhetoric is the craft that makes that joining possible, structuring the institutions of politics and law through the medium of speech, cultivating commitment by connecting our minds and our hearts (707). Weinrib is far less generous than Kronman; referring to the myth of judgment at the end of the dialogue, Weinrib notes Socrates refers to it as "truth" to him, though perhaps not to his listeners. But because myth functions as rhetoric for Weinrib (791), and rhetoric is concerned with effect rather than content (793), the myth is "true" only in a rhetorical sense—meaning, "not because the incidents that the myth recounts are true, but because the persuasion at which the myth aims flows from the rationality of genuine craftsmanship" (797). And even Kronman, who says he wants to point the way toward the beginnings of a more sympathetic account of rhetoric, concludes that rhetoric, because it deals in the "corruptible," is a dirty business (709).

Respondents to both of these keynote texts differed in their assessments of their relative contributions to rhetorical and legal theory. Two respondents to Kronman attempted to figure out what the sympathetic account of rhetoric he pointed toward might look like; one, wrestling with the vagaries of law as a language or a language game, concludes that it would simply delve into what is good and bad about the activities of lawyering (Joseph 725). Another, quoting Miller's *Anatomy of Disgust*, concludes that lawyers, understood as rhetoricians, deal with "moral dirt" (Campos 716). So much for sympathetic accounts. Back in the *Iowa Law Review* of 1989, the three respondents to Weinrib's equation of rhetoric to myth (with its simultaneous divorce from truth) object strenuously without managing to contribute a great deal to rhetorical theory. Two take issue with the Platonic dichotomies, whether of philosophy and rhetoric (Zoeller) or existence and essence (Klemm). Another response posits Callicles as the good guy, the rhetorician who refuses to stoop to what he calls the nihilism of Socrates, his denial of the worth of the world (Nonet 811). Perhaps the most effective response draws on etymology to note the sources of rhetoric, persuasion, and passion in the Greek root for "speech." Not the Latin "sweet talk," persuasion in the Greek refers to the flow of words and emotion that make rhetoric subjective, but not merely private, not self-seeking but community-seeking (Meyer 728, 748–51). Apropos of my own metaphor, this writer points out the pleasure involved in finding the "right fit" between our perceptions of the world and the structure of our minds (739) and suggests that rhetorical flexibility compensates for uncertainty and disagreement by allowing "a generous hem to let the fabric down as we grow" (753), or as the legal world turns.

I have purposely left out of my discussion of these two symposia one common thread to which I have already referred in my more general discussion, the thread of fear that somewhat incongruously (at first blush) becomes paired with the praise of community. These two threads are only lightly touched upon in the two symposia. In 1989, Zoeller notes the egregious nature of legal error while Klemm suggests that "dialogue" can compensate for the loss of "truth" through "historicity," his equivalent of the rhetorical nature of experience. Ten years later this small debate is still barely visible, as Joseph points out that law has "real consequences" while Meyer stresses the role of rhetoric in building communities that can, if necessary, jointly decide to let their skirts down. But in 1994 a collection titled *The Rhetoric of Law* in the Amherst Series in Law, Jurisprudence, and Social Thought, Austin Sarat and Thomas Kearns took up these threads together and followed them through the fabric of law. In the first paragraph of their introduction, Sarat and Kearns note the anxiety that generally accompanies statements about law's inevitable partnership with rhetoric (1). In the essays that follow, anxiety alternates with community, or accompanies it, depending upon the individual writer's preference.

James Boyd White, whose work on law, literature, and rhetoric began in the 1970s and was surely iconic by 1999, but who is cited in neither of the symposia, is the law's foremost advocate of the connection of rhetoric and community. As such, he is often called unrealistic and utopian. But he persists in "imagining the law" as a "system of discourse" that either creates meaning for its speakers or allows them to create meanings of their own (29). Law, he has said in other work, is a "culture of argument" (*Acts of Hope*), a community that is constructed by its language. His contribution to *The Rhetoric of Law* states that one task of the judge, the most frequent object of his scholarly attention, is that of inclusion of the voices before him in his written decisions; understanding that "the barrier between his mind and theirs will . . . never entirely dissolve," he nevertheless claims for the judge a "real and disciplined sympathy" (Sarat and Kearns 53–54) for those whose lives his words will change.

White's usually sunny perspective is followed immediately in this collection by that of Peter Goodrich, who argues at length that rhetoric is not about agreement but about antagonism, or antirrhesis (57–59). Arguing that legal doctrine has historically been structured around a "dialectic of antinomy," he concludes that the turn to rhetoric in legal scholarship "may well have the advantage of translating antagonism into discourse . . . [but is] a return to a fundamentally antithetic dispute. . . . [Law's] object," he says, "is difference, while its figure, image, or emblem, is most properly that of dispersion. Language, as the very term antirrhetic implies, is the sign of plurality and of confusion; it marks the difference of people and the separation or distance that is the object of law" (100).

The essays in this collection merit more attention and in-depth analysis than is possible in this short paper. What is important to note for my purposes is that the writers collected here, all law professors, do not draw on the research of what we tend to think of as the discipline of rhetoric—indeed, only three of the nine contributors provide an explicit definition of rhetoric

(Sarat and Kearns, J. B. White, and Douglas), while implicit definitions abound. Ferguson's fascinating account of the transcripts of the trial of Benedict Arnold's coconspirator, the British Major André, points out that each of the principals in this case, including the absent Arnold, constructs himself through language in a manner appropriate to his purpose; Arnold, he says, affects the "exterior tone of the gentleman," creating character through his language "rather than the other way around," which presumably would be genuine (124). Here rhetoric becomes a "linguistic convention rather than the embodiment of character" (125), a charade that Arnold enacts in his letters to the court. Barbara Johnson's essay on the work of Patricia Williams sees legal "style" as necessarily effacing the subject position Williams attempts to take on. Noting that the voice of the murdered Mary Frug, unlike that of Williams, is permitted in another law review to speak without editorial emendment and proper citation style, she comments that, "It seems that it is only when the author is dead that a law review sees value in the preservation of 'voice'" (266).

But the time has come for me to be more straightforward. If these writers do not provide a satisfactory account of legal rhetoric, what might that satisfactory account be? As I have said earlier, I see the unique capacity of rhetoric, including "legal" rhetoric, to be its role in the production of text rather than in its analysis. In *The Rhetoric of Law*, both Lucie White, in her study of a meeting of a Project Head Start policy council, and Austin Sarat, in his study of the sentencing phase of a murder trial, make a move toward the productive capacity of rhetoric. White, who titles her chapter "Ordering Voice," at first seems to disparage what she calls Head Start's "gesture toward grassroots democracy" (189), the regulations that require parental involvement in policy decisions. Observing the process by which one council votes for its president, she seems to emphasize the lack of empowerment brought about by confusing regulatory language and the council members' relative lack of experience with legal and educational discourses. "The ways that the law conceives the policy council's purpose, constructs its power, and constrains its conversation," she writes, "are but three of the features of the law's order that undo the promise of democracy that its . . . imagery seems to hold out" (219). But she goes on to criticize the familiar image of law's constricting framework, offering in its stead the image of a framework and a group of actor-speakers who "take their meaning from the other's play" in such a way that the legal order is "recast as its subjects repeatedly act out what it means" (221). Sarat, too, notices the construction work of legal language as it confronts its own limits. Relying on Elaine Scarry's *The Body in Pain*, he describes the ways in which the violence of both murder and capital punishment are brought into discourse; that discourse, he says, constructs boundaries around the violence committed by both the criminal and the law in order to create them as qualitatively different (Sarat and Kearns 141).

In both of these accounts, a limitation or boundary enables the construction of meaning at the same time that it constrains it. Rhetoric, in fact, enables through constraint; as Aristotle reminded us, the unlimited is literally unknowable (*Art of Rhetoric*).

Let me return to my metaphor to illustrate what I see as the potential contribution of rhetorical scholarship to legal scholarship. I have been following threads, longitudinal strands of thought that make up the various approaches to "rhetoric" in legal scholarship. These threads, first literally issuing from my printer and then from my scissors, make up the weft of the fabric, what might be seen as its foundation. But, switching metaphors briefly, imagine that these "threads" are the slips of paper created when a page goes through a shredder; once the threads reach their ends, they fall apart and away. While they are still held by the shredder, the farther they get from their source the more they can stray from each other. So, too, the weft of our legal fabric, also known as the "woof," can fall apart without the cohesive function of the horizontal thread, what is called the "warp." And now you realize what I am suggesting, that rhetorical scholarship can function as the horizontal thread, the warp that holds the fabric together and prevents what would otherwise be theoretically unlimited bias.

This image is more than word play on my part. Many legal scholars, including Sarat and Kearns, point out that the problem with a rhetorical understanding of law is that it admits the possibility of legal error—and legal error, as many others have pointed out, can be lethal. I don't intend to be sanguine about such lethal possibilities; rather, I intend to be Aristotelian. In the *Nicomachean Ethics*, Aristotle not only admits the role of error in arts such as rhetoric, but says that "in art, he who errs willingly is to be preferred" (VI.v.7). Not enough has been made of this passage in terms of its implications for rhetoric. Though both David Roochnik and Joseph Dunne have tackled it, it seems clear that Aristotle is not speaking about failures in art because of defects in its material, as Roochnik argues (50), or even about the mastery implied in the face of occasional failures, as Dunne claims (266). In either case, law's material—its language—would simply be held to be somewhat unpredictably inadequate to the task it must take on, a result that is of no use in formulating theories either of legal expertise or legal change. Instead, Aristotle would seem to be saying—what he is (literally) saying: first, that error in art is preferable to error in other endeavors (indeed, he says that error is impossible in knowledge, which would then not be knowledge, and blamable in practice, which would then not be virtuous); next, that error in art actually "is" art. Error here, Aristotle has made clear, is not error in a moral or factual sense—those are within the realm of practice and knowledge, respectively. Artistic error in Aristotle's sense is more accurately thought of as a sort of purposeful wandering among the threads and across the seams of the legal fabric. Working its way over and under the "woof" of legal scholarship, rhetorical scholarship allows the fabric of law to retain a shape that is recognizably legal while tugging along its bias, sizing the fabric not through the imposition of a "solution," as I at first thought, but through testing and stretching its limits.

It is for this reason that I have allowed myself the liberty of writing about the process of writing this paper. Rhetoric is more unique as a heuristic than as a hermeneutic, more useful as invention than as interpretation. But if I have been hard on legal rhetorical scholarship, suggesting that such scholarship needs a little less "woof" and a little more "warp," I also recognize the value of much of the work I have taken on in this very quick glance at a very complex swatch of the legal fabric. And I am reminded of what I am told, probably by legal imperative, about the fabric of some of my most expensive clothing. Variations in color and imperfections in the texture of my raw silk jacket, wrinkles in my linen skirt, even the fraying and fading of my jeans, are not to be taken as flaws, I am told, but as signs of the genuineness of the fine fabrics of which they are made. They are a little warped, perhaps, but that's a sign of their quality. And so it is, I think we can say, with law.

Works Cited

Alexander, Cynthia L. "The Defeat of the Civil Rights Act of 1990: Wading through the Rhetoric in Search of Compromise." *Vanderbilt Law Review* 44 (1991): 595–640.

American Judicature Society. "Listening to Judge Lefkow." *Judicature* 88 (May–June 2005): 240, 242.

Amuso, Peter. "Welfare Realities: From Rhetoric to Reform." *Harvard Journal on Legislation* 32 (1995): 565–71.

Aristotle. *Art of Rhetoric.* Trans. J. H. Freese. The Loeb Classical Library. Cambridge, MA: Harvard UP, 1926.

———. *Nicomachean Ethics.* Trans. H. Rackham. The Loeb Classical Library. Cambridge, MA: Harvard UP, 1926.

Austin, G. W. "The Illusion of Equality: The Rhetoric and Reality of Divorce Reform [Book Review]." *Victoria University of Wellington Law Review* 21 (1991): 417–23.

Bailey, Elizabeth Chambers. "Don't Undermine Persuasiveness: Brief Writing." *For the Defense* (July 2005): 68.

Brown-Scott, Wendy. "Unpacking the Affirmation Action Rhetoric." *Wake Forest Law Review* 30 (1995): 801–17.

Campos, Paul F. "What the Twins Saw." *University of Cincinnati Law Review* 67 (1999): 711–17.

Carelli, Richard. "Not Quite Irrelevant: Rhetoric Aside, Lawyer's Group Still Capital Hill Mover." *Chicago Daily Law Bulletin* 143 (July 18, 1997): 1 col. 3.

Cos, Grant C., and Brian J. Snee. "Robert M. Lafollette and the Rhetoric of Free Speech." *Free Speech Yearbook* 39 (Annual 2001): 26–33.

Dunne, Joseph. *Back to the Rough Ground: Practical Judgment and the Lure of Technique.* Notre Dame, IN: Notre Dame UP, 1993.

"Forming Immigration Policy In the Spotlight: Rhetoric and Reality." *Washington Law Review* 70 (1995): 589–804.

Forsythe, David P. "American Foreign Policy and Human Rights: Rhetoric and Reality." *Universal Human Rights* 2 (July–Sept. 1980): 35–53.

Frost, Michael. "Justice Scalia's Rhetoric of Dissent: A Greco-Roman Analysis of Scalia's Advocacy in the *VMI* Case." *Kentucky Law Journal* 91 (2003): 167–204.

Futrell, J. William. "Superfund and Reactionary Rhetoric." *The Environmental Forum* 11 (Jan.–Feb. 1994): 56.

Gabor, Thomas. "Inflammatory Rhetoric on Racial Profiling Can Undermine Police Services." *Canadian Journal of Criminology and Criminal Justice* 46 (July 2004): 457.

Griset, Pamala L. "Determinate Sentencing and the High Cost of Overblown Rhetoric: The New York Experience." *Crime and Delinquency* 40 (1994): 532–48.

Guttman, George. "IRS Reorganization—Take 29—Separating Rhetoric from Reality." *Tax Notes* 61 (1993): 899–908.

Hing, Bill Ong. "Beyond the Rhetoric of Assimilation and Cultural Pluralism: Addressing the Tension of Separatism and Conflict in an Immigration-Driven Multiracial Society." *California Law Review* 81 (1993): 863–925.

Joseph, Lawrence. "On Kronman's 'Rhetoric.'" *University of Cincinnati Law Review* 67 (1999): 719–25.

Karcher, Alan J. "No More No-Fault: Beyond the Rhetoric toward True Reform of the New Jersey Automobile Insurance System." *Seton Hall Legislative Journal* 8 (1984): 173–92.

Keogh, William J. "The Separate Representation of Children in Australian Family Law: Effective Practice or Mere Rhetoric?" *Canadian Journal of Family Law* 19 (2002): 371–422.

Kevelson, Roberta. "Property as Rhetoric in Law." *Cardozo Studies in Law & Literature* 4 (1992): 189–206.

Klemm, David E. "*Gorgias*, Law, and Rhetoric." *Iowa Law Review* 74 (1989): 819–26.

Klinck, Dennis R. "Evidence as Rhetoric: A Semiotic Perspective." *Ottawa Law Review* 26 (1994): 125–58.

Klooster, Tye J. "Repeal of the Death Tax? Shoving Aside the Rhetoric to Determine the Consequences of the Economic Growth and Tax Relief Reconciliation Act of 2001." *Drake Law Review* 51 (Mar. 2003): 633–65.

Kronman, Anthony T. "Rhetoric." *University of Cincinnati Law Review* 67 (1999): 677–709.

Laufer, William S. "The Rhetoric of Innocence." *Washington Law Review* 70 (1995): 329–421.

"Legal Reform in Russia: Rhetoric Versus Reality." *Wisconsin International Law Journal* 14 (1996): 531–623.

Lisnek, Paul M. "Opening Statement: Getting Past the Barrier in Jurors' Minds." *Chicago Daily Law Bulletin* 141 (27 Feb. 1995): 6 col. 1.

McElhaney, James W. "The Sin of Self-Persuasion: Getting Carried Away with Your Rhetoric Can Be Perilous." *ABA Journal* 85 (Nov. 1999): 92.

Meyer, Linda. "Between Reason and Power: Experiencing Legal Truth." *University of Cincinnati Law Review* 67 (1999): 727–59.

Moris, Halim. "Self-Determination: An Affirmative Right or Mere Rhetoric?" *ILSA Journal of International & Comparative Law* 4 (1997): 201–20.

Moss, Debra Cassens. "The Policy and the Rhetoric of Ed Meese." *ABA Journal* 73 (1 Feb. 1987): 64.

Nonet, Philippe. "In Praise of Callicles." *Iowa Law Review* 74 (1989): 807–13.

"On Abortion . . . Tone Down the Rhetoric." *The Los Angeles Daily Journal* 108:25 (1995): 6 col. 1. Sacramento Bee. <http://www.sacbee.com>.

Peirce, Charles Sanders. *The Essential Peirce: Selected Philosophical Writings 1893–1913*. Ed. Peirce Edition Project. Bloomington: Indiana UP, 1998.

Ranney, Frances J. *Aristotle's Ethics and Legal Rhetoric: An Analysis of Language Beliefs and the Law*. Aldershot: Ashgate, 2005.

"The Rhetoric of Difference and the Legitimacy of Capital Punishment." *Harvard Law Review* 114. (Mar. 2001): 1599–622.

Roberts, Michael T. "The Unique Role of State Trading Enterprises in World Agricultural Trade: Sifting through Rhetoric." *Drake Journal of Agricultural Law* 6 (2001): 287–315.

Roochnik, David. *Of Art and Wisdom: Plato's Understanding of Techne.* University Park: The Pennsylvania State UP, 1996.

Sarat, Austin, and Thomas R. Kearns, eds. *The Rhetoric of Law.* Ann Arbor: U of Michigan P, 1994.

Scarry, Elaine. *The Body in Pain: The Making and Unmaking of the World.* New York: Oxford UP, 1985.

Steuerle, Gene. "From Taxes to Health Care: Inconsistent Rhetoric is Bipartisan." *Tax Notes* 100 (7 July 2003): 93–94.

Teepen, Tom. "Whitewater Hearings: Misdemeanor Deeds and Felonious Rhetoric." *The Los Angeles Daily Journal* 107 (9 Aug. 1994): 6 col. 3.

Tuohey, Seamus M. "Swap Facts for Rhetoric." *The National Law Journal* 16 (30 May 1994): A19 col. 3.

Verhoosel, Gaetan. "Beyond the Unsustainable Rhetoric of Sustainable Development: Transferring Environmentally Sound Technologies." *Georgetown International Environmental Law Review* 11 (1998): 49–76.

Warner, Kate, and Jenny Gawlik. "Mandatory Compensation Orders for Crime Victims and the Rhetoric of Restorative Justice." *The Australian and New Zealand Journal of Criminology* 36 (2003): 60–76.

Weinrib, Ernest J. "Law as Myth: Reflections on Plato's *Gorgias*." *Iowa Law Review* 74 (1989): 787–806.

Weston, Peter. "The Rueful Rhetoric of 'Rights.'" *UCLA Law Review* 33 (1986): 977–1018.

White, James Boyd. *Acts of Hope: Creating Authority in Literature, Law, and Politics.* Chicago: U of Chicago P, 1994.

———. *Justice as Translation: An Essay in Cultural and Legal Criticism.* Chicago: U of Chicago P, 1990.

Wiethoff, William E. "The Logic and Rhetoric of Slavery in Early Louisiana Civil Law Reports." *The Legal Studies Forum* 12 (1988): 441–57.

Wise, Stuart M. "'Quote' from the Best of Them." *The National Law Journal* 5 (24 Jan. 1983): 39 col. 2.

Zagel, James B. "Drug Rhetoric, Courts, and the Law: A Response to Professor Rudovsky." *University of Chicago Legal Forum* (Annual 1994): 275–96.

Zoeller, Guenter. "Is the Life in the Law Worth Living? Some Critical Remarks on Plato's *Gorgias*." *Iowa Law Review* 74 (1989): 815–17.

Getting the Government Out of Farming
Sizing Up Eisenhower's Early Agricultural Policy Rhetoric

Lora Cohn

Although the population was shifting to the cities through the 1950s, agriculture was still a major "industry" in America. Twenty-three million people lived on farms—approximately 15% of the U.S. population (Ulrich). Government spending on farm programs during Eisenhower's presidency was significant. For example, in the budget year ending in June 1952, farm program spending had dropped to a low of $680 million, but by June of 1954 the total was more than $3.5 billion (Cochrane and Ryan). This represents a 500% increase in two years. Although agriculture was not a major issue in the 1952 presidential election (Cochrane and Ryan), the Republican platform accused the Truman administration of "seeking to destroy the farmer's freedom" and claimed the Truman administration's Brannan farm plan "aims to control the farmer and to socialize agriculture" ("Text" 8). Republicans did "not believe in restrictions on the American farmer's ability to produce" and promised to "create conditions providing for farm prosperity and stability, safeguarding the farmers' independence and opening opportunities for young people in rural communities" (8).

Eisenhower had no choice but to address agriculture early in his presidency. Eisenhower's early public addresses on agriculture reveal a man committed to limited government and dedicated to correcting the problems created by continued New Deal style policies. After a brief introduction to the situation and agricultural policy, this paper examines Eisenhower's 1953 Kansas City address, his 1954 Butler University address, and his substantial revisions and notes related to both addresses. Eisenhower was actively involved in the drafting of his early agricultural speeches, as evidenced by his involvement in drafting the Kansas City address. Through these addresses, Eisenhower not only explained his vision for American agriculture, but more importantly, developed his persona as a president for all Americans and a man of action. Eisenhower's agricultural rhetoric emphasized the values of study, balance, interdependence, and partnerships between levels of government, which became hallmarks of his presidency. Finally, the paper explores Eisenhower's use of persuasive strategies such as identification, appeals to patriotism, and parallelism and vivid language to strengthen the appeal of his messages.

Background

Eisenhower was an unusual man elected in unusual circumstances. His war leadership made him a well-known and popular choice for president despite his lack of political connections or qualifications. As a new president, however, Eisenhower had to deal with a complex domestic situation. Truman had left a mountain of debt and the economy went into a recession soon after Eisenhower came to office. Additionally, Americans' view of the role of government shifted while Eisenhower was in the military—they had come to embrace FDR's New Deal programs. Eisenhower's Republican party had limited control of Congress and was not united. Eisenhower's response was a return to the 1948 farm policy passed by a Republican Congress.

Medhurst argued that three books coming out after the war, Kenneth S. Davis's *Soldier of Democracy,* Harry C. Butcher's *My Three Years with Eisenhower,* and Eisenhower's *Crusade in Europe,* along with Eisenhower's public speaking, helped create Eisenhower's public persona. Medhurst said, "Five qualities repeated themselves, in different forms, throughout these works: commonality, dedication, considerateness, humility, and a special sort of moral vision" (5). These characteristics are further developed in his agricultural rhetoric. Medhurst's list is apolitical. Indeed, Eisenhower's military background and personal characteristics enabled his image to be the *antithesis* of a politician. Scheele further noted that "to understand the Eisenhower image one must recognize that through most of his life he worked diligently at avoiding any involvement in partisan politics" (460). No doubt this apolitical persona helped Eisenhower to be elected, but would it help him lead a country deeply in debt and tied to policies that ran counter to Eisenhower's conservative tendencies?

The Truman budget for fiscal year 1954 showed a projected deficit of $9.9 billion, but that was not the worst part (Adams). The deficits of the previous two fiscal years and the additional expenditures Congress made for the Korean War added up to an $80 billion deficit. Budget Director Joseph Dodge analogized the

> financial plight of the departing Democratic administration to that of a family with an accumulated debt four times bigger than its annual income, with never more money in the bank than it needs to cover one month's living expenses, facing a 10 percent reduction in income and with current bills for C.O.D. purchases hanging over its head larger than a year's total income. And these bills would have to be met with cash on the line as soon as the goods were delivered. (153)

Additionally, Saulnier noted that in 1953–54, the economy slipped into a recession (63).

Eisenhower also had to deal with a different America from the one in which he was raised. There is no doubt that the New Deal reshaped politics and American life—especially for farmers. Brinkley explained:

> The New Deal created a series of new state institutions that greatly, and permanently, expanded the role of the federal government in American life. The government was now committed to providing at least minimal assistance to the poor, the unemployed, and the elderly; to protecting the rights of workers and unions; to stabilizing the banking system; to regulating the financial markets; to subsidizing agricultural production; and to doing many other things that had not previously been federal responsibilities. As a result of the New Deal, American political and economic life became much more competitive than ever before, with workers, farmers, consumers, and others now able to press their demands upon the government in ways that in the past had been available only to the corporate world. (34)

The New Deal legitimized special interest groups' ability to shape economic policy (McCraw 37). The overall effect of the New Deal was a new attitude about government. Brinkley noted that the New Deal "created broad new expectations of government among the American people, expectations that would survive, and indeed grow, in the decades that followed" (35).

Ulrich called 1933 "a sort of 'big bang' for farm policy" (58). In 1933, farm policy moved from programs concerned with the general farm situation to direct aid to individual farmers (Bonnen, Browne, and Schweikhardt). World War II increased demand for farm products, reduced surpluses, and drove prices up, but farm policy remained unchanged because officials were afraid that when the war ended the reduced demand would lead to lower prices (Cochrane and Ryan). The Steagall amendment in 1941 locked the price of farm commodities at high levels for two years after the end of World War II. The Hope-Aiken bill kept price supports at 90% of parity from 1948 to 1950, when price supports were supposed to drop gradually below the 90% threshold (Ulrich). Parity is a price determined by a formula that would give a commodity the same buying power as it had during a previous period. The 1910–1914 time period was chosen because it was believed that farm prices were the most unaffected by depression or other restraining conditions at that time (Matusow). Truman's 1949 farm plan, which would have given money to farmers when supply and demand drove prices too low for an acceptable lifestyle, did not pass. Instead, Congress modified the Hope-Aiken bill. The Korean War again drove prices up but that crisis eased in 1952 and Congress extended the high price supports through 1954.

Eisenhower also had to compensate for limited control of the government and a divided party. During Eisenhower's first two years in office he had an eight-vote margin in the House and a two-vote margin in the Senate. Eisenhower also had to contend with a factious Republican party (Lammers and Genovese). The "old guard" Midwestern and Western congressmen who were isolationists and hated New Deal social programs did not work well with the more moderate Eastern Republicans who echoed Eisenhower's acceptance of some social programming and the importance of international cooperation (Pach and Richardson). In 1954, Democrats took over the House, and Republicans did not regain control while Eisenhower was president.

The philosophy Eisenhower and Secretary of Agriculture Arthur Benson applied to agriculture was the same philosophy Eisenhower had applied to business and industry: "Release the farmer from arbitrary government control, regulation and subsidy, then let the laws of supply and demand in an expanding economy work toward full parity prices" (Adams 203). Eisenhower's 1954 agricultural legislation featured: flexible price supports so the administration could raise and lower the percentage of parity to deal with surpluses or increased demand; steps to remove some commodities from the Commodity Credit Corporation (CCC) holdings to use outside normal markets so as not to suppress prices; steps to minimize the use of acreage reductions and increase the number of diverted acres placed into conservation programs; the expansion of markets abroad; and a study of the problems faced by small farmers. Schapsmeier and Schapsmeier suggest that:

> The farm bill President Eisenhower sent to Congress in 1954 was not a
> clarion call for abrogation of the price support system. Instead it com-
> bined a request for more flexibility with a gradualistic approach. There
> were to be distinct (but slow) steps towards reducing price support levels.
> This was to be accomplished by a progressive transition to a modernized
> parity ratio based on contemporary market factors and a step by step
> reduction of price supports from the rigid 90% figure to a flexible range of
> from 82.5 to 90 percent. (151)

Flexible price supports caused conflict (Cochrane and Ryan), but were passed after the administration pressured GOP legislators (Pach and Richardson).

A Food for Peace program (P.L. 480) was passed in July 1954 with little controversy (Cochrane and Ryan). The program authorized CCC commodities to be sold abroad and used in the United States to help the poor. The program did little good in reducing the surplus threatening to overrun the nation's storage capabilities (Peterson). Don Paarlberg, assistant secretary of agriculture under Eisenhower, summed up Food for Peace saying:

> We sold what we could for cash. What we couldn't sell for cash we sold
> for credit. What we couldn't sell for dollars we sold for foreign currency.
> What we couldn't get money for we bartered. What we couldn't get any-
> thing for we gave away. What we couldn't export by any means we
> stored. And still the stocks increased. (qtd. in Peterson)

So, Eisenhower's agricultural speeches in 1953 and 1954 represented his first attempts at articulating a policy that would deal with rapidly growing surpluses and rapidly dropping farm prices. He faced farmers grown used to government assistance. His party had a limited majority in Congress and the party itself was divided. A recession was underway and Eisenhower had to deal with the debt Truman left behind.

Eisenhower's Early Agricultural Addresses

In assessing Eisenhower's early agricultural rhetoric, I examined two speeches: Eisenhower's first major agricultural address at the Annual Convention of the Future Farmers of America (FFA) in Kansas City, Missouri, on October 15, 1953[1] and his address at Butler University in Indianapolis before the National Institute of Animal Agriculture exactly a year after his FFA address.[2]

Additionally, I examined two drafts dated October 12, 1953, bearing Eisenhower's editing changes for the KC Address[3] and the speaking text from the Butler Address (Butler Speaking Text). I also examined six pages of notes dated October 6, 1953, which Eisenhower dictated for the KC Address ("Dictated Notes").

In assessing Eisenhower's agricultural rhetoric, I examined how Eisenhower developed his persona. As a "nonpolitician" with a military background, how would Eisenhower choose to portray himself when dealing with political issues outside of his experience? How much would his philosophy and values shape his speaking considering that the American people remained supportive of New Deal policies? How would Eisenhower construct arguments to move people from their support of New Deal farm policies to support of his more conservative philosophies?

Analysis

In preview, Eisenhower was deeply involved in writing his early agricultural addresses, especially his first major speech at Kansas City in 1953. Eisenhower's speeches further bolstered the independent persona developed in his campaigns. His political philosophy and values were apparent in his early agricultural speeches. Eisenhower's two major recurring arguments were that the existing farm program had caused the problems facing farmers and that his administration had acted to reduce regulation and free farming from government. Eisenhower actively argued about agricultural policy—often with a loose problem-solution organization.

Eisenhower's Involvement in Writing the KC Address

The KC Address is significant because it was billed as Eisenhower's first major agricultural address (Whitman). Eisenhower's brother Milton suggested that this advanced billing made the 1,500 FFA members in the audience not the primary audience. Memos between Eisenhower and his speechwriter Bryce Harlow dated October 5, 1953, indicate the depth to which Eisenhower was involved in drafting the address. Initially, Harlow introduced the conference as a display of action. He suggested that, "Lacking some positive move like this, you are also put in the position of simply echoing, in different words, things that the Department of Agriculture has been saying incessantly, without much beneficial result, since last Spring" (Harlow). In response, Eisenhower said that the "conference idea may evoke more

jeers than anything else." Eisenhower did note: "I like the business of showing interdependence of farm and city. . . . Could we not make the point that it
is a misnomer to say 'farm problem.' There are many farm problems . . .
[such as] cattle vs. corn and grain" ("To Bryce N. Harlow"). Additionally, the
following day, in his dictated notes Eisenhower included the idea that:

> Every young farmer in this audience has a very definite interest in every
> trade agreement that the United States makes with other nations, in all of
> the security arrangements we make to assure that this trade may take
> place, and in all of the State Department activities to assure that other
> nations in the world, inspired by similar need and understanding, may
> and will continue to trade with us. Consequently every man here is just as
> interested in the activities of the Secretary of State as he is in the activities
> of the Secretary of Agriculture. ("Dictated Notes" 3)

In Draft 6, the text read:

> In short, the interests of you young men and women here cannot be
> delimited, isolated, or fully described by any such term as "agriculture."
> The future is yours and as young Americans, you are entitled to expect
> your future to be rich and rewarding. But for it to be so your vision in the
> coming years must range beyond your communities and encompass the
> entire globe. (1–2)

Eisenhower edited it to read:

> The interests of you young men and women here cannot be limited, iso-
> lated, or described by any single term such as "agriculture." Your vision
> in the coming years must range beyond your immediate problems and
> your home communities. Your vision must encompass the entire globe.
> Certainly, for you and your parents, the activities of the Secretary of State
> and the Secretary of Defense are as important as those of the Secretary of
> Agriculture. (1–2)

In the speech this idea became:

> The interests of you young men and women cannot be limited, isolated,
> or described by any single term such as "agriculture." Your study in the
> coming years must range beyond your immediate problems and your
> home communities. Your vision must encompass the entire globe. Cer-
> tainly, for you and your parents, the activities of the Secretary of State
> and the Secretary of Defense are as important as those of the Secretary of
> Agriculture. Your fortunes are and will be as directly and intimately
> affected by the foreign policies of the United States as they will be by any
> farm policy of the government. (KC Address 668)

This idea progressed clearly from notes to draft and final speech.

This speech is interesting because it illustrates that Eisenhower was not
willing to leave the development of such a major address in the hands of his
staff. It leads to the rejection of the image of Eisenhower as an amiable bum-
bler. It also leads to a better understanding of Eisenhower's skills at speech

writing when the extent to which Eisenhower's ideas were integrated into the speech is understood. It illustrates Eisenhower's belief in the interconnectedness of spheres and the strength of that belief since Eisenhower strengthened that image through many edits. Finally, Eisenhower's active involvement suggests an awareness of his situation and a willingness to work within its constraints. Eisenhower took care during the drafting phase to further develop his independent persona.

Persona

Eisenhower's independent persona appeared throughout his agricultural rhetoric. His rhetoric created the image of a man who understood farming and spoke for farmers and nonfarmers alike. He was a man of action who studied before he acted but always avoided partisanship as he worked toward his goals.

In Eisenhower's KC Address, which was his first farm policy speech, Eisenhower established his farm experience. Eisenhower suggested the honorary degree of Farmer of America bestowed upon him by the FFA entitled him to Department of Agriculture pamphlets—and "with my farm in Pennsylvania, I need them" (667). Later in the KC Address, he mentioned that he worked on a farm in Abilene as a boy (667). At Butler University in 1954, Eisenhower said the interdependence between nations was not understood "when I was a boy working on the farms of Kansas" (907). He continued: "In those days we plowed with a team of horses and a one-bottom plow. We stacked our hay by hand. When a calm stopped the windmill we had to pump countless buckets of water for use in home and stable" (907). Eisenhower personally edited this speech passage to simplify it. On his speaking text, Eisenhower changed "We laboriously tramped down our hay in stack and loft" to read "We stacked our hay by hand" (Butler Speaking Text 8). In the Butler Address, Eisenhower explained: "Watering and feeding the stock, and milking the cows, still have to be done right on time. In short, good farming is still sun-up to sun-down work" (907). Emphasizing his farm experience was vital to Eisenhower because he was attacking current farm policy. By showing he understood farming, Eisenhower was able to develop a level of trust in the farming community which, in turn, garnered support for Eisenhower's policy changes.

Beyond his experience with farming, Eisenhower suggested he spoke for farmers and all Americans. Referring to the crises of war and inflation, Eisenhower said: "I grew up among farmers. I know they do not want their future prosperity contingent upon crises of one sort or another" (KC Address 671). In his address at Butler University, Eisenhower said the nation wanted and was working toward permanent peace: "In this I know I speak for every American citizen regardless of partisan or any other considerations" (Butler Address 906).

Eisenhower's persona was also that of a man of action. In his KC Address, Eisenhower showed he would act to help those hurt by the drought affecting much of the country. He touted actions taken already by his administration: "Emergency government programs were quickly set up to provide low cost feed in the disaster areas" (670). This was a simplification of changes Eisenhower had made in Draft 6 of the KC Address from "Within a week after Secretary Benson and I visited [illegible word] disaster areas, emergency government programs were distributing low cost feed there" (6). He added he would be meeting with governors of the states caught in the 1953 drought to get their recommendations. A year later at Butler University, Eisenhower pointed out that the drought continued and the administration continued to help by giving aid in 15 states and negotiated with the railroads to cut shipping costs on hay to the affected areas (910).

Eisenhower also acted to deal with other issues. For example, at Kansas City he noted that many cattle farmers were forced to liquidate herds because it cost more to raise the cattle than they would receive for selling them. Eisenhower said: "One of the first official acts of this Administration dealt with this problem. Price controls were promptly removed, as was the compulsory grading that had been obstructing the market" (669). Further, he said he had kept up with the progress of studies being done by farm organizations on the farm problems. He was "calling together" the National Agricultural Advisory Commission and he would "confer with" farm leaders (KC Address 674). Thus, the image Eisenhower creates is that of a president fully engaged with the plight of farmers and taking firm steps to alleviate their crises.

Eisenhower also emphasized that his farm policy was thoughtful and well researched. In the KC Address he referred to studies the administration had undertaken and said: "I intend to weigh carefully the many recommendations developed by these groups of men experienced in all these phases of agriculture. Based on those views, I will submit my recommendations to the Congress early next year on the kind of program I believe to be in the Nation's best interest" (672). In the Butler Address, Eisenhower again emphasized the research the administration did before proposing policy:

> Twenty-one months ago we set out to develop a durable, logical plan. We sought objective, expert advice from practical farmers, farm groups, commodity specialists. We consulted with educators, law makers, food processors. The final result was a comprehensive program passed by the 83rd Congress, under Republican leadership. (908)

Eisenhower repeatedly emphasized bipartisanship and his desire to avoid partisan political expediency. In Draft 6 of the KC Address, Eisenhower added the statement, "I look upon the formulation of our farm policy as a bipartisan undertaking. The welfare of our farm families knows no politics and I assure you there shall be none in the approach of this Administration" (page between 12 and 13 labeled "Insert A"). In the speech as delivered, the last part of the text was further changed to say, "The welfare of our farm families knows no politics and I assure you there shall be none in the approach to that problem by this administration" (KC Address 672). Thus, Eisenhower presented himself as acting from sound basis and reaching for support outside of his party.

In sum, Eisenhower took care to create identification with farmers by showing them he was one of them. Eisenhower's words also emphasized his willingness to act quickly when needed but also to a dedication to study before determining long-range policies requiring bipartisan support.

Philosophy and Values

Eisenhower's values and philosophy were evident in his agriculture rhetoric. Eisenhower believed in the interconnectedness of political spheres and in limited government. He emphasized partnerships between the federal government and the states.

Eisenhower saw a connection between the rural and urban areas of the United States, between the nations of the world, and between the foreign and domestic policy of the United States. In his KC Address, Eisenhower explained the interdependency:

> Our great cities, our mighty industries, our business and professional accomplishments, our educational institutions, our high living standards, are possible because of the efficiency and productivity of the American farm.
>
> In the same fashion your own agricultural interests and income are inseparably tied up with the health and prosperity of working men and women and the industries in our towns and cities. One element of our Nation can scarcely exist and certainly cannot prosper independently of the others. (668)

This interconnectedness meant one interest group could not receive excess benefits. Eisenhower also said:

> Let us look at your wider interests as Americans and as citizens of the world and at the kind of world in which you may spend your years. And let us not forget that the demands of those wider interests must always be met satisfactorily before specific programs affecting any profession or calling can have validity. (674)

Thus, the interests of the farmer (for example) must be subservient to America's interests.

Eisenhower also saw a connection between foreign policy and farm policy. He said:

> Your vision must encompass the entire globe. Certainly, for you and your parents, the activities of the Secretary of State and the Secretary of Defense are as important as those of the Secretary of Agriculture. Your fortunes are and will be as directly and intimately affected by the foreign policies of the United States as they will be by any farm policies of the government. (668)

The next year, in the Butler Address, Eisenhower noted: "The welfare of 163 million Americans is bound up with our Nation's agriculture—just as every farmer is affected by all national and world affairs" (906). He continued, "We must never forget that the fortunes of all of us are tightly intertwined. This interdependency applies also among the nations of the world—certainly among the nations which are free" (907). This belief in the interconnection of spheres runs throughout Eisenhower's agricultural rhetoric and gives strong justification for many of his agricultural policies. Although Eisenhower recognized the interconnection of spheres, he rejected the New Deal position that interconnection required more federal regulation.

Eisenhower believed the proper role of the federal government was limited and involved partnership with other levels of government. Eisenhower argued that government should have only a limited role in people's lives. The government should take responsibility only for protecting citizens' rights and avoiding widespread disaster. In his KC Address, after noting the problems facing farmers, especially the drought, he said: "Clearly here was a case for action by a government that was concerned with the welfare of all our people" (670). He also said:

> Your own property, your own security, your own opportunity, your own liberties—they must be earned, they cannot be bestowed upon you. It is government's function to preserve your possession of these rights and opportunities and privileges, and to protect you against every disaster which is of such a kind that the individual alone cannot conquer it. (675)

He continued:

> What is promised you is opportunity to get ahead, to make of yourselves what you can. What is promised you, too, is a chance to keep a free government free, a government carrying forward in keeping with the Nation's ideals, a government of limited powers, preserving your freedom, responding to your will, and insuring that the Nation is secure. (675)

At Butler University, Eisenhower spoke against the spread of government regulation and noted that "opportunity is ours if we continue to reject policies that lead to ever higher taxes, to regimentation, to dependence on government far from our homes" (911). Eisenhower wanted to limit government and people's dependence upon it.

Eisenhower emphasized partnerships between the state and federal governments, especially during emergencies. In the KC Address, Eisenhower referred to the drought of 1953 when he said:

> My own conviction is that the principle of partnership between the Federal government and the State governments should govern our approach to such emergency problems. Only in this way can we gain the dual advantages of local knowledge, efficiency and incentive on the one hand, and of wider Federal resources on the other. (670)

In Draft 6 this passage was initially phrased:

> My own conviction in this matter, as in most other areas of governmental activity, is that the relationship between the Federal government and the

State governments should be one of partnership, not domination and pre-emption by the Federal Government. Only in this way can we gain the dual advantages of local knowledge, efficiency and incentives on the one hand, and the vast reservoirs of Federal [illegible word] and resources on the other. (7)

Eisenhower's editing removed all reference to federal preemption while emphasizing the importance of levels of government working together. At Butler, Eisenhower mentioned a new law that gave federal help for local groups for the protection of watersheds. He said: "And very important, these programs will not be planned by an all-wise bureaucracy in far-off Washington. They will be planned at the instance of local level people, with the cooperation and participation of state and local governments" (910). For Eisenhower, the federal government should act to assist other levels of government and other organizations, but not control the decisions.

In summary, Eisenhower believed in the interconnection of spheres, farm and city, domestic and foreign policies, and America and the world. Eisenhower believed the government should protect citizens' rights and act to avoid disaster but avoid overt interference in people's lives. Finally, partnerships, both between government levels and between the government and other organizations, could result in better policy.

Arguments and Argument Structure

Eisenhower's arguments and agricultural rhetoric were consistent throughout his administration. His major arguments focused on farmers' many problems, which began with the old policy and the proper role of the federal government in farming. In both the Kansas City and Butler addresses, he used a variation of a problem-solution format for his arguments.

When Eisenhower came to office, farmers were in economic trouble. He developed the problem element of his speeches by focusing on the causes and effects of the problem. According to Eisenhower, the agricultural policies of the New and Fair Deals, designed to help farmers, had literally created more problems for American farmers. Government control was the root of the problem. In two passages in the KC Address, Eisenhower foreshadowed his future argument that the farm laws in effect had created the current farm problem. He said: "There are difficult problems today in our agriculture—problems deeply rooted in our recent past" (669). He continued that the "major problem" was that "our war-expanded agriculture produces more than enough, in some lines to meet market demands and reserve requirements at present prices" (671). He asked why the problem had not become apparent sooner and answered that the war stimulated inflation and high exports kept agricultural prices high: "It was this series of events that blurred the basic problem and deferred its solution to later years" (671).

At Butler, he is clearer about the cause of the problem. For example, Eisenhower developed the problem with agriculture by saying:

Every farmer knows why his income declined. Agriculture was losing markets. Prices were depressed by uneconomic production which was encouraged by the old farm law. The truth is this vital problem of markets and surpluses had never been faced head on. Two wars had postponed the day of inevitable reckoning. (908)

Farmers' decreased buying power "took place under the old farm law—a law that is still in effect. Yet, some would have our farmers believe that in the future this law will do what it has failed miserably to do in the past" (908).

Also at Butler, Eisenhower used some simple statistics to illustrate the decline in buying power facing farmers:

In 1947, a cotton farmer could buy a pickup truck with 9 bales. By the end of 1952 it took 14 bales.
In 1947, 800 bushels of corn would buy a tractor. By the end of 1952, it took not 800 but over 1,300 bushels, two-thirds more.
In 1947, 930 bushels of wheat would buy a combine. By the end of 1952 it took not 930 but over 1,600 bushels, three-fourths more. (908)

This vividly demonstrated the problems farmers faced. At Kansas City, Eisenhower was less picturesque about the problem. For example, he said: "By last January, farm prices, farm income, and our agricultural exports had all gone into full retreat, while the cost of the things farmers bought were on the increase" (669).

Eisenhower set conditions for the solution. Action should be taken only when the problem affected the entire country, but government action should never infringe on freedom. Eisenhower's KC Address illustrated both facets of the argument. Eisenhower first noted that the drought-induced cattle sell-off was a problem for all Americans: "Clearly here was a case for action by a government that was concerned with the welfare of all of our people" (670). Eisenhower's editing made this passage emphasize government action. In KC Address Draft 6, Eisenhower changed a verb to make the government seem more involved. Initially, a sentence read "Clearly, here was a case for help from a government concerned with the welfare of all our people." Eisenhower changed "help from" to "action by" (6).

Later he argued that:

It is government's function to preserve your possession of these rights and opportunities and privileges, and to protect you against every disaster which is of such a kind that the individual alone cannot conquer it. But in the necessity of constantly adjusting the processes of government so as to always provide for the needed protection to its citizens, while at the same time insuring perpetuation of their economic, political, and intellectual freedoms, here is where we find the great challenges of America. So what is promised you is the opportunity to get ahead, to make of yourselves what you can. What is promised you, too, is a chance to keep a free government free, a government of limited powers, preserving your freedom, responding to your will, and insuring that the Nation is secure. (675)

This contrasts Eisenhower with New Dealers who advocated more control over farmers and agricultural production. Additionally, it pairs with the argument against the old policy to illustrate the correct path for the new agricultural policy.

Eisenhower's solution was to eliminate the old law and introduce new legislation based on the administration's research. First, get rid of the old law. Eisenhower said: "We must continue to free our farmers from paralyzing bureaucratic control" (Butler Address 911). Eisenhower substantially changed the tone of this passage in the speaking draft when he changed it from "We must continue to free our farmers from the dead hand of bureaucratic control." In his final message, the paralysis is a temporary thing; Eisenhower could stop the paralysis and let farmers farm again. The phrase "dead hand" could imply that no change was possible. Second, he also planned to implement legislation based upon the administration's research. He said, "We have a program which attacks our farm problem on both crucial fronts—markets and production. We have a farm program geared not to war, but to peace—a program that will encourage consumption, expand markets, and realistically adjust farm production to markets" (909).

In support of his 1954 farm program, Eisenhower argued that his farm policy was sound because it was developed in response to a report from a broad-based commission on farming. In his KC Address in October 1953, Eisenhower foreshadowed the argument that his administration acted on solid research when he informed the audience that such a commission was studying the issue: "We have established an 18-member commission to help devise programs for the farmers' future—a commission—and please note this well—a commission with 12 active, practical farmers as members, to insure that practical men help form a sound national agricultural policy" (672). At Butler, Eisenhower mentioned this commission again and noted that the results of the commission's findings were worked into the administration's agricultural policy. Eisenhower's argument that his policy was good for farmers and the country is a logical argument for any president to make, and important for Eisenhower because he also emphasized the interconnection of spheres. Additionally, it neatly tied into his arguments against the prior policy.

Eisenhower sometimes moved beyond problem-solution format, adding proof that the administration's solution had worked. For example, in the KC Address, he identified the problem and followed it with examples of actions taken by the administration and the effects of those actions. He followed this general pattern several times in the speech. For example, he began by talking about the current problems and their roots in the past as well as the change in buying power after the war, which especially hurt young farmers and cattlemen. The administration had acted fast, though:

> One of the first official acts of this administration dealt with this problem. Price controls were promptly removed, as was the compulsory grading that had been obstructing the market. Secretary of Agriculture Benson then vigorously attacked the problem from the merchandising standpoint. (669)

The result was a 26% increase in beef sales (669). Eisenhower then began another cycle of problem and action. Eisenhower developed programs to provide low-cost feed, reduced rail transportation rates, increased government purchases, and emergency loans to respond to the drought in the Midwest (669–70). He drew a picture of an administration that acted quickly and decisively.

Eisenhower's general problem-solution organization let him argue that change was warranted and emphasized the positive actions the administration proposed. Eisenhower reinforced his arguments through several rhetorical strategies.

Rhetorical Strategies

Eisenhower used a variety of rhetorical strategies in speaking about agriculture. Eisenhower sought to develop a relationship with the audience through the use of identification and praise; he emphasized alliteration and repeated sounds and words; he used parallelism extensively; and he used some appeals to patriotism as well as interesting sentence structures and vivid language. He edited his speeches carefully to simplify ideas and to make images more dramatic.

Eisenhower used language to develop a relationship with his audience. To do so, he used identification and praised the audience. He used "us," "our," and "we" often to create identification. For example, in the KC Address, he said the "simple fact is that *we* must seek methods of increasing stability and prosperity in all elements of agriculture; and, because *our* national interest is so deeply involved, I think it might be well for *us* to take stock of where *we* are today"; and "let *us* talk first about some disagreeable facts" (668–69, emphasis added). He used similar strategies in his speech at Butler University: "But, my friends, let *us*—all of *us*—strive together for that kind of future for America—a future boundless in opportunity, unlimited in rich promise for *our* farmers, for all of *us*, for *our* children" (911, emphasis added).

Eisenhower also praised his audience. At Kansas City he said: "Our great cities, our mighty industries, our business and professional accomplishments, our educational institutions, our high living standards are possible because of the efficiency and productivity of the American farm" (667). Later in the same speech Eisenhower suggested that the audience understood farming better than young people did in his day: "I know you have a far greater understanding of the factors at work than did young people during my own youth" (669).

Near the end of the speech he said:

> I deeply wish that I could be given the words to express the boundless confidence I have in the ability and character and the stamina of America's young people. I have lived with them and gained inspiration from them in peace and in war in many corners of the earth. . . . I deeply believe that the energy, the courage, the imagination, the readiness to sacrifice, of American youth, when united behind this purpose, will constitute such a force that obstacles will fall and victory finally emerge. (676)

This upbeat tone about the future and praise of youth fit the speaking situation and also reminded listeners of Eisenhower's military experience, which bolstered his credibility. At Butler, Eisenhower praised farmers by pointing out that farming was difficult work. He said: "But just look at what this hard work has done for America" (907). He continued that, "A skilled American farm worker today produces food and clothing for eighteen other Americans. What a contrast with countries where as many as nine must toil to produce food for themselves and one other person" (907). Overall, the strategies of identification and praise were important to Eisenhower because he was attacking policies upon which many farmers had come to rely. To overcome their resistance to change meant his audience needed to see him as one of them. Identification and praise build a relationship between the president and the people, which he can then draw upon for support.

Eisenhower used alliteration and repetition of initial word sounds often in his early agricultural rhetoric. At Butler University he noted that the transition from war to peace did not result in economic problems "so widely predicted last winter by *p*rofessionally *p*essimistic but *p*olitically hopeful *p*rophets" (906). This bit of language was all Eisenhower. The Butler Speaking Text read, "We have moved from war to peace without the economic collapse so widely predicted last winter by hopeful political pessimists" (6). This change is significant because it indirectly pokes fun at a group that obviously wrongly held differing views and it shows his sensitivity to language.

Eisenhower also used parallelism. In the KC Address, he identified the basis of the farm problem with several "it was" statements: "It was World War II inflation . . . it was these emergencies, these calamities, this rampant inflation. . . . It was this series of events that blurred the basic problem and deferred its solution to later years" (671). Later in the speech he said: "Your own property, your own security, your own opportunity, your own liberties, they must be earned" (675). In his Butler Address, he repeated "our farmers" at the beginning of phrases five times:

> Our farmers, just as all of us, want America strongly defended. . . . Our farmers, like all the rest of us, want relief from oppressive taxation. . . . Our farmers, like all the rest of us, demand efficient Government. . . . Our farmers, as all of us, want a trustworthy government. . . . Our farmers, and all of us, want a national economy strong in all parts. . . . (906)

This passage is interesting for more reasons than just the repetition. It also served to reinforce Eisenhower's contention that farmers are first of all Americans—they are not different from any other group of citizens and should not receive special treatment. At Butler University, he said farmers wanted a better agricultural picture, repeating the phrase "a stop to" four times: "They wanted a stop to falling income, a stop to rising farm costs, a stop to the loss of markets, a stop to the piling up of threatening and unmanageable surpluses" (908). In this instance, the parallel structure emphasized farmers' needs. This extensive use of parallel structure reinforced the causes of the problem and the advantages of his suggested program.

Eisenhower also used appeals to patriotism to end his early agricultural speeches. In his speech to the FFA, he said:

> As you till your farms, go to school, plan your futures, raise your families, remember that only he can deserve America who stands forever ready to give America all he has.
>
> To live for America as devotedly, as nobly as so many thousands have died for her is the greatest ambition any of her children can have. Fortified and strengthened by this one truth, there is no problem you will not solve. (676)

In the Butler Address, he said:

> But my friends, let us—all of us—strive together for that kind of future for America—a future boundless in opportunity, unlimited in rich promise for our farmers, for all of us, for our children. For it is given to us to do our part in building and preserving America, an America whose shining faith and hope and freedom will continue to light the way for all in the world who, with us, love liberty and peace. (911)

These endings enlist the audience in Eisenhower's crusade to preserve America's greatness.

Eisenhower also used some unique sentence structures. For example, at Butler University he said: "So, peace, lower taxes, honest government, a strong economy, personal security, these we must seek for every American" (907). In the KC Address, he said: "Your own property, your own security, your own opportunity, your own liberties, they must be earned" (675). He also said: "Our great cities, our mighty industries, our business and professional accomplishments, our educational institutions, our high standard of living—are possible because of the efficiency and productivity of the American farmer" (668). By placing the key idea at the end of the sentence, Eisenhower created anticipation and focused the listener on that idea. He used other interesting sentence structures as well. For example, at Butler, Eisenhower said: "So, at last, we have a program which attacks our farm problem on both crucial fronts—markets and production. We have a farm program geared not to war, but to peace—a program that will encourage consumption, expand markets, and realistically adjust farm production to markets" (908). These interesting turns of phrase are not just rhetorical flourishes. They focus the listener on the key idea expressed in the phrase and make the idea more memorable.

He also used language to create vivid images and worked on careful editing to enhance the images. In talking about farm problems, he said: "A disaster of nature's making came to aggravate the trouble. A drought of devastating intensity blistered the great Southwest. Economic misfortune confronted hundreds of thousands of Americans on ranches and farms. The cattle forced upon the market from the stricken areas further depressed prices" (KC Address 669). "Disaster," "drought," "blistered," and "stricken" are powerful words that emphasized the real plight of farmers in the region. In the Butler Address, Eisenhower suggested war had kept Americans from seeing the root of the agricultural problem—war had "postponed the day of inevitable reckoning" (908). Another vivid image appears in that same address when Eisenhower said: "Our nation extends the hand of friendship to all in the world who will grasp it in honesty and good faith" (906). Eisenhower used language strategically here to create vivid sensory images for his audience.

Eisenhower's editing shows a sensitivity to language and a desire to simplify. Eisenhower eliminated some detail in the Butler Speaking Text that made the speech tighter. For example, he eliminated the phrase "Laws of nature have not been repealed" from this passage: "And yet in many ways . . . [farming] hasn't changed. Laws of nature have not been repealed. Markets and the weather are still unpredictable. Wind and hail, mud and dust, floods and drought still exist" (9). Notice too, the pairings in the last sentence. Eisenhower contrasts mud and dust and flood and drought. He also eliminated the last sentence from the following passage: "A skilled American farm worker today produces food and clothing for eighteen other Americans. What a contrast with countries where as many as nine must toil to provide food for themselves and only one other. How meaningful to all of this makes the skillful work of our farmers" (Butler Speaking Text 10).

He cut the statement that the law was in effect for the year from the passage "this steady decline in farmers' buying power took place under the old farm law—a law which stays in effect until the end of the current crop year. Yet some would have our farmers believe that in the future this law will do what it has failed to do in the past." This simple change placed emphasis on the law's failure by tightening the connection between the old law and the failure (Butler Speaking Text 12).

The Butler Speaking Text illustrates Eisenhower's continued tinkering with speeches to improve their language. He began with:

> For the first time in twenty years, there is no active battlefield anywhere in the world. Today we have peace, and every resource of our country is being tirelessly used to make it a lasting peace. Today our nation extends the hand of friendship to all in the world who will grasp it in honesty and good faith. (3)

Eisenhower then eliminated some repetition, but his edits made the sentences more powerful.

> Today we have peace, for the first time in twenty years, there is no active battlefield anywhere in the world. And every resource of our country is being tirelessly used to make it a lasting peace. Our nation extends the hand of friendship to all in the world who will grasp it in honesty and good faith. (3)

This is a simple change but the rhythm of sentences and the emphasis on peace that the change created is powerful.

In summary, Eisenhower used identification and praise to make his audience feel positive. He used other strategies such as alliteration and repetition of words as well as parallel structure. Eisenhower's appeals to patriotism, interesting sentence structures, and language created vivid images for his audience. He edited to make the language tighter and more vibrant. These language strategies illustrate how Eisenhower used language to sell his ideas. Why is language significant to Eisenhower? Such rhetorical flourishes are the epitome of good, persuasive rhetoric, which is especially important to a president bent on changing a popular policy.

Conclusion

Eisenhower's early agricultural rhetoric showed a keen understanding of the situation he faced. His speeches furthered his independent apolitical persona, initially developed well before the election, by emphasizing his understanding of farming, his role as representative of all Americans, his bias toward action, and his belief in bipartisanship. His identification with the audience made him seem one of them and his praise furthered the relationship between them, making them more willing to accept his suggestions for change.

Eisenhower understood the depth of American support for New Deal farm policy and crafted his arguments against that policy with great care. He attacked the policy by suggesting it had failed to meet its objectives and by illustrating the extent of that failure's effects on all farmers. Eisenhower's repetition, unique sentence structures, and vivid language focused attention on the problems farmers faced. Once the argument against the old policy was developed, it was easier for the audience to accept policy changes. Eisenhower then argued that his policy, developed with the help of both farming experts and practicing farmers, would solve the farm problem. Additionally, Eisenhower offered proof of the administration's ability to solve problems by referencing drought relief and action taken to support beef prices. Because Eisenhower had successfully dealt with crises, it seemed likely that he could solve deeper problems. Eisenhower's use of language also helped emphasize the benefits of the proposed solutions, making them seem more attractive.

Because Eisenhower had such a slim majority in Congress, he needed the support of all his party or the support of some Democrats. His careful arguments and continued development of his independent persona may have allowed him to appeal to both parties. Conversely, it may have bothered Republican congresspersons who felt Eisenhower did not identify with them. The strategy, although perhaps problematic, did reach the American public. It is also important to note that Eisenhower did not introduce radically new policy (perhaps having seen the Brannan plan fail), but instead stuck to plans similar to those passed before by Republicans and even similar to FDR's conservation programs. This also suggests that he understood the situation and chose to develop policy that would be at least acceptable to most Americans.

Eisenhower's belief in the interconnection of political spheres led him to emphasize partnerships between levels of government. Rhetorically, this is a wise argument because it made him seem reasonable. His belief in limited government came, it seemed, from his belief that the government best suited to act is closest to the people. Eisenhower could support state and local efforts without taking away the local control that mollified both conservatives and those seeking government solutions. The interconnection argument was also powerful because he could praise farmers for their work but refuse support that might upset the balance between the spheres. At the same time, it allowed him to appeal to listeners' patriotism because everyone should want to do their part to maintain the balance and thus, the health of America.

In sum, Eisenhower faced a difficult situation. Farmers supported government involvement in farming, which violated Eisenhower's basic beliefs. A limited majority in Congress and a divided party made passing legislation difficult. Eisenhower's efforts in the creation of his first major agricultural address, the KC Address, illustrates his involvement in all phases of policy development and speech writing. Eisenhower pursued flexible price supports and sought to reduce the regulations on farmers and reduce the surpluses that were driving farm prices down. Eisenhower's rhetoric supported his independent persona and illustrated his philosophy of limited government and the interconnectedness of farmer and city dweller. Eisenhower used variations on a problem-solution organization and argued that the surplus and the New Deal/Fair Deal programs were the problem. Eisenhower used language carefully and his editing often reflects this desire. He used identification, praise, alliteration, repetition of key phrases, and parallel structure to persuade. He also often used very vivid language as well.

This paper focused only on Eisenhower's early agricultural rhetoric. The Republican Party lost control of Congress in 1954 and future research should determine if Eisenhower adapted to that situation as well as he did to a Republican-controlled Congress. Additionally, future research should focus on other aspects of Eisenhower's domestic policy rhetoric. Eisenhower managed three balanced budgets during his term in spite of three small recessions. How did Eisenhower rhetorically deal with the recessions and persuade Congress to pass balanced budgets? Additionally, civil rights became an issue while Eisenhower was president. How did Eisenhower deal with the competing demands of civil rights advocates and conservative southerners on the eve of the civil rights movement in the United States? The common belief that nothing much happened during the 1950s and Eisenhower's war record has perhaps pushed scholars away from the study of Eisenhower's domestic policy rhetoric. It is, however, an area worthy of continued study.

Notes

[1] Eisenhower, "Public Papers," 1953, p. 667. Future references to this speech will be "KC Address."

[2] Eisenhower, "Public Papers," 1954, p. 905. Future references to this speech will be "Butler Address."

[3] Eisenhower, "Speech Draft." Further references to this draft will be "Draft 6."

Works Cited

Adams, S. *First-Hand Report: The Story of the Eisenhower Administration.* New York: Harper & Brothers, 1961.

Bonnen, J. T., W. P. Browne, and D. B. Schweikhardt. "Further Observations on the Changing Nature of National Agricultural Policy Decision Processes, 1946–1995." *Agricultural History* 70.2 (1996): 130–52.

Brinkley, A. *Liberalism and Its Discontents.* Cambridge, MA: Harvard UP, 1998.

Cochrane, W. W., and M. E. Ryan. *American Farm Policy, 1948–1973.* Minneapolis: U of Minnesota P, 1976.

Eisenhower, D. D. "Butler Speaking Text, Indianapolis Farm Speech." 15 Oct. 1954. Box 9, Speech Series, Whitman File. Abilene, KS: Eisenhower Library.

———. "Dictated Notes." 6 Oct. 1953. Bryce N. Harlow Records, 1953–61. Folder 6, Box 32. Abilene, KS: Eisenhower Library.

———. *Public Papers of the Presidents of the United States: Dwight D. Eisenhower, 1953–1961.* Washington, DC: Office of the Federal Register.

———. Speech Draft for FFA Speech. 12 Oct. 1953. Bryce N Harlow Records. Box 25, Speech Series. Abilene, KS: Eisenhower Library.

Eisenhower, Milton. "To Ann Whitman." Sunday, Future Farmers, 15 Oct. (1), Speech Series, Whitman File. Abilene, KS: Eisenhower Library.

Harlow, Bryce N. "To Dwight D. Eisenhower." 3 Oct. 1953. Bryce N. Harlow Records, 1953–61. Folder 5, Box 32. Abilene, KS: Eisenhower Library.

Lammers, W. W., and M. A. Genovese. *The Presidency and Domestic Policy: Comparing Leadership Styles, FDR to Clinton.* Washington, DC: CQ P, 2000.

Matusow, A. J. *Farm Policies and Politics in the Truman Years.* New York: Atheneum, 1970.

McCraw, T. K. "The New Deal and the Mixed Economy." *Fifty Years Later: The New Deal Evaluated.* Ed. H. Sitkoff. Philadelphia: Temple University Press, 1985. 37–67.

Medhurst, M. *Dwight D. Eisenhower: Strategic Communicator.* Westport, CT: Greenwood P, 1993.

Pach, C. J., Jr., and E. Richardson. *The Presidency of Dwight D. Eisenhower.* Lawrence: U of Kansas P, 1991.

Peterson, T. *Agricultural Exports, Farm Income, and the Eisenhower Administration.* Lincoln: U of Nebraska P, 1979.

Saulnier, R. J. *Constructive Years: The U.S. Economy under Eisenhower.* Lanham, MD: UP of America, 1991.

Schapsmeier, E. L., and F. H. Schapsmeier. "Eisenhower and Agricultural Reform: Ike's Farm Policy Legacy Appraised." *The American Journal of Economics and Sociology* 51.2 (April 1992): 147.

Scheele, H. Z. "The 1956 Nomination of Dwight D. Eisenhower: Maintaining the Hero Image." *Presidential Studies Quarterly* 17 (1987): 459–71.

"Text of the Republican Party's 1952 Campaign Platform Adopted by National Convention." *The New York Times* 11 July 1952, 8.

Ulrich, H. *Losing Ground: Agricultural Policy and the Decline of the American Farm.* Chicago: Chicago Review P, 1989.

Whitman, Ann. "To Dwight D. Eisenhower." 11 Oct. 1953. Future Farmers 15 Oct. (2), Box 15, Speech Series, Whitman File. Abilene, KS: Eisenhower Library.

Appealing the Divide
Logos, Ethos, and Contemporary American Presidential Campaign Rhetoric

Marc C. Santos

Introduction

The verdict following the first of three presidential debates on September 30, 2004 was virtually unanimous: Senator Kerry bested President Bush. Save for the partisan pundits on the far right, America seemed to agree that Kerry scored a decisive victory. Experts praised Kerry's clarity, consistency, and composure. Although things would get slightly closer in the next two debates, Kerry maintained a clear advantage at the podium.[1]

Conventional rhetorical analysis of the first debate reveals at least one key to Kerry's success: a virtuosic deployment of stasis theory. Kerry consistently scores points by undermining or questioning the conjectural and definitional stasis of Bush's central tenets—particularly the notion of Iraq as "central" to the war on terror. By shifting questions away from Bush's perceived strengths to his weaknesses, Kerry forces Bush into a defensive position; the president spends most of the first debate unsuccessfully stumbling for answers. Simultaneously, Kerry's own responses are textbook examples of classical oratorical deliberative performance; he deftly moves from conjectural and definitional stasis to procedural stasis. One letter to the editor published in the *New York Times* shortly after the first debate captures the sentiments of the left:

> The presidential debate on Thursday night showed a president with an uncomfortably weak grasp of the impact of his own decisions, and a challenger, John Kerry, who had intelligent, well-planned and achievable solutions to the many problems we face abroad. The debate was about substance over ideology, and where Mr. Kerry outlined concrete steps, President Bush had a vague claim that "I just know how this world works." Mr. Bush's lack of focus and surplus of confused misdirection have never been so obvious as now. (Murray)

Despite Kerry's virtuosic performances (and, actually, I will later argue that, perhaps, in part *because* of them), he lost the election. In the wake of Kerry's defeat arose a wave of vituperate responses expounding the ignorance of the red states, responses that signify the left's frustration with the impotence of what it deemed acceptable rational deliberation in the 2000 and 2004 elections. A personal anecdote best represents the tenor of this resentment: I spent election night with a group of colleagues who began the night confident that Kerry would win—certainly people had seen through W's ineptitude—certainly Bush's "surplus of confused misdirection" was *so obvious* to everyone. I remember tracking their growing agitation and incredulity as the night wore on. Several pints into the wee hours of the morning, as the election results grew increasingly clear, one fellow graduate student venomously spat, "Great, now we have to put up with that f---ing grin for four more years."

The comment struck me—in fact, this paper began as an investigation into the rhetorical strategies operating behind Bush's smile. The more I delved into the topic, the more I became concerned with liberalism's dismissive demeanor toward red America and the underlying assumptions grounding the extremely critical critiques of Bush's rhetorical effectiveness. My central concern today lies not in exposing the "deceptive" nature of Bush's rhetoric as it does in exploring the disturbing reactions liberals have had toward this rhetoric, which can be epitomized by Thomas Frank's *What's the Matter with Kansas.*[2] Regardless of postmodern considerations of hospitality toward the Other and critiques on the imperialism and elitism of modern knowledge/power, liberal America increasingly occupies an invective and condescending position opposite "red America." Its rhetoric exposes a continuing attachment to Platonic rationalism and to modern cosmopolitan narratives of teleological progression toward enlightenment along with a general distrust of non-Philosophical rhetoric (stressing the big "P" and the little "r"). This rhetorical disconnect spurs our nation's political divide: liberalism's strong relationship with academia has led to deep rationalist roots, which produces a distrust of ethos and a failure to acknowledge it as a sophisticated or legitimate political appeal.

Critiquing Bush's Use of Ethical Rhetoric

For those who might forget, the president's posture and demeanor grew increasingly "looser" over the course of the three debates. By the third debate he regularly leans lackadaisically over the podium and seems to laugh off every one of Kerry's logical lashings (and, for those keeping score, there are many) with a chuckle and a grin. No wonder it was so frustrating to my embittered colleague: it shouldn't make sense—the more he loses, the more secure he appears. However, behind this chuckle lay an equally virtuosic performance of epideictic rhetoric incorporating an ethical construction that I describe as "the-good-man-of-action-getting-the-job-done." "Losing" the liberal/deliberative political "game" conceivably complements Bush's ethical identity: a new variation of the neoconservative "backlash" posture depicted by Frank:

> While most of us think of politics as a Machiavellian drama in which actors make alliances and take practical steps to advance their material interests, the backlash is something very different: a crusade in which

one's material interests are suspended in favor of vague cultural grievances that are all-important and yet incapable of ever being assuaged. (121)

The neocon backlash politician carefully constructs a populist image diffident to the elitism of the condescending, cosmopolitan liberal—s/he is consubstantial with the authentic American people, united in a struggle against liberalism's tyrannous and unstoppable relativist depravity.[3] Rhetorically considered, such a construction relies more heavily on establishing ethos than logos.

President Bush has always exhibited a unique talent for ethical rhetoric. Reviewing Bush's rhetorical strategies in the 2000 presidential election, Gary Orren refers to Bush as "ethos incarnate," writing that: "The amiable Texan's meteoric rise in American politics is a triumph of personality over policy. Spontaneous and unpretentious, the governor's good-old-boy demeanor and habit of bestowing nicknames on new acquaintances belies his patrician roots." A component of the backlash strategy, the "good-old-boy" persona frames Bush as an outsider attempting to infiltrate the cutthroat liberal political stronghold. Unlike the "good-old-boy" persona of the 2000 election, the 2004 version is anything but unpretentious—his ostentatious displays of confidence are no doubt what triggered such an affective response in my colleague. Responding in the first debate to moderator Lehrer's question whether Kerry's accusations "raise[d] any hackles with you?", Bush casually leans forward and replies with that confident grin, "Oh, I'm a pretty calm guy. I don't take it personally" ("The First"). This projected detachment constitutes a political outsider, an "I'm-not-one-of-them-I'm-one-of-you" rhetorical move dissociating him from career politicians while maintaining his political agency. Consider Bush's statement in response to Kerry's accusation that he has greatly diminished world alliances: "*I know how these people think*. I deal with them all the time. I sit down with world leaders frequently and talk to them on the phone frequently" (15, emphasis added). Notice the subtlety: while Bush is clearly not one of these people (career politicians), he has authentic access to how they operate. He has knowledge of their "logical" exercises and need not take political accusations personally because he (and any "we" consubstantial with that "he") recognizes that "they" have their games, and, as we are all well aware, he (and "we") should not let these games stand in the way of "hard work," a phrase repeated 15 times in the first debate alone (emphasizing "getting the job done"). Bush, then, need not concern himself with "winning" the debate, since Kerry's displays of stasis theory and all the other political masquerading on stage represent nothing more than liberalism's manipulative trickery bent on shadowing and perverting what authentic Americans know to be fundamental "truths."

Critiquing the Critique of Bush's Use of Ethical Rhetoric

Of course, the critical performance above presupposes a narrow, logocentric, Aristotelian conception of ethos, a conception that at its core expresses a fundamental aversion to anything rhetorical. Focusing almost exclusively on credibility, Aristotle's treatment of ethos reflects his teacher's distrust of non-Philosophical (rational, absolute, logically derived) rhetoric by framing awareness and skill with ethos (along with all non-logos forms of persuasion) as necessary evils. Consider his introductory lament in *On Rhetoric*—that in all human affairs "friendliness and hostility and self-interest are often involved, with the result that they are no longer able to see the truth adequately, but their private pleasure or grief casts a shadow on their judgment" (1.1.7). If only the world were properly enlightened (properly committed to logos), then there would be no need to protect Truth from human frailty (by protecting the populace from being duped). Specifically addressing ethos, Aristotle instructs his students that "it is necessary [for a speaker] . . . to construct a view of himself as a certain kind of person and to *prepare the judge*" (2.1.2, emphasis added). This preparatory role subjugates ethos to logos by limiting its approved functions to creating a character that will facilitate logical argument. Aristotelian ethos, stripped of any epistemic function, is not considered as operating in the generation of truth, only as a precondition or accessory for its dissemination.

Ethos receives far more robust epistemic consideration from Augustine, who equates "character" directly with "wisdom." A Christian thinker, Augustine conceptualizes both healthy souls and thoughts as divine rewards from a transcendental authority. Since this authority is beyond the scope of human reason, Augustine inverts the Aristotelian relationship between logos and ethos: logos becomes subjugated to a divine ethos (rather than being itself considered divine). Knowledge is not considered as the fruits of human travail; one receives knowledge only after properly cleansing the soul by first submitting to fear of God and then by unequivocally accepting his holiness (see Augustine 2.17–23). Hence Augustine's proclamation that "[the eloquent] observe the rules because they are eloquent; they do not use them to become eloquent" (4.11). The ability to profess wisdom is reliant on possessing a wise and healthy soul. In such light, one need not be afraid of judgments plagued by what lurks in the shadows. While it might seem circular or mystical from a Platonic perspective, in an Augustinian culture, ethos is not a mere factor in the transmission of truth, it is the embodiment *possession* of truth (see 1.17–26).

In addition to Augustine's inversion of ethos's relationship to logos, both S. Michael Halloran and Dale E. Sullivan demonstrate how conceptions of ethos often overemphasize the primacy of a speaker and thus undervalue the importance of audience and context. In his article "Aristotle's Concept of *Ethos*, or if not His Somebody Else's" (clearly I am in favor of the latter), Halloran argues that in Greek ethos translates more literally to "place" rather than to "person." "In contrast to modern notions of the person or self, *ethos* emphasizes the conventional rather than the idiosyncratic, the public rather than the private. The most concrete meaning given for the term in the Greek lexicon is 'a habitual gathering place'" (60). Halloran describes ethical argument as a coming together of speaker and audience to "share experiences and ideas," noting that "to have ethos is to manifest the virtues most valued by the culture to and for which one speaks" (60). Such "speakings" are requisite for the perpetual (re)constitution of that culture (without which logical exchanges cannot take place). They are what Dale E. Sullivan refers to as "epideictic encounters"—encounters that aim at sustaining and celebrating cultural values (117). The logical truths upon which Platonic forms of deliberation function are themselves grounded upon epideictically maintained "orthodoxies," therefore, as Sullivan puts it, "The speaker is freed up to make stronger value statements because he or she can draw upon cultural assumptions about the good" (129).

This ethical/epideictic rhetorical tradition elaborated by Halloran and Sullivan emphasizes the dynamic, social aspects of rhetorical engagements. Thus, we can make out a strong connection between this classical rhetorical tradition and Kenneth Burke's more contemporary concept of identification. Beyond mere "flattery," for Burke, successful rhetorical engagements require that a rhetor and audience share similar interests and principles—neither should be conceptualized as in absolute control of a rhetorical situation since the two are mutually substantiating. Ethos is not embellishment of a speaker's preconceived, objective truth or the mere adoption of a static persona that an audience will find credible; it is the collaborative crafting (between a rhetor and her audience) of an affective temporal coexistence, a dynamic, mutually constituting exchange, without which there is no truth to embellish (*A Rhetoric of Motives* 57–58). Such is the core of Burke's doctrine of consubstantiality:

> A doctrine of *consubstantiality*, either explicit or implicit may be necessary to any way of life. For substance, in the old philosophies, was an *act*; and a way of life is an *acting-together*; and in acting together, men have common sensations, concepts, images, ideas, attitudes that make them consubstantial. (21)

Of course, Burke's work focuses on the old philosophy's and modern enlightenment's discomfort with this requisite consubstantiality since it problematizes the possibility of a transcendental and static, absolute, pure, perfect objectivity. Such a theme runs throughout twentieth-century post-Nietzschean thinkers—Heidegger, Derrida, Grassi, and Vitanza—who, by attuning our ears to the intonations in our own principles of reason, make audible the nonlogical, foundational archaic speech playing underneath Platonic/philosophic/modern/enlightenment discourse and our perpetual anxiety toward such hysterical play.[4]

Conclusion: " . . . Into the Fire"

Despite these critiques and robust intellectual histories, the 2004 election reveals a continuous dis-ease by those on the left with ethical rhetoric and epideictic encounters (and here I must self-incriminate, since my brief critique of Bush's ethos was drenched in skepticism and condescension). Academia's logological leanings too often predetermine it to view any non-logos-based persuasive appeal as a form of deception. Ethos, epideictic encounters, and identification are framed more as part of a "manipulative strategy that makes the whole senseless parade possible" (Burke, *A Rhetoric of Motives* 242), as a "movement building" full of "hallucinatory appeal" promoting "the derangement of the backlash" (245–46), than as the constitutive requirement of *any* culture. It must come *before* good and evil, before the rational systems separating sense from the senseless. As much as I might agree with Frank's politics, I cannot help but be troubled by the medium of his message. It manifests a discomfort with "politics in ruins," a mourning for enlightenment, a desire to play the game from a position of absolute security, a denial of risk, and an aversion to rhetoric. Consider his closing statement: "American conservatism depends for its continued dominance and even for its very existence on people never making certain mental connections about the world, connections that until recently were treated as obvious or self-evident everywhere on the planet" (248). In Frank's diatribe on "this onrushing parade of anti-knowledge . . ." (248) one can hear the echoes of the superiority with which Plato leads the masses from the cave, or of the resentment buried deep in Kant's proclamation that "the people want to be *led* (that is as demagogues say), they want to be *duped*. But they want to be led not by the scholars of the faculties (whose wisdom is too high for them) . . ." (51). Frank's lament on the ignorance of the neocon is exemplary of Platonic/Kantian philosophy's unrest with "people" as defined by Burke: symbol misusing animals ripe with imperfection ("Definition of Man" 3, 16). It is loquacious chatter on the edge of the abyss (5). Yet, history shows that such enlightened chatter, confident in its superiority, risks the worst. I offer David Hume's proclamation:

> When we run over libraries, persuaded of [modern, logical] principles, what havoc must we make? If we take in our hand any volume, of divinity or school metaphysics, for instance, let us ask, *Does it contain any abstract reasoning concerning quantity or number?* No. *Does it contain any experimental reasoning concerning matter of fact and existence?* No. Commit it then to flames; for it can contain nothing but sophistry and illusion. (425)

Unfortunately, as Vitanza reminds us, "Athens enable[s] Auschwitz" (39). The indignant superiority implicit in the former's divine rationality ignited the first spark in the latter's most horrendous fires, which still burn in the recesses of our collective memory. Fortunately, for many, such rationality still tastes of corpses.

In a feeble attempt to end on a lighter note, as we move into the next election cycle, we should all recall Jon Stewart's appearance on *Crossfire*: we must stop hurting America.[5] While I agree with much of Frank's perspective, I believe it is equally important to recognize that characterizing Republicans as ignorant automatons brainwashed beyond the capability of logical reasoning equally prevents any rhetorical possibility for resolution while insulating Frank's own position from blame for any such impasse.[6] Moreover, as Frank recognizes, such smug and patronizing tones ironically feeds the beast it seeks to destroy, since the backlash machine incorporates such logocentrism into the heart of its identifications of both self and Other.[7] Appealing the divide between liberals and conservatives, then, becomes more an education into what haunts us than an ordered assimilation or reeducation of an ignorant and incompetent Other. It means becoming comfortable with our own faith in the rational and its possession of us, and addressing the Other with the spirit of hospitality rather than with the arms of a violent and imperial totality. And such, of course, is hard work.

Notes

[1] *Newsweek* reported that in a controlled survey, 61% of 1,100 registered voters declared Kerry a clear victor, as opposed to only 19% for President Bush (Braiker). In a less scientific survey of over 1,000,000 voters on CNN's Web site, George W. Bush received only "Cs" for content and delivery whereas Kerry earned a "B" and an "A–" respectively. Even given all the disclaimers regarding reliability, validity, and bias, one cannot completely dismiss CNN's "quick vote" Internet poll, which revealed that 72% of over 875,000 voters deemed Kerry victorious ("Poll: Kerry Tops"). After the second debate, a CNN poll of 550 registered users had the outcome at 53%–37%, which was far wider than the mock election numbers at the time (still slightly in Bush's favor) ("Poll: Bush"). A nonscientific poll on MSNBC's *Newsweek* site, with 42,177 responses, showed Kerry as a 65% victor in the final debate (Wolffe). CNN's snap poll following the third debate showed numbers that were a bit closer, as 52% of 511 registered voters selected Kerry, as opposed to only 39% for Bush ("Early Poll").

[2] Although publication of Frank's book precedes the 2004 election, it epitomizes the spirit and methodology of postelection responses. Frank's stature and ability coupled with the book's rigor and popularity makes it a fitting selection for this discussion. While lesser works of similar popularity, such as Jane Smiley's satiric essay "The Unteachable Ignorance of the Red States" or virtually any of the popular and often anonymous "Letter to the Red States" pieces appearing on the Internet, could be dismissed as simple partisan pedantry, Frank's work warrants careful examination.

[3] Frank repeatedly asserts that neocon politics primarily concentrates on controlling access to the authentic image of the average American who is (perhaps unknowingly) in class conflict with tyrannical, immoral, liberal snobbery. See his sixth chapter, "Persecuted, Powerless, and Blind" for an explication of the role of authenticity in backlash rhetoric.

[4] See especially Grassi's often overlooked work, *Rhetoric as Philosophy*, 18–34.

[5] For those unfamiliar with Stewart's appearance, video and transcripts are readily available on the Internet.

[6] This is the exact charge that Frank levels against liberalism's seeming invincibility in backlash rhetoric. Since it is incapable of being overcome (due to the Other's ubiquity and impregnable stranglehold on discursive power), it provides backlash politicians with a universal scapegoat.

[7] See Frank, 129–31. He notes how the neocon discourse relates liberalism's inherent cosmopolitan elitism to the hegemonic impulses of Nazi Germany (which is, ironically of course, a critique echoed by many on the outer limits of the left).

Works Cited

Aristotle. *On Rhetoric: A Theory of Civic Discourse*. Trans. and ed. George A. Kennedy. New York: Oxford UP, 1991.

Augustine. *On Christian Teaching*. Trans. R. P. H. Green. Oxford: Oxford UP, 1999.

Braiker, Brian. "The Race is On." *Newsweek* MSNBC. 4 Oct. 2004. 10 May 2006. <http://www.msnbc.msn.com/id/6159637/site/newsweek/>.

Burke, Kenneth. "Definition of Man." *Language as Symbolic Action: Essays on Life, Literature, and Method*. Berkeley: U of California P, 1966.

———. *A Rhetoric of Motives*. Berkeley: U of California P, 1969.

"Early Poll Gives Kerry the Edge in Final Debate." CNN.com. 14 Oct. 2004. 10 May 2006. <http://www.cnn.com/2004/ALLPOLITICS/10/14/snap.poll/index.html>.

"The First Bush-Kerry Presidential Debate." 2004 Debate Transcript. Commission on Presidential Debates. 30 Sept. 2004. 25 Oct. 2004. <http://www.debates.org/pages/trans2004a.html>.

Frank, Thomas. *What's the Matter with Kansas? How Conservatives Won the Heart of America*. New York: Henry Holt, 2004.

Grassi, Ernesto. *Rhetoric as Philosophy: The Humanist Tradition*. Trans. John Michael Krois and Azizeh Azodi. Rhetorical Philosophy and Theory. Series ed. David Blakesley. Carbondale: Southern Illinois UP, 2001

Halloran, S. Michael. "Aristotle's Concept of *Ethos*, or if not His Somebody Else's." *Rhetoric Review* 1.1 (1982): 58–63.

Hume, David. *An Enquiry Concerning Human Understanding*. 2nd ed. Oxford: Clarendon P, 1961.

Kant, Immanuel. *The Conflict of the Faculties*. Trans. Mary J. Gregor. New York: Abaris Books, 1979.

Murray, Joe. "After the First Debate, Americans See a Winner." Letter. *New York Times* 2 Oct. 2004. 11 May 2006. <http://query.nytimes.com/gst/fullpage.html?res=9400E2DD1038F931A35753C1A9629C8B63>.

Orren, Gary. "Gore vs. Bush: Why it's All Greek to Me." *The Kennedy School of Government Bulletin*. Autumn 2000. 30 Oct. 2004. 9 May 2006. <http://www.ksg.harvard.edu/ksgpress/ksg_news/publications/gorevsbush.html>.

"Poll: Bush, Kerry Even in 2nd Debate." CNN.com. 9 Oct. 2004. 10 May 2006. <http://www.cnn.com/2004/ALLPOLITICS/10/09/snap.poll/index.html>.

"Poll: Kerry Tops Bush in Debate." CNN.com. 1 Oct. 2004. 10 May 2006. <http://www.cnn.com/2004/ALLPOLITICS/10/01/debate.poll/index.html>.

Smiley, Jane. "The Unteachable Ignorance of the Red States." 4 Nov. 2004. <http://www.slate.com/id/210921817>.

Sullivan, Dale E. "The *Ethos* of Epideictic Encounter." *Philosophy and Rhetoric* 26 (1993): 113–33.

Vitanza, Victor. *Negation, Subjectivity, and the History of Rhetoric*. Albany: State U of New York P, 1997.

Wolffe, Richard. "On the Defense: How They Fared in the Final Debate." *Newsweek* MSNBC. 14 Oct. 2004. 10 May 2006. <http://www.msnbc.msn.com/id/6246889/site/newsweek/#anc_nwk_041014_third_debate>.

Complexity and Ideology in Televisual War Rhetoric

The Ad War Over Iraq in Campaign 2004

Stephen A. Klien

Americans who rely on television to learn about the world have developed an approach to political learning that favors images and personalities over policy issues and political institutions: "With television, there are no disembodied issues. Abortion means abortion protestors. Inner-city decay means Washington, DC mayor Marion Barry. Inflation or AIDS means drugstore interviews with their victims. This is how television brings politics to life" (Hart, 1999, p. 58). Indeed, even print journalism has often adopted televisual norms regarding the primacy of visual images and entertaining, personality-driven content in order to compete with broadcast media for audiences (Cooke, 2003; Gladney, 1993). The implications of such televisual political learning for military and foreign policy issues are easily recognized:

> There is no Defense Department apparatus, there is Donald Rumsfeld; there is no United Nations, there is Secretary-General Kofi Annan; there was no clear and verifiable evidence of weapons of mass destruction in Iraq, or a complex interrelationship of competing religious and political interests in the Middle East, but there were numerous images of Saddam Hussein, a diabolical figure featured centrally in the rhetoric of three American presidents to justify military action against Iraq. (Klien, 2005, pp. 427–428)

Much of the public dispute surrounding the competing Iraq War platforms of President George W. Bush and Senator John Kerry during the 2004 U.S. presidential election involved a clash between those preferring the moral clarity of Bush and those preferring the intellectual complexity of Kerry—argument styles, it should be noted, that were mirrored in the candidates' language use and delivery style.

Critical scholars have often examined the ways in which televisual politics sacrifices (perhaps intentionally, in some cases) complex, logical argument construction in favor of simple, direct, and emotionally charged positions. Most critics of political rhetoric have criticized such oversimplified televisual argument as problematic for the possibility of prudential citizen judgment. In *The Sound Bite Society*, Scheuer goes so far as to argue that the rift between simplex and complex public argument defines the primary distinction between those embracing liberal versus conservative political ideologies. Indeed, television, Scheuer argues, is an inherently conservative medium that favors conservative politicians and policy agendas; liberal ideology and politics, subsequently, are at a profound disadvantage.

In the case of election season policy discourse regarding the Iraq War, the campaign advertising of both major party candidates—in particular, those of President George W. Bush—tended to simplify the construction of the issue in terms of dramatic binary choices, discouraging voters from engaging the complexities of war and national security policy, and constituting a deferential public character for citizens as witnesses to political spectacle. This paper examines a selection of campaign television advertisements from the 2004 Bush and Kerry presidential campaigns that have the Iraq War (and, more broadly, the "war on terror," to the extent it is implicated with Iraq) as a central theme. Elements of videostyle and recurrent lines of argument will be analyzed and compared through close textual reading. This critical discussion explores how the televisual war rhetorics of Bush and Kerry utilize simplex or complex policy argument, and how the patterns suggest broader assumptions of ideology and public character that the candidates invite American voters to embrace. Examining such ideological and character constructions can help us understand how citizens are encouraged to consume, judge, and act upon public policy.

Campaign Advertising, Policy Argument, and Videostyle

It is obvious that campaign advertising is an important venue for public argument, particularly since advertising is positively associated, to a point, with increased voter turnout for elections (Jamieson, 2000, p. 96). Debate among critics of political advertising has occasionally centered on whether campaign ads provide enough content on matters of policy to enable citizen judgment and action, and whether the tenor of such ads affects voter behavior. Jamieson (2000) found, contrary to the assumptions of some critics, that ads attacking opponents involve more policy issue content than do so-called "positive" ads (which focus more on the image of a candidate), and that "the average contrastive ad contains nearly as high a percentage of policy content as do attack ads" (p. 106). Such contrastive ads increase both turnout and vote share (p. 113), more so than positive "advocacy" ads (p. 106). Clearly, because campaign ads often provide at least the appearance of policy content, and they affect the behavior of voters in demonstrable ways, such a medium for public policy argument requires continued attention.

While ads certainly involve issue content, the nature of the argument regarding that content may well not be the sort of argument best suited for public policy deliberation. Johnston and Kaid (2002) advance this argument, citing the emotional focus of "issue ads":

If it is surprising that image ads do not use emotion to appeal to viewers [tending to rely on credibility appeals instead], it may be even more surprising that issue ads do. For over half of the issue ads [sampled between 1952 and 2000], the language was not factual or data laden; it was emotional, designed to make voters feel something, not know something. This does support critics' concerns that televised presidential advertising is not the best place for the discussion of complex issues or details of policy concerns. (p. 298)

Examining the arguments in campaign ads requires attention to the various components of message presentation—what Kaid has referred to as "videostyle."

A sizable literature of videostyle research in political communication has utilized what Kaid (2001) explains as a "tri-component model" of ad content: verbal content, nonverbal content, and video production techniques (p. 27). "Verbal components" include such elements as "issue" or "image" characteristics, "positive" or "negative" content, types of evidence used, types of values articulated, "explicit strategies or tactics" (e.g., partisanship, incumbent or challenger styles), and other language choices (pp. 27–28). "Nonverbal components" involve such "visual . . . and audio elements" as candidate appearance and environmental elements that accompany verbal content. "Production components" are described by Kaid as "[a]spects of production such as camera angles and movement, color, editing, music and sound, lighting, camera shots, staging and setting, special effects, and other techniques" (p. 30).

Johnston and Kaid (2002) conducted a study comparing videostyle trends between issue and image ads from 1952 to 2000. They found that more issue ads attacked opponents than did image ads, that such issue ads attack issue stands and consistency more than do image ads, that they "are dominated by emotional, rather than logical appeals" (p. 288), that they use fear appeals more often, that they are more likely to use formal indoor settings and a formally dressed candidate, that they use significantly more slow motion and superimpositions, and that they are more likely to use what Trent and Friedenberg (1983) identify as "challenger" strategies of "calling for changes," "taking the offensive on issues," and "attacking the record of the opponent" (pp. 293–294). Johnston and Kaid (2002) also found that the 1990s and 2000 saw a decrease in image ads and an increase in issue ads, "but many of them featured a particular issue as the dominant focus of the ad, using the issue as the setting into which they also featured image construction" (p. 296). These findings are instructive for the present study, as such videostyle trends may have important implications for how ad audiences learn about and perceive the public policies discussed in such issue-focused ads.

In 1984, Hart studied political discourse using the DICTION program for quantitative stylistic analyses. He examined patterns of language using the categories of activity, optimism, realism, and certainty. Certainty was defined as language that conveys "resoluteness, inflexibility, and completeness" (p.

16). Using Hart's categories, a study by Ballotti and Kaid (2000) focused on the use of verbal style in presidential campaign ads from 1952 to 1996. They made several intriguing findings regarding the use of "certainty":

- Use of certainty has declined since 1980, with a huge-drop-off in 1992, and only a minor uptick in 1996;
- "Democrats tend to demonstrate less certainty (–.97) than Republicans (–.66), indicating that Democrats are less willing to make firm, resolute positions and are more willing to compromise than are Republicans" (p. 269);
- Losers use certainty less than winners; and
- Challengers use certainty less than incumbents.

Given what is widely known about Senator John Kerry's 2004 presidential campaign—that he was a Democratic challenger with a reputation (perhaps deserved, perhaps a media construction) for difficulty with taking and articulating certain decisions on policy issues and who lost to a Republican incumbent—may shed light on how Kerry's ads on the issues of the Iraq War and the "war on terror" are consistent with broader longitudinal trends in campaign ad videostyle.

For the present study, these findings also raise provocative questions regarding the styling of policy argument in televisual politics, especially the relationship between complexity, certainty, political ideology, and policy argument. Scheuer (1999) argued that the medium of television itself affects the way issues are argued and consumed; specifically, that it favors simplification over complexity.

> The electronic culture fragments information into isolated, dramatic particles and resists longer and more complex messages. These characteristics militate against a vision that emphasizes 1) change, including gradual or evolutionary change; 2) abstraction, an important tool for envisioning and framing change; 3) ambiguity and nonbinary thinking; 4) reasoning that appeals to causal, contextual, or environmental considerations; 5) divergence between appearance and reality; and 6) stronger bonds between individual, community, and nation. The sound bite culture in fact reinforces a contrary vision: one that focuses on the immediate and the obvious; the near-term, and the particular; on identity between appearance and reality; and on the self rather than larger communities. Above all, it is a society that thrives on simplicity and disdains complexity. (pp. 9–10)

Moreover, Scheuer argues that such a media culture has a built-in ideological bias: "Simplicity . . . is epitomically conservative, whereas complexity is quintessentially progressive" (p. 10). He argues that the distinction between simplicity and complexity is at the heart of the distinction between conservative and progressive thought:

> The left and right, in short, tend toward opposite ways of resolving the post-Cartesian dilemma of reconciling matter—or what we might call the

random messiness of experience—and the pristine geometry of the mind. In resolving this primal tension, conservatives (to generalize broadly) characteristically appeal to clear and rigid distinctions and dichotomies, as bulwarks of meaning and intellectual order. Complexitarians pursue a more fluid intellectual balance: not rejecting conceptual absolutes, but seeking to relax and transcend them. (p. 133)

Scheuer equates a "complexitarian" framework with a progressive standpoint on ideology and policy.

He goes on to argue that, because "[t]elevision . . . thrives on action, immediacy, specificity, and certainty" (p. 121), it filters out precisely those elements of abstraction, causality, context, and ambiguity that drive complexitarian thought and discourse. What results is a medium that intrinsically favors those with a "simplex view. . . more disposed to see the world in rigidly dichotomous, black-and-white, either/or terms" (p. 138). Scheuer describes such a mind-set as "conservative," and argues that a televisual politic that inherently favors simplex conservatism is politically problematic: "A mature democracy not only tolerates but demands respectful discourse across a broad range of responsible opinion. . . . Such respectful discourse [between progressive and conservative tendencies] is precisely what television does not deliver for American democracy at present" (p. 11). Of course, one might well argue that Scheuer's position is overly deterministic and itself oversimplified, that the equation of simplex and conservative thought, and of complex and progressive thought, may be a product of late-twentieth-century, post-Reagan political coincidence rather than an intrinsic reality of televisual politics. In any event, pairing Scheuer's argument with the results of campaign ad videostyle research raises important questions for the present study. In brief: (1) Does the videostyle of 2004 presidential campaign "issue ads" concerning the Iraq War and the "war on terror" reflect previous findings regarding the use of contrastive and attack strategies, emotional (especially fear) appeals, or the presence or absence of certainty language? (2) To what extent do these campaign ads reinforce or call into question Scheuer's claims regarding the relationship between complexity, political ideology, and televisual political success?

Analysis of Campaign 2004 Advertisements on the Iraq War and the "War on Terror"

The present study provides an initial attempt at what will be a more comprehensive examination of 2004 presidential campaign issue advertisements concerning the separate yet related (and often conflated) Iraq War and the "war on terror." A sample of ten television advertisements was acquired from the Web site for the Political Communication Lab (PCL) at Stanford University, which includes an archive of all of the ads run during the general election, as well as ads run during the primary campaign by Kerry and Bush from 2003 to October 2004. All ads involving the Iraq War or the "war on terror" as the primary content focus were identified for the sample. The analysis discussed here examined five ads from each campaign that illustrate the primary videostyle and argumentative tendencies of each candidate's televisual war rhetoric throughout the 2004 campaign. Specifically, this analysis examined (1) patterns of verbal style, (2) patterns of nonverbal style, and (3) patterns of production techniques. While research in the videostyle literature uses a process of quantitative coding and analysis to examine a large number of texts, the following analysis uses close textual reading in order to describe and interpret the interplay between these three videostyle dimensions in a richer fashion. The results of this analysis lay a foundation for a more complete analysis of the larger sample, which will be conducted at a later stage in this project.

This analysis explores the ways campaign ad videostyle constructs televisual arguments regarding the Iraq War and the "war on terror"; particularly, I am interested in the extent to which (a) the televisual medium forces the hands of both campaigns to rely on simplex ideological argument and (b) whether either candidate (but presumably Kerry) operates within the strictures of televisual argument to construct a complexitarian ideological message that involves the following characteristics identified by Scheuer (1999): (1) change; (2) abstraction; (3) ambiguity and nonbinary thinking; (4) contingent reasoning; (5) "divergence between appearance and reality"; and (6) "stronger bonds between individual, community, and nation" (pp. 9–10).

Bush Campaign Videostyle for Iraq War Ads

Five ads from the Bush-Cheney 2004 campaign were selected for this analysis: "Troops Fog—Revision" and "Weapons," both airing during April and May of 2004, and "Searching," "Windsurfing," and "Whatever It Takes," all airing during October 2004. Close examination of these ads confirms the claims of Scheuer that ideological conservatives benefit from the norms of televisual discourse.

Verbal Videostyle. While there is much in the verbal content of the arguments presented in these ads, four characteristic strategies in these ads seem especially significant. First, these ads construct the issues and available positions exclusively as "yes/no" or "for/against" binaries. Moreover, the positions presented within these parameters (and they are usually Kerry's positions that are attacked in the ads) are presented without any contextual information regarding the details behind the decisions. This makes the construction of Kerry as a flip-flopper who surfs "whichever way the wind blows" (Bush-Cheney, 2004e) that much easier—because it is enticing to expect that a decision as easy as "yes" or "no," especially one untouched by temporality or contingent circumstances, should remain stable.

Second, Kerry's vocal comments are included frequently with video clips of Kerry from television interviews and rallies, enabling the ads to focus on "Kerry's own words" as the basis for an argument that his positions are inconsistent and incoherent. One notable example is "Searching" (Bush-

Cheney, 2004a), in which six televised Kerry statements are presented back to back, followed by the accusatory question, "How can John Kerry protect us when he doesn't even know where he stands?" At the same time, Kerry's statements are sharply edited, often cutting in mid-sentence to prevent any explanation, while Bush's vocal comments, when presented (and they rarely are), are allowed to play out unfiltered and uninterrupted. The result is that Kerry's comments are both decontextualized and stylistically choppy. The combination leaves the impression that Kerry's statements are ill-considered, often contradictory, and bereft of explanatory detail. By contrast, the "Whatever It Takes" ad (Bush-Cheney, 2004d) provides Bush an uninterrupted sixty seconds to develop a coherent, vivid, and moving narrative.

Third, describing the conflict as the "Iraq War" or "war in Iraq" is rarely done in the Bush ads, unless the words are used to identify an apparent contradiction in Kerry's position, or they are spoken by Kerry himself. Otherwise, the present conflict is identified only as the "war on terror." This gives Bush not only an inherent persuasive advantage in being able continually to rely on post-9/11 fear appeals to solidify emotional support, but also enables him to label Kerry as "soft on terrorism" or, fantastically, one who aids and comforts the objectives of terrorists against American citizens generally and soldiers particularly. Any distinction between the war in Iraq and antiterrorism policy is erased in these ads.

Finally, and relatedly, Bush's pro-war positions are usually phrased in terms of (a) "supporting the troops" and their "families," and sometimes "veterans," and (b) "defending America against terrorists" and "national/homeland security." This naming strategy enables the Bush campaign to more effectively frame Kerry's opposition to the administration's Iraq War policy as "antitroops," and therefore beyond reasonable defense. At the same time, war policy is never discussed as an offensive military action, never discussed in terms of regime change, nation building, and so forth. Because it is always "against terrorists," and always in "self-defense," Bush can make a just war argument without actually identifying the war that is actually being fought.

Nonverbal Videostyle. To complement these patterns of verbal style, three patterns of nonverbal depictions function to establish a close relationship between Bush and his ideal American audience (soldiers, their families, and those who support them), while casting Kerry as a detached outsider at best and an enemy at worst.

First, the nonverbal depiction of Kerry works to isolate him. He is usually in the frame alone (unless shown with dour looking veterans who apparently disagree with him). Moreover, the spots are edited so that Kerry is juxtaposed against soldiers, their families, veterans, and so on as groups from whom he is detached. Visually, there is "Kerry," and there is everyone else. In addition, when Kerry speaks, he is usually in close-up, sounding severe and pointing his finger or is otherwise depicted in a visually distorted and/or unpresidential manner (e.g., extreme close-ups, in surfer attire).

Second, Bush's nonverbal depiction works to shape his character in conventional ways for an incumbent presidential candidate. Bush is either depicted alone, in a presidential context and appearance—dark suits, White House backdrops—dressed casually as a middle-class Everyman with his wife at the ranch, or surrounded by crowds of supporters (e.g., in the middle of an RNC spectacle, or surrounded by loyal, smiling troops). Visually, Bush is both one with his ideal American audience and first among equals, standing out in "presidential" fashion.

Finally, the extras that flesh out the dramatis personae in these ads depict the ideal American audience in ways that reinforce Bush's verbal identification of the beneficiaries of the "war on terror." There are numerous images of soldiers in most every ad (except some of those focused on attacking Kerry), as well as frequent images of families (entire ones, or represented by images of children or middle-aged women) and recurrent images of veterans (who listen raptly to the president, but with disdain to Kerry). The implications are predictable, unsurprising, but nonetheless important for the narrative Bush constructs surrounding Iraq: the president, and the war, are intended to protect and serve the well-being of soldiers, families, and veterans, and anyone who isn't with them is, in a binary world, against them and with the terrorists.

Production Techniques Videostyle. The use of editing techniques and special effects to shape and dramatize the argument are a central feature of videostyle. Bush's ads on the "war on terror" reveal some interesting patterns that function with the verbal and nonverbal patterns to isolate Kerry and his positions on the Iraq War.

First, camera shots that display Bush and his positions positively are longer, lingering, and fade in and out gently. They are presented with sharp, vivid, and colorful visuals and are accompanied by positive, upbeat music. This serves to focus viewer attention on Bush as he articulates his message, as well as to frame that message as an emotionally satisfying one. This tendency is seen especially clearly in "Whatever It Takes" (Bush-Cheney, 2004d), an ad that provides sixty uninterrupted seconds of Bush reaching out to those grieving the sacrifices of soldiers and their families, his face occasionally intercut with the admiring faces of his primary constituent groups, complete with stirring string and horn music and a vividly colorful background.

On the other hand, camera shots of Kerry frequently involve visual distortion (e.g., blurry images, images that appear to be "on videotape," etc.), quick-cuts, and rapidly edited transitions. His spoken comments are usually quick, cut-off sound bites that at times clearly present a statement in a decontextualized state—as evidenced by Kerry's vocal inflection, indicating that the sentence is about to continue. The clearest example of this can be seen in the "Searching" spot (Bush-Cheney, 2004a), where numerous clips of Kerry expressing seemingly contradictory messages supporting and opposing the war are displayed in a television. The clips indicate no temporal sequence, are not presented with any citation information, and a couple of them (including the infamous "I actually did vote for the $87 billion, before I voted against it" line) are cut off before Kerry's explanation can follow.

Second, verbal titles, labels, and emphasized assertions often appear in white text on a black screen. In the "Searching" ad, the effect was punctuated by a slashing blue light. The stark contrast draws the viewer's eyes to the message, conveys a sense of drama (usually foreboding, in the case of Kerry attack ads), and may perhaps connote the "black and white" view of policy controversy advanced by the Bush campaign.

Finally, Bush's ads make frequent use of dramatization via special effects and editing to depict the consequences of Kerry's record and positions on Iraq. "Weapons" (Bush-Cheney, 2004c) does so most cinematically, depicting a desert battlefield in which crucial weapons vanish into thin air as a soldier looks on, concerned. "Troops Fog—Revision" (Bush-Cheney, 2004b) creates a story via editing in which Kerry and the Senate are set in dramatic opposition to combat troops and their families. "Searching" (Bush-Cheney, 2004a) uses a series of Kerry statements to weave a narrative of indecision and contradiction as ominous music plays in the background. "Windsurfing" (Bush-Cheney, 2004e), designed expressly to ridicule, pairs footage of Kerry windsurfing near a large yacht with "Blue Danube" playing in the background and was edited to switch directions rapidly back and forth to correspond with allegedly switching positions on a series of issues. In "Whatever It Takes" (Bush-Cheney, 2004d), Bush's sole positive advocacy ad in this sample (and one of only two such ads in the Stanford PCL archive focused on the "war on terror"), Bush uses dramatic anecdotes about soldiers and their families to construct a compelling encomium of the military that he connects to his strong leadership in defending America.

In short, the videostyle of Bush constructs a televisual argument that assumes that decisions should take the form of "yes" or "no"; that they should endure regardless of circumstance; that, indeed, specific circumstances should not be the subject of deliberation; and that the criteria for decision making should be grounded in principle, but those principles are defined through emotion (particularly fear) and identification with ideal American identities (particularly soldiers, families, and the president). Such a simplex argument is consistent with Scheuer's assumptions regarding both the norms of televisual discourse and the discourse of political conservatives.

Kerry Campaign Videostyle for Iraq War Ads

Five ads from the Kerry-Edwards 2004 campaign were selected for this analysis: "No, Mr. President," airing during the 2004 election preprimary period; "Risk," airing in April and May of 2004; "Different Story" and "Doesn't Get It," airing during September 2004; and "He's Lost, He's Desperate," airing in October 2004. Examination of these ads reveals that, while Kerry's argument is certainly more complexitarian in character than Bush's, the norms of televisual discourse constrain the Kerry argument in ways that make it uncomfortable or unsatisfying for television viewers.

Verbal Videostyle. At least four recurrent characteristics of verbal content in the Kerry campaign ads seem significant. First, Kerry's verbal content provides more policy-oriented detail than Bush's ads. This is done in two ways. The ads provide specific detail regarding the current, worsening situation in Iraq (e.g., mounting casualties, mounting financial costs, etc., with added attention late in the campaign to terrorist attacks on Americans and the benchmark statistic of 1,000 dead U.S. troops) as well as public comments by Bush that seem to fly in the face of evidence presented as journalistically documented fact. The ads also provide an explicit, recurrent set of three policy actions referred to as "the Kerry plan": "getting allies to share the burden," "helping Iraqis protect themselves," and "taking real steps for free elections" (Kerry-Edwards, 2004a, b, d). By contrast, the ads describe Bush's Iraq policy as a nonpolicy. They construct a narrative in which the president rushed the United States to war without a "plan to win the peace," and now has no "plan for Iraq" while Americans die. Of course, the development of "the Kerry plan" is limited solely to a set of four broad, unobjectionable objectives. This "plan" is not only bereft of specific details or explanation, but also is impossible to distinguish from what was most probably the plan of the Bush administration in the first place. Still, Kerry lays out a set of four policy planks, while Bush presents none.

Second, while the Kerry campaign certainly makes use of anonymous off-screen announcers when attacking Bush, Kerry's primary season ads involve Kerry speaking directly to the camera, at length, articulating his argument. Only one ad in the Bush sample, by contrast, does this, however, "Iraq" and war policy is not specifically discussed. This tendency of Kerry's lessens during the general election ads, presumably so he can avoid levying direct, negative attacks on the president himself.

Third, a good deal of Kerry's verbal content is supplemented with graphics that resemble clipped headlines from newspapers, accompanied by on-screen source citations. While a similar tactic is used by Bush in several ads, Kerry's usage involves information specific to the Iraq War, while Bush's use of verbal content from news sources primarily involves attacks on Kerry's personal statements rather than on the objective conditions in Iraq and the specific planning and execution of the war (with the possible exception of "Troops Fog—Revision" from April–May 2004, which includes barely visible citations of specific Senate votes in the Congressional Record).

Finally, Kerry's arguments (both attacking Bush and presenting his own "plan") present elements of verbal content in at least two simultaneous forms—vocally presented by Kerry or an announcer and verbal text displayed on-screen (as a caption or as a simulated newspaper headline clipping, and sometimes both in the same ad). The repetition is sometimes identical or close to it, while in other ads vocal and caption delivery present information while a news clipping graphic displays something related but distinct. For instance, in "Different Story" (Kerry-Edwards 2004, September) the four plan planks detailed above are presented by the announcer and the captions, while a clipping graphic states "Kerry Outlines Plan to Fix Iraq." In this way, the verbal content is presented through multiple modes, hitting the viewer simultaneously from different directions.

Nonverbal Videostyle. As in the Bush ads, nonverbal videostyle is used by the Kerry campaign to establish his ethos as a leader—both directly and indirectly via Bush's depiction in the ads. This is done especially in two recurrent patterns.

First, Kerry simply appears more often in his ads concerning Iraq and the "war on terror." Of the five Bush ads sampled, Bush appears as a key character only in "Whatever it Takes" (Bush-Cheney, 2004d), an ad that presents footage from his nomination acceptance address and mentions neither Kerry nor "Iraq" directly. Kerry is at least nonverbally a key character in all five ads sampled for this study, beyond the "I approved this message" element. One implication of this difference is that Kerry seems more willing to associate himself with his policy positions—particularly by using contrastive ads, in which Bush's record is attacked and Kerry's platform is provided as a preferable alternative. Such a message provides viewers with a clearer sense of choice between options than Bush's ads, which tend to attack Kerry's positions without providing a positive alternative. Another implication of this difference, however, is that Kerry is more easily associated with Iraq-oriented messages, especially attacks. Bush's appearance in attack ads is minimal, and he never makes any reference to Iraq himself in any of his ads. Therefore, Kerry is the only one reminding the audience that Iraq is a mess, while Bush limits himself to vague messages regarding self-defense against terrorists.

Second (and perhaps predictably for a challenger, especially a wealthy northeastern liberal seeking to broaden his appeal), Kerry is frequently presented in intimate settings. Early in the campaign, when he had to establish name/face recognition with primary voters, Kerry speaks directly to voters—either straight into the camera, or to an off-screen focus as if he is being interviewed. These ads involve close-up visual shots that give viewers the impression of being in close proximity. In several other ads, Kerry is shown at rallies and campaign events with numerous audience members in close proximity, in the immediate background or in the off-screen foreground. The strategy gives the impression that Kerry's positions on Iraq are being willingly and personally shared, as opposed to Bush, who is only seen in these ads alone or with close associates or his wife (in the "I approved this message" clips), or speaking to a massive Republican National Convention audience, and then not specifically about Iraq. While Kerry is mixing it up with the people, Bush is leading as president, a strong, solitary figure.

Relatedly, Kerry is frequently presented in shirtsleeves rather than in a suit. Whether the scene is a rally or an intimate talking head spot, Kerry conveys himself as active, perhaps more active than the strictures of a suit can allow. The exceptions to this rule occur in ads immediately following the Democratic National Convention and air late in the campaign, when Kerry apparently wants to appear more "presidential." While Bush is depicted in short shirtsleeves at times, this is only during the "I approved this message" scene in which he stands with his wife on the porch of his ranch. For Kerry, shirtsleeves are presented as a sign of activity and identification with his immediate audience; for Bush, the incumbent president, shirtsleeves are only for home, and reinforce his character as a strong, masculine figure.

Production Techniques Videostyle.   Kerry's ads utilize some elements of editing, special effects, and dramatization in ways similar to Bush's ads. Visual depictions of Kerry are always sharp, focused, and colorful, while Bush is depicted in obvious video footage captures that are often blurry and presented in slow motion. Important verbal content is presented on black screens with white text that often emerges incrementally or is highlighted by flashing light effects. Ominous music accompanies attacks on Bush, while upbeat and pleasing music accompanies Kerry's presence on-screen. However, at least two characteristics of Kerry's production style are distinct from Bush's ads in ways that contribute to a sense of activity and complexity in the messages.

First, Kerry's ads make frequent use of handheld camera shots with wavering and rapid pans, along with quick cuts to a similar shot with a slightly different angle or distance, in a cinema verité style. Even in some of his talking head spots, this style conveys a sense of natural movement, speed, and raw activity. The viewer is given the impression that these images are being conveyed as they happen, without a smooth, polished production style. Not all of Kerry's ads use this cinema verité style, but significantly more of them use this style than do Bush's ads, which tend to be more controlled and stylishly shot ("Windsurfing" from October 2004 is an exception, but this ad depicts Kerry in action, not Bush).

Second, compared to Bush's ads, Kerry's ads often contain multiple verbal and visual elements in the same scene. "Different Story" and "Doesn't Get It" (Kerry-Edwards 2004, September) involve extended sequences when multiple video clips, verbal captions, news headline clipping graphics, and vocal content from an announcer are all present at once, conveying the same broad point with different forms and details at the same time. The viewer is subject to sensory overload, taking in a lot simultaneously and having to process it to apprehend a single central point. These sequences also present a few specific factual points in succession, resulting in a fast flurry of clips, captions, clippings, and narration hitting the viewer with a barrage of information. The fact that these ads feature the horrific situation in Iraq against a black screen background makes the experience all the more intense. By contrast, Bush's combinations of verbal and nonverbal elements is kept relatively cleaner, presenting a single unified image or two juxtaposed images at the most (the exception, "Searching" from October 2004, provides a rapid succession of video clips of Kerry, which is, again, designed to make Kerry seem frenetic).

The dramatization that results from these production patterns involves emotional fear appeal, as do Bush's ads. However, the thematic and argumentative thrust of these ads are different from Bush's in at least two important ways: (1) they deal expressly with the war in Iraq, unlike most of Bush's ads, and (2) they critique and challenge Bush's policy based on the terrible conditions in Iraq at the time. The ads, perhaps by necessity for the argument, must depict violence, destruction, and soldiers in peril. The closest Bush's ads come to this is making weapons disappear on a fictional battlefield. Therefore, the dramatization in Kerry's ads is more concrete, visual, and factual in its connection to the experiences of soldiers at war and depicting policy failure and the need to repair it. Bush's dramatization, by contrast, is focused more on Kerry as an untrustworthy character whose past actions are responsible for putting soldiers, theoretically if not factually, at risk.

Discussion: The Construction of Public Character in Televisual Argument on the War

One important goal for public argument—particularly regarding acceptable approaches to argue about and judge policy issues—is the promotion of a "civic culture, one based on communication and persuasion" (Denton, 1991, p. 5). Walzer (1995) argues that "only a democratic civil society can sustain a democratic state," and "civil society is tested by its capacity to produce citizens whose interests, at least sometimes, reach further than themselves and their comrades, who look after the political community" (pp. 104, 105). To maintain a functional democratic system capable of pursuing the good for its citizens, the citizens within that system must possess political agency: the capacity to act as "authoritative and responsible participants" (p. 105) in public life. The normative goal of civil society provides critics with a central criterion for evaluating political rhetoric: Does the rhetorical performance construct a "citizen" capable of democratic public discourse and efficacious action? Or does it restrain (or eliminate) the capacity of the political subject to participate in public life as a citizen?

"Public character"—the constitution of idealized norms of political agency via the construction of ethos (Klien, 1999, 2000, 2002, 2005)—is a normative argument regarding two connected relationships. A construction of public character enacts an "ideological worldview": a perspective of how the sociopolitical world works and a relationship of political agency between the agent and the larger world (indicating the available, and best, ways to act in public). A construction of public character also enacts a relationship of civic friendship between the rhetor and the audience (indicating a level of respect and identification with other persons within a public community). Ideally, these relationships will be composed of a reciprocal sharing of community values and the possibility for open, interactive ethical conduct through civil discourse and political action, both individual and collective.

Two broad approaches to televisual argument on the Iraq War and the "war on terror" were present during Campaign 2004. The first approach, presented by George W. Bush, constructs an evocative narrative about a broad, vague "war on terror" pitting valorous troops and their families against terrorists who attack America. This narrative emphasizes personal character, imagery, and fundamental values of patriotism and self-defense. In the world of this narrative, to paraphrase the president, one is either with the soldiers or with the terrorists. Bush's opponent is therefore depicted as an unprincipled antagonist who is contradictory and confused at best, antisoldier and proterrorist at worst. This narrative does not mention the war in Iraq specifically, because for Bush Iraq is but one component of a broader war, one nearly impossible to oppose without tolerating terrorism in a post-9/11 world.

The second approach, presented by Senator John Kerry, constructs a very different narrative, one that actually addresses the war in Iraq in a direct manner. This narrative attempts to present the complexities of policy decision making by directly presenting such aspects of war policy as the initial decision to go to war, the case made to the American people to get popular approval, the actual execution of the war (and whether it should involve international involvement), and the presence (or absence) of a plan to conclude the war. This narrative attempts to convince American voters that one can support the war on terror and oppose the war in Iraq at the same time, that one can have a nuanced position that can change as circumstances change, and that one can oppose the commander-in-chief and still support the military.

In a post-9/11 America during a time of war, it may be that Americans prefer stability and reassurance to critical argument. Therefore, a simplex depiction of military policy might make such policy appear more easily understandable and worthy of support by U.S. media audiences, and subsequently make more ambivalent, ambiguous, or otherwise complex depictions appear devoid of foundational principles or a sound rationale. Gauging audience preferences and responses to these ads is beyond the present scope of this study. What does seem clear, however, is that while the videostyle resources of television advertising may be used to communicate substantive policy argument, such argument must be compromised of nuance and complex detail for stylistic and emotional clarity. Moreover, direct engagement of policy issue details can make a candidate vulnerable to attack—either because an opponent can frame the argument negatively via videostyle, and/or because the engagement itself is too complicated to effectively communicate in a thirty- or sixty-second spot. In any event, the articulation of war policy in the presidential campaign advertising of 2004 didn't provide American voters with a clear, direct debate on the issues that they could use to deliberate, judge, and act on in a prudent, informed way. Such a reluctance to engage this debate, particularly on the part of the Bush administration and campaign, relegated American citizens to the position of passive audiences to a simple yet emotionally compelling spectacle. Unfortunately, such a short-term spectacle may displace the critical public discussion necessary to engage in more rational public policy in the first place.

Indeed, at the time of this writing (well beyond Campaign 2004), public support for an American military presence in Iraq has waned dramatically since the successful regime change in Iraq, the apprehension of Saddam Hussein, and a series of revelations regarding the manipulation of intelligence data by members of the Bush administration in order to craft a persuasive but misleading rationale for war. A *Newsweek* poll conducted November 10–11, 2005 revealed that 65% of Americans disapprove of the way President Bush is "handling the situation in Iraq," while only 30% approve. An NBC News/ *Wall Street Journal* poll on November 4–7, 2005 found that 57% of Americans believe President Bush deliberately misled the United States into war with Iraq, 58% believe he has not given good reasons for why troops must remain in Iraq, and 52% now believe that removing Saddam Hussein from power was not worth "U.S. military casualties and the financial cost of the war" (The Polling Report, Inc., 2005). This contrasts against polling in June 2004, when 55% of Americans believed that military action in Iraq was the right decision, while only 39% reported following events in Iraq closely and 35% reported that "people they know are becoming less emotionally involved in the news from Iraq" (Pew Research Center, 2004). These figures also stand in stark contrast to January 2002, when 73% supported military action in Iraq to remove Hussein—56% maintaining support even if it meant thousands of American casualties (Pew Research Center, 2002).

While the presence of simple, vivid campaign advertisements from the Bush campaign in 2004 was certainly not a sole cause for perpetuating American popular support for the war at that time, it is undeniable that these messages and the narrative they constructed provided a rationale for action more comprehensible and compelling to less well-informed audiences than the esoteric complexities of military resource allocation and regional geopolitical stability in the Middle East. As legions of yellow ribbon decorations evidence (as they did in 1991), the average American's closest identification with the U.S. military is with the women and men who serve in it as soldiers and support staff, rather than with civilian politicians and the vagaries of military policy. Since Campaign 2004, however, the absence of Hussein, weapons of mass destruction, and credible links to 9/11 have left a televisual vacuum that was inevitably filled by news reports of U.S. soldiers in Iraq killed and wounded by anonymous, faceless insurgents. It makes sense, then, that support for a U.S. military presence in Iraq has dropped precipitously since Campaign 2004.

An affinity for personalities and visual images in contemporary politics may be seen in relation to another important phenomenon in contemporary democratic political culture, described in various contexts as a "crisis of legitimacy." Sullivan (1986) defines such a crisis as a fundamental inability of the liberal political tradition to provide either a viable justification for political institutions or a basis for social life. Sullivan's argument is that the liberal emphasis on the individual places a premium on the exercise of autonomous self-interest and attempts to organize social life on a market-based equilibrium. However, Sullivan notes at least two complications. First, the pursuit of self-interest is such that political institutions can never satisfy the various competing needs of a nation of isolated individuals. Second, liberal rationality is inherently limited in that it can provide no moral rationale for the exercise of public agency as a community. Citizens in a classically liberal political culture are in it for themselves and their families, not for their communities. The challenge for political leaders and institutions, then, is to establish a compelling answer to the omnipresent "so what?" question that drives liberal democratic political culture.

Since September 11th, however, the "it's the economy, stupid" paradigm that drove American political preferences during the 1990s has been superseded in large part by a paradigm of "it's the war, stupid," featuring principally national security and the safety of Americans from military threats at the hands of terrorists and rogue powers. The American political culture, after September 11th, was infused with a sense of fervent patriotism it has not experienced since the first Reagan term, when Cold War patriotism provided the grounding rationale for military growth, foreign policy choices, and the required government spending. A semblance of community may arise under such conditions to fulfill the void left by the individualism of liberal philosophy. However, the "legitimacy crisis" is still in place, albeit in altered form: Americans approve of their soldier patriots and their national values but view civilian politicians with trepidation and seem to distrust any activity by their political leaders that appears to call into question the patriotic feelings and personal sense of safety felt by American individuals and families.

This ambivalence was reflected in the reluctance of many politicians to risk their political careers in 2002 and 2004 by publicly calling the president's foreign policy platform into question during the debate over invading Iraq and by the painstaking care taken by Bush's political opponents in 2004 to support the American military even as they proclaimed their opposition to the Iraq War. In these years, successful American politicians spoke primarily with one voice opposed to Hussein; dissenters were ousted from office or defeated handily as campaign challengers. For instance, in 2002 former U.S. senator and Vietnam war hero Max Cleland was attacked in television advertisements displaying him with images of Hussein and bin Laden, and in 2004 the outspoken war critic and early media favorite Howard Dean was blasted out of the Democratic presidential primaries at the start.

Hence, as the 2004 election made plain, publicly declared opposition to the war in Iraq (or even guardedly supportive positions that nonetheless critiqued the execution of the policy, such as those articulated by Kerry) was vulnerable to demagogic attacks, especially in advertising from Republican candidates and Republican-friendly independent organizations such as Swift Boat Veterans for Truth and the Progress for America Voter Fund. To oppose the war was to oppose the mission and sacrifices of the American soldier, a patently unpatriotic and dangerous position indeed. With Saddam Hussein no longer an enemy to combat, and an elusive Osama bin Laden downplayed as an enemy by the Bush administration (perhaps due to years of failed attempts to locate him), multiple Purple Heart recipient Kerry was, ironically, vilified as an enemy of the soldier and therefore unworthy to serve as commander-in-chief.

Such discourse patterns raise an important question: When televisual images and patriotic feelings dominate the public discourse at the expense of complex policy details, to what extent are political institutions and critical public discourse actually legitimized? Hart's (1999) treatment of the role of the popular media in televisual political education suggests at least one important implication: Examining how military policy is argued in campaign advertising can shed some light on how contemporary American audiences are engaging in mediated political learning in ways that can impact the conduct of public policy debate on military matters. The media teach the public audience which institutions, thought processes, and values to embrace and engage, and which to distrust and keep distant.

Sullivan's (1986) proposed alternative to the liberal tradition provides an ethical standpoint for evaluating the rhetorical constructions of public character embedded in popular culture texts. Sullivan argues that the traditional (and often overlooked) counterpart to liberalism, a public philosophy of "civic republicanism," provides a superior foundation for political action. He defines "civic republicanism" as denying that "individuality exists outside of or prior to social relationships" (p. 21):

> Instead, the republican tradition has taught that there is an ineluctably participatory aspect to political understanding that develops only through the moral maturation of mutual responsibility. . . . [T]here are qualities of social relations, such as mutual concern and respect, that transcend utility and that can be learned only in practice. (p. 21)

For Sullivan, contemporary republicanism "requires at once a moral culture and an institutional basis" appropriate to the conditions of contemporary society (p. 209). Specifically, a democratic political culture driven by a civic republican ethos requires legitimate political institutions that encourage critical public discourse on policy issues. Such a position is consistent with Scheuer's (1999) argument that televisual discourse fails to provide the "respectful discourse"—a discourse tolerant of ambiguity and complexity—that a "mature democracy" requires (p. 11). To the extent that the American polity is not encouraged by political institutions to develop its interest and critical-thinking skills in policy discourse, what Scheuer describes as a "critical spirit" (p. 190), those institutions may hold less public legitimacy even as they enjoy public emotional approval.

Civic republicanism provides a normative goal that is relevant for the present study as well as for continued critical study in this area. Assuming the desirability of a democratic public condition that is oriented actively toward the critical examination of public policy, such study can examine the extent to which policy arguments in a televisual campaign context function to encourage critical civic engagement of policy issues—or to discourage it, or to repudiate the need for public involvement entirely.

Conclusion

The results of this analysis suggest that the public character constructed by the war-related presidential campaign advertisements in 2004—be it due to the inherent tendencies of television videostyle, or due to the specific ideological agendas of the candidates—diminished the civic importance of tolerating and examining complex, ambivalent, and fluid positions on military policy. Moreover, the oversimplification of policy critique to a reverent depiction of soldiers and the values attached to the soldier culture—duty, professionalism, sacrifice, bravery—also serves to marginalize ethical assessment of policy making on the part of American audiences. Voters in 2004 were presented two options regarding the war in Iraq: the simple choice of supporting soldiers and their values (and therefore supporting the war, and Bush), or the more complex choice of supporting the war in broad principle but opposing Bush's rationale for the war and his execution of military policy. The choice of the U.S. voter tended toward simplicity.

References

Ballotti, J., & Kaid, L. L. (2000). Examining verbal style in presidential campaign spots. *Communication Studies, 51*(3), 258–273.

Bush-Cheney 2004, Inc. (2004a). "Searching." Advertisement. Retrieved from Political Communication Lab, Stanford University Web site: http://pcl.stanford.edu/campaigns/campaign2004/archive.html

Bush-Cheney 2004, Inc. (2004b). "Troops fog—Revision." Advertisement. Retrieved from Political Communication Lab, Stanford University Web site: http://pcl.stanford.edu/campaigns/campaign2004/archive.html

Bush-Cheney 2004, Inc. (2004c). "Weapons." Advertisement. Retrieved from Political Communication Lab, Stanford University Web site: http://pcl.stanford.edu/campaigns/campaign2004/archive.html

Bush-Cheney 2004, Inc. (2004d). "Whatever it takes." Advertisement. Retrieved from Political Communication Lab, Stanford University Web site: http://pcl.stanford.edu/campaigns/campaign2004/archive.html

Bush-Cheney 2004, Inc. (2004e). "Windsurfing." Advertisement. Retrieved from Political Communication Lab, Stanford University Web site: http://pcl.stanford.edu/campaigns/campaign2004/archive.html

Cooke, L. (2003). Information acceleration and visual trends in print, television, and web news sources. *Technical Communication Quarterly, 12,* 155–181.

Denton, R. E., Jr. (1991). Political communication ethics: An oxymoron? In R. E. Denton, Jr. (Ed.), *Ethical dimensions of political communication* (pp. 1–5). New York: Praeger.

Gladney, G. A. (1993). USA Today, its imitators, and its critics: Do newsroom staffs face an ethical dilemma? *Journal of Mass Media Ethics, 8,* 17–36.

Hart, R. P. (1984). *Verbal style and the presidency: A computer-based analysis.* San Francisco: Academic Press.

Hart, R. P. (1999). *Seducing America: How television charms the modern voter* (Rev. ed.). Thousand Oaks, CA: Sage.

Jamieson, K. H. (2000). *Everything you think you know about politics . . . and why you're wrong.* New York: Basic Books.

Johnston, A., & Kaid, L. L. (2002). Image ads and issue ads in U.S. presidential advertising: Using videostyle to explore stylistic differences in televised political ads from 1952 to 2000. *Journal of Communication, 52,* 281–300.

Kaid, L. L. (2001). *Videostyle in presidential campaigns: Style and content of presidential advertising.* Westport, CT: Praeger.

Kerry-Edwards 2004, Inc. (2003). "No, Mr. President." Advertisement. Retrieved from Political Communication Lab, Stanford University Web site: http://pcl.stanford.edu/campaigns/campaign2004/archive.html

Kerry-Edwards 2004, Inc. (2004a). "Different story." Advertisement. Retrieved from Political Communication Lab, Stanford University Web site: http://pcl.stanford.edu/campaigns/campaign2004/archive.html

Kerry-Edwards 2004, Inc. (2004b). "Doesn't get it." Advertisement. Retrieved from Political Communication Lab, Stanford University Web site: http://pcl.stanford.edu/campaigns/campaign2004/archive.html

Kerry-Edwards 2004, Inc. (2004c). "He's lost, he's desperate." Advertisement. Retrieved from Political Communication Lab, Stanford University Web site: http://pcl.stanford.edu/campaigns/campaign2004/archive.html

Kerry-Edwards 2004, Inc. (2004d). "Risk." Advertisement. Retrieved from Political Communication Lab, Stanford University Web site: http://pcl.stanford.edu/campaigns/campaign2004/archive.html

Klien, S. A. (1999). Rhetorical constitution of public character and conservative ideology in the 1996 Republican presidential primary campaign. *Dissertation Abstracts International, 60,* 03A.

Klien, S. A. (2000). Defining "public character:" Agency and the ethical criticism of public argument. In T. A. Hollihan (Ed.), *Argument at century's end: Reflecting on the past and envisioning the future* (pp. 341–350). Annandale, VA: National Communication Association.

Klien, S. A. (2002). Romantic heroism and "public character": Ethical criticism of performative traditions in public discourse. In F. Antczak, C. Coggins, & G. Klinger (Eds.), *Professing rhetoric: Selected papers from the 2000 Rhetoric Society of America conference* (pp. 139–146). Mahwah, NJ: Lawrence Erlbaum.

Klien, S. A. (2005). Public character and the simulacrum: The construction of the soldier patriot and citizen agency in *Black Hawk Down. Critical Studies in Media Communication, 22,* 427–449.

Pew Research Center for the People and the Press. (2002, January 22). *Americans favor force in Iraq, Somalia, Sudan and. . . .* Retrieved July 8, 2004, from http://people-press.org/reports/display.php3?ReportID=148

Pew Research Center for the People and the Press. (2004, June 17). *Public support for the war resilient: Bush's standing improves.* Retrieved July 8, 2004, from http://people-press.org/reports/display.php3?ReportID=148

The Polling Report, Inc. (2005). Iraq. *PollingReport.com.* Retrieved November 13, 2005, from http://www.pollingreport.com/iraq.htm

Scheuer, J. (1999). *The sound bite society: Television and the American mind.* New York: Four Walls Eight Windows.

Sullivan, W. M. (1986). *Reconstructing public philosophy.* Berkeley: University of California Press.

Trent, J. S., & Friedenberg, R. V. (1983). *Political campaign communication: Principles and practices.* New York: Praeger.

Walzer, M. (1992). The civil argument. In C. Mouffe (Ed.), *Dimensions of radical democracy: Pluralism, citizenship, community* (pp. 89–107). London: Verso.

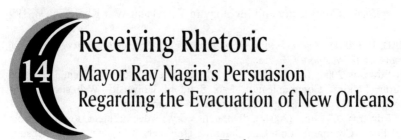

Receiving Rhetoric
14 Mayor Ray Nagin's Persuasion
Regarding the Evacuation of New Orleans

Karen Taylor

For those who live in New Orleans, hurricane evacuation rhetoric is a normal feature of every summer/early fall, a genre that is mostly formulaic. The genre could probably be categorized as part of a broader grouping of "emergency preparation" rhetoric; the most familiar example for many of you probably being winter snowstorm closings. According to Beck, emergency preparation rhetoric seems to be an increasingly frequent characteristic of our modern "risk society." There are differences across occasions, and to some extent there are differences across rhetors, but as a rhetorical act these speeches seem singularly uninteresting because of their formulaity. That is, hurricane evacuation rhetoric seems uninteresting rhetorically until suddenly an event like Hurricane Katrina creates an awareness of how much hinges on successful persuasion. Rhetoric in this context can be, very literally, a matter of life and death: if the rhetors had been more successful, and had successfully persuaded the tens of thousands who remained in New Orleans to evacuate before the storm, it might have saved over 1,500 lives, and would have spared tens of thousands more from the nightmarish experience of being trapped in a drowning city.

For this paper, I have multiple goals. My first is identification and description of the features of the genre of hurricane evacuation rhetoric. My second will be to identify the constraints on rhetors regarding this genre, and also to identify the expectations and constraints of the audience in responding to evacuation rhetoric. My third goal is to analyze the impact of evacuation rhetoric, relying on interviews and autoethnographic data. My final goal is to provide a few tentative recommendations that might improve the links between evacuation rhetoric and audience responses.

Identification and Description

Let me acknowledge initially that my sampling of rhetorical texts in this genre is incomplete. I understand that hurricane rhetoric in Florida is different, in that evacuation is a less-preferred option than sheltering in the part of the residence designated as the "storm hideout." I also cannot speak to the history of the genre, although I've searched I can find no extant texts of the preparatory speeches before key hurricanes such as Camille, Betsy, or George. Therefore, the conclusions here are primarily based on recent Gulf Coast evacuation rhetoric, and as such it's possible that characteristics I identify as genre based belong instead to idiosyncrasies of Louisiana politicians. Indeed, hurricane evacuation rhetoric is certainly influenced by the norms of Southern rhetoric more generally. In 1910, Charles Kent characterized Southern rhetoric "by a freedom approaching volubility and a love of ornamentation temptation to indulgence in high coloring" (qtd. in Braden).

A hurricane evacuation speech is more often mediated by means of the radio than by means of television or newspaper. The choice of channel makes sense when you recognize that the rhetor, assuming s/he is successful, is addressing an audience primarily already in their cars or working around the house on storm preparation. Hurricane preparation requires a forty-eight-hour lead. Homeowners need time to put either tape or boards in place to protect their windows, all household electronics need to be shut down and unplugged, belongings need to be moved away from doors and windows and preferably up off of the floor. Whether the individual is staying or evacuating, errands such as fully fueling the car, stocking up on bottled water, and contacting friends and family require additional time. Further preparations depend on whether the decision is made to evacuate or to remain. The crucial point here for the rhetor is clear: timing is everything. *Kairos* is the key to successful evacuation rhetoric.

Within the speech itself, evacuation rhetoric is dominated by logos. The genre typically opens with a declaration as to what specific areas are to be evacuated, and whether the evacuation is precautionary, recommended, or mandatory. The list of parishes[1] goes in order starting with those expected to be hit first. Details are given regarding the hurricane's current position,[2] its current and projected strength, its current and projected path, and the estimated times of arrival for key places along the projected path. This information must be given out slowly, partly because this array of new facts[3] must be assimilated with previous knowledge and therefore takes longer for the audience to fully understand (and partly because an unhurried presentation provides a sense of calm). It is also possible that the slow pace is evidence of audience adaptation, an appeal to ethos in that audience members who self-identify as residents of "the Big Easy" (the nickname for the greater New Orleans area) often understand this identity as a counterpoint and contrast to the hurry and rush perceived as typical of other large American cities.

The second section of the speech is the most variable, and is the only portion in which appeals to pathos are noticeable. Typically, the rhetor will segue into this fear appeal (the emotion evoked is always fear because the goal is to persuade audience members to be alarmed enough to decide to evacuate while staying calm enough to do so in an orderly manner) by repeating the goal of evacuating the previously named areas immediately, rather than waiting until closer to the estimated arrival time of the hurricane. Some element of novelty is important at this stage of the speech, something to distinguish why this particular occasion is worthy of evacuation. Here I include several examples of this key section from several evacuation speeches, presented in chronological order:

> "This city could be under water all the way up to twenty feet with the storm surge. We are below sea-level, folks, there is no place that's gonna be safe if this is the big one" (Mayor Nagin, prior to Hurricane Charley, 2004).

> "If you're going to stay, then go get a toe-tag so afterwards we can identify your body" (Mayor Nagin, prior to Hurricane Ivan, 2004).

> "We haven't recovered from the damage done by the last storm. If this storm hits us straight on, that water level's already so high, I guarantee you there will be some flooding that you do not want to be here to see" (Mayor Nagin, prior to Hurricane Dennis, 2005).

> "Tonight I'm asking you nicely to leave. Tomorrow might be another story, I might not be so nice about it. I wish I had better news, but we are facing a storm many of us have long feared" (Mayor Nagin, prior to Katrina, Saturday evening 2005).

> "I am gravely concerned about reports coming in regarding those who are choosing not to evacuate. I strongly urge you to get to safety while there is still time to do so" (Governor Blanco, prior to Hurricane Katrina, Sunday evening as contraflow was ended).

> "I'm expecting that some people who are die-hards [about not evacuating] will die hard" (Jefferson Parish President Aaron Broussard, prior to Katrina).

Several observations might be made based on this sample. One point is that the ethos of the rhetor is important to understanding audience reception to this section of the speech. Mayor Nagin's speaking style, for example, seems distinctive to most of the nation. Most of you could probably have guessed, without reading the citation information, which quotes came from him, even if your only familiarity with his rhetoric comes from hearing his statement urging "the feds to get their asses down here" the day after Katrina hit (interview on WWL, Tuesday, August 30, 2005). Nagin's rhetorical style has been characterized by outsiders as "brash," "blunt," "outspoken," and "unsophisticated."

An important point that can be observed by comparing across these evacuation texts is that no correlations after the fact can be observed between hurricane rhetoric and hurricane harm. That is to say, in an ideal world we would expect to see stronger pathos appeals associated with hurricanes that did greater damage. We would also like to see, in an ideal world, an association between stronger pathos appeals and greater persuasive success. Obviously, we live in a world that is far from ideal. The table below gives a ranking of pathos that is assessed in terms of vivid imagery and word-choice connotations (see Lee), a ranking of the hurricane's damage to this region of the Gulf Coast,[4] and a ranking for success assessed in terms of percentage of the population that evacuated. The rankings only include the texts from Nagin in order to control for differences in rhetorical style.

Quote	Pathos	Damage	Success[5]
"20 feet with storm surge"	2	2	4
"get a toe-tag"	1	4	2
"flooding you don't want to be here to see"	4	3	3
"asking you nicely tonight"	3	1	1

You will notice from the table that there is also relatively little correlation between the damage done by the hurricane (as known after the fact) and the probability of evacuation.

A final section of the evacuation rhetoric genre requires providing information about the mechanics of the evacuation. Sometimes this will begin with a list of additional office closings ("I'm closing the city government offices for Monday and Tuesday, with the exception of essential personnel, and I'm evacuating all RTA drivers to the West Bank or another standby location after 5:00 PM tonight," to provide a hypothetical example). Shelter information is sometimes included ("The Superdome is open as of noon today as a shelter of last resort, but if you can get out, go do so, and make sure your neighbors can get out, and the old lady who lives alone down the street, anybody you know, if they can't get out on their own help them out," to quote Nagin again prior to Katrina). The conditions and directions for the evacuation routes will also be included, particularly the information about contraflow. (For example, "Contraflow was initiated at 8 this morning on I-10 and the Causeway, and continues to junction I-12 and to junction I-55. The Causeway will be closed after noon today.") Residents are assumed to know in advance what their local evacuation route is for getting to the main thoroughfares, and also to understand what "contraflow" means,[6] so that the speech ends the way any good motivational speech should, by succinctly providing simple actions that can be remembered and performed. In order to keep this section succinct, however, a great deal is demanded of the audience.

Constraints

The key to successful hurricane evacuation rhetoric, as noted earlier, is *kairos*. Evacuation speeches have to be kept reasonably short because you want the audience acting, not listening. Evacuation speeches need to be done well in advance of the hurricane because evacuation is a slow process. After individuals have completed their personal preparations, there is still considerable time spent in traffic, which seems unavoidably slow. Moreover, the timing is further complicated by the fact that, after evacuating the population, cities sometimes bring in emergency responders from other locations, which means that contraflow has to end well in advance of the hurricane. For New Orleans in particular, the timing must be done well in advance because the storm surge, which arrives ahead of the storm itself, can sweep cars off of bridges, so the bridges must be closed down early (safety margin is twelve hours in advance of the storm) even if those in outlying areas are still evacuating.

The problem is, we don't have the ability to predict the path of a hurricane with accuracy more than twenty-four hours from any given position. Weather systems are too complicated to give more than broad probabilities as to where a hurricane might make landfall. The National Hurricane Center (NHC) uses five different simulation models to predict storm paths, which it refers to as strike probability models. The visual representations of each model's predictions can be viewed on their Web site (www.nhc.noaa.gov), which gets updated every six hours when a storm is actively being tracked. The data to feed into the models comes from both active and passive measurement systems. The television weather coverage privileges the visual images, and the NHC provides both still images representing strike probabilities and a moving image showing the recent path of the storm as well as a prediction for its movement over the next six hours. An example of a still visual of a strike probability is included here:

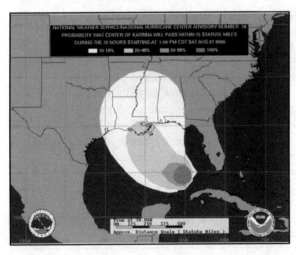

Figure 1
National Hurricane Center. Strike Probability Map. Advisory 18 for Hurricane Katrina. 7 June 2007. <http://www.nhc.noaa.gov/archive/2005/KATRINA_graphics.shtml>.

The visual representations produced by the simulation models gets translated by the NHC into a table of probabilities, which then gets supplied to all of the relevant state emergency management agencies and media representatives that have signed up to receive them. Note that the officials responsible for making evacuation decisions are working primarily from the text-based strike probability tables. The probability tables for a hurricane more than twenty-four hours out typically look like this:

```
PROBABILITIES FOR GUIDANCE IN HURRICANE PROTECTION PLANNING BY
GOVERNMENT AND DISASTER OFFICIALS


AT 5 AM EDT...0900Z...THE CENTER OF FLOYD WAS LOCATED NEAR
LATITUDE 28.8 NORTH...LONGITUDE  78.8 WEST


CHANCES OF CENTER OF THE HURRICANE PASSING WITHIN 65 NAUTICAL
MILES OF LISTED LOCATIONS THROUGH  2AM EDT SAT SEP 18 1999
```

LOCATION	A	B	C	D	E	LOCATION	A	B	C	D	E
33.2N 79.1W	38	2	X	X	40	PROVIDENCE RI	X	X	3	13	16
36.3N 78.0W	X	26	6	X	32	NANTUCKET MA	X	X	2	12	14
40.0N 75.0W	X	X	18	3	21	HYANNIS MA	X	X	2	12	4
COCOA BEACH FL	5	X	X	1	6	BOSTON MA	X	X	2	13	15
DAYTONA BEACH FL	20	X	X	X	20	PORTLAND ME	X	X	1	14	15
JACKSONVILLE FL	5	X	X	X	25	BAR HARBOR ME	X	X	X	12	12
SAVANNAH GA	36	1	X	X	37	EASTPORT ME	X	X	X	11	11
CHARLESTON SC	41	1	X	X	42	ST JOHN NB	X	X	X	10	10
MYRTLE BEACH SC	30	7	X	X	37	MONCTON NB	X	X	X	9	9
WILMINGTON NC	15	17	1	X	33	YARMOUTH NS	X	X	X	9	9
MOREHEAD CITY NC	5	19	3	1	28	HALIFAX NS	X	X	X	7	7
CAPE HATTERAS NC	1	13	8	X	22	SABLE ISLAND NS	X	X	X	2	2
NORFOLK VA	X	11	15	X	26	SYDNEY NS	X	X	X	3	3
OCEAN CITY MD	X	2	19	1	22	EDDY POINT NS	X	X	X	4	4
ATLANTIC CITY NJ	X	X	17	4	21	PTX BASQUES NFLD	X	X	X	3	3
NEW YORK CITY NY	X	X	12	7	19	BURGEO NFLD	X	X	X	2	2
MONTAUK POINT NY	X	X	5	11	16						

```
COLUMN DEFINITION   PROBABILITIES IN PERCENT


A IS PROBABILITY FROM NOW TO 2AM THU
FOLLOWING ARE ADDITIONAL PROBABILITIES
B FROM  2AM THU TO  2PM THU
C FROM  2PM THU TO  2AM FRI
D FROM  2AM FRI TO  2AM SAT
E IS TOTAL PROBABILITY FROM NOW TO  2AM SAT
X MEANS LESS THAN ONE PERCENT
```

Note that no probability for a city on America's coast gets as high as even 50%. The very high probability readings are those that are closer to the hurricane's current position. The probabilities do not add to 100% because a hurricane will hit multiple places along its path.

The information provided by the NHC is, of course, another form of "hurricane evacuation rhetoric," a visual argument that functions persuasively in the decision making of individuals regarding whether or not to evacuate. The visual element is predominant. I would suggest that the table, with its wide range of probabilities, is less likely to persuade in favor of evacuation than the visual representation of strike probabilities. It might seem that the NHC has recognized that the table is ineffective rhetoric: as of May 15, 2006, its use was discontinued.

For the rhetor determining whether and how to persuade residents to evacuate, this constraint is the heart of the challenge. How high must the probability be before you urge a precautionary evacuation? How high must the probability be before you declare the evacuation mandatory? How long do you wait to know what the hurricane is going to do before deciding? The answer is not as simple as saying that the choice should always be better safe than sorry. For one thing, that would mean a tremendous loss economically. But more importantly, that choice would reduce the success rate of your evacuation rhetoric.

From the audience's perspective, evacuation rhetoric is a challenge to evaluate critically. Evacuation is a high cost: a huge amount of time on the road that everybody would prefer to put to some better use, stressed-out pets and kids all stuck in a small space for an extended period of time under difficult driving conditions, the expenses of gas and food and hotels, and an emotional toll from being wrenched out of the daily routine and forced into a high-uncertainty situation. And that high cost has to be weighed against a relatively low probability but highly catastrophic event and the possibility of physical harm resulting from hurricane winds or flooding. Other probabilities weigh into the decision: you're likely to lose power for some period of time, and if there is somewhere attractive to evacuate to (a friend's house), staying there might be more persuasive. Additional factors have to be considered: will your employer expect you to be there? Have they notified you that the office (or whatever) is closed, and if so for how long? Driving out of the affected area and then immediately back because only one day off from work has been declared is a higher cost than driving out and staying away for some short period of time. But there are far more complications to consider: is the car working reliably, or is there the possibility of being trapped on the road in a defunct vehicle with traffic piling up behind you? Are others in your social network evacuating or are they staying? If you have a loved one in the hospital (hospital patients are routinely not evacuated because the stresses of travel are so dangerous for them, and the expectation is that the hospital is equipped with a self-sufficient energy and water supply for the period necessary), then you are far less likely to abandon that sick individual. Do you or a loved one have responsibilities to your employer that would categorize you as "essential personnel," or do you think that you do? Do you have a pet that would be unable to evacuate with you? What do you think the odds are that the rhetor in question knows more about the storm situation than you do?

What this means is that the audience members must individually and critically evaluate their response to the evacuation rhetoric. And if you have heard a lot of evacuation rhetoric before, and if the damage as assessed after the fact has been low, then you are far less likely to be persuaded. The constraints on the audience impact the rhetor, because the more often s/he calls for evacuation *and is wrong*, the *less* likely the audience will be persuaded the next time. This is the same lesson that we all learned as children from fables like the boy who cried "wolf" in jest and then was ignored when a wolf really came.

Audience Response

The magnitude of the disaster caused by Hurricane Katrina sometimes obscures the fact that the evacuation rate was unusually high. Most estimates suggest that around 80% of the greater New Orleans area evacuated, which was a higher percentage than for any previous hurricane and represents a staggeringly large number of people (about 1.3 million) to move in a coordinated fashion with little preparation. For comparison purposes, when Houston was threatened by Hurricane Rita, less than 60% evacuated. The relative success of the evacuation does not excuse responsibility for the suffering and deaths of those left behind, of course. But in assessing the audience response to the evacuation rhetoric, we should keep in mind that 80% is a far larger margin than any president has won in recent elections, or most other examples of rhetorical success.

Though I hate to say it (since it makes our profession seem less central), the truth is that rhetoric makes relatively little difference in individual evacuation decisions. The material and social constraints on an individual are not mediated or removed by any words or images of any public figure. The real determinant of individual decision making regarding evacuation is the social network. Paul Lazarsfeld, Bernard Berelson, and Hazel Gaudet's research on opinion leadership bears out in this situation as well. A recent publication by Susanna Priest and her colleagues in the *Journal of Applied Communication Research* argued on the basis of interview data that approximately 70% of New Orleans evacuees identified interpersonal communication as the determining influence on their decisions. Of the remaining interviews, most spoke of an amorphous "they" who said the hurricane would be severe and influenced the decision to leave. I would hypothesize that the "they" in question refers primarily to the images and probabilities promulgated by the NHC, and particularly the use of the images by weather reporters at television news stations. For example, my department chair, a well-known rhetorical scholar, upon hearing that I was evaluating hurricane evacuation rhetoric declared: "I sure wasn't influenced by the rhetoric!" Then, upon reflection, he backtracked: "Or maybe I was, but I didn't wait around to hear Nagin, maybe NOAA convinced me, but you know that since I sent an e-mail telling everybody to get the hell out." The images alone do not seem to function consciously as the deciding factor (or at least, only in three of 116 interviews[7] does the visual element enter the conversation), and indeed most of us would probably not have the ability to interpret the images well enough to guide our evacuation decisions, but this does not rule out the unarticulated impact such visual rhetoric might wield.

On a note that I as a rhetorical scholar find more encouraging, a statistically significant number of interviewees did mention Nagin by name or by title when asked about their decision whether or not to leave. Seventeen interviewees explicitly referred to Nagin's speeches, and two specific quotes were cited in particular: the speech given on Saturday (at a press conference with Blanco) in which his statement about "asking you nicely" occurred and a speech the following Sunday when the evacuation was changed from advisory to mandatory for Orleans Parish, in which he said, "This is it. Get out now." It is interesting to note that of those interviewed, only one said anything specifically about Governor Blanco, although she was at the same initial news conference, and that reference was to post-Katrina rhetoric.

But the reaction to the mayor's rhetoric was not always straightforward. Five of the respondents who mentioned the mayor's rhetoric expressed distrust. The distrust seems to be not precisely a suspicion regarding Nagin; indeed, Nagin gets exempted from the blanket condemnations expressed regarding authorities, and the very fact of his being singled out for mention is a tribute to his popularity at that time.[8] The suspicion is rather a generalized distrust of messages from the mass media, a belief that anything on mass media has arrived there by some process of negotiation and therefore needs to be interpreted as concealing as much as revealing. Below are some examples:

"There was obviously some fight. And the point whenever the governor and the mayor wouldn't tell the people to go."

"So that's all TV does. You know? Control. A person out there know what the TV doing. That's why I [indecipherable]. You know? But . . . Mayor seen, 20 feet of water was coming. They know it was coming. You hear me? They knew it was coming. Bush knew it was coming. FEMA and them knew it was coming. The mili . . . everybody knew that water was coming, so . . . look what they done, four days later. They all look bad. When you knew it was coming. You all no idea, it was on TV before it came. Talking 'bout it was coming. Now where you at when it did came? You didn't in here, and you no way around it. The people in it, were destroyed. It wasn't destroying you, because you weren't no where in it. But here you're on TV telling us."

Another important element of the audience response to evacuation rhetoric is the mediated nature of rhetoric. During Katrina, the second most frequently named rhetorician is not a politician, but rather is the weatherman for the local Fox affiliate, WVUE. Bob Breck is an elderly, white-haired gentleman, and has reported on weather long enough to be trusted and read in nuanced ways by his community. Respondents would talk about his evacuation rhetoric, though the format of the genre remained the same as in previous cases, but small differences became magnified by years of familiarity. One interviewee commented on his nonverbals: "When his brow gets all furrowed like that, you know it's time." Breck also tried to stress the significance of his message with the use of a rhetorical question, "What else can I tell you that will help you understand the need to leave?" Other weathermen are also well familiar with the dangers of "crying wolf," as Dan Milham of NBC's

WDSU made clear in a later presentation (Milham). He observed that he has a frontstage and a backstage response to hurricanes, wherein he always recommends evacuation while on television, but sometimes encourages family and close friends to not evacuate. He cannot *not* urge evacuation each time a hurricane threatens, yet the numerous false alarms mean that persuasion is made difficult for the times when it is most important (and to the extent that he or any other can judge when it is important in advance).

In a previous paper, we noted that interpersonal influence (opinion leadership) was the key dynamic in understanding decision making. A third type of evacuation rhetoric is oppositional—those who usually speak and decide against evacuation. Longtime residents, those who survived Betsy and Camille, are foremost among these. Also frequently referenced as influential are the fishers (recreational and commercial) and boaters. The phrase that continually recurs in interviews is "so-and-so left, and they *never* evacuate, so I knew it was time for me to go too."

Conclusions and Recommendations

1. The impact of rhetoric is severely and primarily limited by material constraints, such as the inability of residents to leave due to work or financial restrictions. Disbelief and social networks that mitigate against mobilization also contribute to a negative response.

2. The impact of mass-mediated rhetoric is far less than the impact of interpersonal communication.

3. "Crying wolf" is hard to avoid because of scientific uncertainty as well as the desire of officials to err on the side of safe rather than sorry. However, a result of the "crying wolf" phenomenon renders the rhetoricians ineffective. As Cicero said, "These rhetorical fireworks should not be used in petty matters, or with men of such temper that the eloquence can achieve nothing, unless we would be deemed fit objects of ridicule or disgust, as indulging in heroics over trifles" (II: 205). The better response is to change from rhetoric to dialectic at such a point. Given the opinion leadership dynamic, inviting respected community leaders to speak via mass media might improve evacuation rates, but overuse will lead to the same problem. A better solution might be to use a debate format: identify community leaders who routinely persuade against evacuation, and on those occasions when they also agree to evacuation place them in a speaking situation where success in persuasion is likely.

Questions

1. How can we more effectively persuade individuals to evacuate a city prior to a hurricane?

2. Given how much we *do not* know in advance, given our own poor understanding of their situation, and given that every time we "cry

wolf" we lessen the chances of future rhetoric being successful, do we have any business attempting to persuade individuals to evacuate? Whose responsibility is it to decide such things?

Notes

[1] Louisiana does not have counties, operating instead on the basis of smaller units that were based historically on the Catholic church's divisions. Functionally, this is advantageous because it allows greater specificity as to who is under what degree of hurricane threat.

[2] Position is given in terms of latitude and longitude, and only rarely translated into terms of "miles west of Cuba" or whatever. As an audience member who doesn't know what the latitudinal and longitudinal readings mean, I found no significance in this section of the speech. During conversations over the years, however, I've come to appreciate this clever bit of audience adaptation. Longtime residents, particularly in areas south of New Orleans, are almost all boat owners comfortable with navigating in terms of latitude and longitude. The evacuation rhetoric excludes subtly those who do not need to be concerned about the hurricane while out at sea, while sending clear warning to those who do need to be concerned. Pathos is avoided, and the audience members in-the-know are able to take some small sense of pride in that they are trusted to be smart enough to draw the appropriate conclusions on their own.

[3] Another possibility explaining the slow pace was suggested to me by a student, who noted that numbers are harder to process than other information. While the basic argument is sound, I'm not convinced that time is processed in the same ways as other numeric figures.

[4] The difference between the hurricane's damage to the region and the hurricane's overall damage is a very important distinction. Hurricane Ivan, for example, caused no damage to this part of the Gulf Coast, but it caused flooding and hurricane-strength wind damage as far north as Pittsburgh. The constraints section will discuss this issue further.

[5] Statistics on the percent of population evacuating—here referred to as "success rate"—were collected by the Louisiana State Police. They are available at www.lsp.gov/hurricane.html.

[6] Contraflow means using all lanes for traffic going in the same direction. So in New Orleans, for example, I-10 east of the city becomes eastbound-only, even the lanes on the side of the divided highway that normally carry westbound traffic. Similarly, west of the city I-10 becomes westbound-only, so the question of where you want to go must be addressed before entering any of the main thoroughfares, because there's no turning back. The first time one encounters contraflow is bewildering: you see cars going up ramps clearly labeled "wrong way" and "do not enter," and once successfully on the wrong side of the interstate, you see only the metal back of all the road signs that tell you what city you're passing or where the exit is for the next turn.

[7] Interviews with 116 New Orleans evacuees were conducted, primarily within two months after Katrina, by a team of interviewers from the University of South Carolina, Louisiana State University, and Tulane University. Transcripts of the interviews are available by contacting the author.

[8] Interviews were conducted primarily during October, which was probably the high point of Nagin's popularity, as the criticisms regarding his rebuilding plan had not yet begun. Prior to Katrina, Nagin's popularity was high enough that there would have been no challenger in the mayoral elections for that year. His status as a "nonpolitician"—he was the CEO of Cox Cable before running and winning the mayoral race—and his efforts to fight corruption were generally well-received.

Bibliography

Beck, Ulrich. *Risk Society: Towards a New Modernity.* Trans. M. Ritter. Newbury Park, CA: Sage, 1992.

Braden, Waldo. *The Oral Tradition in the South.* Baton Rouge: Louisiana State UP, 1983.

Cicero. *De Oratore.* Trans. E. Sutton and H. Rackham. The Loeb Classical Library. Cambridge, MA: Harvard UP, 1988.

Lazarsfeld, Paul F., Bernard Berelson, and Hazel Gaudet. *The People's Choice: How the Voter Makes Up His Mind in a Presidential Campaign.* New York: Columbia UP, 1944.

Lee, Irving. "Some Conceptions of Emotional Appeal in Rhetorical Theory." *Speech Monographs* 6.1 (1939): 66–87.

Milham, D. Katrina Takes Aim: The View from WDSU-TV Chief Meteorologist. Part of Tulane University's Katrina Lecture Series, New Orleans, LA, Aug. 28, 2006.

Priest, Susanna, Stephen Banning, Kenneth Campbell, Hilary Fussell, and Kim Taylor. "Reading Katrina: Information Sources and Decision-Making in Response to Natural Disaster." *International Journal of Mass Emergencies and Disaster Management* (under review).

Rogers, Everett. *Diffusion of Innovations.* 3rd ed. New York: The Free Press, 1983.

Into Dark Places
15 Violence, History, and the American Militia Movement

D. J. Mulloy

In the final decade of the twentieth century, a fierce rhetorical battle took place in the United States between the newly formed citizens' militia movement and the political mainstream, one which had much to say not just about political extremism, but also about the place of violence in the wider American culture, including its centrality to American patriotic identity. In the broadest terms, the emergence of the militia movement in the 1990s was a product of a widespread sense that the United States was a nation in decline: politically, economically, morally, and spiritually. Concerns over abortion rights, gay rights, gun rights, affirmative action policies, educational standards, immigration policy, environmental issues, the effect of international trade agreements like GATT and NAFTA on the American economy, and the apparent "militarization" of American law enforcement all seemed to be motivating militia members. Yet, it's also the case that the movement wouldn't have emerged when it did without the impact of three very specific events—the siege of Randy Weaver and his family at Ruby Ridge, Idaho, in August 1992; the disastrous assault on David Koresh's Branch Davidian sect in Waco, Texas, in 1993; and the successful passage, in the same year, of the Brady Bill, the most significant piece of federal gun control legislation since the Gun Control Act of 1968.[1]

Responding to these events, militia members saw themselves as the vanguard of a revolutionary movement, one that would wake the American people up to what was going on around them and one that would help return the United States to the kind of nation it was originally intended to have been: a limited republic in which the states predominated, the federal government's powers were radically circumscribed, and the right of the people to keep and bear arms received its due recognition as the very cornerstone of the constitutional system. A crucial part of the militias' endeavor to restore this "lost republic" involved their use of American history, especially the history of the American Revolution, as a means of analyzing and critiquing contemporary U.S. politics and society.[2] As a part of this process, violent, revolutionary-style rhetoric was enthusiastically embraced.

As militia members saw it, they were the "George Washingtons of today." Americans, they argued, had to "throw off the tyrants" again, just as they had in 1776. This was feasible, it was thought, because their forefathers had defeated Great Britain, one of the most powerful nations of the eighteenth century, with the support of "only about 4% of the people" in the colonies. Accordingly, Americans should embrace the example set by the minutemen at Lexington and Concord and take up arms in order to combat the "bullying-bureaucrats and two-bit tyrants" who were intent on stealing their freedom. Indeed, "the primary trigger" for the American Revolution was the same as it is now, which is to say, "You don't mess with a free man's right to keep and bear arms."[3]

It was important in this respect to follow the advice of Samuel Adams and act to resist a government "both tyrannical and lawless," rather than meekly crouching down to "lick the hand" that fed you—such resistance, it was reasoned, was simply being loyal to the spirit of the founding fathers and to the Declaration of Independence. Appearing before Congress in 1995 one militia leader, J. J. Johnson, described the movement as composed of people who had "'Don't Tread on Me' stamped across their foreheads." They were people, he said, who were "drawing a line in the sand," and he warned that at the time of the first Revolution the "British didn't get the hint" about what was really going on "until they saw dead redcoats" lying all about them. The "only thing standing between some of the current legislation being contemplated [in Congress] and armed conflict is time," Johnson said. It was a common assertion. In the view of Norman Olson, another prominent militia leader, armed conflict was all but inevitable "if the country doesn't turn around." For "Joan," a spokesperson for the North Carolina Militia, because the "blood of our ancestors is flowing in our veins" neither the North Carolina Militia nor the militia movement as a whole would be willing to "submit to lives of slavery." On the contrary, she said, "We are willing to die for our beliefs. We will fight to the last man [or woman] because we would rather die than live a life where there is no justice or freedom." In the oft-repeated words of Patrick Henry, it seemed that for many militia members, in the end, it was all a question of "Liberty or Death."[4]

Unsurprisingly, law enforcement officials; civil rights groups; and local, state, and national politicians expressed considerable concern about the militia movement's use of this kind of rhetoric—what the Anti-Defamation League called its "revolutionary posturing."[5] It was taken to provide clear and incontrovertible evidence of the danger the militias posed: of their confrontational and trigger-happy intent; of their unreasonable—and irrational—expectations; and of their frenzied readiness to commit acts of violence, whether in response to specific legislative enactments of which they disapproved (most obviously gun control laws), or in some more generalized future conflict with the federal government. Concern was also expressed about the effect such language could have on the "marketplace of ideas,"[6] especially when it was taken in conjunction with the militias' penchant for camouflage fatigues and paramilitary-style training. Even in the absence of actual violent activity, the militias' rhetoric was seen as intimidating, both to private citizens and to public officials. This was particularly so at the grass-roots level, where local authorities often lacked the manpower and resources to combat the potential threat posed by the militias.[7]

Concerns about the effects of the militias' propaganda understandably took on a new sense of urgency following the Oklahoma City bombing. As Michigan Senator Carl Levin saw it, for example: "Extreme hate rhetoric contributes to an incendiary atmosphere in which an unstable individual will take the rhetoric seriously and light a match or a fuse." President Clinton addressed the same issue during a speech at Iowa State University six days after the bombing. "Words have consequences," he said, "and to pretend otherwise was idle." After all, Patrick Henry hadn't stood up and said "'Give me liberty or give me death,' expecting it to fall on deaf ears," nor had Thomas Jefferson written the Declaration of Independence expecting his words to simply "vanish [into] thin air." Of course words have consequences, and it was incumbent on all Americans to speak out against the kind of violent speech emanating from militia members, speech that might "push fragile people over the edge," speech that had the potential, the president said, to take the United States "into a dark place." Ten days later, in a speech at Michigan State University, Clinton challenged the militias' broader claims on American history. Expressing his outrage that militia members were trying to "appropriate our sacred symbols for paranoid purposes" in comparing themselves to the "colonial militias who fought for the democracy you now rail against," the president declared: "How dare you suggest that we in the freest nation on earth live in tyranny! How dare you call yourselves patriots and heroes!"[8]

Such concerns are legitimate of course. The dangers posed by armed groups spouting violent rhetoric should not be minimized. Acknowledging this, though, shouldn't prevent us from digging a little deeper into what's transpiring when militia members embrace a language of violence or lead us to ignore the fact that militia members are far from alone in applying the language of America's Revolutionary past in the way they do. After all, the unexplored implication of Senator Levin's remark that the real danger lies in unstable individuals taking the militias' rhetoric "seriously" and going out and setting off bombs is that "normal," "stable" people understand that such talk isn't intended to be taken "seriously"—in the sense of its being a direct incitement to violence—that it fulfills other functions within the militias' ideological system. It is worth exploring what these other functions might be.

Most obviously, militia members want to establish a connection with those they see as their revolutionary predecessors. Establishing such a connection is a means of bolstering both their individual and their collective sense of identity. (And, militia members might say, if America's founding fathers spoke in violent terms and undertook violent actions, why shouldn't they?) But by emulating the example of America's founding fathers in this way, militia members were also hoping to call attention to themselves. Ray Southwell of the Michigan Militia made exactly this point during an interview with the *Detroit Metro Times*: "People say, 'Why the camouflage and guns?' And I say, 'Without the camouflage and guns, no one would pay any attention.'"[9] A similar self-consciousness is at play in the militias' revolutionary rhetoric. Militia members are well aware that its use will get them noticed. It is employed precisely because of this. The threats of violent confrontation explicitly and implicitly contained in the militia movement's literature and public pronouncements have the same function as their uniforms, guns, and marches—to a considerable extent they operate as a demand for attention and a call for recognition. Violence, after all, has tended to play very well in American society and culture. Throughout the history of the United States, numerous groups, from the far left and the far right, have deployed violence and its threat in order to advance their political claims: Sons of Liberty, Know Nothings, radical abolitionists, antiabolitionists, Klansmen, anarchists, socialists, Wobblies, Panthers, Weathermen, Christian Identity adherents, and antiabortion activists among them.[10]

In the case of the militias, there are two different audiences for this rhetoric: potential militia members and those in positions of power in the political mainstream. With regard to the latter, we can see the militias' revolutionary language as an attempt to convince local, state, and federal politicians, government officials, and law enforcement personnel that they should take militia members and their concerns seriously. Indeed, it is perhaps an indication of the lack of influence that militia members feel they have through the conventional channels of political activity—their essential *powerlessness*—that they attempt to "shortcut" them in this way,[11] although it could also be argued that such a strategy is based on a realistic assessment of the movement's numerical weakness.[12] As far as potential militia members are concerned—those in the wider patriot movement, in the gun culture, constitutionalists, libertarians, and so on who might be sympathetic to the militias' concerns—the rhetoric of revolutionary action also functions as a call for recruitment to the movement, rather than necessarily being a call to immediate violent action. In most of the examples noted above, the violent talk was followed by an emphasis on the importance of finding "like-minded people" and of "getting organized," with plentiful exhortations for gun owners and others to "stand-up together" and "make a difference."

Getting other people involved means making the issues at stake seem worth standing up for. This is part of the discursive work required when trying to build a political movement. Invocations of violence are a swift and effective way of raising those stakes. The militias' talk of drawing "lines in the sand" provides a richly symbolic illustration of the lengths to which militia members are prepared to go to in order to achieve their aims. It is a strategy with positive psychological benefits, one that reinforces militia members' own sense of worthiness and heroism. What could be more formidable than expressing a willingness to take on the agencies of the state? And to die in the process? What greater indication of seriousness and importance could there be? Unpleasant and uncomfortable as it is, it would be a mistake in this regard to ignore what David Apter calls "the heroic side of political violence," or to downplay the significance of Frantz Fanon's insights on the "positive and creative qualities" of violence—its transformative, cleansing, and restorative functions.[13] All of which is to say that, whatever else it does— or is intended to do—the militias' confrontational rhetoric also serves to dramatize the heroic activities that militia members see themselves involved in, and this dramatization is a key aspect of its use.

Central to this heroic posturing is the notion of patriotism. In *The Roots of American Loyalty*, Merle Curti wrote that although patriotism has meant many things and has been put to many varied uses, it "may nevertheless be defined as love of country, pride in it, and readiness to make sacrifices for what is considered its best interest."[14] The ultimate sacrifice, of course, the ultimate declaration of one's love for one's country, is being prepared to give one's life for it. The militias' revolutionary rhetoric is intended to be a mark of *their* patriotism. We need to understand militia members' expressions of their "willingness to die" within these terms.

Declarations of this kind are simply part of the *lingua franca* of American patriotism (as they are of patriotism worldwide). Patrick Henry's "Liberty or Death" speech is a prime example. Declaimed, anthologized, reproduced, remembered, and revered ever since William Wirt's 1815 biography of Henry detached it from the oral tradition that had sustained it for the previous 40 years, Henry's speech is widely regarded as one of the quintessential texts of American patriotic identity, a hymn to liberty and democracy, "the oratorical essence of the American Revolution," which is why it was chosen to symbolize the nation's "spirit" during its bicentennial celebrations.[15] The very centrality of Henry's speech to the American political canon was presumably one of the reasons why Clinton chose to invoke it, together with the Declaration of Independence, during his "words have consequences" speech at Iowa State University.

There is no little tension, though, between Clinton's invocation of Henry as a member of the patriotic pantheon and the actual content of Henry's speech, which was, after all, a call to arms, a discourse on the necessity of political violence, and a rousing appeal for others to follow Henry's example in forcefully engaging the enemy.[16] It is a tension Malcolm X tried to exploit more than once when defending himself from charges that he was a political extremist during the 1960s. Speaking at the University of Ghana in 1964, for example, he made the case that Americans in 1776 hadn't turned "the other cheek to the British. No, they had an old man named Patrick Henry, who said, 'Liberty or death!'" Malcolm complained that he had never heard his critics refer to Henry "as an advocate of violence." On the contrary, "They say he's one of the Founding Fathers, because he had sense to say, 'Liberty or death!'" Black Americans of the time, Malcolm argued, were reaching the point "where they are ready to tell the Man no matter what the odds are against them, no matter what the cost is, it's liberty or death."[17]

A similar tension is evident in Clinton's use of the Declaration of Independence, a document that underpins much of the militia movement's revolutionary analysis and arguments. When Clinton invoked the Declaration during his speech at Iowa State, he was calling upon the document as it is generally recalled and understood within American society—a "sacred text" that offers a "moral standard by which the day-to-day policies and practices of the nation [can] be judged."[18] He was reaching back through time, to Martin Luther King speaking on the steps of the Lincoln Memorial in 1963 and calling on America to honor the Declaration's promise to the rights of "life, liberty, and the pursuit of happiness"; to Abraham Lincoln at Gettysburg in 1863 declaring that the nation born in 1776 was one "conceived in liberty, and dedicated to the proposition that all men are created equal"; and, ultimately of course, to Thomas Jefferson himself. It is an understanding of the Declaration that forms the basis of a particular strand of American patriotism, one John Schaar has termed "covenanted patriotism." This form of patriotism is "unique to America," Schaar believes, because it is based not on blood, race, religion, or territory, but on political ideas. "Those principles and commitments [of the Declaration of Independence] are the core of American identity, the soul of the body politic," Schaar argues.[19]

There is, however, another, more martial meaning attached to the Declaration of Independence, and it is this meaning that the militia movement relies upon. Militia members have, in the main, sought to return the Declaration to its "original" revolutionary purpose, emphasizing not the right of the people to "life, liberty, and the pursuit of happiness"—the part of the preamble that Clinton was invoking; the part most people remember—but rather their right to "alter or abolish" governments that have become destructive of their citizens' liberties, which was of course the key to the document's significance in the eighteenth century.[20]

This is not to say that militia members are unaware of the basis on which the modern reputation of the Declaration rests, and the document is certainly revered as both "sacred" and central to American identity. But it is this other aspect of the Declaration—its role as a revolutionary manifesto—that militia members attach the most significance to, and draw the most sustenance from.

That Clinton and others in the mainstream should downplay the revolutionary significance of the Declaration is hardly surprising. As Pauline Maier has noted, revolutionary documents are always uncomfortable for established governments to have to deal with. This was especially evident in the United States at the turn of the twentieth century during the campaign for "100% Americanism," when, as Merle Curti points out, legislature after legislature rushed to condemn as "treasonable any expression of belief in the right of revolution" from radicals and socialists. "The fact that the country had originated in revolution and that almost all the notable figures of the nineteenth century had openly expressed their belief in the right of revolution was conveniently overlooked."[21]

Clinton's speech illustrates some of the problems involved in using the past as a political tool in the present. If the president was really intent on encouraging more civility in public discourse, his two examples could certainly have been better chosen. More fundamentally, though, Clinton's and the militias' differing uses of Patrick Henry and the Declaration of Independence also helps to illuminate some of the tensions that exist between the two dominant strands or traditions of American patriotism (as well as how closely intertwined they are). The first strand has already been identified. This covenanted patriotism, to use Schaar's term, is generally seen as progressive and emancipatory, a force for good in the world, based as it is on the expansion of equality, liberty, justice, and freedom for all.[22] The values associated with the second strand of American patriotism are not so unambiguously positive. This is the militaristic strand, and it is built around more troublesome notions of blood, violence, bodily sacrifice, and martial fervor. Of course, the strengths of the latter may be necessary to realize the goals of the former, and few have gone as far as to argue that the militaristic strand of patriotism is completely dispensable.[23] Indeed, its assets may well be essential when it comes to protecting the homeland from external threats. Nonetheless, it is easy to see how the values associated with the militaristic strand of American patriotism can be problematic.

Troublesome or problematic as they may be, however, the values associated with militaristic patriotism are also highly prized and deeply embedded within American culture. Indeed, according to Edward Linenthal, they represent the "primal themes of patriotic orthodoxy: war as holy crusade, bringing new life to the nation and the warrior as a culture hero and savior."[24] The militias' use of Patrick Henry's speech and the Declaration of Independence as revolutionary manifesto both fall within this category. The same is true of a third important component of the militias' revolutionary reconstructions, their invocations of the example set by the minutemen at Lexington and Concord.

From casual allusion to detailed retellings, members of the militia movement have made extensive use of the minutemen as providing a "heroic model for today['s] citizen soldiers."[25] Again, this shouldn't really come as a surprise. As Linenthal has pointed out, the battles of Lexington and Concord in 1775 stand as one of the most important physical and imaginative sites in the American "patriotic orthodoxy," they are "sacred ground" where "memories of the transformative power of war and the sacrificial heroism of the warrior are preserved." Lexington and Concord, he says, are "prime martial centers" in American culture, and the minutemen are the "primal patriots": holy warriors "who killed not out of hate but out of the forceful inspiration of the love of liberty"; sacrificial figures who brought the new republic into being "through the agency of holy war." What's more, the militias' use of these figures—and values and ideals they represent—is barely distinguishable from how many others have used them: from actual participants in the battles to presidents, would-be presidents, military officers, poets, sculptors, painters, advertisers, and political activists; from the Reverend Jonas Clark through Ralph Waldo Emerson and Daniel Chester French to John F. Kennedy, Robert DePugh, John Kerry, and Noam Chomsky.[26]

Critics of the militias in organizations such as the Anti-Defamation League and the Southern Poverty Law Center would bridle at any discussion of the militias within the terms of American patriotism. They do not see the militias' expressions of patriotic identification as genuine. To them the militias are simply "false patriots," their patriotic words and gestures cynical window dressing intended to disguise a deeper racism and religious bigotry[27]—the radical right, it seems, has always known that American patriotism is an effective language to lay claim to within the United States, even if the radical left has largely abandoned it, mostly as a consequence of the Vietnam War.[28] However, distinguishing "genuine" from "false" patriotism is not necessarily a straightforward undertaking. Which version of American patriotism is the most important to adhere to? Can one be a sincere and "genuine" patriot and still have dangerous, stupid, or bad ideas? Can one be a "false" patriot yet still express some of the basic tenets of American patriotic identity? Patriotism, after all, is not some neutral, timeless, or natural concept. It is a construction, a political weapon to be unleashed against one's opponents, or a soothing salve to comfort one's allies.

The "drive to build the nation reveals paradoxical processes of unifying and dividing, consolidating and fracturing, remembrance and amnesia," writes Cecelia O'Leary in her history of American patriotism, *To Die For.*[29] A crucial part of the amnesia accompanying the construction of the American nation centers on the role played by violence—real and imagined, justified and illegitimate, casual and philosophical—in the founding and subsequent development of the United States. Indeed, according to Barbara Ehrenreich, Americans have long tried to maintain an artificial distinction between nationalism—which is seen as essentially "foreign" and prone to "irrational and bloody excess"—and patriotism—which is seen as "quintessentially American," "clear headed and virtuous." This is a useful cultural fiction to maintain, she says, because "by convincing ourselves that our nationalism is unique among nationalisms, we do not have to acknowledge its primitive and bloody side." One of the reasons why so many in mainstream America object so strongly to the militias' use of America's revolutionary past is that they *do* articulate its "primitive and bloody side."[30]

Victor Le Vine provides a particularly apt illustration of how this process works in his discussion of the minutemen as a preeminent patriotic symbol within the United States:

> One hand on the plough and the other grasping his musket, the violence of American beginnings is celebrated—and consecrated—in monument and song. These references are so commonplace, taken for granted, that their other meanings remain submerged; they not only teach and inspire patriotism, but also legitimize both the founding violence and subsequent violent challenges to American democracy.[31]

All of which is to say that words also "have consequences" because the patriotic orthodoxy (the one Clinton was seeking to defend in his speeches in Iowa and Michigan) is vulnerable to challenge and continually needs to be reinforced and protected (*How dare you! These symbols do not belong to you! Who do you think you are?*), and because, as Ernest Gellner puts it, the "cultural shreds and patches used by nationalism are often arbitrary inventions."[32] The militia movement, although not, it must be said, in any systematic or even necessarily fully conscious way, is working at—and in—the fissures and cracks of American patriotic identity, threatening to undermine its arbitrary and tension-ridden constructions.[33] In so doing it provided an uncomfortable reminder of some of the more violent aspects of America's nationalistic or patriotic constructions—the other dark places of American society.

Notes

[1] On the rise of the militia movement and their concerns see Kenneth S. Stern, *A Force Upon the Plain: The American Militia Movement and the Politics of Hate* (Norman: University of Oklahoma Press, 1997); David H. Bennett, *The Party of Fear: The American Far Right from Nativism to the Militia Movement*, 2d ed. (New York: Vintage Books, 1995), 409–474; Morris Dees and James Corcoran, *Gathering Storm: America's Militia Threat* (New York: Harper Perennial, 1996); Richard Abanes, *American Militias: Rebellion, Racism and Religion* (Downers Grove, IL: InterVarsity Press, 1996); David A. Neiwert, *In God's Country: The Patriot Movement and the Pacific Northwest* (Pullman: Washington State University Press, 1999). Although "Oklahoma City bomber" Timothy McVeigh was never a member of a militia, he shared many of their concerns and ideas, and the sense that the militias were also responsible for the bombing remains strong. An interesting discussion of some of the reasons for this can be found in Steven M. Chermak, *Searching for a Demon: The Media Construction of the Militia Movement* (Boston: Northeastern University Press, 2002). On McVeigh see Dan Herbeck and Lou Michael, *American Terrorist: Timothy McVeigh and the Oklahoma City Bombing* (New York: Regan Books, 2001).

[2] On the militias use of this aspect of American history see D. J. Mulloy, *American Extremism: History, Politics and the Militia Movement* (New York: Routledge, 2004); Timothy M. Seul, 'Militia Minds: Inside America's Contemporary Militia Movement' (PhD diss., Purdue University, 1997); Robert H. Churchill, '"The Highest and Holiest Duty of Freemen": Revolutionary Libertarianism in American History' (PhD diss., Rutgers, The State University of New Jersey, 2001); Joshua D. Freilich, Jeremy A. Pienik, and Gregory J. Howard, 'Toward Comparative Studies of the U.S. Militia Movement,' *International Journal of Comparative Sociology* 42, 1–2 (2001): 163–210; and Lane Crothers, 'The Cultural Foundations of the Modern Militia Movement,' *New Political Science* 24, 2 (2002): 221–234.

[3] Linda Thompson, interview, *The Vision Thing*, Channel 4, United Kingdom, 1995, transcript obtained by author; James A. McKinzey, 'H.Q. Bunker,' *Necessary Force* (January 1997): 2; The Kentucky Riflemen Militia, 'What Will You Do?' *The Kentucky Riflemen News* 1 (1995): 4.

[4] 'Editorial, Don't Tread on Me!' *Common Sense*, 'Liberty or Death: Don't Tread on Me' (Kansas City, MO: A Group of Concerned Citizens, 1994), 1; J. J. Johnson, Senate Committee on the Judiciary, *The Militia Movement in the United States: Hearing before the Subcommittee on Terrorism, Technology and Government Information*, 104th Congress, 1st session, 15 June 1995, 102–103; Norman Olson quoted in Anti-Defamation League, *Armed & Dangerous: Militias Take Aim at the Federal Government* (New York: ADL, 1994), 2; "Joan," 'The NC Militia—Just Regular People,' *The Carolina Free Press*, electronic version, 3, 6 (23 August 1997). On the use of Patrick Henry's speech see, for example, Don Gonzales, 'Price of Freedom,' *Patriot's Alert* 1, 2 (September 1994): 5; 'Patrick Henry's Call To Arms,' *Wake-Up Call America* (January/February 1997): 7; and *The Field Manual of the Free Militia*, 'The Heritage of Arming and Organizing,' 1.2–1.2.2, available at <www.publiceye.org/ifas/library/militia/1-2.html>.

[5] Anti-Defamation League, *Armed & Dangerous*, 26.

[6] The American Jewish Committee, *Militias: A Growing Danger* (New York: AJC, 1995), 6. Justice Oliver Wendell Holmes's famous conception of the "marketplace of ideas" was first expressed in his dissenting opinion in *Abrams v. U.S.* 250 U.S. 616 (1919), when he argued that "the best test of truth is the power of the thought to get itself accepted in the competition of the

market." The concept is frequently invoked in discussions of political extremism. See, for example, Seymour Martin Lipset and Earl Raab's classic, *The Politics of Unreason: Right-Wing Extremism in America, 1790–1970* (London: Heinemann, 1971), 4–6.

[7] See, for example, Ken Toole, *What to Do When the Militia Comes to Town* (New York: The American Jewish Committee, 1995), 4–6. Patrick Sullivan, Sheriff of Littleton, Colorado, and Nickolas Murnion, County Attorney for Jordan, Montana, expressed these views before the House Committee on the Judiciary, *Nature and Threat of Violent Anti-Government Groups in America: Hearing before the Subcommittee on Crime*, 104th Congress, 1st session, 2 November 1995, 141–157.

[8] Carl Levin, *Hearing: The Militia Movement in the United States*, 15 June 1995, 44; President Clinton, 'Remarks to Students at Iowa State University,' 25 April 1995, *Weekly Compilation of Presidential Documents*, 31, 17 (1995): 711; 'Remarks at the Michigan State University Commencement Ceremony,' 5 May 1995, *Weekly Compilation of Presidential Documents*, 31, 17 (1995): 773.

[9] Beth Hawkins, 'Patriot Games,' *Detroit Metro Times*, 12 October 1994, in *Militias in America 1995: A Book of Readings & Resources*, eds., Don Hazen, Larry Smith, and Christine Triano (San Francisco: Institute for Alternative Journalism, 1995), 7.

[10] See, for example, Richard Hofstadter and Michael Wallace, eds., *American Violence: A Documentary History* (New York: Vintage, 1971); Richard Maxwell Brown, ed., *American Violence* (Englewood Cliffs, NJ: Prentice-Hall, 1970); and the National Commission on the Causes and Prevention of Violence, *Violence in America: Historical and Comparative Perspectives* (New York: Signet Books, 1969). A more recent and "enjoyable" examination of the appeal, celebration, and destructive capacity of violence in various forms within American society can be found in David Cronenberg's film *A History of Violence* (2005).

[11] Christopher Hewitt's study of the activities of segregationists, black militants, New Left radicals, and militant antiabortion activists in the United States from the 1950s to the 1980s suggests that violence is most likely to occur from those who feel themselves to be losers in the political game—"particularly if they lose consistently." 'The Political Context of Terrorism in America: Ignoring Extremists or Pandering to Them?' *Terrorism and Political Violence*, 12, 3 & 4 (Autumn/Winter, 2000): 325–343.

[12] Between 1994 and 1996 estimates of the number of militia members ranged from 7,000 to 300,000, although when "supporters" or "potential supporters" were included, the figure rose to anywhere between 5 and 12 million. See, for example, John George and Laird Wilcox, *American Extremists: Militias, Supremacists, Klansmen, Communists, and Others* (Amherst, New York: Prometheus Books, 1996), 260; the Anti-Defamation League, *Beyond the Bombing: The Militia Menace Grows* (New York: ADL, 1995), 1; and Jill Smolowe, 'Enemies of the States,' *Time*, 8 May 1995, 25.

[13] David E. Apter, 'Political Violence in Analytical Perspective,' in *The Legitimization of Violence*, ed. David E. Apter (New York: New York University Press, 1997), 3; Frantz Fanon, *The Wretched of the Earth* (London: Penguin Books, 1967), 73–74. Apter sees the heroic side of political violence at work in the role that both actual violence and its threat has played in the "moral teleologies of human betterment," political and social reform, and the "evolution of democracy itself."

[14] Merle Curti, *The Roots of American Loyalty* (New York: Columbia University Press, 1946), viii.

[15] William Wirt, *The Life and Character of Patrick Henry* (Philadelphia: Porter & Coates, 1815); David A. McCants, *Patrick Henry, The Orator* (New York: Greenwood Press, 1990), xi, 58; Steven T. Olsen, 'Patrick Henry's "Liberty or Death" Speech: A Study in Disputed Authorship,' in *American Rhetoric: Context and Criticism*, ed. Thomas W. Benson (Carbondale and Edwardsville: Southern Illinois University Press, 1989), 19. See also Judy Hample, 'The Textual and Cultural Authenticity of Patrick Henry's "Liberty or Death" Speech,' *Quarterly Journal of Speech*, 63 (October 1977): 298–310. Although, as Hample says, the "textual authenticity" of Henry's speech is open to serious doubt—Hample attributes it to William Wirt, while Stephen Olson sees St. George Tucker as the most likely "author"—its "cultural authenticity" is not, and both the militia movement and President Clinton contributed to this.

[16] This is reflected in the accounts we have of the reaction the speech produced at the time, such as Henry Stephens Randall's note of an old man's recollection that, when Henry had finished speaking, "It seemed as if a word from him would have led to a wild explosion of violence." Quoted in Hample, 306. Nor is it a point lost on contemporary militia members that Patrick Henry was a militia leader himself. "A group of concerned citizens" who were attempting to get the militia movement off the ground in 1994, for example, reproduced the imagery of his Culpepper Minutemen's flag on the cover of one of their first publications (*Common Sense*, 1994). On the militias' use of the speech, see also Eugene V. Gallagher, 'God and Country: Revolution as Religious Imperative on the Radical Right,' *Terrorism and Political Violence*, 9, 3 (Autumn 1997): 64–69.

[17] Malcolm X, 'I'm Not an American, I'm a Victim of Americanism,' *Malcolm X Talks to Young People: Speeches in the U.S., Britain and Africa*, ed. Steve Clark (New York: Pathfinder Press, 1991), 18.

[18] Pauline Maier, *American Scripture: How America Declared its Independence from Britain* (London: Pimlico, 1999), 154.

[19] John H. Schaar, 'The Case for Patriotism,' *American Review* 17 (May 1973): 59–100, reprinted in Schaar, *Legitimacy in the Modern State* (New Brunswick, NJ: Transaction Books, 1981), 285–311, 291.

[20] See, for example, Carl L. Becker, *The Declaration of Independence: A Study in the History of Political Ideas* (New York: Vintage Books, 1922, 1942), 8; Stephen E. Lucas, 'Justifying America: The Declaration of Independence as a Rhetorical Document,' in *American Rhetoric*, 68; Wilbur Samuel Howell, 'The Declaration of Independence: Some Adventures with America's Political Masterpiece,' *Quarterly Journal of Speech*, 62 (October 1976): 232–233; and Maier, 209–214.

[21] Maier, 211; Curti, 235. See also Hofstadter and Wallace, *American Violence*, 31.

[22] On these two traditions see Cecilia Elizabeth O'Leary, *To Die For: The Paradox of American Patriotism* (Princeton: Princeton University Press, 1999), *passim*; Curti, *American Loyalty*, 247; and Schaar, 291–297. This is not to argue that the covenanted strand of American patriotism has been an unalloyed success. Schaar himself acknowledges that "American patriotism in practice has failed to live up to Lincoln's teaching of the ideal," not least in its treatment of Native Americans, African Americans, and Mexican Americans. Indeed, although a "covenanted polity might be our finest tradition and our best hope," Schaar argues, "[i]t is not our reality. That reality is nationalism."
Todd Gitlin has also pointed out that, under stress, this progressive tradition can easily break down, turning into an ugly and partisan weapon to be used to weed out the "un-American." Political "extremists" of the 1920s and 1950s suffered from this, as have wartime dissenters throughout U.S. history. The most recent example of the latter is Attorney General John Ashcroft's warning to those who were criticizing the "war on terror": "To those who scare peace-loving people with phantoms of lost liberty, my message is this: Your tactics only aid terrorists for they erode our national unity and diminish our resolve." Todd Gitlin, *The Intellectuals and the Flag* (New York: Columbia University Press, 2006), 130–131, 154.

[23] Cecilia O'Leary argues that it wasn't until World War I "when the government joined forces with right-wing organizations and vigilante groups, that a racially exclusive, culturally conformist, militaristic patriotism finally triumphed"—albeit temporarily—"over more progressive, egalitarian visions of the nation." Ibid., 7. One of the strongest critiques of the militaristic dimensions of patriotism—and of the violence inherent in it—is Emma Goldman's 1908 essay, "Patriotism: A Menace to Liberty" *viz.*:

> Patriotism . . . is a superstition artificially created and maintained through a network of lies and falsehoods. . . . Patriotism requires allegiance to the flag, which means obedience and readiness to kill father, mother, brother, sister. . . . We Americans claim to be a peace-loving people. We hate bloodshed; we are opposed to violence. Yet we go into spasms of joy over the possibility of projecting dynamite bombs from flying machines upon helpless citizens. Such is the logic of patriotism. . . . Patriotism is inexorable and, like all insatiable monsters, demands all or nothing.

Goldman, of course, was deported from the United States in 1919, during the first red scare. Emma Goldman, *Anarchism and Other Essays* (New York: Dover Publications, 1969), 127–144.

On these issues, see also, John Somerville, 'Patriotism and War,' *Ethics*, 91, 4 (July 1981): 568–578; and Michael Parenti, *Land of Idols: Political Mythology in America* (New York: St. Martin's Press, 1994), 26–39.

24 Edward Tabor Linenthal, *Sacred Ground: Americans and Their Battlefields* (Urbana: University of Illinois Press, 1993), 4.

25 'Book Review,' *The Carolina Free Press*, electronic version, 3, 2 (28 February 1997). The book under review was John R. Galvin, *The Minute Men, The First Fight: Myths and Realities of the American Revolution* (Washington, DC: Brassey's, 1967, 1996).

26 Linenthal, 3, 17, 22, 40–43.

27 See, for example, Southern Poverty Law Center, *False Patriots: The Threat of Antigovernment Extremists* (Montgomery, AL: SPLC, 1996); SPLC, 'Racist Extremists Exploit Nationwide Militia Movement,' *Klanwatch Intelligence Report* 76 (December 1994): 1–4; the Anti-Defamation League, *Vigilante Justice: Militias and 'Common Law Courts' Wage War Against the Government* (New York: ADL, 1997), 2–3; Toole, *What to Do*, 2–4.

28 On this see Gitlin, 134 and Schaar, 41.

29 O'Leary, 4. On the constructed nature of patriotism in general, see Benedict Anderson, *Imagined Communities: Reflections on the Origins and Spread of Nationalism*, rev. ed. (London: Verso, 1991); John Bodnar, *Remaking America: Public Memory, Commemoration and Patriotism in the Twentieth Century* (Princeton: Princeton University Press, 1992); John Bodnar, ed., *Bonds of Affection: Americans Define Their Patriotism* (Princeton: Princeton University Press, 1996); Eric Hobsbawm and Terence Ranger eds., *The Invention of Tradition* (Cambridge: Cambridge University Press, 1983).

30 Barbara Ehrenreich, *Blood Rites: Origins and History of the Passions of War* (London: Virago, 1997), 216–217. John Schaar calls nationalism "patriotism's bloody brother," while Michael Lind refers to American nationalism as the "political doctrine that dare not speak its name." Schaar, 285; Michael Lind, *The Next American Nation: The New Nationalism and the Fourth American Revolution* (New York: The Free Press, 1995). On the "dark side" of American nationalism, see also Anatol Lieven, *America, Right or Wrong: An Anatomy of American Nationalism* (Oxford: Oxford University Press, 2004), especially 88–150. On the violence that does not want to remembered, see also Homi Bhabha, who argues that a nation's existence is dependent on "a strange forgetting of the history of the nation's past: the violence involved in establishing the nation's writ. It is this forgetting—a minus in the origin—that constitutes the *beginning* of the nation's narrative." Homi K. Bhabha, ed., 'DissemiNation: Time, Narrative, and the Margins of the Modern Nation,' *Nation and Narration* (London: Routledge, 1990), 310.

31 Victor Le Vine, 'Violence and the Paradox of Democratic Renewal: A Preliminary Assessment,' *Terrorism and Political Violence*, 12, 3 & 4 (Autumn/Winter 2000): 273.

32 Ernest Gellner, *Nations and Nationalism* (London: Blackwell, 1983), 56.

33 The irony of this, however, is that the militia movement is acting in the name of a reimposed unity and naturalness as it fights to restore a past it sees as the "real history" of the United States and the "true legacy" of the founding fathers.

PART IV

Rhetorics of Science

Bio(in)security

16

Rhetoric, Science, and Citizens in the Age of Bioterrorism—The Case of TOPOFF 3

Lisa Keränen

This is not science fiction. The age of bioterror is now.
—Organizer of international counterterrorism exercise Atlantic Storm[1]

The language of risk is itself contagious.
—Joost Van Loon[2]

On April 4, 2005, the "full scale exercise" component of TOPOFF 3, a congressionally mandated weapons of mass destruction (WMD) preparedness drill, commenced across America. Touted as the "most comprehensive terrorism response exercise ever conducted in the United States," TOPOFF 3 involved a two-year cycle of planning, seminars, training, simulation, and post-exercise review geared around five days of simulated simultaneous pneumonic plague attacks in New Jersey.[3] These faux attacks were accompanied by simulated mustard gas and conventional explosive attacks in Connecticut to the tune of $16–18 million dollars.[4] Over 10,000 volunteers, 27 federal agencies, and more than 200 international, national, state, local, and tribal organizations participated. Publicized as "a realistic test of the nation's security," the exercise was designed to "prepare" America for a "complex WMD bioterrorism attack in New Jersey, as well as a kind of dual-header in the state of Connecticut."[5] Over half the participants role-played "victims" by sporting fake pustules, seeping wounds, and brain injuries applied by professional make-up artists. Others played what health care officials called the "worried well" or "hypochondriacs" who showed up at hospitals complaining of vague, unidentifiable symptoms. Still another group acted as emergency first responders, journalists, and law enforcement officials. Although biological weapons themselves were nowhere in sight, their symbolism had become potent and ubiquitous.

TOPOFF 3's elaborate scripting and staging seem an appropriate place to begin a discussion of the rhetorical dynamics of counter-bioterrorism training exercises for they illuminate just how deeply biological weapons have captured our public and institutional imagination. Although experts had warned for decades that a rogue nation or substate actor could deploy biological weapons against a state or its interests, it was only after the circulation of anthrax-laced mailings of unknown origin in October 2001 that the possibility of attack by deadly pathogens acquired pronounced attention in the U.S. public sphere.[6] The resulting profusion of discourses configuring biological weapons, bioterrorism, and the tropes of biodefense, biopreparedness, and biosecurity have triggered an unprecedented wave of counter-bioterrorism spending, training, and policy initiatives.[7] In this essay, I attempt to discern the rhetorical currents that shape recent conceptions of "biopreparedness" by focusing on the rhetorical operations of TOPOFF 3. More specifically, I analyze the rhetoric that scripts and eventuates from TOPOFF 3 as representative of what sociologist Lee Clarke calls "fantasy documents," or functional planning tools that signal organizations' ability to prepare for anticipated disaster.[8] As emblems of rational planning against the irrational, these exercises serve as more than mere tools of impression management for wary publics. As a container for our fears about the great unknown, they encode cultural meanings of self and Other, invoke and reproduce broader cultural discourses of contagion, and reveal some of the dilemmas inherent in the present age of terror and empire.[9]

Although the news media has irregularly covered the TOPOFF exercises, these reports have neither touched off a national debate about biodefense nor have they cued large segments of the population to the post-9/11 biopreparedness drills routinely conducted in their community. Although these exercises may help to prepare small segments of the populace for a biological catastrophe, among their prevailing rhetorical operations, I argue, is their capacity for garnering support among high-level emergency managers for military solutions to complex catastrophic events. By enrolling the fantasy of viral apocalypse and the promise of the technological fix to reify the risk of bioterrorism, exercises such as TOPOFF 3 perform in increasingly self-reproducing or autopoietic ways that promote a powerful interlacing of our public health system and the military industrial complex.

In advancing this argument, I offer rhetorical criticism in the "pragmatic attitude," that is, intertextual interpretation concerned with "the social practices (praxis) of everyday life" and their relation to the institutional and non-institutional structures that influence everyday life.[10] Put another way, criticism in the pragmatic attitude explores the interplay between rhetoric, everyday experience, and social relations. First advanced by Elizabeth Walker Mechling and Jay Mechling, this theoretical perspective on criticism draws from American pragmatism and critical theory to require that the critic "ground public discourse in the practices of every day life" to consider how texts "might replicate, elaborate, or contradict the lived experiences of the audience."[11] I begin by sketching the contemporary landscape in which the threat of bioterrorism looms. I then examine how TOPOFF 3 enrolls the rhetoric of viral apocalypse and the technological fix to reify the risk of bioterrorism and to encourage military solutions to outbreaks. I conclude by considering what this study offers to our understanding of the dilemmas of the present historical moment.

The Contemporary Landscape

It is worth noting that the fear of bioterrorism is related to anxieties about globalization, scientific and technological development, emerging infectious disease, and the primal dread of contamination by the Other. This dread is activated through what Joost Van Loon, drawing from Julia Kristeva, terms the "viral abject."[12] Working through colonization, replication, and contagion, pathogens can become the viral, bacterial, rickettsial, or fungal epitome of Kristeva's "stranger within," and thus have the power to elicit profound existential horror and dread.[13] As Alan Goldstein explains, as "agents of death derived from life," biological weapons "are the most terrifying exactly because they operate far beyond the twilight zone of our collective imagination."[14] Although biological weapons are as ancient as warfare itself, contemporary anxiety about terrorist use of biological weapons is tied up in a postmodern response to the historical contingencies of the post-cold war/post-9/11 political scene coupled with the technological advances of the genetic revolution.[15] No longer operating in the shadow of the nuclear threat, the discourses and material practices surrounding biological weapons are now assuming greater clarity and autonomy in reconfiguring the relationship between the state, biological sciences, and our health care system in ways that deserve scholarly scrutiny.[16]

Despite the inherent importance of the topic to international security and the lives of the global citizenry, and despite the interaction of discursive and material practices that shape our understanding of the threat of intentional pathogen spread, scholars in rhetoric have yet to produce sustained analyses of how discourses about biological weapons are produced, mobilized, and translated into action by various stakeholders.[17] Scholarship that addresses these rhetorical processes can contribute to cold war/post-cold war/post-9/11 rhetorical and organizational studies by uncovering and critiquing neglected cold war rhetorics of biological weapons proliferation, and by engaging biological weapons threat construction and symbolism in the discourse of international relations.[18] As cold war documents about biological weapons increasingly reach the public sphere, rhetoricians can begin to fill in an important aspect of post-cold war history in order to, as Martin Medhurst suggests, "gain a new way of thinking about the Cold War."[19]

Research that addresses the unique rhetorical and communicative dimensions associated with biological weapons can further provide an important counterpart to nuclear rhetorical criticism, for arguments about the uniqueness of biological weapons abound.[20] In addition, Bryan Taylor and Stephen John Hartnett have argued that scholars should expand (post-)cold war scholarship to engage the general cultural circulation of cold war iconography and arguments in contexts such as mass-mediated discourses and commercialized spectacles.[21] Cold war rhetorics of containment, surveillance, and civil defense are encoded in biological weapons' representations in popular culture that further circulate through biopreparedness training exercises—

their role in sustaining particular contamination fantasies deserves analysis. Finally, the rhetoric of biological weapons and bioterrorism provides a site for uncovering institutional and public dimensions of risk construction and mitigation. Rhetoricians, I insist, should be contributing to the growing body of risk scholarship by demonstrating how the rhetorical dimensions of risk construction function as agents of social change and by unmasking the political implications of these processes.[22] The most promising lines of research in this area, I believe, will be those that ground their analysis in an understanding of the recursive relationship between institutional structures and discourses in ways that are sensitive to the institutional context of big science.[23] This essay aspires to this task.

Although they share several features in common with other WMD, the symbolically potent scepter of biological weapons seems to have captivated contemporary public and expert imagination to a greater extent than other WMD. A 2002 report by the Center for Nonproliferation Research at National Defense University noted that of threats posed by nuclear, chemical, biological, and radiological weapons, "a disproportionate share of the literature in the past three years has been devoted to the biological weapon threat."[24] Indeed, the dominant rhetoric of bioterrorism that circulates in policy circles encourages a political reality in which fear of the threat of bioterrorism has ushered in a new era of viral panic among decision makers, accompanied by scientific and technological expansion into more realms of human activity. Cultural commentators and journalists have pointed out the unparalleled changes that have occurred in biodefense since the anthrax mailings of 2001. These "politics of urgency," magnified by growing concern about associated threats from SARS, West Nile, avian influenza, and other emerging infectious diseases, have prompted changes in many aspects of the public and private sector.[25]

In the area of federal funding, for instance, bioterrorism-related research and development has mushroomed over the past four years with considerable, growing, and bipartisan-supported federal monies allocated to counter-bioterrorism initiatives. The federal government spent more than $14.5 billion on civilian biodefense between FY2001 and FY2004 and an additional $7.6 billion in 2005.[26] FY2006 requests of $5.1 billion show increases for all agencies involved with civilian biodefense.[27] The government has thus far allocated more than $6 billion for Project BioShield—twice the amount spent on the Human Genome Project. Funded biological-weapons-related research by the National Institutes for Allergens and Infectious Disease (NIAID) has grown a staggering 1,500% since 2001 with 97% of funding recipients never having worked on biological weapons agents previously.[28] In fact, biodefense funding now tops HIV/AIDS funding by NIAID, a situation that has led some experts to decry a bioterrorism "brain drain" in which health researchers abandon areas of study with high global mortality rates (for instance, malaria and tuberculosis) to study biological weapons agents.[29] Level four biosafety laboratories (BSL-4), where researchers investigate live strains of

the world's most deadly pathogens under conditions of (presumed) heightened security, are popping up at Wal-Mart-sized facilities at universities, military sites, and private pharmaceutical companies across the nation.[30] The
sprawling "biodefense complex," as the Department of Homeland Security
(DHS) refers to its network of laboratories, includes the Plum Island Animal
Disease Control Center, the Biodefense Knowledge Center, national laboratories, and the university-based Department of Homeland Security Centers of
Excellence. Many of these will eventually fall under the purview of DHS's
National Biodefense Analysis and Countermeasures Center (NBACC),
which will oversee the National Bioforensic Analysis Center (NBFAC) and
the Biological Threat Characterization Center (BTCC), which will conduct
pathogen research in BSL-3 and 4 laboratories. Trends in federal funding
have been matched by investments in the private sector with pharmaceutical
companies, defense contractors, and venture capitalists producing technologies designed to aid in the detection of and response to a biological attack.[31]
David Rothkopf estimates the private sector will spend four times as much as
the federal government on homeland security applications, with biopreparedness projects taking a lead.[32] To counter the bioterrorism some experts suggest is inevitable, "biopreparedness" has become the topic *du jour,* spurring a
growing industry of products and protocols that ostensibly seek to protect the
citizenry from biological threats. Enter large-scale counter-bioterrorism preparedness exercises.

　　Although government preparedness exercises are hardly new, their complexity, frequency, and publicity have dramatically increased post-9/11. During World War I, the National Defense Council (NDC) initiated early
preparedness exercises that flared and waned in number and scale depending
on threat perception during subsequent conflicts. During the cold war, civil
defense simulation exercises geared toward a Soviet thermonuclear attack
revealed the tension between preparedness, prevention, and aiding the
enemy. The Federal Civil Defense Administration (FCDA) launched Operation Alert, a series of nuclear attack scenarios between 1954 and 1961 that
President Eisenhower noted might have a deterrent effect on the Soviets. Guy
Oakes has called Operation Alert "an elaborate national sociodrama that
combined elements of mobilization for war, disaster relief, the church social,
summer camp and the fair."[33] Its scenarios involved annual drills that
required citizens in more than 60 participating cities to take cover for fifteen
minutes. Mass evacuations occurred—even Eisenhower and his staff
retreated to the countryside where they issued a report declaring 8 million
predicted deaths.[34] After 1979, the Federal Emergency Management Agency
(FEMA) oversaw civil defense preparedness efforts reflecting the "all hazards
approach" and sponsored large-scale readiness exercises (REXs) involving
agencies with defense responsibilities. A number of FEMA's readiness exercises in the 1970s and 1980s were classified military drills involving cold war
nuclear scenarios, and, after the accident at Three Mile Island, nuclear power
emergency preparedness. Thousands of preparedness exercises have been

held since this time. Elizabeth Walker Mechling and Jay Mechling examined dispersal and evacuation, the fallout shelter, and the naturalization of the bomb to track the evolution of cold war civil defense strategies as a "proxy debate over the larger salient issue of the tension between individualism and community in Fifties America."[35] Following their lead, we might profitably ask what contemporary biopreparedness exercises reveal about the dilemmas and tensions of the present era. As a container for our fears of contamination by the terrorist Other and our rationalist desire to prepare for the unprepara-ble, exercises like TOPOFF 3 are worth examining for their encodings of par-ticular cultural understandings of the risk of bioterrorism and appropriate responses to it on individual and collective levels.

The Coming Viral Apocalypse:
Biopreparedness Exercises as Fantasy Documents

TOPOFF 3, more than two years in the making, was the third in a series of increasingly elaborate, large-scale WMD preparedness exercises con-ducted initially by FEMA and the Justice Department before being trans-ferred to the purview of the DHS. TOPOFF 1, conducted May 20–23, 2000, entailed Denver, Colorado, succumbing to a simulated *yersinia pestis* (plague) attack while Portsmouth, New Hampshire, underwent a staged chemical weapons attack with a $3 million price tag. Between May 12–16, 2003, TOPOFF 2 simulated a plague attack in Chicago with a radiological device detonation in Seattle accompanied by a simultaneous cyber attack. With more than 8,000 participants, it was touted as the most comprehensive coun-terterrorism exercise ever conducted. Total cost: $17 million. TOPOFF 3 was designed, in the words of DHS secretary Michael Chertoff, "to push our plans and our systems to the very limit" and to be larger and more compli-cated than TOPOFF 1 and 2.[36] Organizational rhetors who produced the script for TOPOFF 3 included "a team of exercise planners experienced in WMD, war gaming, law enforcement, intelligence, and international terrorist networks."[37] The exercise scenario featured a simultaneous mustard gas release and explosive detonation in New London, Connecticut, and a biolog-ical release of pneumonic plague from an SUV sprayer system in Union and Middlesex Counties in New Jersey. TOPOFF 3 used "a data source (Univer-sal Adversary) that replicates actual terrorist networks down to names, pho-tos, and driver's license numbers [that] enable[s] exercise players to simulate intelligence gathering and analysis," as well as a virtual news network (VNN) enrolling professional journalists to report events as they unfold on closed-circuit television.[38] Local and national media outlets also covered TOPOFF 3, but its findings, both classified and unclassified, are still being developed by event participants.

That TOPOFF organizers went to the length of enlisting make-up artists, a faux news network, and scores of emergency first responders suggests the seriousness with which organizers take the threat of bioterrorism, while their elaborate staging, vigorous efforts to ensure realism, and recurrent themes suggest the presence of a fantasy, a collectively shared worldview, about what a bioterrorism attack will entail. Because of its invocation of a widespread, collective vision of social reality, the concept of fantasy documents provides a productive lens through which to view these biopreparedness exercises. According to sociologist Lee Clarke, fantasy documents are organizational planning rhetorics aimed at demonstrating to outside audiences that organizations can manage the disasters presented by the technological decisions that support modern life. For Clarke, "Fantasy documents are rationality badges, symbols organizations use to signal they are in control of danger, whether they really are or not."[39] Moreover, "these rationality badges originate in the everyday routines that organizations develop in response to problems, and in the social conditions engendered by organizations that produce them."[40] Fantasy documents "are usually set in a rhetoric of technical competence, and often enough in one of national interest, providing a context that helps persuade (internal and external) audiences of their legitimacy."[41] Documents detailing plans for oil spills, natural disasters, even nuclear accidents, are examples of fantasy documents. TOPOFF 3 documents are fantasy documents in two senses. First, they are used to train emergency managers how to respond to anticipated future disasters. Second, they are used to derive future plans for how to respond to disaster. There is a certain reflexivity built into the genre in that these fantasy documents are then used to script future fantasy documents and policy initiatives.

The rhetorical import of fantasy documents lies in their promotion of particular institutional responses over others through the repeated invocation of shared assumptions and meanings. Fantasy documents achieve this process by setting "terms of public debate by shaping vocabularies within which discussion occurs."[42] Clarke explains, "In this way fantasy documents justify support systems that seem increasingly beyond our comprehension and control."[43] The dramatic elements of fantasy documents and their capacity for shaping deliberative rhetoric are evident in that "fantasy documents read like scripts for plays and movies. They specify relevant actors and the story lines those actors are supposed to pursue."[44] Thus, "fantasy documents supply the scenery, necessarily neglecting much as they construct an organizational stage upon which the fantasy will work itself out."[45] Fantasy documents are an endemic feature of our risk society in which organizational rhetors must plan for the risks associated with modern life.

The concept of fantasy has a rich and tangled history in rhetoric and communication studies, ranging from the work of Ernest Bormann and fantasy theme analysis to the role of fantasy in psychoanalytic approaches to rhetoric.[46] I use Clarke's concept of a fantasy document here to highlight the existence of a genre of technically informed institutional rhetoric that is created primarily for the purpose of reassuring publics of institutional readiness for such disaster, but I maintain that these fantasy documents do evince rhetorical visions worthy of consideration and have structural implications beyond their reassurance function. In invoking the language of fantasy, I am not suggesting that the resultant social visions are "made up." Rather, I assume that they are the collective result of rhetorical processes in which shared assumptions become crystallized and then replicated in discourse. While I am not conducting a formulaic fantasy theme analysis, I am concerned with how the rhetoric of TOPOFF 3 documents forges shared perceptions, scripts, and stock responses to the threat of bioterrorism and how these responses interact with institutional structures to shape the contours of everyday life in the post-9/11 world.

Consistent with Clarke's account of fantasy documents, Christian Erickson and Bethany Barratt argue that WMD preparedness exercises are "explicitly designed forms of information warfare and perception management that are targeted at both reassuring the population of the ability of the state to respond to weapons of mass destruction incidents, and to communicate a message of deterrence to potential enemies."[47] Erickson, Barratt, and Clarke stress the role of these exercises in persuading audiences of organizational competence to plan for the future, while I examine them as cultural artifacts that locate the epistemic "truth" of biological weapons in rhetorical practices that prime elite decision makers to respond to the threats posed by biological weapons in particular militarized ways. My critical interpretation of TOPOFF 3 as a key node in the formation of a shared vision of post-9/11 biopolitics is not meant to suggest that these exercises are not doing the reassurance and credibility work Clarke suggests or to intimate that organizational officials should not be planning for disasters. Rather, I seek to uncover and trouble the "root assumptions" of the technical and mass-mediated public discourse scripting and emerging from these exercises.[48] In so doing, I argue that a major purpose of the exercises is to build consensus among emergency planners and high level officials that the "threat is real," that it is as event planners suggest it will be, and that it is too complex to handle without military intervention. The rhetoric of risk is central to this process.

Reifying the Risk of Bioterrorism and the Reality of Simulation: Autopoiesis and Structure

The biological weapons discourses of TOPOFF 3 do not merely present scientific and technical aspects associated with a biological weapons attack. They structure understanding of the *risk* of bioterrorism. The rhetoric of risk has become a powerful catalyst for social action in the modern world.[49] The 1992 translation of Ulrich Beck's seminal *Risikogesellschaft* into English stimulated a substantial amount of scholarship that investigates how the construction of risk becomes an agent of social change.[50] Many of these studies demonstrate how modern risk societies "manufacture" risk through their institutional attempts to control the natural world.[51] Yet, the social construction of risk entails the selection and definition of particular hazards in ways that effect social order.[52] That is, as we attempt to manage certain risks, we inevitably ignore others; the rhetorical process involved in the selection of particular risks for management often follows elite agendas. A critical rhetorical perspective on risk asks us to move beyond the statistical calculation of risk to consider the ways in which official perceptions of risk are cultivated and transformed into stable rhetorical formations and how these formations, in turn, affect political processes.[53] TOPOFF 3 is the rhetorical creation of self-styled biosecurity experts who occupy an increasingly prominent space in policy circles and who argue for a message of urgency of the risk of bioterrorism (a threat that some outside experts argue is exaggerated) to spread to multiple audiences, from expert political actors to the general citizenry. To a large extent, the threat is hypothetical, although it is constructed around a frightening kernel of possibility. Yet event organizers invite increasing numbers of volunteers to participate in the fantasy that bioterrorism will be as dire as they suggest. "Devastating," "destructive," "disruptive," and "horrifying" are adjectives that cling to descriptions of intentional pathogen spread.

TOPOFF 3 invokes a realist rhetoric of science to normalize biological weapons and direct attention away from the risks made possible by our own extensive biological weapons research programs to those posed by "the terrorists." Organizers of Atlantic Storm, TOPOFF 3, and other biopreparedness exercises symbolically transform the uncertainty of biological weapons attack into a tangible future in which large-scale bioterrorism is a predestined part of our political landscape. Wrapped in the ethos of scientific objectivity, these exercises cloak the contingency of their knowledge claims and derive rhetorical authority by marshalling the language of scientific discourse. TOPOFF 3 features, for example, a realist-technical rhetoric that legitimizes its contingent claims by appeals to science and rational planning. Statements such as "seed stocks of Variola major virus (the causative agent of smallpox) were obtained" and "smallpox virus can be grown in embryonated eggs and a variety of tissue cell culture systems" convert the hallmarks of modern scientific discourse from technical language to passive voice into perceptions of the "reality" of the scenarios.[54] Handouts for participants in the exercises feature footnoted epidemiological assumptions charts, "calculations of final casualties and deaths," and "spread and fatality" assumptions tables. The level of detail includes estimated fatalities of cats and rabbits. Mediated reportage of both exercises echoes the realist rhetoric and often takes the opportunity to offer the citizenry lessons about the symptoms and preventive measures for the biological weapons agents featured in the exercises.

A second mechanism that works to grant legitimacy to the vision of bioterrorism inherent in these exercises presents through the vigorous assertion of the "reality" of the simulation. While in one breath trying to reassure citizens that the simulation is not "reality," biopreparedness exercise organizers and participants go to great lengths to assure auditors of the soundness of the preparedness plans and the simulation's verisimilitude. Comments by officials involved in the TOPOFF 3 exercise, echoed in the media, reinforce the "reality" of the simulation. House Homeland Security Committee Chair Representative Christopher Cox (R-CA) told reporters that "one of the things that really struck me is how hard everyone has to work for an exercise. It's every bit as much work as if it were real."[55] Meanwhile, Connecticut Commissioner for the Department of Emergency Management and Homeland Security James Thomas said, "It definitely feels real. I'm impressed with the way everyone is doing."[56] The Associated Press amplified appeals to realism, quoting New Jersey's acting governor Richard Codey: "We are better prepared than most states in America. We will put New Jersey's terrorism preparedness to a very thorough test. It will be a very realistic exercise." Journalist Wayne Parry stated: "It will be so realistic, in fact, [that] Codey worries about people who haven't gotten word that a drill is underway might think the country is under a real terrorist attack."[57] The stress on realism functions to foster perceptions that disaster planners accurately understand the situation and that a real bioterrorism attack would look indistinguishable from the simulation, but it also works to stifle debate about the broader purposes of biodefense by assuming that the threat comes from a large-scale biological weapons attack.

Jean Baudrillard, one of the most prominent theorists of simulation, describes simulation as "substituting signs of the real for the real itself."[58] Yet, as Barry Brummett notes, "Simulation and reality are confounded in that simulations may speak to, affect, or have relevance for reality."[59] In *The World and How We Describe It*, Brummett distinguishes between reality as lived experience, representation as communication about (that is, a re-presentation of) lived experience, and simulation as "a self contained fantasy that is none of the above, not real or a representation of the real but an experience within a world apart from the world."[60] A paradox of biopreparedness and WMD simulation exercises is that they do link up in some way with broader political conditions at the same time that much of their operations—ironically, given the increasing number of participants in each exercise—are increasingly discursively closed. One of the major rhetorical operations of these exercises is thus an increasing trend toward autopoiesis, or self-reproduction, that, as we shall see in the next section of the essay, enrolls the rhetoric of viral apocalypse and the promise of the technological fix to garner support among elite decision makers for military responses to biological incidents.

The concept of autopoiesis, literally self-creation, was originally advanced by biologists Humberto Maturana and Francisco Varela to capture the way in which systems interact with themselves as they recursively reproduce themselves.[61] Cells, for example, draw from structures such as a nucleus, organelles, and so on, to reproduce themselves. German organization theorist Niklas Luhmann transformed autopoiesis from a metaphor to explain biological systems to a theory of social relations in which "communication" is central to the self-reproduction of a social system.[62] For Luhmann, social systems are communication systems that maintain their boundaries from the larger environment by reducing complexity. Communication systems thus take in information from the outside but organize that information in terms of their overall orientation and purposes. Autopoiesis extended to social systems helps to explain how a system "interact[s] recursively with itself, as new information only makes sense in relation to the structures created by previous information gathering."[63]

As a rhetorician, I am appropriating Luhmann's concept of autopoiesis to point to the increasingly self-reproducing aspects of the biodefense complex that take in information from the larger social environment and interpret it in terms of its own purposes—reproduction of the system. I want to bracket the issues autopoiesis raises for organizational theory to harness the concept's capacity for thinking about rhetorical replication. "The language of risk is itself contagious," explains Van Loon, "it induces everything into its own properties."[64] In this way, fantasy documents are central to a rhetorical process of autopoiesis that authorizes a host of actions in the social structure that make the need for biodefense more likely. According to Robert Cooper, "Autopoiesis tells us that human life is a series of self-constituting acts of creative division, acts which tell us that human life is a continuous process of founding and finding, re-founding, and re-finding, oneself in a world motivated by incompleteness, decay, and disappearance."[65] So in the act of making themselves over again, the organizations that participate in biopreparedness exercises bring together the past to construct a vision of the future that reproduces their system.

Luhmann emphasizes how systems that are open thus rely on communicative closure as a means of producing social order. This strategic insularity, which promotes self-reproduction by blocking off the discourse of those who would challenge its authority, is evident in the tight circle of those who scripted and participated in TOPOFF 3. Those who plan biopreparedness exercises are drawn from a more or less insular pool of war gamers, self-styled biodefense experts, public health officials, and military officials. Furthermore, according to *Slate's* Daniel Engber, "Officials in Connecticut said they tried not to advertise too much for volunteers: About half were military personnel from the local naval base, and most of the rest were recruited by word-of-mouth."[66] Thus, insiders who are already likely to buy into the assumptions of bioterrorism's relation to the war on terror are those most likely to participate in these exercises.[67] That people who role play journalists and other officials are prevented from writing about their experiences in the mock drills further insulates the system from critical challenges of its core assumptions. "Role-playing reporters must not be full-time employees of a real news organization, and they must agree never to write about the mock terror attack in any other context," explained Engber.[68] While the system is discursively open to incorporating information from the life-world, it increasingly supplies its own justification for future policy that its vision recommends. Fantasy documents thus produce self-created fantasies that justify the perpetuation of their creating system. Temporality is important to this autopoietic process for the system needs to draw together events from the past to craft its future vision. In the case of TOPOFF 3, the rhetoric of viral apocalypse supplies the link between past and future.

Scripting Futures: Viral Apocalypse and the Technological Fix

The central rhetorical vision of biopreparedness exercises such as TOPOFF 3 may be expressed as "viral apocalypse." Indeed, these exercises invoke and reproduce a proliferating rhetorical formation that I term the "postmodern viral apocalyptic." For James Jasinski, apocalyptic discourse is "a form of prophesy or prophetic speech that predicts how and when the world will end."[69] The apocalyptic is an enduring and recurrent feature of both the Judeo-Christian tradition and also American culture.[70] According to Barry Brummett, the "apocalyptic is always a response to meaninglessness, failure of points of reference, and bewilderment about how to understand the present."[71] The postmodern viral apocalyptic gathers power from transforming ancient and culturally ubiquitous contagion anxieties into a vivid and horrifying potential future resulting from bioterrorist attack, intentional pathogen spread, or emerging infectious disease. The villain is either a terrorist, a madman, or Mother Nature run amok. The viral apocalyptic combines inventional resources from persistent concerns about emerging infectious disease and heightened awareness of bioterrorism with elements of Joshua Gunn and David Beard's "apocalyptic sublime" to predict the near end of humanity through viral pandemic.[72] Manifest in both popular culture and policy forms, it appears in films like Danny Boyle's *28 Days Later* (2003), where stark aesthetic conventions cement a picture of abjection and despair, best-selling books like Laurie Garret's *The Coming Plague*, and even Atlantic Storm's prediction of hundreds of thousands of casualties and massive geopolitical breakdown.[73] The result is a symbolic displacement of millennial apocalyptic anxieties with concerns about malevolent microbes and contamination by the Other.

In popular fiction, through renditions and even writings of would-be ecoterrorists who seek to expunge the human race of evil-doers, the viral apocalyptic often has a purifying capacity. It purges the earth of the unfortunates and the damned. However, as it manifests itself in exercises like TOPOFF 3, viral apocalypse itself pollutes global civil society and perhaps more menacingly, undermines global economic stability. Pandemic and resultant chaos is understandably, but not inconsequentially, prominent in biopreparedness training exercises. The rhetorical vision of viral apocalypse entails widespread outbreak, usually at multiple sites at once. Yet numerous studies and reviews of attempted bioterrorism by criminals, terrorists, and sects have raised serious questions about the efficacy of biological weapons attacks.[74] Pathogens are fragile. Most die when exposed to sunlight or environmental changes. Explosive means of delivery are unlikely to work since heat and charge are likely to kill the organisms. Previous attempts to kill in large numbers using biological weapons have repeatedly failed. The Department of Defense noted in 1997 that "conventional terrorism was far more prevalent, far more harmful, and far more deadly than chemical or biological terrorism."[75] The report concluded, "If the past is any predictor of the future, terrorist incidents involving chemical and biological substances will continue to be small in scale and far less harmful than conventional terrorist attacks."[76]

Yet, the rhetorical vision that inheres in the viral postmodern viral apocalyptic form entails large-scale suffering, civil unrest, and economic collapse. Although TOPOFF 3's casualty predictions have not yet been publicly released, the scenario was designed to stress the system with panicked volunteers who would overwhelm hospitals and shelters. In the ministerial Atlantic Storm exercise held several months before TOPOFF 3, the scenario resulted in a projected 660,000 victims within two months with "45,000 Americans dead, millions dying worldwide, the global economy at a standstill, and ethnic fighting in many nations."[77] The presence of this fantasy chain of social breakdown can be tracked across the discourse of those who participated in scripting the exercises. In 1999, Tara O'Toole, who has organized a number of international biopreparedness drills, including Atlantic Storm and TOPOFF, wrote an article entitled "Smallpox: An Attack Scenario" in the *Journal of Emerging Infectious Disease*. In this essay "outbreaks" of "civil unrest" require participation of the National Guard.[78] In her TOPOFF 1 exercise, "thousands of panicked persons . . . flood[ed] into emergency departments."[79] In the unfolding drama, "civil unrest broke out." Moreover, "People had not been allowed to shop. Stores were closed. Food supplies ran out because trucks were no longer being let into the state. Rioting began to occur."[80] This trope of the panicked public works to forge participants' perceptions that martial law is required. The Model State Emergency Health Powers Act (MSEHPA), drafted by some of the same people who help plan biopreparedness exercises such as Atlantic Storm and TOPOFF, has been adopted by several states and gives governors the power to declare martial law and force vaccinations, quarantine, and property seizure during a suspected epidemic.[81]

As if pandemic itself was not enough, the imagery of these exercises increasingly presents complex catastrophic events in which bioterrorism is accompanied by other types of WMD or conventional attack. The identity altercasted to the terrorist-villains in these exercises is thus the technologically sophisticated network. It is a dispersed terrorist organization capable of conducting large-scale attacks using chem-bio methods that require careful scientific training and disciplined execution. The hero, by contrast, is rational planning and proper application of technology. Thus, these exercises also enroll the reassuring rhetoric of the technological fix. They are predicated on the shared fantasy theme that these exercises generate powerful knowledge that will help mitigate future attacks. Technology is central to this vision and thus demands a dizzying array of biological detection and containment systems that drive biotech research and development. What might be epidemic then is not biological weapons outbreaks, but responses that suggest that if we just apply enough technology and rational planning we will be able to insulate ourselves at least somewhat from mass casualty chem-bioterrorism, a theme that reveals a central ambiguity in the rhetorical vision inherent in biopreparedness. As President Bush has noted:

> The proliferation of biological materials, technologies, and expertise increases the potential for adversaries to design a pathogen to evade our existing medical and non-medical countermeasures. To address this challenge, we are taking advantage of these same technologies to ensure that we can anticipate and prepare for the emergence of this threat.[82]

Thus, this fantasy pivots on the perilous promise of the technological fix for the United States and her allies and the unseemly saga of the Other's misuse of techno-science on the other. The unprecedented expansion in biodefense industries we are now witnessing is thus justified through the rhetoric of the technological fix without widespread consideration of how they are part of the same system that reproduces risks and uses those risks as a justification for continued production of risk.

Not only is the perceived threat of bioterrorism-induced pandemic amplified by these preparedness exercises that help to drive contemporary biodefense policy and research and development, it is also providing inventional fodder for broader cultural narratives about contagion, pandemics, and viral apocalypse, which, in turn, reciprocally reinforces alarm about biological weapons attacks further. Philip Strong's notion of "epidemic psychology" and Elaine Showalter's "cultural narratives of hysteria" remind us that fear and panic can be contagious.[83] Strong notes that historically when societies have faced novel diseases the resulting panic profoundly disrupts the social order. In the early stages of Albert Camus's *LaPeste,* town residents react to the plague with selfish plans, officials are slow to admit epidemic, and the worried well plot to flee the city. Yet, perceptions of widespread panic might be more a part of our cultural mythos than a historical actuality. Showalter notes that "infectious epidemics spread by stories circulated through self-help books, articles in newspapers and magazines, TV talk shows and series, films, the Internet, and even literary criticism."[84] For Showalter, these "hystories," or "cultural narratives of hysteria," "multiply rapidly and uncontrollably in the mass media, telecommunications, and email."[85] In this way, they may be more persuasive to elite decision makers charged with protecting the population than everyday citizens who may be experiencing what sociologists call "risk fatigue." Thus, while representations of panic abound, actual panic does not. In fact, despite the prevalence of writers writing about cultural panic, empirical evidence of panic from over fifty years of disaster studies is rare.[86] Instead, in times of crisis we witness at the community level what sociologists call the "rational flight response." What we witness at the discursive level, however, is the trope of panicked public, phobic citizens who need to be controlled and disciplined through martial law into what Michel Foucault famously called "docile bodies."[87]

Supporting Discourses:
Militarized Public Health for a Phobic Citizenry

The rhetorical vision contained in viral apocalypse works in conjunction with the techno-realist rhetoric that reifies the risk of bioterrorism to garner support among elite decision makers for military solutions to public health crises that have historically been handled locally at the household and community level. TOPOFF 3 scenario assumptions entailed a "code red alert," which combines a war and military-type command control situation that blurs the lines between civil and military defense in the arena of public health response. Indeed, the distinctions between civilian and military response seem to collapse under the assumptions of the scenarios. Classified operations conducted in tandem with TOPOFF included Department of Defense drills. A second set of classified war game exercises conducted by the United Kingdom and Canada in conjunction with TOPOFF did not receive major press coverage, although they had been previously announced by the DHS. When a reporter asked senior DHS officials during a TOPOFF press briefing, "Can either of you speak to any involvement by Northern Command, and/or DOD's WMD specially trained teams?" the official responded by explaining the process through which unmet local and state needs get filtered into requests to "energize" federal "interagency partners" to "determine if there is a federal solution to the problem."[88] The official also noted:

> I believe that we built in some deliberate Department of Defense play in this exercise, some of it in coordination with the state National Guard units to figure out who might have the best capability and be able to best respond. And we had quite a bit of analysis and assessments in terms of DOD hospital capability where I believe there were some DOD mobile hospital requirements built into each venue that were sourced by DOD. And we were somewhere in the process of those being mobilized, energized and deployed on site. Also there were DOD requirements to, I believe, provide DOD airlift or transportation for some critical care patients out of the Connecticut venue when the New England treatment capacity for some of the more severe casualties that had experienced chemical burns had to be flown to other burn centers across the country. I believe that DOD volunteered for the mission and taskings to transport those patients to those—through the DOD medical system out to those other care centers.

The hesitance of this official in characterizing the role of the Department of Defense in TOPOFF 3 suggests, I believe, the difficulty of separating the classified, military components of TOPOFF from the unclassified, public ones. The interlacing of military and civil defense plans in light of pandemic is masked by the erasure of military plans and purposes from public discourse about these exercises. A "Frequently Asked Questions" section of the TOPOFF 3 press release poses the question, "What are the overarching goals of TOPOFF 3?"

> The stated goals of TOPOFF 3 are to test the full range of existing procedures for domestic incident management of a WMD terrorist event and to improve, through evaluation and practice, top officials' capabilities in affected countries to respond in partnership; to test the handling and flow of operational and time-critical intelligence; and to practice strategic coordination of media relations and public information issues.[89]

The odd inclusion of the term "stated" implicitly begs the question of what the unstated goals of the exercise might be and what the classified military planning documents might suggest.

These exercises also symbolically link biopreparedness to the war on terror, which justifies a military response to a growing number of emerging health threats. Milton Leitenberg argues that "threat assessment, most particularly regarding 'BW terrorism'—the potential for BW use by non-state actors—has been greatly exaggerated."[90] "The U.S. anthrax events in September–October 2001," he explains, "and the demonstration of other capabilities by the Al Qaeda organization, has made it even easier to continue that exaggeration."[91] In response to their scripted frequently asked questions, the following question was posed: "How relevant is the TOPOFF 3 scenario to the war on terrorism?" The DHS responded, "The TOPOFF 3 scenario is based on research of actual terrorist organizations' capabilities and news accounts of events that have transpired since September 11, 2001."[92]

The irony is that there is a tension in the preparedness discourses that converges around these exercises that push, on the one hand, privatized preparedness at the individual and household level and, on the other, militarized responses. When former DHS director Tom Ridge advocated citizens "arm" themselves with duct tape and plastic sheeting, for example, he drew from institutionally derived preparedness plans such as DHS's "Don't Be Afraid, Be Ready" campaign, which "seeks to help American families be better prepared for even unlikely emergency scenarios." According to DHS, "We know from intelligence reports that terrorists are working hard to obtain biological, chemical, and radiological weapons, and the threat of an attack is real."[93] Although preparedness discourses are hardly particular to bioterrorism, much of the current preparedness discourse, like that of previous wars and periods of disaster awareness, privatizes preparedness and further directs attention away from institutional productions of risk. To give a concrete example, I recently attended a tabletop counterterrorism training exercise in Denver, Colorado. While participation was contingent on not discussing the details of the scenario, I can share that after the exercise, when the director of Colorado's Emergency Management Office exalted the virtues of individual responsibility for preparedness, many participants and observers broke into enthusiastic spontaneous applause. I was struck by the disjuncture between the conditions of the scenario (which in my view clearly suggested the need for institutional oversight over certain easily accessible types of WMD) and the solution of individual preparedness. As a disaster sociologist friend of mine later remarked in a voice dripping with sarcasm, "How is bottled water going to help you against [agent]?" The discourse of self-help with its attendant technological solutions, ranging from low-tech surgical masks and provisions to high-tech "sniffer" detection systems and Hazmat suits, mirrors cold war atomic bomb civil defense messages in ways that deserve more scrutiny; these discourses also interact with the discourses of biopreparedness exercises like TOPOFF 3 to locate responsibility at the household level.[94] At this point, we can circle back to Mechling and Mechling's call for criticism in the pragmatic attitude to note the way in which official visions of viral apocalypse do not seem to be spurring the citizenry into action. Thus, there is a disjuncture between the fantasies encoded in the biopreparedness exercises and everyday citizens' perceptions of their social reality.

The Complexity of the Challenge

A central paradox of militarization is that in large-scale modern risk societies, many citizens accept public militarization in lieu of private preparedness activities. Laura McEnaney explains that during the cold war, "most Americans endorsed an arms buildup and heartily supported a resolutely anticommunist diplomacy" while at the same time rejecting "reorganizing their domestic space to fit national security priorities."[95] Similarly, in the post-9/11 era, most Americans are not duct-taping plastic sheeting to their homes (although a few did, to former DHS head Tom Ridge's chagrin). This, then, is one of the tensions between the rhetoric of our institutional discourses that promote visions of viral apocalypse and the ambivalence, apathy, alienation, and "risk fatigue" citizens experience in their every day lives. Despite the complexity, scale, and frequency of our biopreparedness drills, few citizens are aware of their practice. And even fewer are persuaded to take responsibility for protecting themselves and their families from a bioterrorism attack. However, many may accept protection from the military as an acceptable course of action in the event of an outbreak. TOPOFF 3, along with other biopreparedness exercises, then, does not seem to be functioning primarily to prepare everyday citizens for a bioterrorism attack. Rather, it primes decision-making elites to accept military solutions as a desirable recourse following a biological incident while constructing publics as passive, panicked phobics that need to be properly managed.

Another element of decision makers' acceptance of the interlacing of military and civilian life might stem from the "command and control" model adopted in exercises such as TOPOFF and their repeated depictions of civil unrest and breakdown. The War Resisters League of New England held protests in New London, Connecticut during TOPOFF 3. Coordinator Joanne P. Sheldon noted, "We see this as more of a scare tactic than anything else."[96] Sheldon's comment suggests that at least some critics see a connection between these exercises and increased militarization, which is gaining currency. An October 2005 conference of U.S. mayors recommended a "greater role for military in emergency response," noting that the "sheer magnitude" of terrorism or natural disaster makes it advantageous.[97] Similarly, President Bush also recently announced his desire to increase military response to disaster following Hurricane Katrina: "It is now clear that a challenge of this scale requires greater federal authority and a broader role for the armed forces."[98] Considered in conjunction with a patchwork of post-9/11 laws that transfer control to military sources in the event of pathogen spread, the implications for public participation in biosecurity are deeply troubling. Increased surveillance though biometrics, proposed containment through quarantine, and the justification of military interventions for unfolding public health situations as biopreparedness gets swept up under the mantle of the global war on terror are logical outcomes of this rhetoric.

In considering what the present study offers to our understanding of the role of rhetoric in the burgeoning biodefense industry, two key questions, I believe, should animate future research: First, how are defense contractors, pharmaceutical industry representatives, military officials, elected politicians, biosecurity experts, and citizens collectively transforming technical knowledge into a form of bio-insecurity that fuels biodefense research and development? And second, how are perceptions of the risk of bioterrorism mobilized across technical, public, and private spheres of argument? This essay has attempted to provide speculative answers to these questions by charting how biopreparedness exercises such as TOPOFF 3 are key nodes in increasingly self-reproducing discourse systems in which rhetorically facilitated fantasies push military solutions and direct attention away from the institutional production of biological weapons risks. The fantasy documents that script and eventuate from these exercises promote the rhetorical vision of viral apocalypse, which in turn authorizes and legitimates a particular vision of public health subsumed under the security state. Significant to this process is a kind of communicative closure in which the realities of decision-making elites scripting these fantasies do not link up well with the everyday experiences of the citizenry. Apathy, ambivalence, and alienation may result; this may further harm efforts to promote community resilience. These exercises thus point to the paradox of militarism in complex modern risk society and its relation to ambivalence or apathy in the daily lives of citizens.

In trying to offer criticism in the pragmatic attitude, this essay has attempted to show how autopoiesis allows for a perpetuation of conditions at the systemic level at the same time that many citizens do not accept the fantasies of elite decision makers regarding bioterrorism and biodefense. Yet, there are a host of deliberative issues about biodefense that need to be aired. Growth in the biotech industry raises a host of ethical and practical dilemmas related to biodefense that have profound consequences for the lives of the citizenry, and most of these are not being actively debated or attended to in the public sphere. Many of these dilemmas are obscured in exercises like TOPOFF 3 that draw from a slightly modified cold war political script and ignore the risks posed by our own laboratories. These scenarios often minimize the delicate line between offensive and defensive biological weapons research and their connection to weapons proliferation at home and abroad. As the German economist E. F. Schumacher wrote, "It is of little use trying to suppress terrorism if the production of deadly devices continues to be deemed a legitimate employment of man's creative powers."[99]

In a climate where international security is far from guaranteed, the impulse is often to privilege the interests of the state over those of individual citizens. Moreover, some scientists and policy experts have cautioned that the Patriot Act and the 2002 Public Security and Bioterrorism Preparedness and Response Act are examples of "command and control" regulation—a "top down governance system" that threatens scientific research and biosafety.[100] They argue instead for scientific self-governance organic to the culture of biological research. Either scientific self-governance or state control might be politically efficient in a time of crisis, but in the longer haul, they erode the democratic impulse and take decision making out of the hands of the people who have to live with the consequences of particular techno-scientific or political decisions. Perhaps the greatest fantasy is that we can ever adequately prepare for large-scale disaster at all and that our own biodefense research is largely without peril. But such a realization does not undermine the need to plan, nor does it obviate the need to debate the implications of our collective responses to bioterrorism and naturally occurring infectious outbreaks. Despite tremendous growth in the biological sciences and innumerable benefits to human life, the dark side of biological advancement allows for a similar curtailing of human life, agriculture, and ecosystems. The rhetoric of bioterrorism and its attendant scientific and cultural practices participate in a restructuring of the relationship between biology and the public sphere that potentially affects all life on the planet. The consequences of this hostile use of biotechnology, I believe, are too grave for rhetoricians to ignore. If, indeed, as the epigraphs that open this paper suggest, "the age of bioterror is now," rhetoricians can at the very least play a more significant part in explaining how this situation came to be and how it might be reproducing itself in both discourse and the life world. This essay represents the beginning of such a task.

Notes

1. Unnamed organizer of international counterterrorism exercise Atlantic Storm quoted in "Not Science Fiction," *Washington Post*, January 27, 2005: A18. For contrasting commentary on the exercise, compare Anne Applebaum, "Only a Game?" *The Washington Post,* January 19, 2005: A19 to David Ruppe, "Experts Question Merit of Recent Smallpox Exercise," Global Security Newswire of the Nuclear Threat Initiative, March 9, 2005, http://www.nti.org/d_newswire/issues/2005/3/9/77244457-cd48-4284-9410-107a998b5aa6.html (accessed March 10, 2005).

2. Joost Van Loon, *Risk and Technological Culture: Towards a Sociology of Virulence* (New York: Routledge, 2002).

3. Department of Homeland Security, Press Kit: TOPOFF 3 Exercise, http://www.dhs.gov/xprepresp/training/editorial_0588.shtm (accessed November 10, 2005).

4. Department of Homeland Security, Press Kit.

5. Office of the Press Secretary, Department of Homeland Security, TOPOFF 3 Frequently Asked Questions, http://www.dhs.gov/xprepresp/training/editorial_0603.shtm (accessed February 24, 2006).

6. During the Cold War, Robin Clarke's *We All Fall Down: The Prospect of Biological and Chemical Warfare* (London: Penguin Press, 1968) sounded the alarm about these weapons systems in general. For more contemporary works that address bioterrorism as opposed to biowarfare, see Jeanne McDermott, *The Killing Winds: The Menace of Biological Warfare* (New York: Arbor House, 1987); Laurie Garrett, *The Coming Plague: Newly Emerging Diseases in a World out of Balance* (New York: Penguin, 1994); and Jonathan B. Tucker, ed., *Toxic Terror: Assessing Terrorist Use of Chemical and Biological Weapons, BCSIA Studies in International Security* (Cambridge: MIT Press, 2001).

[7] See Ari Schuler, "Billions for Biodefense: Federal Agency Biodefense Funding, FY2001–FY2005," *Biosecurity and Bioterrorism: Biodefense Strategy, Practice, and Science* 2 (2004): 86.

[8] For the major book on fantasy documents, see Lee Clarke, *Mission Improbable: Using Fantasy Documents to Tame Disasters* (Chicago: University of Chicago Press, 1999).

[9] For a discussion of terror and empire, see Stephen John Hartnett and Laura Stengrim, *Globalization and Empire: The U.S. Invasion of Iraq, Free Markets, and the Twilight of Democracy* (Tuscaloosa: University of Alabama Press, 2006).

[10] For a discussion of "criticism in the pragmatic attitude," see Elizabeth Walker Mechling and Jay Mechling, "The Campaign for Civil Defense and the Struggle to Naturalize the Bomb," in *Critical Questions: Invention, Creativity, and the Criticism of Discourse and Media*, ed. William Nothstine, Carole Blair, and Gary Copeland (New York: St. Martins, 1994), 118–154.

[11] Mechling and Mechling, "The Campaign for Civil Defense," 128.

[12] For Kristeva, the abject is not that which is unclean but that which threatens identity by disrupting boundaries. See Julia Kristeva, "Powers of Horror," in *The Portable Kristeva*, ed. Kelly Oliver (New York: Columbia University Press, 1997), 229–63. For the classic discussion of contamination fears, see the recent reprint of Mary Douglas, *Purity and Danger: An Analysis of the Concepts of Pollution and Taboo* (New York: Routledge, 2002); Van Loon.

[13] Rickettsiae are a disease causing type of bacterium that, unlike other types of bacteria, require a host to live. Rickettsiae cause Rocky Mountain Spotted Fever and some types of typhus.

[14] Alan Goldstein, *"Bioterror Hysteria: The New 'Star Wars,'"* December 9, 2003, http://dir.salon.com/story/tech/feature/2003/12/09/bioterror_funding/index_np.html (accessed March 24, 2005).

[15] The condensation of biological weapon and terrorism into the neologism "bioterrorism" does not appear in our lexicon until the late 1980s. The Oxford English dictionary entry for bioterrorism, "the use of infectious agents or biologically active substances as weapons of terrorism," identifies one of the earliest references to the term as occurring in Jeanne McDermott's 1987 *Killing Winds*: "Since the intimidating powers of biological weapons are so uncomfortably clear, bioterrorism is a sensitive subject that few want to discuss or face." See Jeanne McDermott, *The Killing Winds*, 252.

[16] Judith Reppy, "Regulating Biotechnology in the Age of Homeland Security," *Science Studies* 16 (2) (2003): 38–51.

[17] A possible exception is the 2003 special issue of the *Journal of Health Communication* devoted to the 2001 anthrax attacks: Vicki Freimuth, "Epilogue to the Special Issue on Anthrax," *Journal of Health Communication* 8 (2003): 148–51. However, this volume largely offers two types of scholarship: content analyses of mediated messages and CDC communiqués about 2001 attacks and results of public opinion polls. This work is useful but represents a small portion of the kinds of perspective and critical approaches that should be brought to bear on this topic. See, for example: Kathleen Hall Jamieson, Kelli Lammie, Clare Wardle, and Susan Krutt, "Questions about Hypotheticals and Details in Reporting on Anthrax." *Journal of Health Communication* 8 (2003): 121–23; Felicia Mebane, Sarah Temin, and Claudia F. Parvanta, "Communicating Anthrax in 2001: A Comparison of CDC Information and Print Media Accounts," *Journal of Health Communication* 8 (2003): 50–82; and William E. Pollard, "Public Perception of Information Sources Concerning Bioterrorism before and after Anthrax Attacks: An Analysis of National Survey Data," *Journal of Health Communication* 8 (2003): 93–103.

[18] For collections of cold war rhetoric scholarship, see Martin J. Medhurst, Robert L. Ivie, Philip Wander, and Robert L. Scott, eds., *Cold War Rhetoric: Strategy, Metaphor, and Ideology* (East Lansing: Michigan State University Press, 1997); and Martin J. Medhurst and H. W. Brands, eds., *Critical Reflections on the Cold War: Linking Rhetoric and History* (College Station: Texas A&M University, 2000).

[19] Martin J. Medhurst, "Introduction: The Rhetorical Construction of History," in *Critical Reflections on the Cold War: Linking Rhetoric and History*, ed. Martin J. Medhurst and H. W. Brands (College Station: Texas A&M University, 2000), 7. See also Bryan C. Taylor and Stephen J. Hartnett, "'National Security and All That It Implies': (Post-)Cold War Culture and Communication Studies," *Quarterly Journal of Speech* 86 (4) (2000): 465–87.

20 For a review of key works in nuclear criticism, see Bryan C. Taylor, "Nuclear Weapons and Communication Studies: A Review Essay," *Western Journal of Communication* 62 (1998): 300–15.

21 Taylor and Hartnett, "National Security."

22 For recent risk work with a rhetorical flavor, see Beverly Sauer, *Rhetoric of Risk: Technical Documentation in Hazardous Environments* (Mahwah: Lawrence Erlbaum Associates, 2003); and Jeffrey T. Grabill and W. Michele Simmons, "Toward a Critical Rhetoric of Risk Communication: Producing Citizens and the Role of Technical Communicators," *Technical Communication Quarterly* 7 (1998): 415–41. For some of the more recent work in sociology, see Paul Slovic, ed., *The Perception of Risk* (London: Earthscan, 2000).

23 This argument is advanced in William J. Kinsella, "Rhetoric, Action, and Agency in Institutionalized Science and Technology," *Technical Communication Quarterly* 14 (2005): 303–10.

24 Center for Nonproliferation Research, "Chemical, Biological, Radiological, and Nuclear Terrorism: The Threat According to the Current Unclassified Literature: Executive Summary," (National Defense University, 2002), on file with author.

25 See Van Loon, *Risk and Technological Culture,* for a discussion of how the politics of urgency are driving social life.

26 Ari Schuler, "Billions for Biodefense," 86. This figure might be low as monies allocated to the DOE and DOJ were not included in his analysis due to nonresponse of these agencies to requests for information.

27 Ari Schuler, "Billions for Biodefense: Federal Agency Biodefense Funding, FY2005–FY2006," *Biosecurity and Bioterrorism: Biodefense Strategy, Practice, and Science* 3 (2005): 94–101. The increases are seen when adjusted for the advance appropriation for Project BioShield.

28 These figures come from the Sunshine Project's analysis of NIH funding for biodefense of six agents (anthrax, plague, tularemia, glanders, meliodosis, and brucella) using NIH's CRISPer database. These figures can be found at http://www.sunshine-project.org/biodefense/niaidfunding.html. Anthrax-related grants have increased a whopping 3,471% percent from 2001 levels.

29 Merrill Goozner, "Bioterror Brain Drain," *The American Prospect* 14 (2003); Goldstein, "Bioterror Hysteria."

30 See the Sunshine Project for the latest map of a biodefense facility near you at http://www.sunshine-project.org/. The Sunshine Project takes its name from the fact that most biological weapons die when exposed to sunlight. This nonprofit group tries to shed light on biological warfare in the United States and Europe.

31 David J. Rothkopf, "Business Versus Terror," *Foreign Policy* May/June (2002): 56–62.

32 Rothkopf, "Business Versus Terror."

33 Guy Oakes, *The Imaginary War: Civil Defense and American Cold War Culture* (New York: Oxford University Press, 1994), 84–104.

34 "Civil Defense: Best Defense? Prayer?" *Time Magazine* 27 (June 1957), 17–18.

35 See Mechling and Mechling, "The Campaign for Civil Defense."

36 Office of the Press Secretary, Transcript of Press Conference with Secretary of Homeland Security Michael Chertoff on the TOPOFF 3 Exercise, April 4, 2005, http://www.dhs.gov/xnews/releases/press_release_0650.shtm (accessed November 10, 2005).

37 Office of the Press Secretary, TOPOFF 3 Frequently Asked Questions.

38 See Department of Homeland Security Web page, www.dhs.gov.

39 Clarke, *Mission Improbable,* 16.

40 Clarke, *Mission Improbable,* 16.

41 Clarke, *Mission Improbable,* 16.

42 Clarke, *Mission Improbable,* 16.

43 Clarke, *Mission Improbable,* 16.

44 Clarke, *Mission Improbable,* 16–7.

45 Clarke, *Mission Improbable,* 16.

46 See, for example, on the fantasy theme side, Ernest Bormann, "Fantasy and Rhetorical Vision: The Rhetorical Criticism of Social Reality," *Quarterly Journal of Speech* 58 (1972): 396–407 and Ernest Bormann, "Colloquy: I. Fantasy and Rhetorical Vision: Ten Years Later,"

Quarterly Journal of Speech 68 (1982): 288–305. For a psychoanalytic approach to fantasy, see Joshua Gunn, "Refiguring Fantasy: Imagination and Its Decline in U.S. Rhetorical Studies," *Quarterly Journal of Speech* 89 (2003): 41–59.

47 Christian W. Erickson and Bethany A. Barratt, "Prudence or Panic? Preparedness Exercises, Counterterror Mobilization, and Mass Media Coverage—Dark Winter, TOPOFF 1 and 2," *Journal of Homeland Security and Emergency Management* 1 (4) (2004), www.bepress.com/jhsem/vol1/iss4/413 (accessed July 15, 2005).

48 Thomas B. Farrell and G. Thomas Goodnight, "Accidental Rhetoric: The Root Metaphors of Three Mile Island," *Communication Monographs* 1981 (48): 271–300.

49 Ulrich Beck, *Risk Society: Towards a New Modernity*, trans. by M. Ritter (London: Sage, 1992).

50 Beck, *Risk Society*. See also Barbara Adam, Ulrich Beck, and Joost Van Loon, eds. *The Risk Society and Beyond: Critical Issues for Social Theory* (Thousand Oaks: Sage, 2000).

51 See Adam, Beck, and Van Loon, *Risk Society and Beyond*.

52 Van Loon, *Risk and Technological Culture*.

53 For the seminal work on critical rhetoric, see Raymie E. McKerrow, "Critical Rhetoric: Theory and Praxis," *Communication Monographs* 56 (1989): 91–111.

54 See *"Atlantic Storm* Scenario Assumptions: Distributed at End of Exercise," on file with author.

55 Matt Appuzzo, "Conn. Officials Say Terrorism Drill 'Feels Real,'" *Bergen County Record*, April 5, 2005, www.lexisnexis.com (accessed February 24, 2006).

56 Wayne Parry, "Anti-Terror Drill Designed to Spot Weaknesses Begins in NJ, Conn.," Associated Press State & Local Wire, April 5, 2005, www.lexis.nexis.com (accessed February 24, 2006).

57 Wayne Parry, "Largest-Ever Anti-Terror Drill to Begin Today in Union," Associated Press State & Local Wire, April 5, 2005, www.lexis.nexis.com (accessed February 24, 2006).

58 Jean Baudrillard, *Simulations*, trans. Paul Foss, Paul Patton, and Philip Beitchmann (New York: Semiotext(e), 1983), 4.

59 Barry Brummett, *The World and How We Describe It: Rhetorics of Reality, Representation, Simulation* (Westport, CT: Greenwood, 2003), 21.

60 Brummett, *The World*, 1.

61 Francisco Varela and Humberto R. Maturana, "Autopoiesis: The Organization of Living Systems, Its Characterization and a Model," *Biosystems* 5 (1974): 187–96.

62 Niklas Luhmann, "The Autopoiesis of Social Systems," in *Sociocybernetic Paradoxes: Observation, Control, and Evolution in Self-Steering Systems*, ed. F. Geyer and J. van D. Zeuwen (London: Sage, 1986), 172–92.

63 Tor Hernes and Tore Bakken, "Implications of Self-Reference: Niklas Luhmann's Autopoiesis and Organization Theory," *Organization Studies* 24 (2003): 1513.

64 Van Loon, *Risk and Technological Culture*, 31.

65 Robert Cooper, "Making Present: Autopoiesis as Human Production," *Organization* 13 (2006): 59–81.

66 Daniel Engber, "Can I Help With the Terrorism Drill? I Wanna be a Victim!" *Slate*, April 5, 2005, http://www.slate.com/id/2116261 (accessed March 6, 2006).

67 To be fair, the organizers of Atlantic Storm just invited me to a conference called "Democracy and Disaster."

68 Engber, "Can I Help With the Terrorism Drill?"

69 James Jasinski, "Apocalyptic Discourse," in *Sourcebook on Rhetoric: Key Concepts in Contemporary Rhetorical Studies*, ed. James Jasinski (Thousand Oaks, CA: Sage, 2001), 17.

70 See Barry Brummett, *Contemporary Apocalyptic Rhetoric* (New York: Praeger, 1991); Stephen D. O'Leary, "Apocalyptic Argument and the Anticipation of Catastrophe: The Prediction of Risk and the Risks of Prediction," *Argumentation* 11 (1997): 293–313; "A Dramatistic Theory of Apocalyptic Rhetoric," *Quarterly Journal of Speech* 79 (1993): 385–426; and *Arguing the Apocalypse: A Theory of Millennial Rhetoric* (New York: Oxford University Press). For literary studies of apocalypse (thanks to Frank Beer), see Frank Kermode, *The Sense of an Ending: Studies in the Theory of Fiction with a New Epilogue* (New York: Oxford University Press, 2000).

71 Barry Brummett, "Premillennial Apocalyptic as a Rhetorical Genre," *Central States Speech Journal* 35 (1984): 86.

[72] Joshua Gunn and David E. Beard, "On the Apocalyptic Sublime," *Southern Communication Journal* 64 (4) (2000): 268–86 and "On the Apocalyptic Columbine," *Southern Communication Journal* 68 (3) (2003): 198–216.

[73] Bob Drogin, "Smallpox Exercise Poses Big Question: Is Anyone Ready?" *Los Angeles Times,* January 17, 2005: A1.

[74] Tucker, *Toxic Terror.*

[75] U.S. Secretary of Defense, *Proliferation: Threat and Response* (Washington, DC, Department of Defense, 1997).

[76] U.S. Secretary of Defense, *Proliferation.*

[77] John Mintz, "Bioterrorism War Game Shows Lack of Readiness," *Washington Post,* January 15, 2005: A12.

[78] Tara O'Toole, "Smallpox: An Attack Scenario," *Journal of Emerging Infectious Disease* 5 (1999): 545.

[79] Thomas V. Inglesby, Rita Grossman, and Tara O'Toole, "A Plague on Your City: Observations from TOPOFF," Confronting Biological Weapons [Special Issue]. *Clinical Infectious Diseases* 32 (2001): 436–45.

[80] Inglesby et al., "A Plague on Your City," 442.

[81] In the next draft, I am expanding this section to demonstrate all the laws that license military intervention into public health.

[82] U.S. White House, "Biodefense for the 21st Century Press Release," April 28, 2004, http://www.whitehouse.gov/homeland/20020430.html (accessed March 3, 2005).

[83] Philip Strong, "Epidemic Psychology: A Model," *Sociology of Health and Illness* 12 (1990): 249–59; Elaine Showalter, *Hystories: Hysterical Epidemics and Modern Culture* (London: Picador, 1997).

[84] Showalter, *Hystories*, 5.

[85] Showalter, *Hystories*, 5.

[86] Lee Clarke, "Panic, Myth or Reality." *Contexts* (2002, fall): 21–26. I realize Hurricane Katrina response may be an exception, although Slavoj Žižek examined how media coverage may have exaggerated the sense of panic and lawlessness in what was inarguably a terrible situation. This view seems to be shared among disaster sociologists.

[87] Michel Foucault, *Discipline and Punish: The Birth of the Prison,* trans. Alan Sheridan (New York: Vintage Books, 1995).

[88] Office of the Press Secretary, Department of Homeland Security, Transcript of Background Briefing with Senior DHS Officials on TOPOFF 3, April 8, 2005, http://www.dhs.gov/xnews/releases/press_release_0656.shtm (accessed February 28, 2006).

[89] Office of the Press Secretary, TOPOFF 3 Frequently Asked Questions.

[90] Milton Leitenberg, "Biological Weapons and Bioterrorism in the First Years of the 21st Century." Paper presented at the conference on "The Possible Use of Biological Weapons by Terrorists Groups: Scientific, Legal, and International Implications," Rome, Italy, August 16, 2002, 91.

[91] Leitenberg, "Biological Weapons," 91.

[92] Office of the Press Secretary, TOPOFF 3 Frequently Asked Questions.

[93] See www.dhs.gov.

[94] For an excellent volume on nuclear civil defense, see Laura McEnaney, *Civil Defense Begins at Home: Militarization Meets Every Day Life in the Fifties* (Princeton: Princeton University Press, 2000).

[95] McEnaney, *Civil Defense*, 155.

[96] Jeff Holtz, "A Mock Terrorist Attack is Heading to the State," *New York Times,* March 27, 2005: 14CN.

[97] Center for Biosecurity of University of Pittsburgh Medical Center, "Biosecurity Briefing: Mayors Recommend Greater Role in Emergency Response," October 28, 2005, www.upmc-biosecurity.org (accessed October 31, 2005).

[98] Center for Biosecurity, "Biosecurity Briefing."

[99] Eric M. Meslin, "Genetics and Bioterrorism: Challenges for Science, Society, and Bioethics," in *In the Wake of Terror: Medicine and Morality in a Time of Crisis*, ed. Jonathan D. Moreno (Cambridge: The MIT Press, 2003), 199–218.

[100] Gigi Kwik, Joe Fitzgerald, Thomas V. Inglesby, and Tara O'Toole, "Biosecurity: Responsible Stewardship of Bioscience in an Age of Catastrophic Terrorism," *Biosecurity and Bioterrorism* 1 (2003): 27–35.

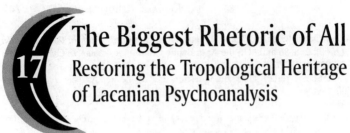

The Biggest Rhetoric of All
Restoring the Tropological Heritage of Lacanian Psychoanalysis

Christian Lundberg

Of the "canonical" techniques in the psychoanalytic interpretive tradition, the idea of the inversion or reversal holds a position of the highest honor. Where would Lacan and his interpreters be without the idea of the object causing desire, language speaking the person, and emptiness generating the subject? This paper proposes a similar kind of inversion in the question, "What does the inclusion of psychoanalysis tell us about the current state of rhetorical theory?" What can rhetorical theory tell us about the current state of psychoanalysis? How might a rhetorically inflected reading of psychoanalysis intervene in contemporary psychoanalytic thinking?

This inversion is productive in two specific ways. First, in highlighting the rhetorical heritage of psychoanalysis as an economy of tropological exchange it is possible to address some substantial problems with psychoanalytic theories of interpretation, notably the problem of a latent structuralism. Second, in restoring the primacy of rhetoric in psychoanalysis, it may also become possible to articulate a warrant for "Big R" Rhetoric as a vocabulary par excellence for thinking the human in language. I will proceed by making the case for psychoanalysis as a rhetorical technology, and then, situating rhetorical exchange as an economy, I argue for the primacy of rhetoric as a more global technology thinking the subject of the sign.

Psychoanalysis

Psychoanalysis is an incredibly contested discourse. As a method and field of study it has been alternately derided as an excuse for making sloppy and nonverifiable claims about psychic life and lauded as a method for thickening accounts of the reception of discourses and the functioning of symbolic action. To understand the possibilities and perils of psychoanalytic interpretation, and its relationship to rhetoric, it is necessary first to lay out the logic of psychoanalytic approaches in the most conceptually minimal sense.

If there is a core instinct that unites psychoanalytic modes of interpretation in the Freudian tradition, it lies in the conceptual triad of the unconscious, repression, and the symptom. Perhaps Freud's greatest insight was that the meaning of a discourse, affective state, or symptomatic display could not be discerned by attention to its immediately perceptible surface: psychoanalysis, for better or worse, is a discourse about secrets. The critical question is the structure and form of the psychoanalytic secret and the secondary problems it implies: psychoanalysis's relation to the doctrine of the subject's interiority and the conditions for its validity as a mode of interpretation.

The secret here is the unconscious. The unconscious has been framed in a number of different ways: as the hidden substrate of an individual's interiority; as a set of social archetypes; or as a way of marking the fact that language outstrips any given individual's employment of it. The unconscious, in its varying manifestations, serves as a placeholder for that which is not immediately apparent in the reception, reading, or interpretation of a discourse—for the secret of speech. As a discourse paying attention to iterations of the unconscious, psychoanalysis stakes its methodological credibility on the necessity of thinking this "beyond" of discourse, namely the structures of enjoyment, desire, and trope, can be understood as the conditions of possibility for specific discursive exchanges.

Why is the unconscious beyond or outside the surface of intentionally mediated discourses? In the classical Freudian account, the unconscious exerts immanent but unspecifiable effects on speech, lying beyond the speech situation in the dark recesses of the individual's inner life. Usually psychoanalytic discourses account for the relative hiddenness of the unconscious by relying on an account of repression: either out of the necessity of avoiding an unspeakable desire or as an inherent function of language. Some process is required to account for the presence of the "secret" of the unconscious, and psychoanalytic schools have applied some repression, or some version of it, to explain the production and functioning of the unconscious. But there are many possible ways of rendering the secret here, and subsequently of rendering both the unconscious and repression.

For a Lacanian (if there is such a beast), both the question and the classically Freudian answer are misguided: the "unconscious," whatever it is, is never "outside" any given discourse. The unconscious always figures discourse, but the way it does so is not always immediately apparent, nor is it "outside" of a discursive exchange. Classical Freudian psychology claims that the existence of repression in the life of subjects is a result of people coming to grips with desires that for various reasons cannot be spoken or acted upon. For the Lacanian, repression is not so much an intentional action by the ego on a discourse or a set of desires as much as it is a phenomenon inhering in structures of signification: here Lacan implicitly relies on the Heideggerian adage that to represent an object in one way precludes other representational possibilities. This account of repression implicitly refers to the maxim of "On the Essence of Truth" that every act of revealing is simultaneously and productively an act of concealing.[1] But what is it that is concealed? Lacan's rereading and subsequent critique of the sign as simple reference hinges on the fact that signifiers are only connected to signifieds by the labor of tropes, specifically of metonymic connections that are subsequently raised to the level of a metaphorical condensation of the signifier in the signified. In Lacan's psychoanalytic conception of the sign, signifiers are by nature overly saturated with meaning. Any given signifier is situated in a semiotic field that contains many such possible metonymic connections, any number of which might inform the other's reception of a subject's speech act. The unconscious, which Lacan also calls "the discourse of the other," represents the field of possible lines of metonymic connection that might stem from the employment of any signifier.[2] Concealment, which is perhaps the best rendering of what Lacan understands as repression, occurs when a subject employs a specific meaning for a signifier at the expense of other possible metonymic connections—these connections are temporarily displaced, but are still operative in the enunciation and reception of a signifier. This is the core insight of the Lacanian maxim that "the unconscious is structured like a language."[3] To say that the unconscious is structured like a language marks two complementary qualities. One, it marks the fact that the unconscious, while a linguistically mediated phenomenon, does not operate along the lines of the structural linguistic account of signification that presumes an unproblematic referential relationship between signifier and signified. Instead, the unconscious is conceived of as the labor that has been done by the subject in sliding a signified under the signifier, or in bringing trope to bear in creating meaning (*glissement*).[4]

The unconscious is structured like a language because it is a result of the structural possibilities for polysemous meaning in any act of signification, but it is not a "language" because it does not obey concrete rules of reference. Here a Lacanian re-reading of Freud's famous "Rat Man" case might be instructive.[5] In reading the signifier "rat," Freud asserts that it does not just invoke the furry rodent, but a whole set of unintended, sedimented metonymic connections: it also invokes the dirtiness of an animal that tends to live in squalor, and the sense of immorality metonymically associated with dirtiness; it invokes discourses of disease and corruption; and because of a phonetic similarity between the German word rat (*raten*) and periodic monetary installments (*ratten*) it invokes a set of associations with money and greed. The unconscious here is not a description of the fact that these associations were latently held in the analysand's interior: instead, Lacan exteriorizes the unconscious by locating it in the materially situated connections implied by past usage of the word "rat," highlighting the metonymic associations it invokes in a signifying chain, even when they are displaced by the metaphorical operation that insists on a specific meaning for the word "rat." The unconscious exists outside of the specific instance of usage of a given sign by a specific subject, and is simultaneously present in the speech subject's usage by simple virtue of repeating a thickly layered signifier with a rich set of possible metonymic associations. As a result, the unconscious is also the speech of the Other, because it is the speech of the "big O" Other (the general symbolic order) and specific others who also speak, producing the chains of signifying associations that are present in any act of speech. Given this characterization of the unconscious, there is a constant tension in the gaps between langue and parole, and the subject and the Other, because the moment of speech always and necessarily contains a set of unexpected, even uncontrollable, associations that belie the possibility of consummating a communicative exchange as a communicative relationship. Speech both says too much and not enough: it says too much because any act of signification is overburdened by a plurality of metonymic connections, and not enough because the mere fact of sliding a signified under a signifier ensures that the connection between the two is never fully saturated or without polysemous possibility.

Whichever way a psychoanalytic critic decides to render the unconscious and repression, there is wide-ranging agreement on Freud's maxim that "the repressed must return." The final element in the triad, the symptom, creates a category for tracking the ways that the repressed comes to life in everyday discourses. Psychoanalytic framings of the symptom have also varied widely: from presenting symptoms as the surface manifestations of unresolved desires or stages of development to treating all speech as symptom in some sense. The idea of the symptom, like its conceptual kin the unconscious and repression, is a placeholder for the general commitment to the idea that discourses can be understood only by framing them as the result of operations in the unconscious, which arise in relation to repression, whether this phenomenon is the result of an intentional and hydraulic economy of desire or an implicit structural operation in all acts of signification. On this reading, discourses are always symptomatic, in that they are produced by the underlying operation of the unconscious, or, the language of the Other, which is nothing more than the metonymic possibilities foreclosed by the metaphor of the sign.

But discourses of the symptom, at least in the more classical Freudian model, had a difficult time standing up to post-structuralist critiques of the unified subject and to critiques of the historicity of the person, both of which challenged the idea of a naturally given interiority of the subject as the playground of the libido. In the same way, critiques that politicized the category of "the normal," such as Foucault's, made it difficult to sustain the symptom as a site of therapeutic intervention. Finally, critiques of language as an instrument disclosing the subject's (now questionable) interiority made it difficult to treat symptoms as discursive fragments of the inner workings of a psychic economy.

Lacan required a vocabulary for dealing with the discursive operations that constitute the subject and its speech in light of these interventions, and this drove him to reframe a theory of analysis. A number of his attempts at rearticulating the subject of analysis are famous (or infamous): topology, algebra, and so on. But the significant thing about each of these attempts is that they are *metaphors*, and the goal of these metaphors is to make the processes of subjects coming to language seem strange. This strangeness is productive in marking the labor inherent in signification and speech, but in thinking out Lacan's theories of signification it is important to meditate on more than just sheer difference among his various models. Each of these metaphors implies substantial similarity between the models, and it is also important to highlight the continuities in Lacan's different attempts to rethink the subject and the analytic situation through the motifs of post-structural thought. Ultimately then, the most significant resources for Lacan in engaging these conversations, despite the plurality of metaphors, are metaphor and metonymy themselves, or a rhetoric of trope.

Rhetoric is one of the few themes that unites both the early and later work of Lacan. There is ample evidence in the Lacanian corpus that one of the central thematics in psychoanalytic work is the restoration of a rhetorically figured model of articulating the symbolic. In his early and pivotal "The Agency of the Letter in the Unconscious or Reason Since Freud," Lacan argues that his theory of signification was inspired by Quintilian's theories of metaphor and metonymy, and that he ultimately differs from the structuralist accounts of the symbolic on the basis of their lack of attention to the function of tropology.[6] In *The Function of Language in Psychoanalysis*, Lacan argues that one of the primary problems of contemporary psychoanalysis is the disregard of "speech."[7] Lacan argues through Freud's *The Interpretation of Dreams* that attention to speech as a manifestation of the symbolic requires attention to "its rhetoric . . . ellipsis and pleonasm, hyperbaton . . . apposition . . . metaphor, catachresis, antonomasia, allegory, metonymy, and synecdoche—these are the semantic condensations in which Freud teaches us to read the intentions . . . out of which the subject modulates his [sic] oneiric discourse."[8]

The rhetorical operation of the symbolic also figures prominently for the later Lacan. By foregrounding the role of the symbolic function in the constitution of the desiring subject, Lacan opens a path to think of the symbolic as specifically tropological and, therefore, as a rhetorical phenomenon. Here, the object of inquiry moves from the reading and interpretation of specific texts or the interior life of the analysand to a broader engagement with the productive circulation of trope. This charge frames the task of rhetoric as a kind of analytic engagement with the conditions of the production of subjectivity, of knowledge, and of the subject's acts of meaning making in encountering other subjects and texts. *Seminar XX* contains an elegant presentation of this task: "The universe is a flower of rhetoric. . . . The ego (*moi*) can also be a flower of rhetoric, which grows in the pot of the pleasure principle. . . . That is what I am saying when I say that the unconscious is structured like a language."[9]

Borrowing inspiration from Lacan, perhaps it would be productive for contemporary theorists of psychoanalysis to meditate on the analytic endeavor as a doctrine of trope. A new psychoanalytic triad that supplements the unconscious, repression, and the symptom presents itself: metonymy (both a displacement and a connection), metaphor (condensation), and exchange. Given this new triad, psychoanalysis could be framed as nothing more than a theory of how subjects negotiate their relationship to language (and as a result to other people, objects, and so on) through trope: through relations of metonymic connection, metaphorical condensation, and what is gained and lost in the exchanges between the two. But to undertake this task requires that the interpreter move beyond individual tropes to think of the broader set of conditions that regulate the exchange of tropes in a semiotic economy.

Economy

Why an economy? Deirdre McCloskey's *The Rhetoric of Economics* frames economics as a specific set of literary or tropological practices that present arguments about exchange, efficiency, and systematic effect.[10] On her accounting, economics is a probabilistic discourse for predicting how inputs in one part of a system create effects in another part of a system. Psychoanalytic thinking has been described as economic by various commentators, though there are different ways of rendering the metaphor. One version, based on a classical clinical reading, perhaps the least "rhetorical" of the readings, holds that psychoanalysis is a kind of "hydraulic economy." Actions in one part of the psyche implied an equal and opposite effect in another part of the psyche. This is one of the standard explanations for a concept such as sublimation. So, by reading psychoanalysis as a hydraulic economy Freud could account for men as the bearers of culture. In a famous example from "Civilization and its Discontents," Freud talks about the sublimation of the urge to urinate on the communal campfire as the generative force in the creation of civilization:

> It is as though primal man had the habit, when he came in contact with fire, of satisfying an infantile desire connected with it, by putting it out with a stream of his urine. . . . Putting out fire by micturating . . . was therefore a kind of sexual act with a male, an enjoyment of sexual potency in a homosexual competition. The first person to renounce this desire and spare the fire was able to carry it off with him and subdue it to his own use. By damping down the fire of his own sexual excitation, he had tamed the natural force of fire. This great cultural conquest was thus the reward for his renunciation of instinct.[11]

Freud continues this line of argument by claiming that it explains why men, and not women, were the bearers of culture: women found it anatomically impossible to micturate on the fire. Here the "hydraulic" (pun intended) character of the classical Freudian psychic economy becomes clear. An *id* impulse to satisfy homosexual competition is repressed by action at the level of the superego. The energy of this impulse does not simply disappear: it must be displaced and will reemerge in another site, in this case it is sublimated to the production of culture.

This "hydraulic" view of the psychic economy has been a source of great embarrassment for psychoanalytic thought, and has rightfully been one of the sites of the most trenchant critique by psychoanalysis's critics. Newer analytic thought replaces the notion of a hydraulic economy with a system of more generalized semiotic exchanges. This more generalized economy of equivalences replaces the one-for-one system of perfect correspondence in the hydraulic model with a more open account of tropological exchange and displacement.[12]

In the place of a hydraulic economy for the relation between the subject and meaning, one might propose the idea of multiple economies, both of a general economy that inheres in the subject's entry into language, and of specific economies that underwrite local and provisional acts of meaning making. On this reading, all speech, and even all signification, are bound up in an economy of rhetorical exchange: this economy is both manifest as a locally provisional set of practices for meaning (a specific economy) be they in speech, image, or in mass mediation, and as a more universal set of operations that underwrite the formation of subjects (a general economy). If this division does in fact describe the subject of speech and of signs, one might ask if it is a productive division to hold as an interpretive maxim.

One of the most common criticisms of the Lacanian reinvention of Freud is that it imports a banal structuralism, popular among some of Lacan's French contemporaries, into psychoanalytic work. This criticism was first forwarded most aggressively by Maria Reugg, though it has reemerged in the recent post-structuralist attempts to characterize psychoanalysis as an old ontology in a new wineskin.[13] For example, Andrew Robinson argues forcefully that psychoanalysis's fascination with "constitutive lack" ontologizes lack, framing it as a new foundation and authorizing the creation of a new structure based mostly on violence: Derrida's criticism of the arche in psychoanalysis works this argument out in a little more careful detail in *Archive Fever*, though he maintains a kind of ambivalence about the "beyond" of psychoanalysis in his later work.[14]

This criticism has some merit. Many employments of psychoanalytic thought, most notably in the work of its most recent and notorious popularizer, Slavoj Žižek, have attempted to read the Lacanian project as an antidote to post-structuralism run amok in American cultural studies. Žižek employs Lacan's symbolic order, account of subject formation, framing of the "name of the father," and his logic of the "real" to argue that psychoanalysis provides an antidote to an endless and unbounded fascination with particularity and difference that he diagnoses in cultural studies. Žižek reads the logic of such employments of post-structuralism as complicit with neoliberalism, in that the refusal of a grand narrative for political struggle implicitly advantages neoliberalism by disarming potential lines of struggle against the "common enemy" of capital.[15] For Žižek, psychoanalytic insights can provide firm ground for the revitalization of Marxist, and even Leninist, politics as an antidote to the complicity of cultural studies with neoliberal capitalism. It is also significant that Žižek reads this model for psychoanalysis as an alternative to a simply rhetorical account of psychoanalysis, as demonstrated in his "The Limits of a Semiotic Approach to Psychoanalysis."[16]

Laclau argues, along similar lines, that there is a set of formal, structural imperatives that inhere in the structure of political demands and in processes of hegemony that provide a positive basis for psychoanalytic politics—though these structures are rhetorical on his reading, they are also squarely rooted in a structural account.[17] On Robinson's diagnosis, these attempts to peg political interventions to the logic of formal "structures" based on a central "lack" ultimately generate a new political ontology founded on constitutive lack. For Robinson and Reugg, the logic employed to think out the concrete implications of a subject founded on lack ends up smuggling in an only slightly revised set of ontological claims for the structure and function of a proper politics.

Can psychoanalytic inquiry be disassociated from this structuralist tendency while maintaining the best interpretive insights of psychoanalytic thinking? If so, what resources lie in the Lacanian corpus that might accomplish such a partial disassociation from structuralism? Careful reading of Lacan's work reveals that there is an often undertheorized metaphor that he consistently employs in dealing with the translation of the subject's lack to concrete action by and interaction between subjects: the idea of an *economy*. Why the choice of the term economy? How does this relate to the accusation of some that psychoanalysis is structuralism by another name—that it borrows the logic of structuralism, with only a facile reference to the emptiness of the subject to distract readers from the surreptitious reformation of a nearly metaphysical ontological center?

A step back is in order here: what are the characteristics of and problems with a structuralist account on Reugg, Derrida, and Robinson's accounts? It seems that there are two interrelated problems with a structuralist account for those who reject psychoanalysis on this basis. One, structuralism is flawed because it overdetermines fields of action and signification—put differently, structure eclipses the arguably central rhetorical category of contingency. In some sense, structuralism reads specific phenomena as epiphenomenal, in that individual phenomena are meaningful only because they reveal the underlying logic of the structure. There are two related problems that stem from the central theme of overdetermination: structuralism implies a kind of automaticity to individual phenomena, and therefore it endorses determinism. There is also an interpretive problem, in that critics of structuralism worry that individual phenomena are always read through the frame of the structure, so that there is a kind of nonfalsifiability built into a structuralist account. Here the structuralist's acts of reading may be tropological, but trope acts at the expense of an account of contingency. This criticism repeats the basic Popperian charge against psychoanalysis: that there are no criteria for testing it because it generates an all encompassing and ubiquitous set of general explanations that are not amenable to empirical testing.[18]

Second, there is the related problem of structuralism revealed by Derrida in the seminal essay "Structure, Sign, and Play in the Discourse of the Human Sciences." Derrida isolates two specific paradoxes for structuralism: that structure is itself a kind of event, and play in structures is governed by a center that is exempted from the rules that govern the rest of the structure.[19] In the final analysis, the force of Derrida's criticism is that structures themselves are historically determined by a field of play that provides them with a kind of intelligibility in their specific epoch, and as a result, references to ahistorical structures are haunted by the specter of their own historicity or eventfulness.

So, the nexus question: is an economy a structure? Economies have a special relationship with structure, or if you prefer, are special kinds of structures: plumbing their uniqueness as structures might generate insight into the problem of psychoanalysis and structure, especially if one has a penchant for a reading of psychoanalysis through the metaphor of economies of exchange. One can render the metaphor of the economy a structure in two senses. One way of calling an economy a structure is familiar to those who study the neoliberal descendants of Adam Smith: the term economy represents an unavoidable logic of material exchange, guided by invisible hands and invariable self-interests. Here, as critics of neoliberalism are quick to point out, the metaphor of the economy seems structuralist in all the most dangerous senses of the term: individual exchanges are expressions of a governing logic that is exempted from the vicissitudes of history and specific context.

But there is a second possible rendering of an economy as a special kind of structure: one inspired by conversations surrounding the question of economics as a discipline within the social sciences. Milton Friedman's "The Methodology of Positive Economics" argues that the goal of a methodologically positivist economics is not the perfect prediction of behavior in every possible instance, nor is it the articulation of hypotheses that mirror reality.[20] Instead, such a mode of economic theorization is more a post hoc heuristic device than a description of the inevitable outcomes of specific economic assumptions in any given case. The core of Friedman's claim is that a truly "realistic" theory of economic behavior that presented a seamless account of all possible inputs and assumptions in an economic exchange and their outcomes is impossible:

> A theory or its "assumptions" cannot possibly be thoroughly "realistic" in the immediate descriptive sense so often assigned to this term. A completely "realistic" theory of the wheat market would have to include not only the conditions directly underlying the supply and demand for wheat but also the kind of coins or credit instruments used to make exchanges; the personal characteristics of wheat-traders such as the colour of each trader's hair and eyes, his antecedents and education, the number of members of his family, their characteristics, antecedents, and education, etc.; the kind of soil on which the wheat was grown, its physical and chemical characteristics, the weather prevailing during the growing season; the personal characteristics of the farmers growing the wheat and of the consumers who will ultimately use it; and so on indefinitely. Any attempt to move very far in achieving this kind of "realism" is certain to render a theory utterly useless.[21]

Instead of thinking of the theory of economics as a structure that mirrors, and perhaps even prescribes economic behavior, Friedman frames economic thought as a kind of discourse in "autobiography . . . maxim . . . and example":

> The construction of hypotheses is a creative act of inspiration, intuition, invention; its essence is the vision of something new in familiar material.

> The process must be discussed in psychological, not logical, categories; studied in autobiographies and biographies, not treatises on scientific method; and promoted by maxim and example, not syllogism or theorem.[22]

Though Friedman still holds out for the eventual promise of a positivist validation of such maxims and examples, the logic of Friedman's point is suggestive in thinking out the status of the metaphor of economy in psychoanalysis. Here, a psychoanalytic economy is not based on uncovering the automatic relationship between a structure and individual events in the operation of the structure (though many forms of psychoanalysis, including the ego-psychology traditions of Freudian interpretation, are explicitly in this mold). Lacan, for example, describes the psychoanalytic interpretation as a strange dialectic between *tuche* and *automaton*. Borrowing from Aristotle, the category of tuche embodies the uncanny randomness of the "real," the category of chance, which situates the automatic operation of the symbolic domain. In other words, for Lacan, the psychoanalytic account of subjects is not about the inevitable unfolding of the automatic structures of the symbolic in the subject's action; instead, it embodies the contingent interface of the subject thrown into the symbolic with the tychic realm of chance.[23] Here the "real" is unruly in the same ways that Friedman's wheat market is—it is inherently unspecifiable and unrepresentable from the vantage point of the symbolic logic of the structure.

The analogy between Friedman's hypothetical wheat market maps nicely over the general interpretive problems ascribed to psychoanalysis. One of the most often cited criticisms of psychoanalysis is that for it to address the specific case of a person, text, or social phenomenon, it requires a degree of interpretive faith in the logic of the system. From this vantage point, the biggest failing of the application of therapeutic psychoanalysis to the individual case is ironically (for reasons that will become clear shortly) that it relies on a set of *rhetorical* sutures in any given case to make the system contain the virtually infinite set of factors that might go into explaining a specific individual's psychic life.[24] In other words, there is an unavoidable suture between the symbolic function of the automaton and the contingency of tuche that does not always hold up to scientific standards for rigor. This problem is also mirrored in efforts to bring psychoanalytic criticism to bear on the practice of literary interpretation. The biggest problem with earlier attempts to appropriate psychoanalytic criticism for literary and rhetorical studies is that they often reduced it to psychobiography, and as such avoided an engagement with the specifics of the text. This problem is much less pronounced if psychoanalysis is read through the metaphor of the economy as a post hoc heuristic, since this theory, born from the analysis of individual cases, is paradoxically at its strongest when it tracks a large field of phenomena as opposed to bringing a specific prediction or interpretation to bear in a specific case.

Here we are bordering on what Lacan identified as a discourse of trauma. How so? In the treatment of tuche and automaton in *The Four Fundamental Concepts of Psychoanalysis*, Lacan frames the relationship between the two as a missed encounter: automaton, which is an iteration of the somewhat structuralist logic of the symbolic order attempts to orient the subject towards its world as a systematic unity. But this systematic account of the logic of the subject's world is constantly thrown against the "heart of experience," the hard "kernel of the real."[25] Every act of the subject's framing of world is a kind of "missed encounter" with the "unassimilable" real, and this produces a kind of trauma for the subject by revealing that the operations of the symbolic are accidental, or rather arbitrary.[26] On Lacan's reading, the symbolic automaton attempts to address this missed encounter through strategies of repetition, constantly attempting to make the symbolic logic map over the contingency of the real.

Here we can come full circle, addressing the concerns with psychoanalysis's structuralism exemplified by Robinson's criticism. Obviously, on this account of the metaphor of psychoanalysis, there are significant resources for addressing the claims to psychoanalytic structuralism as a kind of determinism, and as a form of overdetermined interpretive logic. But this framing of psychoanalysis also hones in on Robinson's most incisive criticism: that the category of lack secretly becomes a positive ontology.[27] This criticism is true if psychoanalytic economies are read as an inevitable outcome of the logic of lack—here the operations that found the subject are not contingent, but are the universal, quasimetaphysical effect of a subject negotiating a nonexistent foundation. But another framing is also possible, that of a set of rhetorical regularities that are generated by a constantly missed appointment with the real. As a post hoc explanation of a set of regularities, the category of lack might maintain a sense of contingency, since the explanation of this metaphor presumes the primacy of the real as an only contingently farmable encounter with reality—lack here is not a positive category, but a negative category capturing the subject's strategies for coping with the lack of a positive ontological foundation.

If all of this seems a bit abstract, Lacan provides an analogy that helps explain the relationship between psychoanalysis and structuralism in his Baltimore address, Lacan's earliest and most significant engagement with the question of structuralism. The lecture, entitled "Of Structure as an Inmixing of Otherness Prerequisite to Any Subject Whatever," employs the analogy of counting to lay out the logic of structure in the psychoanalytic economy.[28] Lacan begins this treatment of counting by distancing himself and psychoanalytic thought generally from the idea of structure as a "unifying unity" of human experience:

> At any rate, it is always the unifying unity which is in the foreground. I have never understood this, for if I am a psychoanalyst I am also a man, and as a man my experience has shown me that the principal characteristic of my own human life . . . is that life is something which goes, as we say in French, *à la dérive*. Life goes down the river, from time to time touching a bank, staying for a while here and there, without understanding anything—and it is the principle of analysis that nobody understands

anything of what happens. The idea of the unifying unity of the human condition has always had on me the effect of a scandalous lie.[29]

This idea of a unifying unity as a scandalous impossibility belied by the encounter with "real" life repeats the dialectic of tuche and automaton. Here, Lacan introduces his treatment of the logic of counting:

> The sameness is not in *things* but in the *mark* which makes it possible to add things with no consideration as to their differences. The mark has the effect of rubbing out the difference, and this is the key to what happens to the subject, the unconscious subject in the repetition; because you know that this subject repeats something peculiarly significant, the subject is here, for instance, in this obscure thing that we call in some cases trauma, or exquisite pleasure. What happens? If the *thing* exists in this symbolic structure, if this unitary trait is decisive, the trait of the sameness is here. In order that the *thing* which is sought be here in you, it is necessary that the first trait be rubbed out because the trait itself is a modification. It is the taking away of all difference, and in this case, without the trait, the first *thing* is simply lost. The key to this insistence in repetition is that in its essence repetition as repetition of the symbolical sameness is impossible.[30]

For Lacan, numbers are a second-order representation of things in the real world: the idea of a number is not naturally contained in the things in a given set. The "sameness" that allows things to be counted is a kind of assigned "mark" that fits them into a conceptual unity. Assigning a mark, and engaging in the conceptual commerce in numbers, can only take place by eliminating the difference in the counted things, presuming their sameness for the sake of founding the logic of counting. This is the dynamic of the symbolic or the automaton in distilled form. But the function of this sameness is only bought by fully transposing the thing into the conceptual automaton embodied in the act of accounting. But there is excess here—the act of assigning consecutive numerals to objects in a set does not fully suppress the difference between the objects, or, "in its essence repetition as repetition of the symbolical sameness is impossible."[31] Put in terms outside the realm of counting, every act of identifying and repeating sameness is inextricably tied to the contingent operation of tuche. Thus, the psychoanalytic economy requires the presupposition of ineradicable difference among different elements integrated into the logic of the symbolic. Far from suppressing plurality under the rubric of economy as a structure, psychoanalytic economies are a mode of articulating the subject's negotiation with the plurality of the real—these economies presume their own failure in fully assimilating any given phenomena into the logic of a structure.

Psychoanalytic economies are a kind of *tertium quid* in the simple binary of structure and particularity for other reasons that flow from this central insight. For example, economies are based on regularities in terms of exchange, but the principles of exchange are constantly malleable. In a monetary economy, the principles of exchange are constantly fluid, for reasons alluded to in Friedman's wheat market example. Extending the analogy of exchange to the psychoanalytic metaphor of the economy, the terms of exchange in a psychoanalytic economy are tied to a set of rhetorical processes that flow from contingency: dynamics of misrecognition, the vicissitudes of the subject's desire, and the inescapability of strategies of trope.

The same is true of the question of circulation in an economy: in any economic exchange the value of a product is dictated by the constantly and uncontrollably variable cost of inputs, labor, and the fluctuation of supply and demand. Although in the psychoanalytic economy the metaphor does not hold fully because of the lack of monetization, there is a similar dynamic in terms of circulation. How so? Again, we are turned to two possible different framings of the metaphor of circulation in psychoanalytic economies. On one reading, prevalent in the Freudian tradition, psychoanalysis is a "hydraulic" economy of the individual subject's flows of desire, where symptoms are the exchange media for unrealized desires. On this reading of the psychoanalytic economy, psychoanalysis does fall prey to the criticism that it is an over-determined structuralist discourse. But in the Lacanian economy, the fundamental units of exchange are not desires and symptoms: they are tropes, an intricate interplay of metaphor and metonymy reaching back to the very moment of the subject's genesis. Here desires, enjoyment, and even specific acts of representation are symptoms, in that they are effects of an underlying tropological economy of exchange.

The concept of an economy implies another consideration besides that of systematically interrelated but contingent conditions of exchange. Economies also imply notions of value and investment. Value and investment are as instrumental in the psychoanalytic semiotic economy as they are in a monetary economy. Tropes are invested, through acts of cathexis, with varying degrees of affective intensity and are of differing value in reproducing practices of enjoyment. In a psychoanalytic economy, as in a monetary economy, changing the value of one investment implies ripple effects in other investments: cathectic investments in specific tropes displace or devalue the level of investment in other tropes, etc.

Consider the cumulative picture of the economy based on the preceding account: economies are a metaphor for the idea that there are regularities in tropological exchange viewed from the broadest perspective, but when tracked at a more specific level, they are about a set of contingent choices, framed by tropological exchange but not predetermined by the logic of a structure as much as by the chance encounter of formal regularities with the messy world of contingency. Such exchanges are probabilistic enterprises, necessarily based on incomplete information and subjective judgments. Economies, and interpretations of such economies, are a way of managing the inherent uncertainties presented by the presence of luck, chance, and contingency: they do not require the formal criteria of validity as much as they must convincingly pay attention to as many of the available means of persuasion (or here the possibilities for generating meaning) as possible.

In other words, the psychoanalytic economy of exchange is another way of reaffirming *rhetoric*, or as Lacan unwittingly defines it: "People talk nowadays about messages everywhere . . . a hormone is a message, a beam of light . . . from a satellite is a message . . . but the message in language is absolutely different . . . our message, in all cases comes from the Other by which I understand 'from the place of the Other.'"[32] Talk of messages and transparency belongs with the categories of the sciences and structural linguistics: the "message" in human language is mediated by a contingent encounter with an other, and with the difficulties in grasping the signifying practices of the other. The message in language is inextricably tied to a messy economy of exchange with an other who is never fully known, and whom we interact with under the charge of both *tuche* and *automaton*. This is the condition of rhetoricity, to the extent that psychoanalysis eschews this focus for a more automatic account of structure, to the extent that it forgets the primacy of "speech" it misses the encounter with chance and contingency, and replicates the problems of structuralism.[33]

Alternatively, in focusing on the rhetoricity of psychoanalysis as an account of all human meaning making, the notion of an economy necessitates the primacy of rhetoric as a set of tropological regularities that work through both contingency and affect. Restored primacy for rhetoric is significant for the evolving debate in critical theory over the place of psychoanalysis, but for the community of rhetoricians the implications are even more important. On this reading, rhetoric, and the preeminently rhetorical categories of trope, affect, and contingency, can reassert a status as a privileged vocabulary within the critical interpretive humanities.

Notes

[1] Martin Heidegger, "On the Essence of Truth," in *Basic Writings: Second Edition, Revised and Expanded*, ed. David Farrell Krell (San Francisco, CA: Harper Books, 1993), 111–39.

[2] Jacques Lacan, "On a Question Preliminary to any Possible Treatment of Psychosis," in *Écrits: A Selection*, trans. Alan Sheridan (New York: W.W. Norton, 1982), Section III.

[3] Jacques Lacan, *Seminar XX, On Feminine Sexuality; the Limits of Love and Knowledge 1972–1973. Encore: The Seminar of Jacques Lacan, Book XX*, trans. Bruce Fink, ed. Jacques-Alain Miller (New York: W.W. Norton, 1999), 48.

[4] For a treatment of the concept of *glissement*, or sliding, see Jacques Lacan, *Seminar XI, The Four Fundamental Concepts of Psychoanalysis, The Seminar of Jacques Lacan, Book XI*, trans. Alan Sheridan, ed. Jacques-Alain Miller (New York: W.W. Norton, 1998), 129.

[5] Sigmund Freud, "Notes Upon a Case of Obsessional Neurosis," in *Three Case Histories*, ed. Philip Rieff (New York: Scribner Paper Fiction, 1963 [1909]), 1–82.

[6] Jacques Lacan, "The Agency of the Letter in the Unconscious or Reason Since Freud," in *Écrits: A Selection*, trans. Alan Sheridan (New York: W.W. Norton, 1982), 156.

[7] Jacques Lacan, *The Language of the Self: The Function of Language in Psychoanalysis*, trans. Anthony Wilden (Baltimore, MD: The Johns Hopkins University Press, 1998), especially the section "The Empty Word and the Full Word."

[8] Lacan, *The Language of the Self*, 31.

[9] Lacan, *Seminar XX*, 56.

[10] Deirdre McCloskey, *The Rhetoric of Economics* (Madison: University of Wisconsin Press, 1998).

[11] Sigmund Freud, *Civilization and its Discontents. The Standard Edition of the Complete Psychological Works of Sigmund Freud,* ed. James Strachey (New York: W. W. Norton, 1972).

[12] For an in-depth treatment of this theme in Lacan's work see Jean-Joseph Goux's *Symbolic Economies: After Marx and Freud* (Ithaca: Cornell University Press, 1990).

[13] Maria Ruegg, "Metaphor and Metonymy: The Logic of Structuralist Rhetoric," *Glyph* 6 (1979): 141–57.

[14] Andrew Robinson, "The Political Theory of Constitutive Lack: A Critique," *Theory and Event* 8:1 (2005). Jacques Derrida, *Archive Fever: A Freudian Impression,* trans. Eric Prenowitz (Chicago: The University of Chicago Press, 1998) and "Psychoanalysis Searches the States of Its Soul: The Impossible Beyond of a Sovereign Culture," in *Without Alibi,* ed. Peggy Kamuf (Stanford, CA: Meridian, 2002).

[15] Slavoj Žižek, *The Fragile Absolute* (London: Verso, 2001).

[16] Slavoj Žižek, "The Limits of a Semiotic Approach to Psychoanalysis," in *Interrogating the Real,* ed. Rex Butler and Scott Stephens (London: Verso, 2005).

[17] Ernest Laclau, *On Populist Reason* (London: Verso, 2007).

[18] Karl R. Popper, *Conjectures and Refutations: The Growth of Scientific Knowledge* (London: Routledge, 1969).

[19] Jacques Derrida, "Structure, Sign, and Play in the Discourse of the Human Sciences," in *Writing and Difference,* trans. Alan Bass (London: Routledge, 1980).

[20] Milton Friedman, "The Methodology of Positive Economics," in *Essays in Positive Economics* (Chicago: The University of Chicago Press, 1966).

[21] Friedman, "The Methodology of Positive Economics," 32.

[22] Friedman, "The Methodology of Positive Economics," 43.

[23] This is a word coined by Lacan to signify the realm of tuche. Lacan, *Seminar XI,* 70–1.

[24] For an exemplary work in this regard see Donald Spence, *The Rhetorical Voice of Psychoanalysis* (Boston, MA: Harvard University Press, 1994). Spence's work is particularly interesting for rhetoricians who engage psychoanalysis, because he argues that the central failing of contemporary psychoanalysis is that it has given up any pretense to scientific validity in relying on *rhetoric* as a supplement to empirical evidence. The remarkable thing is that Spence is using rhetoric in a technical sense, and a good portion of his book is dedicated to locating the Aristotelian roots of the rhetorical tradition.

[25] Lacan, *Seminar XI,* 53.

[26] Ibid., 55.

[27] Robinson, "The Political Theory," 1.

[28] Jacques Lacan, "Of Structure as an Inmixing of Otherness Prerequisite to Any Subject Whatsoever," in *The Languages of Criticism and the Sciences of Man: The Structuralist Controversy,* ed. R. Macksey and E. Donato (Baltimore, MD: The Johns Hopkins University Press, 1970) 186–195.

[29] Ibid.

[30] Ibid.

[31] Ibid.

[32] Lacan, "Of Structure as an Inmixing of Otherness Prerequisite to Any Subject Whatsoever."

[33] Lacan, *The Language of the Self,* esp. section I.

Physicians Who Are Qualified; Women Who Are Not

18

Barbara Schneider

In Monty Python's film *The Meaning of Life*, the viewer zooms in on a pair of physicians discussing the impending arrival of an administrator they wish to impress. They survey the delivery room, find it barren, and order several different machines to be brought into the room. The laboring mother, flat on her back on a delivery table with her legs in stirrups, attempts to address the masked medical personnel, asking, "What should I do?" The chief physician answers, "Nothing! You're not qualified." The anticipated administrator arrives, and the physician secures his own credentials by announcing gleefully, "See here. I have the machine that goes bing!" This scene captures and compresses the long rise of technologized ways of reading the pregnant body that privilege physicians' ways of reading while suppressing woman's ways of knowing.

Prior to the Progressive Era, pregnancy and childbirth were almost exclusively women's domains. Women, endowed with bodily knowledge not available to men, were assumed to be the expert readers of the signs that signaled pregnancy, normal or abnormal fetal development, and imminent birth. Women were also assumed to be the authoritative practitioners, with a few who garnered expertise through experience directing and attending the births of others.

Critical changes in the reading and writing practices of medicine during the Progressive Era affected a redistribution of knowledge and power that eroded the ground upon which women claimed authority and repositioned male physicians as the experts who are assumed to know. A reading of the case histories of pregnant, laboring, and childbearing women, published first in the American Medical Association's *Journal of the Diseases of Women and Children* and then, after 1920, in the *Journal of Obstetrics and Gynecology*, reveal three key changes in medical practice during these years. Increasingly, medicine incorporated industrial technologies, changing the way bodies and diseases are read. These technologies carried with them the values of the scientific management movement holding sway during the era, most notably a regard for standardization and efficiency, which changed the expectations of how bodies will perform. This shift in reading practices was part of medicine's efforts to professionalize itself, in terms legible and thus legitimate, to a culture invested in modernist ideals of rationality and objectivity. Technologi-

cal innovation and professional desire contributed to a shift in medical educa
tion that was further encouraged by the publication of the Flexner report in
1910. Taken together, technology, professionalization, and the regulations
that ensued from that report hastened the closing of women's medical
schools. New reading practices and educational requirements prompted the
third key change. By the end of the Progressive Era, the case histories that
represented pregnant and laboring women in medicine's professional journal,
once multivocal narratives, evolved into a set of discursive practices that cut
women into reproductive parts whose processes were under the management
of expert male physicians.

Prior to the incorporation of industrial technologies into medical practices, medicine was in many ways composed largely of conversation. Patients
came to their physicians with their complaints; physicians elicited descriptions of their symptoms with further questions. During the course of their
conversation, patient and physician constructed a history of the illness and
placed it in the context of the present symptoms. A cursory physical examination might or might not follow. The physician then pronounced a diagnosis
and a plan of treatment, a treatment that, as Susan Wells points out, often
consisted of only more talk: instructions for hygienic care, routines for
strengthening the system, and encouragement.[1] It was through these conversations that the physician read the patient's body. It was a reading created out
of a dialogue with the patient and if the doctor's interpretation was somewhat
privileged, the patient still retained an active voice in the telling. Here is a
case history from 1902, just as the Progressive Era opens. An extended introduction describes the call to come to the patient's home as well as a description of her household before the physician, who writes the case history, gets
to the diagnosis:

> She had the peculiar coloring of the skin so frequently noticed and a col-
> lapsed appearance. On further inquiry it was found that in August she
> had menstruated. In September she had seen very, very little. . . . The
> breasts indicated pregnancy. . . . Was satisfied that the case was one of
> ruptured extrauterine pregnancy. (Ross 1902)

Here, the patient is placed in the context of her home life. The dialogue
replays the conversation between woman and physician as they discuss her
symptoms. She is the one who reports on her menstrual cycle, and it is easy to
imagine her also contributing to the reading of her breasts. Her interpretation
of her body's signs figure into the diagnosis that serves as the basis for action.

The weight the patient's story bears on the diagnosis and treatment of her
body is steadily eroded, however, as the tools and methods of clinical examination add increasing weight to what the doctor finds. The thermometer,
although invented in the late eighteenth century, was not routinely used in
medical care until the late nineteenth century, but it then became both a tool
for diagnosis and for research, as well as a warrant for the physician's claim to
be healing the sick. The stethoscope likewise slowly became a standard

instrument of practice. X-rays, which give physicians a significant advantage in reading the body by allowing them to see what is hidden, were invented in 1895, and were gradually introduced into clinical practices through the Progressive Era. They assumed a special place in obstetrics. Introduced in 1898, X-ray pelvimetry replaced mechanical pelvimetry and was used routinely to take measurements of the pelvis, which were then translated by physicians into predictions of the length and outcome of labor as well as an evaluation of a woman's natural ability to bear children.[2] Wassermann tests first devised in 1906 began increasingly to figure into obstetric examinations. Microscopes and histological readings of tissue samples became more and more sophisticated, even before the introduction of the electron microscope in 1933.

Taken together, the growing instrumentalization of medicine provided the physician with an increasing advantage in the negotiation of symptoms into a diagnosis. These tests reveal to the doctor the presence of a disease or foreign body that may well be either invisible or illegible to the pregnant woman they inhabit. More and more, the history the patient has to tell diminishes in authority; more and more, what the doctor reads through the machines is written as the story of the patient's body. The following case study, written in 1928 at the end of the Progressive Era, demonstrates the ways technology shifted the reading practices of medicine, practices that suppressed the woman's voice in the story of her body:

> Case 2.—Mrs. A.W., aged thirty-eight. Admitted to Lebanon Hospital April 15, 1928, discharged May 2, 1928. Membranes ruptured a few hours before onset of labor. The patient had a flat pelvis, and it was deemed advisable to give her a test of labor. After forty-six hours of labor there was no engagement of the fetal head. I thereupon performed a cesarean section employing the same technic as in Case 1. Temperature at time of operation was 101°. The temperature range during her convalescence was between 98.6° and 101.6°. The tubes were removed eight days after operation. (Rosenfeld 410)

Here, the patient at least has a marital status and initials. In other case histories from this year, women are represented only by case number, age, and number of pregnancies. Nonetheless, the investment in machine readings is clear. This woman has evidently not measured up on the X-ray pelvimetry, as the physician notes that she has a flat pelvis. And according to the clock that runs for forty-six hours as she labors, she fails the test the physician has put to her. It is the physician who manages the delivery process, tests the woman's labor, finds it wanting, and determines the time and type of intervention. His reading of the thermometer serves as a sign of his ongoing authority and as a warrant for his claim to deliver care.

David Armstrong describes this shift as a movement from the patient's story to the doctor's story:

> The old medicine relied primarily on the patient's history, perhaps with the support of some observation, but the new medicine gave the clinical

> examination pride of place (Foucault, Birth of the Clinic). Pathological
> medicine took over the old history but separated sign (what the doctor
> finds) from symptom (what the patient reports); it also continued with
> the process of observation, formalized in "inspection," and added the
> inferential procedures of percussion (tapping the body to listen for areas
> of relative density), palpation (feeling the body with the hands), and aus-
> cultation (listening with the stethoscope). Here then were the great tech-
> niques of medicine—what the patient said, what the doctor saw, and
> what the doctor could infer—first mapped out on a compartmentalized
> body early in the nineteenth century. (236)

This increasing reliance on machine readings diminishes the role of women
in multiple ways. The stories of pregnant and laboring women occupy less
and less of the case histories written into professional journals. The shift also
hastened the movement of women from their homes to the hospitals where
the machines were stationed. And at least as importantly, the increasing reliance on technology contributed to the closure of women's medical colleges.

The elision of women's stories was particularly injurious to women physicians. Concerns that the modesty of the woman might be jeopardized by a
visual examination made by a male physician prompted for many years a
blind examination carried out by touch while the woman remained otherwise
clothed and the physician remained visually out of touch with the body he
read by hand. It was just these conventions of modesty, as they complicated
the reading of bodies, that a number of female physicians invoked to bolster
their argument that they occupied a privileged position as readers of women's
bodies. As Susan Wells recounts in her reading of the texts of the women's
medical schools in the latter half of the nineteenth century, women physicians
claimed that because they were members of the same sex, they could elicit
from their female patients histories that were much less vexed by concerns of
cross-gender modesty and therefore were much more revealing of the patient's
symptoms. While male physicians might find their ability to practice medicine through the traditional art of conversation compromised by this modesty,
no such impediment, women physicians claimed, stood in their way:

> Everyone agreed that it was easy to talk to a woman physician. . . . It is
> not surprising that early women physicians claimed a distinct professional
> practice founded on the unconstrained confidence between patient and
> physician. On this ground, women physicians developed and deployed
> distinct forms of professional authority. Patients were described as telling
> a "heart history" to which the woman physician was an understanding,
> but unswervingly moral, auditor. Her response to the heart history estab-
> lished the exigency of her authority, intimate and inexorable. (Wells 51)

In other words, the female physician, by virtue of her bodily similarity to the
pregnant patient, is endowed with an intrinsic ethos that makes her the privileged recipient and therefore a more expert writer of the woman's body.

The feminine privilege of receiving the heart history unrestrained by the
barriers of modesty was quickly eroded by the incorporation of modernist

and technological values and practices and the standardization of medical education to include access to and experience with technological equipment. The standardization of medical education also centralizes it in colleges associated with long-standing and largely male universities. Graduation from these medical schools, as opposed to graduation from the small and numerous proprietary schools, quickly garnered professional prestige, a prestige that operated to ensure already well-funded institutions even more secure funding. At the same time, it put competitive pressure on the already strained proprietary schools. Medical education became increasingly reserved for those who could afford it and those who could gain admission to institutions that were almost exclusively male.

Women's medical schools, which flourished after the Civil War, lost prestige in the face of this growing acclaim. And when more and more of the powerful universities, perhaps prompted by Johns Hopkins's agreement to admit women at its opening in 1893, opened their doors to women, they attracted the most qualified women students and many of their sources of funding. Once women could attend these formerly all-male institutions, the argument that women had to have their own schools lost authority, eroding the social basis for their existence. This diminished social mission concurs with the increasing reliance on diagnostic machines in medicine, a reliance that increasingly put financial pressure on the already constrained budgets of proprietary schools. Enrollment at women's medical schools fell from 459 in 1893 to 183 in 1904, a decline that continued throughout the Progressive Era.[3] In 1910, the AMA sponsored and released the Flexner report. Flexner recommended rigorous educational standards, extensive clinical training, and expanded laboratory work. The Flexner report dealt another injurious blow to the proprietary women's schools that were already reeling from falling enrollments. One by one, the women's colleges closed. By the end of the Progressive Era, only the Women's Medical College of Pennsylvania remained. The number of women practicing medicine subsequently declined until the female physicians and their alternative ways of reading patients' bodies no longer held any cultural sway.

By the era of the case histories under investigation here, the reading and writing practices of obstetrics and gynecology were shaped by modern configurations of gender in a technologized field. The attending physician was almost exclusively male in a culture that privileged his interpretation. This privilege extended to his reading of the female body. And his reading of that body was further privileged because of the advantages technology granted to him. Technology overcame the reticence of modesty by mediating between the physician's male gaze and the patient's female body. No longer disadvantaged by the reticence of his feminine patients, the male obstetrician, through the instruments of technology, could read a body that remained in many ways invisible and illegible to the woman who was that pregnant body. The importance and sway of the story the pregnant woman had to tell of her own body was even further diminished.

Medicine's adoption of both the instruments and values of industrial scientific management and its application to pregnant women resulted in a third key change. The shift in reading practices prompted by the uptake of technology stimulated a shift in writing practices as texts increasingly incorporated technical rather than discursive forms of representation. Tables, charts, graphs, and labeled photos overtook the narration and description of the case history that preserved the pregnant woman as a subject and reduced her to reproductive parts that become the object of study. The "heavily discursive" practice of medicine that relies on and is constituted by talk, as Susan Wells recounts it, still holds within the early issues under review here. The opening article of the July issue of *The American Journal of Obstetrics and Diseases of Women and Children* in 1902, by James F. W. Ross was written in first person voice and retained the conversational tone from its first presentation as an oral lecture to the Alumni Association of Detroit Medical College. The paper, which ran 42 journal pages, includes a subhead that notes the incorporation of seven illustrations, a notation made because of the rarity of illustration at that time. It also includes what Ross describes as a "tabulated statement," a table that records the 45 cases he discusses (29–41). The table itself displays the negotiation between the tradition of discursive medicine and the emergence of technological ways of reading and writing bodies. The table frames the cases in a standardized way, lining up the cases in regular columns and rows. Each case is separated into seven categories and reported through those categories. The table operates as a machine that regularizes the reporting of the cases. The tradition of medicine as conversation, however, dominates. The content of the seven categories includes reports by the women of their menstrual history, descriptions of their symptoms and pain, and their accounts of the event that prompted them to seek medical attention. The greatest portion of the table was devoted, then, to reporting what the patients said. Their stories abut the stories of the physical examination performed by the physician, along with any clinical findings, notations on the operation performed, results, and a column for remarks (which holds only one, "unruptured"). Reports of temperature readings, heart tones heard through a stethoscope, and measurements are scant or missing altogether. In spite of the technology of the table, the case reporting remains conversational, with patient and physician negotiating her symptoms into a diagnosis that leads to a practical intervention in the form of an operation. The article concludes with remarks suitable to its original oral presentation. Ross thanks his audience for their patient listening and the predecessor from whom he draws much of his research, and closes with a rhetorical bow: "I feel that I have been greatly honored by your Association and will always carry with me a pleasant recollection of its session in 1902" (42).

By 1917, the transition to more technical, textual forms inscribed the increasing reliance on technological ways of reading. Tables and charts, once exceptional, are now routinely part of most articles. Furthermore, tables report findings not in terms of conversation, but in terms of dose measurements, temperatures, and times. Pregnant women are routinely identified by their categorical status as childbearers. "Primapari, pari-ii, pari-iv" immediately follows their initials in case histories. And increasingly, bodies are presented in terms of their participation in statistical categories. This shift in writing practices from a discursive to a technologized way of reading was even more pronounced by 1929.

The opening article of the January 1929 issue of *The American Journal of Obstetrics*, "Radium Therapy of Carcinoma Uteri," by George Gray Ward, MD, FACS, includes extensive tables, and the tables here, unlike those employed in the 1902 article, do operate as a machine that standardizes the bodies and practices represented. Bodies become the disease that inhabits them and diseases become statistical possibilities and probabilities. And what occupies the bulk of this article is not the stories of the women who are being treated, but the relative success and failure of the methods employed. Medicine's focus here is on procedure, not people. This technological form of representation is even more evident in the opening article of the March 1929 issue. Here, the women being treated are reduced through a table to initials, age, and number of births. They are recorded in terms of their method of delivery, febrility, blood and bacteriology counts, and antitoxin tolerance. The traditional discursive portion of the text occupies less than a quarter of the text's 30 pages. Tables, charts, statistical graphs, and slides occupy the rest. The woman once represented in the context of her life, whose story contributed meaningfully to a diagnosis and whose treatment was negotiated reciprocally with the attending physician, is now simply a neatly charted array of measurements and statistics. In these accounts, she does nothing and the textual report of childbirth and delivery becomes the machine that silences her, the machine that goes bing.

The shifts in reading and writing practices that I have traced here produced the biomedical model currently critiqued by a number of feminists for the ways that model atomizes human bodies and disassociates itself in many ways from human experience. The biomedical model is what made possible a procedure called a pubiotomy, recounted by A. J. Rongy, among others, where a woman's pelvic bone was cut in half in order to expedite the extraction of the baby. While the operation left any number of women crippled, it was efficient and assured the delivery of the baby, enacting the values of scientific medical management. In her examination of the intersection of biological and technological systems, Laura Fantone reminds us that "body and life are information" and argues that the reduction of bodies and life into manipulable parts

> [has] not been aimed for women's health; rather [it has] imposed norms
> and disciplines on our bodies. In a modern paradigm, organs had func-
> tions that composed and organized the whole individual. Today, not only
> the integrity or beauty of the body are not valuable, but rather the value
> lies in its subindividual characteristics, namely, the genetic material. The
> importance of genes is inevitably related to digital technologies that
> made possible their representation. (17–18)

One way the research presented here suggests we might proceed to produce complementary and alternative medical practices as advocated by Fantone and other feminist critics of the biomedical model is to return to the women's stories that are suppressed by this model as a source of information that might be mined to produce new answers to persistent questions and to reevaluate and revalue body and life as sources of knowledge.

Notes

[1] This section is richly informed by Wells, *Out of the Dead House.*

[2] From Leavitt, *Brought to Bed.* Pelvimetry has been the object of a number of cultural analyses of the intersections of gender, medicine, and reproduction.

[3] See Bonner, *To the Ends of the Earth* for useful analysis and statistics in this area as well as Wells, *Out of the Dead House.*

Works Cited

Armstrong, David. "The Medical Division of Labor." *Knowledges: Historical and Critical Studies in Disciplinarity.* Ed. Ellen Messer-Davidow, David R. Shumway, and David J. Sylvan. Knowledge: Disciplinarity and Beyond. Charlottesville: UP of Virginia, 1993. 232–42.

Bonner, Thomas Neville. *To the Ends of the Earth: Women's Search for Education in Medicine.* Cambridge, MA: Harvard University Press, 1992.

Fantone, Laura. "From Dissection to Digital Genetics: Representations of the (Female) Body and the Political Implications of Genetic Research." Gender and Power in the New Europe; the 5th European Feminist Conference. Lund University, Sweden, August 2003. May 2006. <http://www.iiav.nl/epublications/2003/Gender_and_power/5thfeminist/paper_542.pdf 23>.

Flexner, Abraham. *Medical Education in the United States and Canada.* New York: Carnegie Foundation for the Advancement of Teaching, 1910.

Leavitt, Judith Walzer. *Brought to Bed: Childbearing in America, 1750 to 1950.* New York: Oxford UP, 1986.

Python, Monty. *The Meaning of Life.* Dir. Terry Jones. 1983. DVD. Universal, 2003.

Rongy, A. J. "The Treatment of Contracted Pelvis, With Special Reference to Pubiotomy." *The American Journal of Obstetrics and Diseases of Women and Children* 75.2 (1917): 208–21.

Rosenfeld, Samuel. "Prophylactic Treatment of Puerperal Infection by Intrauterine Applications of Antiseptic Solutions." *The American Journal of Obstetrics and Gynecology* 17.3 (1929): 408–11.

Ross, James F. W. "Ectopic Gestation." *The American Journal of Obstetrics and Diseases of Women and Children* 46.1 (1902): 1–42.

Ward, George Gray. "Radium Therapy of Carcinoma Uteri." *The American Journal of Obstetrics and Gynecology* 17.1 (1929): 1–22.

Wells, Susan. *Out of the Dead House: Nineteenth-Century Women Physicians and the Writing of Medicine.* Madison: U of Wisconsin P, 2001.

Limited Prevention, Limiting Topos
Reframing Arguments about Science and Politics in the HIV Prevention Policy Debate

J. Blake Scott

In April 2003, the U.S. Centers for Disease Control and Prevention (CDC) announced a new initiative—Advancing HIV Prevention (AHP)—that shifted the focus of prevention efforts and funding to more widespread, routine HIV testing and the prevention case management of persons living with HIV (CDC, 2003a, p. 331). In justifying its initiative, CDC officials argued that existing prevention strategies focusing on those at high risk, such as community-based education, had stalled, creating the need for other, more proven public health approaches to combat the epidemic (p. 331).[1] Expanded HIV testing, in particular, was touted as the key to reducing the rate of new infections. This argument assumed that the implementation of testing as a routine part of medical care and the targeted expansion of rapid testing in nonmedical settings would lead to the identification, education, and preventive action of HIV-positive persons, an assumption that exaggerates the power of testing and glosses over the contingencies of its practices and effects (see Scott, 2003). In several of its publications, the CDC emphasized the preventive power of testing and, to a lesser extent, the simplified and more efficient "science-based" prevention counseling and education (see, for example, CDC, 2003b). As part of defining its new initiative as grounded in "science-based public health principles and practices" rather than a "political agenda" (CDC 2003c), the CDC cited several scientific studies that, at best, yielded mixed results about the effects of testing and counseling on risk behavior (e.g., Colfax et al., 2002).[2]

The CDC's attempts to define its policy shift as scientific rather than political were echoed, attacked, and defended in what Paula Treichler (1999) might call a larger, ongoing "epidemic of signification," or an outbreak of arguments about U.S. prevention policy in which rhetors on both sides attempted to use science and its discursive traditions to control the debate but only further exacerbated it, spawning new claims about the science behind their arguments and those of their opponents (p. 39). Following this analogy, this paper presents a partial epidemiology or mapping of the (mostly flawed) arguments framed by the science versus politics topos, a conceptual vantage point that made certain lines of argument possible and others less possible.

Rhetors supporting *and* opposing AHP and other shifts in U.S. prevention policy aligned themselves with sound, effective science and the goal of protecting the public health; both sets of rhetors characterized competing arguments and approaches as invalid, inaccurate, ineffective, and, most of all, motivated by political, nonscientific goals. Each side used the science versus politics topos to argue that its prevention approaches were good, effective, beneficial, or promising because they are driven by science while, in contrast, the approaches of their opponents were bad, ineffective, harmful, or dangerous because they are driven by politics or ideology. Although this rhetorical epidemic generated a vigorous debate among public health officials, community activists, politicians, and other rhetors, the arguments both for and against prevention policy shifts relied on oversimplified, nonnegotiable positions that prevented rather than contributed to a robust, ethical deliberation about the best course of action.

A few responses to the AHP wholeheartedly endorsed the policy shift as a long overdue move toward science. For example, Joe McIlhaney (2003), president of the Texas-based Medical Institute for Social Health (which received federal prevention funding for abstinence-only education), argued in a commentary titled "AIDS a Disease, Not a Political Issue" that throughout the epidemic "traditional infectious disease control methods" have been in "direct conflict" with the individual rights of gay men and others, with the latter prevailing. In contrasting public health and science on the one hand with politics and individual rights on the other, he hailed AHP as a desperately needed "first step toward treating HIV/AIDS like a public health challenge, not a political issue."

Other responses, particularly those by HIV prevention workers, met the CDC's new initiative with caution, skepticism, or outright disapproval. Many of these responses accused the CDC of usurping local control of prevention programs, of taking a too narrow approach to prevention efforts, of privileging more expedient but less effective forms of testing and counseling, of not calling for additional funding for prevention and treatment services (so that infected individuals identified through testing actually get connected to such services), and, above all, of being driven by politics rather than science.

Community-based organizations and other groups complained that the new initiative would take funding away from locally developed, culturally relevant prevention approaches, especially those targeting minority and men who have sex with men (MSM) communities. In their place, the CDC would fund programs that privilege testing and standardized prevention messages for infected individuals, both were simplified and streamlined so that physicians and other health care providers might be more willing to offer them (see CDC, 2003d). In arguing that local expertise and experience were necessary to ensure the validity and efficacy of science-based prevention programs, such critiques drew on what Lawrence Prelli (1989) has identified as the scientific topos of observational competence.

Those wary of the new initiative also protested the CDC's either-or argument for choosing one set of prevention approaches over another; the CDC should be adding to existing approaches rather than cutting them, they argued, as HIV prevention requires a full, varied range of efforts that target both infected and at-risk individuals. Some critics further accused the CDC of privileging testing not in the interest of public health but out of pressure from conservative politicians critical of safer sex programs (Ornstein, 2003). In the words of Terje Anderson, executive director of the National Association of People with AIDS, expanded testing would function "as a backdoor way of defunding" more controversial efforts (Ornstein, 2003).

In June 2003, not long after the CDC's AHP announcement, over 150 AIDS organizations sent a letter to President Bush, the 2004 Democratic presidential candidates, and members of Congress complaining about the new initiative's shift of already inadequate resources away from community-based strategies, the latter proven effective by "overwhelming scientific data" (Arnold, Harrington, & Baker, 2003). The letter also put the initiative in the larger context of "a series of events which appear to prioritize political ideology over sound science and public health policies," events that included the shift toward abstinence education, political censorship of prevention programs and research deemed controversial by conservatives, and continued flat funding for U.S. prevention efforts. The letter ends by calling on the president to "protect science" and public health policy from the "divisive politics of a few politicians." In addition to attacking the motives of conservative politicians, the authors position their comprehensive prevention efforts as benefiting the larger public health.

The longer trajectory of politically motivated policy making condemned by the letter began soon after President George W. Bush took office in 2001 and began appointing conservative politicians, such as former U.S. Representative Tom Colburn, to key positions in public health agencies and on advisory boards.[3] As President Bush and his appointees increasingly promoted a national HIV prevention policy around HIV testing and abstinence-based education, the CDC channeled more and more of its domestic prevention funding into programs, including many run by faith-based organizations, focusing on these efforts.

Under pressure from conservative lawmakers and officials, the Department of Health and Human Services (HHS) and the CDC joined what some HIV health care workers and activists have called a "war against condoms" and, by extension, the science showing their efficacy. In 2001, the CDC's condom fact sheet was removed from its Web site; the new fact sheet that appeared over a year later emphasized abstinence and lacked important information about condom use and efficacy. The CDC was also pressured to delete a document called "Programs that Work," which described effective and comprehensive (rather than abstinence only) STD, HIV, and pregnancy prevention programs (U.S. House of Representatives Committee on Government Reform, 2003, pp. 6, 11–12).

Conservative activists, lawmakers, and others supporting the government's shift toward abstinence-only education argued that science was on their side (*Sex*, 2003). Foreshadowing the CDC's argument in its AHP announcement, supporters argued that stalled prevention progress indicated that existing community-based prevention approaches, such as social marketing campaigns, peer outreach and counseling, and safer sex education workshops, had not been working.

Critics of the policy shift disputed this argument, attacking the methodology and validity of the studies cited by their opponents and citing studies showing the efficacy of condoms and comprehensive sex education. As Human Rights Watch (2004) pointed out, the same National Institutes of Health (NIH) study cited by conservatives backing abstinence education showed an 85% decrease in risk of HIV transmission among consistent condom users versus nonusers (see HHS, 2001). The HIV Prevention Defense Working Group (2002) cited scientific reviews by the NIH, CDC, and United Nations that confirmed the efficacy of existing prevention programs, including those involving condoms. Critics also countered that the biggest reason for stalled prevention success in the United States and world was the gross underfunding of such efforts.

In their efforts to shift funding away from programs they deemed "controversial," conservative lawmakers pressured HHS and the CDC to scrutinize the programs' efficacy and morality. In 2001, U.S. Representative Marc Souder began pressuring the HHS to audit government-funded safer sex workshops targeting MSM by San Francisco's Stop AIDS Project, claiming that the workshops were obscene and promoted sexual activity in violation of the Public Health Service Act. HHS Secretary Tommy Thompson and his inspector general began auditing the Stop AIDS workshops and similar programs by other organizations. After CDC head Julie Gerberding confirmed that the programs were in line with government policy, Souder demanded to see scientific proof of the programs' efficacy, invoking what Prelli (1989) calls the topos of skepticism, which suggests lines of argument about the "emotional attachment and systematic doubt" of those doing or using science. In what one journalist called a "blatant victory of politics over public health," Gerberding soon reversed her position, notifying Stop AIDS that their workshops did indeed appear to promote and encourage sexual activity and therefore must be changed or lose federal funding (Block, 2003).

Stop AIDS was joined by other organizations in expressing outrage at the CDC's about-face. Anderson of the National Association of People with AIDS warned that the decision would have a chilling effect on prevention organizations, sending them the message that a "group of right-wing jihadists with political power will be looking over their shoulders as they attempt to meet the prevention needs of their communities" (Connolly, 2003). Marsha Martin (2003) of AIDS Action protested in a letter to HHS Secretary Thompson that the audits of Stop AIDS and similar organizations suggested "an unacceptable shift away from scientifically based programs that deal realistically with sexual activity." In charging conservative policy makers with politically motivated censorship, including the censorship of science, these critics argued, in part, from the scientific topos of disinterestedness, which enables the rhetor to challenge the legitimacy of science based on the nonscientific motives of those producing or advocating it (see Prelli, 1989, p. 132). In such an argument, the intentions of those claiming to use science become a major way to assess the value of this use.

Prevention-related research was also under attack by conservatives. In April 2003, the *New York Times* revealed that scientists were being advised to avoid "controversial" terms such as "sex workers," "men who have sex with men," and "needle exchange" in their NIH grant applications ("Certain Words," 2003). Another New York newspaper pointed out that studies of these topics were politically, not scientifically, controversial because they dealt with what conservatives thought to be unacceptable modes of transmission ("Mixed Signals," 2003). Later, along with conservative U.S. House members, a coalition of conservative church groups called the Traditional Values Coalition pressured HHS to investigate how certain sex-based research studies were awarded NIH funding. The head of the coalition called the topics of the research, which included the sex practices of Mexican immigrants, truckers, and African American teenage girls, "smarmy" and "prurient," arguing that "reasonable people" would find them inappropriate for taxpayer funding (Wahlberg, 2003). Although these conservatives questioned the NIH's peer review process and the public health importance of such "controversial" topics, they also protested the studies on explicitly moral grounds. In arguing that taxpayer-funded prevention programs should be assessed by moral as well as scientific criteria, these conservatives illustrated what Sharon Crowley (2006) calls "ideologic" at work. Crowley coins this term to name "connections that can be forged [and disconnected and reconnected] among beliefs within a given ideology and/or across belief systems," in this case among values coming out of the authoritative traditions of science and religion (p. 75). As Crowley explains, ideologic can work to cover up such connections, presenting a falsely coherent set of beliefs and arguments and making them more difficult to disconnect and realign.

Efforts to censor prevention research prompted another round of accusations of politics and ideology driving public health policy.[4] U.S. Representative Henry Waxman fired off two angry letters to HHS Secretary Thompson, calling the church coalition group's efforts "scientific McCarthyism," a witch hunt driven by political motives rather than scientific ones. Alan Leshner of the American Association for the Advancement of Science echoed this response, arguing that "we can't have moralizing and ideology trump science when it comes to protecting the public health" (Weiss, 2003). Here, again, critics of conservative scrutiny and censorship focused on the political and ideological motives of their opponents, accusing them of attacking rather than supporting science and HIV prevention. The government's scrutiny of "controversial" prevention programs and studies mobilized the HIV Prevention Defense Working Group (2002), comprising over 80 AIDS-related organizations, to circulate the policy paper *HIV Prevention Saves Lives* on Capitol

Hill. Like earlier responses, this document accused the CDC of allowing policy makers "driven by political agendas rather than scientific imperative" to hold the "nation's commitment to prevention . . . hostage to politics." The science versus politics binary pervades the entire paper, which first presents scientific studies that show the efficacy of existing HIV prevention approaches and then critiques the government's shift toward abstinence-only education and increased scrutiny of sex-based prevention research as driven by politics rather than scientific evidence and analysis.

A frequent critic of HIV/AIDS policy under the Bush administration, Waxman extended his criticism of the administration's "attack" on science in a report published by the U.S. House of Representatives Committee on Government Reform (2003) and titled *Politics and Science in the Bush Administration.*[5] Embodying perhaps the most striking use of the science versus politics binary, the report documents "numerous instances where the Administration has manipulated the scientific process and distorted or suppressed scientific findings" about a wide range of issues, including abstinence-only education, condom efficacy, reproductive health, stem cell research, global warming, wetlands policy, oil and gas energy policy, and workplace safety (p. i). In its executive summary, the report states, "The Administration's political interference with science has led to misleading statements by the President, inaccurate responses to Congress, altered web sites, suppressed agency reports, erroneous international communications, and the gagging of scientists." In addition to their alarming treatment of science, the report goes on to explain, these actions share another attribute: "The beneficiaries . . . are important supporters of the President, including social conservatives and powerful industry groups" (p. i). Thus, the report suggests that those attacking science are motivated by economic gain as well as ideology. The report concludes by contrasting the necessity of "objective input of leading scientists and the impartial analysis of scientific evidence" with the current crisis involving the suppression, distortion, and obstruction of science "to suit political and ideological goals" (p. 32).

The president has legal authority to appoint leaders of federal agencies and help shape the agenda of these agencies, the report acknowledges, but "this prerogative should not extend to manipulating scientific research, controlling the advice provided by scientific advisory committees, or distorting scientific information presented to decision makers and the public" (p. 1). Although the report recognizes that politics cannot be totally absent from policy making, it argues that such policy making should be shaped by Science with a big "S" and politics with a small "p." In critiquing more recent conservative efforts to block FDA approval of a vaccine for the human papilloma virus, or HPV, renowned scientist and Nobel laureate David Baltimore similarly acknowledged the roles of politics and belief in science but drew the line at what he called "religious zealotry masked as politics" (Specter, 2006).

The mostly sharp but occasionally more nuanced distinctions between science and politics in the arguments I've been discussing illustrate how a rhetorical topos can be disabling as well as generative. In framing their arguments with the science versus politics topos and grounding these arguments almost solely in scientific values, reasons, and evidence, critics of the shifts in prevention policy relied on what Crowley (2006), via William Connolly, might call a fundamentalism or "imperative to assert" an unquestionable source of authority, even as they accused their opponents of doing the same (p. 12).

The line of arguments framed by the science versus politics topos depended on narrow views of the political and ideological as nonscientific and even antiscientific, as hindrances to scientific validity and effectiveness. Instead of relating to power relations, the political is described as the influence of politicians and/or activists seeking to shape policy for partisan, often economic, gain. Rather than a network of interpretation, ideology is described as a limited, usually irrational, viewpoint. Both politics and ideology are linked to closed, limiting perspectives and already-set, nonnegotiable agendas; as a result, they contaminate and compromise science's objective search for knowledge and the policy-making process of determining the most effective applications of scientific knowledge and technology.

The idealized notions of science and prevention made possible by the science versus politics topos are similarly limited and limiting. Science is presented as an objective source of truth, and prevention policy is driven (or should be driven) by scientific values and data. Such a framework limits the conceptual and rhetorical resources of those involved in science-related disputes, a limitation encapsulated in the words of a prominent scientist and critic of Bush administration policy: "As a scientist, the answer has to be *I believe in data*" (Specter, 2006).

Most science studies scholars and many scientists (e.g., Lewontin, 1991) would reject the easy distinctions between science and politics that permeate much of the HIV prevention debate. Rhetoricians (e.g., Condit, 1996; Doyle, 1997; Lessl, 1988), sociologists and anthropologists (e.g., Latour & Woolgar, 1986; Martin, 1994), feminist critics (Fox Keller, 1985; Haraway, 1991; Spanier, 1995), and cultural critics (Terry, 1999; Treichler, 1999; Waldby, 1996) working in science studies have argued, to varying degrees, that scientific practice and knowledge are linguistically, socially, and culturally constructed and that, consequently, science is always contingent, partial, ideological (i.e., shaped by interpretive frameworks), and political (i.e., shaped out of power relations). Some of these scholars have, more specifically, shown how harmful, discriminatory ideologies such as sexism and homophobia have helped shape scientific practice and knowledge.[6]

To borrow a term from Bruno Latour (1987), the science versus politics binary problematically black boxes science, covering up the messy practices of science-in-the-making to make it appear clean, coherent, and ready-made. But science is not a pure, stable, and separate cultural domain free of politics or ideology, and viewing it as such can overlook the full range of cultural actors and forces that shape it and, consequently, limit our ability to assess, mobilize, and participate in it. Neither is science free of ambiguity, contradiction, or disputes; scientists often disagree, of course, about how to interpret data and conduct, evaluate, and apply research. CDC scientists and their critics interpreted the stalled prevention progress differently, even though both groups recognized that several factors contributed to the stable numbers of HIV and AIDS cases. Researchers have not reached a consensus about the effects of HIV testing and counseling on prevention behavior, even though the CDC's rhetoric assumes that they have.

The debates over HIV prevention policy also illustrate how the science versus politics topos can be used to limit the aims, methods, participants, and applications of science. Thus, another related problem with the topos is that it can lead to a dangerous privileging of science and scientific discourse that excludes other participants, their "situated knowledges" (to borrow a term from Haraway, 1991), and their forms of knowledge making. As Condit (1996) and Treichler (1999) have argued (and demonstrated), if we enable those speaking in the name of science to dismiss other, contradictory viewpoints, methods, interpretations, and applications as ideological and therefore nonscientific, we risk reinforcing the black box of science and privileging one set of partial knowledges over other potentially enriching and beneficial knowledges.

Although, upon close scrutiny, the arguments of those opposing the AHP initiative and other even more clearly problematic policy shifts seem to have science on their side, we must still acknowledge the relative ineffectiveness of such arguments in redirecting policy. To be sure, this ineffectiveness can be explained by the power dynamics of the debate and the "inartistic proofs" of conservatives in power. But it might also be explained by critics' persistence in making their arguments almost solely on scientific grounds. The debate over the direction of HIV prevention policy illustrates that arguments framed by the science versus politics topos can be just as easily wielded to argue for shortsighted or risky policy as against it, even if such arguments might not always stand up to scrutiny. Given that those arguing on either side of the debate can appropriate the topos in problematic and possibly harmful ways, critics of the policy shifts would be wise to consider alternative conceptual frameworks and networks of arguments.

One alternative, embraced by some rhetoricians of science, would be to resist judging science as good or bad and simply accept it as always partial, incomplete, and limited. Science would be viewed as another ideology, and not a wholly separate or coherent one. This alternative would enable critics of HIV prevention shifts to avoid the trap of fundamentalism and to more effectively articulate connections between scientific concerns and other, more explicitly normative beliefs, values, and desires, as some conservatives have done. By recognizing the ideological nature of their own and others' arguments, critics would also be better positioned to rearticulate and reappropriate these arguments as needed.

One problem with this alternative is the difficulty it can present in distinguishing good science from bad science, however these terms are defined. In "How Bad Science Stays that Way," Condit (1996) proposes that we assess science's goodness based on its openness to alternative perspectives and ability to produce rich results and explanations. We might also begin to assess science, as a set of material practices and rhetorical constructions, according to the locatable knowledges in which it is grounded, the ethical purposes by which it is driven, and the responsiveness of its applications. My own preference is to focus on the applications and effects of scientific constructions, asking, "Who benefits and who loses from acting on these constructions in particular ways?" Science may be partial and limited, but that does not make its power any less potent, and sometimes this power works to neglect, oppress, or otherwise harm those whom it could serve.

Condit (1996) argues against the choice of either privileging science as the purveyor of truth or dismissing it as relative and just another form of knowledge making; "It is possible," she writes, "to portray language uses, including statements of 'fact,' as being responsive to a complex interplay among the three components of external material forces, social forces, and linguistic structuration" (p. 85). In other words, we can recognize the constructedness of science while also recognizing its "unique forms of contact with material realities" and also assess these forms of contact and the interpretations that they enable or disable (p. 101). Haraway (1991) similarly argues that relativism can be the other side of totalization, as "both deny the stakes in location, embodiment, and partial perspective" (p. 191). The stakes of HIV prevention are too high to not critique a policy characterized by a shortsighted and narrow focus on testing, limited prevention approaches, and questionable science.[7]

In my view, Haraway (1991) offers the best explanation of how to grapple with the disjunction between recognizing science's constructedness and partiality and recognizing its usefulness in interpreting the material world. In "Situated Knowledges," she proposes that we simultaneously juggle "an account of radical historical contingency for all knowledge claims and knowing subjects, a critical practice for recognizing our own 'semiotic technologies' for meaning-making, and a no-nonsense commitment to faithful accounts of a 'real' world" (p. 187). In this formulation, it is not enough to account for the constructedness and contingency of scientific knowledge (in part by tracing its conditions of possibility), we must also be inclusive of and responsive to the situated knowledges and embodied objectivities of the various stakeholders of this knowledge. We can assess these various knowledges, Haraway explains, according to their locatability, their effects, and their reflexivity (p. 191). Although strategies by Condit, Haraway, and others cannot help us escape the quandary of defining, assessing, and acting on science, they can at least help us recognize it as a quandary with which we, including those recognized as scientists as well as other stakeholders, must continuously grapple, not through the either-or logic of the science versus policy topos but by building arguments around a wider network of beliefs, values, and desires.

Notes

[1] In characterizing its proposed approaches this way, the CDC implied that existing approaches were relatively less proven and haphazard, a distinction that alludes to the long-standing accu-

sation of "AIDS exceptionalism"—the claim that, because of the over-politicization of AIDS, the public health response to the epidemic has been muted and has not treated it like other public health emergencies. This distinction of some prevention approaches as more proven and standardized than others also suggests a distinction between some approaches as more grounded in and verified by science.

² For the most comprehensive meta-studies of this relationship, see Wolitski (1997) and Higgins et al. (1991).

³ None of Bush's appointees to his Presidential Council on HIV and AIDS were scientists specializing in the disease, prompting one critic to call it a "freak show of fringe ideology, not science or sound judgment" (Salyer, 2003). Members included Patricia Ware, who had lobbied against including AIDS in the Americans for Disabilities Act, and, before he withdrew, Jerry Thacker, who had called AIDS a "gay plague."

⁴ These efforts also prompted two protests. In August 2003, a group of advocacy organizations led by ACT UP staged a protest of the Bush administration's HIV prevention policies outside the meeting of the President's Advisory Council of HIV and AIDS. Demonstrators urged the president to stop cutting proven prevention efforts that serve gay people and drug users in favor of "ideologically driven, scientifically unproven" measures, including abstinence until marriage programs ("Activists," 2003). The week before World AIDS Day, on November 24, 2003, a larger group of activists marched on the White House to protest Bush's global and domestic AIDS policies ("Stop," 2003). This group later released and circulated a report titled "HIV/AIDS Federal Policy Year in Review" (2003) that called for the Bush administration to "adequately invest in [U.S.] HIV treatment, care and prevention infrastructure" and to "prioritize sound science and public health . . . strategies" over "conservative religious values."

⁵ Waxman's report foreshadowed some of the attacks on Bush during the 2004 presidential campaign. An October 2004, *USA Today* article titled "Science, Ideology Clash on AIDS Prevention" explained that the "tension between science and ideology has emerged as one of the central issues . . . in the campaign" (Sternberg, 2004). The article cites John Kerry's claim that Bush "puts ideology ahead of science" as well as the Bush campaign's reiteration that previous prevention efforts were not effective. Even after the election, Bush opponents would continue to attack his policy making through the science versus politics framework, as illustrated by the book *The Republican War on Science* (Mooney, 2005).

⁶ Treichler (1999), for example, explains how homophobia shaped many early biomedical (mis)conceptions of AIDS that were taken as fact and that guided various cultural practices.

⁷ The effects of the CDC's policy shift are mostly yet unknown, but we can hypothesize, based on good science, that the narrowing and standardization of prevention efforts will make prevention messages less accessible to and effective for more at-risk people, that the defunding of community-developed prevention programs will exacerbate risk within these communities, and that the simplification and expansion of testing will function more as a means of case identification than as an opportunity to provide prevention messages or link people to needed care. In June 2005, the CDC announced its latest estimate of Americans living with HIV—an increase from around 900,000 to 1.18 million. The increase was not shocking, argued the head of the Community HIV/AIDS Mobilization Project, given the "potent mix . . . of insufficient funding for science-based HIV prevention and an overdose of ideologically driven policy" ("Number of Americans," 2005).

References

Activists march on white house: Bush lies on AIDS! (2003, November). ACT UP. Retrieved October 3, 2005, from www.actupny.org/reports/03WAD.html

Arnold, W. E., Harrington, M., & Baker, A. C. (2003, June 20). Letter to President George W. Bush. Retrieved December 9, 2004, from www.thebody.com/tag/oct03/bush_letter.html

Block, J. (2003, September 1). Science gets sacked. *The Nation*. Retrieved October 5, 2005, from www.thenation.com/doc/20030901/block

Centers for Disease Control and Prevention (CDC). (2003a). Advancing HIV prevention: New strategies for a changing epidemic—United States, 2003. *Morbidity and Mortality Weekly Report, 52*(15), 329–332.

Centers for Disease Control and Prevention (CDC). (2003b). *Advancing HIV prevention: The science behind the new initiative.* Retrieved March 21, 2005, from www.cdc.gov/hiv/partners/ahp_science.htm

Centers for Disease Control and Prevention (CDC). (2003c). *CDC's new HIV initiative: Questions and answers.* Retrieved March 21, 2005, from www.cdc.gov/hiv/partners/question.htm

Centers for Disease Control and Prevention (CDC). (2003d). Incorporating HIV prevention into the medical care of persons living with HIV. *Morbidity and Mortality Weekly Report, 52*(RR-12), 1–16.

Certain words can trip up AIDS grants, scientists say. (2003, April 18). *New York Times.*

Colfax, G. N., Buchbinder, S. P., Cornelisse, P. G., Vittinghoff, E., Mayer, K., & Celum, C. (2002). Sexual risk behaviors and implications for secondary HIV transmission during and after HIV seroconversion. *AIDS, 16*(11), 1529–1535.

Condit, C. (1996). How bad science stays that way: Brain sex, demarcation, and the status of truth in the rhetoric of science. *Rhetoric Society Quarterly, 26*(4), 83–109.

Connolly, C. (2003, June 14). U.S. warns AIDS group on funding; CDC cites S. F. programs that "appear to encourage" sex. *Washington Post,* p. A14.

Crowley, S. (2006). *Toward a civil discourse: Rhetoric and fundamentalism.* Pittsburgh: University of Pittsburgh Press.

Department of Health and Human Services (HHS). (2001, July 20). Scientific review panel confirms condoms are effective against HIV/AIDS, but epidemiological studies are insufficient for other STDs. Press Release. Retrieved October 10, 2005, from www.hhs.gov/news/press/2001pres/20010720.html

Doyle, R. (1997). *On beyond living: Rhetorical transformations of the life sciences.* Stanford: Stanford University Press.

Fox Keller, E. (1985). *Reflections on gender and science.* New Haven: Yale University Press.

Haraway, D. J. (1991). Situated knowledges: The science question in feminism and the privilege of partial perspective. In D. J. Haraway (Ed.), *Simians, cyborgs, and women: The reinvention of nature* (pp. 183–201). New York: Routledge.

Higgins, D. L., Galavotti, C., O'Reilly, K. R., Schnell, D. J., Moore, M., Rugg, D. L., & Johnson, R. (1991). Evidence for the effects of HIV antibody counseling and testing on risk behaviors. *Journal of the American Medical Association, 266*(17), 2430–2431.

HIV/AIDS federal policy year in review. (2003). November 24 March on White House Coalition. Retrieved September 1, 2005, from www.aidsinfonyc.org/yearinreview.pdf

HIV Prevention Defense Working Group. (2002). *HIV prevention saves lives.* Retrieved February 10, 2005, from www.gmhc.org/policy/prevention/prevention_defense.pdf

Human Rights Watch. (2004). The United States' "war on condoms." Retrieved February 10, 2005, from hrw.org/backgrounder/hivaids/condoms1204/2.htm

Latour, B. (1987). *Science in action: How to follow scientists and engineers through society.* Cambridge: Harvard University Press.

Latour, B., & Woolgar, S. (1986). *Laboratory life: The construction of scientific facts.* Princeton: Princeton University Press.

Lessl, T. M. (1988). Heresy, orthodoxy, and the politics of science. *Quarterly Journal of Speech, 74,* 18–34.

Lewontin, R. C. (1991). *Biology as ideology: The doctrine of DNA.* New York: HarperCollins.

Martin, E. (1994). *Flexible bodies: Tracking immunity in American culture from the days of polio to the age of AIDS.* Boston: Beacon Press.

Martin, M. A. (2003, June 16). Letter to Secretary Tommy Thompson. Retrieved October 3, 2005, from www.aidsaction.org/communications/letters/get_real.htm

McIlhaney, J. S. (2003, June 23). AIDS a disease, not a political issue. *St. Paul Pioneer Press.*

Mixed signals; Bush administration works at cross-purposes on AIDS research. (2003, May 4). *Buffalo News*, p. H2.

Mooney, C. (2005). *The Republican war on science.* New York: Basic.

Number of Americans living with HIV exceeds 1 million, illustrating failure of federal government to implement prevention plan. (2005, June 13). Community HIV/AIDS Mobilization Project. Retrieved October 5, 2005, from www.thebody.com/press/hiv_prevalence.html

Ornstein, C. (2003, April 18). Federal spending on HIV prevention to shift course. *Los Angeles Times*, p. A30.

Prelli, L. J. (1989). *A rhetoric of science: Inventing scientific discourse.* Columbia: University of South Carolina Press.

Salyer, D. (2003). Why the presidential advisory council on HIV and AIDS should be disbanded. AIDS Survival Project. Retrieved on October 5, 2005, from www.thebody.com/asp/mar03/lazarus.html

Scott, J. B. (2003). *Risky rhetoric: AIDS and the cultural practices of HIV testing.* Carbondale: Southern Illinois University Press.

Sex, condoms and STDs: What we know now. (2003). Austin, TX: Medical Institute for Social Health.

Spanier, B. (1995). *Im/partial science: Gender ideology in molecular biology.* Bloomington: Indiana University Press.

Specter, M. (2006, March 13). Political science. *The New Yorker*, 58–69.

Sternberg, S. (2004, October 28). Science, ideology clash on AIDS prevention. *USA Today*, p. 8D.

Stop Bush's war on HIV prevention. (2003, July). ACT UP. Retrieved October 5, 2005, from www.actupny.org/reports/cdc7-03.html

Terry, J. (1999). *An American obsession: Science, medicine, and homosexuality in modern society.* Chicago: University of Chicago Press.

Treichler, P. A. (1999). *How to have theory in an epidemic: Cultural chronicles of AIDS.* Durham, NC: Duke University Press.

U.S. House of Representatives Committee on Government Reform—Minority Staff. (2003, November 13). *Politics and science in the Bush administration.* Retrieved October 5, 2005, from http://democrats.reform.house.gov/features/politics_and_science/pdfs/pdf_politics_and_science_rep.pdf

Wahlberg, D. (2003, November 9). Conservatives accuse NIH of wasteful health research. *Atlanta Journal-Constitution*, p. A21.

Waldby, C. (1996). *AIDS and the body politic: Biomedicine and sexual difference.* New York: Routledge.

Weiss, R. (2003, October 30). NIH faces criticism on grants; Coalition assails "smarmy" projects. *Washington Post*, p. A21.

Wolitski, R. J. (1997). The effects of HIV counseling and testing on risk-related practices and help-seeking behavior. *AIDS Education and Prevention, 9*(3 suppl), 52–67.

PART V

Rhetorics
of Religion

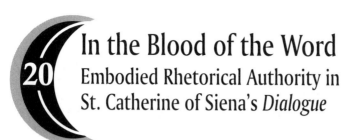

In the Blood of the Word
Embodied Rhetorical Authority in
St. Catherine of Siena's *Dialogue*

Kristie S. Fleckenstein

"I am one who is pleased by few words and many works," God tells Catherine of Siena (1347–1380) in the *Dialogue*, a mystical conversation between Catherine's soul and God (42). Throughout the *Dialogue*, this medieval saint emphasizes the importance of balancing discernment, or knowledge of God acquired through contemplation and prayer, with charity, or embodying one's knowledge through specific actions in the world. Both discernment and charity require agency: the belief in one's ability to effect change in one's life and in the world. Catherine, a dyer's daughter with no formal literacy or ecclesiastical training, exercised a unique and powerful agency through which she affected secular and ecclesiastical policies.

In this presentation, I argue that Catherine of Siena enacts an embodied rhetorical agency: her ability to use language to bring about political transformations among Italy's warring city-states and ecumenical transformations in her church and her religious order results from her bodily authorization of language. As humanity is saved through "the blood of Christ the Word," so Catherine acquires and deploys rhetorical power in ways that mirror her holy espoused: she fuses words and deeds, contemplation and action, prayer and charity.

An exploration of this medieval saint's rhetorical agency is valuable for three reasons. First, it enlarges our understanding of medieval religious rhetoric. It highlights one woman's ability to transform a conundrum of her age—the contemplative versus the active life—into an opportunity for rhetorical action. Catherine reconfigured the contemplative-active binary into a single unit: prayer had no meaning outside of the action of charity. As God tells Catherine, sin and evil are in the *not* doing more than in the doing. "For if you are not doing good you are necessarily doing evil," God warns Catherine in the *Dialogue*. So Catherine, like her beloved Christ, becomes the blood of the word (34).

In addition, this exploration of one medieval woman's agency enlarges our understanding of issues that plague rhetoric on the cusp of the twenty-first century. For instance, an exploration of Catherine's agency renews our understanding of the embodied nature of rhetorical authority. This is valuable

in a postmodern era when bodies as well as any kind of transcendental reference point have been eroded. As Naomi Scheman in *Engenderings* argues,
"Putting flesh back on our bones" would "allow us to be responsible" even if
only to ourselves and, through ourselves, to others (192).

Finally, a third reason for the value of an exploration of Catherine's configuration of agency is that it reveals the disruptive power of embodied authority for voices marginalized by gender, class status, and education. Although
her theology might have been conventional, her goals for the political face of
Italy, for the Holy Catholic Church, and for her own Dominican order were
nothing short of radical. The transformatory power of embodied authority
informs our current era where activists such as Gloria Anzaldúa call for
women of color to dismantle the status quo by writing as embodied agents:
with eyes like painters, ears like musicians, feet like dancers, and tongues of
fire (173). Only when they write the words "chanting in their bodies,"
Anzaldúa warns, will they, like Catherine, write to change the world (171).

While I believe that a close examination of Catherine's rhetorical authority informs troublesome issues with twenty-first century agency, it is important not to lose sight of the specificity of Catherine's fourteenth century
situation. Many scholars, myself included, are tempted to sift through history
to find lessons and insights that can be applied to our current dilemmas.
However, Elizabeth A. Dreyer warns twenty-first century scholars to take
care in our reading of medieval women mystics. While these women "provide early examples of female agency and voice in the western Christian tradition" (155), she says, we must be cautious not to make of these women and
their writing "foils for the presentation of [our] own late twentieth-century
philosophy" (154). According to Hollywood, it is absolutely essential to "give
careful attention to the specificity of their writing and understanding" (qtd. in
Dreyer 155). Therefore, before moving to an analysis of Catherine's agency, I
want to "give careful attention" to the unique challenges that Catherine confronted at the end of the fourteenth century in Tuscany. By better understanding her response to those challenges, we can better understand what we might
learn from Catherine about her situation and our own.

The late Middle Ages presents a variety of complications for human
agency. To begin, this era teeters on the cusp between the early modern
period, a time when humans rather than God were positioned as the center of
the universe, and the medieval period, where "human acting in the world"
was—or was supposed to be—another way of saying "human acting for God"
or "God working through human" in the world. This orientation resonates to
Christ's plea in Gethsemane before his crucifixion. He prays, "Yet not as I
will, but as you will" (Matt. 26.39); so were the people of the Middle Ages
expected to surrender agency to God. In fact, exercising agency required, paradoxically, yielding agency because authority was derived from God.

Clearly evident in Catherine's words and life is the extent to which God
and Catherine work together. God tells Catherine that "every one of you has
enough light to know the truth if you but will," underscoring the importance

of human free will, human agency (70). When the soul "wills to see," then the "will is fulfilled" (92). God says to the soul, "Vision and knowledge fills their [the faithful's] will," and they become one with God (92). Human will and Divine will join. Thus, Catherine, whom Evelyn Underhill in *Mystics of the Church* describes as "one of the most thoroughly institutional and yet profoundly transcendental of all the mystics of the Church," exercises her free will in conjunction with God's, finding in that conjunction an imprimatur to act in the world (158).

The blurring of individual will and God's will is integral to the second complication for late medieval agency: the confusion of religious and political authority, both of which the church wielded. The conundrum arises out of the paradox of the active and contemplative life. In the theological writing of early church scholars, the active life and the contemplative life were represented as distinct and oppositional. Despite the Gospel's emphasis on agape, which is a "working and merciful charity dedicated to the active and eager service of one's brothers" (Camelot and Mennessier 647), the contemplative life was privileged as the way by which the believer gained knowledge of and oneness with God.

The problem with contemplation and agency is that agency in the contemplative life is turned not toward the world—acting in it either physically or politically—but toward God. In fact, agency is exercised in material and psychological isolation so that one is separated from the distractions of life lived in the world. Agency operates only in reference to one's pursuit of unity with God. The quintessential example of this lifestyle—and the troubling of agency, defined as one's ability to act *in* the world—is the fourth century hermits of the Egyptian desert, who presaged what Underhill calls the "mysticism of the cloister" (*Mystics* 57).

The importance of contemplation and prayer are clearly evident in Catherine's life choices. She experienced her first vision at six, resisted her parents' efforts to arrange a marriage for her, and dedicated her life to Christ before she was 16. She joined the Sisters of Penance, a Dominican lay order whose members followed religious rule in their own homes, and, in defiance of the order's charitable work, cloistered herself in a cell-like room in her home, engaging in prayer and practicing bodily austerities with the specific end of discerning God's will and then responding to that will.

And yet even as contemplation—the means by which one knows/unites with God—is privileged in the early life of the church, political activity—acting in the world as God wills—also extensively characterized the life of the church. This mix of contemplation and action is not a binary but a union. Underhill argues in her landmark work *Mysticism* that contemplation and action are inextricably linked in Western mysticism: contemplation is a necessary precursor to action because one must know God's will—be united with God—before one can act as God wills (172–75).

Again, Catherine confronts this contemplative-active conundrum. For instance, in 1366, during her self-cloistering period, God speaks to her in a vision known as her "Mystical Marriage with Christ" (Underhill, *Mystics*

154). In that vision God tells Catherine that she can best serve his will by acting in the world; that insight draws Catherine out of her cell into what Underhill calls "an active and altruistic mysticism" (154). From this point, until her
death in Rome at 33, Catherine created a public career that Underhill
describes as almost "sensational in character" (162). This career was sensational not because of any lurid events but because of the vast power wielded
by Catherine in three arenas: mediating peace among insurgent city-states
and between those city-states and the papacy; persuading Gregory XI to
move the papal seat from Avignon to Rome; and reforming the Dominican
order. Even as she worked indefatigably among the poor and sick, Catherine
dictated an overwhelming number of letters, more than 400 of which are
extant, to political leaders and friends. She established Genoa's first hospital,
traveled through Italy as a preacher, served as a special envoy to Pope Gregory in Avignon, and created in the last two years of her life the *Dialogue*, an
outpouring of a series of ecstatic visions. Within the isolation of contemplation, Catherine found the impetus to act in and on the world.

The question of agency during the Middle Ages is rendered even more
convoluted when gender is factored into the equation. "Let the woman learn
in silence with all subjection. But I suffer not a woman to teach, nor to usurp
authority over the man, but to be in silence" (1 Tim. 2.11–12). So writes Paul
in his first epistle to Timothy, articulating a role for women that resonates
with Eve's original sin, a sin that was very much a rhetorical act. Eve was
deceived by words, and, in the grip of that transgression, she uses her voice,
her body, to persuade Adam to a like sin. Thus, the command from Paul is to
subdue a woman's voice as a means of subduing her body.

While a few well-educated and well-connected women finessed this dic-
tum to rise to eminence through their position within the church and through
the support of politically astute male allies, Catherine lacked the cultural capital of education, aristocratic family, and patronage.[1] She possessed scanty literacy, no spiritual allies, no formal theological training, no powerful family,
and no political connections. Yet, despite these drawbacks, this medieval
Dominican tertiary configured agency so that she could act in the world
without sacrificing her oneness with God. In an era when women had few
liberties and less power, St. Catherine changed the face of Italy's secular and
religious life. She created and exercised a unique rhetorical agency.

I believe that Catherine juggled the paradoxes and complications of
agency in the Middle Ages by "inventing an agency," to use Karlyn Kohrs
Campbell's words, based on the consubstantiality of words and deeds, contemplation and action, prayer and charity: she gives birth to words as deeds.
This unique construction of rhetorical authority can be traced through Catherine's embodied language in the *Dialogue* and through her commitment to living the words of the *Dialogue* in her own life choices. In both text and life,
Catherine's body becomes her word.

Throughout the *Dialogue* (c. 1378), the most sustained articulation of her
theology, Catherine presents the active-contemplative binary as a symbiotic

relationship: contemplation exists in action; action constitutes contemplation. Agency emerges from the interaction of both. A fusion of language, embodied imagery, and action characterizes all 167 sections of the *Dialogue*, but it is especially evident throughout two recurring themes: prayer and charity. To tease out the nature of Catherine's agency, I analyze her presentation of prayer and charity in two ways: first, as an explicit statement of the importance of the action-contemplation/body-word fusion and, second, as a metaphoric enactment of that fusion through the embodied images she uses to articulate God's beliefs about discernment, charity, and prayer.

A central tenet that God reiterates throughout his conversation with the soul is the necessary reciprocity between discernment, knowledge of God and knowledge self-acquired through prayer, and charity, followed by enacting that knowledge of God through service to one's neighbors. Here is the nexus point of Catherine's rhetorical authority.

Prayer is the vehicle by which the faithful acquire discernment, or knowledge of God and of self. "For discernment is nothing else but the true knowledge a soul ought to have of herself and of me, and through this knowledge she finds her roots," God counsels the soul (40). Without discernment, the faithful "cannot arrive at virtue" (72), and discernment is the outgrowth of "opening the mind's eye" and "seeing with the mind's eye": that is, the internal vision necessary for discernment is gained via prayer. Thus, God promises Catherine that the soul will come "to the house of self-knowledge, where she shuts herself up in watching and continuous prayer" (122) and through that watching and continuous prayer she will gain discernment. The *Dialogue* is in fact a manifestation of that promise. It is one long revelation—the direct result—of staying "inside the house of self-knowledge, in holy prayer" (123).

The watching and continuous prayer that God advocates possesses an active component. It exists as something much more than vocal prayer, especially rote repetition of Pater Nosters sans affection (123). In addition to vocal prayers in their assigned time, God asks of the faithful a kind of continuous embodied or mental prayer, a constant, ongoing physical expression of "holy desire": "having a good and holy will," God tells Catherine, is "continuous prayer" (126). Vocal and embodied prayer "stand together like the active life and the contemplative life" (126).

That fusion of action and contemplation in prayer is further underscored by charity as prayer. Acts of charity, God reminds Catherine, are a kind of prayer. Deeds are words. "Whatever you do in word or deed for the good of your neighbor is a real prayer," God counsels Catherine, "everything you do can be a prayer" (127). Thus, the discernment that is acquired through prayer is tied to action through charity. God makes this reciprocity explicitly clear: discernment is joined to charity—to acting in the world—like "an engrafted shoot" (41). In addition, he repeatedly tells Catherine that discernment without charity is not truth, not love, because "it is charity that gives life to all virtue" (35). Every virtue is "put into action by means of your neighbors" (33) because love of God and love of neighbor are the same (36). Therefore, God warns Catherine, "The soul in love with my truth never ceases doing service for all the world" (37).

The explicit articulation of theological truths concerning the contemplative life through which one acquires knowledge of God and self and the continuous outpouring of prayer through charity to one's neighbors provides insight into Catherine's rhetorical agency. Word in prayer and body in charity unite. The unity of word and body is further emphasized through the embodied word images that characterize the *Dialogue*.

Michel de Certeau argues that mystics were drawn to what he calls a language of the body. "In a new interplay between what they recognized internally and the part of their experience that was externally (socially) recognizable, mystics were led to create from this corporeal vocabulary the initial markers indicating the place in which they found themselves and the illumination they received" (15). Catherine exemplifies this language of the body. For example, prayer and charity are linked to embodiment. Prayer is the "food which is the body and blood of my only-begotten Son"; it is potentially a way to "communicate in the body and blood of Christ" (126). Charity is similarly articulated by means of embodied word images. Virtue is no virtue without action, without charity, God warns Catherine. "Virtue, once conceived, must come to birth," he says. "Therefore, as soon as the soul has conceived through loving affection, she gives birth for her neighbor's sake" (36).

In addition, Catherine uses equally forceful physical images to highlight the fusion of discernment and charity: "For discernment and charity are engrafted together and planted in the soil of that true humility which is born of self-knowledge" (41). They are like the vessel and the water: "Sacrifice in act and in spirit joined together as the vessel is joined with the water offered to one's lord" (46).

By fusing contemplation and action, words and deeds in the *Dialogue*, Catherine implicitly authorizes both the saying and the doing. The disciples' mouths—their words—are conduits for the Holy Spirit, God shares with Catherine. "The Holy Spirit is on their tongues to proclaim the truth" (79); therefore, words in prayer to God and in reproof to the world are important. Words are deeds. But deeds also become words, they become a means of persuasion in and of themselves. And here is the second source of Catherine's rhetorical authority.

God points out to Catherine, "First he [Christ] acted, and from his actions he built the way. He taught you more by example than with words, always doing first what he talked about" (69). Taking Christ as her example of ultimate agency, Catherine makes of her own flesh a partner and testament to her faith. Her embodied actions—her bodily austerities, her indefatigable service to the poor, and her apostolic preaching—coupled with her embodied words in the *Dialogue*, her letters, and her ministries contribute to the invention of her rhetorical agency. She authorizes—sanctions and sanctifies—her words through her deeds.

De Certeau argues that mystics were already predisposed "by the life they lived and by the situation that was given to them, toward a language of the body" (15). I would go one step further and contend that in Catherine's case the language of the body—the embodied verbal images she relies on in the *Dialogue* to articulate her embodied theology—wielded spiritual and political power because of a literal language of the body. To return to de Certeau, "Meaning is written through the letter and the symbol of the physical body" (22), and Catherine makes this point explicitly clear in the *Dialogue*: "Just as a mirror reflects a person's face, just so, the fruit of their labors will be reflected in their bodies," God tells Catherine. Virtue was inseparable from the body of Christ, the holy word; it is, as God describes, "hewn on the body of the Word" (66). The implication, then, is that spiritual power derives from one's physical testimony to faith.

The *Dialogue* constitutes a "word deed," a prayer in action, and that prayer is hewn on Catherine's body. Her life is an embodied articulation of the fruits of discernment. She becomes the blood of the word through the self-discipline she exercised on her own body.

First, Catherine made a word of her body through acts of penance. Beyond regular flagellation, especially intense during her early self-cloistered years, Catherine practiced ritual starvation. Suzanne Noffke points out that Catherine was "relentless in her ascetical demands on herself." While self-cloistered in her home between the years of 16 through 21, Catherine practiced sleep deprivation and ate only raw vegetables with a little bread. This severe fasting in her early years resulted in continued difficulties with eating throughout her entire life. In a letter to a "religious person," who apparently accused her of fraud and rebuked her for her bodily austerities, Catherine confesses that she too worries about her problems with eating, consciously striving to take food once or twice a day. However, she quickly points out that she trusts in the will of God. She prays, "and will continue to pray to God for the grace to live as other people do in this matter of eating—if it is his will, for it certainly is mine" (*Letters* 160–61). Raymond of Capua, her confidante and biographer, claims that toward the end of her life Catherine relied almost solely on the Eucharist for sustenance, consuming and becoming the body and blood of Christ.

Second, Catherine authorized her words through her indefatigable service to the poor and ill. She acted in the world through her body, abandoning the contemplative solitude of her teenage years to use her body relentlessly in service among Siena's poor. Her devotion to plague victims in Siena brought her to the attention of the head of the Dominican order, who assigned Raymond of Capua to her as confessor and advisor. It was Raymond who urged her to become involved in the crises confronting the church, drawing her further into her work in the world. Throughout her life, Catherine carried out an itinerant ministry whose mission, in accordance with Jesus, was the healing of the world and the church through one's physical involvement with both world and church.

The paradoxical authorizing of her textual body through the waning of her physical body provided Catherine with a secular and spiritual influence that defied the New Testament dictates silencing women. Catherine's life and words offered women in the late Middle Ages a transformative image to mirror, an identity that was voiced, proactive, and physically present in the world. "Her writings mirror her person, and what we know of her life supports her writings," Noffke attests. But more important for Catherine, in creating out of her body a word, she becomes more like her beloved espoused. God promises the faithful: "You will all be made like him in joy and gladness; eye for eye, hand for hand, your whole bodies will be made like the body of the Word my Son" (85). Here is the ultimate goal of Catherine's agency and her impetus for acting so completely in the world.

Through the light of discernment and charity as prayer, through a fusion of word and deed, contemplation and action, prayer and charity, Catherine fashioned an embodied rhetorical agency that enabled her to unite with her God by working in the world. She highlights the degree to which women have consistently challenged a culture's dominant prohibitions against teaching, preaching, and exercising authority in the world. As a result, Catherine offers us insights both into medieval agency for women and into troubling issues with agency that we currently face today. I believe that Catherine's spiritual and political activism suggests the necessity of considering agency as body and text, image and word. She reminds us that we are agents in the world only through the blood of the word, whether we live on the cusp of the early modern period or on the cusp of the twenty-first century. "Set my will ablaze in your charity's fire," Catherine pleads with God. "Let that fire burst the seed of my body and bring forth blood; then with that blood, given for love of your blood, and with the key of obedience, let me unlock heaven's gate" (364). Her agency was directed toward God through the world. Our agency can be directed to the world through the word, through an embodied rhetoric that unlocks the promise of equitable and compassionate living.

Note

[1] Nancy Bradley Warren illustrates this point in *Women of God and Arms*. For instance, Warren points to St. Colette of Corbie as a "profoundly political saint" (13), who wielded both spiritual and political power in early fifteenth-century France. Founder of a reformed branch of the Poor Clares, St. Colette was educated, politically connected to the Duke of Burgundy, and spiritually enfranchised as a Franciscan nun with papal authorization to establish reformed houses of Claresses. Out of these qualities she fashioned and exercised extraordinary agency. Thus, despite Paul's prohibition, female rhetorical authority was possible for those who possessed education, family, and patrons. A few women did successfully exercise agency through the balance of contemplation and action, prayer and politics.

Works Cited

Anzaldúa, Gloria. "Speaking in Tongues: A Letter To Third World Women Writers." *This Bridge Called My Back: Writings By Radical Women of Color.* Ed. Cherríe Moraga and Gloria Anzaldúa. 2nd ed. New York: Kitchen Table, 1983. 165–74.

Camelot, P. T., and I. Mennessier. "The Active Life and the Contemplative Life." *The Virtues and States of Life.* Ed. A. M. Henry. Chicago: Fides, 1957. 646–83.

Campbell, Karlyn Kohrs. "Agency: Promiscuous and Protean." *Communication and Critical/Cultural Studies* 2 (2005): 1–19.

Catherine of Siena. *The Dialogue.* Trans. Suzanne Noffke. New York: Paulist P, 1980.
———. *The Letters of Catherine of Siena.* Vol. I. Trans. Suzanne Noffke. Tempe: Arizona Center for Medieval and Renaissance Studies, 2000.
De Certeau, Michel. "Mysticism." Trans. Marsanne Brammer. *Diacritics* 22 (1992): 11–25.
Dreyer, Elizabeth A. "Whose Story Is It?—The Appropriation of Medieval Mysticism." *Spiritus: A Journal of Christian Spirituality* 4.2 (2004): 151–72.
Noffke, Suzanne, O. P. "Catherine of Siena and Ecclesial Obedience." *Spirituality Today* 41.1 (1989): 4–17.
Scheman, Naomi. *Engenderings: Constructions of Knowledge, Authority, and Privilege.* New York: Routledge, 1993.
Underhill, Evelyn. *Mysticism: The Preeminent Study in the Nature and Development of Spiritual Consciousness.* 1911. New York: Image Books, 1990.
———. *Mystics of the Church.* Harrisburg, PA: Morehouse, 1925.
Warren, Nancy Bradley. *Women of God and Arms: Female Spirituality and Political Conflict, 1380–1600.* Philadelphia: U of Pennsylvania P, 2005.

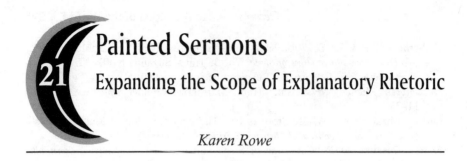

Painted Sermons
21 Expanding the Scope of Explanatory Rhetoric

Karen Rowe

Robert Connors contributed two articles on this subject to *Written Communication* in 1984 and 1985.[1] In the first of his articles, he contends: "Explanatory discourse, however, has been given hardly any historical or theoretical attention at all" ("Aristotle" 27). He goes on to remark in his purpose for his survey article, "If this essay is in some ways an admission of how little we know about it [explanatory discourse], I hope it will also be taken as an invitation to delve into the many issues surrounding explanatory discourse that are as yet unresolved" (28). While his subsequent article in 1985 addresses the concept of explanatory rhetoric from 1850 to the present and finds its presence in the work of James Kinneavy and Frank J. D'Angelo, Connors nonetheless bemoans the lack of history associated with explanatory rhetoric: "Our rhetorical knowledge of explanation is much less developed than our knowledge of persuasion" ("Present" 58). In his essay, Connors characterizes explanatory rhetoric as the following: rhetoric primarily in written form with an informative purpose that aims at communication or instruction, which in turn leads to works. This didactic function of rhetoric is one that has been relatively overlooked in rhetorical studies, Connors contends, though it has its roots as far back as Augustine, who encouraged his preachers to take on a teaching role.

Explanatory Rhetoric Defined by Campbell and Blair

For both the eighteenth and nineteenth century, the advocates of explanatory rhetoric were the rhetoricians of the day: George Campbell and Hugh Blair. In light of explanatory rhetoric's Augustinian ties, it is not surprising that both advocates of this type of rhetoric were preachers as well as rhetoricians. The rhetorical avenue of preaching lent itself admirably to explanatory rhetoric in part because of religion's dual purpose: to persuade people of the necessity of salvation and then to instruct those converts in the tenets of their new faith. As Connors notes: "By 1772 most Europeans were Christians and most Englishmen were Anglicans. They did not *need* to be persuaded to join the faith; the element of persuasion was not lost, but it had been undermined by attacks on the Doctrine of Works and increasingly was less important to pulpit orators than was the explanation of doctrine" ("Aristotle" 34). This instruction in doctrine was accompanied by instruction in duty and forms the essence of explanatory rhetoric.

George Campbell spent a great deal of time developing the constraints and principles of explanatory rhetoric in the form of sermons. Five of the twenty-two lectures in his book, *Lectures on Systematic Theology and Pulpit Eloquence*, concern themselves with the rationale for and structure of explanatory sermons. He lists three main purposes for this type of rhetorical approach: (1) "to explain something unknown," (2) to "prov[e] something disbelieved or doubted" (228), and (3) to "illustrat[e] one point of doctrine or duty" (233). He proposes that the "antagonist" of the preacher/orator is the "ignorance" of the listeners, and the final goal is "to dispel ignorance" (243). This cognitive shift from primarily achieving audience action to achieving audience knowledge is what sets explanatory rhetoric apart.

Hugh Blair also addresses explanatory sermons though not in the detail that Campbell does. Blair sums up his position:

> To explain the doctrine of the text with propriety; to give a full and perspicuous account of the nature of that virtue or duty which forms the subject of the discourse, is properly the didactic part of preaching. . . . Consider what light other passages of scripture throw upon it; consider whether it be a subject nearly related to some other from which it is proper to distinguish it; consider whether it can be illustrated to advantage by comparing it with, or opposing it to, some other thing; by inquiring into causes, or tracing effects; by pointing out examples, or appealing to the feelings of the hearers; that thus, a definite, precise, circumstantial view may be afforded of the doctrine to be inculcated. (117)

The in-depth examination of the doctrine is the necessary first step to explaining it to the hearers and relies on the preliminary understanding of the preacher, a fact that Augustine insisted on centuries earlier.

But more important than merely the historical discussion of explanatory discourse is the versatility of the genre. Campbell and Blair advocated the arena of preaching as appropriate and fundamental to this variety of rhetoric. However, it is my contention that just as preaching found its way outside the cathedral to the camp meeting grounds, so explanatory rhetoric had already found its way into other venues of communication in the service of religion.

A History of Explanatory Rhetoric

Robert Connors lays out a timeline of the major figures of explanatory rhetoric, but it is possible to insert other practitioners and commentators whose discussions add valuable insight into the components and principles of this branch of rhetoric. Aristotle, Cicero, and Quintilian all included a *narratio* section in the prescribed format for rhetoric; however, this section was to be brief and followed immediately by a lengthy and fully developed argumentative section. Thus, these fathers of ancient rhetoric admitted a kind of explanatory element into their rhetoric, but downplayed it in two ways: first, by its cursory nature and secondly, by emphasizing the next segment of the oration. This privileging of persuasion over information remains throughout most of the history of explanatory rhetoric even though later rhetorical authorities give explanation a higher value.

Complementing Connors's survey, George Kennedy traces the history of classical rhetoric specifically in the Christian arena. In doing so, he called third century Origen "the greatest Christian thinker between Paul and Augustine" (157). Origen's *On First Principles* considers scripture to have three levels: the first is "corporeal," or a literal level that "imparts edification (knowledge of religious law and history, for example)" (qtd. in Kennedy 158). Origen's ranking of edification as the most basic level is commensurate with the emphasis that the ancients give to explanation. While the upper levels of scripture are the primary domain of the preacher, they rest on the foundation of knowledge though little attention is given to how that knowledge is imparted. The homily, Origen's specialty, points to this hierarchy of presentation: "The speaker is mindful to persuade his audience not only to understand and believe the text but to live in accordance with it" (qtd. in Kennedy 160). Even in definition of the speaker's roles, persuasion is privileged over teaching, but that call to action is inextricably linked with instruction.

Fourth century Augustine is the next major figure to address the nature of explanatory rhetoric. This rhetorician-turned-preacher makes clearer the dependence that persuasion has on information. Augustine's major work, *On Christian Learning*, begins Book One with the statement: "There are two things necessary to the treatment of the scriptures: a way of discovering those things which are to be understood, and a way of teaching what we have learned" (7). The preacher is first taught himself; then in turn he teaches his flock. The foundational assumption about the role of teaching in rhetoric is elaborated on in Book Four with Augustine's quoting of Cicero's injunction: "To teach is a necessity, to please is a sweetness, to persuade is a victory" (136). The thread of the rhetorical fathers is referenced and then applied to preaching. Augustine emphasizes: "Instruction should come before persuasion" (137). This ordering of the rhetorical process clearly places teaching before persuasion. He continues: "It is necessary therefore for the ecclesiastical orator, when he urges that something be done, not only to teach that he may instruct and to please that he may hold attention, but also to persuade that he may be victorious" (138). Clearly, Augustine gives more weight than his predecessors to the teaching aspect of rhetoric. Earlier, he notes that "if those who hear are to be taught, exposition must be composed, if it is needed, that they may become acquainted with the subject at hand" (121). Only after the necessary knowledge is expounded does Augustine address "those who hear [who] are to be moved" (121). So, Origen's "understanding" becomes fully implemented by Augustine's directions to preachers.

Another rhetorical historian, Harry Caplan, surveys rhetoric and the *ars praedicandi* and notes that "a ninth-century manuscript . . . progresses as far as to list seven *modi* of preaching"; the first is "by teaching disciples" (79). As disciples, the audience is clearly already converted. In this role, they need instruction in the tenets of the faith, not a missionary sermon. The usefulness of classical rhetoric is acknowledged in Rabanus's *De clericorum instructione,* which states: "Rhetoric . . . is not extraneous to ecclesiastical discipline, for skill in this art is useful to the preacher for fluent and proper teaching, as well as for apt and elegant writing, and for delivering a sermon" (qtd. in Caplan 81–82). This teacher of preachers clearly considers teaching to be a crucial part of the preacher's office; indeed, it seems to be set apart from sermonizing as a separate duty of the preacher. Caplan continues his survey with Alain de Lille whose definition of preaching is as follows: "Preaching is open and public instruction in faith and morals, devoted to the informing of men, originating in the way of reason and proceeding from the source of authorities" (qtd. in Caplan 86). This preacher of the twelfth century plainly continues the thread of teaching as a fundamental aspect of preaching, going so far as to define preaching as instruction.

He is followed in the thirteenth century by John of Wales, who says: "Preaching consists of invoking God's aid and then suitably, clearly, and devoutly expounding a proposed theme by means of division and concordance; its aim being the catholic enlightenment of the intellect and the enkindling, with grace, of emotion" (qtd. in Caplan 87). The introduction of the divisions of a sermon, a division that bears a likeness to that of the classical oration as set forth by the ancients, uses the term "expounding" rather than "explanatory." But the goal is still first education of the intellect, then generated motivation by appeals to the passions. This structured approach echoes the address to the disciples as seen in the ninth century's seven *modi* of preaching.

The next major figure of the *ars praedicandi* is Robert of Basevorn, whose work follows the upsurge of sermons during 1230–31. Murphy records that "a number of Latin sermons were preached at the University of Paris using a new and remarkably standardized format employing a 'theme' (Scriptural quotation) and a complex process of division and amplification worked out from the opening quotation" (xviii). This introduction of the "thematic" sermon was much more stylized and formal than the homily of Origen's day. This structured approach was also called the "university-style sermon" because of its direct connection to the educational system. It is significant, I think, that this development in a branch of rhetoric, which gives new standing to the instruction of the congregation, is labeled with a title so distinctly educational. After this flood of newly styled sermons, there was a "rapid spread of the specialized manuals of the new *ars praedicandi* during the thirteenth and fourteenth centuries" (xviii). This new development in preaching was popular enough to generate "nearly three hundred authors of such manuals," although Murphy notes that "very little is known of the immediate antecedents of the formal *ars praedicandi* as a preceptive form" (xvii). Though Connors considers that there were "no advances in any conception of a theory of informative discourse" ("Aristotle" 29) for 1,500 years after Augustine (fifth century), Murphy states that Basevorn (the writer of the major treatise on preaching in the fourteenth century) "provides so 'typical' an *ars* that his *Forma praedicandi* is sometimes seen as the exemplar of the whole theory" (xx). Like Connors, Murphy notes that there was a gap of more than a millennium after the Christian era began without "a specialized body of rhetorical precepts to aid preachers" (xvii–xviii). Basevorn's work was apparently the first to begin to fill this gap.

Though the thirteenth through sixteenth centuries had advocates of preaching and teaching such as Augustine, there was no real formal manual of preaching until that of Robert of Basevorn. And indeed, Basevorn does little to emphasize the instructive nature of preaching, though he states: "Since preaching and teaching are necessary for the Church of God, that science which presents the form of preaching artistically is equally necessary, or even more so" (114). He continues with a definition of preaching that reverts to the persuasion emphasis of the rhetorical past: "Preaching is the persuasion of many, within a moderate length of time, to meritorious conduct" (120). Here, though he gives the nod to teaching as an integral part of the church, he nevertheless considers preaching to be primarily persuasion to action.

Thus, Basevorn significantly contributes to the art of preaching through his influential manual of the art, though he does not broaden the purposes of preaching as greatly. His contribution to this study lies in his detailed instructions about the parts of a sermon, specifically the choice of theme (or text) and its discussion. In his elaborate discussion of the introduction, Basevorn lays out a variety of methods for its creation. First, he allows authority for the introduction to come "from something original, from a philosopher, a poet, or someone with authority" (155). Then he discusses the actual construction of the introduction. Under the method "by argument" he permits "example," detailing three possible sources: "in nature, in art, in history" (155). It is this example from art, which Basevorn then delineates with the example of a doctor healing the sick, that hints at the possible inclusion of illustrative art in a sermon. The authority of the poet as well as the example of the art of medicine leaves the possibility of the artist as yet another source of material for the introduction. At the end of Basevorn's work, he addresses "two other methods [of preaching], which must be set apart by themselves because they are extraordinary" (205). He notes that the first method "belongs in part to the Parisian method and in part to that of Gregory" (205). In this method, the preacher develops his theme, again through "examples, [but now] in nature, in figure, in history" (206). As an example for "in figure," Basevorn details an "example in art [that] is some pinnacle built too high, especially if the base or column supporting it is too slender or weak" (206). This preaching manual recommends the field of architecture as a source for developing the truths of a sermon. Consequently, it is no great stretch to expand the possibilities for sermon construction from architecture to art.

A History of the Visual in Sermons

Concurrent with the thread of the development of explanatory rhetoric is the integration of the visual into the field of rhetoric itself. Classical rhetoric used the visual as part of its persuasive power from the time of the ancients onward. Gorgias's *Encomium of Helen* presents a slight twist on the myth: it is not Helen's beauty that causes the Trojan War, but rather it is Paris's beauty that attracts the attention and causes the actions of Helen. And it is the power of sight that serves as her defense. This power, Gorgias says, is actually greater than the power of speech. So, the conjunction of sight and beauty is a tool of history and the shaper of man's destiny. And in the case of this classical rhetor, the visual is the capstone of his argument and the means of his persuasion.

The term *ekphrasis* is another instance of the power of sight being harnessed to the reason of rhetoric. Vivid word pictures within an oration stir the passions of the hearers and make the rhetor's job more successful. The visual can stir more than the emotions; it can also stir the memory, a point which Gorgias also makes: "Through sight the soul receives an impression even in its inner features. . . . The sight engraves upon the mind images of things which have been seen. And many frightening impressions linger, and what lingers is exactly analogous to <what is> spoken" (46). Remembrance of terrors is not the only thing the visual stimulates. That power can be made positive as well. Mary Carruthers and Francis Yates thoroughly develop the prominent part that the visual played in the medieval scholastic tradition. These rhetors in the spiritual field rather than the secular used visual images to organize their *copia,* a vast store of knowledge, which, due to the scarcity of books, they had to memorize in order to possess. Without a good memory, a monk or preacher was useless as an orator, for he was naturally limited in the scope and sequence of his speech. Even the description of an orator's memory is a visual image: "The memory of an orator is like a storehouse of inventoried topics" (Carruthers 26). The "inventoried topics" are arranged in a visual pattern that allows the orator to locate any idea at any time in any order. Examples of common patterns include banqueting tables with the facts arranged as guests around them, gardens laid out in logical and orderly fashion, and even the geographical features of a town. To aid retention, the "arts of memory" are vitally connected "to manuscript painting conventions, the *Bestiary,* and various conventions of pictorial diagrams" (123). Carruthers states that "the Bestiary [sic] was thought of as a beginner's book, an entertaining way of retaining moral precepts" (126). In the Middle Ages, as Carruthers points out, is the connection of the visual and moral training; rhetoric is not merely the ability to remember and deliver a speech, but is actual instruction in moral doctrine.

An extension of the role that the visual played in medieval times is presented in a collection of essays entitled *Preacher, Sermon and Audience in the Middle Ages* (Muessig). Augustine Thompson notes that: "Artistic motifs and models as a window into hearers' visualizations remain relatively unexplored" (34). In addition, Phyllis Roberts discusses the idea of the "medieval *exemplum* as an illustrative story" (54). These rhetorical tools were like the commonplaces of Aristotle's topoi, places the preacher could go to for the material of his sermon. Now the preacher has not only a topic suggested by the topoi, he also has a way to make that topic seem real to his audience through a developed example.

More telling is Nirit Ben-Aryeh Debby's research on the uses of the visual arts themselves in the fourteenth and fifteenth centuries by Italian preachers. He has located sources that not only describe the use of or references to visual artwork in sermons of the time but also sources that prescribe how artwork should be used. According to Johannes Balbus: "An image had three functions: the first was to instruct the ignorant and the illiterate, the second was to keep alive the memory of the mysteries of the faith and the examples of the saints, and the third was to act as a means of inspiring devotion" (qtd. in Debby 129). The first two uses are not new: a knowledge of stained glass cathedral windows will evidence the idea of visuals as teaching devices; medieval memory techniques have already been discussed; and the idea of the visual as a devotional aid is also obvious considering the portrayal of divine figures in the great works of art (such as the Sistine Chapel) from this period. So the preacher who considers referring to artwork in his sermon must determine which, if any, or how many of these purposes his reference will serve.

However, it is important to note that the visual is an aid to communicate truth, it does not take the place of truth. Dominici (1356–1419) advocated that "a mother should keep pictures and sculptures of biblical figures in her house in order to educate her children" (Debby 133). He warns, however, "that painting of the angels and saints is permitted and ordained, for the mental utility of the lowest . . . but the sacred scriptures are mainly for the most perfect" (133). This established hierarchy clearly places the image lower than the Bible, though it can be useful to explain that text.

The reformer Savonarola was also quite interested in art for its own sake as well as for its uses in the pulpit: "The place of the fine arts in Savonarola's technique and philosophy of preaching is twofold. On the one hand, he lectured on the Bible in a simple manner that excluded descriptions of artworks as sermon *exempla*; on the other hand he used art in a unique way, to explain his philosophy of religious rhetoric" (Debby 149). This conjunction of the visual and rhetoric, now theory as well as illustration, is balanced by a warning like that of Dominici's: art is inferior to the scriptures, though it may convey a scriptural message. Debby points out that "Savonarola constantly drew parallels between the vocation of the preacher and that of the artist and suggested a kind of rivalry as well as identification between the two professions" (150). Clearly, in medieval times the concept of "art for art's sake" was tempered by an understanding of its powerful role in communicating ideas vital to man's aesthetic and spiritual soul.

Lest it seem that only the Italians made this connection between preaching and art, between the rhetor and the artist, Miriam Gill examines the presence of artworks both in the sermons and in the churches of the late Middle Ages in England: "Medieval apologists sometimes described monumental art such as wall paintings as '*muta predicatio*' or 'silent preaching'" (155). As evidence of the propriety of using art in sermons, Gill offers Robert of Basevorn's suggestion that sermon illustrations could come from "nature, in art [and] in history," a reference that has already been made in this paper (163). The authoritative nature of Basevorn's preaching manual adds weight to his teaching about both of these subjects. Gill goes on to pull in yet another medieval thread: according to a sermon by Hugh Legate, which referred to several detailed descriptions of artworks, the viewers were supposed to be well able to understand "hybrid images" created by the preacher from accepted iconography. Thus, they "were expected to have a good visual memory of religious art . . . and also expected to assemble complex images in their imagination, possibly in order to help them remember the theme of the sermon" (164–65). The art becomes not only illustration, but also content and memory device.

Another important stepping-stone is Gill's discussion that poems were used in sermons to raise the audience's passions and reactions to the sermon. The telling detail is that lines from poems were placed in close relationship to artwork on cathedral walls. For example, one popular couplet appeared "in St. Alban's Cathedral beneath a painting of Doubting Thomas" and was "probably displayed beneath an image of the Crucifixion . . . in Westminster Abbey," as well as "beneath, 'a curious picture representing the whole Passion of Christ' recorded in Hatfield Parish Church in the West Riding of Yorkshire" (Gill 168). Here verbal inscriptions and visual images are paired in order to reinforce the sermon in the minds and hearts of the hearers. The placement of some of these images and texts is significant. Gill discusses their placement "on the north side of the church . . . [which] was the side of the church frequently, although not exclusively, associated with the pulpit" (175). In placement, in reference, and in content, instances of pictorial rhetoric were prominent in the religious world of the medieval citizen. Gill summarizes her research with the following:

> Preachers allegorised religious images, enlivened their sermons with verbal echoes of visual representations and presented strategies for interpreting images or constellations of images. Murals deployed didactic images derived from sermon *exempla* to address important concerns. They shared the catechetical and Christological emphasises of sermons, and may even have presented the visual equivalent of sermon form. They were not mere "sermon illustrations." (179)

So by the end of the Middle Ages, artworks were an integral part of the religious life of both preacher and audience. The cooperation between image and text functioned to reinforce as well as communicate biblical truth, truth that instructed parishioners in the doctrines and teachings of the church. This usefulness of art would resurface later in rhetorical history as so many other elements of the Middle Ages also made their way back into teaching and preaching.

During the Renaissance, the visual became a part of the structure of orations as well as functioning as their illustrations. Walter Ong notes that the Renaissance orator Ramus devised a "method" for organizing a speech, a scheme designed to improve delivery and effect: "And in its resort to diagrams and other visual models to establish the idea of order—a procedure encouraged both by scholastic logic and by typography—it marked a significant movement away from the world of voice favored by the rhetorical tradition" (64). But there is more to the foundation of the visual in rhetoric, not only in organization, but also in content. Ong continues: "Related to commonplace collections and the rhetoric of invention is a special genre combining literature and the visual arts: the emblem books . . . accompanied by appropriate mottoes, verses, and elaborate prose analyses" (61). This conjunction of the visual and the rhetorical brings into play more than mere visual locations as the building block of a speech; here the speech is actually constructed of both verbal and visual elements. "The emblematists' concern with iconography and all sorts of symbolism is intimately related to rhetorical and dialectical word play and to rhetorical 'ornament'" (61). This secular juncture of word and image will find its way into the religious realm as well.

The Spanish friars also utilized the visual in their efforts to convert and proselytize the colonies of the New World. In particular, Diego Valadés, a native of New Spain, wrote *Rhetorica Christiana* (1579), a discussion of rhetorical practices as amended for the specific purpose of missionary work. The work records the principles used in the New World as well as those taught to the students of rhetoric resulting from the friars' educational and missionary work. The importance of Valadés's work is obvious from its appearance; it is amply illustrated with his own engravings. These engravings demonstrate the crucial nature of the visual in the culture of the Mexica. The friars learned through a grounding in and appreciation of the culture of their charges that the visual was an integral part of the lore maintenance of these people. So, the "preachers made use of large illustrated screens (*lienzos*, literally 'linens') as a backdrop to their sermons, allowing the speaker to point to the particular concept or event under discussion" (Abbott 48). This method incorporated the concepts of illustration, memory, and instruction for a populace that was familiar with the visual and already relied upon it to communicate their own history. Valadés and his fellow missionaries found that "the use of pictorial representations proved to be a 'graceful and fruitful' way to present the word of God to an indigenous audience" (Abbott 49). As Abbott concludes: "Actual images must be joined with mental images for persuasion to be more effective. Again, among the Indians the screens used by the Franciscans were more than clever devices; they were essential to the rhetorical process. They worked where words alone could not" (56). This passage reflects the power that Gorgias assigned to sight as well as the memory devices of the monks.

By the Victorian age, we have several concepts resurrected from the Dark Ages. Among them is the joint office of preacher and artist. In a series of lectures at the end of the nineteenth century to the Cambridge Divinity School, W. Boyd Carpenter urges, "There is illumination in illustration" (126). This return to the medieval exemplum is recommended for the same reason it was used centuries before: anything that the rhetor/preacher can do to help his audience understand the theme of the oration is welcome. Using illustrations that the audience can relate to is among these techniques. Carpenter continues extolling the virtues of illustrations: "Imagination links thought with life, translates for the audience the abstract into the concrete, and shows how the principles which were strong and vivid in the sacred story have their living message for our own day" (127). This theoretical approach to sermon construction links not only the visual and the verbal, it also links the past with the present—how the ages-old scriptures have a relevance to those living in the present. And what else would the preacher want to make relevant but doctrine and duty, the core teachings of the Bible? Carpenter sums up his recommendations with (what else?) a visual illustration: "Let him [the preacher] bethink himself whether his sermon is not all walls and no windows; and if so, let him take pains by illustration or example or story to let in the light" (127). Enlightenment, for the church congregation of the Victorian age, comes as much through visual illustration as biblical revelation. Another preaching manual of this period sums up these ideas perfectly:

> Does anyone ask, for instance, what on earth pictures can have to do with sermon-making? I answer (may I say from long experience?), a very great deal indeed, since many of the qualities that go to make an artist, or that help us to appreciate his art, are invaluable aids to a sermon. The way, for instance, in which a great picture strikes the imagination with the breadth and width of the world . . . helps you almost for the first time to appreciate, and ever afterwards to retain,—all go to quicken the sensibilities, to open the pores of the entire spiritual being. (Ellicott 13–14)

This preacher connects the threads of art, preaching, and memory in order to help the preacher fulfill his responsibility to make the biblical teaching relevant to the audience and even more so, to make it efficacious through having a lasting effect. Using the visual not only helps the congregation understand the principles of scripture; the visual helps them remember the principles in order to facilitate change in their actions. Given the success of medieval preaching around the world, instruction about doctrine when combined with the visual proved to bring about lasting rhetorical effects.

The role of artist-preacher is aptly illustrated by a major figure of the pre-Raphaelite brotherhood, William Holman Hunt, a Victorian whose inscribed frames embody explanatory rhetoric and turn his artwork into painted sermons. His work follows most directly in the tradition of priest and painter Giovanni Canavesio. As the subject of Véronique Plesch's study of the *ars praedicandi* in paintings of the fifteenth century, his work clearly reveals that there is no fixed demarcation between preaching with words and preaching with visual art. Her study situates the work of Canavesio within the rhetorical framework of Alan de Lille's preaching manuals, which acted as guidebooks that advocated, among other principles, the basic content of preaching and presented the best methods for delivering that content. Plesch defines preaching as having a "two-fold purpose: to teach about faith and about behavior, or, as Alan put it, 'preaching sometimes teaches about holy things, sometimes about conduct'" (174). Quoting de Lille's definition of preaching once more—"an open and public instruction in faith and behavior" (174)—Plesch analyzes a series of murals in a French church. She states: "Canavesio shaped his pictorial idiom—his visual *elocutio*—in order to capture the attention of the viewer, and to involve him or her" (181). Her study also draws on the works of other scholars who have investigated the role of the *tituli,* or "Latin inscriptions that run below each scene and number and describe them," as reflective of the Latin quotations that were inserted in sermons (182). According to Plesch, Canavesio

> translated verbal signs into visual ones when he rooted the subject of his depictions in a text. . . . [The] paintings' narrative and message are a crystallization of an enduring and multifaceted tradition comprising not only the four Gospels, but also apocrypha, glosses, dramatic adaptations, and other religious texts—a common textual repository from which preachers, dramatists, and painters alike drew their inspiration and their materials. (183)

Within this context of correlation between the verbal source and the visual painting, I believe that the Victorian artist William Holman Hunt turns to preaching, using inscriptions much as Canavesio did. In keeping with the legacy of preaching manuals, Hunt's works address exactly the same issues: doctrine and duty, each serving as the impetus and the inspiration for the other.

A Sermon on Doctrine and Duty

An example of the relationship between doctrine and duty as cause and effect is Hunt's work, *A Converted British Family Sheltering a Christian Priest from the Persecution of the Druids.* The representatives of Christ—both missionary and convert—must risk their very lives. The missionaries risk theirs to communicate religious teachings such as the doctrine of Christ. The converts risk theirs as evidence of the impact that doctrine has had on them. Both of these groups appropriately "love the Lord [their] God" and their "neighbour as [themselves]." No other motivation would account for the self-sacrificing nature of missionary work. Hunt himself says that he "was designing [his] 'Christian' picture to honour the obedience to Christ's command that His doctrine should be preached to all the world at the expense, if need be, of life itself" (160). Clearly Hunt has as his rhetorical purpose the espousing of biblical doctrine both of Christ and of Christian duty.

A Converted British Family Sheltering a Christian Priest from the Persecution of the Druids.
William Holman Hunt. Ashmolean Museum, Oxford.

Hunt portrays men who have executed their duty properly by following
the example of Christ. The inscriptions on this frame reflect several more
truths about duty. First, the inscription on the top frame—"They shall put
you out of the synagogues: yea, the time cometh, that whosoever killeth you
will think that he doeth God service" (John 16.2)—informs the viewer that
there are false understandings of duty. Killing those who tell others of what
Christians hold to be the truth of Christ's death is no service to God. Yet in
the words of Christ: "The servant is not greater than his lord. If they have persecuted me, they will also persecute you" (John 15.20). The Romans 3.15 reference—"Their feet are swift to shed blood"—only intensifies the irony.
Rather than loving God with all their heart, the falsely dutiful (the druidic
priests in the background of the painting), with the same degree of dedication,
destroy those who do. Keeping in mind Hunt's proclivity for creating chains
of biblical reasoning, the reference could also be to King Solomon's admonition to his son to avoid "sinners [who] entice" him, "for their feet run to evil,
and make haste to shed blood" (Pro. 1.10, 16). Thus, those who pursue only
the mirage of duty are sinners, not saints emulating their Saviour's example.
    Those saints are reflected in the quotations at the bottom of the frames
and placed in the foreground—"For whosoever shall give you a cup of water
to drink in my name, because ye belong to Christ, verily I say unto you, he

shall not lose his reward" (Mark 9.41). Hunt then finishes the chain of reasoning with Matthew 25.35: "For I was an hungred, and ye gave me meat: I
was thirsty, and ye gave me drink: I was a stranger, and ye took me in." The
hospitality of the Christians and the context of the scriptures clearly equate
the "taking in" as a life-saving act, equal to giving food and water. Here Hunt
portrays proper duty in action: the salvation of God's missionaries from
death, which in the church's view is the clear emulation of God's actions
toward the converts. The converts risk the same danger as the priests. But
they follow the doctrine that Christ has set down: they love their neighbor as
themselves. They go well beyond the "cup of water" that Christ commends,
showing that they have understood the principle he taught: the servants of
God minister in his place and thus deserve the same treatment that would be
given to Christ himself. Here again is doctrine resulting in duty: the Christian
is Christ's representative on earth; it is imperative that he reflect Christ's
nature as revealed in the scriptures, both in how he acts and reacts to others.
These converts demonstrate that the proper fulfillment of a Christian's duty
recognizes the person of Christ in others and mirrors the example he lived
while on earth. The reference to "taking in" Christ is from Matthew 25 where
Christ describes the last judgment of the world; the righteous protest that they
have never seen Christ hungry or thirsty or naked, but "the King" tells them:
"Inasmuch as ye have done it unto the least of these my brethren, ye have
done it unto me" (40). As a result of their actions, the righteous are accorded
heaven. So the Bible teaches that one reward of properly followed duty is
everlasting fellowship with God, a facet of the doctrine of Christ in yet
another form. This painting teaches that the source of duty lies in doctrine,
regardless of whether or not that doctrine is sound, for the druidic priests are
dutifully following doctrine as well. But the purpose of explanatory rhetoric—and Hunt's picture—is to educate the viewer on proper Christian doctrine. The natural conclusion of properly taught doctrine is a properly
executed duty. Hunt's converts illustrate that doctrine; his work prompts the
viewer to emulate them.

Conclusion

This survey brings together several crucial threads. One, the history of
explanatory rhetoric is richer than has been discussed. The ancient rhetorical
fathers may have had little to say directly about such rhetoric, but the medieval fathers developed its importance more than has been fully recognized.
Second, the visual has been a crucial part of sermons for many centuries and
in many cultures. Today's emphasis on visual rhetoric in this electronic age
only revisits and expands practices already in place. Third, just as the
preacher was urged to construct sermons carefully with the needs of his audience in mind by using the best approach, so the artist-preacher used the
frame to instruct his viewers about the message of the work as well as the
overarching truth behind it: paint like a priest, preach like a pastor. Hunt's

application of the medieval visual and rhetorical approaches shows how firmly his duty was founded in the Middle Ages and how effectively the old was made new again, not unlike the work of God he wished to see in his "congregation" of Victorians.

Note

¹ Due to the similarity of the titles, the articles will be cited "Aristotle" and "Present," respectively.

Works Cited

Abbott, Don Paul. *Rhetoric in the New World: Rhetorical Theory and Practice in Colonial Spanish America.* Studies in Rhetoric/Communication. Columbia: U of South Carolina P, 1999.

Augustine. *On Christian Doctrine.* Trans. D. W. Robertson, Jr. Upper Saddle River, NJ: Prentice-Hall, 1997.

Blair, Hugh. *Lectures on Rhetoric and Belles Lettres. The Rhetoric of Blair, Campbell, and Whately.* Ed. James L. Golden and Edward P. J. Corbett. Landmarks in Rhetoric and Public Address. Carbondale: Southern Illinois UP, 1990. 30–137.

Campbell, George. *Lectures on Systematic Theology and Pulpit Eloquence.* Boston, 1810.

Caplan, Harry. "Classical Rhetoric and the Mediaeval Theory of Preaching." *Classical Philology* (Apr. 1933): 73–96.

Carpenter, W. Boyd. *Lectures on Preaching: Delivered in the Divinity School, Cambridge, in April and May, 1894.* London: Macmillan, 1895.

Carruthers, Mary. *The Book of Memory: A Study of Memory in Medieval Cultures.* Cambridge, MA: Cambridge UP, 1990.

Connors, Robert. "The Rhetoric of Explanation: Explanatory Rhetoric from Aristotle to 1850." Ede and Lunsford 25–42.

———. "The Rhetoric of Explanation: Explanatory Rhetoric from 1850 to the Present." Ede and Lunsford 43–61.

Debby, Nirit Ben-Aryeh. "The Preacher as Goldsmith: The Italian Preachers' Use of the Visual Arts." Muessig 127–53.

Ede, Lisa, and Andrea A. Lunsford, eds. *Selected Essays of Robert J. Connors.* Boston: Bedford, 2003.

Ellicott, C. J. *Homiletical and Pastoral Lectures. Delivered in St. Paul's Cathedral before the Church Homiletical Society.* New York: A.C. Armstrong & Son, 1880.

Gill, Miriam. "Preaching and Image: Sermons and Wall Paintings in Later Medieval England." Muessig 155–80.

Gorgias. "Encomium of Helen." *The Rhetorical Tradition: Readings from Classical Times to the Present.* Ed. Patricia Bizzell and Bruce Herzberg. 2nd ed. Boston: Bedford/ St. Martin's, 2001. 44–46.

Hunt, William Holman. *Pre-Raphaelitism and the Pre-Raphaelite Brotherhood.* Vol. 1. London: Macmillan, 1905.

Kennedy, George A. *Classical Rhetoric & Its Christian and Secular Tradition from Ancient to Modern Times.* 2nd ed. Chapel Hill: U of North Carolina P, 1999.

Muessig, Carolyn, ed. *Preacher, Sermon and Audience in the Middle Ages.* Leiden: Brill, 2002.

Murphy, James J., ed. *Three Medieval Rhetorical Arts.* Berkeley: U of California P, 1971.

Ong, Walter J. "Tudor Writings on Rhetoric." *Studies in the Renaissance* 15 (1968): 39–69.

Plesch, Véronique. "Pictorial *ars praedicandi* in Late Fifteenth-century Paintings." *Text and Visuality: Word & Image Interactions 3.* Ed. Martin Heusser, Michèle Hannoosh, Charlotte Schoell-Glass, and David Scott. Amsterdam: Rodopi, 1999.

Robert of Basevorn. *The Form of Preaching (Forma praedicandi)*. Trans. Leopold Krul. Murphy. 114–215.

Roberts, Phyllis B. "The *Ars Praedicandi* and the Medieval Sermon." Muessig 41–62.

Thompson, Augustine. "From Texts to Preaching: Retrieving the Medieval Sermon as an Event." Muessig 13–37.

Yates, Francis. *The Art of Memory.* Chicago: U of Chicago P, 1966.

PART VI

Nineteenth-Century Discourse

The Prophet of Abolition

22 Ambiguous Prophecy and Rhetorical Echoes in the Rhetoric of David Walker's *Appeal*

David C. Bailey

To most casual observers, the United States during the first half of the nineteenth century could be characterized by one word—growth.[1] The nation was growing in nearly every way imaginable—its territory had expanded well beyond that of the thirteen original colonies at the time of the Revolution; its population had risen exponentially; and, despite some early setbacks, the economy was growing to such an extent that the United States was becoming a genuine player on the world's economic stage.[2] Despite this success, the year 1829 also saw the revival of a contentious moral debate that had been seething just below the surface since the days of the nation's founding, one that many believed could tear the country apart. The publication of African American abolitionist David Walker's *Appeal to the Coloured Citizens of the World* thrust the issue of slavery into the limelight and placed it at the center of public debate in both the North and South. Although some in both regions attempted to limit the distribution of Walker's *Appeal*, its powerful statements against slavery on both religious and republican grounds "reverberated throughout Antebellum America and beyond."[3]

This essay seeks to uncover the distinctive features of Walker's *Appeal* by: (1) briefly describing its contents and historical context, (2) identifying Walker's modified use of the American jeremiad (a religious rhetorical form dating back to Puritan New England), (3) noting Walker's use of rhetorical echoes from the Declaration of Independence, and (4) discussing the effects of Walker's *Appeal* on both the abolitionist movement and the subsequent national discourse over slavery. Although both historically and rhetorically significant, Walker's *Appeal* has received relatively little scholarly attention in either discipline. This essay hopes not only to rectify this oversight, but to demonstrate how powerful discourse of this type has the potential to exercise great political and historical influence.

Context and Content of David Walker's *Appeal*

Little is known about David Walker's early life. He was born near the Cape Fear River in Wilmington, North Carolina, sometime around 1796.[4] His mother was a free African American and his father a slave—making him free according to the American slave codes of the time.[5] Walker's early life was likely dominated by two powerful influences—his attendance at the local African American Methodist church and constant reminders of the injustice and brutality of slavery. Small-scale slave rebellions occasionally flared up near Wilmington. When they occurred, Peter Hinks notes that the leaders of such rebellions "were often summarily executed, after which their severed heads were placed on long poles that were displayed prominently on a point of land directly across the Cape Fear River . . . brazenly called 'Nigger Head Point' by the locals."[6] This environment imbued the young Walker with a deep hatred of slavery, while his religious beliefs instilled in him the conviction that a just God would surely not allow such a horrible institution to endure.

Around 1820, Walker relocated to Boston, Massachusetts, where he opened a used clothing store and began a long-standing affiliation with the city's fledgling abolitionist community.[7] Although a long way from Wilmington, the attitudes of many Bostonians toward African Americans were often little better. For instance, as the proprietor of a used clothing store and an African American, Walker was investigated and brought to trial in 1828 (one year before writing the *Appeal*) on suspicion of selling stolen goods. Hinks explains that "the popular assumption was that most of their wares were stolen, so these black merchants were thus regularly harassed by the police."[8] Although exonerated by the proceedings, Walker's trial was one more personal reminder that bigotry and prejudice were not confined to the South.

In 1829, Walker wrote and published his famous *Appeal to the Coloured Citizens of the World*. The pamphlet (approximately 80 pages in length) was published in three editions between 1829 and 1830 and consisted of four articles and a preamble.[9] In the *Appeal*, Walker harshly criticized white American society for its deplorable treatment of blacks. He was especially scornful of the fact that slaveholding American society was dominated by "Christian Americans!"[10] Walker's preamble began his rhetorical attack on "Christian Americans" by identifying African American slaves as "the most degraded, wretched, and abject set of beings that ever lived since the world began."[11]

The remaining four articles were loosely arranged by topic. The first described the terrible inequality endured by slaves at the hands of their masters and American society as a whole. Walker also discussed the deleterious effects of slavery upon his people. At several points in the first article, he excoriated his fellow African Americans for "aiding them [the whites] to keep their hellish chains of slavery upon us"[12] by acting as informants to their masters about upcoming slave revolts, performing their duties without protest or complaint, and generally refusing to demand a greater share of social equality. Walker's description is consistent with William Freehling's analysis that North American slave uprisings usually died in their infancy because "some black domestic almost always alerted some white patriarch in time."[13]

In the second article, Walker attacked the ideological heart of slavery—racial prejudice—citing it as the root cause of the afflictions suffered by his people. Walker plainly laid much of the blame for the ignorance with which whites viewed blacks at the feet of Thomas Jefferson, offering that: "Mr. Jefferson, a much greater philosopher the world never afforded, has in truth injured us more, and has been as great a barrier to our emancipation as any thing that has ever been advanced against us."[14] Walker argued that Jefferson's comments about African Americans in his *Notes on the State of Virginia*[15] were not only damaging, but "have sunk deep into the hearts of millions of the whites, and never will be removed this side of eternity."[16] Jefferson's opinion that "the blacks, whether originally a distinct race, or made distinct by time and circumstances, are inferior to the whites in endowments of both body and mind"[17] was not only emblematic of the beliefs espoused by many whites, it was also a significant factor explaining why he favored colonization of blacks if they were ever emancipated.[18] Walker's second article also contains a challenge to his fellow African Americans:

> Men of colour, who are also of sense, for you particularly is my APPEAL designed. . . . I call upon you therefore to cast your eyes upon the wretchedness of your brethren, and to do your utmost to enlighten them—go to work and enlighten your brethren!—Let the Lord see you doing what you can to rescue them and yourselves from degradation.[19]

Walker was light on specifics with regard to recommendations for mobilizing the race toward ending slavery, yet the second article also makes clear (as will be discussed later) Walker's belief that slavery and inequality must and would end someday because of God's justice.[20]

In the third article Walker's focus quickly turned toward two religiously oriented arguments: (1) that white American Christians were being hypocritical since they claimed to believe the teachings of the Bible, yet had no biblical basis supporting the institution of slavery, and (2) that God would eventually judge the nation for its practice of slavery. Both of these features will be explored later in this analysis. However, it must now be noted that both of these arguments were not confined exclusively to Walker's third article, but appeared throughout the entire *Appeal*.

The fourth article of Walker's *Appeal* purported in its title to address "Our Wretchedness in Consequence of the Colonizing Plan,"[21] yet it provided very little explicit discussion of colonization, instead serving to summarize all of the major arguments found within the rest of the *Appeal*. Walker did employ one new rhetorical turn of great importance to this analysis—he cited the Declaration of Independence's sweeping coda that "all men are created equal" as further evidence of American hypocrisy regarding slavery.[22] Walker's use of this rhetorical echo allowed him to take an immediatist rather than gradual posture toward abolition. As Eric Foner notes, the abolitionist movement in David Walker's time "was very moderate and cautious."[23] In this regard, Walker was far ahead of his time. By invoking the Declaration of Independence, Walker was able to challenge his readers with the notion that these high ideals were yet to be realized and that they should not be sought in the distant future, but immediately.

Walker's Modified American Jeremiad

Although Walker's *Appeal* is certainly noteworthy given its standing as a strong and confident antislavery statement by an African American, it would be a great mistake to regard it worthy of analysis only for this reason. The rhetorical complexity of Walker's *Appeal* reveals that he, like other significant antislavery rhetors such as William Lloyd Garrison and Frederick Douglass, employed his own adaptations of a culturally accepted rhetorical form—the jeremiad. The jeremiad is a rhetorical form dating back to the early days of Puritan preaching in the American colonies. It was reminiscent of the Old Testament prophets who tended to use a common argument pattern to chastise their people for failing to abide by their special covenantal relationship with God. The jeremiad has received extensive scholarship as a recognized pattern of discourse. Perry Miller first noted the presence of the jeremiad in the sermon of Governor John Winthrop preaching to the colonists of what would become the Massachusetts Bay Colony as they lay anchored just offshore preparing to land.[24] Winthrop's sermon argued that he and the colonists with him represented God's effort to restore a new utopia based upon what they believed to be their special relationship with God: "Thus stands the cause between God and us: we are entered into covenant with Him for this work; . . . He ratified this covenant and sealed our Commission, [and] will expect a strict performance of the articles contained in it."[25] Winthrop further argued that they and their colony would be blessed if they followed the covenant; however, failure to follow the covenant would result in harsh retribution from the Almighty:

> For we must consider that we shall be as a city upon a hill, the eyes of all people are upon us. So that if we shall deal falsely with our God in this work we have undertaken, and so cause Him to withdraw His present help from us, we shall be made a story and a by-word through the world: . . . till we be consumed out of the good land whither we are going.[26]

Winthrop's sermon is quite ambiguous as to the specific terms of the covenant, allowing for a great degree of adaptability to whatever exigencies might arise. However, one may infer from his message that the covenant primarily involved uncompromising adherence to the tenets of Puritanism, including: church attendance and proper observance of the Sabbath, an attitude of Christian charity toward their fellow colonists, and obedience to the proper (as they believed, divinely ordained) local authorities.[27] Robert N. Bellah and Sacvan Bercovitch agree that Winthrop's remarks were based upon two central premises found in American Puritan theology: (1) that they (the Puritans) were a chosen people, set aside by God to enjoy a special covenantal relationship, and (2) that God would reward or punish them based upon their faithfulness to the covenantal relationship.[28, 29]

The jeremiad is far more than a religious form; in fact, some of its greatest rhetorical impact has been felt in American political discourse. The jeremiad's cognate doctrine of American exceptionalism was used by some rhetors to justify the American Revolution, the belief in westward expansion in the name of manifest destiny, and the abolitionist movement.[30] In these and other instances where the jeremiad was used in political discourse, the covenantal relationship alluded to was of a political rather than religious nature. Kurt Ritter notes this evolution of the form as employed in the nomination acceptance speeches of modern presidential candidates, offering that: "As American culture evolved from religious to secular concerns, its Biblical past was replaced by an American past, and the Puritan faith was replaced by an American civil religion."[31] Based on the robust scholarship of the jeremiad, one may identify the typical features of the American jeremiad as some combination of the following:

1. A reminder of the people's covenantal obligations, coupled with an injunction against the people for violations, or potential violations, of the covenant.

2. A statement promising either national ruin or reward based on proper adherence to the covenant.

3. An appeal to the people to reform their errant ways.

Having established the typical argument pattern of the American jeremiad, it is necessary to analyze David Walker's rhetorical adaptation of this form in his *Appeal*.

Walker's *Appeal* clearly asserted that Americans had a twofold national covenant to which they had pledged themselves: (1) a commitment to the equality of all, and (2) a commitment to practice their Christian faith with regard to equality. Walker used the very words of the Declaration of Independence as a proof text to remind Americans of their special civic covenant. After quoting the entire preamble of the Declaration, Walker writes:

> See your Declaration Americans!!! Do you understand your own language? Hear your own language, proclaimed to the world, July 4th 1776—"We hold these truths to be self-evident—that ALL MEN ARE CREATED EQUAL!! that they are endowed by their Creator with certain unalienable rights; that among these are life, liberty, and the pursuit of happiness!!" Compare your own language above . . . with your cruelties and murders inflicted by your cruel and unmerciful fathers and yourselves on our fathers and on us—men who have never given your fathers or you the least provocation!!![32]

Walker found slavery to be particularly offensive since it was practiced in the "Republican Land of Liberty!!!"[33] Walker identified the "inhuman system of slavery" as the "source from which most of our miseries proceed. . . ."[34] He clearly established his belief that American slavery was far worse than any form of slavery ever practiced in the world: "Those [slaveholding] heathen nations of antiquity, had but little more among them than the name and form of slavery; while wretchedness and endless miseries were reserved . . . to be poured out upon our fathers, ourselves, and our children, by Christian Americans!"[35] He indicted the nation for failing to live up to its professions of republican liberty and inalienable rights—the same principles Americans had used to justify the American Revolution. Walker plainly asked: "Was your sufferings under Great Britain, one hundredth part as cruel and tyrannical as you have rendered ours under you?"[36] Although he found any form of human slavery at any time in human history to be reprehensible, his argument was directed toward the fact that it was being practiced in a land that claimed to love liberty. Thus, he provided strong injunctions against the American nation for failing to extend its creed of liberty to African Americans.

His condemnation of American slavery and inequality was equally strong on religious grounds. Walker asked, "Have not the Americans the Bible in their hands? Do they believe it? Surely they do not. See how they treat us in open violation of the Bible!!"[37] Again, Walker's primary complaint was that America was failing to live up to its self-professed Christian creed. The strength of his condemnation on religious and moral grounds would have been painfully clear to his biblically literate audience. For example, Walker argued that America's sin of slavery was worse than that of Sodom and Gomorrah:

> I cannot but think upon Christian Americans!!!—What kind of people can they be? Will not those who were burnt up in Sodom and Gomorrah rise up in judgment against Christian Americans with the Bible in their hands, and condemn them? . . . Who have a revelation from Jesus Christ the Son of the living God? . . . The Christians of Europe and America go to Africa, bring us away, and throw us into the seas, and in other ways murder us, as they would a wild beast.[38]

Throughout the pamphlet, Walker reinforced his injunctions with anecdotes of American cruelty toward slaves, including vivid retellings of instances where slaves were forced to beat to death members of their own families.[39]

Walker's jeremiad diverged from the typical jeremiad in the second movement, which foretells either a nation's ruin or renewal based on its choice to either abandon or rediscover its special covenant and correct its infractions. In fact, Walker largely discounted the possibility of national renewal:

> I tell you Americans that unless you speedily alter your course, you and your country are gone!!! For God Almighty will tear up the very face of the earth! . . . I hope that the Americans may hear, but I am afraid that they have done us so much injury, and are so firm in their belief that our Creator made us to be an inheritance for them forever, that their hearts will be hardened so that their destruction may be sure.[40]

While the idea that a nation can reach a point of irredeemable sin is common in prophetic literature and theology, even Jeremiah himself (often known as one of the harshest Old Testament prophets) allowed for some small hope of redemption and eventual restoration through repentance.[41] Throughout the *Appeal*, whenever Walker referenced a slight possibility of hope, as above, he always followed with the notion that it was too late for the nation to change:

"Their cup [of divine judgment] is nearly full."[42] In this way, Walker diverged from the typical pattern of the American jeremiad by focusing almost exclusively on the coming judgment to the exclusion of any hope of eventual restoration.

Walker further diverged from the pattern by completely disregarding any type of direct appeal to the nation to reform its behavior. While he obviously wanted the nation to change by immediately abolishing slavery and treating African Americans as equal human beings, he (as above) discounted the possibility that American society would attempt any reform at all. One simple rhetorical factor may be given as an explanation for Walker's divergence from the typical pattern with regard to reform. Walker's immediate audience was not white American society, but the "coloured citizens of the world," as the pamphlet's title specifically states. Because Walker was addressing an African American audience, his jeremiad forecasted divine judgment and calamity for white Americans: "Can the Americans escape God Almighty? If they do, can he be to us a God of Justice?"[43] Similarly, Walker prophesied that slavery would come to an end one way or another:

> When this [emancipation] is accomplished a burst of glory will shine upon you, which will indeed astonish you and the world. Do any of you say this never will be done? I assure you that God will accomplish it—if nothing else will answer, he will hurl tyrants and devils into atoms and make a way for his people.[44]

However, one must note that an appeal for reform did indeed take place, yet this appeal was directed toward African Americans. Walker offered that African Americans should "go to work and prepare the way of the Lord."[45] Although some of Walker's eloquent exhortations to his black brethren lacked an appeal to specific actions, he did specifically mention education for slave children, devotion to religious practice, the dissemination of his own *Appeal* throughout the country, and the rejection of the complacency of some to live in slavery.[46] In this way, Walker proclaimed two different messages for two different audiences. The white, slaveholding nation, which was violating its sacred covenant on both religious and republican grounds, was bound for God's harsh judgment; while the oppressed African American slaves received a message of the future hope that God would intervene on their behalf, provided that they take proactive steps toward their own liberty. In short, Walker adapted the essential features of the American jeremiad (truncating some and extending others) to address two distinct audiences on the evils and consequences of permitting chattel slavery and to provide hope and exhortation to his fellow African Americans.

Rhetorical Echoes in Walker's *Appeal*

In 1957, sociologist John F. Wilson conducted an analysis of the influence of President Woodrow Wilson's rhetoric regarding the ideal role of the proposed League of Nations, forerunner of the United Nations. Wilson discovered that subsequent political figures such as Franklin D. Roosevelt, Harry S. Truman, and Adlai E. Stevenson all echoed Woodrow Wilson's rhetoric in their speeches about the United Nations.[47] The echoes manifested themselves in these rhetors' use of key terms and arguments employed by Woodrow Wilson.[48] John Wilson argued that this was more than coincidence, but rather a case of one discourse inspiring subsequent discourses. Although John Wilson never developed the concept of rhetorical echoes into a formal method for conducting rhetorical analysis, Walker's *Appeal* provides an excellent example of the use and effects of rhetorical echoes.

For purposes of this analysis, a rhetorical echo is defined as the repetition of key words, phrases, or argument patterns from a prior discourse by a subsequent rhetor in order to address a similar type of exigency. For example, Walker's previously noted use of a modified form of the American jeremiad must be considered a type of rhetorical echo since he used a historically recognized argument pattern to address a situation with notable similarities to the original discourse. The Puritan preachers of colonial America used the jeremiad to demonstrate how their congregations were in danger of failing to live up to the covenant; Walker used it to condemn a nation and forecast its impending judgment for failing to follow either its religious or civic covenants.

In addition to the echo of the jeremiad form, Walker used another clear example of a rhetorical echo to reinforce his argument: America's own stated principles as revealed in the Declaration of Independence.[49] Eric Foner recognizes Walker's use of this technique: "He utilized the rhetoric of the nation, the rhetoric of liberty, of equality, the Declaration of Independence, and threw it back in the face of white America, charging the nation with being hypocrites, with violating their own professed ideals."[50] The rhetorical impact this echo would have had upon the American mind in 1829 must not be passed over lightly. Stephen Lucas asserts that the Declaration "has become not only the charter of America's political faith, but a timeless document whose appeal cuts across national borders and political divisions."[51] The Declaration was not only a soaring statement of American ideals, its provision that a people, when oppressed, had the God-given right to overthrow their oppressors and take back their liberty was a world-altering idea for both the American colonists in 1776 and for African Americans in 1829. While arguments from principles such as those found within the Declaration and other revolutionary rhetoric are, by nature, somewhat ambiguous, they are no less powerful. For instance, Stephen Lucas offers: "Ambiguous liberty and other rights claimed by the Whigs . . . were held to be absolute in the sense of being inalienable, unalterable, and eternal. They were God-given."[52] Thus, the power of these principles stemmed, in large part, from both their ambiguity and universality—the same features that made them so palatable and effective for David Walker. As such, Walker's use of the Declaration as a major lynchpin of his overall argument was more than mere rhetorical artistry or evidence gathering; it was a declaration in its own right that the privileges of liberty and equality due to other Americans were also due to the members of his race. In this way, Walker sought to bring African Americans into what Pauline Maier calls the "American covenant."[53] This was not only a compelling rhetorical strategy; it was consistent with his previously noted use of a modified American jeremiad.

Some scholars such as Stanley Harrold and James Stewart opine that Walker's *Appeal* must be considered a call for general slave revolt throughout the South.[54, 55] While this is a seductive interpretation (shared by many Southerners after the pamphlet's publication) in light of Walker's harsh condemnation of whites and his predictions of forthcoming judgment, Walker's use of prophetic form combined with the absence of any direct endorsement of violence to gain their freedom places this interpretation upon purely speculative grounds. At most, he encouraged slaves to defend themselves when necessary, but stopped well-short of advocating armed revolt.[56] Walker prophesied both the eventual downfall of slavery and that the nation would have to suffer dreadfully for practicing it, yet he never actually encouraged slaves to take up arms. In short, Walker's *Appeal* is ultimately prophetic rather than revolutionary despite the fact that its core message was unsettling to slaveholders.

The Influence of Walker's *Appeal*

Walker's *Appeal* is certainly a noteworthy rhetorical artifact from a pivotal era in American history. While it is difficult to demonstrate the full extent of one piece of rhetoric during such an era of great political and social upheaval, both historical events and subsequent discourses reveal that Walker's *Appeal* certainly had an effect. Among the most immediate effects were the efforts by officials in Southern seaports to stop its dissemination. Knowing that Southern officials would attempt to prevent the *Appeal's* distribution via the mail, Walker plotted to have white merchant sailors smuggle it into cities such as Charleston and Wilmington in the Carolinas and Savannah, Georgia.[57] These clandestine efforts prompted Savannah Mayor William Thorne Williams, and the governors of Georgia and Virginia, to appeal to Boston's mayor, Harrison Gray Otis, to censor Walker's publication—an appeal that Otis tactfully declined.[58] Some Southern officials responded by passing ordinances forbidding black sailors from leaving their ships while in port and strengthening existing laws that prohibited the distribution of antislavery literature.[59] There were even reports from North Carolina that some free blacks were either killed or sold into slavery as punishment for reading the pamphlet themselves or aloud to others.[60] Despite these efforts, the pamphlet continued to circulate throughout the South. In the ensuing years, Walker's *Appeal* added to the South's heightening anxieties over the Nullification Crisis and the growing strength of abolitionist sentiment in the North.[61]

As previously noted, abolitionism was in its infancy at the time of Walker's *Appeal*. Hinks believes that Walker's pamphlet had a profound impact upon the ideology of the abolitionist movement, reporting that significant African American abolitionist figures such as Maria Stewart, Frederick Douglass, and Henry Highland Garnet all praised his efforts and identified him as one of the fathers of radical abolitionism.[62] Hinks also offers: "Nothing even vaguely resembling this vehement manifesto had ever been published before, and its boldness heralded a new and confident movement among blacks to end slavery and racial discrimination."[63]

The previously described notion of rhetorical echoes is also an appropriate concept with regard to assessing the rhetorical effects of Walker's *Appeal*. Not only did the *Appeal* circulate throughout the South in its own right, Henry Highland Garnet, one of Walker's self-professed ideological progeny, republished it in his own *Address to the Slaves* in 1848.[64] While this is a clear example of a rhetorical echo, Harrold suggests a possible connection between these two discourses and that of William Lloyd Garrison (the white abolitionist who published his own *Address to the Slaves* in 1842) because of "similarities in subject matter and phraseology"[65]—the very essence of a rhetorical echo. Additionally, it must be noted that by the late 1830s and 40s, abolitionists were consistently drawing parallels between the spirit of independence based upon liberty and equality manifested in the American Revolution and the abolitionist movement.[66] Although it is impossible to prove conclusively that this parallel originated with Walker, the vast dissemination of his *Appeal* throughout the nation, coupled with its first appearance in 1829, raises the distinct possibility of such a connection. In any case, Walker's powerful and prophetic voice certainly resonated throughout the nation and the abolitionist movement.

Ironically, David Walker did not live to see either the fulfillment of his prophecy of slavery's eventual abolition or the historical and rhetorical impacts of his *Appeal*. Walker died in Boston on August 6, 1830. Hinks trenchantly observes that this was not the end of his influence:

> But even as his body was lowered into the ground, slaves were reading his book in the towns and swampy backwaters of North Carolina and running his message up and down the coast. Walker continued to traverse America, imploring his afflicted brethren not to abandon their homeland and to hold the nation to account for its ideals and mission.[67]

This analysis has examined David Walker's *Appeal to the Coloured Citizens of the World*, particularly noting his use of a modified form of the American jeremiad and rhetorical echoes from the Declaration of Independence to create one of the earliest and most compelling antislavery discourses in American history. Although Walker's influence has been either forgotten or marginalized for many years, his words and ideas remain with us. Perhaps this is because some of his radical ideas were the same as those used to proclaim the birth of this nation. Hopefully, the full extent of Walker's prophecy will someday be realized, and his nation will hear its own words and live out its declaration that all "are created equal."

Notes

[1] James M. McPherson, *The Battle Cry of Freedom: The Civil War Era* (New York: Oxford University Press. 1988), 6.

[2] McPherson, 6.

[3] Peter P. Hinks, *David Walker's Appeal to the Coloured Citizens of the World* (University Park: The Pennsylvania State University Press. 2000), xli.

[4] Hinks, xv. For an alternative date see: James S. Peters, *The Spirit of David Walker: The Obscure Hero* (Lanham: University Press of America. 2002), 3.

[5] Hinks, xv.

[6] Hinks, xviii.

[7] Peters, 3.

[8] Hinks, 83.

[9] All quotations from Walker's *Appeal* used in this analysis are from the third edition originally published in 1830 and republished in Hinks. (Hereafter cited as *Appeal.*)

[10] *Appeal*, 3.

[11] *Appeal*, 3.

[12] *Appeal*, 13.

[13] William W. Freehling, *The Road to Disunion: Secessionists at Bay 1776–1854* (New York: Oxford University Press. 1990), 78.

[14] *Appeal*, 29.

[15] Jefferson's comments about blacks are less than flattering—even by the standards of 1781. See Thomas Jefferson, "Notes on the State of Virginia," *Avalon Project/Yale Law School*, <http://www.yale.edu/lawweb/avalon/jevifram.htm> (30 April 2005). (Hereafter cited as *Notes.*)

[16] *Appeal*, 30.

[17] *Notes*.

[18] Roger G. Kennedy, *Mr. Jefferson's Lost Cause: Land, Farmers, Slavery, and the Louisiana Purchase* (New York: Oxford University Press. 2003), 116.

[19] *Appeal*, 30.

[20] *Appeal*, 32.

[21] *Appeal*, 47.

[22] *Appeal*, 78.

[23] Eric Foner, "Modern Voices: Eric Foner on David Walker," *Africans in America: Judgment Day—Resource Bank*, <http://www.pbs.org> (15 March 2005).

[24] Perry Miller, *The American Puritans: Their Prose and Poetry* (New York: Columbia University Press. 1956), 79.

[25] Miller, 82.

[26] Miller, 83.

[27] Harry S. Stout, *The New England Soul: Preaching and Religious Culture in Colonial New England* (New York: Oxford University Press. 1986), 61–62.

[28] Robert N. Bellah, *The Broken Covenant: American Civil Religion in Time of Trial.* 2nd ed. (Chicago: University of Chicago Press. 1961), 36–37.

[29] Sacvan Bercovitch, *The American Jeremiad* (Madison: University of Wisconsin Press. 1978), xi.

[30] Bercovitch, 132, 142. See also: James Darsey, *The Prophetic Tradition and Radical Rhetoric in America* (New York: New York University Press. 1997), 68–84.

[31] Kurt Ritter, "American Political Rhetoric and the Jeremiad Tradition: Presidential Nomination Acceptance Addresses," *Central States Speech Journal* 31 (1980): 158.

[32] *Appeal*, 78.

[33] *Appeal*, 5.

[34] *Appeal*, 5.

[35] *Appeal*, 3.

[36] *Appeal*, 79.

[37] *Appeal*, 40.

[38] *Appeal*, 61–62.

[39] *Appeal*, 24.

[40] *Appeal*, 40.

[41] Jeremiah 15.19 New International Version. Jeremiah writes: "If you repent, I will restore you that you may serve me. . . ."

[42] *Appeal*, 41–42.

[43] *Appeal*, 24.

[44] *Appeal*, 32.

[45] *Appeal*, 32.

[46] *Appeal*, 32.

[47] John F. Wilson, "Rhetorical Echoes of a Wilsonian Idea," *Quarterly Journal of Speech* 43 (1957): 271.

[48] Wilson, 272.

[49] *Appeal*, 78–79.

[50] Foner.

[51] Stephen E. Lucas, "The Rhetorical Ancestry of the Declaration of Independence," *Rhetoric & Public Affairs* 1 (1998): 173.

[52] Stephen E. Lucas, *Portents of Rebellion: Rhetoric and Revolution in Philadelphia, 1765–1776* (Philadelphia: Temple University Press. 1976), 86.

[53] Pauline Maier, *American Scripture: Making the Declaration of Independence* (New York: Random House Publishing. 1998), 21.

[54] Stanley Harrold, *The Rise of Aggressive Abolitionism: Addresses to the Slaves* (Lexington: University of Kentucky Press. 2004), 6.

[55] James B. Stewart, *Holy Warriors: Abolitionists and American Slavery* (New York: Hill and Wang. 1976), 42.

[56] Hinks, xxxvii–xxxviii.

[57] Hinks, 100.

[58] Hinks, 98–99.

[59] Hinks, xxxix.

[60] Hinks, xl.

[61] Stewart, 42.

[62] Hinks, xli–xlii.

[63] Hinks, xli.

[64] Harrold, 28.

[65] Harrold, 28.

[66] Harrold, 26.

[67] Hinks, xliv.

What about Sex?
Reconsidering Histories of Nineteenth-Century Women's Public Reform Discourse

Inez Schaechterle and Sue Carter Wood

While a growing body of rhetorical and historical research about American female reformers and the movements in which they were involved exists, little or nothing has been done focusing on the sexual aspects of reform speech. This is a significant omission; reform movements led by female activists, such as suffrage and temperance, were fundamentally rooted in sexual discourse. Much of the legislation sought by women reformers in the late nineteenth century revolved around women's sexual availability within and outside of marriage. Liberalization of divorce and child custody laws and of property rights within marriage, for example, were not simply about a woman's ability to leave a drunken or adulterous husband; reform newspapers of the day were replete with accounts of marital rape, which was not legally recognized as a crime. Reforms calling for female supervision in women's prisons or for raising the age of consent were primarily concerned with protecting vulnerable women from sexual abuse. Likewise, many reformers viewed prostitutes as victims of a system that denied women adequate employment, forcing them into a sexual service for which they, but not the men who frequented them, were legally and socially punished. Discussion of any of these issues, as well as discussion of pregnancy, contraception, abortion, infanticide, bigamy, adultery, seduction, sexuality education, maternal health, or even women's ability to find employment as an alternative to marriage, therefore constituted sexual discourse. In short, women reformers were often obliged to speak publicly about sex and sexual issues, sometimes explicitly, often obliquely, which added an additional element of risk to the challenges of female public speech.

This paper is part of a larger study that examined the public sexual discourse of three female reformers. Examining these women and their public sexual discourse separately and in relation to each other allowed us, among other things, to hypothesize a model of late nineteenth-century women's sexual reform speech. We then interrogated that model by considering how white women's sexuality was depicted in the antilynching rhetoric of Ida B. Wells. That model and the interrogation are the focus of this essay.

"Public sexual discourse" is a term we created specifically for our study, based on the evident sexual assumptions of our three primary rhetors. It refers to (1) reform-oriented speech or text produced for and delivered to an audience that (2) discussed either the physical aspects of heterosexual, vaginal intercourse, the environments in which such intercourse occurred (marriage, rape, etc.), or the possible results of such intercourse (pregnancy, sexually transmitted disease, the need for preventative measures, etc.). The political conditions under which this discourse occurred should also be noted here. Beginning in 1872, and with increasing power, federal and state Comstock laws regulated much of the public discourse of sex. Because all sexual language was by definition obscene, any reform discussion of sexuality could be charged as a crime if it occurred in print and was mailed, and violators, regardless of their purpose in mailing sexual discourse, could be sentenced to up to five years in prison at hard labor with fines from $100–$2,000 (Langley and Fox). Thus, although all public speech throughout the nineteenth century presented women reformers with a number of sociocultural challenges and consequences, public sexual discourse in the final 27 years of that century carried legal penalties as well. The subjects of this study made the decision to distribute their sexual discourses under these conditions and were aware of the possible costs.

Individual Discourses

A brief introduction to the public sexual discourses of Frances Willard, Victoria Woodhull, and Ida Craddock may be made by examining their comments about rape in marriage. While a woman of that time could attempt divorce on the grounds of cruelty or brutality, marital rape was not in itself a crime; the law considered it a woman's duty to have intercourse with her husband, even if she were ill, afraid of pregnancy, or forced to participate (D'Emilio and Freedman 79–80). Because marriage was generally regarded as the foundation of society, as well as a legal and a religious concern, how each rhetor approached marital rape may function as a microcosmic view of her public sexual discourse.

As head of the highly visible and respectable Woman's Christian Temperance Union (WCTU), Frances Willard both performed and shaped public reform speech. Adopting a strategy that so well served female abolition speakers and earlier temperance leaders, Willard and her followers presented themselves as True Women, applying women's virtuous, maternal touch within and beyond the home. When speaking of sexual issues, this womanliness dictated the use of euphemism and circumlocution. In "A White Life for Two," a speech and pamphlet extolling socially pure marriage, for example, Willard referred to the legal and physical power a husband held over his wife as "mediaeval continental and harem philosophies" (323). This description was the closest Willard came in the text to admitting the problem of marital rape. Euphemisms Willard employed for the crime of rape—meaning forced sexual intercourse outside of marriage—were "awful deeds," "brutal relations," and "unspeakable atrocities" (329). By employing such terms, Willard condemned the crime of rape without ever speaking the word, and she linked sexual violence within marriage to a fading, decidedly non-American perspective. Her reticence to say the word "rape" assured her conservative audience of her status as a True Woman; more importantly, by touching so slightly on the problem of marital rape in a speech praising marriage, Willard seemingly confirmed her allegiance, and the allegiance of the WCTU, to the existing social order of white, middle-class America.

While Frances Willard was the consummate True Woman, Victoria Woodhull, depicted in a Thomas Nast cartoon as Mrs. Satan, represented everything the True Woman was not: of dubious background, divorced and remarried, an advocate of free love, and unabashed seeker of public recognition. As a free lover, Woodhull made a point of discussing sex and sexuality in common terms. Thus, in an 1872 speech and pamphlet titled "Tried as By Fire; or, The True and The False, Socially," Woodhull named and defined marital rape:

> Of all the horrid brutalities of this age, I know of none so horrid as those that are sanctioned and defended by marriage. Night after night there are thousands of rapes committed, under cover of this accursed license; and millions . . . of poor, heart-broken, suffering wives are compelled to minister to the lechery of insatiable husbands, when every instinct of body and sentiment of soul revolts in loathing and disgust. (8)

In this speech, Woodhull did much more than bluntly state that husbands habitually raped wives. She spoke from the common free love standpoint that marital sex was necessarily coercive. In a social system that designated marriage as a woman's main financial support and as her only acceptable sexual relationship, a wife who "ministered" to a husband's sexual demands was as abused as one who submitted or was forced. Because marriage was viewed as the very basis of all social and religious order, *Mrs.* Woodhull's words and her willingness to speak them in public simultaneously functioned as her critique of late nineteenth-century society and as that society's critique of her. In fact, the martyrdom of her socially outcast status, willingly borne for the betterment of women and society, was a secondary focus of Woodhull's text.

As representatives of True Womanhood and free love, Willard and Woodhull may be viewed as opposite poles of nineteenth-century women's reform discourse. Ideologically, Ida Craddock occupied a position between the two. In terms of sexual speech, for example, Craddock employed the free love philosophy of using correct terms for genitalia and the sex act, yet she positioned heterosexual intercourse firmly within Christian marriage. Among other works, Craddock authored two sex-in-marriage pamphlets, "The Wedding Night" and "Right Marital Living." Blending advice about the physical act of heterosexual intercourse and the emotional and spiritual relationship between husband and wife, these pamphlets-for-sale were distributed through doctors, through the mail, and through Craddock's personal consultations with men and women.

The main purpose of "The Wedding Night" was to guide couples through what was assumed to be the wife's (and perhaps the husband's) first experience of intercourse. By following Craddock's advice, "every newly married couple . . . would never descend to the methods commonly practiced among married people today—methods which involve loss of sexual self-control, tigerish brutality, persistent rape of the wife's person, and uncleanness" (Craddock, "Wedding" 5). Like Woodhull, Craddock named rape as a common occurrence in marriage, yet, like Willard, she believed a loving, cooperative union would transcend such indecencies. However, whereas Willard referred to marital rape via circumlocution ("harem philosophies") and Woodhull employed dramatic terms ("accursed license," "lechery of insatiable husbands"), Craddock discussed marital rape and related issues in everyday language. These differences highlight Craddock's position relative to Willard, Woodhull, and many of the iconic nineteenth-century female reformers who have been studied by feminist rhetoricians. For all their differences of social philosophy and self-representation, Willard and Woodhull were similar in that their public discourses occupied the same plane, encouraging audiences to support broad sociocultural reforms for the good of all. Craddock's speech, in contrast, was delivered directly to the individuals it was meant to benefit and described specific sexual activities in plain, practical language. In terms of public sexual reform discourse, then, Craddock was neither a True Woman nor a free love radical, but an early sexuality educator, allied more firmly with the people she wished to help than with a single social ideology.

Nineteenth-Century Public Sexual Reform Discourse: A Model

To create our model of women's public sexual reform discourse, we divided the issues of sexual reform into three categories: Women, Marriage, and the Sex Act; Women's Sexual Rights; and Sexual Reform. Within each category we listed conditions or ideals about which all three rhetors agreed and conditions or ideals about which two rhetors agreed, based on their texts. Individually held opinions were not included because they could not be generalized toward a model of reform (see table 1).

According to the most generalizeable points of the model, nineteenth-century women reformers' public sexual discourse was based on the perception that men sexually victimized women and that contemporaneous marriage could trap women into sexual, financial, and reproductive abuse. Sexual reform, in contrast, would protect women's rights to control their own bodies within sexual relationships and to choose when to become pregnant. Reform would also encourage couples to form intimate relationships founded in supportive religious or spiritual belief systems, and those relationships would, in turn, improve the entire culture. Sexual reformers themselves held radical religious beliefs relative to the Protestant Christian norm. One integral component of sexual reform was sexuality education and discussion.

Sexual reformers practiced this component, delivering their public sexual speech to large audiences and to individuals.

The model's secondary points explicate the major points and illustrate areas of disagreement between the rhetors. For example, all three agreed that marriage could be harmful to women. Willard and Craddock would have solved the problem by improving marital relationships, while Woodhull would have solved it by abolishing marriage altogether. Similarly, while all three found reasons to criticize contemporaneous marriage, it fell to Craddock and Woodhull to recognize that husbands raped wives. One intriguing feature of the secondary points is illustrated by Craddock's appearance in both explications discussed here. In the sections titled "Women, Marriage, and the Sex Act," and "Women's Sexual Rights," Craddock always appears as one of the two rhetors in agreement, paired with either Willard or Woodhull. That in itself does not surprise, since Craddock incorporated tenets from social purity and free love into her personal ideology. In contrast, however, in the secondary points section of "Sexual Reform," the paired rhetors are Woodhull and Willard exclusively. Despite the fact that these women may be constructed as polar opposites—Willard's virtue versus Woodhull's promiscuity, Willard's social purity versus Woodhull's free love, Willard's fame versus Woodhull's infamy—the women agreed on three ideals. Both socialists, Willard and Woodhull envisioned perfected societies resulting from sexual reform. Both also held an elevated, essentialist view of women, believing that women must be responsible for creating sexual reform and were better able to pursue such reform than men were. Finally, both women agreed that women's sexual freedom depended upon their ability to earn a living, a fundamental tenet of American feminism. It must be noted that Craddock's absence from this conversation did not necessarily indicate her disagreement with these ideals; Craddock's public sexual discourse was centered in relationships between individuals, whereas Willard and Woodhull addressed larger social issues. Craddock's beliefs aside, however, the fact that Willard and Woodhull, despite their many differences, agreed on the shape and results of sexual reform indicates that their matching ideals were a significant aspect of nineteenth-century women reformers' public sexual discourse.

Public Sexual Discourse and Uses for the Model

Public sexual discourse was, indeed, an integral feature of the late nineteenth-century reform landscape and, based on these findings, it was clearly a discrete component or genre of nineteenth-century women's reform rhetoric. Aligned with suffrage, temperance, social purity, free love, and other reform movements of the time, public sexual discourse nonetheless was based in a distinct set of premises that was shared across the spectrum of participating rhetors' reform ideologies and yet was not necessary or foundational to participation in those ideologies or reform efforts. Thus, public sexual discourse, like suffrage, temperance, and other reform speech, may be separated or winnowed away from the larger topic of nineteenth-century women's reform for examination and theorizing. We believe that the model presented in table 1 will help us to further explore women reformers' public discourse. A first step, however, might be to examine the reform speech of rhetors who, though similar to the three women discussed in this study, did not discuss sexual relationships in any overt or recognizable manner. That is, just as Willard's "A White Life for Two" would seem, at first glance, to have little to do with sexual intercourse, other women reformers' speech on other topics may fit the model and reveal previously uncovered elements of sexual reform discourse.

In addition to using the model to further explore women reformers' discourse, we hope that our colleagues in women's rhetoric will revise, reimagine, reinterpret, and redefine the model and the assumptions that underlie it. In that spirit, then, we offer our own interrogation of the model, a comparison between the public sexual discourse of Ida B. Wells and that of Willard, Woodhull, and Craddock.

Interrogating the Model: The Public Sexual Discourse of Ida B. Wells

Ida B. Wells is one of the most widely recognized black women reformers of the late nineteenth century. Coowner and publisher of the weekly Memphis, Tennessee, newspaper *Free Speech*, she began her international antilynching campaign in the spring of 1892 (Royster 1). In an editorial printed on May 21, Wells reported the lynching of eight black men. After describing the victims and the circumstances, she commented on "the old threadbare lie" that such lynchings were punishment for raping white women: "If Southern white men are not careful, they will over-reach themselves and public sentiment will have a reaction; a conclusion will then be reached which will be very damaging to the moral reputation of their women" (qtd. in Royster 1). This early implication that white women willingly engaged in sexual intercourse with black men was amplified in Wells's later antilynching discourse. Because the rape of white women was used as a justification for lynching, a justification that otherwise liberal whites might accept, Wells tried to dispel the myth of black-white rape. One way she addressed the problem was to research and report who was lynched and why. In "A Red Record," published in 1892, Wells listed the allegations used to justify actual lynchings, which included burglary, arson, and insolence, to show that rape was very often not the charge (Royster 29). In the cases where rape was the allegation, she reported evidence showing that many of the sexual encounters were consensual and that some had been long-term (29). In doing so, Wells produced a pointed critique of white female sexuality.

Through her comments and stories, Wells created a definite image of white women's sexuality. In this portrait, white women enjoyed sexual intercourse and actively sought it, even to the point of seduction. Occupying the position of power within a sexual relationship, white women would sacrifice their partner's well-being in order to preserve their own. In some ways, this depiction confirmed aspects of our model. Wells's white woman obviously enjoyed sexual intercourse, a benefit claimed for women by Woodhull and Craddock. Given the social ramifications of bearing a mixed-race baby, Wells's white woman must have mentally separated sexual intercourse from procreation, again confirming Woodhull's and Craddock's ideologies. Finally, a white woman having consensual intercourse with a black man was exercising choice in the disposition of her body, a right claimed for women by all three rhetors. In a single, highly significant aspect, however, Wells's white woman differed sharply from that agreed upon by Willard, Woodhull, and Craddock. Their white woman was never the sexual aggressor, but rather suffered at the hands of men; men hurt women through sexual violence and also by wielding certain social and legal powers over women. This construction of women as sexual victims was absolutely foundational to the public sexual discourse of all three rhetors. Women's victim status and men's sexual aggression created the need for sexual reform and provided a counterpoint for Craddock's image of perfected sexual relationships and Woodhull's and Willard's perfected societies. In a very real way, then, Wells's sexually aggressive, sexually selfish white woman not only threatened the three rhetors' sexual views, but their worldviews as well. And more than that, Wells's white woman challenged the underpinnings of entire social reform movements: social purity, free love, spiritualism, and suffrage arguments based on expediency were all heavily invested in the purity and selflessness of white women.

It is doubtful that Woodhull, Craddock, or Willard would have welcomed any description of white women's sexual relations with black men as support for their own ideologies, and Willard emphatically rejected Wells's claims of white women's sexual aggression and sexual enjoyment relative to black men. Their public sexual discourse was built on assumptions, laws, and personal experiences rooted in white, middle-class, heterosexual, Northeastern and Upper-Midwestern culture; a comparison to Wells's depiction of Southern white women's sexuality confirms the regional and racial centeredness of the three rhetors' discourse and of the model based upon it.

We are aware that in briefly using Wells's antilynch law texts to critique our model we have simplified her arguments and elided the greater part of her work. A more detailed study of Wells's public sexual discourse and its depictions of white and black women's sexuality is needed. Also necessary is a larger study of nineteenth-century black women reformers' public sexual discourse, which might exist as discrete texts or may be embedded in the larger discourses of women's rights, civil rights, mob violence, self-help, or racial uplift. Such studies would provide a new point of comparison between white and black women reformers' perceptions, agendas, and rhetorical strategies, and would contribute to the atmosphere of conversation and critique that is central to feminist rhetorical inquiry.

Table 1   Model of Nineteenth-Century Women Reformers' Public Sexual Discourse

	Craddock	Willard	Woodhull
Women, Marriage, and the Sex Act			
Men hurt women through sexual violence	•	•	•
Contemporaneous marriage could be harmful to women in a number of ways	•	•	•
Intimate female-male relationships benefited from a religious/spiritual aspect	•	•	•
Sexual education/discussion was necessary and appropriate	•	•	•
Sexual intercourse belonged within marriage	•	•	
Sexual violence/rape occurred in marriage	•		•
Discussions of sex should be carried out in plain terms*	•		•
Women's Sexual Rights			
Women should have the right to choose what happened to their bodies	•	•	•
Women should have the right to choose when to become pregnant	•	•	•
Women could and should enjoy intercourse	•		•
Sexual intercourse could be independent of pregnancy	•		•
Responsibility for pregnancy/prevention belonged to both partners	•	•	•
Sexual Reform **			
The current state of female-male sexual relationships made sexual reform necessary	•	•	•
Sexual reform would improve the entire culture	•	•	•
Sexual reform was the first step toward a perfected citizenry and society		•	•
Women's sexual freedom would occur when they were no longer financially dependent on men		•	•
Women were responsible for creating sexual reform and were better able to do so than were men		•	•

* Although Craddock did not specifically state that plain or exact language use was necessary, her own use of explicit terms implied this opinion.
** Sexual reform speech required some degree of radical religious belief. It was delivered to large audiences and to individuals.

Works Cited

Craddock, Ida. "Right Marital Living." ~1900. *Ida Craddock: Sexual Mystic and Martyr for Freedom.* 23 Feb. 2004. <http://idacraddock.org/right.html>.

———. "The Wedding Night." ~1900. *Ida Craddock: Sexual Mystic and Martyr for Freedom.* 23 Feb. 2004. <http://idacraddock.org/wedding.html>.

D'Emilio, John, and Estelle B. Freedman. *Intimate Matters: A History of Sexuality in America.* 2nd ed. Chicago: U of Chicago P, 1997.

Langley, Winston E., and Vivian C. Fox, eds. "Document 58: The Comstock Law (1873)." *Women's Rights in the United States: A Documentary History.* Westport: Greenwood P, 1994. 147–48.

Nast, Thomas. "Get Thee Behind Me, (Mrs.) Satan!" Cartoon. *Harper's Weekly* 17 Feb. 1872. 14 June 2005. <http://www.harpweek.com/09Cartoon/BrowseByDateCartoon.asp?Month=February&Date=17>.

Royster, Jacqueline Jones, ed. *Southern Horrors and Other Writings: The Anti-Lynching Campaign of Ida B. Wells, 1892–1900.* Boston: Bedford, 1997.

Willard, Frances. "A White Life for Two." *Man Cannot Speak for Her: A Critical Study of Early Feminist Rhetoric.* Vol. II. Ed. Karlyn Kohrs Campbell. Westport: Praeger, 1989.

Woodhull, Victoria. "Tried as By Fire; or, The True and The False, Socially." *The Victoria Woodhull Reader.* Ed. Madeleine B. Stern. Weston: M & S P, 1974.

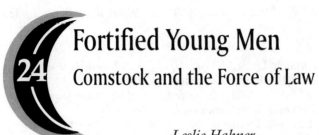

Fortified Young Men
Comstock and the Force of Law

Leslie Hahner

In the late nineteenth century, the vice panic heralded a deafening cacophony of troubled, worried, and adamant voices. From legislators and government officials to educators and physicians, public officials and private citizens expressed concerns that indulgence in vice—gambling, drinking, drug abuse, and sexual activity—was destroying the health and well-being of America's citizenry. Amid the shrieks of this panic, hundreds of societies for vice regulation were founded in cities and states throughout the 1870s.[1] One of the most visible and powerful of the period was the New York Society for the Suppression of Vice (Boyer, *Purity*). Founded in 1871 under the auspices of the Young Men's Christian Association (YMCA), by 1873 the newly incorporated society was put in charge of regulating vice throughout the state of New York (Horowitz 383). That Anthony Comstock, secretary of the New York society, was able to shut down establishments, ban books, and regulate "vice" as he saw fit, and given that hundreds of these organizations were determined to examine those things that led to vice, seduced people to vice, or enticed people to commit vice, is proof positive that the public believed the American citizen was in moral jeopardy.

In tandem with this new fervor about wayward conduct, the U.S. Congress approved a federal regulation against vice in the spring of 1873. To hurriedly pass a number of bills before adjournment on March 4, the House passed S.R. 1572 in the early morning hours of Sunday, March 2, with little discussion or objection (Tone 3). The Act for the Suppression of Trade in, and Circulation of Obscene Literature and Articles of Immoral Use amended an 1872 postal search and seizure statute (2004). It regulated any "obscene, lewd, or lascivious book, pamphlet, picture, paper, print, or other publication of an indecent character, or any article or thing designed or intended for the prevention of conception or procuring abortion, or any article or thing intended or adapted for any indecent or immoral use or nature . . ." that was publicly sold or shipped through the mail (2005). Any individual with the intention to "sell, or lend, or give away, or in any manner exhibit" these materials could be convicted of a misdemeanor, imprisoned for up to ten years, or fined up to $5,000 (2005). Popularly known as the Comstock law, this legislation was used to prosecute free-love advocates, shut down brothels, ban novels, and generally legislate any public "vice."[2]

Comstock, the proponent of this new law, was a former clerk who had risen to notoriety by self-proclaiming his status as a vigilante against vice. In 1873, he traveled to Washington, DC with a suitcase of notecards, books, photographs, and contraceptives he believed were obscene (McGarry). Exhibiting his "Chamber of Horrors," he grabbed the attention of the vice president and other influential legislators (DeGrazia 647). He lobbied prodigiously on Capitol Hill, and S.R. 1572 made it successfully into Congress. Indeed, with the passage of S.R. 1572, the late-night schemes of the House granted federal authority for the suppression of "immoral" materials circulating in the public and by post.

The Comstock law has been treated as a noteworthy moment in our regulative history. The force of this law was unique insofar as it granted tremendous jurisdiction over publicly sold and shipped materials labeled as "obscene" (Horowitz 442; McGarry 9; Tone 13). Many scholars mark the Comstock law as significant because it inaugurated a new mode of regulation for national morality (Boyer; Bates; Haney; Tone; Horowitz). There is no small sense in which this law codified an exigence about vice and provided the necessary legal authority to regulate said problem. In the words of this rhetorician, the Comstock law was constitutive of the vice panic. But, what does it mean to constitute a problem? What exactly is the rhetorical force of this law?

Many scholars have identified the force of the Comstock law as regulative: the law polices the immoral behaviors and individuals of the Progressive Era. Communication scholar John Peters argues that this law regulated a fundamental anxiety about how mediums of circulation spread the seeds of sexuality (172). Historian of medicine Andrea Tone claims that this bill enforced the immorality of contraceptives (10). Professor of History and American Studies Helen Lefkowitz Horowitz contends that the Comstock law legislated with a combination of evangelical zeal and physiologically rooted social reform (441). Historian Molly McGarry suggests that this law buttressed the public and private divide and protected the privacy of "women and children" from public "male vice" (17–19). Each of these authors argues that the Comstock law is significant as it regulates certain people and practices. Problematically, these critics take the basis of the Comstock law as their own: they claim that the law was an authoritative code that regulated the supposedly immoral members of the United States. Which is to say: to theorize the Comstock law as purely regulative is to take the problem and its perpetrators as *a priori* to the law itself—a fallacy that fails to recognize the rhetorical force of the law and its potential to fundamentally legislate or constitute.

Unfortunately, critical rhetorical scholarship on the law doesn't offer us a variant perspective with which to theorize the constitutive force of the Comstock law. Focused on the performative functions of courtroom adjudications, our current understanding about the rhetoricity of law centers on the way in which law provides or performs a hegemonic narrative. The law works, then, by dramatizing a powerful story about rights that citizens must negotiate.

Indeed, as Marouf Hasian has cleverly argued, the intersection of legal and public discourse is the playground of identity formation. The courtroom dramatizes both public and legal discourses and legitimates certain narratives of law ("Performative Law" 60). Of course, the law is not the only legitimizing narrative recognized by critical rhetorical legal scholarship. Much contemporary work, Hasian the most notable, attends to the way in which vernacular publics present competing legal narratives that influence public understanding ("Vernacular" 90; "Legal Argumentation" 184). However, the theoretical lynchpin of these claims assumes that law acts upon and is negotiated by a preexisting public comprised of preexisting subjects. The failure of this claim is that it does not account for the possibility that law does not tell us "who we are," but rather constitutes the very *who* and *we* of that identification (Hariman 17). Particularly when it comes to federal regulation (not courtroom adjudication), it is a mistake to theorize the law as a regulative or performative resource that subjects identify with or against as it assumes that subjects enter into the law from a former state of being. To suggest that there are citizens subject *to* the law is to contend that these subjects do not simply enter into the social contract from a former identity, but rather are constituted in the proclamation of the law itself. To argue otherwise is to disavow the very authority articulated in the sovereignty of law. This is not to imply that legal rhetoric is divorced from public discourse, but rather that the form of legal rhetoric is significant, indeed, constitutive of particular subjects. Nor does this indicate that the law "exists apart" from its playing out in judicial arenas, but rather that the law produces the way in which courtroom drama will proceed (Lucaites 435). Given these limitations, current rhetorical scholarship on the law cannot help us comprehend law's rhetorical force.

To supplement the current rhetorical theorizations of the law and our historical understanding of the Comstock law, this essay will attend to the ways in which S.R. 1572 constituted the vice panic and its own subjects. This law was not simply an authoritative (top-down) code or performative narrative against which certain bodies are regulated, but rather worked within a constitutive logic of governmentality. Michel Foucault explains that governmentality functions by promoting the welfare of a population as the end of governance. Like many other nineteenth-century aims of governance—a period when the logic of governance radically shifted—the law is not imposed upon citizens, but is a tactic working to "arrange things in such a way that, through a certain number of means, such and such ends may be achieved" ("Governmentality" 95). The purpose of law is not the "act of governance itself," but rather, governance is achieved via tactics that promote the "welfare of the population" (101). For our purposes, what is significant is that within a logic of governmentality, the law disciplines the population, it arranges subjects in such a way so as to achieve both sovereignty and discipline (Passavant 116). In this arrangement, the law produces new subjects and consequently invites the training of citizens to fulfill this subjectivity and promote the vigor of the state. Thus, the point of this essay is to engage the constitutive and rhetorical force of the Comstock law as that which produced subjects capable of exercising a right to public decency and demanded the production of subjects for these rights.[3] Using young men as my case study— those who were supposedly uniquely able to carry out the project of proper governance—I contend that the Comstock law produced certain virtuous subject positions that young men were trained to fulfill.

This essay will identify the way in which the threat of vice was articulated to anxieties about democratic order and young men's future as leaders. Next, I will turn to the regulation of vice and the constitutive functions of the Comstock law. Finally, I will analyze those technologies working, alongside a plethora of other discourses, to produce moral citizens who could govern the nation properly.

Anxious Democracy: The Republic Amid Immorality

At the end of the nineteenth century, the terms and functions of democratic governance were radically changing. Orators, educators, legislators, city planners, and reformers all assumed that individual liberty was a problem when it was juxtaposed with the administration of an industrializing metropolitan population. How to govern was often a question put into play with how one should live; or, the ideals of democratic social control were put up against the idea of self-rule.[4] As part of this restructuring, urban governments took on new and unprecedented responsibilities.[5] These maneuverings were met with a general anxiety about the status and functions of metropolitan democracy. As will be shown, many lamented the shifting tides of economic and social realignments (e.g., the creation of a middle class, the rise of tenement housing); still others were hopeful that the city was entering a golden age. Regardless of their level of optimism, these texts registered a certain amount of anxiety about the order and governance of the city and its citizens at a time of dramatic change.

At a fevered pace large numbers of governmental and nongovernmental agencies emerged to provide services and welfare to the populations of the city. First, a number of changes were happening to and under city governance that fundamentally transformed the perception of city responsibility. While disease and poverty have always been a "problem," at the turn of the twentieth century, these issues began to be dealt with through careful city government protocols.[6] All of these organizational and political maneuverings marked the transformation of previously community or familial "problems" into a problem of city governance. The troubles of citizens increasingly became the domain of the government. Second, in addition to governmental intervention, private organizations emerged to combat the (seemingly) ever-growing tide of poor, stricken, and elderly. Settlement houses, charity organizations, and nongovernmental agencies surfaced at an unprecedented pace (Boyer, *Urban*). In short, at this time there was the emergence of what we now call liberalism, or the transformation of government into social services.

As the Public Charities, Welfare, Almshouse, and Health Departments systematized their labors, they also codified the populations they served as disorderly. That is, the order provided by these agencies was not simply a solution to the chaos of the metropolis. It also was a discourse that proved there *was* disorder in the city that needed remedy. Agencies justified their labors (e.g., garnered their budget) by claiming the need for order—an order they provided that simultaneously confirmed the problem of disorder. Further, the increasing number of social services produced an anxiety: the proliferation of social services underscored the shifting functions of governance within a disorderly metropolis. In effect, citizens began to question the necessity and strength of their liberties in relationship to the marked increases in government size and responsibilities.

As evidence of this anxiety, a plethora of writers and orators began to situate the notion of liberty against the governmental management of social issues. Interestingly, these discussions did not fuse the binary between individual liberty and social control, but instead the split between these terms produced more anxieties about control and containment in the city. Elocution instructors, as an example, justified their instruction on the idea that oratory provided freedom. S.S. Curry (elocution instructor) demonstrated in 1907:

> The Muse of Eloquence and the Muse of Liberty, it has been said, are twin sisters. A free people must be a race of speakers. The perversion or neglect of oratory has always been accompanied by the degradation of freedom. The importance of speaking to a true national life, and to the forwarding of all reforms, can hardly be overestimated; but it is no less necessary to the development of the individual. (3)

For Curry, eloquence (as attained by the study of elocution) engendered liberty. If liberty was to continue, or even flourish, citizens must also be great orators. This idea was not new, as Curry echoed the sentiments of Plato, Isocrates, and Aristotle. But unique to Curry was the idea that speaking was important for the "forwarding of all reforms." Oratory provided a balance that ensured the careful cooperation among individual freedoms, the "development of the individual," and "a true national life." Nation building required freedoms for the individual and social reform—elocution served both ends. It was the assumed split between social control and personal license that produced more discourses (in this instance, training in elocution) to redress the anxiety this split perpetuated.

The balance between individual liberty and social reform was a significant concern for young men. That is, while many subjects were feared to risk contagion from vice (e.g., young women could become prostitutes with improper influence; husbands were led away from home by the seductions of alcohol and gambling), the young man was articulated as the agent whose preoccupation with vice threatened the future of democratic governance. Period authors and speakers were quite concerned that young men besmirched by immoralities could not become proper democratic leaders.

Both Jane Addams (founder of Hull House and reformer in Chicago) and Anthony Comstock argued that the corruption of young men put democracy at risk. Addams claimed that the selfishness of young people would leave them unfit to govern their fellow citizens. Addressing the problems between freedom and social reform, Addams wrote:

> [T]he great principle of liberty has been translated not only into the unlovely doctrine of commercial competition, but also has fostered in many men the belief that personal development necessitates a rebellion against existing social laws. . . . Fortunately, however, for our moral progress, the specious and illegitimate theories of freedom are constantly being challenged, and a new form of social control is slowly establishing itself on the principle, so widespread in contemporary government, that the state has a responsibility for conditions which determine the health and welfare of its own members; that it is in the interest of social progress itself that hard-won liberties must be restrained by the demonstrable needs of society. (206)

Addams bemoaned the disparity between personal liberty and government by the people. She advocated social governance as an effort to stave off the threats unrestrained liberty posed for democracy. The man who valued his own personal life above that of the collective threatened this liberalism. His selfishness had the potential to tip the scale of liberty and social control and thereby ruined both "hard-won liberties" and "social progress."

Anthony Comstock repeated a concern for young men's liberties in and against social welfare. He stated:

> Let no patriot, no person who has the welfare of the rising generation at heart, patronize any person who exposes to public view or keeps for sale the vile and crime full illustrated papers of the day. There are plenty of illustrated papers to be had which are free from these evil influences, *and these have first claims upon respectable patronage.* (19, italics in original)

Comstock outlined a difference between patriots as those who have a general public welfare in mind, and those who read these vile papers. He turned the laws of supply and demand against consumption to cast the purchaser of these so-called vile materials as disrespectable and unpatriotic. Comstock positioned individual rights up against the demands of social altruism—the right of purchase was juxtaposed with the true patriot. A patriotic young man kept the welfare of the collective in mind in his purchasing habits.

Still other authors lamented the immoral influences that contaminated young men and thereby polluted the social. Max Exner, writing in *Physical Training*, a YMCA magazine about gymnasiums and athletics, suggested that young men must be trained to avoid certain selfish indulgences. According to Exner, while the "sex instinct" is normal, its misdirection "tends to physical decay, intellectual confusion and spiritual ruin" (274). The end result of this abuse is not simply the degradation of the boy, but also creates "one of the greatest sources of economic and social loss in modern civilization" (274). For

Exner, the boy must learn to quell his indulgences or risk his consumption with vice. On a larger scale, the results of this disastrous preoccupation included the proliferation of unfit citizens, venereal disease, and economic costs.

The notion that young men must be trained to avoid vice in order to become proper citizens pervaded the culture of the Progressive Era. As part of this fervor, a group of sexual education handbooks entitled the *Self & Sex Series* began publication in the 1870s and continued with multiple reprints and language translations into the 1920s. Within this series, four books were directed at males: *What a Young Boy Ought to Know, What a Young Man Ought to Know, What a Young Husband Ought to Know, What a Man of Forty-five Ought to Know.* At the supposedly age-appropriate time, the author, Dr. Sylvanus Stall, guided young men in the knowledge of their own bodies, the avoidance of vice, and the rules for proper behavior. Much of the first two texts were directed at the suppression of masturbation. They suggested that the young man was led to "solitary vice" (masturbation) by outside influences, including "evil books" and "vicious pictures" (33, 35). By averting his eyes from this illicit material, the young man helped to balance his triune nature. According to Stall, "Men's highest culture is found in the symmetrical development of his threefold nature—the physical, intellectual and spiritual" (24). To attain this pinnacle of culture, then, was to renounce the lures of vice. In so doing, the man sustained himself as a truly respectable and civically minded individual, able to become the balanced democratic gentleman.

In short, period authors and speakers voiced anxieties that individual liberty may corrupt democracy. All of these authors preferred the confines of regulation to an unordered and selfish society of individuals. Similarly, each assumed there was a division between individual opportunity and social constraint—a dialectic threatened by the selfish rebellion of young men caused by evil influences. Young men were particularly important as their moral failures endangered the liberties of others. Thus, it was these men who must be managed, taught, and coaxed into civic responsibility. Amid these discourses, the Comstock law produced a new kind of subjectivity for young men, a position imbued with the right to decency and the will to vice suppression.

Federal Legislation and Young Men: Producing Moral Subjects

To promote the morality of the nation, the enforcement of the Comstock law attempted to suppress the trade in published vice. Comstock and his cadre of cohorts worked with vehemence, prosecuting authors of immoral novels, destroying circulars about birth control, disposing of illicit pictures, and closing the doors of brothels throughout the nation.[7] But, one need not simply read S.R. 1572 as legislating Progressive Era Puritanism, or as protecting Americans from themselves. Rather, by reading this law rhetorically, I will argue that this law both constituted the vice panic as *bona fide* and produced particular subject positions. The Comstock law had rhetorical force—within a logic of governmentality, it composed subjects able to claim the right to public decency.

First, the constitutive force of the Comstock law is found in the way it materialized and codified anxieties about vice. Certainly, "vice" had been a moral, social, and governmental problem for centuries. The Comstock law is noteworthy insofar as it granted unprecedented U.S. *federal* authority to search and seize all public goods and privately mailed materials that might be labeled obscene (McGarry 9). Thus, to the extent that the war against vice required federal legislation to police its supposedly ubiquitous trade, that very same legislation proved the necessity of a war on vice. It offered citizens a legitimate right to make claims against the legality and morality of vice. The law embodied and legitimated the panic described in period discourses and declared a right to public decency.

Second, the Comstock law exhibited a logic of governmentality. It was not simply a majestic regulation, but rather promoted proper governance via the management of the nation's populace. As the Comstock law penalized those who sold, exhibited, lent, gave away, or published "obscene" or "immoral" materials, it promoted the welfare of the population as justification for the suppression of vice. The logic of its governance was not a regulative appeal based on the sovereign authority of the state, but was warranted by the general welfare of America's citizenry. Indeed, vice reform societies, social purity organizations, and state laws modeled on the federal regulations proliferated in the 1870s and 1880s (McGarry). Citizen groups and representatives kept a watchful eye on the best interests of the populace, and further encouraged citizens to suppress vice in order to promote the moral well-being of the United States.

Third, the law worked by sequestering moral rights for individual citizens. As such, the management of public morality was entrusted to the individual, who must be shielded from those vices circulating in public and by post. With the Comstock law, governance was not achieved by top-down authority regulating the nation as a whole, but rather by granting protection from so-called immoral materials to individuals. The well-being of the individual—his ability to claim a right to decency—was produced as the domain of federal legislation. In short, the constitutive force of this law was not that it regulated a former problem, but that it made the problem, it calculated the terms of justice to proceed in the courtroom, the public welfare to be protected, and the rights to be proclaimed by citizens (Derrida 947).

But, of course, the manufactured jurisdiction of this law is not its only constitutive force. The law also produced subject positions, those individuals subject to and of the law. Justice is still to come in this inauguration as those under the law are beholden to its proclamation (969). Yet, the founding moment of the law articulates and invites subjects who belong at the behest of its right.[8] The law delimits those subjects with the ability to claim a right to public decency and those subjects who violate such standards. First, the law produced a subject to be protected from the manufacturer, distributor, or publisher of these materials ("Act for the Suppression" 2005). The consumer of vice—the individual who purchased, borrowed, or obtained such illicit material—was not the offender regulated by the Comstock law. Instead, the prohibition was placed upon the individual who "shall sell, or lend, or give away, or in any manner exhibit . . . article[s] of immoral use" (2005). As such, the law produced a subject who was to be protected from the vile seller of smut—the virtuous citizen. This was the subject able to claim a right to decency, to be protected from public and postal obscenity.

But, of course the "tautology" of the "phenomenal structure" of the law is that it declares an "outlaw" anyone who refuses its authority (Derrida 987). With the Comstock law, the text of the bill announced that those with the intention to distribute or exhibit "obscene," "immoral," or "unlawful" materials could not claim the right of the First Amendment ("Act for the Suppression" 2005). It articulated an improper citizen, a scoundrel who preyed upon the prurient interests of the public by spreading obscene materials.[9] Thus, the manufacturer or exhibitor of "immorality," an individual without civility, had "no claim upon . . . law or morality" (Passavant 121). This citizen embodied the limits of free speech; he threatened the very well-being of the nation as he promoted obscenity and immorality. The vice peddler is the very subject who "threatens the law," "belongs to it," outlines the limits of its founding authority—an authority both defined and delimited by the idyllic subject of the law and the criminal subject to the law (Derrida 989).

To suggest that the Comstock law performatively produced different subject positions is to read this law rhetorically, insofar as it suggests the way in which the law founds a certain kind of moral order. Within this moral order, the inlaw and the outlaw are defined and articulated. The inlaw is produced as a citizen who can claim a right to public decency. The outlaw is manufactured as a he who both threatens and refuses the authority of law. Both the moral subject (the virtuous citizen) and the immoral subject (the vice peddler) are necessary to this moral order and to the law itself. There must be a subject to prosecute and a subject to protect to uphold the phenomenal structure of law. The fundamental authority of the law is based upon its rhetorical ability to constitute its jurisdiction and limits. Those limits are not given by federal law alone, but in the law's ability to produce subjects who dialectically inscribe the law in the contours of citizenship by creating proper citizens and improper criminals.

Significantly, the outlaw is not an aberrant subject, a rogue individual living outside the law, but he is necessary to the law as it is he who threatens the order of democratic governance. Given this threat, it is he who demands the production of moral subjects. That is, to offset the threat of this immoral subject—he who threatens the very authority of law itself—the law demands individuals to answer the call to proper citizenship, to come into the law, to promote the welfare of the populace. The constitution of this position—the subject able to claim a right to decency—also demands the production of a subject to embody such claims. One of those subjects able to demand such a right was the young man. Indeed, this individual could be molded into a particularly moral citizen, able to negotiate the contours of radical change. He alone could perform the governance needed—he could control his selfish urges and promote the welfare of the population. Now fully authorized by the rhetorical force of law, the young man could be produced as a future steward of the burgeoning American democratic project.

To prove the ways in which young men were disciplined to take on the demands and rights of virtuous citizens, I turn to technologies that trained young men as moral citizens, as citizens who would not become the vile peddler or possessor of smut, but would become the virtuous citizen able to claim decency. Indeed, I argue that not only could young men claim such a right, they were guided into a leadership position, as shepherds of the flock helping to set obscenity standards.

Technologies of the Self: Training Young Men to Demand Decency

In order to produce such moral subjects, several discourses, including athletic education, elocution, and moral education, proposed ethical and physical instruction. Young men were made into virtuous subjects who proclaimed the necessity of public decency. Moreover, this kind of education redressed anxieties about young men and their future role as leaders and citizens—young men would be trained to balance individual liberty and social welfare, to become virtuous citizens and defenders of public decency. This section will detail several educational programs designed to make young men into moral and respectable citizens.

Frequently, social reformers and sociologists argued that education must be reshaped to fit the lives within a bustling metropolis. This reshaping would intercept the newly budding problems of industrializing cities. Sociologist Simon N. Patten claimed, "In order to emancipate him in the industrial world, it is necessary to educate him by methods radically different from systems that succeeded with men living in the country and working under the conditions of nature itself" (123). In other words, young men must be taught to properly navigate the new, industrial city. New forms of navigation, or education, manufactured young men as virtuous, decent citizens. To provide new methods of navigation, curriculum ideas were modified and routine became a "new" technique of learning.[10] This system focused on daily habits as places to instill proper behaviors and encouraged young men to practice them as virtuous subjects, to take on the moral behest of decency.

One routine supposedly able to teach young men virtue was exercise. Posited as a primary solution to subduing the passions of young men, physical exercise and games became increasingly common. Athletic "inventions" during this time period include marathon running, calisthenics, and Pilates. Many authors claimed these forms of exercise as preventative solutions to vice. For example, Simon Patten asserted physical labor as a "renewing force" that ended the "sedative pleasures of smoking and saloon card-games" (123). This mode of self-governance suppressed pleasure and regulated the body. The young man of routine was vigilant in his own care; he was aware of his own passions and controlled them (Foucault, *The Care of the Self* 274). Therefore, through daily exercise, young men learned to counter those "sedative pleasures" that aroused their passions. They regulated their own bodies via daily physical routines.

Physical routine was also encouraged by the Anti-Saloon League (founded in 1893). It produced large numbers of flyers and handouts to persuade young men to choose athletics as a common routine and avoid the perils of alcohol. Around the turn of the century, members of the Anti-Saloon League handed out cards to young men. Many of these cards were used to encourage young men to participate in athletics and to discourage drinking, gambling, and masturbation. The cards reminded young men that skills in football would be diminished by alcohol; it was a moral medium against the ever-present threat of vice (see figure 1 for an example).

In order to instill routine, proponents of physical education encouraged moral activities. By practicing proper athletics, the young man avoided vice. In *Physical Training*, the YMCA laid out the ways the young man might train his body in order to control his excitements or passions. YMCA members understood themselves as *the* organization to tutor boys in conduct free from the ill effects of vice (Seerley 7). Thus, members of the YMCA debated the *kind* of sex education and physical training they should offer within their walls. In the journal, YMCA member Max Exner argued that sex education should teach physiology, chastity, the effects of venereal disease, and engage young men in athletics (279). Exner claimed that young men's knowledge of their bodies and physical exertion would save them from a life of "the lowest abuses" (274). The YMCA provided training in these routines in order to mitigate the lures of these abuses for young men.[11]

Just as reform advocates encouraged routine in young men, elocution deployed routine in pedagogy. Lessons in elocution instructed young men to practice daily speaking drills so as to make the "body a FIT instrument" (Fulton and Trueblood 1, capitals in original). For example, elocutionists contended that the mind, body, and soul of the young man should be managed through particular exercises. The young man (most commonly the student of

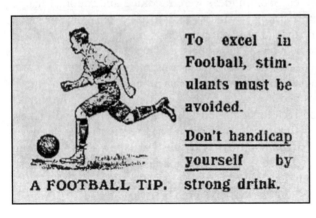

To excel in Football, stimulants must be avoided.

Don't handicap yourself by strong drink.

A FOOTBALL TIP.

Figure 1
Anti-Saloon League. "A Football Tip." Westerville Public Library. 30 Apr. 2004. <http://www.wpl.lib.oh.us/AntiSaloon/>.

elocution) was most persuasive or grand when he learned how to carefully manage every inch of his body. Nearly every elocution book from 1880 to the 1910s began with a diagram of the lungs and larynx. After this diagram, the functions of these organs were explained. This diagram documented the ways in which the body should be understood and regulated. In other words, the body came under self-scrutiny as a way to master the appetites. The student of elocution was persuaded to practice different breathing, speaking, and bodily exercises to keep his body in perfect alignment. The young man who performed such exercises would feel no lure of vice—he would not desire alcohol or narcotics as they would destroy his speaking voice. Elocutionary routine disciplined the body of the speaker to produce *"higher spiritual and magnetic effects"* (Fenno 9, emphasis in original). These higher spiritual and magnetic effects were the result of a highly disciplined body that balanced its triune character; the body of the elocutionist avoided the perils of vice by inculcating daily habits that balanced his body, mind, and spirit.

Once balanced, the young man was encouraged to manipulate his body so as to demonstrate his interior state. Like other proponents of elocutionary gestures, Frank Fenno's 1912 edition of *Science of Speech* provides multiple photographs of body poses for the young student of elocution. These body positions supposedly demonstrated the speaker's interior state—posturing illustrated "higher spiritual and magnetic effects." Fenno's "Expression of the Feet" diagram shows readers the ways in which the feet might be stanced in order to convey an emotion (see figure 2). For example, feet facing away from one another communicate "Weakness with a Strong Attitude." The goal for the student of elocution was to learn these feet positions with the accompanying hand, head, and torso positions in order to correctly convey proper emotions as he was speaking or reciting. Again, the young man was tutored in how to represent particular emotions or practices through his body postures. The young man who properly regulated his body (e.g., learned the proper emotive movements of the feet) represented himself as respectable (not immoral) and would easily perform such gestures and thereby display his own interior balanced state. Elocution taught

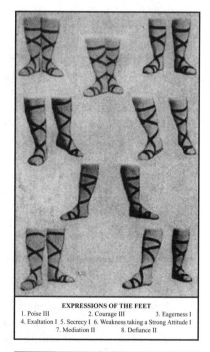

EXPRESSIONS OF THE FEET
1. Poise III   2. Courage III   3. Eagerness I
4. Exaltation I 5. Secrecy I 6. Weakness taking a Strong Attitude I
7. Mediation II   8. Defiance II

Figure 2

Fenno, Frank H. "Expressions of the Feet." *Fenno's Science of Speech.* Chicago: W. Fenno, 1912.

the young man to manage his body and how to demonstrate his own composition of character—he was trained to show himself as a virtuous citizen.

Yet another new training mechanism for young men was moral education—a Progressive Era pedagogy that tutored students in virtues such as honesty, fairness, and altruism. Moral education similarly situated young men by training them to be virtuous citizens who not only digested moral lesson plans (e.g., honesty, fairness), but also demonstrated such virtues for others. For most moral education systems, weekly and daily lessons instilled habits in children. Elocution instructor F. H. Ellis elaborates the goal of these lessons:

> The ideal has been given, and throughout the week, and whenever possible in every lesson, the Thought is reiterated, until the desire to *be* as the Ideal has become a habit. "As a man thinketh, so is he." The child thinks about the Ideal, desires it and then expresses the thoughts in conduct. (1)

Ellis marks these ideals as significant to daily habits—children learn by daily practice. For example, the Brownlee System for Moral Education (1908) used mock city governments to teach children the quotidian propriety of civics. Photographed in the center of the Brownlee volume were two mayors for one school township. Edward Buerke, one of the mayors pictured, was quoted on his philosophy of governance, "I will do the best I can for all the people of Lagrange City [the school], all the time" (Brownlee 18). Edward, an example par excellence, had taken on the lessons of moral education and become devoted to his fellow citizens. He did his "best" "all the time" and showed himself a proper ruler and citizen.

Indeed, the objective of moral education was to manufacture young men as stewards, to proffer their guidance as moral individuals. Sir Oliver Lodge (a British educator whose works were reprinted in the United States through Funk & Wagnalls) details such aims:

> Preparation of the child for individual life,—this is the main object of education. And its chief aim must surely be the formation of a personal character, a will, the separate individuality of a free being. The faculty of acquiring and worthily utilizing real freedom,—that is the object of education. And to this end self-discipline, self-control, is the main factor. (31–32)

Young men trained in their proper role practiced self-control. They balanced their own liberties with social welfare. Such moral countenance delivered the young man's worthy freedom to proper governance. He was produced as the principled citizen able to demand a right to public decency.

Ultimately, the young man learned to control his own interests and thereby learned true devotion to the welfare of the social. Moral educator John King Clark argued that the boy who "reigns within himself, and rules passions, desires and fears, is more than a king" (88–89). The boy was not simply in control of himself, nor was he simply a good governor; instead, the boy did both: he controlled himself in order to become a good governor of the collective. Many other moral educators argued that education in individual conduct was necessary for the preservation of "social union" or "public welfare" (Griggs 81; Sneath and Hodges 2). Young boys were invited to scrutinize and control their bodies, mind, and selves to promote the "nation's moral welfare" (Palmer xiv). By learning the will of mind necessary to govern their own bodies, they learned how to become good governors of the social union.

However, these educational practices were not simply to be done anywhere. Young men were offered a particular space for their practice in proper habits—the city park. Focused on improving public parks, creating art societies, and the ornamentation of the city, the city beautiful "movement" offered citizens a pristine environment from and in which to learn proper behavior.[12] There were multiple types of city beautification. From municipal art societies spread in cities throughout the nation to city planners who wrote treatises on the aesthetic improvement of civic spaces, creating beautiful cities became a priority.

According to Charles Mulford Robinson (a self-avowed planner of beautiful cities), art appreciation was municipal in nature: "If men seek it they seek not for art's sake, but for the city's; they are first citizens and then, in their own way, artists, and artists in this way only because they are citizens" (26). Robinson demonstrated the devotion expected of men. As well-trained citizens, responsible men sought civic beautification for the sake of other citizens—not for their own pleasure. The proper man was indebted to his fellow humans, not his own artistic sensibilities. Further, according to Robinson, a beautiful civic space trained young men for moral adulthood.

> The Juvenile Court would not have business enough to keep it going; the saloon would have its vigour sapped by a substitute [sic]; the hospitals would not require constant multiplication. There would be more of manliness; there would be purer souls, for there would be less temptation; there would be saner minds because of stronger bodies. (245)

If civic spaces were of the right aesthetic sensibility, young men could not be led astray. They would be "purer souls" facing "less temptation." For Robinson, beautiful cities bred true men that could rule with a strong body and a pure soul. Taking this deployment of beauty as premise and the large amount of space offered to young men, the city parks can be read as a civics training ground for boys.[13]

The St. Louis city plan of 1907 strongly advocated parks throughout the city as places of rest, recreation, and preventative reform. City planners asserted (citing a report by the St. Louis Board of Police Commissioners that claimed habitual criminals are those who begin their first offense under the age of 16), "The tremendous value of the parks and playgrounds, merely as a preventive agency in minor juvenile crime, becomes obvious" ("A City Plan" 41). Indeed, the value of parks was held as supreme—they molded proper behavior by offering a space for proper activities.

More specifically, the St. Louis city plan detailed the different activities that were needed for the reformation of different peoples. Factory workers required a "breath of fresh air" after "their confining day's work" (49). Young

men (presumably not factory workers) needed active recreation in these parks
(49). The plan for a typical city park (the St. Louis report references a typical
park from Chicago) in St. Louis was divided into five sections: the ball field,
the children's outdoor gymnasium, the women's outdoor gymnasium, the
pool, and the men's outdoor gymnasium.[14] The park offered young men a
sizable amount of space for play. In addition to the very large outdoor track
and gymnasium provided, the ball field was also available to young men.
This play was not simply recreational, but allowed young men to enact virtuous activities in a beautiful environment.

Indeed, many lauded the park's potential to teach virtue and asked the
city to take on the role of instructor. The St. Louis report argued that in order
to combat the evils of child labor, the corruptions of political life, and the
weakening of home ties,

> the government must employ every resource in its power. Schools' librar-
> ies, playgrounds and public baths, by developing their minds, training
> their bodies and up-building the character of a people, furnish the foun-
> dation upon which a nation's welfare depends. Self-preservation is a law
> of nature for nations as well as individuals, and upon the character of its
> people depends the preservation of the State. (53)

This short quotation demonstrates the weight placed upon the reformatory
power of the parks. Parks were building blocks in the creation of the nation. The
welfare of the entire nation depended upon self-preservation as built and taught
by those public sites that constructed the character of the nation's citizens. Character was not simply something taught to citizens in public parks. Parks, as
beautiful sites and sights, trained and built the proper character of citizens.

The young man was part and parcel of this nation building. Given the
largest amount of space in the park, he was a crucial subject for whom the
beautiful park was necessary. It was his propriety that developed the nation.
Upon him the nation was built and its character morally fortified. The actual
allocation of park space in St. Louis marks the young man, indeed the privileged young man, as the subject who was able to actually use parks to their
so-called civic potential. A map of St. Louis from 1917 (ten years after the
printed plan) shows the location of all city parks. Interestingly, primarily
wealthier neighborhoods had access to the expansive Forest Park while
neighborhoods commonly inhabited by poorer immigrants had very small
parks. Moreover, the Hill (a traditionally African American neighborhood
northwest of the city's center) shows no parks. As such, the privileged young
man was given a scene in which to enact his moral and virtuous subjectivity—a scene delimited from poorer and marginalized peoples.

City beautiful planners created spaces for play, activity, and rest. Yet, this
was not simply the encouragement of exercise—the promotion of this activity
had an end in mind. Planners positioned these locales as training grounds.
Therefore, the privileged young man would learn to negotiate his body by
playing in the park. Exercise and play in parks developed the minds and bod-

ies of citizens. Repetitive physical action trained the young man to manage his own body and to devote himself to the good of the social. He enacted such virtue in the park and the playground. If he was able to enact quotidian practices of moral and physical education, he would become a moral citizen, able to guide the nation through the precarious balance between individual liberty and social control and thereby demand decency and morality for the nation.

Conclusion

While conventionally rhetorical scholars have read the law as a legitimizing discourse for identity formation, this essay has suggested that the law must be read as constitutive of rights-bearing subjects. Specifically, I have argued that the Comstock law produced citizens with a right to public decency and demanded the training of individuals for these rights. My analysis not only supplements the current theorizations of the law, but also refocuses the historical debate about the Comstock law. This reading suggests that the Comstock law should not be viewed as purely regulative, but rather as a law with a particular rhetorical force—a force that imbued privileged subjects with a right to public decency.

Given that the balance of individual liberty and social reform presented a dilemma to turn-of-the-twentieth-century citizens, it seems appropriate that one citizen trained to take up such rights was the young man. His instruction ensured those anxiety-ridden social reformers that democratic citizens would keep the interest of the populace at the forefront of their minds. With this education, young men became moral stewards for the leadership of the nation—individuals trained to forward the well-being of the social and demand public decency.

In sum, the law is not simply one discourse among many, but has rhetorical force. The law authorizes, produces, and invites the discipline of particular subjectivities. While my analysis has unfortunately ignored the dialectical other of this law—the criminal—I have tried to argue that the law is not just one plurality among the infinite, but has authority relevant to our daily practices of subjectivity. Indeed, the rhetoricity of law is not only sovereign power or storytelling, but the law's ability to constitute a singular plural—subject(s) *to* and *of* the law.

Notes

[1] Examples of these societies include the New England Watch and Ward Society, the Minneapolis Vice Commission, the Little Rock Vice Commission, the Hartford Vice Commission, the Chicago Vice Commission, etc. For a detailed description of these commissions, see: Boyer, Paul S. *Purity in Print; the Vice Society Movement and Book Censorship in America.* New York: Scribner, 1968; Boyer, Paul S. *Urban Masses and Moral Order in America, 1820–1920.* Cambridge, MA: Harvard UP, 1978.

[2] Comstock prosecuted Victoria Woodhull and Ezra Heywood for voicing their views on free-love or spiritualism. Woodhull and Heywood argued that marriage stifled spiritual attachments and promoted what we would now call "open" marriages. For more information, see: Helen Lefkowitz Horowitz, *Rereading Sex: Battles over Sexual Knowledge and Suppression in Nine-*

teenth-Century America. New York: Knopf, 2002; Helen Lefkowitz Horowitz, "Victoria Woodhull, Anthony Comstock, and Conflict over Sex in the United States in the 1870's." *Journal of American History* 87.2 (2000); Paul S. Boyer, *Purity in Print; the Vice-Society Movement and Book Censorship in America.* New York: Scribner, 1968.

3 In "The Governmentality of Discussion," Paul Passavant reads the First Amendment of the United States. He argues that "rights are given meaning within a discourse that embodies subjects who can make legitimate rights claims" (115). Using the premises and logic of his argument, I read the Comstock law similarly. My departure from Passavant is that I work to historicize the law as constitutive of particular subject positions—rather than the more general subject positions (i.e., civil subject) of Passavant—and then turn to read the way in which subjects were trained to embody such positions. See: Passavant, Paul. "The Governmentality of Discussion." *Cultural Studies & Political Theory.* Ed. Jodi Dean. Ithaca, NY: Cornell UP, 2000. 115–31.

4 Richard Sennett has written a considerable amount of work detailing the history of democracy and liberal governance. He claims that the history of democratic cities is beset by a loss of individual rights up against city governance. To be sure, I am not claiming that the ideas I cite here are necessarily "new," but rather that this is a time of shift in the United States and that this shift became *positioned as* a balance between individual liberty and liberal administration. See Sennett, Richard, *The Fall of Public Man.* New York: W.W. Norton, 1974; Sennett, Richard, *Families against the City: Middle Class Homes of Industrial Chicago, 1872–1890.* Cambridge, MA: Harvard UP, 1984; Sennett, Richard, *Flesh & Stone: The Body and the City in Western Civilization.* New York: W.W. Norton, 1994.

5 For example, as the populace became more dependent on city governments for water, electricity, and sewage (all services previously provided for by the property owner), citizens began to question what they should have to give up (e.g., property rights, adherence to city codes) in order to have access to social services. Machinations such as these forever changed the economic infrastructure, employment systems, and social stratifications of turn of the century cities.

6 New York City is just one example of the massive changes in the administration of charities and public works. The Department of Public Charities & Correction and Almshouse Department governed the allocation and administration of city funds to work houses, orphanages, sanitariums, etc. In 1895, the Department of Public Charities split from the Department of Corrections as part of a massive reorganization of city government. By the 1920s, the Department of Public Charities was renamed to the Department of Welfare, signifying both a huge shift in governance and its status as a new umbrella organization for hundreds of public service projects. See: Almshouse Department, "Records, 1759–1947," New York City Department of Records and Information Services.

7 By 1885, twenty-four state legislatures had passed "little Comstock laws" that were modeled on the federal statute or on a more stringent New York obscenity law passed shortly after S.R. 1572. See: McGarry, Molly. "Spectral Sexualities: Nineteenth Century Spiritualism, Moral Panics, and the Making of U.S. Obscenity Law." *Journal of Women's History* 12.2 (2000): 8–29.

8 The force of law I am engaging is the foundational moment, which is different from the force of adjudication. As Derrida so eloquently writes, there is a difference between the "founding violence" of the law, that which "institutes and positions law," and the "violence that conserves, the one that maintains, confirms, insures the permanence and enforceability of law" (981). While I laud efforts to engage the rhetoric of courtroom drama, I feel our field must also criticize the rhetoricity of founding law. See: Derrida, Jacques. "Force De Loi: Le Fondement Mystique De L'autorite/Deconstruction and the Possibility of Justice." *Cardozo Law Review* 11.5–6 (1990): 920–1046.

9 Thus, the prosecutions conducted under the banner of the Comstock law. Most of the defendants prosecuted under S.R. 1572 were small manufacturers of pornographic pictures, birth control devices, or other "obscene" materials. For more information on these prosecutions, see: Tone, Andrea. *Devices and Desires: A History of Contraceptives in America.* New York: Hill & Wang, 2001.

10 In *The Care of the Self,* Foucault notes that routine was positioned as a kind of self-governance. See: Foucault, Michel. *The Care of the Self: The History of Sexuality,* Vol. 3. 3rd ed. Trans. Robert Hurley. New York: Vintage Books, 1988.

[11] George Chauncey offers an important history of gay culture in New York, citing the YMCA as a gay cruising ground. It seems that the training offered by the YMCA did not necessarily impact or "reform" all audience members as Chauncey argues that these men did not feel ashamed nor remorseful about their sexual acts. See: Chauncey, George. *Gay New York: Gender, Urban Culture, and the Making of the Gay Male World, 1890–1940.* New York: Basic Books, 1994.

[12] In turning to the public park, I will not cede the particularity of location to simply a privileged discourse enacted by practices. Instead, I have drawn on the public park precisely because its value within systems of capital, sociality, and civics was already circumscribed as a place of reformation, recreation, and rest. The park could be taken up as a civics training ground as its rhetorical function was already delimited as a site in which lessons could be learned. Or more generally, I am pulling on circulatory systems as a way to frame the materiality of those sites promised to train young men.

[13] Landscape planners Frederick Olmsted, Charles Mulford Robinson, and Ebenezer Howard argued that parks were critical for the proper training of city residents. Indeed, parks became a crucial site for training citizens. The park and other sites of beauty were situated as the antitheses of the vice district—it trained the boy as a moral (instead of immoral) citizen. While parks were not *always* a moral training ground, they nevertheless became a way for citizens to be taught respectability. See: Schuyler, David. *The New Urban Landscape: The Redefinition of City Form in Nineteenth-Century America. New Studies in American Intellectual and Cultural History.* Baltimore: Johns Hopkins University Press, 1986.

[14] Historian Edward C. Rafferty explains that the Civic League in St. Louis was a largely unsuccessful bourgeois organization. Created by elite, wealthy citizens in 1895, the Civic League pushed for many measures in the city that, Rafferty claims, were voted out by working-class populations. Such measures included highway construction, park creation, and public transit rerouting. Rafferty asserts that the Civic League lost such electoral battles by failing to appeal to working-class voters who saw Civic League projects as in the best interests of the elite. See: Rafferty, Edward C. "Orderly City, Orderly Lives: The City Beautiful Movement in St. Louis." *Gateway Heritage* 11.4 (1991): 40–62.

Works Cited

Act for the Suppression of Trade in, and Circulation of Obscene Literature and Articles of Immoral Use, S.R. 1572. *Cong. Globe,* 42nd Cong., 3rd Sess. 2004–5 (1873).

Addams, Jane. *A New Conscience and an Ancient Evil.* New York: Macmillan, 1923.

Bates, Anna Louise. *Weeder in the Garden of the Lord: Anthony Comstock's Life and Career.* Lanham, MD: UP of America, 1995.

Boyer, Paul S. *Purity in Print; the Vice-Society Movement and Book Censorship in America.* New York: Scribner, 1968.

———. *Urban Masses and Moral Order in America, 1820–1920.* Cambridge, MA: Harvard UP, 1978.

Brownlee, Jane. *Moral Training in the Public Schools.* Springfield, MA: The Holden Patent Book Cover Co., 1908.

A City Plan for Saint Louis: Reports of the Several Committees Appointed by the Executive Board of the Civic League to Draft a City Plan. Civic League of St. Louis, 1907.

Clark, John King. *Systematic Moral Education with Daily Lessons in Ethics.* New York: The A.S. Barnes Co., 1910.

Comstock, Anthony. *Traps for the Young.* 1883. Ed. Robert Bremmer. Cambridge: The Belknap P of Harvard UP, 1967.

Curry, S. S. *Foundations of Expression: Studies and Problems for Developing the Voice, Body, and Mind in Reading and Speaking.* Boston: The Expression Co., 1907.

DeGrazia, Edward. *Girls Lean Back Everywhere: The Law of Obscenity and the Assault on Genius.* New York: Random House, 1992.

Derrida, Jacques. "Force De Loi: Le Fondement Mystique De L'autorite/Deconstruction and the Possibility of Justice." *Cardozo Law Review* 11.5–6 (1990): 920–1046.

Ellis, F. H. *Character Forming in School.* New York: Longmans, Green, and Co., 1907.

Exner, Max. "A Tentative Statement of Problems and Principles of Sex Education for Men and Boys." *Physical Training* 10.9 (1913): 274–88.

Fenno, Frank H. *Fenno's Science of Speech.* Chicago: Emerson W. Fenno, 1912.

Foucault, Michel. *The Care of the Self: The History of Sexuality,* Vol. 3. 3rd ed. Trans. Robert Hurley. New York: Vintage, 1988.

———. "Governmentality." *The Foucault Effect: Studies in Governmentality.* Ed. Graham Burchell, Colin Gordon, and Peter Miller. Chicago: U of Chicago P, 1991. 87–104.

Fulton, Robert I., and Thomas C. Trueblood. *Practical Elements of Elocution.* Boston: Ginn & Co., 1893.

Griggs, Edward Howard. *Moral Education.* New York: B.W. Huebsch, 1903.

Haney, Robert W. *Comstockery in America; Patterns of Censorship and Control.* Boston: Beacon P, 1960.

Hariman, Robert. "Performing the Laws: Popular Trials and Social Knowledge." *Popular Trials: Rhetoric, Mass Media, and the Law.* Ed. Robert Hariman. Tuscaloosa: U of Alabama P, 1990. 17–30.

Hasian, Marouf. "Legal Argumentation in the Godwin-Mathus Debates." *Argumentation & Advocacy* 37 (2001): 184–97.

———. "Performative Law and the Maintenance of Interracial Social Boundaries: Assuaging Antebellum Fears of 'White Slavery' and the Case of Sally Miller/Salome Muller." *Text and Performance Quarterly* 23.1 (2003): 55–86.

———. "Vernacular Legal Discourse: Revisiting the Public Acceptance of the 'Right to Privacy' in the 1960s." *Political Communication* 18 (2001): 89–105.

Horowitz, Helen Lefkowitz. *Rereading Sex: Battles over Sexual Knowledge and Suppression in Nineteenth-Century America.* New York: Knopf, 2002.

Lodge, Sir Oliver. *Parent and Child: A Treatise on the Moral and Religious Education of Children.* New York: Funk & Wagnalls, 1910.

Lucaites, John Louis. "Between Rhetoric and 'the Law': Power, Legitimacy, and Social Change." *Quarterly Journal of Speech* 76 (1990): 435–66.

McGarry, Molly. "Spectral Sexualities: Nineteenth Century Spiritualism, Moral Panics, and the Making of U.S. Obscenity Law." *Journal of Women's History* 12.2 (2000): 8–29.

Palmer, George Herbert. *Ethical & Moral Instruction in Schools.* Boston: Houghton, 1908.

Passavant, Paul. "The Governmentality of Discussion." *Cultural Studies & Political Theory.* Ed. Jodi Dean. Ithaca, NY: Cornell UP, 2000. 115–31.

Patten, Simon N. *The New Basis of Civilization.* 1907. Cambridge, MA: Harvard UP, 1968.

Peters, John. *Speaking into the Air: A History of the Idea of Communication.* Chicago: U of Chicago P, 1999.

Robinson, Charles Mulford. *Modern Civic Art, or, the City Made Beautiful.* New York: The Knickerbocker P, 1903.

Seerley, F. M. "Suggested Methods for Giving Instruction in Sexual Hygiene." *Physical Training* 6.1 (1908): 3–11.

Sneath, Elias Hershey, and George Hodges. *Moral Training in the School and Home; a Manual for Teachers and Parents.* New York: Macmillan, 1913.

Stall, Sylvanus. *What a Young Man Ought to Know.* Philadelphia: Vir, 1897.

Tone, Andrea. *Devices and Desires: A History of Contraceptives in America.* New York: Hill & Wang, 2001.

PART VII

Contemporary Rhetorical Cultures

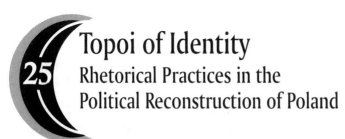

Topoi of Identity
Rhetorical Practices in the
Political Reconstruction of Poland

Cezar M. Ornatowski

It may be taken for granted today that communities are in some sense "imagined" or symbolic entities. In his *Imagined Communities*, Benedict Anderson suggests that a nation is "an imagined political community" because "members of even the smallest nation will never know most of their fellow members, meet them or even hear of them, yet in the minds of each lives the image of their communion" (6). Such communities inhere, Anderson suggests, largely in a state of consciousness: a sense of "horizontal comradeship," a temporal simultaneity existing in and moving through history (7). Such communities are qualitatively different from religious or dynastic communities, which rely on entirely different sorts of relationships and affiliations. Between the decline of the latter and the rise of the former, Anderson suggests "a fundamental change" had to have taken place in "modes of apprehending the world" in order to make it "possible to 'think' the nation" (22). He suggests that this change was brought about by the popularization of such "forms of imagining" as the novel or the newspaper, which "provided the technical means for 're-presenting' the *kind* of imagined community that is the nation" (horizontal-secular, transverse-time), mass literacy, the spread of administrative vernaculars, capitalist relations of production, technologies of communication, travel, the rise of an intellectual class, mass schooling, and textbooks (25). In fact, Anderson goes on to claim that "all communities larger than primordial villages of face-to-face contact (and perhaps even these) are imagined"; communities, he suggests, "are to be distinguished, not by their falsity/genuineness, but by the *style* in which they are imagined" (6).

For the past several years, during the course of work on rhetorical aspects of the political transformations in Poland and South Africa, I have noted the diversity of forms of symbolic representation of identity along with their transformations and permutations as part of the processes of national reconstruction. I have seen statues pulled down, crosses erected, streets renamed, buildings altered, plaques rewritten, maps redrawn, emblems redesigned, museum reinvented. I became fascinated with souvenir plates with the image of Pope John Paul II, place mats with the map of South Africa, and coasters with royal emblems. Finally, I could not help recalling Anderson's remark about the differences in the "styles" in which communities are imagined while on a recent visit to Yerevan, Armenia, where I toured the national war and Karabakh museums; they are virtual shrines to a narrow and defensive conception of collective identity under siege.

I began to suspect that there may be no limit to the human capacity to make any kind of object or medium grist for the expression of collective identity. I also began to reflect on the relationship of this capacity to rhetoric and rhetorical action. In this paper I want to share some preliminary observations and reflections on this relationship; I offer them less in the spirit of a systematic account than a rough outline of a complicated terrain still seen only from ground-level and only in the course of a few forays.

A Foray in the Rhetoric of Nation Building

Let us begin by looking at a concise, official verbal statement of collective political identity. The preamble to the July 22, 1952, "Stalinist" constitution of the Polish People's Republic (the name of the polity erased in the wake of the 1989 transformation) reads:

> The Polish People's Republic is a republic of working folk. The Polish People's Republic harks back to the most progressive traditions of the Polish Nation and realizes the liberatory ideas of the Polish working masses. The Polish working folk, under the leadership of the heroic working class, basing on the worker-peasant alliance, has struggled for decades for liberation from national enslavement imposed by Prussian, Austrian, and Russian conquerors-colonizers, just as it has struggled for the abolition of the exploitation of Polish capitalists and landowners.

This short passage articulates some basic outlines of the political community of the Polish People's Republic. Membership in this community is limited to "working folk." Even though it refers to "traditions of the Polish nation," actual historical continuity is reserved only for certain "ideas" of a specific segment of the population. The text also establishes the basic social relationships in its emphasis on the "leadership of the heroic working class" and the concept of the "worker-peasant alliance" (this relationship was never reversed to "peasant-worker alliance"). Finally, it also names its "others": Prussian, Austrian, and Russian conquerors-colonizers and Polish capitalists and landowners.

The passage articulates in a particularly compact form four out of six basic dimensions of collective identity that I have been able to observe in the wide variety of symbolic objects, including "identity junk" (such as plates with Abraham Lincoln or place mats with the Golden Gate Bridge), as well as in the pronouncements of politicians and in public discourse during the course of the Polish transformation: membership (who belongs to the community, who are we), origin (where we come from, what are our antecedents, including narratives of collective history), internal relationships (how our community is ordered, structures of authority), and the community's "other" (who we are not, who does not fit).

A denizen of communist Poland actually experienced each of these dimensions in daily life through an array of symbols embodied in a wide variety of objects, artifacts, and media. Thus, "membership" was symbolized through depictions of hardy proletarians, bucolic peasants, or professionals busily working at their respective work stations for the common good (if you did not see yourself in any of these roles, you probably did not belong); holidays and events (such as May Day) celebrating labor or specific segments of the "laboring masses" (there were state holidays and official celebrations for miners, steelworkers, and shipyard workers); films and exhibits devoted to labor and the proletarian life; visits by state leaders to factories and "great construction sites of socialism"; achievements in science and technology; erection of entire cities as symbols of socialist industrialization; official display of specific working-class clothing and paraphernalia on appropriate occasions; and so on. Origin was symbolized through narratives, histories, films, portraits of past communist activists and the ubiquitous duo of Marx and Lenin hanging in classrooms and public buildings; displays of copies of symbolic documents of socialism; historic films and documentaries depicting the struggle for social and national liberation that led to socialism; and so on. Internal relations were symbolized through portraits and statues of leaders; artwork depicting social transactions in which those in uniform or wearing red ties (indicating party or Young Pioneer membership) were shown in positions of authority or leadership; as well as films depicting daily encounters and situations at work and in public and private life that illustrated models of social conduct and dealing with people and situations. Finally, the community's "others" were depicted in films showing West German or CIA spies, saboteurs, criminals (such as, for instance, possessors of Western currencies), provocateurs, or ideological enemies of all stripes.

A 1972 amendment to the constitution wrote in a clause about the "friendship" with the Soviet Union, which represents another dimension of collective identity construction: external relations. This dimension was symbolized in cultural practice through programs about the Soviet Union and other socialist countries, organizations such as the Association for Polish-Soviet Friendship, statues and place names devoted to heroic Red Army troops, portraits of Soviet and allied leaders, and the largest symbol of them all: the Palace of Culture—a sky-piercing monstrosity in the very center of Warsaw modeled on an identical structure in the center of Moscow, a gift from Stalin to the Polish people and a symbolic link between the center of the communist world and the periphery. External relations were also symbolized by routine visits of Polish leaders, especially newly appointed ones, to Moscow.

One of the critical aspects of the reconstruction of Polish collective identity during the course of the political transition immediately preceding and following 1989 has been a change in official collective symbols. I will cite as one example a lengthy and important parliamentary debate that took place on February 9, 1990, six months after the installation of the first non-communist government in Poland in Central/Eastern Europe. The debate concerned changing the national emblem from a communist white eagle to a differently shaped white eagle with a crown.

In Polish history, the eagle had at various periods been represented with two types of crown: a "closed," hat-like crown (like the royal crown of England worn by Elizabeth II on state occasions) topped by a cross, and an "open" crown of the type represented, for example, in Burger King commercials. During the debate,[1] the chamber divided into proponents of the open or closed design. Minister of State Piotr Nowina-Konopka, who presented the motion to the chamber, believed that the open design symbolized the new democratic nation's "openness to the diverse religions and nations present in the Republic" (8). Proponents of the "closed" design argued that that design represented a self-contained, unified national community morally united by the thousand-year tradition of Christianity in Polish history. According to Stefan Bielinski, a proponent of the "open" design, the object of the emblem was to achieve a "graphic summary of Poland's historic glory, a visual connection between a post-partition, sovereign Poland and an array of emblems of Poland's most outstanding kings" (12). Thus, Bielinski concluded, the redesign of the national emblem was not to be regarded as "an abstract exercise in heraldry" but as "a summation of history and a treasury of national tradition" (11–12). Opponents such as Kazimierz Czerwinski, however, questioned the design's implicit "direct continuation of [communist] time, the time that had passed" (13). Proponents of the "closed" crown, on the other hand, argued that the emblem should lead into the "future," as well as connect with the past; they argued that the Polish struggle against communism, like past struggles for sovereignty and freedom, were carried out under certain "constant motifs," including the crown (a closed crown as a symbol of complete sovereignty) and the cross on the crown. These symbols, as Marek Jurek put it, were symbols of "values, for which it is worth giving something in life, for which it is worth giving up one's life," as well as a "reminder, that over state power, over human power, there is a transcendent moral order" (14–15).

Proponents of the "closed" design also cited, and in fact intoned, an old Polish patriotic song from the days of Poland's national oblivion that went: "Only under the Cross, only under this symbol, Poland is Poland and a Pole is a Pole" (the jingle rhymes in Polish). The song enacted through still another medium, that of music, the historical continuity of patriotic struggles that has continued to undergird, through Poland's turbulent history, the nation's sense of self, the continuity between struggles against foreign occupation, communism, and now political struggles in the democratic parliament and a democratic polity. In the latter context, the song introduced a divisive element, putting proponents of the "open" design implicitly in the position of the "others," of enemies of some eternal essence of Polishness. In fact, just such division quickly began to mark the political scene, as political debates about identity and democracy in the early 1990s degenerated into arguments about what the "real" Poland was and who was a "real" Pole. Such categories appropriated and exploited the "us" versus "them" rhetoric of the anti-communist struggle, in effect substituting "us" (the nation opposed to communism) in pre-1989 rhetorical struggles with the "real Poles" (right-wing Catholic, anti-European Union nationalists) and putting liberal, center and left-of-center oriented, pro-European Poles in the rhetorical position of "them" (the designation reserved for the regime before 1989). Paradoxically, Marek Jurek, a proponent of the "closed" crown, as part of his argument in parliament suggested that "the national emblem should unite and not divide" (15). Clearly, however, what is capable of uniting (a national symbol) is also capable of dividing in various times and contexts (unity along certain lines and division along others) down to the smallest symbolically readable detail.

An example will show how the smallest detail can become an object of political contention. The design for the eagle, finally adopted after the stormy debate on February 9, 1990, has two swirls within its wings that resemble five-pointed stars. These "stars" became another major object of contention; some members saw in them a reflection of "Bolshevik stars" and advocated an alternative design for the eagle without the "stars." The "stars" were in fact decorative flourishes of feathers and part of the original design predating communist Poland. However, they were preserved in the communist-era eagle (which was otherwise still quite different in shape) precisely *because* they resembled the Soviet symbols and thus constituted a symbolic link between the socialist "brotherly nations."

In another important study that lays the foundation for rhetorical approaches to collective (national or community) identity, British anthropologist Anthony Cohen argues that communities are symbolic constructs. Similarly to Anderson, Cohen calls them symbolic not because they are less than real; rather, they are symbolic because they coalesce around symbols. Symbols, however, Cohen argues, do not so much express meaning or tell us what to mean as "give us the capacity to *make* meaning" (16, emphasis added). Communities share symbols, but they do not necessarily share their meanings. "The quintessential referent of community," Cohen suggests,

> is that its members make, or believe they make, a similar sense of things generally or with respect to specific and significant interests, and, further, that they think that that sense differs from one made elsewhere. The reality of community in people's experience thus inheres in their attachment or commitment to a common body of symbols. . . . But it must again be emphasized that the sharing of symbol is not necessarily the same as the sharing of meaning. (16)

The debate over the national emblem showed that while after 1989 there was little debate about the need to reject the communist emblem there was disagreement about the specific emblem to adopt as well as the meanings of every potentially symbolically significant detail. No such disagreements were felt before 1989. Only when collective political identity began to change did the emblem regain political currency and become the object of intense rhetorical action. The debate over the eagle also shows that even accidental resemblances harbor, under the right circumstances, the potential for political meaning. Signs may become symbols (i.e., "stars" on feathers), and symbols may be appropriated in the service of multiple meanings, often distant from their intention and origin. Such appropriations are integral to, form part and parcel of, politics, just as arguments based on them constitute an essential part of political rhetoric. (Witness, for instance, the debate over the Spanish-language U.S. national anthem in the context of the current debate on immigration reform.)

The debate over the eagle emblem, however, also shows another aspect of national identity construction. The debate over elements of the "eagle's" meaning were not debates about the eagle per se; rather, they were debates about specific aspects of collective identity, in this case whether this identity should be "open" to "others," and to whom specifically, and whether it should be grounded in the spiritual foundation of Christianity. In this respect, the eagle spanned two dimensions of national identity: membership (who belongs to the "imagined" community) and origin (what is the foundation, point of departure, principle of coherence) of the community. The debate over the "star-like" feathers also concerned both the dimension of "origin" and "external relations": the connections of the community with other communities and the relationships that help define it. The evolving, democratic Poland rejected its association with both the communist past and the Soviet Union; this rejection was reflected, or better enacted, by some members' objections to the design that appeared to contain star motifs. Defenders of the star motifs, however, argued that the motifs came from a pre-World War II design, not just from the communist-era design, and that this was the design that the Polish diaspora, especially in the United States, "has continued to live under," in the words of one member of parliament. The design with the "stars" thus represented national continuity to those Poles who had emigrated during the communist times. This symbolic connection with the diaspora was worth preserving (in fact, this connection was an essential part of the emerging extended, more inclusive, concept of Polish nationhood), and thus the "star" design was worth preserving, in spite of the potential "Bolshevik" connotations of the "stars" themselves.

A historic leap forward to the preamble of the constitution of the Republic of Poland dated April 2, 1997 (the post-transitional constitution that replaced the 1952 one) will show the final results of such negotiations, now enshrined in the "authoritative" articulation of national identity in the foundational document of the new democratic polity. The preamble reads:

> Having regard for the existence and future of our Homeland, which recovered, in 1989, the possibility of a sovereign and democratic determination of its fate, we, the Polish Nation—all citizens of the Republic, both those who believe in God as the source of truth, justice, good and beauty,

as well as those not sharing such faith but respecting those universal values as arising from other sources, equal in rights and obligations towards the common good—Poland, beholden to our ancestors for their labours, their struggle for independence achieved at great sacrifice, for our culture rooted in the Christian heritage of the Nation and in universal human values, recalling the best traditions of the First and the Second Republic, obliged to bequeath to future generations all that is valuable from our over one thousand years' heritage, bound in community with our compatriots dispersed throughout the world, aware of the need for cooperation with all countries for the good of the Human Family, mindful of the bitter experiences of the times when fundamental freedoms and human rights were violated in our Homeland, desiring to guarantee the rights of the citizens for all time, and to ensure diligence and efficiency in the work of public bodies, recognizing our responsibility before God or our own consciences, hereby establish this Constitution of the Republic of Poland as the basic law for the State, based on respect for freedom and justice, cooperation between the public powers, social dialogue as well as on the principle of aiding in the strengthening the powers of citizens and their communities. We call upon all those who will apply this Constitution for the good of the Third Republic to do so paying respect to the inherent dignity of the person, his or her right to freedom, the obligation of solidarity with others, and respect for these principles as the unshakable foundation of the Republic of Poland. (Preamble)

One can readily identify four out of the six dimensions of identity here. First dimension: membership. In contrast to the 1952 constitution, the "democratic" Polish political community includes "all citizens of the Republic." In addition, in what was intended as a deliberate contrast to the 1952 text, the 1997 preamble opens with the plural pronoun "we," symbolizing the "authentic" voice of the political community (the 1952 constitution was written in Moscow and, following a review in Warsaw, was hand edited by Stalin and handed to the Polish parliament for endorsement). The community characterizes its members as both believers and nonbelievers, although the former appear to be privileged, at least by syntax (but everything is symbolic here). Membership is also extended to Poles living elsewhere (who were, under the previous dispensation, considered traitors and enemies, and thus among the "others"). Second dimension: origin. The community traces its origins to the Christian tradition and the thousand-year history of Poland (Christianity coincides with the existence of Poland as a recognizable political entity). It pointedly erases the communist republic from its antecedents. Third dimension: internal relations. The preamble posits social and political relationships among members based on solidarity, social dialogue, freedom, and justice in contrast to the class-based relations characterizing the community of real-socialism. Fourth dimension: external relations. The 1997 text refrains from naming its political "others" (although it may be read as implying moral "others," or those who do not share the universal human values). By explicitly calling for the "cooperation with all countries," the text distances itself from the multiple divisions that defined the geopolitical positioning of the socialist community.

Topoi of Identity: Symbols and Rhetoric in Nation Building

Let me suggest that the "dimensions" of nation building I identified in the two constitutional preambles constitute basic "topoi" of collective identity. I am using the term "topoi" here in its Aristotelian sense as "universal topoi," that is, as common places (in this case constituting common aspects of collective identity) and as lines of argument "applicable to a large number of inquiries of diverse sorts" (15). There is a sixth such topos, which was not represented in the preambles cited above: the topos of location, which relates to the community's sense of place, of geographic or geopolitical localization. This topos is best illustrated symbolically by three globes I observed in the hallway of the South African parliament building in Cape Town: one globe was positioned on its vertical axis; another was turned sideways so its axis ran horizontally (making Europe and South Africa parallel to the United States and Argentina); and the third was turned upside down, with the North and South Poles reversed, leaving South Africa to "dominate" the rest of its hemisphere. The globes link with many other expressions of South Africa's ongoing self-redefinition from a (past) cultural and ethnic satellite of Europe and the outpost of the West to a (projected future) dominant cultural and economic power in Africa. In the Polish context, debates concerning Poland's location have shifted from a conception of Poland as part of the "east" to arguments about whether it should be "imagined" as part of the "west" or a "bridge" between east and west—these are debates with major political and economic stakes.

What I have called here "topoi of identity" represent, in Radcliffe and Westwood's words, "key sites [in a rhetorical sense] in which national identities are generated and sustained" (7). These reference points are variably embodied in an array of symbols (flags, coats of arms, music, names, and so on). Portraits of famous members of the community, past or present, belong to the topos of "membership": they show who "we" (in our collective "imagination") are. Landscapes on place mats are symbols belonging to the topos of "location": they symbolically identify places that constitute and help define our collective character and that circumscribe us (similarly to songs such as "America the Beautiful"). Such symbols, in turn, provide the storehouse of meanings that in turn, especially in times of political instability, become grist for rhetorical action, for negotiation, debate, and redefinition. In the wake of such redefinition, collective identity may become represented by other symbols. A political leader arguing that Poland is positioned next to Russia and far from the United States and therefore needs a defensive pact with the former is arguing from the topos of location. A member of parliament who hung a cross in the Polish parliamentary chamber in 1997 (the cross remains; nobody has yet had the political courage, or capital, to remove it) was implicitly activating, and "arguing" from, the topos of "membership."

Symbols that enact topoi of identity open up potential spaces for negotiation, for rhetorical action and transformation. They are the "vehicles" (an appropriate term, since symbols are ultimately metaphors and a vehicle is the "object" aspect of metaphor) for the embodiment, preservation, and transformation of collective identity. In periods of political stability, such symbols simply circulate largely unnoticed in a wide variety of forms, both official (statues, buildings, portraits, museum displays) and vernacular (or "vulgar"): plates with George Washington or Lenin, or place mats with maps of Capri. In periods of instability, when collective identity is challenged or changes, they become "active," they regain their status as enactments of topoi of identity and repositories of meaning. (The topoi of identity are, for instance, rhetorically deployed in the current immigration debate in the United States.)

Gerard Hauser, in his discussion of the vernacular rhetoric of cultural memory in Poland, has suggested that "the political odyssey of Central and Eastern Europe following the mostly bloodless revolutions of 1989 provides an object lesson in the material process of discursive reconstruction of society from its own extant symbolic resources" (120). He argues that stories from the past, in the context of Central/Eastern European transformations, provided models that were "appropriated" in the turmoil of current politics "not as patterns to be reproduced but as stock of resources with which to reframe political realities" (157). He concludes that "the political upheavals in Poland, the former Yugoslavia, and the other Central and Eastern European nations generally suggest that the self-producing activity of a society's rhetoric depends less on forging consensus than on sharing a *common reference world*" (152).

In the post-1989 reconstruction of Poland, the constant "structuring the present through acquisition and reacquisition of its tradition" appears to have proceeded in a more chaotic, fragmented, and contestatory manner than Hauser's description would imply. The "stock of cultural resources" that is circulated to reframe political realities consists not of stories, but of symbols and fragments of symbols: stories, crowns, eagles, feathers, buildings, architectural fragments, ornaments, figures, expressions, turns of phrase, pictures, trees, landscapes, maps, paintings, design elements, and so on.

The process of Polish transformation also included imported symbols and elements: the American flag or its motifs and colors, a poster of Gary Cooper from *High Noon* going to vote for "Solidarity" in the watershed June 4, 1989 elections (with a ballot instead of a gun in his hand), pictures of politicians, both communist and oppositional, on dollar bills. Poland thus did not just, as Hauser suggests, transform itself out of its own symbolic resources. Rather, politicians of all provenances appropriated and cannibalized symbolic resources and invested them with meanings for their own contingent use. With globalization and technologies of instant communication along an increasingly wider spectrum of media, such circulation of symbols, significations, and potential materials for symbols is perhaps becoming ever more rapid.

Political transformation is (besides the enactment of new legislation, establishment of new institutions, issuance of new decrees, and signing of new treaties) to a large extent, at its heart, a symbolic transformation, a trans-formation in the kinds and meanings of symbols that constitute the community's sense of itself, its identity. The common expression "identity politics" suggests that there may be a politics that is not identity related. The case of Poland and other countries under transformation, as much as that of the United States in the early stages of its national formation (as shown, for instance, in the remarkable collection of visual representations of democracy gathered in David Hackett Fisher's monumental *Liberty and Freedom*), suggests that "politics" (most explicitly under conditions of social destabilization and perhaps implicitly at other times) is bound up with identity. In fact, the United States has also been undergoing a quiet transformation as a result of the massive immigration of the last two decades. The current immigration debate indeed foregrounds issues of identity and engages all six "topoi of identity" discussed in this paper.

Topoi of identity constitute a specific rhetorical ecology of community. This symbolic system, according to Josep Llobera, "mediates between the past and future, while providing an effective dimension for the present" (20-1). They constitute the privileged locus (to paraphrase Llobera) where a variety of discourses converge or are reflected. It is in this respect that from the standpoint of rhetoric it may be said that such topoi open the royal path (again borrowing from Llobera) to understanding the ends of any given rhetoric.

Focus on community or national identity helps to broaden discussions in rhetoric and composition studies that in the United States have focused primarily—although for understandable reasons—on ethnicity and race. Examining processes of transformation in countries such as Poland also provides a different lens on these issues than postcolonial studies and provides a balance to the latter's often Marxist bias. Finally, the perspective outlined here may be useful in view of the attempts at many universities—including my own— to "internationalize" the rhetoric and writing curriculum. Focus on issues of identity along symbolic and rhetorical lines may form a foundation for rhetorically based curricula that combine political discourse, community studies, and international relations (three "hot" areas today) and thus push beyond the traditional—and perhaps divisive—politics of race and ethnicity to look at the constitution of human political communities at all levels, from local communities to national, international, transnational, and global ones.

Note

[1] In this section quotations are from the stenographic record of the twenty-first sitting of the Sejm conducted on February 9, 1990. It is available from the Sejm Library, Warsaw.

Works Cited

Anderson, Benedict. *Imagined Communities: Reflections on the Origins and Spread of Nationalism*. 1983. London: Verso, 1991.

Aristotle. *The Rhetoric of Aristotle*. Trans. Lane Cooper. Englewood Cliffs, NJ: Prentice-Hall, 1960.

Cohen, Anthony P. *The Symbolic Construction of Community. Key Ideas.* London: Routlege, 1985.

Fisher, David Hackett. *Liberty and Freedom: A Visual History of America's Founding Ideas.* New York: Oxford, 2005.

Hauser, Gerard A. *Vernacular Voices: The Rhetoric of Publics and Public Spheres.* Columbia: U of South Carolina P, 1999.

Llobera, Josep R. *Foundations of National Identity: From Catalonia to Europe.* Oxford: Berghahn, 2004.

Preamble. The Constitution of the Republic of Poland. As adopted by the National Assembly on April 2, 1997. 13 July 2007. <http://www.kprm.gov.pl/english/106_104.htm>.

Radcliffe, Sarah, and Sallie Westwood, eds. *Remaking the Nation: Place, Identity, and Politics in Latin America.* London: Routlege, 1996.

"Sorry Seems to be the Hardest Word to Say"
Official Apologia and Rhetorical Agency in Contemporary Danish Politics

Lisa Storm Villadsen

The May 4, 2005, Speech

Every year in the evening of May 4, a ceremony is held at Mindelunden ("Memorial Grove"), north of Copenhagen to mark the anniversary of the 1945 BBC radio broadcast that German troops had surrendered. This news meant that five years of Nazi occupation had come to an end.

In 2005, it was 60 years since Denmark celebrated its liberation. On the occasion of the anniversary Prime Minister Anders Fogh Rasmussen gave a speech at the annual memorial ceremony. In attendance were representatives of the royal family, former resistance members and their descendants, as well as invited British war veterans who participated in the Allied forces' arrival in Denmark in May 1945.

Rasmussen begins by recalling the joy over the liberation of most of Denmark, mixed with the sorrow over the bombing of two cities on the island of Bornholm in the Baltic Sea and the continued occupation of that island for almost another year. Ryvangen, where Memorial Grove is located, was used by the Nazis as an execution site for Danish resistance members, and the prime minister takes his starting point here to comment on the courageous acts of these individuals. By means of five named personal examples, the prime minister portrays the breadth in social background and ages among resistance members and underscores the personal suffering they all went through, most of them with fatal consequences, on Danish soil, at sea, or in prison camps in Germany.

Through a series of antithetical phrases the prime minister underscores the courageous and noble initiative in mounting active resistance: "They did not worry about what would be useful but about what was truthful. They did not just take care of themselves. They took action. They gave their lives for our freedom."[1] The resistance members are thanked for "saving Denmark's honor" and for "secur[ing] the self-respect of the Danish people." A special section of the speech is in English and comprises a thank you to the British soldiers who participated in the liberation of Denmark, and a thank you to Great Britain for that country's part in the defeat of Hitler-Germany.

The prime minister's speech corresponds well with the usual Aristotelian markers of an epideictic speech: the audience is primarily present as onlookers witnessing the celebration of the anniversary, and the prime minister employs the traditional strategies of a ceremonial speech. The use of examples and amplification to praise the individuals are the focus of the ceremony.

But about halfway through the speech we also find embedded an element of a different genre: the official apology. Over the course of four paragraphs, Rasmussen discusses the role of Danish public authorities in the treatment of Jewish refugees seeking refuge in Denmark from Nazi persecution, and a number of other innocent people whom the Danish authorities expelled "to suffering and death in concentration camps" or "abandoned to an uncertain fate in the hands of the Nazi regime." The prime minister calls the Danish authorities' participation in these "shameful events" a "stain on the . . . otherwise good reputation of Denmark" and continues "on behalf of the government and thereby on the Danish state" to "regret and apologize for these deeds."

The speech caught public interest for two reasons: primarily because the prime minister included an official apology to Jewish refugees from Nazi Germany (and also some other refugees) who were turned away by Danish authorities. There is virtually no precedent for such a gesture in the history of Danish government rhetoric.[2] An important aspect of this issue was that the very thought of finding points to criticize in the treatment of Jews in Denmark during the occupation was shocking to a nation that for a very long time basked in a rather unequivocal collective memory of the Danes as being heroic protectors of Danish Jews. Who hasn't heard of the nightly sea passages across to Sweden with Jews hidden in the bottom of fishing boats or seen such a boat on display at the Yad Vashem museum in Jerusalem?

Second, there was a sense that the prime minister was using the celebration of the resistance during World War II to bolster his own government's policy of supporting the war in Iraq.[3] I shall return to both the issues.

Official Apologia

My reading of the speech will focus on its element of official apology, so let me offer a brief sketch of what I understand this to be. In their famous article on the rhetoric of self-defense, Ware and Linkugel proclaimed apologia as a genre to itself.[4] They suggested a terminology for description and categorization of the factors and modes a rhetor may employ in self-defense against attacks on his or her person with the aim of restoring his or her public image. Along with Koesten and Rowland,[5] I would suggest that there are significant differences between apologias presented in one's own name, what we might call *personal apologia*, and apologia presented in a public collective's name (such as a nation-state), what we might call *official apologia*. The official apology resembles the individual's apology in that it is also a response to criticism and works toward restoring strained relations. But on two points the official apology differs from the personal, namely that it is forwarded on behalf of a collective, and instead of dispelling criticism it acknowledges it. This calls for very different responses from those studied by Ware and Linkugel. Thus, Harter, Stephens, and Japp have criticized the usefulness of Ware and Linkugel's terminology when it comes to official, ritualized, and institutional apologia.[6] Koesten and Rowland have pointed out that ordinary strategies of apology are beside the point when guilt is indisputable. They argue that rhetoric that aims at apologizing for wrongdoing comprises a particular subgenre of apologia, namely what they term "the rhetoric of atonement."[7] The function of the official apology is "purgative-redemptive," i.e., to serve as a symbolic gesture where the rhetor wipes the slate clean and establishes the ground for a new beginning that can restore balance and health in the community.[8] Time does not permit me to engage in more particular arguments concerning the problems and benefits of identifying subgenres or their cousins, nor to discuss Rasmussen's speech as an instance of the rhetoric of atonement. Rather, I wish to contemplate wider theoretical questions regarding the ontology of the rhetoric of official apologia and its rhetorical agency.

Rhetorical Agency

Before I proceed with the analysis of the speech, I would also like to offer some thoughts on the notion of rhetorical agency and its relevance to this project. Such an explication may be necessitated by my choice of rhetorical artifact: an official statement by a prime minister is perhaps not the most likely candidate to push the limits of our understanding of how rhetorical agency is constituted and manifested. After all, the concept of rhetorical agency seems to have made the most headway in studies of the rhetoric of subaltern and other traditionally silenced groups.[9] Nevertheless, I suggest that it may be a constructive starting point for appreciating the aspects of a type of rhetorical action that seems to be on the rise, not just in the United States but around the world, namely the official apology.[10] What's more, the absence of an official apology—as in the crisis regarding cartoons of Mohammed in Danish newspapers—may serve as a case for studying the perceived need for and function of such rhetorical action.

I shall abstain from any attempt to define rhetorical agency, but I would like to offer a few comments on my understanding of the term. My approach to questions of rhetorical agency reflects my training in close reading, and I therefore tend to hover near the verbal ground when I read rhetorical texts. In my approach I am influenced by several of the thoughts put forth in position papers for the Alliance of Rhetoric Societies (ARS) conference in 2003.[11] As an overall frame I am sympathetic to Lynn Clarke's call for a focus on the way rhetorical agency allows and/or constitutes intersubjective speech, i.e., "creating and performing the potentials of language and reason in particular situations and processes of invention, thought, and choice." Second, I find

Carl Herndl's way of thinking of rhetorical agency as "contingent on a matrix of material and social conditions" and "a social location into and out of which social subjects move uncertainly" appealing. Finally, I see my paper as a partial response to John Louis Lucaites's call to "begin by identifying the wide range of ways in which the modalities of action are constituted and implicated in particular rhetorical performances."

I also found inspiration in Lundberg and Gunn's *Rhetoric Society Quarterly* essay in response to Cheryl Geisler's report from the ARS conference.[12] While perhaps a bit too provocative for some tastes, Lundberg and Gunn do an entertaining job of pointing to some challenges for our thinking on the nature and role of rhetorical agency. While I no doubt overlook and simplify important and complex arguments in their piece, I take one of their main points to be that there is a tendency among rhetoricians to speak of rhetorical agency in terms of "possession," and that this is problematic because it reifies rhetorical agency into "a quantifiable ectoplasm" that can be possessed and even transferred from one agent to another.[13] This is closely connected with another main point in their critique of Geisler and others: when we speak of rhetorical agency as something that can be possessed, it becomes difficult to escape the exact mode of thinking the concept was seen as an antidote for: namely a relationship between agent and agency resembling a more traditional modern/ humanist understanding of the autonomous and self-transparent subject and his or her more or less instrumental use of rhetoric as means to an end. As I understand Lundberg and Gunn, one point in their essay is to question the link between rhetorical effect and rhetorical agent, and they propose a reframing of the question "in terms of subjectivity and effect" instead.[14]

While I am not prepared to follow Lundberg and Gunn in their radically "hospitable" conceptualization of rhetorical agency as something that possesses an agent, I take from the essay a couple of thoughts: First, by means of the Ouija board metaphor, the invocation of the concept of "ontotheology" and the flippant talk of "ectoplasm." The two authors brought into focus for me a sense that much of the discussion of rhetorical agency has an almost metaphysical aura about it that is both inspiring and intimidating. Lundberg and Gunn take this observation as a cue to what they see as the unproductive element of "ontotheology" in rhetorical theory and criticism, but I just take it as a point from which to comment on the need, especially in pedagogical contexts, for more accessible discussions of rhetorical agency in rhetorical criticism. Second, I think their critique suggests that metaphysical sounding or not, some of this theoretical discussion is perhaps old ideas about rhetoric and its workings shrouded in a new vocabulary. While this suggestion would seem to undercut the significance of the notion of rhetorical agency, that is not my aim. Rather, I would like to find in it a constructive element.

In this paper I will attempt to come to terms with both these thoughts. I will forward the modest argument that discussing even such conventional rhetorical practice in terms of rhetorical agency is a fruitful way to develop our understanding of rhetorical interaction. I believe there is a truth to the thought that a changed vocabulary can have dramatic effects on one's per-spective, and looking at the prime minister's speech through the concept of rhetorical agency brings into focus some of the arguments for and against its justification and constructive contribution.

I want to suggest that the rhetoric of official apologia is a promising locus for interrogating issues of rhetorical agency. First, the very presence of such utterances attests to the notion of the ability of language to affect personal relations, regardless of whether one understands apologia as symbolical expressions writ large or if one favors a more narrow understanding of them as a kind of performative speech act. Either way, the official apologia fore-fronts the potential in rhetoric to act in a social setting.

Second, a schism may lie in the fact that in an official apology the speak-ing subject rarely has any personal responsibility for the wrongful action. This we may expect to have significance for his or her ability to present an actual apology. When speaking by proxy for agents in the past, the question becomes can a contemporary rhetor speak to the guilt of others? If so, how can a speaker constitute him or herself as capable of speaking on behalf of the past *and* of the contemporary collective? Is an officially sanctioned position—such as heading a government—sufficient? How clearly should the rhetor appear as an individual and a spokesperson for a group in order to secure credibility? And how does one on behalf of others deal with possible resis-tance to an apology from the group and/or collective associated with the wrongdoing? I shall return to the relationship of rhetorical agency in official apologia and epideictic rhetoric.

Third and finally, the increase in the number of official apologia (in the Western Hemisphere at least) might be evidence of a more widely emerging rhetorical agency, that is, that groups formerly barred from formulating their thoughts in the public sphere increasingly have the opportunity to gain a hearing in public fora, exert pressure on their governments, and thereby make them publicly accountable for policies deemed suppressive, racist, or other-wise condemnable.[15]

Rhetorical Agency in Rasmussen's Speech

Since I am studying a rhetor whose agency is taken for granted, I find it interesting to begin with his own understanding of it. Rasmussen in fact makes several references to his own role in relation to the situation and the message of the speech, and, I will suggest, in somewhat ambiguous ways. I see the ambiguity played out in terms of personal closeness/distance to the time and the events mentioned in the speech.

As for the epideictic aspect of the speech, Rasmussen very early on com-ments on his personal relation to the situation and the topic: "I did not expe-rience the occupation and liberation myself. But it moves me deeply to stand among these graves. It is overwhelming to think of the many fates behind the names on the gravestones." I read this comment as a response to a perceived expectation of a measure of personal involvement in the occasion—that it is not possible to remember the dead in a suitable manner without, for lack of personal witnessing, at least being emotionally affected. However, as he turns to the discussion of the resistance members' sacrifices, Rasmussen transcends the personal and historical levels and frames the discussion in a distinction between "what is right and what is wrong." By thus inscribing the issue as a moral one, the prime minister frames the issue as immediately available for him to comment on and interact with. In this way, I see him carving out rhetorical agency for himself on a topic that he in some sense has no stock in.

Rasmussen also uses another strategy through which he gains rhetorical agency. In connection with the apology for the Danish authorities' expulsion of Jews and other persecuted individuals to the Nazis, Rasmussen proposes a collective rather than an individual, personal recognition of the problem: "Worse [than the knowledge that some of the victims of the resistance did not even receive a proper grave] is that we, today, know that Danish authorities in some instances contributed to the expulsion of people to suffering and death in concentration camps." Rasmussen said that a "recollection of the dark sides of the occupation" was a necessary part of the marking of the 60 year anniversary of the liberation. Is this passage, Rasmussen appeals to collective memory and thus assigns the responsibility of remembering to the Danish public. It is, of course, important that the nation as such remember, but I find it noteworthy that at this point, he steps back from the issue personally, and perhaps also institutionally.

Yet, in the following passage, Rasmussen returns to the rhetoric of a general moral responsibility. He steps forward in his role as state leader and underscores the institutional aspect of his rhetorical agency with the words: "On behalf of the government and the Danish state I would therefore—at this particular occasion and in this place—regret and apologize for these deeds." From this point in the speech Rasmussen clearly assumes the role as spokesperson for Denmark as a nation with phrases such as, "Tonight we must not forget," "In Denmark we may not forget," "And we can never forget," "Denmark will never forget," "In Denmark, too. We are all eternally grateful," "Tonight we remember all the freedom fighters who gave their lives so that we may live in freedom, peace and progress," and "We are deeply indebted to them."

From a rhetorical vantage it is interesting that Rasmussen seems to be aware of the various aspects—personal and institutional—of his speaking position, and that he so explicitly anchors his rhetorical agency in time and place. We might see this meta-communication as evidence of the great symbolic significance ascribed to an official apology from a state leader—a significance that is likely to be exacerbated by the scarcity of precedent in Danish political tradition. This is underscored by the fact that the prime minister even raises questions about the rhetorical agency of the speech as he explicitly comments on its value as a speech act: "An apology cannot change history. But it can serve to acknowledge historical mistakes. So that current and coming generations hopefully will avoid similar mistakes in the future."

When we see how Rasmussen thus qualifies the rhetorical agency of his statement and very carefully words the speech act ("I would therefore . . . on behalf of the government and thereby the Danish state regret and apologize for these actions"), we might find that Rasmussen does all he can to signal sincerity and thereby forestall possible criticism for paying lip service or eschewing "real" responsibility. It would thus seem that he does not just leave it at *regretting* (which involves a lesser degree of personal responsibility and mortification), but successfully completes the speech act of *apologizing*. Moreover, he forestalls predictable criticism that an apology cannot undo the wrongs of the past by expressing the wish that the apology will not only have an influence on contemporary understanding of the occupation of Denmark, but also may serve as inspiration for more proper behavior in the future. All in all there is good reason to consider Rasmussen's speech a successful official apology, even, in the terminology of Koesten and Rowland, a rhetoric of atonement.

There are, however, at least two aspects that might be taken into consideration that problematize the rhetorical agency of the prime minister's official apology: the apology's placement in the context of a speech of praise and the connection to the prime minister's political agenda as a whole.

With regard to the context of the apology, it would arguably have sent a more distinct message of sincere regret and disgust had it been presented in an independent statement and not just worked into a larger context.[16] With regard to the issue of the prime minister's political agenda in general, it could be argued that the very careful wording notwithstanding, its credibility is severely undercut by Rasmussen's other public statements regarding that era. In this context it is significant that the actions apologized for were committed by the so-called "cooperation government,"[17] which Rasmussen previously had criticized on several occasions, and in fact criticized again in a speech given the following day. In light of Rasmussen's very clear disapproval of the previous government's policy and his own sharp distinction between right and wrongful deeds during the occupation, a question of how much of the responsibility he really is willing to assume presents itself: he might regret the handing over of Jewish refugees, but given his moral disapproval of the responsible government in general, the question remains whether he had distanced himself so much from those historically responsible that his appeal to collective, and not institutional, memory and apology simply does not ring sincere. In other words, the lesser the degree of identification with the responsible party, the "cheaper" it is to apologize for their actions. This may in the end be a matter of political opinion, so let me close with a few more theoretical comments about the rhetorical agency of the rhetor of official apologia.

On a concrete level, it seems to me that the nature of rhetorical agency is an aspect where official apologia differs from personal apologia. The official apology raises, so to speak, the issue of "mandate": if sincerity or mortification is a litmus test of the rhetoric of atonement, as Koesten and Rowland would have us believe, we might ask with what right and to what extent an official apology can be said to express the historically responsible parties' sentiments.

One way of approaching this question is through the work of Brooke Rollins, who in analyses of several funeral orations by Jacques Derrida has shed light on a central challenge in epideictic rhetoric, namely the question of how one, in an ethically defensible manner, can speak to "the other," that is, to a fellow human being in all of his or her inviolable and fundamental authenticity.[18] In relation to the rhetoric of apology, the question is with what right does the rhetor speak on behalf of a collective and is it even justifiable to attempt to put into words other people's hardship and suffering? Does one risk trivializing or in some other way distorting the authentic, individual experience?[19] While Rollins does not mention rhetorical agency this seems to me to be a central theme in the article because it questions what one can say about and to others and with what right.[20]

The Official Apologia and Epideictic Rhetoric

On a more general level, I would argue that the epideictic genre is particularly suited to throwing light on questions regarding rhetorical agency because it reminds us of the importance of language in relation to creating, maintaining, or questioning communal values. The symbolic importance of language is especially noticeable in this genre, and the genre in itself has some functions (celebratory, communal, etc.) that highlight the fact that rhetoric in itself is a form of action and thus a form of agency.

By pointing to theories of epideictic rhetoric as relevant for the analysis of the rhetoric of apologia, and especially the official apology, I am merely saying that genres—Aristotelian or not—do not exist in isolation from one another. Rather, the rhetoric of the everyday tends to blend elements from different genres as well as presuppose the existence of other genres.[21] In this manner they are based on a measure of intertextuality (e.g., when an elected official's ceremonial speech celebrates values that happen to also make up the foundation of a policy proposed by the same person in a deliberative setting). Moreover, the official apology seems interesting from an epideictic perspective because compared to other apologia it employs argumentation aimed at changing the audience's perception of the problem to a lesser degree, taking for granted that there is no real ground from which to argue (at least not about facts). The wrongful deed is, so to speak, acknowledged, and the rhetorical act is meant to demonstrate one's recognition of the error, assumption of responsibility, and distancing from the act as well as possibly showing a will to prevent it from happening again. Rarely is there a developed argument about why the act was wrong. It seems to suffice that it is acknowledged.[22] In other words, there is not so much a need for a reformulation of a norm, but rather for a symbolic recognition that one has been violated and that it must not happen again.

Finally, I would argue that certain types of apologia do not merit much attention unless regarded from an epideictic angle (e.g., when strategies like Ware and Linkugel's *bolstering* and *transcendence* are put to use with the aim of solidifying or recontextualizing the values of the audience). This is interesting because it offers insight into the values prevalent in a society at a given time. In this way, one might rather crudely consider the official apologia an example of epideictic rhetoric of blame because it decries a certain behavior and thus identifies something considered unacceptable. Further, it indicates a way to remedy a harmed relation and thus indicates which goals and ideals are deemed acceptable in the given social context. Thus understood, the rhetoric of official apologia serves epideictic functions. And via the ritualizing that a publicly pronounced apology may be said to represent, the apology marks a symbolic transfer from one understanding or self-image to another.

In order to elaborate on the way epideictic rhetoric can illuminate the rhetoric of official apologia I shall mention three theorists who have made valuable contributions to this question. Both Oravec and Hauser emphasize the significant function vested in a rhetor's ability to put into words shared norms in such a way that the audience recognizes their values within the rhetor's text, whereas Beale is more interested in the performative aspects.[23]

Epideictic as the Basis for Public Life

Christine Oravec analyzes Aristotle's discussion of the role of the audience in relation to epideictic speeches and concludes that there is more to the concept of *theroroi* (the term used by Aristotle to refer to the listeners to the epideictic genre) than merely passive observation and entertainment.[24] I would like to emphasize Oravec's focus on the dialectical relation between rhetor and audience: if a rhetor does not present the topic in a manner experienced as adequate by the audience, his or her credibility will suffer. When making such a presentation a rhetor must obviously have a clear understanding of the values and experiences of the audience, and the challenge lies in formulating them in a discourse that makes them obvious and accessible to the audience, thus actualizing or concretizing what otherwise exists only on an unspoken level. To the extent that a rhetor is able to express the norms and values common to an audience he or she will establish a ground for a shared recognition and experience of a social, cultural, or ethical nature among the audience.[25]

Gerard Hauser, too, argues that a significant function of the epideictic genre is to create a frame of understanding for the interpretation of reality. He stresses the pedagogical and thereby socially significant aspect of Aristotle's treatment of epideictic rhetoric:

> Aristotle's notion of a properly ordered rhetoric assumes that responsible persuasion translates the theoretical contents of politics into the praxis of statecraft and citizenship. . . . In this respect, then, epideictic occupies a unique place in celebrating the deeds of exemplars who set the tone for civic community and the encomiast serves an equally unique role as a teacher of civic virtue.[26]

Although Hauser discusses rhetoric of praise, I believe that his argument holds for the kind of rhetoric of blame that official apologia arguably represents. He continues on the role of epideictic as the rhetoric that puts into words the basic values of society: "It can educate us in the vocabulary of civic virtues that may constitute citizens as an active public, and communicate principles on which responsible citizenship may be based and a vibrant public sphere can thrive."[27]

In addition to this dialectical/didactic function, one might also point to the audience's role as judges of the aesthetic and emotive effects of the speech as significant to the rhetoric of official apologia because the rhetor's ability to present a convincing apology is crucial.[28] Only the audience can decide if their collective set of values has been given an appropriate form. In this way the rhetor's dependence on the audience's support is apparent.[29] I won't go more into these thoughts except to just mention that they, too, indicate the relevance of speech act theory to the rhetoric of official apologia, especially when it comes to felicity conditions, of which I will mention but two of the most obvious. First, a rhetor must have a "mandate" to offer an apology, that is, public support in the shape of more or less explicit adherence to the values presented as grounds for the apology. Second, there has to be an audience that consists of individuals representing both the harmed party and the perpetrators' group to witness the pronouncement of the apology for it to be "official."

Walter H. Beale takes much inspiration from J. L. Austin's speech act theory and emphasizes as the most characteristic trait of the epideictic genre "the epideictic or 'rhetorical performative' act [as] one that participates in the reality to which it refers."[30] He argues that the epideictic genre both says and does something and thereby exists in the present in a more complex manner than other rhetorical utterances that primarily concern something outside themselves.[31] The rhetorical performative, according to Beale, gathers the commonly recognized traits of epideictic: oratorical performance, a connection to literature, ceremony, "presentness," praise and blame, and reinforcement of traditional values. Although Beale actually rejects the common linking of epideictic rhetoric with the present as a significant genre trait, he makes the following observation regarding the anchoring of epideictic rhetoric in a concrete situation:

> Epideictic performances tend to be informed by the "present" in very special ways, often taking their very subjects and forms from the "present" actions or ceremonies in which they are embedded, and often serving to bolster faith or pride in the ideals of the "present system," or assessing "where we are now" as a community.[32]

Again, we see a tendency to place epideictic rhetoric in a frame of cultural analysis. It is this wider function of reflecting the surrounding society that I see as most interesting in relation to Anders Fogh Rasmussen's speech.

Conclusion

I believe that by viewing the rhetoric of official apologia in an epideictic perspective we come closer to being able to answer the question of what kind of rhetorical agency it calls for and is characterized by. An official apology is presented in terms of its own particular time and must be understood and evaluated thus. In an official apology the rhetor places the topic in relation to the values and norms of his or her own time. Condemnation of the actions of the past is therefore put forward in terms of the present, but not in order to correct the past but to create the possibility of a new beginning, wiser through the mistakes of the past. This puts rather high demands on the audience, for, as Kiss has made the point in her study of Hungarian civic responsibility, in order for a collective responsibility (as opposed to collective guilt) to make sense, it requires the audience to identify with a particular group or nation, it asks that they be honest and accept that the moral and political future of their community/society depends on the present-day actions of its members to influence it.[33]

This throws in relief the ways in which the role of the rhetor of official apologia resembles the classic epideictic role: to be the interpreter of one's time and its values and to confirm the community and its course through speech or other symbolic action. A ceremonial setting may also be argued to lend an official apology a measure of rhetorical agency because it is addressed to a wider circle of people than those originally harmed, and because it must be presumed to be more or less reflective of and thus sanctioned by the larger community the rhetor represents. Finally, and beyond the scope of this paper, rhetorical agency in the epideictic genre would seem to play itself out in the more or less explicit guidelines for action to be engaged in by the audience.

By regarding official apologia in the light of rhetorical theory about epideictic rhetoric, the potentially valuable rhetorical functions and ethical orientation of this type of discourse is brought into focus. Further, the epideictic genre seems particularly promising in examining questions of rhetorical agency because it hones our attention to the importance of language in matters of creating, maintaining, or questioning communal values and because it poses functional questions about the possibilities of rhetoric to serve as symbolic action: can one really *apologize?*

Notes

[1] This and all following translations from the speech are my own.

[2] A possible exception is former Prime Minister Poul Nyrup Rasmussen's apology to the indigenous people of Thule, Greenland, for the expropriation of their hunting territory and forced relocation to make room for an American air base in 1953. The Danish government repeatedly declined to apologize for the relocation until, following a court case that decided that the relocation was forced, the Danish prime minister gave an apology in a private telephone conversation with the president of the Inuit Circumpolar Conference (ICC), Aqqaluk Lynge, on September 2, 1998, in which he uttered the Inuit word for "I'm sorry": *utatserquatserpunga*. The prime minister also issued a written statement saying: "On behalf of the Danish state I apologize to the Inuit, the population of Thule, and to the whole population of Greenland for the way the decision about the move was taken and carried out" (www.nunatsiaq.com/archives/nunavut990930/nut90910_12.html).

[3] He addressed this issue in a speech given the next day, May 5, 2005, at the Town Hall of Copenhagen (www.statsministeriet.dk). Contact author for further information.

4 Ware, B. L. and Will Linkugel (1973): "They Spoke in Defense of Themselves" *Quarterly Journal of Speech* vol. 59: 273–283.
5 Koesten, Joy and Robert C. Rowland (Spring 2004): "The Rhetoric of Atonement" *Communication Studies* vol. 55: 68–87.
6 Harter, Lynn M., Ronald, J. Stephens, and Phyllis M. Japp (2000): "President Clinton's Apology for the Tuskegee Syphilis Experiment: A Narrative of Remembrance, Redefinition, and Reconciliation" *The Howard Journal of Communications* vol. 11: 19–34. Hearit has argued that corporate apology represents a type of apology that warrants special consideration: Hearit, Keith Michael (1995): "'Mistakes Were Made': Organizations, Apologia and Crises of Social Legitimacy" *Communication Studies* vol. 46: 1–17.
7 Koesten and Rowland (2004). I won't go into an examination of Rasmussen's speech according to the five requirements of genuine atonement rhetoric forwarded by Koesten and Rowland, but merely suggest that the speech pretty well lives up to them with the possible exception of the need for proof of "mortification." One possible explanation for the lack of concrete suggestions aimed at avoiding a similar problem in the future may be tied to the constraints of the situation. For example, a discussion of Denmark's policy on refugees would displace the focus of the ceremony. Koesten and Rowland also mention that where expectations regarding mortification are clear when it comes to personally responsible rhetors, a nation or an organization's expression of mortification may lie more in the choice of words and not reparation, showing that one will compensate for/prevent repetition of the sins of the past (p. 74).
8 Ibid., pp. 69 and 71.
9 See, e.g., Geisler, Cheryl (2004): "How Ought We to Understand the Concept of Rhetorical Agency? Report from the ARS" *Rhetoric Society Quarterly* vol. 34: 9–17.
10 Cunningham, Michael (1999): "Saying Sorry: The Politics of Apology" *The Political Quarterly* vol. 70, no. 3: 285–293.
11 Unless otherwise noted, all references in this paragraph are to the position papers as posted on www.rhetoricalalliance.org.
12 Lundberg, Christian and Joshua Gunn (Fall 2005): "'Ouija Board, Are There Any Communications?' Agency, Ontotheology, and the Death of the Humanist Subject, or Continuing the ARS Conversation" *Rhetoric Society Quarterly* vol. 35, no. 4: 83–105.
13 Ibid., p. 89.
14 Ibid., pp. 88–89.
15 This is Michael Cunningham's point when he writes that: "The greater emphasis on the concepts of community or cultural identity . . . may also facilitate or encourage a politics of apology which, as I argue above, can reflect a recognition of, and sensitivity towards, both past wrongs and their contemporary resonances" (pp. 292–293).
16 In this respect, the Danish prime minister seems to have learned from the American presidency, specifically Clinton, who framed several apologies in the context of ceremonial occasions so as to leave "on a happy note," as it were.
17 A government that decided to work with the Nazi occupation force in order to secure as much influence as possible in the hope that it all in all would be beneficial to the Danish people. This government, incidentally, contained several members of the same moderately right wing political party that Anders Fogh Rasmussen belongs to: Venstre, Danmarks liberale parti.
18 Rollins, Brooke (2005): "The Ethics of Epideictic Rhetoric: Addressing the Problem of Presence through Derrida's Funeral Orations" *Rhetoric Society Quarterly* vol. 35, no.1: 5–23.
19 This is what Harter, Stephens, and Japp in part conclude in their reading of an apology issued by former president Clinton (pp. 29–30).
20 According to Rollins, Derrida handles these challenges by beginning in and circling around the present as a frame for the witnessing that makes it possible for rhetor and audience to have a shared experience. In this, she finds inspiration in Rosenfield's phenomenological take on epideictic rhetoric: see Rosenfield, Lawrence W. (1980): "The Practical Celebration of Epideictic Rhetoric" *Rhetoric in Transition*. Eugene E. White, ed. University Park: Penn State University Press: 131–155.

[21] See, e.g., Jamieson, Kathleen M. and Karlyn Kohrs Campbell (1982): "Rhetorical Hybrids: Fusions of Generic Elements" *Quarterly Journal of Speech* vol. 68: 146–157; Jamieson, Kathleen M. (1973): "Generic Constraints and the Rhetorical Situation" *Philosophy and Rhetoric* vol. 6, no. 3: 162–170 and (1975): "Antecedent Genre as Rhetorical Constraint" *Quarterly Journal of Speech* vol. 61: 406–415.

[22] Instead it seems that narrative strategies often replace or supplement more formal argumentation. See, e.g., Achter, Paul J. (2000): "Narrative, Intertextuality, and Apologia in Contemporary Political Scandals" *The Southern Communication Journal* vol. 65, no. 4: 318–333; and Harter, Stephens, and Japp.

[23] See Oravec, Christine (1976): "Observation in Aristotle's Theory of Epideictic" *Philosophy and Rhetoric* vol. 9: 162–174; Hauser, Gerard A. (1999): "Aristotle on Epideictic: The Formation of Public Morality" *Rhetoric Society Quarterly* vol. 29, no. 1: 5–23; and Beale, Walter H. (1978): "Rhetorical Performative Discourse: A New Theory of Epideictic" *Philosophy and Rhetoric* vol. 11: 221–246.

[24] Oravec.

[25] Oravec, p. 171. See also, Sullivan, Dale L. (1993): "The Ethos of Epideictic Encounter" *Philosophy and Rhetoric* vol. 26, no. 2: 113–133.

[26] Hauser, p. 14.

[27] Ibid., p. 20. Jasinski, too, mentions that several theorists, among Perelman and Olbrechts-Tyteca, have worked with a much more nuanced conception of the genre and pointed to its massive significance as a basis for political rhetoric because its primary function is to gain adherence to values that later make up the grounds for action: see, Jasinski, James (2001): *Sourcebook on Rhetoric. Key Concepts in Contemporary Rhetorical Studies.* Thousand Oaks: Sage, p. 210.

[28] Cicero, M. T. (1987): *De Oratore.* Book II ix. 35. Trans. E. W. Sutton and M. Rockham. Cambridge, MA: Harvard University Press. See 2.9.35, where he stresses the didactic element of epideictic rhetoric.

[29] Harter, Stephens, and Japp call for a more systematic discussion of audience reactions in the evaluation of the apologic rhetoric.

[30] Beale, p. 227.

[31] Beale tentatively defines a "rhetorical performative" as "the composed and more or less unified act of rhetorical discourse which does not merely say, argue, or allege something about the world of social action, but which constitutes (in some special way defined by the conventions or customs of a community) a significant social action in itself. . . . The performative rhetorical act participates in actions, and in doing so may be appropriate or inappropriate, seemly or unseemly" (p. 225).

[32] Beale, p. 223.

[33] Kiss, Elizabeth (1998): "Saying We're Sorry: Liberal Democracy and the Rhetoric of Collective Identity" *Constellations* vol. 4, no. 3: 387–398.

27 Rhetoric and Resistance in Lu Yin's Feminist Essays

Bo Wang

At a time when it was uncommon for Chinese women to write and publish their writing, Lu Yin was a major figure in writing on various social issues, in particular women's issues. A prolific writer who composed in a variety of literary genres, Lu Yin reached a large number of readers in an effort to advocate women's emancipation and to transform the traditional patriarchal culture. Lu Yin, born in 1899, just as the late Qing reformers promoted women's education and set up the first Chinese-run women's school in Shanghai, came of age when the May fourth movement was beginning to brew.[1] In 1919, Lu Yin enrolled in Beijing Women's Normal College. Like other *xinnüxing* (new women),[2] Lu Yin was fascinated and inspired by feminism, humanism, individualism, democracy, and other Western ideologies newly introduced to China. Recounting her life in college, Lu Yin recorded what she perceived to be her spiritual change:

> I was busy with societal affairs—attending mass meetings in front of Tian'anmen Square, petitioning at the presidential office, and giving public speeches—all these were new to me; I was so zealous and occupied as to forget food and sleep. . . . I made a big rapid progress in my thoughts; I came to know the great responsibility an individual has for the society. (Autobiography 198, 201)[3]

In her rather short life, Lu Yin broke a broad path in the public arena. She opened up a unique space for herself within the public discourse of her day as a fiction writer, an essayist, a public speaker, and a social activist. Perhaps more important for this analysis, by doing so, she would be among the first group of modern Chinese women who would use their pen to make social and cultural change in the early twentieth century.

Over the two decades of her public life as a writer, Lu Yin was extraordinarily productive. As the founder of the youth organization Social Reform, Lu Yin frequently attended its meetings and discussed new ideas with young people who cherished the same ideals. As a fiction writer, Lu Yin was affiliated with Wenxue yanjiu hui (Literary Research Association) as its first female writer.[4] Her short stories regularly appeared in the influential journal *Xiaoshuo Yuebao* (Fiction Monthly) and the literary supplement of Beijing's

Chenbao (Morning Daily). As an essayist, Lu Yin wrote enthusiastically for progressive journals advocating women's liberation and cultural transformation. Lu Yin published her first *zawen* (argumentative essay), "Egoism and Altruism," in *Wenyi Huikan* (Literature and Art Society Journal), edited by the Literature and Art Society at Beijing Women's Normal College in 1920.[5] During this time period, she penned a series of essays that explored issues regarding women, literature, philosophy, politics, nation, and the promotion of the idea of women's liberation and social reforms. Lu Yin's audience included young men as well as young women who could read and write and were receiving the new ideas in the early twentieth century.

Despite the fact that Lu Yin produced a large number of written texts as well as participated in the women's movement as an activist, her written works were denigrated and ignored both in her era and in her profession. Although she was involved in the issues of social and cultural concern, neither this modern woman writer's contribution to history nor her contributions to the making of public discourse were recognized. Like many other women writers of her time, Lu Yin was set aside in histories of modern Chinese literature. Only in recent years have some literary scholars recovered Lu Yin's literary works. Her essays and fiction have been made available through reprinted editions (e.g., *Selected Works of Lu Yin*, 1983; *Modern Chinese Writers—Lu Yin's Masterpieces*, 1998), and she has now received more recognition from the field of literature in China. Several literary scholars have written about her as a fiction writer; however, Lu Yin's written work has another aspect that deserves more public acknowledgement and study. Lu Yin was not only a fiction writer but also a rhetor whose use of language in public exerted a significant impact on the thinking and attitude of the audiences of her time and on the formation of a new culture. She left a rich legacy of using language creatively to inform, communicate, and change attitudes.

In analyzing this legacy, I would like to look at two points that are essential to her rhetoric. First, Lu Yin's feminist discourse was shaped by a specific social and cultural context relevant to the historical period. Second, an analysis of her rhetorical strategies reveals that not only did she write to change minds, but also that she, like many other modern women writers, did so with what should be recognized as a hybrid of rhetorical modes. These modes were created through the clash between Chinese and Western cultures given her position as a writer within a complex social and cultural environment. My analysis of Lu Yin's writing is a response to the recovery of women's rhetoric in the field of rhetorical studies; this project also intends to size down rhetoric by examining the particular rhetorical practices of a woman rhetor in a non-Western culture.

The Rhetorical Context of Lu Yin's Writing

In the late nineteenth and early twentieth century, under the influence of various Western ideologies, a new public discourse was developed by Chinese new intellectuals.[6] Although the new intellectuals promoted Western thought as part of the iconoclastic assault on traditional culture and literature, they also modified Western rhetorical concepts to situate them in the Chinese social and cultural context. They found classical modes of writing, including models of argument and means of literary expression, highly formalistic and abstruse, and therefore insufficient support for the new culture. The rhetoric they articulated was distinctly modern in its aims. Thus, they judged classical thoughts and modes of writing inadequate because classical writers did not provide what they needed to know. Consequently, the new intellectuals, grounded in studies of Western ideologies and scientific approaches to writing, were heavily invested in the prospects of scientific methods and democratic ideals and saw the possibility of modifying imported rhetorical and literary theories and concepts to further their cause: to promote a new culture and move the country toward modernity.[7] The earlier work of new intellectuals opened up social space for Lu Yin to have her voice heard in public.

During the May fourth period, Chinese new intellectuals ardently advocated women's emancipation as part of their effort to attack the Confucian tradition and build a new democratic nation. To the new intellectuals, the unequal gender relationship had trapped women into inhumane situations such as footbinding and female chastity. Moreover, feminist movements launched in the United States and Europe in the early twentieth century provided theoretical reference for the new intellectuals to discuss and solve Chinese women's problems. Thus, the connection between women's emancipation and the nation's modernization made women's rights, education, and emancipation a major theme in the new public discourse. The development of modern education in China at that time prepared a large group of young men as well as young women for reading and receiving new ideas. It is within this social and historical context that Lu Yin wrote and published her essays. Viewed from the perspective of a rhetorical situation, Lu Yin was writing to address the problems in a cultural background in which her audience's experiences and needs were entwined.[8] Her discourse, shaped by the social and political crises in early twentieth-century China, responds to the urgent social issues that women as well as men were facing at that historical juncture. Educated in both Chinese classics and Western knowledge, Lu Yin was able to discern the drawbacks of the old tradition and to appropriate Western ideas and rhetorical modes to provide fitting responses to the exigence in which women were severely oppressed by feudal, patriarchal ethics and norms.

Much of Lu Yin's work on women's liberation was influenced by Chinese and Western thinkers and writers widely read in universities at the turn of the century. Lu Yin's allusions to Hu Shi, Ye Shengtao, and other new male intellectuals suggest the great influence they had exerted on her thoughts and writing.[9] For instance, in "Women's Issues" (1921), Hu Shi criticizes the old customs that bind women's limbs as well as their minds—women not being counted as descendants and having no inheritance rights, one-sided female chastity, and women's major responsibility for taking care of husbands and children (*Speeches of Hu Shi*). Hu Shi points out that in order to gain liberation, women have to break these ancient customs and become independent human beings. Hu Shi believes that self-reliance, independent spirit, and a sense of responsibility as pioneers will help Chinese women liberate themselves from old mores and habits.

Receiving these new ideas, Lu Yin made a further move toward critiquing the patriarchal tradition and constructing a new discourse that perceives and describes the world from a feminist perspective. By "feminism" here I mean the feminist ideas Chinese intellectuals borrowed from the Western culture in the late nineteenth and early twentieth century.[10] Hence, feminism within the Chinese social context in the May fourth period had a close tie with the Western liberal feminism that focuses on the attainment of equality with men in the public arena and freedom from the bonds of gender-biased custom or prejudice.[11] To advocate women's liberation, Lu Yin employed new genres such as *zawen* (the argumentative essay) as a means of creating a discourse of resistance—a discursive strategy of writing against the patriarchal ideology. Lu Yin's texts enable us to see how she challenges the gender hierarchy from a feminist perspective by exploring women's living conditions as well as women's roles and images in a modern society. This textual exploration could be reread as a Chinese feminist rhetoric that forms an important strand in the new public discourse.

Given her engagement in developing the new public discourse, Lu Yin cannot be seen as echoing all that the new male intellectuals (the leaders of the May fourth movement) had to say. For example, while adopting some of their theories and concepts, she adapts them to the promotion of women's self-emancipation. In her essay titled "The Women's Improvement Society's Hopes for Women" (1920), she writes:

> Why do women need men to solve their problems for them? Why don't women recognize their own suffering? Women have brains, and also four limbs and five senses, so why don't they have feelings? Women need men's initiative and guidance in everything. This is truly unthinkable! . . .
> If women themselves lack consciousness and blindly follow men, they will not only fail to achieve their goal of emancipation but also produce endless impediments to the future of women's liberation. Thus, I believe that the issue of women's emancipation must be resolved by women themselves. (qtd. in Lan and Fong 171–72)

Lu Yin questions her countrywomen who waited for men to help them achieve the goal of emancipation and prompts women to take action. She also shows her critical attitude toward men's benevolence to liberate women. Asking questions such as, "Why do women need men to solve their problems for them?" Lu Yin challenges the male intellectuals' sense of superiority and the male assumption that women are the weak sex who need men's guidance. Thus, Lu Yin as a feminist writer intends to subvert the male-dominated discourse and create strategies women could use to express themselves, a move consistent with the major principles of the new public discourse but resistant to the power of patriarchy.

Rhetorical Strategies in Lu Yin's Feminist Essays

Lu Yin's discourse shares similar characteristics with the works of other new intellectuals in the May fourth period, but also has its own distinctive features. Four rhetorical strategies can be identified in her writing: (1) a tendency to redefine the traditional Confucian classics and the traditional culture that perpetuated the patriarchal ideology; (2) the use of new terms and phrases adapted from Western humanist and feminist concepts; (3) the use of vernacular combined with classical Chinese words and phrases in essays and speeches to claim the intellectual authority of the author and to persuade male as well as female readers; and (4) the use of modified Western literary genres including *zawen* (the argumentative essay), *xiaopinwen* (the lyrical essay), and *wenti xiaoshuo* (question fiction) to critique the old culture and to spread new ideas. These strategies, to a certain degree, involve using what I call a hybrid of rhetorical modes based in the Chinese vernacular but integrated with Western thoughts and rhetorical and literary approaches.

While a short essay does not provide enough space for a detailed explanation of each of these strategies, what I intend to emphasize here is that our ability to understand the rhetorical strategies of Lu Yin and other modern Chinese women writers depends to a large degree on the task of thinking more deeply and broadly about the way we define rhetoric, the different assumptions about rhetoric in different cultures, and the possibility of enriching the repertoire of the rhetors in a given culture through creative modifications of the rhetorical modes from another culture. To have a better understanding of Lu Yin's rhetoric, we need to recognize that rhetoric, as a use of language to inform, communicate, and change attitudes, occurs through the reading of a complex social and cultural system that provides a context within which we deploy, negotiate, and resist different social discourses to make changes. Viewed from this perspective, Lu Yin's writing becomes a powerful rhetorical action.

Here, I will focus on Lu Yin's strategies of redefining old, traditional culture and using new terms and phrases translated from Western humanist and feminist concepts. In many of her feminist essays, Lu Yin uses redefining to question the assumptions in the classics and to form a new discourse that legitimized women's needs in a modern society. For example, what had in the past been considered as normal and praiseworthy was now labeled with a negative phrase. I see redefining as an important part of Lu Yin's rhetoric because it is a textual strategy she uses to critique the dominant patriarchal discourse, or in Ratcliffe's words, it is a strategy she employs in her "critiques of language" (4).[12] In "On Women's Mass Education," a treatise published in 1928, Lu Yin critiques the Confucian classics and the feudal cult of womanhood that perpetuated the feudal codes of proper feminine conduct. Lu Yin opens her first section with these words:

> In China, due to the old customs and prejudice, people have believed that *"nüzi wu cai bian shi de"* [lack of talent and learning is a credit to a woman's virtue]. Once this prejudice against women was rooted in the culture, women simply lost any opportunities and wishes to be educated, which has turned the society into an abnormal state. (2)

The traditional Confucian ideal of womanhood is that a woman should practice *nüde* (women's virtue), which includes chastity and physical confinement but excludes learning and intellectual pursuits. The saying *"nüzi wu cai bian shi de"* (lack of talent and learning is a credit to a woman's virtue) is a case in point. Hence, the traditional ideal of womanhood excluded most women from writing and other culture-making activities. Lu Yin views the feudal cult of womanhood as the root of the oppression and dehumanization of women. By associating *"nüzi wu cai bian shi de"* with the negative word "prejudice," Lu Yin uses redefining to negate the traditional ideals of womanhood and reveals that the patriarchal discourse invaded people's consciousness so much so that women even lost their wishes to be educated. This situation, obviously, paralyzed the society. Therefore, it is essential to develop women's mass education in the country so as to raise women's consciousness and enable them to liberate themselves.

Lu Yin also uses redefining to critique the old lifestyles sustained by the gender-biased discourse. For instance, Lu Yin takes on the problem of women's lack of education and women's needs most extensively in the first section of the essay. She details three types of lives experienced by women from different social and economic backgrounds: "parasitic lives" of women from wealthy families who depend on fathers and husbands for a living, "monotonous lives" of middle-class women who live only to take care of their husbands and children, and "miserable lives" of women from poor families who have to worry about food and drink on top of doing all kinds of chores. Lu Yin delves into this problem and laments:

> In today's society, although neither men nor women should ignore familial life, they should value social life as well. . . . But in reality most women, Chinese women in particular, only attend to family life. Bound by old rites and customs, women are separated from the society. It seems that the various social activities have been designed specially for men. Hence, the only life a woman has is to do trivial and tedious housework and become a child-bearing *jixie* [machine], and a *nupu* [slave] of the husband. Meanwhile, men wield economic power and have the authority to *nushi* [enslave] women. Under this condition, many women have lived a dull, miserable, and meaningless life. (10)

Lu Yin points out that such a life is pointless and valueless no matter what kind of family background a woman comes from. Phrases such as "a child-bearing *jixie*" and "a *nupu* of the husband" are used to redefine women's lifestyles, which attach to women's traditional roles a negative meaning and create a strong emotional appeal among the audience. This redefining is essential to envisioning a new life, a life different from the past. In this section Lu Yin uses the same strategy twice to castigate old maxims handed down from the Confucian classics, such as *"nan zhi wai, nü zhi nei"* (Men's stage is in the society; women's stage is within the household). While these sayings might at first seem innocent, Lu Yin thinks that their damage to people's, especially women's, consciousness could be significant and sustained.

Another feminist essay that illustrates Lu Yin's use of redefining to challenge traditional ethical codes and define women's new life is "Huaping Shidai" (The Age of Flower Vases). Lu Yin writes in a highly sarcastic tone:

> We have to thank heaven for showing mercy and moving arrogant and self-respected men to lift their hands and release women from slavery. The so-called modern women can feel complacent in *huaping shidai* [the age of flower vases]. Although flower vases are only a plaything, compared with being locked behind a door as a broom or as a machine to satisfy men's sexual desire and produce children, being a flower vase is not unsatisfactory. (373)

In this essay, Lu Yin uses the metaphor "flower vases" to describe the status quo Chinese women were put into in a patriarchal society.[13] The flower vase metaphor is another form of redefining—an association of the negative connotation of a Chinese phrase with what was valued in a patriarchal society. Here, Lu Yin proposes a further step in the Chinese women's movement, that women should emancipate themselves. Lu Yin uses flower vases to refer to some middle-class women who were happy to attach themselves to men without seeking real independence. She notes that many middle-class women were considered as little more than beautiful decorations for the workplace, rather than as men's equal. By employing flower vases as the controlling metaphor, Lu Yin criticizes those *xinnüxing* (new women) who were relying on men to gain liberation. Lu Yin does not hold naïve beliefs about men's gesture of liberating women, but rather reveals the insidious implications of patriarchy—a power that penetrates into both men's and women's lives. As a beautiful but ornamental plaything, the image of flower vases points sharply to the reality women from different social backgrounds had to face in the process of women's liberation: in order to achieve real gender equality, women must transcend illusions and fantasies and liberate themselves. Here, Lu Yin creatively uses redefining to critique the oppressive patriarchal social norms and encourage women to become their own emancipator. A decision to "break the age of flower vases" implies a rebellion against the patriarchal norms, norms that could be maintained through sexist social structures and sexist language and discourse (374). The flower vase metaphor and two other metaphors—"a broom" and "a machine"—paint a vivid picture of women's life in a society in which women were oppressed by the feudal ethical codes. The language Lu Yin uses here demonstrates her constant endeavor to critique the patriarchal discourse and establish a new discourse that claims women's rights and needs in a modern society.

Because language is crucial in forming and maintaining gender relationship, language is also important to transforming the old gender relationship into a new one. *Renquan* (the rights of human beings), *duli renge* (independent character), *nannü pingdeng* (equality between men and women), *huifu nüquan* (recover women's rights), *nüxuesheng* (women students), *xinnüxing* (new woman), and others—all these new terms and phrases empowered Chinese women in this historical period and provided them with a new language to reexamine women's lives. Using this new language entails using concepts or terms modified from the translations of Western feminist texts. As a rhetorical strategy, it provided Lu Yin with a new language to critique the old traditional culture and construct a new culture.

Lu Yin uses the new language to define what the term "modern women" means and what they need in a modern society. In the conclusion of "On Women's Mass Education," Lu Yin envisions the development of women's education and women's future. She writes:

> If this plan comes true, women who have bowed their heads and begged for pity for over four thousand years will leap from their subordinated position and become *duli de "ren"* [independent human beings]. . . . After we develop women's mass education, women will be able to realize their *renge* (personality) and responsibility; they will work with men to build a healthy society based on the cooperation of both sexes. (25)

In this passage phrases such as "leap from their subordinated position and become independent human beings" and "build a healthy society based on the cooperation of both sexes" depict for men as well as women a prospect of a modern society based on gender equity. Like men, women should participate in various cultural and political activities. The reason why women have no opportunities is that men almost monopolize the social political arena and that the majority of women are not prepared for such activities due to their lack of literacy. Therefore, what modern women in this country need is the ability to attain all kinds of opportunities to improve their life. The new language Lu Yin used in her writing helped women of her day to establish their new identity and claim the legitimacy of their need in a modern society.

This tendency to use new terms and phrases to depict that which constitutes women's life in a modern society can be found in Lu Yin's other feminist essays. In "Jinhou funü de chulu" (Women's Opportunity in the Future), in response to the call for women to go back to the household, Lu Yin refuted the conservatives, noting:

> [M]any educators holding a patriarchal attitude fear that once women have increased their ability and skills men will lose their privilege. Therefore, they do their best to persuade women from going to the society. . . . They put on women the label of "virtuous wife and good mother" and force women to go back to the household. (367)

Lu Yin again questions the traditional ideal of womanhood and boldly claims that such a label or image is part of the patriarchal conspiracy against women. She further analyzes the serious consequences of women being restricted in the household. At the end of the essay, Lu Yin points out a road for her countrywomen: "The fundamental way out for women lies in breaking the boundary of the household, going to the society, leaving *kuilei zhijia* (the doll's house), and living a real human life. A woman should not only live as a woman, but also as a human being—this is my sole viewpoint" (369).[14] Phrases such as "breaking the boundary of the household" and "leaving the doll's house" are fresh as well as powerful in defining women's future in a modern society. In the latter Lu Yin alludes to Ibsen's play *A Doll's House* and uses *"kuilei zhijia"*—a Chinese version of the "doll's house"—to critique the old family system perpetuated by the feudal ethical codes. In a sense, this new language opened up a vision of a new life, a life beyond the gender boundary.

Influences and Implications: Conclusion

In articulating a feminist rhetoric, Lu Yin illuminates for us a period of renovation in Chinese rhetorical history, a period distinguished by the import of Western thoughts, the rise of women's schools and coeducation, and, later, women's movement into the professions. Despite the denigration of Lu Yin's work by critics during this era, she and other modern women writers experimented and started practices that remain influential as we move into the twenty-first century. We can, for instance, recognize the rhetoric and ideology of modernity in the improvement of women's social position and the rise of new generations of women writers: namely, a discursive practice that resists and disarms hostility in conservatives and permeates everyday Chinese life. The rhetoric in Lu Yin's feminist essays could be viewed as a way of creating a new public discourse that challenges deeply held cultural values.

My study of Lu Yin's feminist essays illustrates that her unique perspective of the world around her gave her rhetoric its own distinctive features. Her discourse in the May fourth period offers an awareness of gendered and culturally specific rhetorical concepts and strategies that can inform current studies of language, gender, and culture. Specifically, her adoption of the new genre of *zawen* and her rhetorical strategies (such as redefining old, traditional culture and using new terms and phrases translated from Western humanist and feminist concepts) enabled her to appeal to a large audience and inscribe women's power through literature. My reading of Lu Yin's *zawen* also indicates that creative modifications of rhetorical modes from another culture can enrich the repertoire of the rhetors in a given culture. Studies of the rhetorical practices and concepts of another culture can provide rhetors with a perspective outside of their native culture and enable them to critically view and possibly revise their own tradition. Thus, a rhetorical encounter between two cultures does not necessarily weaken or cause the demise of a culture; instead, such a clash can empower and strengthen a culture that is caught in an unfavorable position in power relations.

Notes

[1] On May 4, 1919, students in Beijing demonstrated in protest against the Chinese government's humiliating policy toward Japan. There resulted a series of strikes and associated events amounting to a social ferment and an intellectual revolution. This rising tide was soon dubbed by the students the May fourth movement, a term that acquired a broader meaning in later years.

[2] *Xinnüxing* (new women), one of many new phrases created in the May fourth movement, referred to educated young women who often came from middle- or upper-class family backgrounds. In 1926, a journal named *Xingnuxing* was published as a sequel to *Funu Zazhi* (The Ladies' Journal), which hosted discussions of love, marriage, sexuality, and other topics on gender and women's issues.

[3] The passages quoted from the original works in this paper are translated into English by me unless noted otherwise.

[4] Wenxue yanjiu hui (Literary Research Association), 1920–1932—one of the most important literary groups in modern China, founded by Zhou Zuoren, Zheng Zhenduo, Ye Shengtao, and Mao Dun, among others. The association advocated realism and humanism in literature, viewing writing as a form of engagement with life and society. Their manifesto criticized the stale moralizing of traditional Chinese literature as well as the "frivolous" attitude of Mandarin Ducks and Butterfly fiction. Among the literary journals founded by this group were *Xiaoshuo Yuebao* (Fiction Monthly) and *Wenxue zhoubao* (Literature Weekly)—many of the best-known Chinese modern writers published in these journals. For a detailed discussion of the Literary Research Association, see Tang, Tao. *Zhongguo xiandai wenxue shi* (History of Modern Chinese Literature). Beijing: Renmin wenxue chubanshe, 1987. 56–67.

[5] *Sanwen* (the essay) is a traditional literary genre in China. Before the May fourth era, the traditional essayists represented by *Tongcheng* school attended to strict rules in organization and diction; as a result, even though their prose was elegant and concise, it was lacking in the writer's individual personality. During the May fourth period, *zawen* (the argumentative essay) as a new vernacular literary genre and a special type of *sanwen* was first experimented and adopted by the new intellectuals to argue against the conservatives and promote the new culture. Lu Yin and other women writers all composed *zawen* to express their opinions on various social issues.

[6] By "new public discourse" I mean the kind of discourse encompassing speeches, essays, letters, short stories, and other genres employed in the early twentieth century in China; a discourse that was preoccupied with critiquing the old, traditional culture and advocating a new culture informed by various Western ideological principles; and that opposed the classical written form and advocated the vernacular.

[7] In this essay, modernity refers to a cluster of notions such as progress, newness, enlightenment, science, democracy, and gender equality that Chinese new intellectuals employed in cultural transformation in response to a specific historical context of imperialism and domestic social crisis. For a detailed discussion of modernity in the Chinese social context, see Leo Ou-fan Lee, "In Search of Modernity: Some Reflections on a New Mode of Consciousness in Twentieth-Century Chinese History and Literature." *Ideas Across Cultures: Essays on Chinese Thought in Honor of Benjamin I. Schwartz.* Ed. Paul Cohen and Merle Goldman. Cambridge, MA: Council on East Asian Studies, Harvard University, 1990, 109–35.

[8] Lloyd Bitzer's essay "The Rhetorical Situation" lays a useful foundation for discussing the rhetorical situation. Bitzer, Lloyd. "The Rhetorical Situation." *Philosophy and Rhetoric* 1 (1968): 1–14. As Roxanne Mountford notes, Bitzer's definition of the rhetorical situation was criticized by Vatz in 1973 for ignoring the rhetor's interpretation and subjective point of view, but has been extended by such scholars as Larson, Consigny, Davie, Jamieson, Hunsacker and Smith, Biesecker, Garret and Xiao, and Gorrell. Mountford, Roxanne. "On Gender and Rhetorical Space." *Rhetoric Society Quarterly* 31.1 (2001): 41–71. It is presented as a standard category of rhetorical analysis in Crowley, Sharon. *Ancient Rhetoric for Contemporary Students.* New York: Macmillan, 1999.

[9] Hu Shi, born in Shanghai, studied Chinese classics in his childhood but attended Western-style secondary schools in China. Later Hu received a BA from Cornell University and did his graduate work with the philosopher John Dewey at Columbia University. In 1917, Hu became a faculty member at Beijing University, where he coedited the influential journals *Xin Qingnian* (New Youth) and *Xingqi Pinglun* (Weekly Review). He was a leading advocate of the new culture movement and the vernacularization of Chinese language and literature.

[10] According to the feminist historian Karen Offen, the term "feminism" spread from Europe to North America and Asia in the early twentieth century. See Offen, Karen M. *European Feminisms: 1700–1950: A Political History.* Stanford, CA: Stanford University P, 2000. The term "feminism" did not appear in Chinese until the May fourth era when the new intellectuals translated feminist texts from Europe, the United States, and Japan. As the historian Wang Zeng observes, in the May fourth period, several Chinese terms—*nüzizhuyi, nüquanzhuyi,* and *funüzhuyi*—were used by Chinese writers to refer to feminism. Wang, Zheng. *Women in the Chinese Enlightenment: Oral and Textual Histories.* Berkeley: U of California P, 1999. Since *nüquan* (women's rights) had been used to denote Euro-American women's movements before the term "feminism" was introduced to China, and also women's rights were the major concern in the Chinese women's emancipation movements, *nüquanzhuyi* was more frequently used during the May fourth period. Without *zhuyi* (-ism), *nüquan* could mean both "women's rights" and "feminism" (7–8).

[11] For a detailed discussion of liberal feminism, see Chris Beasley, *What Is Feminism?* London: Sage, 1999.

[12] I draw on Western feminist rhetorician Krista Ratcliffe's work on Anglo-American women writers and employ methodologies such as rereading and extrapolation to recover Lu Yin's contributions to the Chinese rhetorical tradition.

[13] In Chinese, *"huaping"* (flower vase) has a connotation of being beautiful but useless and unpractical.

[14] Lu Yin was influenced by Ibsen, whose play *A Doll's House* engaged many Chinese new women to break through the restrictions of the old family system in the May fourth period.

Bibliography

Chow, Tse-tsung. *The May Fourth Movement.* Cambridge, MA: Harvard UP, 1974.

Eide, Elisabeth. *China's Ibsen: From Ibsen to Ibsenism.* London: Curzon P, 1987.

He, Yubo. *Zhongguo xiandai nu zhuojia* (Modern Chinese Women Writers). Shanghai: Fuxing shuju, 1925.

Hu, Shi. *Hu Shi jiangyanlu* (Speeches of Hu Shi). Ed. Du Chenhe, Han Rongfang, and Geng Laijin. Shijiazhuang: Hebei renmin chubanshe, 1999.

Lan, Hua R., and Vanessa L. Fong, ed. *Women in Republican China.* Armonk: M. E. Sharpe, 1999.

Lin, Weimin, ed. *Haibin guren—Lu Yin* (Seaside Friend—Lu Yin). Beijing: Renmin wenxue chubanshe, 2001.

Lu, Yin. "Huaping shidai" (The Age of Flower Vases). *Zhongguo xiandai baijia—Lu Yin daibiaozuo* (Modern Chinese Writers—Lu Yin's Masterpieces). Ed. Dai Jinhua. Beijing: Huaxia chubanshe, 1998.

———. "Jinhou funu de chulu" (Women's Opportunity in the Future). *Lu Yin Xuanji* (Selected Works of Lu Yin). Tianjin: Baihua wenyi chubanshe, 1983.

———. *Lu Yin zizhuan* (Lu Yin's Autobiography). Shanghai: Shanghai diyi chubanshe, 1934.

———. *Lun funu pinmin jiaoyu* (On Women's Mass Education). Shanghai: Shangwu chubanshe, 1928.

Mao, Dun. "Lu Yin lun" (On Lu Yin). *Mao Dun lun chuangzuo* (Mao Dun's Work on Creative Writing). Shanghai: Shanghai wenyi chubanshe, 1980.

Qian, Xingcun. *Dangdai Zhonguo nuzuojia lun* (On Contemporary Chinese Women Writers). Shanghai: Shanghai guanghua shuju, 1933.

Ratcliffe, Krista. *Anglo-American Feminist Challenges to the Rhetorical Traditions: Virginia Woolf, Mary Daly, Adrienne Rich.* Carbondale: Southern Illinois UP, 1996.

Shi, Pingmei. "Gei Lu Yin" (To Lu Yin). *Shijie Ribao—Qiangwei Zhoukan* (World Daily—Wild Rose Weekly), No. 9, 1927.

Su, Yuelin. "Guanyu Lu Yin de Huiyi" (Some Reminiscences of Lu Yin). *Wenxue* (Literature) 3.2 (1934).

———. "*Haibin guren* de zuozhe Lu Yin nushi" (The Author of "Seaside Friend"—Ms. Lu Yin). *Haibin guren—Lu Yin.* Ed. Lin Weimin. Beijing: Renming wenxue chubanshe, 2001.

Zhang, Yanyun. *Chunhua qiuyue* (The Spring Flowers and the Autumn Moon). Beijing: Renmin wenxue chubanshe, 2002.

PART VIII

Rhetorical Pedagogy

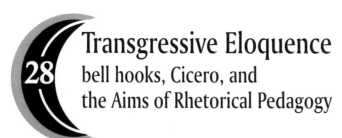

Transgressive Eloquence
bell hooks, Cicero, and the Aims of Rhetorical Pedagogy

Antonio Raul de Velasco

In this paper, I want to discuss a few links between Cicero and the contemporary critical theorist bell hooks. Specifically, I want to use these disparate figures in order to explore the basic aims of rhetorical pedagogy. In my own teaching these aims have come to seem vague and, at times, uninspiring; I am searching for a more coherent and provocative vision of what exactly it is that I do and who it is that I am trying to reach.

I came to these concerns about a year ago as I transitioned out of graduate school and into my current job at the University of Memphis. At about that time, I began to read *Teaching to Transgress* by bell hooks, a moving book in which she offers a series of essays centered on her vision of "education as the practice of freedom." Although I'd read other works of "critical pedagogy" in graduate school, reading hooks last summer hit me in a totally different way. Hooks made me reflect on a basic question that Cicero himself tried to answer on many occasions: What good does the teaching of rhetoric do? Rhetoricians are, of course, armed with an array of stock answers to this question, most of which cluster around the virtues of civic engagement, public speaking, deliberation, and the like. But lately, these stock answers haven't worked as well for me as before. Indeed, hooks's basic premise—that teaching can be a kind of liberatory and healing practice for students and professors alike—now seems to me a fresher and more sincere answer to the question of the "good" of rhetoric than any of those that rhetoric, as an informal discipline, typically offers.

Putting hooks and Cicero into conversation is no easy task. After all, what does a Roman orator and statesman who died more than 2,000 years ago have in common with a contemporary black intellectual who once wrote a critique of Madonna titled "Power to the Pussy"? Nevertheless, while the differences between these thinkers could not be clearer, they do complement each other in ways that have surprised and enlightened me.

In both *De oratore* and *Orator*, Cicero offers readers not merely handbooks in rhetoric, but a far more substantial, Isocratean defense of the ideal orator. As Thomas Conley says about *De oratore*, it is a work "in which the true dimensions of the notion of the 'good man skilled in speaking' are mapped and measured" (37). In today's parlance, Cicero was mapping and measuring the pedagogy of a rhetorical-political subjectivity for his time. Cicero strived to imagine and exemplify a kind of person and this striving led not only to greatness, but also to a horrific death. As we all know, after Cicero's enemies captured and dismembered him, Antony's wife Fulvia yanked his tongue from his severed head, and jabbed it repeatedly with a hairpin. The apocryphal tale of Cicero's gruesome end is appropriate, given the line in Book III of *De oratore* when Crassus laments Socrates' "reprehensible severance between the tongue and the brain, leading to our having one set of professors to teach us to think and another to teach us to speak" (61). That famous passage is telling in light of Fulvia's rage. For she was too mad to see that it was not that formidable tongue that threatened her any more. Rather, it was the synthetic vision that Cicero had of the ideal orator that would endure his own passing. More precisely, it was not the tongue of any single orator that mattered in the end. It was, instead, the multiplication and diversification of a kind of training that sought to transform docile and frightened human subjects into critical orators. In other words, subjects for whom rhetoric is not merely a set of words or thought formulas, but a way of being that directs one towards some kind of ideal fulfillment. This is a fulfillment that shuffles between an inwardly personal and outwardly political sense of freedom and possibility. It is a kind of self-actualization that sparks our embrace of the plenitudes and multiplicities that loom in public discourse. And it is here that a hinge point between bell hooks and Cicero appears.

For hooks, teaching to transgress requires believing that our work as teachers "is not merely to share information but to share in the intellectual and spiritual growth of our students" (14). Along these lines, she endorses what Paulo Freire called "conscientização." Conscientização is the coming to critical awareness of the social, political, and economic contradictions that make up our everyday lives. Teaching from this perspective, we invite students to transform their actual experiences in society into primary pedagogical topoi. And yet, more than simply exhorting students to question the conventions of class, race, sexuality, and gender that govern their lives, what hooks counsels is an attitude that integrates this mode of teaching and learning into a matrix of healing. On this count, transgressive questioning becomes covalent with becoming a complete and compassionate social being. Drawing from Thich Nhat Hanh's notion of "engaged Buddhism," she thus makes a connection between critical awareness, political action, and self-actualization. For hooks, in other words, the central objective of all teaching is to foster a lived experience of theorizing that extends beyond the classroom and that is always linked to processes of self and collective liberation.

Now, all of this talk about transgressing conventions and collective liberation seems decidedly un-Ciceronian, to be sure. But hooks and Cicero do have some mutual resonance, I believe, on this count: *They share a vision of political agency whose fulfillment arises from the rhetorical and ethical exigencies of our experience as individuals.* For them both, political theorizing is not simply integrated with political practice. It arises out of practice and is part and parcel of a certain relationship to what is deemed appropriate in the various social contexts of public life. In other words, Cicero and hooks both zero-in on that territory in which discourse, politics, and decorum all come together. And it is this overlapping concern that I find most inspiring for rhetorical education.

Cicero's notion of the ideal orator elevates decorum into a master term. Centralizing the capacity to ascertain and then act on what is appropriate (re)synthesizes the severance between the tongue and the brain. In this vision of eloquence, decorum becomes, as Robert Hariman points out, architectonically expanded into "the quality whereby speech and thought, wisdom and performance, art and morality, assertion and deference, and other elements of action intersect" (204). As Hariman puts it, decorum for Cicero "operates not merely as a set of rules but as the process of invention in the art of self-fashioning" in which "apprenticeship and reflection on political life" are vital (205). The concept of decorum, and its link to eloquence, would undergo several shifts after Cicero. Still, it is the dynamic combination of political, ethical, and personal dimensions of Ciceronian decorum that I find ironically fascinating in light of hooks's framing of transgression as the pedagogical-political linchpin of self-fulfillment.

For hooks, strong political agency is consistent with the capacity to interrogate the very terms of decorum. The primary sites for critical transgression entail those norms that designate when speech is appropriate, who is authorized to speak, what one should say, and how one should say it. We become free, as it were, when we start to loosen the fixity of these norms in our daily lives and are able to rebuild community around more fluid and democratic axes. The first step in this process is often called "critical awareness" by hooks; but she offers little in the way of counsel on the second step and, for me, not enough on how to make the first step—transgression itself—rhetorically effective (or even how to measure effectiveness at all).

In many regards, this incompleteness finds its reverse image in Cicero's notion of eloquence. For him, the orator's political agency is not, of course, consistent with the transgression of decorum. Rather, eloquence arises precisely from one's ability to grasp and exploit what is appropriate in a range of situations. And yet, in his work on rhetoric at least, Cicero places little priority on the politically performative defiance of what is historically deemed appropriate, on the possibility of cultivating indecorous eloquence as a political tactic or as an ethical obligation in cases when decorum precludes compassion and innovation. Like Cicero, one can easily imagine decorum as a contingent dimension of social coordination and consensus that we tinker with on the way to newer and better senses of "the proper." And yet, like hooks and many of her contemporaries, one can also imagine decorum as a stifling aspect of discourse, one that, more often than not, silences our most creative and benevolent impulses; the fear factor that pins your tongue to the bottom of your dry and anxious mouth.

But, of course, neither Cicero nor hooks wants us to hold our tongues. Both advise and exemplify a politically potent loquaciousness that springs from the recognition of a most powerful truth: How we enrich the self is always tied to how we negotiate the dominant political norms of our existence. My desire here has been to set the groundwork for a first glimpse into how from this truth, we might imagine some kind of a pedagogical vision for rhetoric. This is a vision that takes both hooks's prioritizing of transgression and Cicero's foregrounding of eloquence seriously.

On these grounds, the ideal rhetorical critic—that subject we aspire to become and to have our students become—would not simply be a skilled evaluator of texts. She would also be an eloquent transgressor of contexts, one whose highest calling would be to bridge the critical, antihegemonic aims of transgression with the inventive, aesthetic aims of classical eloquence. This explicit attention to the subjectivity of the rhetorical critic marks a return to rhetoric as a way of being and acting in the world, and not simply as a way of knowing language. Our task, as teachers, would therefore entail folding rhetorical knowledges and skills into a larger narrative of our students' self-discovery and growth.

In addition to these larger, abstract provisions, let me close by offering four concrete, though largely speculative, requisites for how training ourselves and our students in Ciceronian-hooksian transgressive eloquence could proceed. First, as I've already suggested, the goal of such training must always be the cultivation of an ideal subjectivity. Like Cicero and hooks (as well as, of course, thinkers such as Rousseau and John Dewey), we should see ourselves as moved to create a certain kind of person. Second, we must draw our textual examples with an attention to acute cases in which normativities are circulated and enforced in the lives of our students and ourselves—what I call "localized vectors of power." Whether it be in the home, the school, the workplace, or whatever, students would be asked, as hooks says, to "interrogate habits of being" as a path of learning (43). Third, we must reincorporate decorum into rhetorical training through declamatory practices based in an expanded notion of code switching. Though code switching is typically defined as a natural, mid-discourse alteration in language (for instance, into and out of Spanish and English), the emphasis in transgressive eloquence would be different. In practicing decorum, the key would be developing inventional strategies for bridging code conflicts and for articulating the political and ethical implications of conflicting rhetorical combinations of code and context. Finally, transgressive eloquence would entail aesthetic as well as critical criteria. It would be treated, that is, as a kind of political art that we practice in the interest of arousing and pleasing our listeners—and ideally our adversaries—and not simply for the sake of berating or defeating them as is often the case today.

These various provisions, of course, need further qualification. They are only tangentially Ciceronian, I must admit. Still, I am tempted to give Cicero the final word on this matter. Indeed, there is a passage from the start of the *Orator* that has stuck with me lately. Cicero says this to Brutus on the difficulty of delineating the properties of the great orator: "We must not despair of attaining the best, and in a noble undertaking that which is nearest to the best is great" (II. 6). It is seldom clear to me that teaching rhetoric today is a truly noble undertaking. And yet, perhaps trying to enrich and renew its basic purposes might at least get us closer to making it a more relevant and exciting one.

Works Cited

Cicero, Marcus Tullius. *De Oratore*. Books I–III. Trans. E. W. Sutton and H. Rackham. Cambridge, MA: Harvard UP, 1942.

———. *Orator*. Trans. H. Rackham. Cambridge, MA: Harvard UP, 1942.

Conley, Thomas. *Rhetoric in the European Tradition*. Chicago: University of Chicago Press, 1990.

Hariman, Robert. "Decorum." *Encyclopedia of Rhetoric*. Ed. Thomas O. Sloane. Oxford: Oxford UP, 2001.

hooks, bell. *Teaching to Transgress: Education as the Practice of Freedom*. New York: Routledge, 1994.

Arguing War and Facing the Other
Critical Pedagogy in the Post-9/11 Classroom

Kevin Kuswa and Briann Walsh

> The fundamental difficulty at present is that moral conviction and senti-
> ment have no channels of operation. Almost everyone is opposed to war
> in general.
>
> John Dewey (1923)

Teachers today spend so much time and effort teaching to prepackaged
tests and national standards that room for discussion and research over issues
like terrorism becomes essentially nonexistent. In an attempt to take stock of
the effects of 9/11 and the war on terrorism in the classroom, we find ourselves asking: Where do civics and citizenship fall into the curriculum? In
what type of classroom do teachers and students communicate on a similar
or secure emotional platform? Susan Giroux (2002) writes: "There seems to
be a growing interest in the rhetoric—if not the practice—of civic education,
or what it means to teach students to participate as citizens in the moral and
political life of a democracy" (p. 57). Questions surrounding education, citizenship, and democracy are proliferating wildly, but the changing context of
the world around us is difficult to introduce into the equation in a meaningful
way. If events such as the spread of nuclear weaponry, the globalization of
capital and finance, or even the hijacking of a commercial airliner can alter
the planet we all inhabit, then the unique effects of these events must also per-
colate into the classroom and vice versa.

Two of us, both as teachers and as students, have come together to pose a
series of questions involving terrorism, violence, and critical pedagogy. One
of us, having recently completed a fifteen-week student teaching experience
and now embarking on a career in education, found herself pondering particular issues surrounding the war on terrorism that could arise in the classroom. The other one of us, having just completed his first decade of teaching
rhetoric and argumentation, found himself concerned about issues of violence and terrorism that were not being addressed in the classroom at all. We
began to ask, for example: In the face of global disasters such as the 2004 tsu-
nami or the ongoing AIDS epidemic in Africa, how should teachers attempt
to communicate effectively in order to address the different reactions/
responses of students? How is education different during wartime? How does

a teacher create a classroom environment that supports clear communication and leaves room for the discussion of terrorism, global disaster, and even warfare in general? Has President George W. Bush's No Child Left Behind (NCLB) legislation addressed teachers' abilities to create an environment that challenges fear and blame? The idea of citizenship—how it is taught, what it means—advances the query: How does a teacher teach/role model citizenship while at the same time leave room for debate over those definitions? Teachers find themselves in a conundrum that involves the teaching of global citizenship and the appearance of being unpatriotic.

Toward unraveling the conundrum suffocating citizenship and pedagogy, this essay will move through three sections: a general introduction to critical pedagogy, a contextual assessment of education in an era of conflict and terrorism, and a quest for ethical foundations within a critical pedagogy that is positioned in history yet also aware of its antecedents. We will work through the contributions of some of the key scholars in contemporary education by way of laying out five tenets for a renewed critical pedagogy in an era of terror and security. The second section dives into the context and specificity of terrorism, counterterrorism, and the formation of new stereotypes, new geopolitical divisions, and an ever-evolving clash of cultures. How can the five tenets of critical pedagogy weave a tapestry capable of resisting the normalized constructions of patriotism that are attempting to deploy the forces of education under the signs of security and counterterrorism? If such a tapestry of resistance is possible, though, it may offer the precise opening sought after by more sophisticated bio-politics—pressures from the state that would co-opt critical pedagogy by reinforcing the production of a democratic citizenship rooted in eloquent communication (Greene, 2003).

The third section of the essay seeks a response to the seemingly intractable choice between education as overt social control and education as the velvet glove of democracy covering greater and greater injustices in the name of counterterrorism and national security. Our argument begins and ends from the position that practices of critical pedagogy mark an ethical site of struggle implicating responses to global violence and a polarized Other. A rigorous cartography of our current location in history must remain on the agenda, however, for the methods and practices of education are tied up in the knots of terrorism, security, and the tug-of-war between an American citizenship and the meaning of the West's Other. The stakes are nothing short of apocalyptic in that the underlying issue is how to address local and global strategies of fear, oppression, control, annihilation, and extermination. This essay concludes with hope for an open-ended, yet ethical, critical pedagogy that works to isolate and reject any "mediating rhetoric" (Zulaika & Douglass, 1996), particularly any mediating rhetoric that acts to distance and sterilize sincere and expressive engagements between selves and Others, between us and them. Such an ethical stance requires a genealogical method that retraces the present through past events that both define and distinguish our existing context. As a means of "arguing war" in the classroom, a broadly conceived critical pedagogy—a call to address emerging conceptions of citizenship and democracy with passionate skepticism—can encourage thinking actors capable of ethical rhetorical practice.

I. Critical Pedagogy

Simply to open up space in the classroom teachers are often faced with the risks of appearing unpatriotic and hence alienating students and parents. Is it possible to be a role model for all students, leaving room for ongoing dialogue and discussions in an environment that is now overrun with testing stemming from NCLB legislation, not to mention the challenges of reaching a student body in which television remains the paramount source of information and opinion formation? Supporters of NCLB maintain that standardized tests hold teachers accountable for how well they are teaching students, while opponents believe that standardized tests transform the classroom from a place of exploration and growth into a place of rudimentary regurgitation. In a more ideal setting, teachers would act as guides alongside students' subtle interactions with truth and the ability to make change. Critical pedagogy, as a method and a practice, opposes an environment wherein both teacher and student preexist one another as separate entities. Within this opposition to top-down learning, a number of alternative strategies have developed to facilitate a meaningful transition, step-by-step, from an educational process dominated by the logics of globalization and national security to one of understanding and nonviolent change.

While the view of education as the importing and exporting of information is becoming arcane in some quarters, the process is slow and it is often difficult for a new critical pedagogy to emerge that would fill the methodological void and preempt the state's deployment of education's potential. Paulo Freire (1990), a trailblazer in the field of critical pedagogy, maintains that education includes and moves beyond the notion of schooling. Freire and Henry Giroux (1985) note that education is a crucial site of struggle—a place where power and politics link together with desire and what it means to be human. Our experiences with rhetoric and communication have confirmed Giroux's link between education and the struggle for a particular future, linking certain paths of inquiry with certain professional tracks. Early on in the process of schooling, language and language skills become central to understanding the complexities of curricula and instruction. A large part of the elementary school curriculum focuses on the acquisition of language skills at the most basic level.

The significance of experiential learning rests on a conception of education as an ongoing process. The process should be distinct from "organization" and should move beyond problem-solution models of learning. Education takes place throughout the process of engagement, not exclusively at the moment a problem is resolved. Education intertwines with human curiosity and should be broadened to encompass the ever-shifting human dialogues with life. Adding to Freire, Elizabeth Ellsworth (1989) is a postmodern critical pedagogue who urges educators to teach their students to "name the world" as they experience it, hence taking control of their own lives. Taking control of a radical individuality allows momentary escapes from social normalization, urging a post or "counternormative" pedagogy.

Peter McLaren (1994) claims that critical pedagogy does not comprise a finite set of homogeneous ideas. It is more accurate to say that critical theorists are united in their efforts to empower the powerless and transform preexisting social inequalities and injustices. Rochelle Harris (2004) asserts that the goal of critical pedagogy is to have students take ownership of their own agency and become active participants in critiquing and transforming unjust social institutions. Critical educators and theorists strive to make the issues of voice and empowerment available to students, thereby enabling students to critique and transform themselves and unjust social institutions surrounding them. Thus, critical pedagogy offers a potential solution to challenges faced in today's classroom through opinion retrieving, citizenship, and social realization and transformation (2004).

As one of us embarks on a new journey into the field of education and the other struggles to continue to bring change to the classroom, we wonder if the idealism of critical pedagogy will outweigh its practical utility. Initially, it has become necessary to arrange the many elements of critical pedagogy into a loose collection of points of emphasis—goals and themes of education. Consequently, we have marked five tenets or pillars of critical pedagogy that, when used in conjunction with one another, summarize many of the ideals of this movement: cultural respect, an interdisciplinary nature, resistance to binaries and polarized categories, space for dissent, and critical-rational thinking as a cornerstone of democratic citizenship.

The first tenet of critical pedagogy comes out of the works of Paulo Freire, and at its core has three basic components—culture, difference, and tolerance regarding social classes and different races and ethnicities. Freire (1990) conceives of culture as everyday life, the whole range of human activity, and the discovery of differences and essential characteristics through everyday life. It is through these differences—these daily essences—that we live and understand. The second tenet of critical pedagogy is that critical pedagogy is radically interdisciplinary.

McLaren's (1994) work related to individual and societal empowerment informs the third tenet of critical pedagogy that education must call into question an "us versus them" mentality and the entrenchment of a polarized Other. School is often viewed in terms of being a holding pen for the community—a place where working parents drop off their children during the day and remain disengaged from the child's educational experience. If education is to succeed in expunging the idea of "a polarized Other" from learned belief structures, then education must be a holistic experience in which community, culture, and individual interpretations are considered and even challenged. By placing a lens on these items, teachers are able to show students why they hold certain interpretations, hence making for a more just and empowered individual. This third tenet of critical pedagogy calls for asymmetry in expunging the essences of self and Other.

The fourth tenet calls for critical space—a communicative opening that allows for deliberation and debate. Seeking such space, Susan Giroux (2002) argues that it is the task of radical educators, which she calls critical pedagogues, to secure "not only a space for free inquiry and dissent—especially in times of global crisis—but also the conditions for their own autonomy within the academy" (p. 87). Room for students to call into question long-standing traditions and beliefs, even societal conventions and global injustices, creates a process of critical education by developing a stronger sense of autonomy and empowerment. Educators must also perpetually strive for their own independence as a means of securing a critical space without hiding their own ideological agendas. This fourth tenet of critical pedagogy contends that education should create and support a space for students' questions about, and grievances with, long-standing societal constructs.

The fifth tenet of critical pedagogy concerns citizenship as it is taught and generated in schools. Encouraging independent and rational thinking is the cornerstone of a sound citizenry and rational thinking must be developed in students in order to ensure responsible citizenship. The five tenets of critical pedagogy: awareness of and respect for diversity, an interdisciplinary nature, the need to challenge a polarized Other, the creation and support of space for dissent and grievances, and rational and critical thinking as the cornerstones of responsible citizenship, all overlap as a site where progressive thinking intersects the need to question current educational policies. Teachers are not given enough freedom or equipped with enough tools to teach students to disagree with a textbook, to refute a lecture, or to generally think otherwise. Students need to develop an interactive sense of individuality in order to empower themselves to create necessary social change. This impasse in pedagogy has become even more severe when faced with the consequences of September 11th and a global war on terrorism. It is not hard to recognize that the moves to expand national testing and standardized evaluation are contrary to the goals of a critical pedagogy. Now we are beginning to recognize, as a new teacher and as an experienced critic of argument, that the long-term implications of this global war will magnify the importance of our educational practices, making moves for or against a rigorous critical pedagogy inextricably linked to the future of radical democracy and global citizenship.

II. Context and Conflict in Critical Pedagogy

The abstract project of outlining the five tenets of critical pedagogy, combined with the general call to implement such practices across the educational spectrum, desperately requires some specificity. What is unique about our present era? What heightens the need for a more rigorous critical pedagogy? This era—one of security and terror—was not ushered in by the events of September 11th, 2001 as much as it was marked by them. Authors like Jean Baudrillard (1983, 1994) and Noam Chomsky (1983, 1993) have been theorizing terrorism for decades, and perspectives on lawlessness, piracy, and organized crime stretch back centuries, if not further. Within late capitalism and the globalization of state-sponsored market expansion, geopolitical formations have continued to center themselves on enemy construction and their spheres of influence, often boiling down to opposing ideologies. American interests, often standing in for the "West," have fought against fascism, and then against communism, and now against terrorism. Allegiances and proxies shift back and forth over time, but the current war against terror, especially terrorism associated with radical Islamic groups, has clearly become a defining trait of "the times."

The events of September 11, 2001, do force a closer look at current educational policies because teachers are suddenly in the position of needing to discuss the tragic events of that day and its aftermath. In actuality, the climate of the classroom needed to be established in such a way so as to support discussions about terrorism before such an attack occurred. Without a doubt, terrorism is in the classroom and will continue to be a silent feature of a "repressed-patriot" form of student citizenship as long as the global war on terrorism is governing our space for criticism. This section will relate the five tenets of critical pedagogy to this "era of terrorism" as it affects our classrooms and our polity. Incorporating the five tenets of critical pedagogy in the classroom may be one effective tactic in the ideological war against violence and militarism. At the very least, students and teachers alike will be better equipped to deal with crisis as it occurs in the world.

Audrey Kirth Cronin (2003) discusses the difficulties in trying to define terrorism and responses to it. Cronin writes that terrorism is especially difficult to define because the term has "evolved and . . . because it is associated with an activity that is designed to be subjective" (p. 32). Cronin asserts that the targets of terrorism are not only, or even primarily, the victims who are killed or harmed in the attack. The secondary and perhaps more significant targets are "the governments, publics, or constituents among whom the terrorists hope to engender a reaction—such as fear, repulsion, intimidation, overreaction, or radicalization" (p. 32).[1] Terrorism is a matter of perception and can be interpreted differently, making rigid determinations of "us" and "them" even more pernicious.

The events of September 11th shocked the United States as well as the world. In the wake of the tragedy, U.S. citizens wanted answers regarding who was responsible for this act of terror as well as how something like this could happen on American soil. The idea that terrorists were (and are) residing in the United States heightened peoples' consciousness and suspicion of people of Middle Eastern descent. This suspicion, manifesting in violent ways, stretched to those who were law-abiding residents and were not connected to violent groups. If these generalizations remain unaddressed in the classroom, they will lead to unfounded prejudice and the belief that all people with a certain "look," or a certain ethnic background, or a certain religion, are terrorists and are somehow linked to indiscriminate violence. The tenet of critical pedagogy that calls for awareness of and respect for diversity is necessary to guide teachers in discussing culture and difference with students. The argument that cultural difference is what constitutes the strength of this country and that such differences rely on a vigilant tolerance needs to be both demanded and modeled in the classroom. The notion that critical and rational thinking is the cornerstone of citizenship adds new magnitude to the need for a widespread movement based on critical pedagogy. Students now need to develop critical and rational thinking skills in order to deal with acts of terrorism and counterterrorism so that society can come to the understanding that geopolitical factors are intimately connected and have counteracting effects.

After watching what happened to the Twin Towers and to our nation's capital on September 11th, we were all trying to comprehend why anyone would want to cause such horror and destruction to innocent civilians. Our attempts to understand, however, have been overwhelmed by a sense of vengeance and the constitution of a global "Other." How does a child come to understand the cause of Islamic militants, or the Taliban's or any other people's hatred for the United States? Instead of letting an instance like this pass by in the classroom, teachers should explicitly create a space for students to inquire about terrorism, tragedy, and crisis. Within this space, students should be allowed to disagree with the ideas set forth by others and come up with their own conclusions and interpretations based on their questions and hypotheses. Howard Stein (2003) maintains that many students' questions often go unasked and unanswered because "they do not correspond to official and popular narrative accounts, and to the group fantasy and cultural mythology they sustain" (p. 198). There must be a space in the classroom in which students feel free to ask questions and disagree with the causes and the implications of terrorism.[2]

Globalization leads to an increased awareness of other cultures, and students are often faced with the challenge of discerning who is good and who is evil. The Bush administration's response to the terrorist acts of September 11th is based on "not only a definition of U.S. interests but also on ideals which allowed that response to be framed as a struggle of good against evil" (Anderson, 2004, p. 305). How are students going to be able to discriminate between good and evil on grounds other than those that assume that people from the Middle East or of similar origin are evil and average Americans are good? In the days following September 11th, Bush stated that the perpetrators would be brought to justice, a statement that seemingly fell upon the shoulders of all Americans as a widespread effort to find terrorists and put a stop to their evil deeds. The United States' reaction seemed to mirror the days following the attack on Pearl Harbor—"Freedom has been violated" became the common theme (Stein, 2003). Alongside this national sentiment during World War II, the Supreme Court legitimized the detention and internment of thousands of Japanese Americans using "national security" as a justification in the *Korematsu* decision. Someone must be to blame for these violations of "our" freedom and retaliation is expected. The tenet of critical pedagogy that identifies and discards the polarized Other or the idea of "us versus them" is (and had been) crucial to developing a healthy and equitable framework for looking at the world and the peoples that reside in it.

Closely related to the tenet of the polarized Other is the theme of cultural awareness and respect. Living in a world that is so global in nature exposes us to a plethora of different peoples, nations, customs, and religious beliefs. These differences are built into a recurring paradox defining the American identity—the paradox of having migrated from elsewhere yet attempting to limit entrance to others who would do the same. In their essay entitled "We Want Americans Pure and Simple: Theodore Roosevelt and the Myth of Americanism," Dorsey and Harlow (2003) suggest: "The same culture that traced its beginnings from the colonization of the North American continent by foreign-born settlers also fights a recurring apprehension—if not outright fear—of immigrants" (p. 55). Associated with this nativist view of immigrants or people who don't "look American" is the widespread practice of shunning those who are different. Reinforced in school settings, children over time begin to look at other children who are different as bad. Dorsey and Harlow maintain that "public schools aggressively [seek] to acculturate and to assimilate immigrant children, using varied approaches such as discouraging students from speaking their parents' native language, to emphasizing the concepts of democracy and capitalism in school curricula" (p. 56). School settings often force students to take on a set of ideologies that contradict their own cultural standards.

How can democracy be practiced in a setting that forces children to act against difference, often difference that defines particular students? The classroom needs to become a place where different cultures are studied for more than a few weeks in a social studies unit; rather, cultures and differences need to be celebrated as the very fabric that makes America what it is. Individuals are being categorized by broad generalizations that breach overall respect for humanity. Critical citizenship is being disregarded for stereotypical thinking. Howard Stein (2003) writes:

> People died on that terrible day because people could not be recognized as people. They could only be recognized as symbols, embodiments, part objects. People were killed and people killed others because who and what they represented consumed their existence as distinct, differentiated, and integrated persons. (p. 198)

Teachers need to teach tolerance to students and vice versa in order for critical citizenship to emerge. For students to recognize injustices around them and have the tools and the drive to transform widespread societal inequity, tolerance is necessary. Students must be taught at an early age to look at people as more than extensions of a certain race or religious belief.

The implementation of critical pedagogy in the classroom is interdisciplinary wherein identity transcends content. Our era is identified by many scholars as one of globalization that spans across Westernization, secularization, democratization, consumerism, militarism, and the growth of capitalism (Cronin, 2003). Students are currently being exposed to many conflicting forces that challenge them to adopt sets of thinking skills that may clash with certain values, beliefs, and ideals. Cronin further asserts that "globalization . . . represents an onslaught to less privileged people in conservative cultures repelled by the fundamental changes that these forces are bringing" (p. 45). Moreover, analyzing terrorism as something disengaged from globalization is misleading because they are inextricably intertwined forces that characterize international security in the twenty-first century.

Currently, terrorism is being studied at "an uncomfortable intersection between disciplines unaccustomed to working together," including sociology, theology, psychology, economics, political science, international relations, anthropology, history, and law (Cronin, 2003, p. 57). By looking at terrorism as an extension of globalization, which infuses so many areas of academia and society, we begin to see that terrorism cannot be taught in a vacuum—it must be conceptualized as a direct and indirect result of the forces that are occurring in the current economic and political spheres, thus warranting the application of interdisciplinary approaches.

III. Genealogy and a Search for Ethics

Going beyond and within the five tenets of critical pedagogy, we must scour the intersection between our current era—or cluster of interlocking events—of terrorism and the history of education in the United States. What does education produce? What kinds of subject positions are generated by and through education in this country? Clearly the experiences of individual students are varied and diverse—perhaps so singular that we cannot make any pronouncements about a universalized critical pedagogy in the post-9/11 era. On the other hand, holding together the multiplicity of educational contexts and experiences—public or private, rural or urban, elementary or secondary, homogenous or diverse, and vocational or preparatory—is the concept of exchange or personal growth. Communication is inherent to education. We are all learning and teaching what the "we" itself is and what the "we" can be. We are all learning and teaching about our roles within the larger collective and within ourselves. The "we" is always in contention, yet always implicit.

Joseba Zulaika and William Douglass, authors of one of the most insightful and prophetic books on terrorism, *Terror and Taboo*, approached the topic from rhetorical and anthropological perspectives. Written primarily in the 1980s and updated in 1996, Zulaika and Douglass (1996) state that "this merging terrorism 'reality' appears to be already a blooming, self-fulfilling prophecy in the United States" (p. 233). They knew at the time that the outlook for the counterterrorism industry was "bullish" and that the term terrorism had been "enshrined . . . into late-twentieth-century global consciousness" (p. 233). Richard Clarke penned in 2005 that "today's loosely affiliated Islamic terrorist groups are part of a trend dating back to at least 1928, when the Muslim Brotherhood was founded to promote Islam and fight colonialism." The global arena is more than, or conceivably beyond, the new world disorder and post-cold war flux, for we can no longer depict our context without the omnipresent figure of terrorism. The associated question, then, is what ethical stance is mandated by the intensification of global security and global terror?

As Ashton B. Carter (2001) writes: "On September 11th, 2001, the post-Cold War security bubble finally burst" (p. 5). In one way, the cold war and the era of terrorism are inextricably linked in our country's history because many scholars argue that post-cold war complacency was one of the main reasons that the United States found itself so surprised by and unprepared for terrorism and the need for homeland security. In the same way that questions concerning violence, terrorism, and security now transcend the curriculum, so too does the necessity to involve genealogy—a critical history—as a practice connecting the five tenets of critical pedagogy.

Engaging the effects of the global war on terrorism in the classroom requires rethinking previous ideological and global conflict. In his essay entitled "The Politics of Cold War Culture," Tony Shaw (2001) claims that "all wars, especially cold wars, are fought in part through words and images" (p. 59). The words and images deployed during the cold war resulted in unparalleled psychological and cultural conflict.[3] Students during the cold war would have benefited from a broad employment of critical pedagogy inasmuch as they would have been better able to discern between justice and injustice as they applied to societal constructs during that time. The pervasiveness of "us" versus "them" links the cold war to a rigid division between East and West as distinct from, yet parallel to, the cultural and religious conflict between the Judeo-Christian and Muslim worlds. Perhaps during the cold war there was a clearer sense of "us" versus "them" because of the physical separation of the United States and the Soviet Union (Stein, 2003), but those divisions were also constructed and reinforced by the actions of both sides. These are the types of historical juxtapositions that can aid in the multidimensional practice of critical pedagogy. In the era of terrorism students are faced with much more ambiguity in terms of distinguishing between "us" and "them." Such ambiguity, a consequence of an unclear physical separation, leads to students resorting to racial, ethnic, and religious categorizations between groups of people in order to distinguish between "us" and "them" and between good and evil.

Overt and omnipresent, cold war propaganda infused all areas of life, including school textbooks and literature selected for school readings. Students were taught to believe that patriotism and citizenship required internalizing the belief systems of people in positions of authority and power, such as J. Edgar Hoover, director of the Federal Bureau of Investigation. Shaw (2001, p. 61) writes: "Was all culture, on both sides of the Cold War, merely an extension of politics? If so, how could this alter our perception of the conflict?" In his speech "outing" communists in the U.S. State Department given in February of 1950, Senator Joseph McCarthy questioned: "Can there be anyone here tonight who is so blind as to say that the war is not on . . . and will only end when the whole sorry mess of twisted warped thinkers are swept from the national scene so that we may have a new birth of national honesty and decency in government?"

The cold war did not give birth to the inculcation of an "us versus them" social dynamic any more than the openness of the 1960s and the civil rights movement gave birth to critical pedagogy. Arguing war and teaching alternatives to violence foreshadows the importance of critical pedagogy and its ability to adapt to new constraints and possibilities for citizenship. The missing piece in this intersection is provided by a champion of democracy during an earlier period of conflict, John Dewey. Few other figures of contemporary education so represent the tenets of critical pedagogy, particularly opening space for dissent and a concern for critical/rational citizenship. Beginning as early as 1916, John Dewey espoused the importance of imagining democracy as a form of communicative action (Greene, 2003). Dewey's uptake in argumentation studies (Greene, 2003) may fill in the gaps left open by the five tenets—the gaps involving economic exploitation, militarism and the security establishment, and violence as politics. In 1923, John Dewey advocated a stance against war. He literally lobbied for legislation to outlaw war, not to think "in terms of gradual approaches" or to emphasize "educating the moral sentiments of the people," but to unconditionally and unilaterally abolish the act of war.

Certainly the concept of abolishing war raises practical objections and intractable feasibility and verification. As a demand on and toward the state, demonizing war may offer a sensitizing solution well-suited to the goals of critical pedagogy. As a response to the need for specificity, turning back to Dewey does more than reintroduce protest as a cornerstone of democracy, it also joins theory with practice and positions critical thinking as the vanguard of a new and unmediated trajectory of citizenship. Here is how Dewey (1923) defends a "plan of outlawing war" by gesturing to the potential of not only thinking outside the box, but of cutting different lines along uncharted angles:

> The reasons, however, are psychological rather than practical or logical. We have been thinking for a long time along other lines. The scheme seems too simple and too thorough-going. It seems almost like a trick, a magic wand. . . . The new plan moves along different lines. It is not opposed to the others, but it does cut across them. It attacks the problem of war from a different angle.

Dewey's virtually utopian claims do come with their own risks—risks that threaten to derail the entire project of critical pedagogy. For the claim that educational practices must re-think the way in which the Other is conceived and approached in the classroom to be successful, such a claim must prevent itself from legitimizing the very system of normalization it attempts to critique.

Ronald Walter Greene (2003) addresses Dewey's appropriation by rhetorical studies for the purpose of generating an aesthetic-moral citizenship built on political reasoning, eloquence, and communicative action. Greene contends that Dewey's link between communication and democracy rests on a community that can "overcome the fragmentation of multiple publics" (p. 190). The risk, however, as Greene aptly notes here and elsewhere (Greene & Kuswa, 2002) in his meaningful warning, is that "the tendency to translate communication into an aesthetic-moral theory of eloquent citizenship puts argumentation studies to work for, rather than against, new forms of bio-political control." Paving over fragmentation often means homogenizing difference and sanitizing dissent. Is eloquence always at the service of radical democracy or can it also mask the machinations of an oppressive state apparatus? Even so, can we abandon the productive energies of the quest for a deliberating community? Might it be possible, instead of accepting the totalizing critique of education and packing up our toys, to combine the spirit of Dewey's call to outlaw war with his seasoned reflection on a democratic education? Again, the ethics of encountering the Other offers the best detour for assessing the space between communicative action and a more contextualized critical pedagogy. An ethical stance that forces a break with any mediating rhetoric may be the only way in which critical pedagogy can drive a wedge between cultural difference and cultural opposition.

Greene (2003) worries that a pedagogy infused with moral purpose and the conviction that communication can promote democracy will position education, in particular education involving communication and argumentation studies, "as a transcendental authority commanding the subject to speak" (p. 198). Critical pedagogy broadly, though, can partially avoid the state's attempt to use the education of communicative democracy as a way to propagate its own value structure. While on one hand the "speaking subject" is an inevitable outcome of the practices of critical pedagogy, subject-position need not be constituted as an authoritative agent of bio-political norms. Subject-position can inhabit a space of questioning—a reflective empowerment based on critical and rational thinking. Instead of allowing education to become a tool of Westernization, it becomes a process of displacement where mediating judgment is asymmetrically withdrawn and rejected. An ethical and rhetorical stance against the mediating ideologies that turn self and Other into "us versus them" is one that heeds Greene's encouragement of "harder work" by rhetorical scholars "to abandon the view of the eloquent citizen as a moral solution to the crisis of democracy" (p. 199).

Part of the defining characteristic of an era is the consistency of a mediating term between self and Other. A consistent mediating term such as the label "terrorists" to describe Muslims creates a homogenizing binary between self and Other. During the cold war, mediating concepts found ways to demonize communism and create a sense of fear that became the red scare or the fear of red spread. Red fear has slowly evolved into, and been replaced by, a different type of mediating term—a term that goes deeper to the core of insecurity, violence, and the interplay between symbolic and immediate action. The communist Other is now the insurgent, the detainee, the Islamic militant, or the terrorist suspect. But who is in and who is out? A struggle over what "we" means and how best to strengthen an identification with an American value structure is surging through the "global war on terror" and trickling down into all levels of education as another means to transmit and instill the "freedom" implied by the imperative for counterterrorism.

Zulaika and Douglass (1996) recognize that encounters with the Other take many forms, but they also contend that these forms represent significant locations for change: "Whether we turn the encounter into scholarship, inquisition, literature, aesthetics, or expertise, in the final analysis we are all struggling with truth while describing the Other" (p. 221). Despite the many limitations on academic interventions into the practice of education, let alone state-sponsored security policy, we remain committed to the possibilities of a contextualized critical pedagogy. Even if new means of teaching and learning about culture and difference do not translate into a less violent and more equitable world in the years to come, local or micropolitical challenges to intolerance are intrinsically worth pursuing. Pedagogy should be informed by an ethical stance "best captured by the exorbitant and asymmetrical responsibility toward the Other" (p. 221). An asymmetrical mandate requires suspicion—even a refusal—of a mediating term that describes the relations between self and Other prior to their interactions. This also necessitates a drive and desire to accept the Other's humanity "without mediation of a concept" (p. 221), without the resistance of "moral indignation" (p. 218), and without "ignoring our own implication with the violent actors" (p. 218).

Because terrorism has taken the role of representative alterity, a sign of the Other's descent into evil and violence, it is terrorism that must receive the next blow. A blow of expansive justice, living dialogue, and an unmediated embrace of the Other can help critical pedagogy emancipate our polarized productions of citizenship. "The relationship between politics and ethics in the present world is decided, at times emblematically, in the recreation and manipulation of terrorism" (Zulaika & Douglass, 1996, p. 219). Thus, even in a context where suspected terrorists are considered subhuman, evil, or otherwise worthy of extermination, critical pedagogy would still demand a face-to-face encounter without mediating descriptors—an encounter premised on a unconditional hospitality (Borradori, 2003) and a willingness to feel love for and as the Other (Hand, 1989). When confronted with events like 9/11, citizenship cannot collapse into a product produced by the educational system that serves to strengthen state control and legitimize an unquestioning patriotism. This risk of normalization, joined with previous periods of global conflict, simply points to the ongoing need to advocate critical pedagogy.

Conclusion

This essay has traversed three sections, one on critical pedagogy, one on the current context of terrorism, and one on the ethical call to rethink our conceptions of the Other. These sections narrate our desire to update the insights of critical pedagogy by rethinking the way the Other is conceived during times of conflict and the way these stereotypes contribute to a dangerously unthinking citizenship based on "us versus them" stereotypes. Most importantly, the emerging era of terrorism and security intensifies the importance of reinvigorating our educational priorities, striving to achieve tolerance for cultural difference, an interdisciplinary perspective, a critique of a polarized and preexisting Other, space for dissent, and citizenship built on critical and rational thinking. These five priorities of critical pedagogy come together under an ethical stance that would join Greene's (2003) critique of communicative democracy and Zulaika and Douglass's (1996) imperative for asymmetrical justice.

Terrorism is a crucial concept to think through as an object of teaching and learning, but so are its roots of unorthodox warfare and the creation of widespread fear. It is only appropriate to conclude by returning to John Dewey. In a passage that should humble the view that the present is always moving ahead of the past, Dewey (1923) speaks equally poignantly to educators and citizens in the 1920s as he does to us today:

> When wars were waged chiefly by governing classes and hired soldiers it was much easier to salve individual conscience. Under present conditions the moral dilemma is forced home to every civilian, man or woman. When war is a crime by the law of nations, conscience is on the side of the law of one's community and law is on the side of conscience. The warlike people will then be the non-patriotic and the criminals. The pacifist then becomes the active patriot-loyal citizen, instead of an objector, a nuisance and a menace, or a passive obstructionist. The appeasement of the world can never be brought about as long as the public conscience and public law remains at odds with each other.

We can take Dewey as a utopian messenger with a call to nowhere, but then we might miss the underlying call to link our political lives with our sense of morality. The bridge is citizenship, but it cannot hide behind the divisions enforced by nationalism and state competition. Education is uniquely global and local if intertwined with a critical and cultural sensibility to transverse the ongoing mediation of the Other. Teachers find themselves in a conundrum that involves the teaching of global citizenship and the appearance of being unpatriotic.

To continue the necessary resuscitation of citizenship and pedagogy, this essay has briefly introduced critical pedagogy in an era of conflict and terrorism. The aim has been to resist the normalized constructions of patriotism that are attempting to deploy the forces of education under the signs of security and counterterrorism. Our argument ends and begins from the position that practices of critical pedagogy mark an ethical site of struggle implicating responses to global violence and a polarized Other. Once again, the stakes are nothing short of apocalyptic in that the underlying issue is how to address local and global strategies of fear, oppression, control, annihilation, and extermination. An open-ended, yet ethical, critical pedagogy can work toward expressive engagements between selves and Others, between us and them. World war, cold war, globalization, war on poverty, war on drugs, terrorism, war on terror, us versus them, self versus Other—all events that require more than just schooling, but an ethical connection to teaching and learning that argues war to transcend it.

Notes

[1] "The term 'terror' was first used in 1795, when it was employed to describe a policy systematically used to protect the fledging French republic government against counterrevolutions" (Cronin, 2003, p. 34). Terrorism by its very nature has a political component. "It involves the commission of outrageous acts designed to precipitate political change . . . at its root, terrorism is about justice, or at least someone's perception of it" (p. 33). By adding perception to the mix, terrorism becomes a prism of ideas in which each facet needs to be questioned and considered in an effort to achieve understanding. In her essay entitled "Shock and Awe: Interpretations of the Events of September 11," Lisa Anderson (2004) examines a small sampling of the academic and political literature that appeared in the wake of the attacks in New York City and Washington, DC. Anderson asserts that "university-based academics are part of the problem . . . the vocabulary of justification for this militarism has long been provided on both sides of the Atlantic by those factory 'scholars' who have taken the humanity out of the study of nations and congealed it with a jargon that serves the dominant power." Too often students are taught to think mechanically in order to succeed on standardized tests and this style of education has specific effects—it produces a certain stagnancy and willingness to accept authority.

[2] The idea of the polarized Other, or "us versus them," becomes a central feature in the era of terrorism as messages of the enemy and George W. Bush's "axis of evil"—North Korea, Iraq, and Iran—inundate our media. The tenet of critical pedagogy that urges teachers to explicitly address the creation of an "us versus them" in the classroom deserves close attention. In a lecture presented at the University of Richmond in February 2004, Muqtedar Khan asserts the importance of finding a dominant global theme in order to gain a structural understanding of history. Indeed, we are living in a world that is now much more global in terms of economics, foreign policy, and national security.

[3] Shaw (2001) observed that "virtually everything from sport to ballet to comic books and space travel, assumed political significance and hence potentially could be deployed as a weapon to both shape opinion at home and to subvert societies abroad" (p. 59).

References

Anderson, L. (2004). Shock and awe: Interpretations of the events of September 11. *World Politics, 56,* 303–325.

Baudrillard, J. (1983). *Simulations.* New York: Semiotext.

Baudrillard, J. (1994). *The illusion of the end.* Chris Turner (Trans.). Palo Alto, CA: Stanford University Press.

Borradori, G. (2003). *Philosophy in a time of terror: Dialogues with Jürgen Habermas and Jacques Derrida.* Chicago: University of Chicago Press.

Carter, A. B. (2001). The architecture of government in the face of terrorism. *International Security, 26,* 5–23.

Chomsky, N. (1983). *The fateful triangle: The United States, Israel and the Palestinians.* Boston: South End Press.

Chomsky, N. (1993). *The prosperous few and the restless many.* Berkeley, CA: Odonian Press.

Clarke, Richard A. (2005, February 6). No returns. Why democracy won't mean less terrorism. *New York Times Magazine,* p. 20.

Cronin, A. K. (2003). Behind the curve: Globalization and international terrorism. *International Security, 27,* 30–58.

Dewey, J. (1923, April 25). American Committee for the Outlawry of War: If war were outlawed. *New Republic,* pp. 1–8.

Dorsey, L., & Harlow, R. (2003). We want Americans pure and simple: Theodore Roosevelt and the myth of Americanism. *Rhetoric & Public Affairs, 6,* 55–78.

Ellsworth, E. (1989). Why doesn't this feel empowering? Working through the repressive myths of critical pedagogy. *Harvard Educational Review, 59,* 297–324.

Freire, P. (1990). *Pedagogy of the oppressed.* New York: Continuum Press.

Freire, P., & Giroux, H. (1985). *The politics of education: Culture, power, and liberation.* South Hadley, MA: Bergin & Garvey.

Giroux, S. (2002). The post 9/11 university and the project of democracy. *Journal of Academic Communication, 11,* 57–89.

Greene, R. (2003). John Dewey's eloquent citizen: Communication, judgment, and postmodern capitalism. *Argumentation and Advocacy, 39,* 189–200.

Greene, R. W., & Kuswa, K. D. (2002, Fall) Governing Balkanization: Liberalism and the rhetorical production of citizenship in the United States. *Controversia, 1*(2), 16–33.

Hand, S. (1989). *The Levinas Reader.* Oxford: Basil Blackwell.

Harris, R. (2004). Encouraging emergent moments: The personal, critical, and rhetorical in the writing classroom. *Pedagogy, 4,* 401–418.

Khan, M. (2004). *Teaching in the era of terrorism.* Lecture given at the University of Richmond, February 2, 2004.

McCarthy, J. (1950). *Speech on communists in the State Department.* Retrieved March 14, 2005, from http://www.cnn.com/SPECIALS/cold.war/episodes/06/documents/mccarthy/

McLaren, P. (1994). Multiculturalism and the postmodern critique: Toward a pedagogy of resistance and transformation. In H. Giroux & P. McLaren (Eds.), *Between borders: Pedagogy and politics of cultural studies* (pp. 192–294). New York: Routledge Press.

Shaw, T. (2001). The politics of cold war culture. *Journal of Cold War Studies, 3,* 59–76.

Stein, H. (2003). Days of awe: September 11, 2001 and its cultural psychodynamics. *Journal for the Psychoanalysis of Culture & Society, 8,* 188–199.

Zulaika, J., & Douglass, W. (1996). *Terror and taboo: The follies, fables, and faces of terrorism.* New York: Routledge.

AFTERWORD

Remembering Wayne Booth

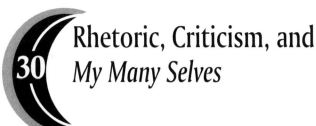

Rhetoric, Criticism, and My Many Selves

Gregory Clark

Wayne Booth finished revisions of this book, which he assigned to the genre of a "life," in March 2005, about the time he was diagnosed with the aggressive dementia that led to his death six months later. Two months earlier, in January, I was reading the manuscript for Utah State University Press and talking to Wayne about it on the phone. In those conversations he was uncharacteristically hurried, and responded to my suggestions for revisions with an abrupt: "I'll change it." I guess he knew.

A year and a half before that, Wayne and I had talked for awhile quite intimately at the ARS conference at Northwestern. We had talked like that occasionally over the last twenty years, sharing as we did the common cultural origin and experience that seemed to diminish our thirty-year difference in age. On that early autumn evening in Evanston we were talking about the joys and sorrows of faith and of fatherhood, and Wayne was listening as I told him about trying to find the faith to sustain me through some of my fatherly sorrows. When I mentioned an autobiographical sketch I had recently written and read at the request of my church group, he asked me to send him a copy. I did, and got this note in response:

> Oct 17, 2003
>
> Dear Greg,
>
> I find your account moving—though of course much too heavily loaded with LDS-influenced self-blame. You and I have been taught since day one that we gotta strive for perfection, and we've never yet made it.
>
> One way of putting that would be to say how much the persona of your talk differed from the one I felt I was meeting when we had our chat at Northwestern. Not that you were being dishonest in either moment, but that I did feel you blaming yourself too much in the speech. The man whom I "met" at NW at the reception, as we chatted privately, made me almost envious of the way he has coped with his various intellectual (and personal) problems. The man I "meet" in your talk sounds too much like—well, too much like me in my many self-blaming moments.
>
> Enough of that. I think you should write up your autobiography—but one trouble would be that to do it honestly you would have to report too many of the problems with the Church that led to your self-wrestling.

> In my autobio, which has just been turned down by the U. of C. editor,
> I have had to wrestle with the same problem: how much do I want to say
> about precisely what "faults" in the Church have led to my becoming a
> fringer? I surely don't want to disturb my many active-devout relatives . . .
> and so on.
>   Hope we can chat again sometime soon.
>
> Yr admirer,
> Wayne

I offer this bit of self-disclosure as a way into Wayne's book, *My Many Selves*. It is, of course, an autobiography. But he chose deliberately not to call it that. Rather, he called it a "life." Perhaps that is because it is a story of one man—a profoundly honest and eloquent man—working his way through and perhaps beyond what he described in his note to me as "self-blame." A life, it seems, is constituted of conflicts—conflicts of ideals and actions, of expectations and actualities, of hopes and of failures to realize them—and of the relationships that one attempts to nurture through those conflicts. *Writing* a life, it seems, then, is a project of, if not resolving those conflicts, at least understanding them and trying to work through them in ways that don't hurt and, perhaps, even help those one loves. And that, it seems to me, might serve as a usable description of what Wayne Booth understood rhetoric to be—a project of reducing if not resolving conflict toward the end of sustaining caring and constructive personal relationships.

I want to suggest that *My Many Selves* can be read as his culminating statement about rhetoric in the sense that it locates this essential rhetorical project—of reducing if not resolving conflict in order to sustain and nurture relationships with others—where it must, finally, both begin and end: within the self, or more accurately for Wayne as for most of us, in the interaction of our conflicting selves. Consequently, his subtitle: "The Quest for a Plausible Harmony."

Here is another way into *My Many Selves,* Wayne's final book, his description of its project:

> My hope for this LIFE is that, by revealing how my quite ordinary Selves
> have confronted—sometimes even battled with—one another, I can show
> how *all* lives, even the least colorful, not to mention *yours*, can be seen as
> dramatic in a sense quite different from the usual plot expectations. . . .
>   In short, instead of tracing my life chronologically from an undra-
> matic birth in 1921 to my scores of undramatic experiences yesterday . . .
> I hope to engage you into thinking hard about my conflicts of "Selves," of
> "Personae," of "Voices"—my "Splits" both deep and shallow—create
> another kind of drama: the quest for harmony, or chorus, among those
> splits. (xi–xii)
>   [Some] of us, old or young, some of the time—part of each day, part
> of each season, part of each year—discover, by conducting our internal
> disputes openly, the sheer fun of signing a treaty among the rival Selves
> or even settling on a genuine federal union of the rival states. Actually, by
> the end, as I've already hinted several times, I go even further toward har-
> mony. My discovery, as a Mormon missionary, of what I now call rhetor-

ology, has granted me . . . a splendid tool for conducting dialogue among
the split Selves.

My hope is that as you read along, or even skip along, you will discover how, by confronting the rivalry in your Voices, the quest can finally
prove to be worth it. (xiii–xiv)

My Many Selves is, then, a book with a mission. And for this good missionary, it is a fitting final book because, again, it brings his primary doctrine
home. That doctrine is what he took to calling "rhetorology," a term he
coined to describe what he considered to be the essential rhetorical act: the
"systematic probing for common ground" (*Rhetoric* 10–11). That home is the
self and the ongoing and unending project of composing from the conflict
and complexity that is the self what the *Oxford English Dictionary* describes in
its definition of integrity as "something undivided; an integral whole." It is
for that reason I think this book can be read as Wayne Booth's culminating
contribution to rhetorical studies.

Let's look again at the definition of rhetoric that Wayne presented in the
introduction to his *Modern Dogma and the Rhetoric of Assent.* "If philosophy is
defined as inquiry into certain truth," he wrote, "then what I pursue here is
not philosophy but rhetoric: the art of discovering warrantable beliefs and
improving those beliefs in shared discourse" (xiii). I have always read that
definition in the interpersonal context of ongoing rhetorical exchange, and
that's likely the context in which Wayne wrote it. But since reading *My Many
Selves* I have begun to read that definition differently, now in an *intra*personal
context, in reference to that highly personal and lifelong project of discovering within the self what beliefs and consequent actions might be put into
interpersonal practice. Indeed, a statement he made in his recent *The Rhetoric
of Rhetoric* suggests this reading:

What has been too often overlooked or understated in rhetorical studies
is that when our words and images remake our past, present, or future,
they also remake the personae of those of us who accept the new realities.
You and I are remade as we encounter the remakings. And that remaking
can either be beneficial or disastrous. (17)

In *My Many Selves,* Wayne exemplifies the project of attending closely to
that process of remaking. Indeed, it is this process that Wayne recounts as the
story of his life. Consequently, this is a story that brings the resources of rhetoric back from the public to the private, from the social to the self, reminding
us throughout that the rhetorical—understood as the project of improving
our beliefs by working with others through our differences and our problems—is, finally, first engaged in the primary work in which each of us is
engaged: the development and improvement and refinement of ourselves in
the context of our ongoing relationships with others for whom we care. That
is the way this book brings rhetoric home.

Let's return to the book that preceded this one, *The Rhetoric of Rhetoric,*
and his definition of "rhetoric" there as "the whole range of arts not only of

persuasion but also of producing or reducing misunderstanding." His preferred subset of those "arts" is what he called "listening-rhetoric," defined as "the whole range of communicative arts for reducing misunderstanding by paying full attention to opposing views." But his focus in that book as well as this one, and what he worked quite deliberately both to preach and to practice throughout his life, is that notion of "rhetorology," that "the deepest form of listening rhetoric: the systematic probing for common ground" (10–11), what I am calling Booth's doctrine. And in all of his work he sought to offer explanations (as well as exhortations) about how we might, as communicators or audiences, as writers or readers, work to reduce misunderstanding and conflict and find common ground. *My Many Selves* focuses finally on what may be the primary rhetorological project in which we are all each engaged: reducing misunderstanding, finding common ground, creating a kind of harmony and, finally, a sort of peace, within ourselves and those with whom we live. Rhetoric, that highly social, essentially political project, here becomes private and personal and primary, for it is from selves that societies must be made.

Booth's work in rhetoric and in rhetorical criticism of literature and life focuses on the project of sustaining and improving human relationships. And his work develops some of our best lessons about how to learn to live together better. A few years ago I was asked to write a reference essay synthesizing his work, and because Wayne liked the result, I will use some of my summarizing statements to review that work here. Here is one:

> Booth's body of work can be read as asserting and explaining his belief that to live well requires individuals to commit themselves deliberately to careful and critical communication of this sort—that, as he once put it, "talking together critically, really trying to be open and honest, is your best defense against misjudgment" ("Art and the Church" 25). His persistent concern throughout his work is to understand and explain how communicative encounters in general, and the encounter of writer and reader in particular, can be sustained in ways that enable people to progress. And Booth means *progress* in an ethical sense, for he does believe that living well requires people to learn to live well *together.* That is why, for him, ethical progress is necessarily a collaborative act. (Clark 49)

But that collaborative effort is built upon the efforts individuals exert in their relationships with others. And individuals are not, it turns out, all that individual (which is why he liked Bahktin). For Wayne, that realization was the beginning of his initial introduction to a rhetorical reality, the occasion for which was his experience as a young Mormon missionary in Chicago. To quote myself again:

> Daily he found himself trying to talk his way onto common ground with people whose worlds seemed incommensurable with his. That required, in his words, "having to 'translate,' hour by hour, what *I wanted to say* into *what I presumed could be heard*" (emphasis in original). And because of his own doubts about aspects of the doctrine he was teaching, the necessity of this constant translation engaged him in what he came later to under-

stand as the practice of rhetoric—experienced then and defined now as "the art of mediating between your own views and the world, the art of discovering in your circumstances what the possibilities for transformation are—including the possibilities for your own increased understanding." ("Three Unfinished Projects" 48) (Clark 50–51)

These possibilities for personal transformation, pursued with the conviction and courage that follows from nothing less than a lifelong leap of faith in the possibility of individual integrity and interpersonal harmony, constitute the personal project that was always the ground and the guide for Wayne's professional work. Indeed, as *My Many Selves* makes quite clear, that personal project is the fuel that powered his work in rhetoric and criticism. If we are going to live well together with others, if we are going to contribute to a reduction in our sphere of influence of the pain and the sorrow that follow from misunderstanding and conflict, his last lesson to us seems to be that we must attend with discipline and honesty and unrelenting effort rhetorologically (remember his definition of that term as "the systematic probing for common ground") to ourselves. We must each make ourselves the primary site of our work as "rhetorologists" who, in his words, persist at the practice of "rhetorology, pursuing common ground on the assumption—often disappointed—that disputants [particularly those that reside within ourselves] can be led into mutual understanding" (*The Rhetoric of Rhetoric* 11).

My Many Selves documents a life of such attention, a life of bringing the demanding critical project of rhetorology home to self-criticism, if not self-blame, in order to press forward despite the disappointments that follow the ongoing disputes that constitute the fractious self. Not that this attention to self is selfish. Rather, the practices of rhetoric and criticism that Wayne engages here are practices that involve some personal pain as the work proceeds to render the self more worthy of society. Remember what Wayne wrote to me: that, in his words, "You and I have been taught since day one that we gotta strive for perfection, and we've never yet made it." Well, that perfection we were not to strive for is not of a selfish sort. It is the intention of our attempt at perfection to make others' lives better. And, that, finally, is the consequence of the "plausible harmony" within the self that is, as this last book of his explains, the quest that was at the core of the life Wayne lived. This personal quest is messy, contradictory, confusing, compassionate, and honorable, and its progress makes possible the success of that interpersonal quest that he named as the subtitle of his next-to-last book, *The Rhetoric of Rhetoric: The Quest for Effective Communication.*

There were a number of memorial services held for Wayne Booth. I attended one of them, a Mormon funeral held just prior to his burial in a church near the place where he was born. I was honored to be asked by his family to read a poem at that service. Someone had brought it to read at the memorial service held in Chicago, and the family found it fitting and asked me to read it at home in Utah. It is Stephen Spender's poem:

I think continually of those who were truly great.
Who, from the womb, remembered the soul's history
Through corridors of light where the hours are suns
Endless and singing. Whose lovely ambition
Was that their lips, still touched with fire,
Should tell of the Spirit clothed from head to foot in song.
And who hoarded from the Spring branches
The desires falling across their bodies like blossoms.
What is precious is never to forget
The essential delight of the blood drawn from ageless springs
Breaking through rocks in worlds before our earth.
Never to deny its pleasure in the morning simple light
Nor its grave evening demand for love.
Never to allow gradually the traffic to smother
With noise and fog the flowering of the spirit.
Near the snow, near the sun, in the highest fields
See how these names are fêted by the waving grass
And by the streamers of white cloud
And whispers of wind in the listening sky.
The names of those who in their lives fought for life
Who wore at their hearts the fire's centre.
Born of the sun they traveled a short while towards the sun,
And left the vivid air signed with their honor.

If you knew him, or if you have read *My Many Selves*, you will recognize
Wayne in some of those lines, particularly those two, toward the end, that
talk about "the names of those who in their lives fought for life/Who wore at
their hearts the fire's centre." Like us, Wayne did his work and worked hard
to do it well. And he did it better than most of us. His work teaching us about
rhetoric and criticism is some of the most important of the last fifty years.
And it was work that was rooted in his life—in the things that troubled him,
and in the things for which he cared deeply. That is true for most of us, I
think, but I also think that Wayne might have managed to root that work far
more deeply than most of us are able, or willing, to. *My Many Selves* documents a lifetime of the most rigorous applications of rhetoric and criticism,
and some of the keenest of Booth's theorizations and critiques, to *himself*. It
documents his life as held accountable to the principles he would have prevail
in those who would constitute the sort of society he seeks. In his introduction
to *The Rhetoric of Rhetoric*, Wayne wrote this: "The quality of our lives, especially the ethical and communal quality, depends to an astonishing degree on
the quality of our rhetoric" (xii). In *My Many Selves*, the book that followed
his quest for effective communication with the narrative of his quest for plausible harmony, Wayne seemed to be saying that the quality of our rhetoric,
which is another way of saying the quality of our relationships, depends to an
astonishing degree on the quality of our lives. Wayne lived a life of immensely
high quality, ethically, communally, and, as *My Many Selves* shows, personally.
His was a life refined, publicly and privately, by rigorous and relentless rhetorical work, a life that stands for us as a model and example.

Works Cited

Booth, Wayne C. *Modern Dogma and the Rhetoric of Assent.* Chicago: U of Chicago P, 1974.

———. *My Many Selves: The Quest for a Plausible Harmony.* Logan: Utah State UP, 2006.

———. *The Rhetoric of Rhetoric: The Quest for Effective Communication.* Oxford: Blackwell, 2004.

Clark, Gregory. "Wayne C. Booth." *Twentieth-Century Rhetorics and Rhetoricians: Critical Studies and Sources.* Ed. Michael G. Moran and Michelle Ballif. Westport, CT: Greenwood P, 2000. 49–61.

Oxford English Dictionary. <http://www.oed.com>.

Spender, Stephen. *Collected Poems, 1928–1985.* London: Faber and Faber, 1985.

 Contributors

David C. Bailey is a doctoral candidate in the Department of Communication at Texas A&M University. His scholarship focuses on historical and contemporary presidential rhetoric, the intersection of religious and political rhetoric, and the interaction of rhetorical form and genre. He wishes to thank Jennifer R. Mercieca for insightful comments on an earlier draft of his essay.

Elizabeth Benacka is a Lecturer in Communication at Lake Forest College. She was the Assistant to the Conference Planning Coordinator for the 2006 Rhetoric Society of America biennial conference while completing her doctoral studies at Northwestern University.

Patricia Bizzell is Professor of English at the College of Holy Cross and was President of the Rhetoric Society of America in 2004–2005. Among her publications is *The Rhetorical Tradition: Readings from Classical Times to the Present,* coauthored with Bruce Herzberg, which received the National Council of Teachers of English Outstanding Book Award in 1992. Research for her paper in this volume was conducted in the Masters in Jewish Liberal Studies Program at Hebrew College.

Gregory Clark is Professor of English at Brigham Young University. Among other publications, he is the author of *Rhetorical Landscapes: Variations on a Theme from Kenneth Burke* (2004). From 2000 through 2007 he served as editor of *Rhetoric Society Quarterly.*

Lora Cohn is Assistant Professor of Communication Arts, Undergraduate Program Coordinator, and Director of the Master's Program in Communication and Leadership at Park University.

Ann Dobyns is Professor and Chair of the Department of English at the University of Denver. She is coauthor of *A Meeting of Minds: A Brief Rhetoric for Writers and Readers* (2nd ed., 2007) and *Literary Conversation: Thinking, Talking, and Writing about Literature* (1996), among other publications.

Kristie S. Fleckenstein is Associate Professor of English, Florida State University. At the time of the conference, she was Associate Professor of English at Ball State University. Among her publications is *Embodied Literacies: Imageword and a Poetics of Teaching,* which won the Outstanding Book of the Year Award from the Conference on College Composition and Communication in 2005. She thanks Nancy A. Myers for comments on early drafts of this essay.

Leslie Hahner is Assistant Professor of Communication at Truman State University. She is a recent doctoral graduate of the University of Iowa. She thanks Barbara Biesecker for her comments on earlier drafts.

Beth L. Hewett is an independent scholar, coeditor of *Kairos,* and a Professional Development Consultant with the National Council of Teachers of English. She recently completed a manuscript, *Teaching through Text: Conferencing with Students in Online Settings* and guest edited a special issue of *Technical Communication Quarterly*, among other publications. She thanks George Lengyel for inspiring her interest in contemporary eulogies and how classical rhetoric can contribute to an understanding of this genre.

Susan C. Jarratt is Professor of Comparative Literature at the University of California, Irvine, where she served as Campus Writing Coordinator from 2001 through 2006.

Lisa Keränen is Assistant Professor of Communication and faculty affiliate of the Center for Science and Technology Research, University of Colorado at Boulder. Her publications concern rhetoric of science, medical rhetoric, and bioethics. She serves on the Board of Directors of the Association for the Rhetoric of Science and Technology. She would like to thank Bryan Taylor, Karen Tracy, and members of UCB's interdisciplinary rhetoric workshop for their intellectual engagement with this essay.

Stephen A. Klien is Associate Professor of Speech Communication at Augustana College (Illinois).

Manfred Kraus is Akademischer Oberrat in the Department of Classics at the University of Tübingen, Germany. He serves on the Executive Council of the International Society for the History of Rhetoric and as Associate Editor of *Rhetorica*. He has published widely and lectured in many countries on the history of rhetoric. He thanks David Zarefsky and Michael Leff for the invitation to conduct the seminar on Aphthonius at the 2006 Rhetoric Society of America meeting and Lawrence D. Green for organizing that seminar.

Kevin Kuswa is Professor of Rhetoric and Communication Studies at the University of Richmond, where he also serves as Director of Debate. He has recently published on the relationship among terrorism, rhetoric, and cultural studies.

Christian Lundberg is Assistant Professor of Communication at the University of North Carolina, Chapel Hill. When he presented this paper, he was a doctoral candidate at Northwestern University. He received the Rhetoric Society of America's Charles W. Kneupper Award in 2006.

Steven Mailloux is Chancellor's Professor of Rhetoric, Professor of English, and Director of the Critical Theory Emphasis at the University of California, Irvine. His books include *Disciplinary Identities: Rhetorical Paths of English, Speech, and Composition* (2006), *Reception Histories: Rhetoric, Pragmatism, and American Cultural Politics* (1998), and *Rhetorical Power* (1989).

D. J. Mulloy is Assistant Professor of American History at Wilfrid Laurier University, Waterloo, Ontario, Canada. He is the author of *American Extremism: History, Politics, and the Militia Movement* (1994).

Lester C. Olson is Professor of Communication and Women's Studies, University of Pittsburgh. His award-winning books include *Benjamin Franklin's Vision of American Community: A Study in Rhetorical Iconology* (2004) and *Emblems of American Community in the Revolutionary Era* (1991).

Cezar M. Ornatowski is Associate Professor of Rhetoric and Writing Studies, San Diego State University.

Ellen Quandahl is Associate Professor of Rhetoric and Writing Studies at San Diego State University. Her publications include articles on ancient rhetoric, rhetorical theory and composition studies, and Kenneth Burke.

Frances J. Ranney is Associate Professor of English and Director of the Women's Studies Program at Wayne State University. She is the author of *Aristotle's Ethics and Legal Rhetoric: An Analysis of Language Beliefs and the Law* (2005).

Karen Rowe is a member of the Department of English at Bob Jones University. She thanks Sue Carter Wood for her insightful comments on an earlier draft.

Marc C. Santos is a doctoral candidate in Rhetoric and Composition at Purdue University. He is the coauthor of "Playing with Ourselves" and "Saving Ourselves," two articles addressing the postmodern psychoanalytic aspects of survival horror video games.

Inez Schaechterle is Assistant Professor of English, Buena Vista University (Iowa). Her essay is based on her dissertation, chaired by Sue Carter Wood. She received the Distinguished Dissertation Award from Bowling Green State University.

Barbara Schneider is Associate Professor of English at the University of Toledo.

J. Blake Scott is Associate Professor of English at the University of Central Florida, where he teaches rhetoric and technical communication. He is the author of *Risky Rhetoric: AIDS and the Cultural Practices of HIV Testing* and coeditor of *Critical Power Tools: Technical Communication and Cultural Studies.* He has received two research awards from the National Council of Teachers of English.

Craig R. Smith is Professor of Communication Studies at California State University, Long Beach. He is the author of *Rhetoric and Human Consciousness: A History.*

Karen Taylor is Assistant Professor of Communication at Tulane University. She thanks her audience at Los Alamos National Laboratory for their helpful questions on an earlier version of this essay.

Antonio Raul de Velasco is Assistant Professor of Rhetoric at the University of Memphis.

Lisa Storm Villadsen is Associate Professor in the Department of Media, Cognition, and Communication at the University of Copenhagen.

Briann Walsh graduated from the University of Richmond in 2005 with a bachelor's degree in rhetoric. She now teaches high school in North Carolina.

Bo Wang is Assistant Professor of English at California State University, Fresno. She teaches and researches rhetorical theory and criticism, comparative/ethnic rhetoric, women's rhetoric, and writing in multicultural spaces.

Kirt H. Wilson is Associate Professor and Director of Graduate Studies in the Department of Communication Studies, University of Minnesota. He is a McKnight Presidential Scholar and a recipient of the National Communication Association's Winans-Wichelns Award for his book *The Reconstruction Desegregation Debate.* He thanks David Zarefsky and Michael Leff for their support in the preparation and presentation of this essay.

Sue Carter Wood is Associate Professor of English at Bowling Green State University.

David Zarefsky is Owen L. Coon Professor of Communication Studies at Northwestern University. Two of his books received the National Communication Association's Winans-Wichelns Award: *President Johnson's War on Poverty: Rhetoric and History* (1986) and *Lincoln, Douglas, and Slavery: In the Crucible of Public Debate* (1990). He is a past president of the National Communication Association and is the 2006–2007 President of the Rhetoric Society of America.

Name Index

Abbott, D. P., 304
Adams, S., 154, 156
Addams, J., 339
Agapitos, P. A., 103
Agricola, R., 64
Alexander, C. L., 143
American Judicature Society, 143
Amuso, P., 142
Anderson, B., 355
Anderson, L., 404
Anderson, T., 275
Anzaldúa, G., 288
Aoki, E., 124
Aphthonius, 52, 54–57, 60, 62–65
Apter, D., 215
Apuleius, 71, 77–87
Aristotle, 72, 74, 82, 84, 91, 95, 142, 149, 176
Armada, B. J., 25, 28
Armstrong, D., 267
Arnheim, R., 130
Arnold, W. E., 275
Augustine, 77, 176, 298
Aune, J. A., 145
Austin, G. W., 142
Austin, J. L., 145, 375

Badiou, A., 15–16
Bailey, E. C., 143
Baker, A. C., 275
Balbus, J., 302
Ballotti, J., 184
Barbatsis, G. S., 123
Barratt, B., 234
Barthes, R., 130, 145
Bates, A. L., 335

Baudrillard, J., 130, 236, 403
Baym, N., 22
Beale, W. H., 375
Beals, M. P., 33–34
Beard, D., 238
Beck, U., 200, 234
Bellah, R. N., 316
Ben-Aryeh Debby, N., 302
Benjamin, W., 130, 145
Benson, T. W., 122, 125
Bercovitch, S., 316
Berelson, B., 207
Berger, J., 130
Bielinski, S., 358
Biesecker, B. A., 25, 123
Birdsell, D. S., 123
Black, E., 22, 35
Blair, C., 25, 28, 123
Blair, H., 296–297
Blair, J. A., 123
Blight, D. W., 24
Block, J., 276
Bonfini, A., 64
Booth, W., 145, 417–422
Borradori, G., 410
Bosmajian, H. A., 122
Boyer, P. S., 334–335, 337
Boyle, D., 238
Boyle, M. O., 41
Braden, W., 201
Breck, U., 208
Brinkley, A., 155
Brock, B. L., 128
Brouwer, D., 131
Browne, S., 22
Brownlee, J., 346
Brown-Scott, W., 143
Brumberger, E. R., 131

Brummett, B., 123, 236, 238
Bryant, D., 128
Buckler, G., 101
Bumiller, E., 20, 35
Burchard, A., 64
Burke, K., 17, 110–116, 118, 121–122, 130, 144, 177
Burstein, A., 22, 26, 30
Bush, G. H. W., 13
Butcher, H. C., 154

Caecilius, S., 84
Camelot, P. T., 289
Camerarius, J., 64
Campbell, G., 296–297
Campbell, K. K., 290
Campos, P. F., 146
Camus, A., 240
Canavesio, G., 305–306
Caplan, H., 298–299
Capote, T., 121
Carelli, R., 143
Carpenter, W. B., 305
Carrier, J., 24
Carruthers, M., 301
Carter, A. B., 407
Carter, J., 35–36
Catanaeus, 64
Catherine of Siena, Saint, 287–294
Cattaneo, G. M., 64
Chapman, M., 25–26, 30
Chappell, K., 20
Cherney, J. L., 127
Chertoff, M., 232
Chicago, J., 123
Chomsky, N., 11, 403
Choniates, N., 102

Christiansen, A., 121
Cicero, 71, 74–77, 82, 84, 92
Clark, D. L., 63–64
Clark, G., 121
Clark, J. K., 346
Clarke, L., 228, 233–234, 368
Clarke, R., 406
Clinton, W. J., 26–29, 214, 217
Cochrane, W. W., 153, 155–156
Cohen, A., 359
Colfax, G. N., 273
Comstock, A., 334–335, 339–340
Condit, C., 279–281
Conley, T. H., 101, 393
Connolly, C., 276
Connolly, W., 279
Connors, R., 296–297, 299
Connors, R. J., 52
Conti, N., 64
Cooke, L., 181
Cooper, R., 237
Copeland, L., 20–21
Corbett, P. J., 52
Cos, G. C., 143
Cowley, M., 110–111
Craddock, I., 327–329, 331
Cronin, A. K., 403, 406
Crowley, S., 14, 16, 52, 127, 277, 279
Curry, S. S., 338
Curti, M., 216–217
Czerwinski, K., 358

D'Angelo, F. J., 52–53, 296
D'Emilio, J., 326
D'Orso, M., 29
Danforth, J., 13
Danto, A., 123
Darrouzes, J., 104
Darwin, T. J., 127
Davis, D., 14
Davis, K. S., 154
Davis, T., 24
de Certeau, M., 292–293
de Lille, A., 299, 306
Decker, J. L., 31
DeGrazia, E., 335
DeLuca, K. M., 127
Demo, A., 121
Dennis, M. R., 93–94, 99

Denton, R. E., 193
Derrida, J., 9, 145, 256–257, 341–342, 373
Desmet, C., 52
Dewan, S., 20, 24–25, 35
Dewey, J., 398, 408–409, 411
Dickinson, G., 124
Dodge, J., 154
Donne, J., 49
Dorsey, L., 405
Douglass, F., 316
Douglass, W., 399, 406, 410–411
Doyle, R., 279
Dreyer, E. A., 288
Dunne, J., 149
Dyck, A. R., 103, 105–106

Edwards, J. L., 123–124, 130
Ehrenhaus, P., 127
Ehrenreich, B., 219
Eisenhower, D. D., 153–171
Ellicott, C. J., 305
Ellis, F. H., 346
Ellsworth, E., 401
Engber, D., 237
Erickson, C., 234
Evers, M., 24
Evers-Williams, M., 25
Eves, A., 123
Exner, M., 339–340, 344

Fanon, F., 216
Fantone, L., 271–272
Farr, C. K., 30
Fenno, F. H., 345
Finnegan, C. A., 123, 126, 129
Fish, S., 40, 145
Fisher, D. H., 364
Fleming, D., 123
Florescu, V., 61
Foner, E., 315, 320
Forsythe, D. P., 142
Foss, S. K., 123, 131
Foucault, M., 11, 17, 130, 145, 240, 268, 336, 344
Fox, V. C., 326
Fox Keller, E., 279
Frank, T., 174, 178
Frankopan, P., 101
Freedman, E. B., 326
Freehling, W., 314

Freire, P., 394, 401
Freud, S., 250, 252, 254–256
Friedenberg, R. V., 183
Friedlaender, D., 44, 50
Friedman, M., 258–259, 262
Fulton, R. I., 344
Futrell, J. W., 143

Gabor, T., 143
Gadamer, H.-G., 7
Gallagher, V., 25
Garnet, H. H., 322
Garret, L., 238
Garrison, W. L., 316, 322
Gaudet, H., 207
Geisel, T. S., 113
Geisler, C., 369
Gellner, E., 220
Genovese, M. A., 155
Gerberding, J., 276
Gill, M., 302–303
Giroux, H., 400
Giroux, S., 398, 402
Gladney, G. A., 181
Glenn, C., 101
Goldstein, A., 229
Goodman, B., 20
Goodrich, P., 147
Gorgias, 301
Gouma-Peterson, T., 101
Green, L., 63
Greene, R. W., 399, 408–409, 411
Gregg, R. B., 121–122
Griggs, E. H., 347
Griset, P. L., 143
Groarke, L., 123
Gronbeck, B., 125
Gross, L., 122
Gunn, J., 238, 369
Guttman, G., 142

Halloran, S. M., 176–177
Hand, S., 410
Haney, R. W., 335
Hanh, T. N., 394
Hanson, J., 121
Hansson, S., 53
Haraway, D. J., 279–281
Harbart, B., 64
Hariman, R., 124, 130–131, 336, 395
Harlow, B. N., 157–158
Harlow, R., 405

Harnett, S., 35
Harold, C. L., 127
Harrington, M., 275
Harris, R., 401
Harrold, S., 321–322
Hart, R. P., 181, 183, 197
Harter, L. M., 368
Hartnett, S. J., 22, 229
Hasian, M. A., 25, 123, 336
Haskins, E. V., 123
Hassett, M., 124
Hauser, G. A., 127, 363, 374
Hawhee, D., 52
Heath, M., 53–54, 56
Helmers, M., 128
Hendler, G., 25–26, 30
Herndl, C., 369
Hero, A. C., 104
Hill, B., 102–104
Hill, C. A., 128
Hing, B. O., 143
Hinks, P. P., 314, 322
Hodges, G., 347
Holmes, O. W., 145
hooks, b., 393–395
Hope, D. S., 121, 129
Horowitz, H. L., 334–335
Hu Shi, 381–382
Hubbard, B., 123
Hume, D., 25, 178
Hunger, H., 101
Hunt, W. H., 305–308

Isocrates, 74
Ivie, R., 14

Jamieson, K. H., 182
Japp, P. M., 368
Jasinski, J., 238
Jay, P., 110–111
Jefferson, T., 315
Jeffreys, E. M., 101
Jeppeson, M. S., 123
Johnson, B., 148
Johnston, A., 182–183
Joseph, L., 146–147
Jost, W., 41–42, 51
Jouvancy, J., 64
Jurek, M., 358–359

Kaid, L. L., 182–184
Kaplan, S., 123
Karcher, A. J., 143
Kearns, T., 147–149

Kennedy, G. A., 53–54, 59, 61, 101, 298
Kent, C., 201
Kent, M. L., 91–94, 99
Kenyon, F. G., 57
Keogh, W. J., 142
Kevelson, R., 144
Kiewe, A., 127
King, C. S., 21–22, 23, 26, 35–37
King, K. S., 21
King, M. L. K., Jr., 21
Kinneavy, J., 296
Kiss, E., 376
Klemm, D. E., 146–147
Klien, S. A., 181, 193
Klinck, D. R., 144
Klinkner, P. A., 27
Klooster, T. J., 143
Koesten, J., 367–368, 372
Komnena, A., 101–108
Kostelnick, C., 124
Kristeva, J., 229
Kronman, A. T., 146
Kuhn, T., 41
Kunkel, A. D., 93–94, 99
Kustas, G. L., 101
Kuswa, K. D., 409

Lacan, J., 130, 251–252, 254, 257, 259–261
Lammers, W. W., 155
Lan, H. R., 382
Lancioni, J., 125
Langer, S., 130
Langley, W. E., 326
Langsdorf, L., 123
Latour, B., 279
Laufer, W. S., 143
LaWare, M. R., 123
Lazarsfeld, P., 207
Le Vine, V., 219
Lee, I., 202
Legate, H., 303
Leitenberg, M., 242
Leshner, A., 277
Lessl, T. M., 279
Lewis, J., 27, 29–30
Lewontin, R. C., 279
Linenthal, E., 218
Linkugel, L., 368
Linkugel, W., 367, 373
Lisnek, P. M., 143
Ljubarskij, J., 103, 107

Llobera, J., 364
Lodge, O., 346
Long, E., 20
Lorich, R., 64–65
Lowery, J., 35–36
Lu Yin, 379–387
Lucaites, J. L., 124, 130–131, 336, 369
Lucas, S., 320
Luhmann, N., 236–237
Lullus, A., 64
Lundberg, C., 369
Lyotard, J-F., 9

Mackenzie, H., 26
Magdalino, P., 101–104, 106
Magoulias, H. J., 102
Maier, P., 217, 321
Mailloux, S., 10, 16, 21
Mandela, N., 28
Martin, E., 279
Martin, M., 276
Masen, J., 64–65
Maturana, H., 236
Matusow, A. J., 155
Mbembe, A., 14–15
McCloskey, D., 255
McCraw, T. K., 155
McElhaney, J. W., 143
McEnaney, L., 243
McGarry, M., 335, 341
McIlhaney, J., 274
McLaren, P., 401
McWilliams, C., 117
Mechling, E. W., 228, 232, 243
Mechling, J., 228, 232, 243
Medhurst, M. J., 122, 125, 154, 229
Mendelssohn, M., 43–50
Mennessier, I., 289
Meyer, L., 146–147
Michel, N., 25, 28, 123
Micraelius, J., 64–65
Milham, D., 208–209
Miller, P., 316
Mitchell, W. J. T., 126, 130
Moris, H., 142
Morris, C. E., 127, 130
Mosellanus, P., 64
Moss, D. C., 143
Mouffe, C., 16
Muessig, C., 301

Mullett, M., 101, 103–104
Murphy, J. J., 40, 63, 299–300
Murray, J., 173
Myra, N., 54

Nagin, R., 200
Noffke, S., 293
Nonet, P., 146
Noonan, P., 35

O'Connor, S. D., 13
O'Leary, C., 219
O'Toole, T., 239
Oakes, G., 231
Oldenburg, A., 30
Olmsted, W., 41, 46, 51
Olson, L. C., 123–124, 127
Ong, W., 304
Oravec, C., 374
Origen, 298
Ornstein, C., 275
Orren, G., 175
Ott, B. L., 124
Owen, S., 127

Paarlberg, D., 156
Pach, C. J., 156
Palczewski, C. H., 123
Palmer, G. H., 347
Panofsky, E., 130
Parks, R., 23, 25
Parry-Giles, S., 27
Parry-Giles, T., 27
Passavant, P., 336, 342
Patillon, M., 57
Patten, S. N., 343
Peck, J., 31
Peirce, C. S., 130, 144
Perelman, C., 144
Peters, J., 335
Peterson, T., 156
Pezzullo, P. C., 127
Plato, 145–146
Plesch, V., 305–306
Pollack, K. M., 16
Pomey, F., 64–65
Praetorius, C., 64
Prelli, L. J., 121, 129, 274, 276–277
Priest, S., 207
Pucci, E., 123

Quintilian, 54, 58, 75

Radcliffe, S., 362
Raiford, L., 24
Rainey, J. H., 24
Randolph, A. P., 27
Ranney, F. J., 145
Rasmussen, A. F., 366, 370–372
Rasmussen, P. N., 367
Ratcliffe, K., 383
Reagan, R., 13
Reagan, R., Jr., 94, 96
Reed, T. V., 22
Reeve, C., 97
Rehnquist, W., 20
Reinhard, K., 15
Reinsch, D., 104
Richardson, E., 156
Ricoeur, P., 145
Ritter, K., 317
Robert of Basevorn, 299–300, 303
Roberts, M. T., 143
Roberts, P., 302
Robinson, A., 256–257, 260
Robinson, C. M., 347
Robinson, J., 24
Rohan, L., 124
Rollins, B., 373
Romano, R. C., 24
Roochnik, D., 149
Rorty, R., 9, 145
Ross, J. F. W., 270
Rothkopf, D., 231
Rowland, R. C., 367–368, 372
Rowson, S., 22
Royster, J. J., 330
Rueckert, W., 110–111
Ruegg, M., 256–257
Ryan, M. E., 153, 155–156

Said, E., 11
Saporta, M., 35
Sarat, A., 147–149
Saulnier, R. J., 154
Savonarola, G., 302
Scarry, E., 148
Schaar, J. H., 218
Schapsmeier, E. L., 156
Schapsmeier, F. H., 156
Scheman, N., 288
Scheuer, J., 182, 184–186, 197
Schiller, F., 103
Schmitt, C., 15

Schumacher, E. F., 244
Scott, B., 123
Scott, J. B., 273
Scott, R. L., 102, 126, 128
Seerley, F. M., 344
Selby, J., 52
Selzer, F. J., 36
Selzer, J., 127
Sewter, E. R. A., 102–108
Shakespeare, W., 73
Shaw, T., 407
Sheldon, J. P., 243
Shelley, C., 123–124
Showalter, E., 240
Shuger, D. K., 42, 46, 49
Sloan, T. O., 118, 125
Sloop, J. M., 127, 130
Smith, A., 25–26, 28, 258
Smith, R. M., 27
Smith, S. M., 120
Sneath, E. H., 347
Snee, B. J., 143
Socrates, 146
Sontag, D., 32–34
Sontag, S., 130
Spanier, B., 279
Specter, M., 278
Spencer, E. C., 94–96
Spender, S., 421
Sprat, Bishop, 40, 49
Stafford, B., 130
Stall, S., 340
Stein, H., 404–405, 407
Stephens, R. J., 368
Stephenson, P., 101–102
Steuerle, G., 143
Stewart, J., 321
Stormer, N., 124, 127
Stowe, H. B., 22
Strong, P., 240
Sullivan, D. E., 176–177
Sullivan, W. M., 195, 197

Tatum, W., 21
Taylor, B. C., 123–124, 229
Teepen, T., 143
Terry, J., 31, 279
Thomas, J., 104
Thompson, A., 301
Tom, G., 123
Tompkins, J. P., 22, 30
Tompkins, P. K., 121
Tone, A., 334–335
Tornikes, G., 102–103

Torpy, B., 35
Torrens, K. M., 127
Toulmin, S., 144
Treichler, P. A., 273, 279–280
Trent, J. S., 183
Trickey, M. B., 34
Trueblood, T. C., 344
Tuohey, S. M., 143
Turner, K. J., 126

Ulrich, H., 155
Underhill, E., 289–290

Valadés, D., 304
Van Loon, J., 227, 229, 237
Van Mulken, M., 123
Varela, F., 236
Verhoosel, G., 142
Vitanza, V., 178

Wahlberg, D., 277
Waldby, C., 279

Walker, D., 313–322
Walker, J., 101, 104
Walzer, M., 193
Ward, G. G., 271
Ware, B. L., 367–368, 373
Warner, K., 143
Warner, M., 130
Warnick, B., 124
Waxman, H., 277–278
Weinrib, E. J., 145–146
Weiss, R., 277
Weld, T. W., 22
Wells, I. B., 325, 330–331
Wells, S., 266, 268, 270
Weston, P., 143
Westwood, S., 362
White, J. B., 144, 147–148
White, L., 148
Whitman, A., 157
Wiethoff, W. E., 143
Willard, F., 326–331
Willerton, R., 123

Williams, P., 148
Wilson, J. F., 319–320
Wilson, S., 31
Winfrey, O., 30–34
Winkler, C. K., 123–124,
    130
Winthrop, J., 13, 316
Wise, S. M., 143
Woodhull, V., 327–329, 331
Woodson, C. G., 23
Woolgar, S., 279
Worth, S., 122, 130

Yates, F., 301

Zagel, J. B., 142
Žižek, S., 256
Zoeller, G., 146–147
Zonaras, J., 102
Zulaika, J., 399, 406,
    410–411

Subject Index

Abolitionism, prophetic, 313–322
Academic intellectuals, 11–12
Acts of Hope (White), 147
Address to the Slaves (Garnet), 322
Advertising, political, image vs. issue in, 182–193
Aesthetic sensibility and avoidance of vice, 347
Agency, and contemplative vs. active life, 289–292
Agonistic pluralism, 16
Alexiad (Komnena), 101–108
Altruism, social, 339
Analogy, 82, 114
Anatomy of Disgust (Miller), 146
Ancient Rhetorics for Contemporary Students (Crowley & Hawhee), 52
Anna Komnene (Gouma-Peterson), 101
Antilynching campaign of Ida B. Wells, 330
Antinomy, dialect of, 147
Antirhetoricism, 9
Anti-Saloon League, 344
Apologia
  contemporary Danish, 366–376
  forensic, 71–87
  official, 373–375
  personal, 367
  personal vs. official, 367–368
Appeal to the Coloured Citizens of the World (Walker), 313–314

Archive Fever (Derrida), 256
Argumentation and Advocacy (Birdsell & Groarke), 123
Argumentative essay, 383
Aristotle
  on automaton, 259–261
  on epideictic rhetoric, 374
  on ethos, 176
  on three forms of public address, 71
  on tuche, automaton, and techne, 142, 259
Ars praedicandi, 298–300
Art of Rhetoric, The (Aristotle), 91
Artistic motifs in preaching and sermons, 301–306
Athletics, avoiding vice through, 343–344
Atonement, rhetoric of, 368, 372
Attitudes toward History (Burke), 111
Audience
  for epideictic speeches, 374–375
  hurricane evacuation rhetoric perspective/response, 206–208
  for militia-based rhetoric, 215
Authority, rhetorical, 287–294
Automaton, Aristotle on, 259–261
Autopoiesis (self-creation), 228, 236–237, 244

Bio(in)security, rhetoric of, 227–245
Bioterrorism
  autopoiesis and, 236–237
  biopreparedness exercises/fantasy documents, 231–234
  command and control regulation of, 245
  contemporary landscape of, 229–232
  institutional discourses vs. social reality, 243–245
  militarized public health discourse/technorealist rhetoric of, 240–243
  politics of urgency on, 230–231
  realist-technical rhetoric of, 235–236
  reifying the risk of, 234–237
  scripting futures of rhetoric on, 238–240
  viral apocalypse rhetoric of, 232–234
Blame, 56, 58–59, 61, 65
Blessing, eulogistic, 95–99
Body in Pain, The (Scarry), 148
Brown v. Board of Education, 32
Brownlee System for Moral Education, 346
Burke, Kenneth
  doctrine of consubstantiality, 177
  Progressive press and, 110–117

on rhetorical power of
fantasy, 111
on technology, 111, 115
visual rhetorical scholarship of, 121–122,
130
Bush, George W., videostyle
of, 187–189
Bush-Kerry presidential
debates, 173–175,
181–182
Byzantine rhetoric, 101–108

Campaign advertising,
182–197
issue vs. image ads, 183
videostyle of, 184–188
Care of the Self (Foucault), 344
Catherine of Siena, rhetorical authority of,
287–294
Celluloid rhetoric, 125
Ceremonial/ritual law, 49–50
Certainty, language of,
183–184
Character
Aristotle on, 74
building, beautification
sites attributed to,
348
collective, and topos of
membership, 362
moral education and for-
mation of, 346
propriety/ethical con-
duct linked to, 74
public, construction of
in televisual war
arguments, 193–197
Charlotte Temple (Rowson),
22
Chinese new intellectuals,
382
Chreia (anecdote), 55, 57–58,
60–61
Cicero
on analogy, 82
on elements of eulogy, 92
on ethos, 84
on the good of teaching
rhetoric, 393–395
on humor, 76–81
on metaphor, 75, 82
on mimicry, 77

City beautification, 347–348
Civic virtue, 74, 84
Civil education, rhetoric of,
398–412
Civil rights movement
commemoration, rhetor-
ical norms of, 34–37
memorial rhetoric on,
20–37
sentimental rhetoric
regarding, 22–30
*Classical Rhetoric for the Mod-
ern Student* (Corbett), 52
Code switching and deco-
rum, 396
Cold war rhetoric, 229, 232,
244, 407, 409
Collective identity
political, 360
relation to rhetoric and
rhetorical action,
356–361
topoi/symbols of, 362
Coming Plague, The (Garret),
238
Commentators as hybrid
intellectuals, 12
Common ground, 419–421
Commonplace, 55–56, 59–60
Community, symbolic con-
struct of, 359
Comparison, 56
element of progymnas-
mata, 56, 59
*Composition in the Classical
Tradition* (D'Angelo),
52
Comstock law, 326, 334–335,
337, 340–342
Confessions (Augustine), 41
Confirmation element of
progymnasmata, 56,
58, 60
Conscientizacão, 394
Conservative simplicity vs.
progressive complex-
ity, 184–185
Consubstantiality, Burke's
doctrine of, 177
Contemplation and rhetori-
cal agency, 289
Contemplative vs. active life,
and agency, 289–292
Contingent eternal truths, 47

*Converted British Family Shel-
tering a Christian Priest
from the Persecution of
the Druids, A* (Hunt),
306–307
Counter-bioterrorism, rhetorical dynamics of,
227–245
Counting, Lacan's logic of,
261
Courage, eulogizing, 95–98
Credibility
Apuleius's, 85
Cicero on, 74
self-disclosure enhanc-
ing, 84–85
style and, 82–84
See also Ethos
*Critical Literacy in a Digital
Era-Technology, Rheto-
ric, and the Public Interest* (Warnick), 124
Critical pedagogy
context and conflict in,
402–406
ethical stance against
mediating ideologies
of self and Other, 409
five tenets of, 401–402
genealogy and a search
for ethics, 406–410
John Dewey on, 408
mediating between self
and Other, 409–410
on terrorism and vio-
lence, 398–412
tolerance of cultural difference and, 404–405
Critical space, 402
Crusade in Europe (Eisenhower), 154
Cultural memory, vernacu-
lar rhetoric of, 363
Cultural narratives of hysteria, 240
Culture
contemporary, image-
dominated nature of,
126
diversity, awareness of
and respect for,
402–406
material, visual rhetoric
in, 119–121, 124

of media, built-in ideological bias in, 184–185
popular, visual rhetoric in, 123
vernacular, 120, 123–124, 130

De clericorum instructione (Rabanus), 299
De inventione (Cicero), 75
De oratore (Cicero), 74, 76, 393–394
Decline and Fall, The (Gibbon), 103
Decorum, 76, 395
Defining Visual Rhetorics (Hill & Helmers), 129
Delight, dangers of, 51
Democracy and America's War on Terror (Ivie), 14
Dialogue (Catherine of Siena), 287, 290–293
DICTION program, 183
Dinner Party, The (Chicago), 123
Dispositio, 60
Disserere in utramque partem (arguing for both sides), 56
Doctrine and duty, sermon on, 306–308
Dogmas, Mendelssohn on, 45, 50
Dramatism, Burke's, 110

Echoes, rhetorical, 319–322
Economic behavior, Friedman's theory of, 258–259
Economy
Lacan's psychoanalytic, 257
psychoanalytic, metaphor of, 259
structuralism and, 258
Education
critical pedagogy, 398–412
oratory as essential to, 74
Eisenhower's agricultural rhetoric
arguments/argument structure, 163–166

background of, 154–156
early addresses, 157–159
independent persona and, 159–161
rhetorical strategies, 166–170
values and philosophy in, 161–163
Ekphrasis, 101, 301
Elaboration, 56, 76
Electronic rhetoric, 125
Elocutio (pictorial idiom/putting into language), 61, 75, 306
Elocution, avoiding vice through, 344–345
Eloquence
eloquent citizenship, 409
importance of, in reform rhetoric, 338
transgressive, 393–397
Emblem, national, 359–360
Empirical commonalities, universals as, 16
Encomium of Helen (Gorgias), 301
Engenderings (Scheman), 288
Epideictic rhetoric
as basis for public life, 374–375
official apologia, 366–376
Eternal truths, 46–47
Ethical progress, collaborative effort of, 420
Ethical rhetoric
critical pedagogy and, 406–410
G. W. Bush's use of in presidential debates, 174–177
Levinasian, 14
politics/ethics of the neighbor, 14–15
Ethopoeia (speech-in-character), 55–56, 60–62, 65
Ethos
Apuleius's arguments based on, 79
Aristotelian relationship with logos, 176
Aristotle on, 176
Cicero on, 84
early Greek and Roman, 84–87

presidential campaign rhetoric and, 175, 177
Ray Nagin's, 202
See also Credibility
Eulogy, 90–100
Aristotle on, 95
audience perspective of, 91–92
blessing/praise of virtue in, 95–99
literature on, 91–94
rhetorical action in, 99–100
Exercise, as preventive solution to vice, 343–344, 348
Exergasia, 56
Explanatory rhetoric
Augustine on, 298
definitions of, 296–297
history of, 297–300
Hunt's sermon on doctrine and duty, 306–308
visual, history of, in sermons, 301–306

Fable, Aphthonius's, 55, 57–58, 61
Fantasy
Burke on rhetorical power of, 111
documents, in biopreparedness exercises, 228, 232–234, 237, 239, 244
Feminine sentimentality, American, 30
Feminist rhetoric, 101, 108
criticism of biomedical model, 265–272
nineteenth-century women's public sexual discourse, 325–331
visual, 123, 127
Figured discourse (*echematismenos logos*), 101
Film, rhetoric of, 125
Forensic apologia, 71–87
Forma praedicandi (Basevorn), 300
Four Fundamental Concepts of Psychoanalysis, The (Lacan), 259

Gender-based rhetoric, Anna Komnena's rhetoricity, 101–108. *See also* Feminist rhetoric

Globalization, 125, 404, 406

God of Socrates, The (Apuleius), 77

Golden Ass, The (Apuleius), 78, 81

Good man (*vir bonus*), 74

Good Words: Writing and Delivering a Eulogy (Hewett), 100

Gorgias (Plato), 145

Governmental intervention into private problems, 337

Governmentality, 340–341 Comstock law, 336

Greek sophists, 71–87

Headings of purpose (*teliká kephálaia*), 60

Hermeneutical logic, 21

Historical truths, 47–48

HIV prevention policy, scientific vs. political topos on, 273–281

Homily, 298. *See also* Preaching; Sermons

Humor Apuleius's, 82–83 Cicero on, 76–77

Hurricane evacuation rhetoric audience response to, 206–209 constraints on, 203–207 Hurricane Katrina, 202–204, 207–209 identification and description of, 200–203 logos and pathos in, 201–203 mediated nature of, 201, 208 Nagin, Ray, rhetoric of, 202–204, 207–208 NHC information on, 204–205 oppositional, 209

Hybrid intellectuals, 12

Hyperbole, 83

Hysteria, cultural narratives of, 240

Icon, varying definitions of, 130–131

Iconography/iconology, rhetorical, 122–124

Identity formation collective, 356–361 in legal and public discourse, 336, 349 national, 355–364

Ideologic, Crowley's, 277

Illumination, 76

Imagined Communities (Anderson), 355

Immutable eternal truths, 46–47

In Cold Blood (Capote), 121

Individual liberty vs. social reform, 338–340

Intellectuals hybrid, overlapping roles of, 12 public vs. academic, 11–12 universal vs. specific, 11

Inventio (finding of arguments), 60, 75–76

Inventors as hybrid intellectuals, 12

Iraq, televisual war rhetoric over, 181–198

Jeremiad, American, 313, 316–319

Jerusalem (Mendelssohn), 43, 45

Jewish religious rhetorical practice, 43–50

Kairos, in hurricane evacuation rhetoric, 201, 203

Kerry, John, videostyle of, 184, 186–193

King, Coretta Scott, eulogy for, 20–37

Lacanian psychoanalysis, restoring the tropological heritage of, 250–263

Language of certainty, 183–184

communicating eternal truths through, 51 gender relationships and, 386–387 transmitting absolute truths through, 40, 48, 51 volitional and creative choice of, 74

LaPeste (Camus), 240

Law, rhetoricity of, 334–349

Lectures on Systematic Theology and Pulpit Eloquence (Campbell), 297

Legal rhetoric Comstock law, 326, 334–335, 337, 340–342 jurors' persuasion through, 143 law from the outside in, 141–150 possibility of legal error in, 149 property as bearer of meaning in, 144 restorative justice, 143 rhetorical research in law, 144–148

Liberalism, nineteenth-century rise of, 337

Liberty and Freedom (Fisher), 364

Listening rhetoric, 420

Little Rock Nine, 31–34

Lochner v. New York, 145

Logos Aristotelian relationship with ethos, 176 evacuation rhetoric and, 201 figured discourse and, 101 presidential campaign rhetoric and, 175

Lyrical essay, 383

Man of Feeling, The (Mackenzie), 26

Marital rape, 326–328

Masking, 78

Material culture, visual rhetoric in, 119–121, 124

Maxim (proverb), 55, 58, 60–61

Media
culture, built-in ideological bias in, 184–185
rhetorical dimensions of, 122
suspicion of messages originating from, 208
televisual war rhetoric over Iraq, 181, 198
Membership, topos of, 362
Memory, sentimental, 20–37
Mendelssohn, Moses, on truth and knowledge acquisition, 46–50
Metacritics as hybrid intellectuals, 12
Metamorphoses (Apuleius), 77, 81
Metaphor
Apuleius's use of, 82–83
Cicero on, 75
economy, psychoanalytic interpretation, 258–259
pictorial, Kaplan's interest in, 123
Methods of Rhetorical Criticism (Brock & Scott), 128
Militaristic patriotism in militia movements, 218–219
Militia movement
audiences for rhetoric of, 215
Clinton on rhetoric of, 214–219
criticism of rhetoric of, 218–219
history of, 212–213
patriotism in rhetoric of, 216–219
powerlessness of, 215
revolutionary posturing of, 213–216
Modern Dogma and the Rhetoric of Assent (Booth), 419
Moral education, avoiding vice through, 346
My Many Selves (Booth), 418–422
My Three Years with Eisenhower (Butcher), 154
Mysticism (Underhill), 289

Mysticism, and language of the body, 292–293
Mystics of the Church (Underhill), 289

Narration element of progymnasmata, 56–58, 61
Narrative, essential components of, 61
National identity/nation building, rhetoric of, 355–364
Nations, as imagined political communities, 355
Necessary eternal truths, 46–47
New Republic, The (Burke), 112
New York Society for the Suppression of Vice, 334
Nicomachean Ethics (Aristotle), 142, 149
Nonverbal rhetoric, visual, 118–133
Notes on the State of Virginia (Jefferson), 315

Official apologia, 366–376
On Christian Learning (Augustine), 298
On First Principles (Origen), 298
On Rhetoric (Aristotle), 176
On the Philosophy of Plato (Apuleius), 77
On the World (Apuleius), 77
Oprah Winfrey Show, 30–33
Orator (Cicero), 75, 393, 396
Ornatus (ornamental rhetorical style), 76, 82

Painting as silent preaching, 303
Panentheism, elitist, 44
Paradox
Apuleius's use of, 83
Burke's use of, 116
Greek sophists' use of, 76
Parallelism, Apuleius's use of, 83
Parks, reformatory power of, 347–348

Pathos
Anna Komnena's use of, 103
hurricane evacuation rhetoric and, 202–203
in progymnasmata, 60
Patriotism, militia movement rhetoric on, 216–220
Permanence and Change (Burke), 111
Phaedon (Plato), 46
Phaedrus (Plato), 79, 145
Philosophy of Literary Form, The (Burke), 111
Photography on the Color Line (Smith), 120
Phronesis, Cicero on Aristotle's, 74
Physical Training (Exner), 339
Picturing Poverty (Finnegan), 126
Pluribus modis tractare (treatment in multiple ways), 57
Poems, use of, in sermons, 303
Poland, political reconstruction of, 355–364
Political rhetoric
campaign advertising, 182–197
militia movements, 212–220
personalities over policy issues and political institutions, 181
simplified televisual argument in, 181–182
tri-component model of ad content, 183
Political theology, 12–16
Political transformation, symbolic nature of, 363
Politics
psychoanalytic, 256
rhetorical disconnect in, 174
See also Political rhetoric
Politics and Science in the Bush Administration (Waxman), 278

Postcolonial theory, 14–15
Praise
    eulogistic, 95–99
    protogymnasmatic,
        56–59, 61, 65
*Preacher, Sermon and Audi-
    ence in the Middle Ages*
    (Muessig), 301
Preaching, rhetorical avenue
    of, 296–297, 299–303
Presidential campaign rheto-
    ric, American, 173–179
Progressive press, Burke
    and, 110–117
Progymnasmata, 52–65
Prudential judgment (*sum-
    maque prudentia*), 74
Psychoanalysis
    psychoanalytic econ-
        omy of exchange,
        260, 262–263
    rhetorical heritage of,
        250–255
    and structuralism, rela-
        tionship between, 260
Public address, forms of,
    71–72
Public character, construc-
    tion of in televisual war
    arguments, 193–197
Public intellectuals, 11–12
Purity (Boyer), 334

Question fiction, 383

Race, American experience
    of, 20, 24–25, 31–37
Race, in the American expe-
    rience, 22–23
Rape, euphemisms for, 326
Rashness (*temeritas*), 74
Reality vs. simulation, Bau-
    drillard on, 236
Redefining, rhetorical tool
    of, 383–385
Refutation element of pro-
    gymnasmata, 56, 58, 60
Religious art, silent preach-
    ing through, 303
Religious persuasion, 40–51
Religious rhetoric
    Catherine of Siena's,
        287–294
    Jewish practice of, 43–50

medieval, 287–294
political theology, 12–16
reason, emotion, and the
    sensory in religious
    persuasion, 40, 51
use of visual images in,
    301–306
Renaissance Rhetoric (Green
    & Murphy), 63
Restorative justice, rhetoric
    of, 143
Rhetoric
    canon of, 10
    contingent universality
        of, 7–17
    ethical, 174–177
    explanatory, 296–309
    postmodern viral apoca-
        lyptic, 227, 238–245
    remaking process in, 419
    Roman system of, 72–76
    sizing up as taking
        inventory, 8–10
    sizing up by sizing
        down, 10–17
    universality of, 7–17
    visual, intellectual, and
        conceptual resources
        for, 118–133
Rhetoric (Burke), 17
Rhetoric of Economics, The
    (McCloskey), 255
Rhetoric of Eulogies, The
    (Kent), 91, 94, 99
Rhetoric of Law, The (Sarat &
    Kearns), 147–148
Rhetoric of Motives, A (Burke),
    118, 121, 177–178
*Rhetoric of Nonverbal Commu-
    nication, The* (Bosma-
    jian), 122
Rhetoric of Rhetoric, The
    (Booth), 419, 421
Rhetorica ad Herennium
    (anon.), 61, 71–72,
    74–75, 78
Rhetorica Christiana (Val-
    adés), 304
Rhetorical agency
    Catherine of Siena's,
        287–294
    contemplation and, 289
    medical, of women,
        265–272

medieval, women's, 287,
    295
official apologia, 366–376
political, of Cicero and
    bell hooks, 393–397
*Rhetorical Dimensions in the
    Media* (Benson &
    Medhurst), 122
Rhetorical echoes, 319–322
*Rhetorical Landscapes in
    America* (Clark), 121
Rhetorical questions, 82, 114
Rhetorical studies, transdis-
    ciplinary potential of,
    10
Rhetorical theory
    eulogy, 90–100
    forensic genre, 71–87
Rhetorics of Display (Prelli),
    129
Rhetorology, Booth's,
    418–421
Ridicule, destroying credi-
    bility through, 85
Risikogesellschaft (Beck), 234
Risk, social construction of,
    234–237
Ritual
    eulogy, rhetorical action
        in, 99
    learning from demon-
        stration rather than
        reading, 49
    observance, truths
        expressed through,
        45, 48–49
Roman rhetorical system,
    72–76
*Roots of American Loyalty,
    The* (Curti), 216
Ruth Hall (Fern), 22

Sarcasm, 76, 78, 83
Science of Speech (Fenno),
    345
Scientific rhetoric
    bioterrorism, 227, 245
    HIV prevention policy
        debate, 273–281
    Lacanian psychoanaly-
        sis, 250–263
    medical rhetorical
        agency of women,
        265–272

Security, rhetorics of, 16–17
Self & Sex Series, 340
Self and Other, consistency of mediating term between, 409–411
Self-disclosure, enhancing credibility through, 84–85
Semiotics, 144, 252, 255–256, 262, 281
Sensibility (*summaque prodentia*), in Greek forensic speaking, 74
Sentimentalism/sentimental memory/rhetoric, 22–30
Sermons
  artistic illumination/illustration of, 305–306
  explanatory rhetoric in, 297, 301–308
  history of visual images in, 301–306
  See also Preaching
Sexual reform discourse
  Ida B. Wells vs. Willard, Woodhull, and Craddock, 330–331
  nineteenth-century women's public discourse on, 325–332
  sexual and monetary/economic freedom, 329
  sexuality education and discussion, 328–329
Shaping Information (Kostelnick & Hassett), 124
Simplex conservatism in televised war rhetoric, 185
Simulation vs. reality, Baudrillard on, 236
Slavery, 313, 322
Social reform vs. individual liberty, 338–340
Social services, transformation of government's role in, 337–338
Soldier of Democracy (Davis), 154
Sound Bite Society, The (Scheuer), 182
Speech act theory and epideictic rhetoric, 375

Stasis system, 75, 78–81
Structuralism, 257, 260
Style, 75–76, 81–84
Symbolic Inducement and Knowing (Gregg), 122
Symbols
  of community/collective identity, 355–364
  memorial, 25
  nation building and, 362–364
  rhetorical operation of, Lacan's, 254
  sharing, vs. sharing of meaning, 359
  topoi and, 362–364
  visual rhetoric and, 122
Synecdoche, 22

Teaching to Transgress (hooks), 393
Techne, 10, 142
Technology, Burke on, 111, 115
Television, inherent conservativism of, 182
Televisual war rhetoric
  analysis of presidential campaign issue advertisements, 185–192
  attack ads vs. policy/issue content, 182–183
  campaign advertising, image vs. issue ads, 183
  campaign advertising, policy argument, and videostyle, 182–185
  construction of public character in, 193–197
  personalities over policy issues and political institutions, 181–182
  simplification favored over complexity in, 184
Temporal historical truths, 47–48
Terror and Taboo (Zulaika & Douglass), 406
Terrorism, critical pedagogy of, 403–412. *See also* Bioterrorism

Theory of Moral Sentiments, The (Smith), 26
Theroroi (epideictic audience), 374
Thesis, 55–56, 58, 60, 62
To Die For (O'Leary), 219
TOPOFF 3, 227–244. *See also* Bioterrorism
Topos
  of identity, 355, 362–364
  of location, 362
  of membership, 362
  scientific, of disinterestedness, 277
  scientific, of observational competence, 274
  scientific vs. political, 279–281
  of skepticism, 276
Tourism, civil rights, 24
Toward a Civil Discourse (Crowley), 14
Towards a Better Life (Burke), 111
Transfiguration of the Commonplace, The (Danto), 123
Transgression, critical, 395–396
Transgressive eloquence, 393–397
Translators as hybrid intellectuals, 12
Traveler's Guide to the Civil Rights Movement, A (Carrier), 24
Truth
  communicating through art, 302–303
  ethos as possession of, 176
  rhetorical conveyance of, 41–42, 45–49
  visual, as an aid to communicating, 302
Tuche, 142, 259, 261
28 Days Later (Boyle), 238

Universalism, 7–17

Vernacular culture, 119–121, 123–124
Vernacular publics, competing legal narratives from, 336

Vice regulation, nineteenth-
century, 334–349
Videostyle
Bush-Cheney, 186–189
campaign ads and televi-
sual arguments,
182–186
definition of, 183
issue and image ads,
trends between, 183
Kerry-Edwards, 184,
186–193
language of certainty in,
183–184
nonverbal, 187–188,
191–192
production techniques,
188–189, 192–193
trends between issue and
image ads, 183
tri-component model of
ad content, 183
verbal content of,
186–187, 190–191
Viral apocalypse, fantasy/
rhetoric of, 228–234,
236–240, 243–244
Virtue, eulogistic praise of,
95–99
Visual Communication
(Hope), 129

Visual images, history of, in
sermons, 301–306
Visual rhetoric
argument/advocacy in,
123
changes in nomenclature
of, 124–125, 127
history of, 118–120
intellectual reservations
about, 128
lack of theory on, 131
in material/vernacular
cultures, 119–121
in popular culture, 123
scholarship, future of,
131–133
scholarship since 1950,
121–130
in sermons, 301
symbolic inducement in,
122
of televised war rheto-
ric, 182–185
Visual Rhetoric (Olson,
Finnegan, & Hope),
129
Voyage to Lilliput (Burke),
113

Walking with the Wind
(Lewis), 29

War, Dewey on abolishing,
408–409
Weapons of mass destruc-
tion (WMD), 227–245.
See also Bioterrorism
Weary Feet, Rested Souls
(Davis), 24
"Wedding Night, The"
(Craddock), 328
What's the Matter with Kansas
(Frank), 174
Womanhood, Confucian
ideal of, 384
Women
American, sentimental-
ity of, 30
erosion of medical
power/biomedical
model, 265–272
medical rhetorical
agency of, 265–272
medieval, rhetorical
agency of, 287, 294
nineteenth-century pub-
lic sexual discourse
of, 329–332
rhetoricity of Anna
Komnena, 101–108
*World and How We Describe
It, The* (Brummett),
236